ECOLOGIES OF THE MOVING IMAGE

ENVIRONMENTAL
HUMANITIES

ECOLOGIES OF THE MOVING IMAGE *Cinema, Affect, Nature*

ADRIAN J. IVAKHIV

WILFRID LAURIER
UNIVERSITY PRESS

This book has been published with the help of a grant from the Canadian Federation for the Humanities and Social Sciences, through the Awards to Scholarly Publications Program, using funds provided by the Social Sciences and Humanities Research Council of Canada. Wilfrid Laurier University Press acknowledges the support of the Canada Council for the Arts for our publishing program. We acknowledge the financial support of the Government of Canada through the Canada Book Fund for our publishing activities.

 Canada Council **Conseil des Art**
for the Arts **du Canada**

 ONTARIO ARTS COUNCIL
CONSEIL DES ARTS DE L'ONTARIO

Library and Archives Canada Cataloguing in Publication

Ivakhiv, Adrian J.

    Ecologies of the moving image : cinema, affect, nature / Adrian J. Ivakhiv.

(Environmental humanities series)
Includes bibliographical references and index.
Issued also in electronic formats.
ISBN 978-1-55458-905-0

    1. Motion pictures—History. 2. Nature in motion pictures. 3. Ecology in motion pictures.
4. Affect (Psychology) in motion pictures. I. Title. II. Series: Environmental humanities series

PN1995.9.N38I93 2013   791.43'66   C2012-907197-8

———

Electronic monograph.
Issued also in print format.
ISBN 978-1-55458-906-7 (PDF).—ISBN 978-1-55458-907-4 (EPUB)

    1. Motion pictures—History. 2. Nature in motion pictures. 3. Ecology in motion pictures.
4. Affect (Psychology) in motion pictures. I. Title. II. Series: Environmental humanities series
(Online)

PN1995.9.N38I93 2013   791.43'66   C2012-907198-6

Cover design by Martyn Schmoll. Front-cover image from *Stalker* (1979 USSR). Directed by Andrei Tarkovsky.
Text design by Janette Thompson (Jansom).

RECYCLED
Paper made from
recycled material
FSC® C103567

This book is printed on FSC recycled paper and is certified Ecologo. It is made from 100% post-consumer fibre, processed chlorine free, and manufactured using biogas energy.

Printed in Canada

Every reasonable effort has been made to acquire permission for copyright material used in this text, and to acknowledge all such indebtedness accurately. Any errors and omissions called to the publisher's attention will be corrected in future printings.

CONTENTS

PREFACE

The world around us contains a wild phantasmagoria of images. Put more provocatively: the world around us *is* a wild phantasmagoria of images. We live and move in a world that swirls with tempestuous currents made of a kind of audiovisual image-substance. Photographs, films and television programs, videos and computer games—these and other moving images blend and mix with images of the external and internal worlds produced by a global array of instruments, from satellites that face down at us, to telescopes that face away from us, to MRIs, EEGs, and ultrasound sonographs that face into us, to the personal computers, cellphones, and iPads that have become our bodily and mental extensions. Together these make up imagescapes full of motion. These images move us, and we move with them. And as we do, we may realize that we too are moving images, seen and heard and perceived by others who are seen and heard and perceived by us. A world increasingly filled with moving images has remade itself into a world *of* moving images.

This book examines how images move us. It is not a treatise on the physics of this movement, nor is it an ethnography of ourselves in the midst of these currents. It is not particularly concerned with distinguishing between images and the supposedly "real things" represented, signified, or perhaps masked by those images. Rather, this book steps back from the immersive image-worlds in which we live in order to get a sense of what the moving image *is* and of what one particular history of it—the cinematic—can tell us today, at this juncture between a photographic and celluloid past and a digital future. "Cinema" refers to one form of moving image, a form that consists of structured sequences viewed by audiences and that emerged in a particular time and place (industrial-era Europe and North America) and has captivated the world over the course of the past twelve decades.

This book presents an ecophilosophy of the cinema. My goal is to think through the ecological implications of the moving images—films, videos, animations, and motion pictures of various kinds—that have proliferated in our world since the late nineteenth century. The "eco" in its philosophy does not restrict itself to the material impacts of the production of those images.

It also delves into their social and perceptual effects. This book is about how moving images have changed the ways we grasp and attend to the world in general—a world of social and ecological relations—and about how we might learn to make them do that *better*.

This project is an eco*philosophy* in the sense that it develops a philosophical framework for reconceiving our relations with moving images. This framework is intended to be pragmatic and empirical, rooted in actual experience, but it is also metaphysically speculative and radical in its implications. The works of the two philosophers on whom I draw most deeply, Charles Sanders Peirce and Alfred North Whitehead, have never to my knowledge been brought together for the task of a detailed analysis of cinematic images. To this combination, I bring insights from a broad array of other sources. These include the ideas of other philosophers, such as Henri Bergson, Martin Heidegger, Gilles Deleuze, and Félix Guattari, and a range of post-Deleuzian thinkers; as well as cultural historians' and geographers' studies of visuality and landscape, ecocritics' analyses of representations of nature and the "ecological sublime," feminist and post-colonial critiques of the "imperial gaze," cognitive and neuropsychological studies of affect and perception, neo-Marxist theorizations of film's political economies, and the work of scholars in animal studies, trauma studies, psychoanalysis, and depth psychology, among other fields.

In its essence, this book proposes and applies a model of cinema that I refer to as "process-relational." Such a model sees the world as consisting of relational processes—socio-semiotic-material events, encounters, and interactions that produce and reproduce the world anew in every moment. Of the modern art forms, I suggest that it is cinema—the art of the moving image—that comes closest to depicting reality itself, because reality is always in motion, always in a process of becoming. Cinema not only mirrors and represents reality but also shadows, extends, reshapes, and transforms it. Describing how cinema does this, and how different kinds of cinematic works do it in different ways, is the task of this book.

This book's argument takes its structure from American philosopher C.S. Peirce's categorization of things into their "firstness," "secondness," and "thirdness." Respectively, these refer, at their most basic, to a thing as it is in itself, which is its purely qualitative potency—or, in Peirce's words, its *firstness*; a thing in its actual, causal and existential relation with another thing—its *secondness*; and a relation between these two as mediated by a third so as to form an observation or logical or relational pattern—its *thirdness*. Following these three categories, the argument I present can be visualized as three interlocking rings, with each of the rings in turn consisting of three intertwined braids. The three rings correspond to (1) the *film-world*, which is the world that a film makes available to viewers, (2) the *cinematic experience*, which is the way that world is encountered by an actual viewer in the experience of watching and responding to a film, and (3) the *context of socio-ecological relations* within which a film is made, shared, encountered, and made sense of, and which is in turn changed by the experience.

Let us take these and break them down into further triads. Cinema, I argue, produces and discloses worlds. It is cosmomorphic: it provides for the morphogenesis, the coming into form, of worlds. Following Peirce's triadism, I distinguish among three dimensions of a film-world: its *object-world*, which expresses cinema's "geomorphism," its taking on the form of a seemingly stable, material-like world that is there, given for agents like us to act within; its *subject-world*, which is its "anthropomorphism," the world of those who are recognized—and who recognize themselves—as active subjects and agents shaping their lives within it; and its *life-world*, the "interperceptive" and "biomorphic" world of things that are lively and dynamic, that see and hear and respond to one another, and that are constituted by an interactive to and fro between subject- and object-making. This is the first ring of our three-ring circus.[1]

The second ring, the cinematic experience, has three layers as well. There is, first, the thick immediacy of cinematic spectacle, the shimmering texture of image and sound as it strikes us and resounds in us viscerally and affectively; this is the moving image that *moves* us most immediately and directly. Second, there is the sequential unfolding of film's narrative "eventness," the one-thing-after-anotherness that we follow in order to find out what happens next and where it will lead. And third, there is the proliferation of meanings that arise once our already existing worlds are set into motion by what we see, hear, witness, and follow in watching a film or video. I call these three layers or dimensions cinema's *spectacle*, its *sequentiality* or *narrativity*, and its *signness*; and the results of each of these as they impact us are, respectively, the affective, the narrative, and the referential or semiotic.

The third ring consists of the ways in which cinema affects and interacts with the broader ecologies within which films and moving images are produced, consumed, and disposed of. These include cinema's *material* ecologies, such as the physical and biological relations necessary for the production of films and the material impacts of that production; and its *social* ecologies, namely, the social interactions that go into film production and the effects on society of depictions of social actors and groups. But they also include an intermediate realm that I call cinema's *perceptual* ecologies, a realm in which images and sounds, *looks* and *listens*, are exchanged and transmitted among the elements of a world that is communicative by its very nature. Each of these sets of ecologies has been radically altered as moving image media have become established as perhaps the most powerful currency of communication in our world.

This book, then, attempts to understand the nature of the worlds that cinema creates; the ways we are drawn into those worlds, cognitively and affectively, by following their lures and negotiating relations with them; and how those worlds relate to the extra-filmic world—the world that exists *before* cinema as well as alongside it, and one that continues to exist—albeit in a changed way—after cinema has done its work upon it.

An ethical imperative underlies the model of cinema presented here: the imperative to revivify our relationship to the world. In the second of his *Cinema* volumes, philosopher and cineaste Gilles Deleuze argued that the point of cinema is "to discover and restore belief in the world, before or beyond words."[2] Cinema, Siegfried Kracauer said, is our way of "redeeming physical reality."[3] The world as we experience it and the world as cinema portrays it are not two different things—they are *many* different things. But to the extent that a shared world underlies the many, that world calls for a different and more sensitive involvement on our part than that which industrial-capitalist modernity has promoted and practised for quite some time. In the readings of films that make up the bulk of this book—films that cover a broad spectrum, from westerns and road movies to science fiction blockbusters and art films to ethnographic and nature documentaries to animation and experimental films—I highlight films and film styles that have set precedents—and those that have challenged precedents—in the cinematic creation of object-worlds, subject-worlds, and life-worlds. I will be positing a specific synthesis of ideas and approaches by which we might think about film and the world and applying these ideas to the history of cinema.

This book is directed at several distinct audiences. I hope to entice other film theorists and critics to recognize the virtues of an approach to cinema that is ecological in its sensibility and that is rooted specifically in the process philosophies of Whitehead, Peirce, Deleuze, and others. I hope to entice other *eco*critics—and environmentalists more generally—to think ontologically and philosophically and to grapple with cinema in more ambitious ways than they have typically done. I hope to attract students of diverse fields—including film, media, and cultural studies, as well as philosophy and environmental studies—to the task of thinking deeply about the relations among cinema, nature, and humanity. And I aim to satisfy those film lovers who simply want an interesting read about many films they have seen and some they have not seen, and who are willing to take up the intellectual challenge that any novel philosophical approach requires. If this book can provide new tools for taking up that challenge, then it will have succeeded.

ACKNOWLEDGEMENTS

Parts of this book have been presented at numerous conferences and in teaching and speaking venues, and segments have appeared in books and in journals, but all of these have been modified, some extensively, for this publication. Portions of the first two chapters appeared in "The Anthrobiogeomorphic Machine: Stalking the Zone of Cinema," *Film-Philosophy* 15, no. 1 (2011); and in "An Ecophilosophy of the Moving Image," *Ecomedia Theory and Practice*, ed. Stephen Rust, Salma Monani and Sean Cubitt (New York: Routledge, 2012). Three different segments of Chapter 6 appeared, respectively, in "Stirring the Geopolitical Unconscious: Toward a Jamesonian Ecocriticism?," *New Formations* 64 (2008); "The Wound of What Has Not Happened Yet: Cine-Semiotics of Eco-Trauma," *Umelec* 11, no. 2 (2012); and "What Can a Film Do? Assessing *Avatar*'s Global Affects," *Moving Environments: Affect, Emotion, Ecology, and Film*, ed. Alexa Weik von Mossner (Waterloo: Wilfrid Laurier University Press, forthcoming). Brief segments from Chapters 1, 3, and 4 made their way into "Cinema of the Not-Yet: The Utopian Promise of Film as Heterotopia," *Journal for the Study of Religion, Nature, and Culture* 5, no. 2 (2011); and smatterings from throughout the book were first presented in print in "Green Film Criticism and Its Futures," *Foreign Literature Studies* 29, no. 1 (2007); and in *Interdisciplinary Studies in Literature and Environment* 15, no. 2 (2008). I am grateful to the publishers of all of these articles and chapters for allowing me to reprint material here, and to their anonymous reviewers for their most useful comments during the development of those pieces.

I am particularly grateful to those who read, heard, commented on, and contributed to the development of the materials presented herein. They include students in my course "Ecopolitics and the Cinema," which I taught four times between 2005 and 2010, including as an open-to-the-public lecture and film series at the Main Street Landing Film House in Burlington, Vermont. They also include many friends and colleagues in the worlds of ecocriticism, ecomedia studies, film and communication studies, philosophy, and cultural and religious studies, whom I have met at conferences, in online conversations (including through my blog *Immanence*, where many of the theoretical ideas underpinning this book were first presented), and elsewhere. Of these, my conversations with the following have been particularly meaningful: David Ingram, Alexa Weik von Mossner, Pat Brereton, Stephen Rust, Salma Monani, Sean Cubitt, Todd McGowan, Wendy Wheeler, Greg Garrard, Steven Shaviro, Michael O'Rourke, Karin Sellberg, Bron Taylor, Robert Mugerauer, Leo Braudy, Kevin von Duuglas-Ittu (kvond), Paul Ennis, Levi Bryant, Chris Vitale, Mark Crosby, Paul Bains, Jeremy Trombley, Michael Pyska, Tim Morton, Shane Denson, Adam Robbert, Leon Niemoczynski, Jason Hills, Dirk Felleman, and Ian Bogost. I am most deeply grateful to David Brahinsky, who read and generously commented on the entire manuscript in its early stages, to Pat Brereton for his detailed and incisive comments on the near-final manuscript, and to two anonymous referees from Wilfrid Laurier University Press.

I must also express deep gratitude for a Research Opportunities Grant from the University of Vermont, which greatly facilitated the development of this project, and for a one-year sabbatical from that university during the course of the book's writing. In addition, speaking invitations and travel grants from the Rachel Carson Center at Munich's Ludwig-Maximilian-Universität, the Arts at Bucks Lecture Series at Bucks College in Pennsylvania, and the International Society for the Study of Religion, Nature, and Culture helped propel the development of these ideas.

Finally, I am most grateful to the many talented elves and mages at Wilfrid Laurier University Press, whose interest, patience, perseverance, and general helpfulness made this book possible. They include acquisitions editor Lisa Quinn, who shepherded the project from its inception, managing editor Rob Kohlmeier, copy editor *extraordinaire* Matthew Kudelka, marketing coordinator Leslie Macredie, publicist Clare Hitchens, and the Environmental Humanities book series team led by Cheryl Lousley.

This book is dedicated to Zoryán, who will grow into a world whose cinemorphologies I can barely imagine.

1

⁘

INTRODUCTION
Journeys into the Zone of Cinema

From *Stalker* (1979 USSR). Directed by Andrei Tarkovsky. Credit: Media Transactions/Photofest. Shown: Aleksandr Kajdanovsky (as the Stalker).

The cinema was a machine that, exploring the world, preserved it and made it available […], but also a machine that has revealed how the world is becoming ever more indistinct […] a device that offered us images so that they might perpetuate the presence of the real; yet one that, reducing the world to its images, also revealed how it was by then a tender or cruel illusion.

Francesco Casetti, *Eye of the Century: Film, Experience, Modernity*[1]

Evocation, invocation: the two functions of the moving image can be complementary. On the one hand, mechanical evocation of events that have already taken place or that will take place, that belong to other worlds even if these other worlds themselves are films, gods already dead or waiting to be born. On the other, invocation of eternal events (*cf.* Whitehead): perpetual recreation in a state of constant regeneration or decay. In this commerce with the beyond, the film invites us on a voyage along a subterranean river; from our boat we glimpse figures bodied forth from the other world, deformed figures that would be invisible without the darkness. Illuminated figures whose epiphany dwells in the shadows, in shadowy forms whose origin is in forms darker still; shadows bearing the seeds of all forms.

Raúl Ruiz, Poetics of Cinema 1: Miscellanies[2]

If you could only see what I've seen with your eyes.

Replicant Roy Baty, in Blade Runner (1982)

WE LIVE IN A VISUAL WORLD, a world dominated by technologies that have given us the clearest, starkest, and most seemingly objective picture of the universe ever known to earthly life. To an extent never before encountered, we know what things look like. We are surrounded by images and representations, and our imaging capacity extends farther than ever before: outward to the stars, inward to our constituent cells and atoms, across and at a distance toward those we share this planet with, and into our very selves, from so many angles of vision.

At the same time, our inundation and even saturation by images has made it difficult for us to make meaningful sense of the "image-worlds" that, as one commentator has put it, "cover the planet like a sheath." These image-worlds make up a "bath of sounds and pictures"—one that simultaneously connects us to others around the world and distances us from those close by, that communicates more information than humans have ever amassed in one place even as it renders us dependent on experts to interpret that information for us.[3] Information is never purely visual, but visual and *televisual* media are at the core of information's spread. Films and cable television, video and computer games, webcams and streaming video, global satellite imagery, technologies enabling the visualization of atoms, cells, internal bodily organs, and galaxies—all of these stream together in a televisual sea of images and sounds.

Historians and philosophers have long associated the predominance of visuality, our contemporary "ocularcentrism," with the emergence of the modern world. Humans have always told stories, and visual representations have often been used to project those stories across the vast universe—the stars and planets, the mysteries of the earth and the depths of the sea. But most societies have, of necessity, lived in close relation with their physical surroundings. Where social hierarchies and empires have arisen, spreading systems of rule over large distances, these have required techniques for mastering space. This is what the development of linear-perspectival representation in fifteenth-century Europe gave that continent's rising maritime powers. Linear perspective made it possible to accurately represent landscapes as they were seen by stationary observers. This facilitated the development of navigation and mapping techniques that led to the conquest of space and the colonization of new lands—lands that were in turn represented as empty spaces to be mapped, measured, and carved up according to the distributive logic of colonization. It also contributed to the development of a scientific gaze, which shifted the European cosmos into a much more distinctly visual or optical register. Perspective acted, in effect, as midwife to the birth of modernity—a modernity that, philosopher Martin Heidegger argued, has given us "the world as picture."

As a result of this shift in sensory orientation, the world we live in is no longer structured according to the meanings and values ascribed to its constituents—in the way, for instance, that God was granted topmost place in Medieval religious iconography, with angels and archangels congregated below him and with humble humans somewhere lower but still above the animals and underworld beasts. It is structured, rather, as it is seen—measured and parcelled out according to a geometrical grid: it is a world viewed with a detached and external, seemingly objective eye. Vision, according to this model of the neutral observer, distances and objectifies: it turns things into objects and renders them passive, inert, manageable, and controllable. What colonial cartography did to territory, it has been argued, the "magisterial gaze" of nineteenth-century landscape art did to the American West, and pornography and the "masculine gaze" does to women today.[4]

This view of visuality as objective, or objectiv*izing*, and at the same time as controlling, as an exercise of power masquerading as knowledge, is rivalled by a second view that has re-emerged forcefully in recent visual and cultural theory. According to this alternative view, while visuality *can* stabilize the world and render it a manageable and inert object, it can also destabilize, dissemble, and jostle. It can set off oscillations in the viewer and the viewed, flood the subject with emotion, and set off ripples around the object and between the object viewed and the viewing subject. Vision, in other words, can move its beholders in ways that leave nothing stable and inert. Visual images provoke, stir, invoke, incite, inflame, and move to tears. They manufacture desire, possess us and claim us—one only need think of the passions generated by national flags, team colours, or global brands. They give rise to "iconoclashes."

They are alive, and we are caught in their grip. At its extreme, this second view leans toward suggesting that images may even be primary and that we, individual subjects, are their ghostly effects: we swim in a sea of images—visual representations providing "subject positions" for us to insert ourselves into, spatial configurations, habituated bodily comportments and cognitive schemata that shape the ways we think, move, look, and act. Images and pictures set us into motion, channel our emotions, and evoke and redistribute our desires, fears, and affects like so much viscous putty.[5]

Both of these perspectives offer valuable insights to a student of visual media, and they are not mutually incompatible. If, as theorists such as Guy Debord, Jean Baudrillard, and Jonathan Beller have suggested, we live in a postmodern world characterized by an increasing circulation of images, spectacles, and simulacra—copies that no longer bear a clear relationship to any original—the possibility for a just and viable politics is all the more difficult, or at the very least, those politics must take on completely new forms.[6] If image technologies can be used to control what is imaged, this control is gained at the expense of acknowledging the actual dynamic by which one term in the relationship (the seer) escapes being seen and denies its connection with the other term (the seen). Seeing is always a relationship, and even if the audience receiving the camera's view is not seen by those subjected to the camera's gaze, the world today, with its global circulation of images, is leaving fewer and fewer places for either to remain hidden from the other. We see our television networks' versions of what *they* are doing over *there* (in Syria, Pakistan, Somalia, or China); then someone "over there" finds out what we are seeing and saying and speaks back to us; then someone "here" returns their call. The circulation between here and there creates a ripple of energy that is affective—emotionally impacting and generative of action—and that flows in both or several directions at once. We are in danger of drowning in a sea of images, spectacles, and simulacra; yet at the same time, our audiovisual media are opening up new possibilities for patching together cognitive life rafts, as well as providing new materials for stitching together, on an ever more global scale, creative and affective alliances.

If paintings, pictures, and photographic images move us, then *moving* images, from Thomas Edison's Kinetoscope to silent and sound films to YouTube videos replicating at near light-speed across computer terminals around the planet, move us further, projecting our imagination more extensively across the territory of the world. They draw viewers into their movement and engage us in the storyline—in the actions and reactions unfolding in and through and around the places and characters portrayed. They immerse us in the flow of sensations felt or imagined in the viewing—in the flow of sounds, words, bodily movements, and performative gestures as these are received by us from the images viewed on movie screens, televisions, computer terminals, and portable media players.

And if moving images move us, those movements unfold in a series of contexts—that is, in relational ecologies that connect us all the way back to the places from which their raw materials were sourced and where they were crafted into manufactured works. And all of this takes place through a process that moves from minerals to photographic chemicals, plastics, and silicon chips, to shooting locations and sets, to editing suites and film distributors, who deliver images to screen and desktop, where they resonate within us so that we subsequently insinuate them into conversations, symbolic narratives, figures of speech, and bodily gestures modelled on screen heroes and heroines. These ecologies entail the material production and consumption of those produced images; the social or intersubjective relations of people whose efforts shape and inform those images; the people and things portrayed or represented by them; those delivering, receiving, interpreting, and being moved by them; and the cognitive, affective, and perceptual relations connecting bodies, sensations, desires, sensory organs, and media formations.

While each of these categories overlaps and interacts with the others, distinguishing among these three sets of ecologies—the material, the social, and the perceptual—will keep us from losing the distinctiveness of each of these layers of the world around us. Calling them "ecologies" is intended not only as an echo of the science of relations between organisms and their environments interacting somewhere out "in nature," but also as a reminder that the nature "out there" is always "in here" as well.[7] To produce a film or video is always to take and shape materials that set off wide arcs of impact in their production and in the trails they leave behind, from the waste products stuffed into landfills around the planet to the trails of desire and movement they may elicit toward the places portrayed—say, in the scenery of a western, a national epic, a landscape documentary, or an advertisement for a place in the sun or a vehicle to drive us there. Nature *as an idea* is always with us in each portrayal of people onscreen where there is any suggestion of how things should be or once were, of how the world has changed (moving us, the story often goes, away from what's natural and good), and of how some of us—men, women, children, whites, blacks, natives, suburbanites, blue-skinned aliens, or talking cats—live or ought to live in relations of greater or lesser proximity with "the natural" than others. There is, finally, the nature of perception itself: the making sense of images, the systemic networks of imagery in circulation, perception in motion, emotion in excitation, and the cognitive and bodily fields that connect individuals and communities as much as they divide them internally and externally.

Cinema as World-Making

This book presents an account of cinematic experience based in its relationship to these three co-implicated layers of the world.[8] The model I present and develop is grounded in the experience of viewing a movie, which in its essence is an organized sequence of moving images. To its viewers, a film presents a finite series of sequentially organized visual and auditory moments or events—a continuous series of moving sound-images, things that happen before us as we watch. These, in turn, are composed of more basic elements, such as (depending on how we parse them) shots and sequences, signs and signifiers, the flicker of light or pixelation of data on a screen, and so on. And they are organized into generalizable braids or threads. These are, minimally, a title reflecting and evoking some organizing idea, but typically they include a set of characters and events, scenes or episodes, an overarching narrative, and a set of connections—which bring with them a set of expectations—to broader contexts such as generic conventions, recognizable authors and actors, geographic places and historical events, and viewing conditions past and present. A film itself is finite in that it has a beginning and an ending, even if the beginning is missed or if sleep obscures the ending. And between these two boundaries the world of the film unfolds in temporal sequence, if not necessarily a linear or chronological one. Viewers of a film enter and follow along into the world of the film in ways that are specific to their own expectations, motivations, and unconscious predilections, and their engagement is always a negotiated one. But when a film works on an audience, that audience is taken to places within the world opened up by the film.

Because cinema is a *visual* temporal-sequential medium, it takes us places through what it shows us. Because it is an *auditory* temporal-sequential medium, it takes us places through what it sounds and speaks to us, auditorially, musically, and linguistically. Within these parameters there is an almost infinite set of possibilities for how cinema can combine its visual and auditory elements into spectacle and narrative, arrange its temporal and spatial coordinates and the complexities of relations between them, and otherwise build its filmic world. Each such world is structured by a set of dimensions or parameters of meaning and affect—dimensions along which viewers' cognitive and affective responses, our thoughts and our feelings, are engaged and set in motion.

Cinema, then, is a form of world-production or, as Heidegger called it, of *poiesis*, the bringing-forth of a world. It is *cosmomorphic*: it makes, or takes the shape of, a world, a cosmos of subjects and objects, actors and situations, figures moving and the grounds they move upon. For something to be such a world, it must have structural dimensions holding it in place or, better, keeping it in motion. The physical world has its three dimensions of space (up–down, left–right, forward–back) and a fourth dimension of time. Similarly, cultural worlds, those made up of meanings, values, and practices, are held together through structural oppositions. These oppositions are typically the sorts of binary pairs or categorical sets that have been identified by structural analysts and their post-structural heirs in countless studies of cultural texts and narratives. Fictional worlds are simplified yet intensified versions of actual cultural worlds. Classical Hollywood westerns, for instance, commonly feature a dimension or axis of virtue, with "good guys" pitted against "bad guys"; an axis of stability, as seen in the search for order, community, and the settled cultivation of land, versus disruption, chaos, and wilderness; and others pitting East against West, cowboys against Indians, men as distinct from women, and so on. These sets of polarities do little on their own. It is what the film *does* with them—how it sets them into motion, combining and overlaying them with and against each other in novel and engaging ways—that makes it possible for the film's narrative to generate the tensions and resolutions that structure an enjoyable film experience for its viewers.

Structuralists have focused on describing a cultural object's narrative in terms of its dependence on such structuring oppositions; other approaches to film—including psychoanalytic, cognitive, and Deleuzian analyses (those inspired by philosopher and cineaste Gilles Deleuze)—have delved into the affective dynamics that draw viewers into the cinematic experience. In effect, viewers are drawn into the filmic world's structural and relational dimensions or "axes." A viewer's movement along the axis of virtue might follow that viewer identifying or empathizing with an apparently virtuous character (played by, say, John Wayne or Sean Penn) only to experience tension or discomfort as that character is seen to cross a line between virtue and vice. In the narrative's negotiation of such tensions—as for instance when a gangster movie's lead character struggles to balance familial obligations against the expectations of mob leaders—any such structural dimension may become affectively charged in a positive, negative, or morally ambivalent way. Boundary lines become charged in a way that draws viewers' emotional and affective investments into the world of the film, and when these intersect in novel ways, viewers experience the distinct forms of tension and pleasure that films are so effective at generating.

Three particular dimensions—spaces making possible certain vectors of movement—along with the respective forms of boundary making and negotiating they entail, are the focus of this study. The first of these I call the *geomorphic* dimension of cinematic experience, because it deals with cinema's production of territoriality, of hereness and thereness, homeness and awayness, public and private spaces, alluring destinations and sites of repulsive abjection—the objectscapes that make up the world and the ways these frame, envelop, highlight, and mark the action of a film narrative. If films produce worlds, this productivity is rooted to some degree in a reproduction of the existing pre-cinematic or "profilmic" world. But cinema only reproduces fragments of that world, features or elements of it disconnected from their original milieu and reconnected to form a new, cinematic one. If the cinematic experience is a form of journeying, the world produced through cinema is one in which there is a *here*, a starting point, and a *there*, which can be an ending point, or a place journeyed to and returned from, or some complex mixture of the two. The world outside the film already has its many uneven textures of meaning and value—centres and peripheries, places of power and marginal hinterlands and backwoods—but films, in displaying and beckoning us into cinematic worlds that refer to places in the "real" world, charge these uneven geographies with film's conjuring magic, amplifying differences or minimizing them, strengthening stereotypes or challenging them. Cinema's powerful production of worlds in relation to *the* world has been assessed, here and there, by students of media geography and of cultural productions of identity, nationalism, empire, and globalization, but rarely have these assessments been brought into the centre of film theory. This is something I will endeavour to do here, particularly in Chapter 3.

Second, because film, with its "illusion" of movement among objects and images, shows us things that see, sense, and interact, and that therefore appear animate, it is *biomorphic* or *animamorphic*. It produces the sensuous texture of what appears to be life—an interperceptive relationality of things, which span a continuum from the barely alive to the recognizably social. With their speaking animals and monstrous hybrids, the animation and horror genres, in divergent ways, specialize in a kind of "animamorphism" that blurs boundaries between humans and living or lifelike non-humans. Insofar as film is primarily visual, it is specifically the *optical* axis, comprising the relationship between seer and seen, subjects and objects of the act of seeing, that is central to film's meaning and impact. Film is seen by its viewers, so in an obvious way we are its unseen subjects; our existence is factored into film by scriptwriters, producers, and distributors, but when we watch, we remain unwatched. This subjectivity, however, is far from straightforward. At its most elemental, film is the result of the camera's seeing of the world. Filmmakers from Dziga Vertov to *cinema verité* documentarists and experimental filmmakers have strived to turn the camera into an instrument of pure vision, a *Kino-Eye*, or into a note-taking pen or *caméra-stylo* capable of documenting the struggles of real people and of raising these into public consciousness. But the camera is never free to explore on its own; it is always an instrument of an individual filmmaker or, more commonly, a diverse and fractal production collective. Film also shows us people (and sometimes other beings) seeing a world. More than a static photograph or painting, which may include eyes that are looking somewhere or at something, film shows us eyes—and then it shows us what those eyes are seeing. If those eyes are seeing another pair of eyes, the back-and-forth movement between the two sets becomes a visual or optical circulation that, interrupted or augmented by the (invisible) cinematic apparatus, sets up a series of lines of sight in temporal and spatial relationship with each other and with us, its viewers. At its most basic, this becomes the "shot–reverse shot" combination that is . the standard building block of classic Hollywood cinema, which cognitivists have argued is as close as anything to being a cinematic universal.[9] In effect, film becomes a tool *for* seeing and for learning *how* to see a moving-image world. Examining these visual and interperceptual dynamics in films as diverse as ethnographies, self-reflexive documentaries, and experimental films, will take us well beyond any simplistic understanding of "the gaze" (or, for that matter, the trained ear) and allow us to consider the different ways in which film shapes our seeing and sensing of the worlds it produces and, in turn, of the world we live in. This biomorphic dimension of film will be the focus of Chapter 5, but articulating film's biomorphic dynamism is a central task of the book as a whole.

Third, because film shows us human or human-like subjects, beings we understand to be thrown into a world of circumstance and possibility like us, it is *anthropomorphic*. It produces subjects more like us and those less like us, characters and character types we relate to in varying degrees. This third register is that in which the human and recognizably social is distinguished from the non-, in-, sub-, or other-than-human, and in which the "cultural" or "civilized" is distinguished from the natural, wild, savage, alien, barbaric, or monstrous. It is this production of an understood boundary between humans and the non-human that philosopher Giorgio Agamben has called "the anthropological machine" because it continually churns out a category of "the human," even as this category changes in relation to the technologies and practices that inform it, challenge and threaten it, and disperse its benefits unevenly across the social world.[10] Those deemed human benefit from the designation, while those deemed less than human, be they animal and beastly, or savage, mad, or criminal (with their humanity suspended as a penalty for deviant behaviour), do not. Furthermore, distinctions between different groupings of humanity are always being drawn and redrawn to populate the terrain between the polar terms, with, for instance, women, non-whites, and indigenous peoples being posited as closer to nature than white European males. By calling this productivity "anthropomorphic," I do not mean that it extends human characteristics to non-human entities, but rather that it posits certain qualities as normatively human and thereby creates the human, the *anthropos*, as distinct from the rest of the animate and inanimate world within which it continually emerges. Chapter 4 in particular will look into this production of a set of relations defining *our* humanity, *others'* humanity, and the relations between both and the non-human nature that is understood to precede and delimit them.

Describing film's dimensions in this way sounds more "social constructivist" and representationalist than I intend. That is, it suggests that what matters is whether and how certain objects are assigned to one category and others to another, as if the production of these three categories were equivalent to cinema's production of a world, with that world being simply another representation of how things are. But this is not exactly my goal. Rather, the crucial difference between the geomorphic and the anthropomorphic is that the first pertains to the way in which a world is presented *as given*, while the second pertains to the way in which a world is presented *as open to action and change*. Put more forcefully, the first presents the world *as givenness*, while the second presents the world *as agency* or capacity for action and creativity. The object-world, in other words, is the way it is; it is the world that we take to be objectively present, capable of being transformed or acted upon, but not itself capable of acting intentionally. The subject-world, on the other hand, is open to the actions of a subject; it is *about* this very capacity to act and bring about change, about both the experience of agency and the negotiated distribution of that experience within the world. These, together, are two ends of a continuum, between which spreads a field of possibilities within which action and reaction, perception and response, take place. In this sense, the geomorphic, biomorphic, and anthropomorphic are not distinct layers of the world. Rather, the geomorphic, or *objectomorphic*, and the anthropomorphic, or *subjectomorphic*, are two ends of a stretched continuum that is itself made up of interperceptivity and interactivity. It is here, in the middle, where the action of world-making takes place—which is why the term *animamorphic* is perhaps more resonant than *biomorphic*, since it suggests an animacy, an interactivity, the to-ing and fro-ing of open encounter, that the latter does not necessary entail. This space within which the subject–object continuum opens up is, finally, one that takes place in every image, every moment of cinematic world-making. It is, therefore, one that can be remade in every instant. Alternatively, it is one that can be fixed and strengthened over the course of a film and, subsequently, over the course of countless films, genres, and traditions of moviemaking and viewing.

Much of what follows will examine the ways these three dimensional axes or dynamics interact in the cinematic experience. Though these are not the only dimensions along which cinema works, each of them is central to what cinema is and does. Because cinema *shows us things*, it works in the registers of opticality, audiality, and interperceptivity. It produces a world that we see and hear; it sets up a series of relations of seeing and being seen, hearing and being heard, feeling and being felt. In the process it tells us what seeing, hearing, and feeling *are*. Because cinema shows us *places* or *objectscapes* (in specific kinds of sequences), it sets up a "background geography" of relations between the places it shows and the movements and distances between them. And because it shows us *subjects* and *subjectscapes*—beings we understand to be experiencers of the world and actors within it, like us to a greater or lesser extent—it is "subjectomorphic," which means that it takes on or provides the elements of subjectivity, recognized by us as the capacity to act and to *become*. In humans this latter quality tends toward "anthropomorphism," just as, for dogs, subjectivity is really a kind of "canomorphism," for dolphins it is "delphimorphism," and for birds, "avimorphism." The point is that it involves a recognition of one's own and others' capacities to act toward the actualization of potentials.

Together, these three morphisms, these related morphogenetic, or form-generating, registers, produce a world that is seemingly objective and material at one end, subjective and experiential at another, and interperceptual in the middle: a world of subjects, objects, and things in between. One could say that film, like other forms of world-making, is *subject/objectomorphic*: it produces a world for us that is at once subjective and objective, made up of both "subjectivating" and "objectified" entities, a world suspended between the poles of agency and conditionality, becoming and being, openness and givenness, featuring a range of potential interactive entanglements on the continuum stretched out between these poles. Put another way, there are things that interact with us and that in so doing model the possibilities for our own actions; and there are things that are simply there for us to act upon. The first are the subjects, the second are the objects; both, however, are "there for us" in particular shapes and formations. But then there are the things we are not sure of, which at the outset—say, at the hypothetical zero point before an infant learns to distinguish between them—include everything. If life is a process of taming the open wildness of the "blooming, buzzing confusion" (in William James's words) that greets us as we enter the world (this world, a world, any world), the perspective I develop here is one that insists there is value in finding that untamed openness not only at the outset of things but in their very middle, in each and every moment that makes up the process of living and becoming. This insistence will sound mystical to some, and indeed it is shared with certain mystical traditions of the world, but it is consistent with traditions of philosophy and of science that are well established, if not widely known as such.[11]

Thinking of the world as made up of processes of subject- and object-making, processes that are dynamic, temporal, and relational, is a form of ontological thinking: it involves reflection on the structure of the world, on its fundamental constituents and how they interact. To understand the moving image as genuinely *moving*, and as doing so within a world of relations laid out at multiple levels and scales, from the molecular to the organismic to the social and ecological, will require that we expend a little effort establishing the philosophical and ontological underpinnings of the model applied in this book. That model is one that I call *process-relational*: it is a model that understands the world, and cinema, to be made up not primarily of objects, substances, structures, or representations, but rather of relational processes, encounters, or events. As we watch a movie, we are drawn into a certain experience, a relational experience involving us with the world of the film. In turn, the film-viewing experience changes, however slightly, our own experience of the world *outside* the film. Both of these unfold over time and in the midst of other, broader sets of relational processes, which I will describe in terms of "three ecologies": the material, the social, and the perceptual.

The process-relational model I develop in this book takes its inspiration from a broad range of thinkers, but most especially from Alfred North Whitehead, Charles Sanders Peirce, and Gilles Deleuze. The intent of this book, however, is not primarily to develop a philosophy of the cinema, but to apply it in ways that reveal film's potentials for articulating interesting and innovative socio-ecological meanings and capacities. Films, I will argue, can *move* us toward a perception of the world in which sociality (or the anthropomorphic), materiality (or the geomorphic), and the interperceptual realm from which the two emerge are richer, in our perception, than when we started. This goes against the claims of those who have argued that technological mediation is more a part of the world's ecological problem than of its solution.

It will be the task of Chapter 2 to delineate the place of cinema within the "three ecologies" and to develop the process-relational model of the film experience that underpins the book. For now, it is enough to point out that a process-relational model takes a film to be not just what comes out of the studio or what is visible on a screen. Rather, a film *is* what a film *does*. And what it does is not just what occurs as one watches it. It is also what transpires as viewers mull it over afterwards and as the film reverberates across the space between the film world and the real world, seeping into conversations and dreams, tinting the world and making it vibrate in particular ways, injecting thought-images, sensations, motivations, heightened attunements to one thing or another, into the larger social and ecological fields within which the film's signs, meanings, and affects resound. To understand the socio-ecological potentials of a film—its capacity to speak to, shape, and challenge the sets of relations organizing the fields of materiality, sociality, and perception, the three ecologies making up the world—we need to be able to conceive of these as being connected, open-ended, and dynamically in process, with ourselves implicated in the processes by which they are formed. This is the goal of the process-relational, socio-ecological approach presented in this book.

To understand the cinematic experience, it is also hardly enough for an analyst to watch films and analyze them as if such understanding were an objective science. It is important also to study the reception of films by audiences, including the different reactions and interpretations of different audiences, the ways in which these reactions change over time, and the various ways in which they infiltrate and affect thinking, sentiment, and action long after a film has been viewed. The later chapters in this book, with their close readings of specific films and genres, will delve into audience responses as well as critical analyses, though the audience research underlying this book is necessarily limited. My hope is that the concepts will prove useful and inspiring for others to do precisely that kind of work. Before further developing the theoretical underpinnings of this approach, which is the task of the next chapter, it would benefit us to examine a film that can serve as an inspirational paradigm for the model I will develop.

The *Stalker* Effect: Stalking the Cinema, Tracking the Psyche

In *The Solaris Effect: Art and Artifice in Contemporary American Film,* Steven Dillon reads recent American cinema through a prism modelled after the relationship between film and fantasy presented in Andrei Tarkovsky's 1972 film *Solaris.*[12] Tarkovsky's film, like Steven Soderbergh's 2002 remake of it, portrays a space station circling around a planet that seems to materialize the contents of its human visitors' dreams and nightmares. Dillon sees "the archetypal relationship of audience and screen at the cinema" exemplified in the relationship between the astronaut Kris and his dead (by suicide) but seemingly rematerialized wife: "There is photographic reality, sensual and emotional immersion, but also a concurrent knowledge that the reality is all along an artifice, a constructed hallucination." Film, in Dillon's reading, is both real and a "copy, a reproduction, an alien, a ghost." Tarkovsky's self-conscious framing of nature—the rustic setting that is Kris's home on Earth, and the more general parallelism by which the two planets, Earth and Solaris, are set against each other, with the latter effecting a ghostly, nostalgically permeated duplicate of the former—provides, for Dillon, a paradigmatic commentary on the relationship between nature and art. The cinematic representations of nature and home are "built out of desire," and it is this desire, according to Dillon, that is self-reflexively mobilized in the work of filmmakers as diverse as David Lynch, Steven Soderbergh, Todd Haynes, Stanley Kubrick, and (at times) Steven Spielberg.[13]

Dillon's desire to weave a path between nature and simulacrum parallels some of my own thinking in this book. *Solaris*, in particular, provides a useful model for a meditation on nature in a globalized and telecommunications-rich world, a world seeded by Apollo, Sputnik, and the Whole Earth visions (such as Stanley Kubrick's *2001, A Space Odyssey*) that are the collective legacy of those missions into space. The apparently telepathic communication between the planet Solaris and the minds or consciences of its human visitors provides a kind of endorsement of a strong form of Gaia theory, biochemist James Lovelock's and bacteriologist Lynn Margulis's suggestive hypothesis that the biogeochemical makeup of the Earth acts as a single organism. In its more spiritualistic interpretations, Gaia theory suggests that humans may be part of the Earth's nervous system and that the planet may be something like our conscience, so that when we do not abide by our stewardly obligations, our ecological conscience nags at us and haunts our dreams and nightmares.

Where *Solaris* is about the relationship between its human characters and their deepest fantasies and traumas, which are set into motion through the medium of an alien planet—following Dillon, we might call it Planet Cinema—Tarkovsky's later film *Stalker* (1979) reflects more directly on the material engagements of the medium. *Stalker* is loosely based on the novel *Roadside Picnic* by the Russian science fiction writerly duo of Arkadii and Boris Strugatskii. The novel's title refers to the debris left behind by an extraterrestrial visit, which creates a "Zone" where people are known to have disappeared and which contains unusual artifacts and phenomena that defy science. The Zone is cordoned off behind an army-patrolled border, and travel into it is prohibited; but over time, guides known as "stalkers" begin to lead risky expeditions into the Zone's interior. At the centre of the Zone is an artifact that is said to have the power to grant its visitors' deepest wishes. (In Tarkovsky's film version, it is a Room at the centre of the Zone that has this reputed power.) What had been random, forgettable remains for the extraterrestrial visitors, ironically, become sources of wonder and mystery that enthrall their human seekers, in part, no doubt, because of the Zone's very prohibition.

In his adaptation of the novel, Tarkovsky pays little attention to the science-fictional elements, just as he paid only nominal attention to those elements in his adaptation of Stanislav Lem's *Solaris*. Instead, he turns the tale into a metaphysical inquiry. The main character, a stalker, leads two men, known only as Writer (an author) and Professor (a scientist), into the Zone and to the Room that is at its centre. The journey becomes a circuitous perambulation, with the Stalker explaining to the men that in the Zone nothing is as it appears and everything can change from moment to moment. "I don't know what it's like when there is no one here," he says,

> but as soon as humans appear everything begins to move. Former traps disappear, new ones appear. Safe places become impassable, and the way becomes now easy, now confused beyond words.... You might think it's capricious but at each moment it's just what we've made it by our state of mind. Some people have had to turn back empty-handed after going half-way. Some perished at the threshold of The Room. Whatever happens here, depends not on the Zone, but on us.

The Stalker leads the men through tunnels, passageways, and other detours, and these become opportunities for Tarkovsky to visually indulge us in his famous long takes, which are filled with an exquisite attention to the material detail of the landscape where the shooting takes place—in this case, the vicinity of an abandoned power plant outside Tallinn, Estonia. As the Writer and Professor bicker, challenging each other on their relative sincerity, speculating on each other's worldly fortunes and misfortunes and what they hope to gain from the Room, the camera depicts a landscape of time and decay, where vestiges of human activities are slowly being reclaimed by nature. The Stalker recounts the story of his mentor and predecessor, known as Porcupine, who, upon reaching the Room on one visit, wished unsuccessfully that his brother's life be saved, but after his return to the outside world, found himself getting wealthier and even winning a lottery. Realizing, guiltily, that the Zone had read his deeper wish of personal wealth, he committed suicide.

By the time the men reach the Room, the Professor unveils his plan to detonate a bomb in order to destroy it so as to prevent malicious men from gaining the means to carry out evil deeds. In any case, he reasons, if the Room does not actually make dreams come true, it serves little purpose. The Stalker and Professor struggle, and eventually the latter relents. The exhausted men, seated at the boundary of the Room, watch as a gentle rain begins to fall through the apparently dilapidated ceiling (not visible to us). We, the audience, see only the edge of the Room; the camera, it seems, has moved into the Room itself, but all it reveals to us is the men seated in the adjacent room's opening, and drops of rain, lit by sunlight filtering into the Room, in the space between the (unseen) camera and the men. While the Stalker had repeatedly warned the men of various dangers, no harm has come to them, and little evidence has been presented that the Zone in fact defies nature or that the Room contains miraculous powers. The secret, or lack thereof, has seemingly concealed itself. The process of rendering a secret, however—a metaphysical Zone created through prohibition, through narrative, or through cinema—sets up a dynamic between a "here" and a "there"—that is, between an outside world (which we can imagine ourselves more or less sharing) in which these men may have attained respectability but not happiness and a Zone that remains, in the end, a *tabula rasa*, a kind of empty screen onto which the men's, and our, hopes and fears can be projected.

In reality, however, the screen is far from empty. Describing this as Tarkovsky's greatest contribution to cinema, Slavoj Žižek refers to the Russian director's "cinematic materialism," an attempt, "perhaps unique in the history of cinema," to develop a "materialist theology" in which the texture and "heavy gravity of Earth" exerts "pressure on time itself." In Tarkovsky's universe, he writes, "the subject enters the domain of dreams not when he loses contact with the sensual material reality around him, but, on the contrary, when he abandons the hold of his intellect and engages in an intense relationship with material reality."[14] The landscape of the Zone is a landscape in which the remains of human history are in the process of being reclaimed by nature in decomposition. As James Quandt describes it, Tarkovsky deploys

> the four elements like no other director before or since. Swathed in fog and aquatic with spas, needled with drizzle, sluicing, stream-ing, coursing and dripping with rain and snow, indoors and out, Tarkovsky's terrain is terrarium. The mottled forest flora of mold, ferns, lichens, and toadstools traversed by his slow camera are lushly entropic. The crumble and rust, detritus and dilapidation of his watery ruins ... signal both the remnants of past cultures and ecologi-cal calamity.[15]

In a sepia-tone, dream-like sequence, as the three characters have laid down for a temporary rest, the camera pans slowly across the murky, algae-tinged surface of water, showing us objects decaying and rusting on the tiled floor beneath it: a syringe, coins, a mirror, a revolver, an icon of John the Baptist, torn pages from a calendar, mechanical parts. While this presence of the earthy and material in Tarkovsky's films could be taken as mere aestheticism or symbolism, as something added by the filmmaker to embellish the story that is its core, my argument—and Tarkovsky has insisted on this point himself—is that what we see is what we get: the rain is rain, the rust is rust, the mould is mould. They are not mere stand-ins for something other than what we see, but are images and sounds intended to insinuate themselves into our consciousness, resonating on multiple levels that are irreducible to a single interpretation. The Zone, then, can be taken to refer to the meeting ground of images and sounds, as they are organized for us by cinema, with the dense texture of perceptual response, bodily affect, and the multiple layers of memory, desire, and the interpretive capacity that we bring to viewing a film or artwork.

The film echoes, in several registers, the themes I have laid out so far. It represents a journey from the everyday world into a Zone that may be the zone of cinema, or of dreams, of hope and imagination, or of an affective connection with the Earth that subtends both cinema and dreams. The film's world-productivity registers in each of the three dimensions I have discussed. It is *geomorphic* in its production of an imagined geography that relates in several ways to the actual world. This geography is structured around a journey between an outside world, the world of everyday life from which Writer and Professor set out, and the enclosed yet now partially open (to us) world of the Zone. In the precarious, pilgrimage-like movement between the two, the Zone becomes a kind of toxic, abject, and sacred landscape all at once, a liminal space that nevertheless presents itself as matter, seen (but not fully revealed), sounded (if ambiguously), perambulated, but never quite mastered.

It is *biomorphic* in that the film is about the dynamics of seeing and of animate interperceptivity. The bodily movement of the characters across the landscape, first as they pass through the military barricades and later as they encounter the rather amphibious and somehow mysteriously inhabited landscape of the Zone, suggests a certain kind of animatedness of the space in which they move. In the Zone, what at first appears as simple "nature," we are told (by the Stalker) is not at all simple, and appears to be alive in some sense. Tarkovsky's use of black-and-white for most of the scenes outside the Zone and of colour for most of the scenes within the Zone (with exceptions indicating dreams and a certain convertibility between the two worlds) sets up a parallel between the geographic here/there and the respective seeing involved in each. For the Stalker, it would seem, and for us who are encouraged to see the world through his eyes, the world only comes into colour upon entry into the Zone. Yet what is seen and heard is not always clear, and what we see through the eyes of the camera is often different from what we are told, leaving us uncertain amidst divergent interpretations. When the Stalker and Writer emerge from the Dry Tunnel, so named as an ironic comment on the violent watery currents that sometimes engulf it, and discover Professor, whom they had taken for lost, sitting safely enjoying a quiet snack, the Stalker, as Robert Bird puts it, "treats this fold in space as a 'trap' and their survival as proof of the Professor's benevolence, but it is difficult to rid oneself of the suspicion that he [the Stalker] was actually leading the Writer, so to speak, up the garden path. The Stalker's strictures," in this interpretation, "are improvised, not to protect his visitors from unknown dangers, but solely to stamp his authority on their quest."[16] When the men finally arrive at the Room, the prize of their difficult journey, it becomes clear that the prize is no prize at all; we, the viewers, do not even see the Room, and the men refuse to enter it or simply lose their motivation to do so. Yet Tarkovsky draws our attention to material reality—the raindrops and sunlight, the clouds of dust spreading in the water from the pieces of the dismantled bomb the Scientist discards into the pool at the entrance to the Room—so that if we are not sure whether what we see is real, what we do see clearly *matters*.[17]

The film's *anthropomorphism*, or subjectomorphism, lies both in this suggestion of a sentience or will in the non-human world and in the relations among the three men and the film's more peripheral characters. Regarding the three main characters, the film represents them as seekers of something, though it is not entirely clear to us, or indeed to them, what that something is. The Stalker has apparently found enough to make him choose to guide others to the Zone. The film is, in this sense, about the capacity to seek what one believes will grant happiness or satisfaction, and therefore about the power of hope. Insofar as one of the men plans to blow up the Room, it is also about the capacity to foreclose others' capacities for hope. The dialogue among the men invites us to entertain variable positions on the Zone and on the outside world: What is of value in worldly affairs? What would *my* deepest wish be if I was in their position? What is the appropriate role of desire—which is what drives the men on this quasi-spiritual quest—in one's negotiation with the world? Žižek and others have pointed out that Tarkovsky's ethic is the one that Martin Heidegger had described as *Gelassenheit*, a "letting-be" that relinquishes control over the world. The Stalker is often taken to be Tarkovsky's own stand-in as a socially misplaced figure—"the last of the Mohicans" as Tarkovsky described him—who sacrifices himself to lead others to faith in the midst of a faithless world. But even he is driven and tormented, hardly a perfect emissary for an ethic of letting-be. His wife, who is only seen in the film's opening and closing scenes, offers another position regarding the Zone: namely, that it is a distraction from the simple bonds of human love. If the journey into the Zone is the journey into cinematic art, then Tarkovsky may be suggesting that art may ultimately be irrelevant; and, at the same time, not so. Her role; that of their mute child, an apparent mutant who demonstrates what appear to be telekinetic abilities; the black German shepherd met on the journey and brought back to the Stalker's home; and the nature of the Zone itself to the extent that it seems to have a mind of its own—all of these play a role in the film's production of a subject-world.

It is in the relationship between the film-world and the extra-cinematic world, however—and particularly in the material conditions and political-ecological resonances surrounding the film during its production and for years following its release—that the more specific significance of the film becomes evident. Produced during the late Brezhnev era of the Soviet Union, its theme resonated on several levels with its Soviet audiences. In a perceptive account of these meanings, Žižek has noted several analogies to the Zone: the Gulag, a carceral territory set aside for political prisoners (which was in fact sometimes referred to as "the zone"; the Stalker's shaved-head appearance is much like a zek's, or prisoner's); the possibility of technological catastrophe, as emblematized by the 1957 nuclear accident at Chelyabinsk in the southern Urals; the walled-off West, and in particular West Berlin, access to which was prohibited for most East Germans and Soviet citizens; the secluded domain of the Communist Party *nomenklatura*; and a territory, such as Tunguska in Siberia, that had been struck by a random "act of God" (in its case a meteorite). Hungarian critics Kovács and Szilágyi interpret the Zone as "the Secret," that is, as a taboo area of memory that any social order requires in order to maintain its authority, while Robert Bird adds to this list of suggestive parallels the Battle of Stalingrad, "where soldiers stalked through ruins, crawling over the dust of bombed-out buildings, only to be confronted by incongruous reminders of the civilization that reigned there so recently."[18] Following its Cannes premiere, the film was commonly perceived by Western critics as a barely veiled critique of the Soviet regime, though Tarkovsky judiciously denied any such intent.

After the 1986 Chernobyl nuclear accident, the film took on even greater resonance. The Chernobyl disaster led to the almost immediate death of several dozen people, the radioactive contamination of large parts of Ukraine, Belarus, and Eastern (and Western) Europe, the evacuation of tens of thousands of people from an area some 30 kilometres across, and a legacy of radioactivity-related diseases and illnesses affecting thousands. The evacuation area around Chernobyl was called "the Zone" (as was a later film by Ukrainian director Yuri Illienko, *Swan Lake—The Zone,* which riffed on both Chernobyl and the Gulag), and unofficial tour guides to the evacuated area referred to themselves as "stalkers." Biblical resonances within the film emerged in interpretations of Chernobyl as "wormwood"—the literal meaning of "Chernobyl" and, according to Russian and Ukrainian interpretations of the Book of Revelation, the site of the Apocalypse. A video game called *S.T.A.L.K.E.R.: Shadow of Chernobyl*, created by a Ukrainian design team and now with more than two million copies distributed worldwide and a few sequels, combines all of these themes and adds its own mutants, physical anomalies, radioactive wastes, and more.[19] The film, then, served as a source of imagery and as a template for the hopes and fears of Soviet citizens in the wake of an ecological catastrophe, a catastrophe that catalyzed an environmental movement that was to contribute powerfully to the demise of the Soviet Union itself.[20] In its often cited prescience, *Stalker's* cinematic materialism can thus be taken as both a symptom and an affect-laden carrier of hopes and fears that would ultimately bring the Soviet Union to its end.

The making of the film contributed to this layering of political and environmental overtones. It was filmed twice, both times under challenging conditions, since Tarkovsky was considered somewhat of a dissident and was not always allowed to film what he wanted; yet the respect and international admiration for his work provided him a measure of protection. The first version of the film was destroyed during processing. Rumours circulated that it was destroyed by Soviet censors, though it seems likelier to have been a matter of ineptness and defective film stock.[21] It took several months for Tarkovsky to convince Mosfilm, the state filmmaking agency, to fund and allow a refilming, which they did on the principle that this was not the same film but a sequel to the (missing) original. Tarkovsky later conceded that this was fortunate, since the second version veered even further away from the science fiction themes into the metaphysical. Both productions took place in and around an abandoned Estonian power plant and downstream from a chemical plant that, unbeknownst to the crew, was releasing toxic pollution into the environment in which they would spend months filming. At one point, the film shows foam floating inexplicably on the river; and at another, it shows snow—reportedly a form of chemical fallout—falling in summertime. The penultimate scene of the Stalker and his wife and child walking home shows, in the background, a power plant that in retrospect eerily prefigures the Chernobyl nuclear plant, and that represents the Soviet industrial sublime at its most uncanny. The presence of toxins in the water and air left its effects on the bodies of the film crew: several crew members reported allergic reactions during the filming, and a number, including the actor Anatolii Solonitsyn, eventually died prematurely from cancer and related illnesses. Tarkovsky himself died of cancer of the right bronchial tube in December 1986, the same year as the Chernobyl accident, at the age of fifty-six. His wife died of the same cause twelve years later.[22]

The film is often compared to *Solaris*. The Zone is a space of nature, prohibited and thus set apart from "the world," but it, or the Room at its centre, exercises a magnetic or strongly ambivalent pull on the psyche. Similarly, the ocean that covers the surface of Solaris exercises a powerful effect on its human visitors, who remain locked in its orbit as if they are compelled by it to relive their deepest traumas. Both seem to trigger an encounter with conscience, a conscience that is shown to be inter-human (dealing with the ethics of how we relate to others) but that is also suggested to be ecological (the ethics of how we relate to nature and the cosmos). The Zone, and the zone within which the planet Solaris exercises its hold on its human visitors, in this sense may be taken to represent an Other within the individual or collective psyche, but an Other made up of the ethical and material relations and emotional entanglements that confront individuals and force them to face their pasts and account for their lives, loves, failures, and misgivings. Both films also suggest that nature— though in *Solaris* it is the nature of another planet—may be an active and even sentient agent, one that precedes us and that in some sense gives rise to us, but also one that follows us and covers us over, as earth covers earth in its sedimentation of memories, meanings, and elemental cycles. In the case of *Stalker,* the long takes and camera movements portray a visceral gravitational pull toward the Earth, as Žižek describes it. In *Solaris*, this is represented both by the apparent pull toward the planet's surface (no longer resisted by Kelvin in the near-psychedelic climax of the film, and more so in Soderburgh's remake) and by Kelvin's seemingly real reminiscences of his rustic earthly home, which is revealed in the end to be floating on an island in the ocean of Solaris.

Ultimately, the meaning of the Zone, like that of Solaris, is left open. And it is this semiotic underdetermination, this openness to interpretation combined with a resonant use of imagery and cinema technique, that makes it a particularly good example of film's ability to produce multiple meanings and affects. The Zone may be extraterrestrial in origin, supernatural, or simply natural. It may represent the archetype-laden depths at the centre of the psyche, in a Jungian interpretation, or the unrepresentable and ungraspable void at its core, in a Lacanian one (the difference between the two will be discussed in Chapter 6). It may represent the sheer contingency at the heart of life, a contingency that haunts us and that reminds us (in a Buddhist interpretation) that our grasp on our very selves is illusory, fleeting, and ultimately empty of self-sufficient existence—that is, the kind of existence we can hang on to and keep separate from the ever-passing flux and flow of experience. Or it may be taken, in more conventionally Christian terms (which, in its Eastern Orthodox form, is the tradition closest to Tarkovsky), as the call of conscience in the midst of material grasping and social pretense. To the extent that *Stalker* gestures toward a transcendent zone that is outside the grasping ego, or outside the all-too-human world of civilizational rises and falls, it does this by means of the world itself—by displaying the world in the sheer facticity of its ongoing becoming, florescence, and deliquescence. Cinema works by representation, so to the extent that it can show us the world at the same time as it gestures toward its disappearance, film can make it possible to *think* the interaction between the representable and the unrepresentable.

The journey that takes us, as viewers, into the zone of cinema is much like this, and we are free to make of it what we will (though it is never entirely a matter of our rational choosing). At its best, cinema exercises a compelling tug on the imagination. It charges or magnetizes the psyche in ways that may not be fully evident to our awareness. What we get out of films depends, to a large extent, on our dreams and desires. As in *Stalker*, however, what cinema shows us is real objects, artifacts from the material world: landscapes and places, mortal bodies and organisms, all caught in the grip of the cycle of living, dying, and decomposition. These *shown* worlds—not the fictional worlds portrayed by them, though the two are necessarily related—are intimately involved in the essence of cinema. Cinema is neither a mirror nor a window; it is neither purely reflecting nor perfectly translucent. As *Stalker's* cinematic surface suggests, it mixes opacity with a certain semi-transparency and mirror-like diffraction of the world outside. It captures images and sounds from the material and social worlds, but then it rearranges them, assembling them into new configurations to produce new or different meanings. In the digital era, even the originals are not always originals, yet they are *based* on something original, and built out of elements—glimpses, ideas, neural explosions, gestures, movements of the wrist on a computer mouse, electrons, silicon chips, and visual data bits—as real as any other bits of an ultimately ungraspable earth that provides for the disclosure of worlds, but ever eludes those worlds into self-concealment.

An ecologically inspired ethic of cinema, such as I develop in this book, advocates for greater attention to be paid to the relationship between the worlds produced *by* cinema and the world(s) *from* and *within* which they are produced—worlds that are material and biophysical as well as social and epistemological. In the case of *Stalker,* the extra-cinematic Real includes the centrally managed cultural industry of the Soviet administrative state, under the auspices of which the film was produced, as well as that state's shadow side of suspicion, paranoia, and interest in the paranormal, all expressed in the film and in the meanings it has engendered. (In this sense, the film could be usefully compared to *The X-Files*, a television series I will discuss briefly in Chapter 6.) It includes the world of industrial technology, represented in the film by the power plants both real and fictional, which, as Heidegger suggested, turn the world into "standing reserve," and which were developed to do this with maximal urgency by the Soviet state in its anxious quest to keep up with its capitalist rivals. The Real, then, includes the Cold War system itself, with its race to the moon and its quest for the bomb, which ultimately delivered to us both Chernobyl and the downward, Earth-b(e)aring gaze from Sputnik and Apollo. And it includes the perceptions of filmgoers—among them those who interpreted Chernobyl through reference to the film (and to the Bible)—and the artistic and religious imaginary of late modernism, which could be taken as the encounter of Enlightenment rationalism with its own limits—an encounter into which seep all manner of spiritual and romantic longings.

Tarkovsky himself breathed the heavy atmosphere of late Soviet industrial modernism. We, today, may be inhaling (if not hyperventilating) something distinctly less heavy—the lighter oxygen of transnational, digital, "fast capitalism." Yet the material world featured in Tarkovsky's long takes—in which signs of human history are covered over by the passing of and return to elemental time—is not all that different from our material world, the shadow side of which is also populated with toxic waste dumps, landfills, hypodermic needles, and disfigured icons of various kinds. Siegfried Kracauer subtitled his influential 1960 treatise on film theory *The Redemption of Physical Reality* in part to indicate that cinema is uniquely qualified to record reality in a way that allows its viewers to experience that reality more fully. Cinema can do far more than record reality, and not all of Kracauer's ideas have withstood the test of time, but the ethic of redeeming physical reality remains worth pursuing. While this book makes some dramatic departures from the realist aesthetic promoted by Kracauer, the ideas and interpretive strategies I develop are ultimately aimed at this project of redeeming the material reality of the world, a world that is shared by humans and non-humans, and shaped by both, at a time of precarious relations between them. The virtue of films like *Stalker* is that they attempt to redeem the sidelined, forgotten, or shadow side of material reality, and it is this side that must feature as central in any ecologically minded filmmaking and theorizing today.

The Argument and the Book

This study's central premises, which I have begun to outline, can be summarized as follows.

(1) Images *move;* they affect their viewers and "take us places." Cinematic moving images, through their melding of temporally sequenced visual display and sound, move us all the more forcefully. They take us on journeys—at least on metaphorical or metaphysical journeys—and through the movement they exhibit and elicit, they give shape to imagined or perceived worlds. Cinema is, in this sense, a form of world-production.[23] In the process of creating worlds,

films generate spaces of hereness and thereness, a certain range of projected, potential, or experienced movements into and across those spaces, a certain set of optical, sensorial, and interperceptual relations, and a certain set of agential powers that relate, in some way, to our own power to act in the world.

(2) Cinematic worlds are kept in motion through an interplay of constituent structural dimensions or parameters along which viewers are invited to cognitively and affectively situate themselves and "travel," and along which the tensions and resolutions of cinematic experience unfold. Viewers are drawn, or lured, into cinematic worlds in a multitude of ways. In my analysis, which follows the phenomenological explorations of C.S. Peirce (described in Chapter 2), these can be said to have three main registers. The first of these is the immediate texture of the cinematic experience, the absorptive, spectacular "thingness" of the cinematic event. The second is the sequential thread of filmic narrative, the way in which one thing follows another, and how that thread engages us in making meaning out of how things follow each other. The third is the resonance and referentiality of cinematic elements—sounds, images, words, and combinations of each—in relation to the world that precedes the film while remaining outside it. As a film draws us in, employing each of these registers to variable effect, it opens a series of vectors, or potential movements, along the axes, parameters, or dimensions it supplies. Along these vectors, cinema also constructs boundary or "bifurcation points"—points of tension or intensification, such as the dividing line between humanity and primeval wilderness in *Tarzan, King Kong, Apocalypse Now,* or *Jurassic Park*—and "basins of gravitational attraction" for the movement between and around these boundaries. (These terms are taken from non-linear dynamical systems theory, which I will not develop in depth, but which will feature in my discussion of the human–animal boundary in Chapter 5.)

(3) As suggested in my reading of *Stalker*, films vary in terms of the multiplicity and potency of affective positions or movements that are made available—structurally or by invitation—for viewers to occupy and move through. A film is in principle more open or dialogical when it makes available a broader range of positions with respect to the main vectors of affective engagement it sets into motion. And while the range of variation depends on the type of film being made, this variation is generally a good thing. A film is also more *resonant* to the degree that the images, sentiments, affects, and narrative resources it makes available carry out their work along multiple and more widely distributed lines. The remainder of this book will show a bias toward specific films that accomplish more in these two respects: they have resonated with audiences and have left behind marks of their resonance in the world; or they have made available alternative readings that have resulted

in some interesting conflicts of interpretation; or, in some cases, they have done both.

(4) The worlds constituted through film relate in various ways to the world *outside* cinema. They mirror that world, refract and diffract its meanings, infuse (or diffuse) meaning and aura into (or out of) the people, objects, and places portrayed. They borrow from the non-cinematic world, selecting bits and pieces that are then assembled and fused into temporal sequences. The many and varied forms of cinematic figuration—lighting and shadowing, the expansion and constriction of time and of rhythm, the back-and-forth movement between faces and eyes in the "shot–reverse shot" sequence, the montage splicing one image to the next, the overlaying, underscoring, and propelling of images by sound and music, the use of voiceovers, and all the other features of cinematic world-building—all of these give rise to a world that is different from the pre-cinematic world because it has been articulated, highlighted, extended, compressed, refigured, transfigured, and reshaped.

If cinema produces worlds—or, as Heidegger would say, if cinema *worlds*—then this worlding also sets off resonances, diffractions, and rippling interactions with the world out of which it produces those worlds. Moving images now pervade our everyday lives. The world has become altered, othered from within, by cinema—that is, by the layered and mobile imagery that presents that world to itself, reflects it, diffracts and refracts it. As John Mullarkey argues in *Refractions of Reality*, "Moving pictures move us because movement is what is Real."[24] The world has become a world *of the motion picture*. As the most synthetic of the arts, cinema may bring us closest to the dynamism of the world outside cinema even while it adds dynamism to it.

The relationship between cinema and the world outside cinema includes the ways in which film is a material medium with material effects. Both ends of the chain of cinematic production and consumption are ultimately grounded, and simultaneously resisted, by the self-subsistent and active materiality that Heidegger calls "earth"—a materiality that gives itself to us as territory, as land, as nature, as resource, and that simultaneously takes away from us as time, as death, and as mystery. The relationship between this earth and the filmic world is central to the ecocritical agenda of this book. While my focus will not be primarily on the material impacts of cinematic production, this is certainly one line of research that an ecocritical form of analysis can and should take.[25]

(5) Moving (sound-)images are moving *increasingly* in this era of digital technology, one that is reshaping, transforming, and absorbing the originals, then recirculating and distributing them through all manner of vectors, flows, channels, webs, and nets. This movement of images and affects is reshaping the ways viewers perceive themselves (as individuals and as groups), the world

(including its landscapes, places, nations, civilizations, and ecologies), the earth that subtends them, and the relationships connecting all of these. The forms taken by these relations among cinema (the film-world), affect (perceptual and bodily response), and nature (the pro-filmic and pre-cinematic material world) will be the focus of this study. As the analysis of *Stalker* suggests, cinema stalks the world, shadowing it, refracting it, and changing it in the process. It turns the world into a *stalked* world. This stalking is not necessarily a bad thing. As Tarkovsky's idiosyncratic use of the term indicates, it is also a "raising" of the world into art (as one might raise a building); in Heideggerian terms, it is a raising of the *earth* into *world*, such that culture dwellers like us may find a home in it. This book will explore some of the ways in which cinema stalks the world to co-create *its* worlds for us in the midst of an ultimately unknowable earth that provides support and foundation for those worlds.

My argument will fall somewhere partway between the idea that cinema has reshaped the world, altering our experience of territory (or geomorphy), sociality (anthropomorphy), and livingness (biomorphy), and the more specific idea that while a few great films have done this, most simply follow along or reproduce things without change. Cinema reshapes the world in many directions, and I wish to focus on films, or film capacities, that move things in the direction of a more fluid, more animate, more process-relational understanding of the world.

What follows, in the next five chapters and the mini-chapter that concludes the book, constitutes an exploratory journey toward understanding how cinema, affect, and nature relate to one another. I develop the theoretical foundations of the argument in Chapter 2. These foundations include an account of how and why it is useful to think in threes—with three ecologies (material, social, perceptual), three registers of the cinematic world (geomorphic, anthropomorphic, biomorphic), and three moments in the viewer's experience of cinema (spectacle, narrative, "signness" or "exoreferentiality"). And they include a brief but hopefully sufficient account of the process-relational metaphysics that underpin this onto-epistemological model.

Chapters 3 to 5 are in-depth analyses of the three dimensions of cinematic worlds: their geomorphism, anthropomorphism, and biomorphism. Each begins with an account of how these dimensions emerge in life and follows with explorations of their emergence in film. The first of this trio of chapters is the longest, as it lays out some primary groundwork, including a discussion of Western pictorial representations of nature and how they have helped shape cinematic depictions of landscape and territory. It covers a range of styles of cinematic landscape depiction, from westerns, road movies, and documentaries celebrating or critiquing the "control of nature," to the cinematic pantheism of Aleksandr Dovzhenko and Terrence Malick, to the deconstruction of the gaze in experimental and art films such as Peter Greenaway's *Prospero's Books*. Chapter 4 deepens the analysis of cinema's production of "us" and "them" by probing the ethnographic impulse that can be found in all cinema, but especially that which contrasts cultural groups that are differently positioned with respect to nature. The cinema of "first contact," which depicts the Western discovery of other people—"primitives," "aliens," and other "others"—represents this ethnographic impulse at its most pure. And while this cinema has traditionally been characterized by what E. Ann Kaplan has called an "imperial gaze," there are alternatives to such stereotypical representations. Films discussed here run the gamut from proto-ethnographic films such as *Nanook of the North* to their commercial and more spectacular progeny (such as *King Kong*) through to more recent ethnographies, mockumentaries, postmodern and post-colonial revisionings of encounters between Europeans and Natives, and indigenous productions themselves. The ethnographic metaphor is extended, in Chapter 5, to the perceived boundary between humanity and the animal or wild, a boundary that can be rendered fixed and stable, or dynamic and malleable, and that can be imbued with positive, negative, or more ambiguous valences. The range of films examined here includes popular nature documentaries, fiction and animation features, and films focusing on boundary-crossing individuals such as Timothy Treadwell (*Grizzly Man*) and Mark Bittner (*Wild Parrots of Telegraph Hill*).

While separating these three registers of cinematic "worlding" may suggest that each is autonomous, a process-relational view insists that they are ultimately part of the same process. Carving them into three chapters can only be taken as provisional, since the goal of a process-relational ethic is to render the boundaries fluid and permeable. This means that, in a very real sense, there is no geomorphology and no anthropomorphology—except to the extent that living, relational beings take it as such in their relational, experiential encounters with others. It is these encounters, these moments of experience, that make up the universe. I am making a distinction here between the "world"—which is the perceptual and conceptual *Umwelt*, or life-world, of any given entity—and the "universe," which is simply *what is*, along with the "earth," which is its local variant. The world, in this sense, is the subjectively perceived life-world of meanings, habits, and taken-for-granted assumptions according to which action proceeds (for someone or other). It is a product of semiosis, or meaning-making. For humans, it is always to a large degree intersubjectively shared, though this sharing is never wholly and perfectly

6

rendered between any two individuals. In contrast, the universe (globally) and earth (more locally) make up the sets of relations that undergird and subtend the worldhood of any world.

There are times when relations between a cultural world and the earth that subtends it become fraught and troubled. Ours is such a time. Chapter 6 brings together threads from the previous chapters to focus on the psychodynamics of this fraughtness, or of what we can generically call the ecological crisis. This chapter examines films that deal with the perception or recognition of eco-trauma both directly (as in *The Day After Tomorrow, Children of Men*, and *Avatar*) and indirectly (as in films depicting social dislocation in the midst of environmental "strange weather," such as *Short Cuts, The Ice Storm*, and *Magnolia*). Here I contend with theories of the sublime, Fredric Jameson's notion of the geopolitical, and the "traumatic kernel" at the heart of ecological consciousness. The latter term is taken from Slavoj Žižek's Lacanian film critique, which brings me back to the cinematic materialism explored in the present chapter in relation to *Stalker*. I suggest that what psychoanalysis reads as the psyche, and Žižek as "the Real," can also be read, through a process-relational detour, as "earth," that is, as the set of material and bodily metabolisms and inter-corporeal relationalities that underpin conscious experience and that serve as its material "undergrowth of enjoyment." Returning here to the architectonic of C.S. Peirce, but with deep nods to the image-centred archetypal psychology of James Hillman and the metaphysics implicit in Tarkovsky's Zone, I develop an aesthetics, ethics, and "ecologics" of the "image-event" that will help us think ecophilosophically about the task of viewing and living with moving images. This final chapter concludes with a reading of two recent films, Terrence Malick's *The Tree of Life* and Lars von Trier's *Melancholia,* as lucid examples of a cinema that can be rendered ecophilosophical when approached through the perspective this book develops.

Much of this book assumes a cinema in which, for all the activity within, the journey remains framed within a single arc (from beginning to end) and the visual frame remains singular. Occasionally, however, I refer to some of the ways in which television and digital media are blurring and dissembling such basic reference points. In the afterword, I deal with arguments that we are seeing the end of cinema, or at least the end of film, and that the digital is bringing an entirely new image sensibility upon us. The interconnectedness of the digital media world is creating a new geography; it is geomorphing a technologically mediated world, one that is layering itself onto the pre-cinematic world in a much more complete and complex way than cinema *as a medium of single films* ever did or could. But cinema is not going away; if anything, it is intensifying.

That intensification is making of our world an ever-moving world, but one in which the movement is not merely from here to there, or from a central place toward its peripheries and back. Cinema is motion; life is motion. And with the intensification of motion through the potentialities being unlocked within digital media, it is becoming clear that the universe *has been motion all along*. Where that takes us is up to us. I hope this book offers tools for moving it toward an appropriate *elsewhere* from where it is today.

2

ECOLOGY, MORPHOLOGY, SEMIOSIS
A Process-Relational Account of the Cinema

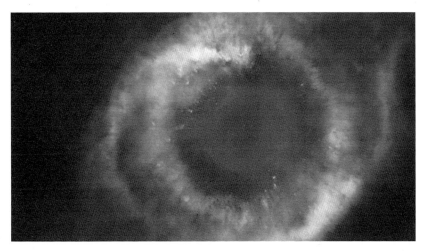

From *The Tree of Life* (2011). Directed by Terrence Malick. Credit: River Road Entertainment/Fox Studios.

The actualities of the Universe are processes of experience, each process an individuated fact. The whole Universe is the advancing assemblage of these processes.

A. N. Whitehead, *Adventures of Ideas*[1]

Subjectivity and objectivity are not only superimposed but endlessly reborn, the one from the other, in a ceaseless round of subjectivizing objectivity and objectivizing subjectivity. The real is bathed, bordered on, crossed, swept along by the unreal. The unreal is molded, determined, rationalized, internalized by the real.

Edgar Morin, *Cinema, or the Imaginary Man*[2]

Activist philosophy concerns the ecology of powers of existence. Becomings in the midst. Creative change taking place, self-enjoying, humanly or no, humanly and more.

Brian Massumi, *Semblance and Event:*
Activist Philosophy and the Occurrent Arts[3]

IN AN INFLUENTIAL ESSAY on the politics of environmental media imagery, cultural theorist Andrew Ross distinguished between "images of ecology" and "the ecology of images." The first category includes the shopworn clichés that populate the modern environmental imaginary:

> belching smokestacks, seabirds mired in petrochemical sludge, fish floating belly-up, traffic jams in Los Angeles and Mexico City, and clearcut forests; on the other hand, the redeeming repertoire of pastoral imagery, pristine, green, and unspoiled by human habitation, crowned by the ultimate global spectacle, the fragile, vulnerable ball of spaceship earth.[4]

As Ross's list indicates, environmentalist visuality typically counterposes a positive or ecotopian imaginary to a negative, dystopian and apocalyptic one. The former inspires, while the latter enjoins us to action or to despair. I will examine some of the cinematic extensions of these tropes in the chapters to come.

The "ecology of images," by contrast, is a term by which Ross intended to capture the much broader kinds of relations—social, economic, political, ethical, and technological—surrounding the production, circulation, and consumption of images. As an example of how one might approach this broader ecology, Ross cited Susan Sontag's argument that photography has, in its effects, reduced the world to "a set of potential photographs" and turned people into "image junkies."[5] The medium, in this case, has changed its users. This broader ecology, however, covers a potentially unlimited terrain, one that it would be helpful to organize into workable categories. I will do this, in what follows, with the help of Félix Guattari's notion of "three ecologies," where the material and the social are supplemented by a third, the mental or perceptual.[6] Cinema is embedded in each of these and affects each in turn. One goal of this chapter is to outline the relationship between cinema and these three ecologies.

But cinema also *produces* a version of each of these ecologies. This is cinema's *cosmomorphism*—its geomorphism, anthropomorphism, and biomorphism— through which it gives us worlds that are material, social, and perceptual in the ways they appear to us. These are, of course, *cinematic* worlds, film-worlds, and their effect is primarily on viewers' perceptions. Through most of this book I will be focusing on this perceptual dimension of cinema, because that is where the essential work of cinema takes place. It is the perceptual, or more broadly the mental, that provides the best opening, the Archimedian hinge, for understanding the power of cinema.[7] A second goal of this chapter is to develop an analysis of this perceptual encounter with cinema, an account of how cinema works on us and draws us into its worlds. Our experience of a film has its own structure, which I will distinguish into three moments. There is, first, the immediacy of cinematic spectacle—the images, sounds, and sensations that are exhibited in our presence. Second, there is the way we are drawn into cinematic narrative, whereby we follow the movement of a story or set of stories as these unfold in time. And third, there is the proliferation of meanings that occurs as we make sense of what we see and hear, bringing our expectations, immediate responses, and previous experiences to the process of interpreting the film we are watching. Cinema is, in this sense, a matter of spectacle, of narrative, and of referential semiosis. While these three moments could be considered consecutive components of any moment of cognition, we experience them simultaneously: they are the three kinds of vectors along which we are drawn into the world of a film.

You will have noticed, by now, a certain fondness for threes in this book: three ecologies within which cinema is embedded, three "morphisms" by which the cinematic world takes its form, and three moments or vectors in the viewer's experience of the film-world. This triadism is inspired by the work of philosopher and logician Charles Sanders Peirce, for whom triads circumvent the kinds of problems that dualities or oppositions tend to ingrain. All three of these triads relate to processes that are relational and dynamic. My analysis of them relies on a philosophical understanding of the world, and of cinema, which I call a *process-relational ontology*. As this framework underpins both the analysis of cinema presented here and the examination of specific films in the chapters that follow, a third goal of this chapter is to elaborate this philosophical framework in sufficient depth to provide a viable foundation for the analyses that follow.

Cinema's Three Ecologies

Cinema, like every artistic medium, is a material process. It requires bringing together material elements both to create the images themselves—strips of light-encoded chemicals, digital laser disks, and the like—and to film the scenes that are rendered in those images. Raw materials are in each case turned into physical objects, which are distributed, experienced (consumed), and released. That consumption, whether we think of it as literal or figurative, takes place in movie theatres, in front of televisions or hand-held viewing devices, on airplanes, in art museums, and elsewhere, and it leaves behind a trail of effects in the material world. These are cinema's material ecologies, which span the entire production cycle from the ecosystems and factories where minerals, plastics, silicon chips, and other resources are extracted, processed, and manufactured, to the locations and sets where narrative ideas and shooting scripts are shot and crafted into cinematic works, which are then distributed and viewed, with waste products emerging at each step of the way.

Cinema is also a social process, one that unfolds among humans, who collaborate in particular ways to produce, distribute, and make use of cinematic images and texts. Cinema's social ecologies include the social relations by which films and their meanings are made, the representations of social life they carry, and the social and cultural uptake and transformation of those meanings in their numerous contexts, from film festivals, multiplexes, and living rooms and bedrooms, to blogs, chat rooms, bodies (gestures, expressions, T-shirts), and dreams. Movies—both their making and their viewing—have long been a way of gathering people together, either for commercially or artistically productive work or for recreation, social mobilization, and other purposes. Commercial and national film industries bring together nations (while setting them apart from one another) and help shape the meanings we find in an increasingly globalized world.

Focusing on the material and the social alone, however, is likely to reinforce the notion that there is a "nature" and a "culture," with an irreducible gap between the two. This habit of dividing the world into two autonomous realms—culture and nature, mind and matter, humans and everything else—is deeply ingrained in Western thought. It is part of what Bruno Latour has called the "modern constitution," a tacit agreement by which social relations are taken to be the exclusively human realm of the socium or the polity, with material "facts" relegated to the sciences that study "nature" and speak on its behalf.[8] A process-relational view rejects this dichotomy. It argues instead that nature and culture are conceptual abstractions by which we make sense of things and that the things we are making sense of are changeable, evolving, and caught within an ongoing exchange of properties. Far from describing the structure of the world, the ascription of the "natural" and the "cultural" emerges out of a rich set of processes by which the world renews itself from moment to moment. To disrupt this nature–culture binary, we need a third, intermediary element that would highlight the dynamic relationality of the first two.

In *The Three Ecologies*, Félix Guattari distinguished among "environmental" or "natural" ecologies, "social" ecologies, and "mental" ecologies. The first two are fairly straightfoward: the first refers to what is commonly called "ecology" (the biophysical), while the second refers to the social, cultural, and human domain. For the third, Guattari drew on anthropologist Gregory Bateson who, influenced by ecology, cybernetics, general systems theory, gestalt psychology, and process metaphysics, defined "mind" as an interactive system characterized by the exchange of information; the latter he defined, in turn, as "difference that makes a difference." Mind, for Bateson, is not located within a person, a brain, or a body; it is immanent to relational systems, circulating within them, as it were. Bateson's work has significantly influenced the field of biosemiotics, which has developed from the semiotics initiated, to an important degree, by the logician and philosopher C.S. Peirce. For both Peirce and Bateson, the living universe consists of relational systems that produce meaning or significance. Semiosis, or sign-production, is in this sense writ through the world "all the way down."[9]

As I argued in the previous chapter, the material and the social, or more precisely the interobjective and the intersubjective, emerge out of an interactive process that consists of a dynamic exchange of affect, perception, and meaning.[10] When things encounter each other, there is an exchange between them, a response or ripple that is affective or "emotional" in nature (as Whitehead argued) and that has to do with a "taking account of," a meaning-making and responding to what is encountered. Between the social and the material, then, is the intermediary register of the mental-perceptual. The idea of a mental *ecology* is intended to suggest that we humans are embodied agents and interpreters of a world that is not only there to be perceived, but also perceptive and communicative in its nature. Perception or mind, understood as the sense- and world-making capacity intrinsic to all experience, is the interactive dimension through which a world comes into being for world-bearing beings. It can be culturally shaped, through the aesthetic and sensory modes extant in a society, but it in turn shapes the interactions of social groups with their environments. An environment is itself comprised of perceptual and communicative relations; from this, it follows that perceptual ecologies constitute the interactive milieu within which the material or "objective" becomes the social and "subjective," and vice versa. That milieu is where sensations and sensory organs, bodies and desires, social groups and mediating formations become connected in specific ways. Perceptual ecologies are the interrelations that arise in the zone between things, the space that Maurice Merleau-Ponty described as the fleshy, interpenetrating *chiasmus* of self and world.[11] They are the spaces of "contagion, contamination and inspiration," as Connolly and Bennett put it, where force and affect flow "across bodies" and are communicated "by looks, hits, caresses, gestures, the bunching of muscles in the neck and flushes of the skin."[12] If we follow the processual ontology suggested by Whitehead, Deleuze, Bergson, and others, and take the universe to be fundamentally active and communicative—experience all the way down—then it is precisely this mental ecology that is central to things, and it is through perceptual experience that subjects and objects, and thus a subject-world and an object-world, are possible at all.[13]

The perceptual or mental realm is not the realm of ideas or meanings *as distinct from* matter. It is the interactive dimension among living things, which are material bodies perceived, or "imaged," and responded to by other material bodies. The word "image" in this sense comes close to the way philosopher Henri Bergson deployed it. For Bergson, the universe is a vibrational whole made up of a stuff that is image, matter, and movement all at once.[14] Humans and other organisms are gaps within this matter-flow, nodes or "centers of indetermination" at which the flow gets momentarily suspended, synthesized, and potentially redirected. We do not simply relay the impacts that strike us, the way a billiard ball passes on kinetic energy to the next billiard ball in a sequence of strikes, losing only a certain quantity of force to friction along the way. We act on those impacts, resist or counteract them, and we do this by virtue of a systemic means of responding to them—a cognitive-affective nervous system, in our case. The perceptual interactions among image–matter bodies are where this action occurs, and it is out of those relations that the specifically material, or interobjective, and social, or intersubjective, dimensions emerge.

With a phenomenon as perceptual as cinema, however, one must keep in mind that the material and the social effects of the medium are autonomous from the perceptual interactions that involve us as viewers. So even though a film may tell us little or nothing about its own production, mineral and chemical substances were moved from one place to another, and mixed together and manufactured into cinematic objects, and material waste was produced in the process. Similarly, what a film shows us may tell us nothing about the social relations that went into its production, such as who had a say in its making and funding, and whether the people or cultural groups portrayed had any influence in their own depictions. All of these relations are interconnected in complex ways. Marxist political-economic analysis would contend that they together make up a "mode of production," a way of organizing the relations among humans, technologies, and ecologies. While culture may be autonomous from the material and economic base of a society, a good case can be made that cinema is—and has been from its outset—intimately linked to the reproduction of capitalist social and ecological relations. In *The Cinematic Mode of Production,* Jonathan Beller argues that cinema is not just related to the late-capitalist mode of production—it is central to that mode. Beller maintains that cinema, defined as the systemic industrial-capitalist organization of "image/consciousness," manages the "attention economy" of its consumers. In the process, it draws us into the circulation of "image-commodities" that structure our identities, our affects, and our sensibilities as consumer-subjects.[15] But

Beller's analysis, like other Marxist analyses, posits such an overwhelming level of coordination between the parts—the material-economic, the social, and the perceptual—that little room is left for understanding how change occurs or how people, individually or in groups, can act to ameliorate the world from within the conditions that determine them. Furthermore, these analyses do not sufficiently discriminate between the studio-centred "classical Hollywood mode of production" and the more hybrid modes—still capital-intensive, but more diverse in terms of funding and distribution networks—that shape film production across the world today.[16] Thus, any project that would articulate forms of creative resistance to "cinematic capitalism" must distinguish between levels, or between moments in the processes that structure the world.

Cinema, then, can be considered in relation to three ecologies. Each of these implicitly suggests criteria by which filmmaking can be judged as contributing to better or worse socio-ecological relations. A useful tool for understanding the process by which cinematic meanings are produced and consumed is the "cultural circulation" model developed by Stuart Hall, Richard Johnston, and other Birmingham School theorists. According to this model, the "cultural circuit" flows through a series of "moments," which include the *production* of cultural products and texts, during which meanings are "encoded" into them; the *texts* themselves, including both their form and content; the *consumption*, reception, use, or "decoding" of their meanings by audiences; and the subsequent *reproduction* of these meanings as they filter into everyday life, which then serves as the ground for further production. At each moment, the object is connected to a larger social and technological world: its production, transmission, and reception are enabled and constrained by available media and production networks, financial capital, and audience mobilization mechanisms, as well as by available cultural discourses, hopes and expectations shaped by recent successes in the medium, and so on. Crucially, as Hall has argued, the moment of decoding does not "follow inevitably from encodings"; rather, it provides audiences with the option of a range of "negotiated" or "oppositional" readings to the dominant reading of a text.[17]

At each moment in the cultural circulation of meanings, critical questions can be raised. Regarding production and distribution, Marxist analysts focus on the political economy of the film industry and on the constraints and possibilities in specific social conditions of film production. The extent to which film production is accessible to the average person serves as a measure of the democratic nature of a society's media ecology. At the level of the text, a variety of analytical traditions have probed the following: the form, the content, and the discourse of film—its representations of gender, race, class, ethnicity, nation, sexuality, power and agency, normalcy and deviance; the generic, semiotic, and ideological codes by which these meanings are mediated; intertextual relations between this film and others of the same genre, author, or cinematic tradition; and so on. And at the point of reception and consumption, ethnographers and audience researchers have asked questions about viewership—for example, how audiences use the media product in their everyday lives—as well as questions about identification with actors, spectatorship, gaze and psychological formation, and the formation and development of specific reception cultures.

To these more generic questions, ecocritical or socio-ecological approaches add several of their own.[18] Regarding production and distribution, ecocritics have asked: What is the ecosystemic impact of the production systems utilized in making, marketing and distributing, exhibiting, and conserving (or eliminating) the film object? Are ecological relations (in terms of resource consumption, production of waste, and effects on socio-ecological relations) taken into account by the producers, and if they are, to what extent are these relations different from normal practices? Regarding the film text, ecocritics ask: How are non-human animals, landscapes, environments and places, ecological relations, and the Earth in general portrayed and represented? How are relations between humans and non-human nature represented? More specifically, how are intra-human and human–non-human relations shown or assumed to interact, if at all—that is, how are social relations mapped out against socio-natural relations? What meanings are conveyed about environmental issues, about environmental actions and practices, and about who bears responsibility and agency for resolving such issues? What is represented as natural and unnatural, and how are these ethically inflected? Does a film draw attention to and reveal the relationship between its making and the world from which it was made, or does it conceal and mystify that relationship? And regarding reception and consumption, ecocritics ask: What are the short- and long-term effects of these media on social and ecological relations? Do they tend to reproduce existing forms of subordination or oppression and to co-opt or contain social ambitions for change? Or do they enable or facilitate the questioning or reframing of existing relations, opening them up in terms of desire and the imagining of alternative possibilities?[19]

Each of these three moments within the cultural circuit of cinema can be captured by a tri-ecological framework. Film, when this approach is taken, unfolds within a series of ecologies. Its material ecologies, or *ecologics*, concern the technologies by which images are made, as well as the ecologies from which resources are extracted to make them and to which waste materials return following their use. Film has always been among the most heavily *mediated* of media because of its reliance on a complex and integrated array of producers, artists, agents, actors, and marketers, on immense and sophisticated technological apparatus, on colossal sums of money and capital, and on the consumption of tremendous material resources (with all the resulting waste). In this, it is without parallel in the arts. "Green" cinematic practices are only now being developed by filmmakers, but they do exist and are rapidly spreading. The Environmental Media Association (EMA) was formed at the end of the 1980s by a group of Hollywood producers, directors, actors, and agents to "promote 'greener' practices in Hollywood film production," including by encouraging recycling and waste management by studios, and "to educate people about environmental problems and inspire them to act on those problems."[20] Along similar lines, the Shambhala Ranch was founded by producer-director Noel Marshall and actress Tippi Hedren to care for animals used in Hollywood film production.[21] Manuals of "green" filmmaking practices have been developed and are being used increasingly by environmentally conscious filmmakers.[22] While they are only a tiny fraction of the total number of films made, a growing number of films claim to have been carbon-neutral productions. These include *The Day After Tomorrow, Syriana,* and *An Inconvenient Truth,* the latter two in cooperation with the Native American-owned company NativeEnergy. Claims about "carbon neutrality" are a complicated matter—difficult to monitor and subject to criticism on a variety of grounds.[23] But strengthening and promoting such efforts should surely be one of the prongs of ecological commitment among film artists in Hollywood and in independent and international settings.

There is also the question of what happens to films themselves over the long run. Echoing a theme set forth poignantly in Paolo Cherchi Usai's elegiac volume *The Death of Cinema,* Scott MacDonald, in an ecocritical account of experimental film, ruminates on the inherent fragility of the film medium. Many of the films he discusses were made for 16mm screening facilities, which are increasingly rare; also, such films exist only in handfuls of copies and have already begun to decay. All of this has put their economic and material viability in jeopardy.[24] In "Toward an Eco-Cinema," MacDonald laments that the screening and viewing of films is helping bring about their physical demise—paralleling the ecological fact that the use of nature's resources can bring about irreversible changes to the systems they comprise. Film's structural impermanence is at once specific and general: every projection erodes the original photochemical image, and time slowly but relentlessly dissolves every film's material substance. Digital cinema may seem to make possible the permanent storage of cinematic works, but digitality multiplies the material forms such storage requires. Digital data always need to be stored somewhere, which may mean on distant computer servers that are vulnerable to hacking, viruses, and unintended erasure. Also, digital storage and projection devices erode notoriously quickly and are replaced by new generations of equipment at a much faster rate than film ever was. The material foundation of cinema—both its analog and digital forms—is ineluctably time-bound and wasteful.

Film's social ecologies—its *sociologics* or, more simply stated, its politics—raise questions about differential access to production, consumption, inter-pretation, and control. Questions of access are most relevant to socially differentiated groups such as women and minorities, which have long been subjected to the camera gaze without being well represented in decisions about how they should be filmed and portrayed. And because cinema is increasingly a global medium, its social ecologies are global. The map of world cinema has always been dramatically uneven, having been shaped by capital and power but also in some measure by national policies and by public enthusiasm for the medium. Since the 1920s, "Hollywood" has been the ubiquitously accepted currency of film throughout the world. Stamping its films with studio logos, imperial Hollywood, as Dudley Andrew puts it, "coloni[zed] countries and continents and [set] up administrative institutions to govern these." Hollywood's dominance has since been challenged to various degrees by India's Bollywood, which produces some 800 films a year and distributes them around the world, and more recently, for African audiences, by Nigeria's low-budget, direct-to-video industry, affectionately known as Nollywood. Andrew has proposed a historical "map of cinematic power," one that would use a grey-scale of production density keyed to Hollywood as a "dark constant" but also showing dark-grey shades over India, Japan, France, Egypt, Turkey, Greece, and Brazil (highly variable over time, depending on the regime in power), and, more recently, Hong Kong, Iran, Taiwan, and Denmark, among others.

A more complicated map would show the distribution of images from near and far (in any given place); variable distributions of genres; interactions over time between imported styles, such as Hollywood's, and indigenous narrative and image styles; and so on.[25] There have also been those movements of filmmakers and cultural elites calling for an anti-imperialist "Third Cinema" or, more recently, a "Fourth Cinema" of indigenous film production. The development of indigenous media production studios and networks and the emergence of internationally recognized women film directors are two of the more promising phenomena of recent years (see Chapter 4). Alternative and independent film distribution venues, such as the Sundance Channel (and Festival) and the Independent Film Channel in the United States and analogous channels elsewhere, have increased distribution possibilities for films by minority filmmakers, community arts collectives, and the like. To build audiences for independent, foreign, experimental, intercultural, and other kinds of non-mainstream cinema remains an uphill struggle in a world of big-budget blockbusters and the transnational control of film screens. Moreover, access to cinematic power also relates to the distribution of exposure to the "negatives" of filmmaking, such as the production *costs* in human and environmental health in terms of the chemical and industrial by-products of the filmmaking process. This is where cinema's material ecologies meet its social ecologies, and much work remains to be done in addressing differences of power with regard to this meeting of the two.

Finally, cinema's perceptual ecologies, or its *epistemologics*, concern its effects on perception and culture. Many have argued that film is the paradigmatic medium of the industrial world and that its epistemological contours are critical to the world that has evolved over the past century. Walter Benjamin called cinema a "mode of perception" that has come with a particular (commodity-capitalist) mode of production: it responds to a desire for nearness and immediacy; it fetishizes *things* even as it subjects the world to a levelling that renders all objects equally in thrall to its gaze. Film has changed our awareness of the world; it has taught us how to see things—faces, emotions, gestures, movements, actions, landscapes—even as it has elicited a range of aesthetic and visual styles in human behaviour and values. It is these perceptual ecologies that will be the primary focus of the analyses in this book.

These three ecologies are ultimately overlapping; at the same time, each has its own material, social, and perceptual aspects. At the risk of multiplying our triads to the point of absurdity, we could delineate three materialities, three perceptualities, and three socialities. Regarding materialities, there is, first, the *materiality of matter*: the physical ecologies and actual material relations (chemical, industrial) making up the production of film, from mining and manufacturing through to waste disposal. Second, there is the *materiality of perception*: the perceptual apparatus, which is technological (cameras, animation and graphics software, projection and viewing equipment), social-situational (viewing contexts such as a movie house, multiplex, living room, or portable video player), and bodily (eyes, ears, a certain bodily orientation). And third, there is the *materiality of the social*: the relations of cinematic production, distribution, and reproduction, and the rituals and rhythms of moviegoing, home movie viewing, review searching, blogging, and so on. Regarding perceptualities, there are those of matter, of perception itself, and of the social; these are, respectively, cinema's geomorphism, its bio- or animamorphism, and its anthropomorphism (see Chapter 1). And regarding socialities, there are those of matter, of perception, and of the social. The first of these is the subjectivity of matter itself: film's real potential for vitalizing the object-world. Cinema embodies a certain sociality of the material world, with certain things—landscapes, animals, objects—typically, but not always, denied social recognition and others granted greater or lesser degrees of it. The *sociality of perception* is the subjectivity of the vital, interperceptual world; it is the way in which the interperceptivity of cinema embodies a sociality, an ethics, and a biopolitics of relations between us and the vital world of living things. (More on that in Chapter 5.) And the *sociality of the social* refers to the subjectivity of social relations and the ways in which the sociality of cinema—cinema-viewing as a collective process—embodies, conveys, and facilitates the processes of subjectivation of persons, selves, possibilities, as well as new relations between them.

In a process-relational view of the world, cinema, like other media, is understood to mediate between a communicative humanity and a larger world that is also communicative and signifying. "To be a world," as Sean Cubitt puts it in his wonderfully provocative *EcoMedia*, "is to effervesce with an excess of signification"; human communication is thus "only comprehensible in relation to the universe of communication that enfolds, contains and speaks with it."[26] The universe, following Peirce's semiotic philosophy, is communicative in nature, with signification happening all the way down, from the interpretive acts of organisms (like us) reading signals in their surrounding worlds, to the decoding of genetic sequences and atomic impulses. Because, as I have been arguing, materiality and sociality arise ultimately out of the same interperceptual processes, they are not separate but constitute a continuum. In between the interobjective material ecologies and the intersubjective social ecologies of the world, there is a spectrum of possibilities: interperceptual relations that can potentially take the form of subject–object, object–object, or subject–subject relations but that are in principle open and emergent at every moment. This is where the things of the world, the processual entities, encounter and perceive one another, showing some faces of themselves to others and being taken account of in one way or another. In the next section, I deepen this understanding of the world as made up of relational processes. Then I will apply that understanding to our experience of the cinema.

A Process-Relational Ontology

Process-relational thought is not new. It can be found in philosophies around the world, from ancient times to modern: in the pre-Socratic Greek philosopher Heraclitus and in the later Hellenistic Stoics, in Nagarjuna and the Madhyamika philosophers of India, and in Zhuang Zhu and the T'ian-t'ai and Hua-Yen Buddhists in China, but also, in one form or another, in such Western philosophers as Giordano Bruno, Baruch Spinoza, Gottfried Leibniz, Friedrich

Schelling, Henri Bergson, Charles Sanders Peirce, William James, John Dewey, Alfred North Whitehead, Charles Hartshorne, Gilbert Simondon, Gregory Bateson, Gilles Deleuze, Félix Guattari, Nicholas Rescher, Michel Weber, Roland Faber, William Connolly, Isabelle Stengers, Brian Massumi, and Bruno Latour. It also characterizes significant aspects of the thought of Hegel, Marx, Nietzsche, and Heidegger, and of many who have followed in the wake of these four giants of modern philosophy.[27]

While not often articulated as a single, unified tradition, certain common themes justify our identifying process-relational thought as an alternative to two other forms of thought that have become dominant in Western philosophy.[28] These rival traditions are *materialism*, which views matter as fundamental and human consciousness or perception as a by-product or "epiphenomenon" arising out of material relations; and *idealism*, which takes perception, consciousness, thought, spirit, or some other non-material force as fundamental and material relations as secondary, if not illusory. A range of interactive and dialectical philosophies have been proposed to mediate between the material and the ideal, but many of these presume either a relatively closed binary structure of one kind or another, such as matter versus spirit, or idea, or mind; or, alternatively, a conception of opposites, such as *Yin* and *Yang*, with homeostatic balance rather than evolutionary change as the baseline norm. Process-relational thought, by contrast, focuses on the dynamism by which things are perpetually moving forward, interacting, and creating new conditions in the world. Process-relational thought rejects the Cartesian idea that there are *minds*, or things that think, and *bodies*, or matter that acts solely according to strict causal laws. Rather, the two are considered one and the same, or two sides or aspects of the same evolving, processual reality.

At the core of the process-relational thought on which I draw, which is grounded in the work of Whitehead, Peirce, and Deleuze, is a focus on the world-making creativity of things: on how things *become* rather than what they are, on *emergence* rather than structure. According to this understanding, the world is dynamic and always in process. As Søren Brier puts it, describing the ontology of Peirce, reality is a spontaneously dynamic "hyper-complexity of living feeling with the tendency to form habits."[29] This is another way of saying that reality is emergent, evolutionary, and creative—a view that, not coincidentally, finds much resonance in twentieth-century developments in physics and biology including quantum mechanics, ecology, and chaos and complexity theories. This reality is constituted, at its core, not by objects, permanent structures, material substances, cognitive representations, or Platonic ideas or essences, but by relational encounters or events.

In Whitehead's process philosophy, reality is made up of moments or occasions of experience—of "acts of existence" in which entities relate to things in their environments through selectively "prehending" or "taking into account" those things.[30] These moments, these "drops of experience," are not necessarily discrete or isolable; they flow into one another, at least in our perception of them. Furthermore, the entities that are the subjects of these encounters are not themselves stable, unchanging things; rather, their subjectivity is formed in and through their encounters. To the extent that we can abstract any single such moment or actual occasion, it will be characterized by a co-emergence of subjectivity and objectivity: that is, by a dimension of *interiority*, a "prehension" or reaching out and taking account of things, which becomes a "concrescence" or "gathering together," an experienc*ing* to which might be ascribed a sense of subjectivity (which will always be a moving target); and, simultaneously, a dimension of *exteriority*, a *thingness* that is *there* being encountered or responded to.[31] Each moment, then, is a moment of becoming, with relationality and "worldness" being co-produced at multiple levels and scales. Relational moments—or what Whitehead calls "actual occasions"—make up the substance of the universe "all the way down." All actual occasions, from the motion of an electron or subatomic particle to the sensate acts of an amoeba and upward, contain this dipolar relational structure.[32] This does not mean that all subjectivity is alike—for instance, that it is all self-conscious or sentient, as it may be in the case of human subjectivity. But what is *real* is that which contains some dimension of experiential, relational process, this taking account of things in an environment through a process of prehension and concrescence, which in turn becomes data for novel instances of prehension and concrescence.[33]

Neither subjects nor objects, then, are pre-given. The two arise out of what feminist philosopher of science Karen Barad calls "intra-action," the performativity by which the agents making up the world co-emerge into existence through what they do, moment to moment.[34] Sociality, or *intersubjectivity*, is what comes out of processes of subjectivation: it is the world at its most open, active, and dynamic. Materiality, or *interobjectivity*, is what comes out of processes of objectivation: it is the world in its most dense, sedimented, settled, and habituated forms. As Whitehead puts it, "an occasion is a subject in respect to its special activity concerning an object; and anything is an object in respect to its provocation of some special activity within a subject." This "special activity," which he calls prehension, involves three factors: the "occasion of experience within which the prehension is a detail of activity"; "the datum," or object, "whose relevance provokes the origination of this prehension"; and "the subjective form," which is the emotional or "affective tone" that originates "from things whose relevance is given" to the experience.[35] Peirce, whose account of experience is loosely congruent with Whitehead's, writes that "viewing a thing from the outside, considering its relation of action and reaction with other things, it appears as matter. Viewing it from the inside, looking at its immediate character as feeling, it appears as consciousness."[36] Both these views result from the fact that what is real, in Peirce's terms, is *semiosic process*: a continual taking account and making sense of, or responding to, that which is encountered. This semiosic process consists of what I have described as the *interperceptivity* of secondness—things encountering other things—and the world-bearing character of thirdness, which is what emerges from the encounters for things that accrue, that form habits, that take on persistent forms. Objectivity and subjectivity, or matter and ideality (consciousness), thus arise mutually, with part of their arising being the durational continuity—the force of habit and memory—of existent forms.

The same entity can, furthermore, be treated as both subject and object. When I think about something, I am the subject and the thought-about is the object. But when I think about myself, "I" become the object of my own thought, which creates a circular or recursive, self-referential loop in my experience. In actual moments of experience, subjectivation and objectivation occur within a milieu of distinct entities interacting as ensembles (for instance, as "persons" or "selves") characterized by relative stability. Certain of the recurrently identifiable others with whom we interact are granted the status of subjects more or less like us, such that we relate to them in ways that assume that they will relate in turn to us with some mutuality. So even if we have objectified them, of necessity, we understand them to possess subjectivity; they hold a claim on us. Other entities are relegated to the status of objects, such that they are not taken to claim or hold us to any relationship of mutual obligation. The distribution of what will count as a subject and what will count as an object varies from one context to the next. For one person or social group, for instance, "Mother," "Father," "you," "my teddy bear," "society," "the nation," or "God" might all be taken as subjects, while toys, beds, cars, trees, dead bodies, or thoughts might be taken as objects. For another person or society, gods might be relegated to the status of objects or illusions, while dead bodies and thoughts or internal voices might be included in the subject category. For subjects or agents, the object-world, in ecological psychologist J.J. Gibson's terms, presents "affordances for action," while the social or subject-world presents "affordances for interaction."[37] Between the two poles—of things understood to be subjects and things understood to be objects—is a continuum of shades of grey, an in-between realm in which subjectness and objectness are negotiated against the background of uncertain potentiality. The negotiation of these relationships—of who or what will count as an acknowledged party to a transaction—makes up the realm of what philosophers of science Bruno Latour and Isabelle Stengers have called "cosmopolitics."[38]

In addition to objects that serve us for other, generally instrumental, purposes and subjects that are interactively responded to (or at least perceived to be of the nature of things one would respond to), there are also objects that mediate—things that serve to signify *other* things for a subject or that serve to extend the possibilities for semiotic relations among many things. Following Peirce's writings on signs and semiosis (or, as he called it, *semeiosis*), we can even claim that *all* actual occasions are occasions of mediation, or of *sign relation*. Anything that takes the role of the object within a subjective moment, the physical pole to the occasion's mental pole, is "standing in" for something beyond the mere direct perception of that object. That is, anything that is being responded *to* by another thing, a subject, becomes an object of perception and therefore a sign of something *else* that remains outside the perceptual field. For instance, my perception of a sunset is not the actual sun, nor is it me; it is a third, perceived object created at their interface. Any event of signification or meaning-creation, as Peirce maintained, is thus a triadic relationship: there is the *representamen*, which is the form, medium, or vehicle that carries meaning (such as the appearance of that sunset, for a human observer); there is the semiotic *object*, which is the absent or inaccessible referent that is being pointed to by the sign (in this example, the sun or, rather, the changing relationship between the sun, the Earth, and an observer on the Earth); and there is the sense or meaning made of the sign by an observer at a given moment, which Peirce called the *interpretant* (which may be an idea such as "The sun is setting," "It's getting late," "What splendour!," "How great the view from this window," or a poetic "All things pass").[39]

An organism, which is a relatively stable and reflexively self-constituting entity, dwells within a perceived world of relative regularities, consistencies, and relational dynamics—a subjective world that ethologist Jakob von Uexküll called the organism's *Umwelt*. That *Umwelt* is, in turn, characteristically built out of mediations, or out of interpretations of signs "from the world" about objects in that world. The world is therefore relational, dynamic, and full of signification. For a worlded being, the world is always already meaningful—which is to say, in processual terms, that for a becoming-subject, the worldhood of the world is always in progress. This is not only the case for humans. The key insight of biosemiotics, which builds on a Peircian semiotic foundation to assess the semiotic nature of the biological world, is that all living things engage in the interpretation of signs, or in "world-modelling."[40] The difference with humans is that the complex, syntactically organized form of communication we call language—along with other self-reflective forms of representational knowledge such as art and cinema—enables us to generate, imagine, discuss, and struggle over the modelling of complex worlds that are different from the world we may have started with. If language is, as Heidegger put it, the "house of being," that house is continually being constructed and deconstructed. The verbal, visual, and performative arts are potent forces in that process of ongoing world-construction.

Before connecting this ontology more directly to cinema, I offer a brief example of how a moment of experience can be described according to the dipolar structure just outlined. As I write, I recognize things: a sharp, rough sound is recognized as that of a motorcycle starting up and driving off; footsteps are recognized as a person coming toward me; verbalized thoughts are recognized as "my thoughts," "what I am thinking now." Sitting outside a café on a summer day in Amsterdam, I recognize a tram driving by, its bell-like sound indicating an upcoming turn, the flashing orange light on its side indicating that it is now beginning its turn. Mediation, or signification, is part of each of these moments of recognition: the streetcar's blinking light, the words used to carry meaning in "my thoughts," and so on. The sound of the motorcycle is not necessarily *intended* to convey meaning, whether by the motorcyclist or by the motorcycle, though it does this *in effect*. It acts as a meaningful sign in that it is interpreted by an observer as such-and-such a sound. If we treat the relationship between the motorcycle, its driver, and the world of other drivers, pedestrians, vehicles, and roads, as an intentional co-production, then the sound of the motorcycle carries an "intentionality" that produces meaning. This meaning is, in Peirce's terms, an *interpretant*, insofar as it conveys information about something to someone (me) at a certain point in time. To this level of intentionality we can add others, such as when a motorcyclist revs his engine conspicuously to draw attention to himself and the style of his vehicle.

Signness, communicativity, or semiotic mediation, is thus not always a product of subjective intent by an agent. It can be a product of a perceptual relationship in which agency is diffuse but historically and materially produced. (This is one way in which a Husserlian, human-agent–centred phenomenology is considered imprecise from a process-relational perspective.) Meaning is simply the result of something being taken as meaningful in a relational moment of experience. The "subjectivation" of a subject hearing and responding to the motorcycle engine is accompanied directly by the "objectivation" of that sound, so that the system

| *Sound of* | → *Me hearing and getting* | → *"Crazy biker on* |
| *motorcycle engine* | *annoyed at the sound* | *a joyride!"* |

comes into being in this moment of experience. Within this process, the sound is a quality, or what Peirce calls a "first"; my startled and annoyed reaction to it is a "second"; and the meaning that is generated from the exchange is a "third." (I will expand on this triad in the next section.) All forms of mediated signification, especially those involving complex combinations of communicative signs, present to their beholders a world such that the perception of that world integrates with, confirms, or transforms those perceivers' experience of themselves and *the* world (or, if we choose to follow Heidegger, their experience of worlded elements of the foundational, subsistent "earth"). Cinema, like all the arts, produces or discloses worlds in this way, but cinema does it with an intensity and affective immersion that makes it more powerful than most other art forms. In drawing us into its worlds of perceived subjects, objects, and relations, it produces worlds with the power to deeply confirm or radically alter our perception of the extra-cinematic world.

In practice, of course, it is only the rare film that produces an earth-shattering shift in a viewer. But in principle, films *can* bring about such shifts; and cinema as a series of ever-modifying forms has the power to do so over time—indeed, it *has* done so. My interest in this book is to delve into the dynamics of how cinema specifically helps formulate relations between *subjectscapes* and *objectscapes*—which generally means between human subjects of one or more classes or categories, with a certain order organizing the relationships between them, on the one hand, and a world of things, places, locations, sites, territories, and extra-human geographies or ecologies, on the other. But it sometimes means something more complicated than that, where the dividing line between the subjects and the objects is not as clear as this human–non-human division suggests. Between the poles of subjectivation and objectivation—the poles of settled categories, as it were—there is an uncertainty gap, a space of interperceptive flux in which, I would suggest, *everything of significance happens*: it is here that categories get unscrambled, that relationships are challenged, and that old, stale truths are overturned into new ones.

This is, perhaps, oversimplifying things. But as mentioned earlier, the central point of a process-relational approach to cinema is that a film *is* what a film *does*. And what it does occurs throughout the entire process by which cinema *does* cinema: from its making to its viewing to its after-effects, including its reverberation in viewers' perceptions, sensations, conversations, motivations, and attunements to one thing or another in the social and material fields that constitute the world. At the core of this cinematic process is the experience of viewing a film. It is this which the remainder of this chapter will explicate.

Peirce's Categories and the Film Experience

Film presents a world to its viewers. That world can be delineated by the dimensions that hold it together, which the previous chapter articulated as three: the geomorphic, the biomorphic, and the anthropomorphic. These are, in turn, related to the ecologies that make up the extra-cinematic world—the material, the perceptual, and the social—both in the ways that film depicts these and in the ways it utilizes and affects them. The three terms in each set should not be taken as a graduated, analog series, since in each case the second term plays a crucial role in the relational dynamic that we might think of as stretching out between the other two.[41] Between these two sets of three terms, there is the intermediary triad of the cinematic experience, where everything in cinema happens. It is through this experience that we are emotionally and cognitively drawn into a film. In what follows, I will set film's three ecologies into motion, as it were, by presenting a phenomenology of the ways in which our experience of cinema is rooted in a processual, interactive, and communicative world.

Some accounts of film proceed from the assumption that images had always been *still* until their mobilization, late in the nineteenth century, by cinematic technologies. The truth, though, is that moving imagery has always been with us. The hunt for an antelope on the plains of Africa would have been full of movement, and even a sunset or the silhouette of a massive rock outcropping seen from below, while appreciated in stillness, can be both *moving* in its effect on us and never quite still in its reality. Sean Cubitt writes that "before [the moving image] was technological, before history began, there were firelight and shadows, gestures of the shaman, strides of the dancer, puppetry of hand-shadows cast on the walls at the rough dawn of consciousness. In these oldest arts, the immediate world became image, an altar, for a god or a throng of gods to inhabit." Film, he continues, "begins in the public scale of torchlight processions through Altamira, the play of sunlight, moonlight, and dappling cloud on the stained glass windows of medieval Europe, the fireworks and waterworks of the Baroque."[42] Alexander Kluge argues that even when considered as a narrative art, "cinema has existed for over ten thousand years in the minds of human beings," in the form of "associative currents, daydreams, sensual experiences and streams of consciousness. The technical discovery only made it reproducible."[43]

In a process-relational view of the world, neither matter, nor sociality, nor the interperceptive realm from which the two emerge, are ever quite still. The material and the social are more like two ends of a continuum that continually emerges out of a single perceptual and relational process. This process is found in all moments of experience but is particularly vivid in the case of the kind of experience of which cinema is an example: the experience of being drawn into and making one's way through a world—the experience *of experiencing*. The world presents us with objects, events, and encounters, and these are made sense of by us, its participating observers. Cinematic experience is both perceptual (we see and hear things) and hermeneutic (we interpret them). Unlike the everyday experience of embodied movement through the world, cinema does not elicit direct and multi-sensorial physical interaction; this possibility is muted when we watch a movie. But we still register physical effects while doing so, and mental and perceptual responses actively occur in us.

Following a triadic formula similar to those already laid out, the experience of being drawn into the film-world can be subdivided into three elements or moments. These follow the phenomenology of signs and meanings developed by C.S. Peirce, whose semiotics are a fruitful starting point for a process-relational understanding of cinema because of the way they draw attention to the connections between signs and material reality. In this they present an alternative to Saussurian linguistics, which lies at the root of most structuralist and post-structuralist cultural criticism. Where the latter, founded on the linguistic analysis of Ferdinand de Saussure, focuses on representations, which are seen as connected to material reality only through an arbitrary and convention-based form of signification, Peircian semiotics explicitly allocates a place for a real materiality that exists outside the sign, but that is also incorporated into the sign in one way or another. For Peirce, the world is "perfused with signs" through and through. These signs signify insofar as they are made up of three interrelated elements (as described above): a sign vehicle, an object, and an interpretant, all three of which must be present for signification to occur. The sign vehicle, which means the object that we would typically recognize as a sign, is in this way simultaneously connected "backward" to the object and "forward" to the interpretant. The interpretant, in turn, begets further interpretants in a potentially endless multiplication of meanings. As Wendy Wheeler observes, semiosis is "both endlessly open at one end (signs beget more signs) and constrained, at the other end, by the finite resources of the real earth from which, with living things, semiosis emerges. You can build castles in the air out of smoke, but earthly finitude will catch up with you in the last instance."[44] This is the way in which, as Stanley Cavell puts it in another context, "objects participate in the photographic presence of themselves; they participate in the re-creation of themselves on film; they are essential in the making of their appearances. Objects projected on screen are inherently reflexive, they occur as self-referential, reflecting upon their physical origins.

Their presence refers to their absence, their location in another place."[45] There is, in other words, a displacement, a movement from one time and place to another, that is part of every semiotic event. Each cinematic presence is indicative of this move from an original point, a profilmic reality, even if that profilmic reality is itself a result of relational, semiotic processes. The *particular kinds* of displacements found in film are what give it both its meanings and its elusive liveliness; they are what give the best cinematic art its ability to continue generating meaning.

Peircian semiotics has come to play an important role in film and media studies, but its appropriation has largely been limited to Peirce's distinguishing of three kinds of signs: icons, indexes, and symbols.[46] Each of these is related to what it stands for in different ways: icons through resemblance, indexes through causation, and symbols through convention. Film, like photography, has been widely viewed as an indexical medium insofar as there is a direct relationship between what is photographed or filmed and the photograph or film itself: a piece of the world is transmitted, via the interaction of waves or particles of light and chemical substances, onto film, so that the representation is not just *conventionally* related to the thing it is representing, but directly, causally, and existentially related. Like other visual media, however, film is also *iconic*: it gives us images that resemble certain things in the real world. And it is *symbolic*, insofar as we translate what we see according to culturally patterned regularities of interpretation. A sunset that we see on a movie screen, then, is at least three things: it is something that looks like a sunset (and thus, an icon); it is the direct residue, a few times removed, of the solar rays that struck the camera at an earlier point in time (an index); and it connotes certain diegetically specific meanings, such as a moment of romantic unity, or the impending end of something good and its replacement by the unknown (a symbol).

These three sign–object relations—icon, index, and symbol—are grounded in a more primitive set of categories, a phenomenological–ontological triad that provides the conceptual core for the process-relational approach to the cinematic experience developed in this book. Meaning, for Peirce, *is* process. In floyd merrell's words, meaning is "engendered when signs are in their act of becoming signs, a becoming that includes sign interpreters as participating agents in the very *semiosic* process of becoming." Meaning is not *in* "the signs, the things, or the head; it is in the processual rush of semiosis; it is always already on the go toward somewhere and somewhen."[47] The work of philosopher Gilles Deleuze, which has brought renewed attention to Peirce within cinema studies, is more faithful to this processual articulation of semiosis as Peirce conceived it. Drawing heavily on Peirce's analysis of signs and on Henri Bergson's philosophy of movement, images, and becoming, Deleuze's two books on film, *Cinema 1* and *Cinema 2*, present a detailed and finely tuned classification of different kinds of film-images. Deleuze's overarching ontology, rooted in Bergson, is broadly compatible with my own. For Deleuze, all being is, as Schwab puts it, "image-being": "Everything that appears is 'image' [and] all images are motional through and through."[48] Everything that takes on form, or that is continually taking on form, consists of such movement–image–being. Similarly, in the framework I develop here, all experience is at heart an inter-active and interperceptive process. Subjectivation and objectivation emerge in and through this process of interactive image-being. But the point in the cinematic process at which I will apply a Peircian phenomenology is different from Deleuze's. To grasp this difference, I must delineate the fundamentals of Peirce's phenomenology, or what he called *phaneroscopy*.

Peirce's phaneroscopy is a phenomenology of the logical categories into which all experience can be classified.[49] Peirce was convinced that dyads tend to be misleading and that the dynamism of the world requires thinking in terms of threes; and in his understanding of phenomena, he distinguishes between three types depending on the number of *relata* they involve. *Firsts* are the raw immediate things that present themselves to us in and of themselves: for instance, the colour red, or a sensation of piercing pain. *Seconds* are dyadic in that they incorporate a causal or existential connection between one thing and another: the redness visible on a human face, the pain felt on that face immediately following a vigorous slap from another person's hand. And *thirds* incorporate a third, mediating element that makes sense of a dyad, rendering it meaningful for someone or something: the recognition that a person is blush-ing or that they transgressed an understanding and were punished by another's slap on the face. *Firstness* refers to the indivisible "thisness" or *haecceity* of a thing, its thereness, its quality of feeling, "the immediate as it is in its immedi-acy," "the present in its direct positive presentness."[50] It is the purely possible, the undetermined, the virtual. Firstnesses include "the color of magenta, the odor of attar, the sound of a railway whistle, the taste of quinine, the quality of the emotion upon contemplating a fine mathematical demonstration, the qual-ity of feeling of love, etc."[51] As Cubitt puts it, "firstness names the perception of a phenomenon before its source is separated out as an object ('secondness') and named ('thirdness')."[52] *Secondness* names the relationality between two entities, the "brute action" of one substance on another. It is actualization, individuation, energetic determination; it is dyadic, involving a pre-semiotic relationship between two elements, typically an action and a reaction arising from the action, with effort met by resistance. *Thirdness* is the dimension of mediation, signification, and meaning. It is the meaning that is beheld, the "I" and the "other" as having *become* through a process of encounter, mutual positioning, mutual taking into account of each other to create a third. It is the basis for recognition of habit, pattern, and lawful regularity.

Firstness can thus be taken, initially, as roughly analogous to the material or objectal domain, the phenomenal thing as it is given; in cinematic experience, it is our direct immersion in the audiovisual image (in the sense that there is no distinction yet between perceiver and perceived, but only the image-event itself). Secondness is the interperceptive domain: it is perception and response, reflexive but unreflective action, direct causal connectivity as it circulates within a temporally or spatially linked network or set. Thirdness is the social and subjectal domain, that of hermeneutics and meaning; in film experience, it refers to *meaningful* action, the synthesis of action/reaction/reflection, the sense made *in* a film for a viewer who herself makes sense *of* the film. Materiality, in other words, is a kind of firstness, the thingness, givenness, beingness, or positivity of what is there; interperceptivity is the dynamic perceptual or imagistic relationality, consisting of the action of things on other things; and subjectivity is what becomes, the meanings—including the "I-ness" and the "otherness"— that are beheld as existing in relationship to one another.

Each of these levels or registers—the geomorphic, the biomorphic, and the anthropomorphic—additionally has its own firstness, secondness, and thirdness. In a sense, once it has morphed into a world, each has come into thirdness, with the geomorphic being a coming-into-thirdness of firstness, the biomorphic a coming-into-thirdness of secondness, and the anthropomorphic a coming-into-thirdness of thirdness. If each of these is a form that arises out of an experiential or relational process, with subjects emerging at one end and objects at the other, then interperceptivity is both the *milieu* within which the tension between the two is negotiated and the *momentum* that pushes the process forward in time. While this secondness of the interperceptive provides the forward "push," it is in thirdness that meaning emerges, so it is thirdness that "pulls" or draws out the significance of the encounter.

In *The Cinema Effect*, media theorist Sean Cubitt derives a typology of moving-images from Peirce's ontological triad. This typology comes closer than Deleuze's does to my own framework, so I will elucidate it in order to distinguish a few key features and a point of divergence with mine. Cubitt's goal is to provide a "retrospective historiography of images in motion from the standpoint of the digital era," so his terms for this triad—pixel, cut, and vector—are taken from the digital world. The *pixel* is a "directionless flux of pure movement" or, as Garrett Stewart describes it, "the pinpoint glisten of luminosity on the first film screens," "sheer scintillating image," "what suture theory would see as the bliss of spectation before the fall into editing, into system, into plot, or, in other words, into the scission that makes for variable temporality and narrative direction."[53] It is "the balmy limitlessness of the newborn child, bathed in the world," the "eternal now of nonidentity," the "oceanic primal temporality" that "becomes navigable only once the cut instigates endings: a delimited field of vision, composited spatial relations, and the spatiotemporal assemblage of shots into sequences."[54]

The *cut* institutes the first distinction between "film, retina, and mind," presenting "the world as object over against the spectator as subject" in a repetition of the Lacanian moment "in which the infant first distinguishes itself from the world." This loss of immersion is a gain of orientation: "The organizational power of the cut controls flux by reconstituting it as space-time, as figures on a ground, as objects in a world."[55] The cut "spatializes the timeless time of the pixel," producing temporal relations including causality and point of view, "objects, worlds, and identities" that are organized into a "hierarchy of expectation and recall."[56] In the "aesthetic of organic unity"—as developed, for instance, in the Hollywood scriptwriter's goal of making every detail "pay off," as in "the gun we see in the drawer must at some point later be fired"—we get a "cinema of predestination" premised on a narrative causality that is ultimately closed in on itself and the stories it has always already told.[57]

Drawing a correspondence between Peirce's terms and Jacques Lacan's phases of psychosocial development, Cubitt writes that "immersion in the pixel's commotion corresponds to Peirce's firstness, the Lacanian Real; the cut to Peirce's secondness, the Lacanian Imaginary." The vector, corresponding to Peirce's thirdness and the Lacanian symbolic, is what provides "concept and meaning, socialization, the paradigmatic axis of film."[58] Like the Deleuzian "line of flight," the vector "takes us one step further: from being to becoming, from the inertial division of subject, object and world to the mobile relationships between them." "The pixel grounds us in the film as a present experience, the cut in the preexistence of the filmstrip to consciousness of it, the vector in the film as the becoming of something as yet unseen. It is the principle of transformation, the quality of changing what we expect from moment to moment."[59] Cubitt locates the emergence of this third step in the early history of animation, particularly in a film like Emile Cohl's 1908 *Fantasmagorie*, which with its animated "line that draws itself" follows an unpredictable journey through "unfinished, unending, undecidable metamorphoses of expectation."[60] "Flowers become bottles become a cannon; an elephant becomes a house; Pierrot becomes a bubble, a hat, a valise." The vector of Cohl's animating line "disrespects the frame edge and equally ignores the syntax of layering."[61] Crucially, it is not only the subjects or figures that change, but the ground as well (a point I will come back to when I discuss animation in Chapter 5).

Both Cubitt and Deleuze draw on Peirce to classify cinematic images and, at the same time, to make an argument about the historical development of cinema. For Deleuze, this concerns the difference between two general kinds of moving images: the "movement-image" and the "time-image." In his analysis, a set of conditions in the period following the Second World War stimulated a shift from a cinema rooted primarily in the movement-image, where the organization of images followed a cause-and-effect logic premised on the necessities of action, to one increasingly marked by a disjunction between the succession of images and causal narrative logic. This disjunction, according to Deleuze, freed cinema to explore the nature of time itself, rather than a time that is locked into the causal distribution of movement and action. In Deleuze's estimation, this shift to the time-image was an important advance for cinema. His argument, however, has been criticized by some as overly generalized and deterministic. Cubitt, for instance, points out that no technique, be it deep focus, the long take, or Deleuze's time-image, "is essentially avant-garde, progressive, or subversive: every technique is capable of becoming merely technical, a tool for further and repurposed productions."[62]

Like Deleuze's historical argument about the time-image as an advance over the movement-image, Cubitt's schema leads to an implied hierarchy of film styles, with the more narratively open metamorphoses of Cohl and his descendants being valued over the narrative closures and "organic totalities" of classical Hollywood film, Sergei Eisenstein's historical-materialist cinema, and Jean Renoir's organic realism. But Cohl's film is no less open in reality than any other: once it has been created and distributed as a finished film, it remains a finished film. Once we have seen it, we know what to expect from it the next time we see it. A second viewing may reveal things we failed to *notice* the first time, but it will not reveal things that were not *there*. What the film provides is elements or *affordances* (to again use James Gibson's useful term) that can be taken up by viewers and communities of interpreters. In the end, what a particular viewer or audience takes up is a matter of conscious choice, unconscious predilection, and social and historical contingency. Films that are narratively more open—more *vectoral* in Cubitt's sense—may result in broader and more interesting social effects than films that are narratively closed, but whether or not they do so depends in part on how the films engage viewers in all three of the ways that Cubitt has outlined. I will, therefore, revise Cubitt's terms so that they describe three distinct qualities of the film experience without presuming a specific history of the emergence of these qualities, or stages of development in which the next transcends the previous. I will rename them in perhaps more conventional terms—as spectacle, narrative, and sign; or imageness, narrativity, and signness. I will make no claims about their relative superiority or inferiority to one another: each is found in almost every film, to varying degrees.

It should be clear that my use of Peirce's categories is not the only possible one, nor is it intended to be authoritative. The difference in my approach relates to the point in the cinematic process at which his semiotic theory is applied. For Deleuze, Peirce's categories apply *within* and *among* cinematic images themselves: a "first" is an affection-image, the image of the affective impression in a face or body of a received movement; a "second" is an image showing reaction of one thing to another (an action-image); and a "third" is a mental- or relation-image, "an image that takes as its object, relations, symbolic acts, intellectual feelings."[63] The latter two correspond to Francisco Casetti's differentiation between the plane of "the world," on which actions happen, and that of thoughts, on which there is reflection on the action itself. Casetti's example, from *The Man Who Shot Liberty Valance*, involves a differentiation between the plane of the film on which "the history of the West is made" and the plane on which "the story of Liberty Valance is recounted."[64] To Casetti's two planes, Deleuze adds a third, which is neither that of action nor that of its recounting, but the virtual thing itself, its primary force or charge, as it is revealed in an image. Another possible application of Peirce's categories, however, would be one that applied them to the relationship between a *single* image (as opposed to a whole film) and a viewer. Firstness in this sense would be the image itself. Secondness would be the impact of that image on the viewer—for instance, the way it arouses me, elicits shivers down my spine, or reminds me of some specific previous event. Thirdness would be the mediation of that impact through an interpretation of the film.[65]

My approach in what follows comes closest to Cubitt's, with the difference that Cubitt is concerned more with the evolving technology of cinema, whereas my interest here is solely in the experience of watching and being drawn into a film. That experience is complex, and my use of the three categories is more functional or even metaphorical. Firstness, in this sense, refers to the spectacular dimension of cinema; secondness, to the serial and (very generally) narrative dimension; and thirdness, to the referential dimension.[66] In the remainder of this chapter, I will elaborate this framework into an analysis of film that encompasses many insights of other film historians and scholars: insights on narrative, spectacle, spectatorship, gaze, cognition, affect, character identification, and much else. Exploring the work of these scholars in detail would require a separate book, so the following can be considered a synthesis whose individual segments are less important than the overall form. Hopefully, the segments are grounded well enough in the work of others. The form, on the other hand, is the original synthesis being proposed here, which is the triadic, process-relational framework derived largely from Whitehead and Peirce.

Spectacle, Narrativity, Signness

In historical analyses of cinema, narrative and spectacle have often been pitted against each other. Film theory in the 1960s and 1970s, especially among critics gathered around the influential British journal *Screen*, focused largely on critical analyses of narrative. In what became the most widely cited article in the field, Laura Mulvey developed an extended feminist analysis of how classic cinema narratives represented men as engaged in a movement taking them from one situation to another, in the course of which they overcame obstacles and vanquished villains.[67] Women, on the other hand, were portrayed as passive subjects of the male (and viewerly) gaze. In Mulvey's argument, men were narrative agents while women were pure spectacle. Conventional narratives, for Mulvey, were ideologically shaped toward closure, and this made for an Oedipal trajectory along which the masculine protagonist found his place within a patriarchal social order by learning to control the disruptive power of the feminine. Narrative, in this sense, tamed and contained spectacle.

The critical response to Mulvey's argument developed into an extended debate over the presumed passivity of the viewer, and eventually, Mulvey herself was persuaded by the possibilities offered by open narratives, by a broader variety of gender role depictions, and by the viewer's certain degree of freedom to interpret and refashion narratives to her own needs. But it was not until the late 1980s that theorists such as Tom Gunning began to revisit the early history of cinema to seek out an alternative tradition to this narratively focused one. Gunning called this tradition the "cinema of attractions." In his argument, cinema before about 1906 was devoted exclusively to the "harnessing of visibility," the "act of showing and exhibition" that constituted the new medium's presentational dimension. In Bart Testa's words, the cinema of attractions was about sensation, "something that happens in a short span of film time that demonstrates the capacities of the cinematic device in a forceful, novel and compressed way."[68] This spectacularity of attraction, wrote Wanda Strauven, "grounds itself on the literal and physical sense of the term, namely 'the force that draws or sucks in.'"[69] Spectacle was what the medium inherited from the magic lantern shows that preceded it; it was what made cinema *cinema* in its early years.[70] Gunning argued that cinema's spectacularity had been demoted for the same reasons that it has been devalued elsewhere in the arts for centuries, going back to Aristotle and the ancient Greeks. The spectacular, in this tradition, was seen as the lowbrow realm of emotionally impacting effects and sensations, less substantial and more "empty" than the cognitive and more meaningful dimensions of artistic expression. Avant-garde films, however, and certain popular genres such as musicals, science fiction, and chase films, have maintained a persistent interest in filmic spectacle. In tandem with Gunning's call for more attention to the cinema of attractions, film theory in general has undergone a shift since the late 1980s away from the semiotic and structuralist theories that dominated in the 1970s and toward a renewed interest in spectatorship, viewer response, cultural identity, and more historical lines of inquiry.

This contrast between spectacle and narrative, or the spectacular and narrative modes of spectatorship, is more or less what Cubitt aligns with Peircian firstness and secondness.[71] Neither term, however, tells us much about what film *means* for its viewers or about the open-endedness of the meaning-making process; and it is the latter that constitutes cinema's thirdness. *Spectacle*, then, is cinema's firstness. It is the immediate felt quality of the film image, the objectness, presentness, and thingness of what we see, hear, and feel as we watch a film. It is film's thickness, viscosity, and texture—its "exhibitionist confrontation" with us, in Gunning's words.[72] If we follow Deleuze's Bergsonism, we ourselves *are* images, which means not that we are visual objects, but that we are material entities that are sensorially perceived by other material entities. Like Peirce's firstness, filmic spectacle is the *image* of the film, the direct meeting of ourselves-as-image with film-as-image. It is the felt quality of our direct embeddedness in the audiovisual image. It is the dimension of film to which our verbal response is little more than a "there!," "look!," "wow!," or "ugh!," which upon reflection might become "cool!," "I'm enjoying this," "Isn't this great?," or "how creepy!" At its extremes this response can be enthralling, but film's imageness, its texturality, can also elicit a slowly brewing sense of congruence, or dissonance, or some other kind of unreflectively felt, tangible visceral orientation of one kind or another toward—or in some kind of rhythm *with* or *against*—what is being experienced. This visceral register is the body's most direct registration of a film. It is what first fascinated so many Lyonnaise when, in 1896, the Lumière brothers screened a short film of a train arriving at a station, which, according to legend (and probably not in reality), its viewers drew away from in horror, as if the vehicle were actually coming toward them. It is also our immediate response to facial expressions, close-ups, unusual objects and actions (such as the slicing of an eye in Salvador Dalí's and Luis Buñuel's *Un chien andalou*), and, significantly, to the music and other sounds that accompany the image. It is the affective turbulence that spreads through an audience by emotional contagion. Cinema's uniqueness lies in part in this ability to present *presentness*—that is, to show us, directly, the moving-image nature of the world. It is this that film theorists are referring to when they describe cinema as an "art of presence."[73]

Film's *narrativity*, or what arises directly out of the horizontal sequentiality of filmic images, is its Peircian secondness. The filmic narrative is what unfolds in and through the movement between images—that is, in the sequence of occurrences that are connected, one to the next, in the temporal displacedness that urges us to seek connections within and between those images. We experience this by getting caught up in the film's story and by asking, "So what will happen next? What will he or she do?" Retrospectively, film's narrativity takes the form "And then ... and then ..." Where spectacle is the thickness or vertical dimension of cinematic experience, narrativity is its serial and horizontal dimension. It is what tends toward linearity, but only because while many virtual roads might be taken by a narrative trajectory, in most films *only one* of these is ultimately taken: the hero vanquishes the villain (or gets killed by him), the killer is found out (or escapes), the mystery is unravelled, and so on. The horizontal, in principle, could be episodic, digressive, non-linear, multiple, and open-ended. There could be many overlapping, parallel, or unrelated fragments of narrative, and more than one ending to the story, or even none at all. At the extreme, such fragmented or alternately convergent and divergent "network" or "hypertext" narratives may be difficult to follow, so such films tend to be unpopular (though an appreciation for them can grow as they become fashionable). But they are possible, and their popularity or impact on viewers depends on other cultural and historical factors than whether they are easy to follow.

Whatever narrative form a film takes, the experience of viewing it normally involves an active seeking of connections, an openness or orientation toward the film's sequential plottedness. As viewers we are generally on the lookout for meaningful connections from one shot to the next. How is this scene different from the last? Who is this new character? Is that the same person we saw before? Film's secondness, in this view, provides us with the possibility of piecing together storylines as we make interpretive connections between the things we see and hear. Because films show us events, one following another through the sequential movement of the plot or narrative, rather than showing us everything at once, they trigger our desire, as Todd McGowan puts it, "to experience what comes next."[74] They keep us effectively suspended, yet in motion with the movement of the images, which offer a promise of resolution at some point ahead of us. Narrativity is what draws us forward as if to satisfy a lack that can only be filled when the last question has been answered, a point we hope will arrive by the end of the film. The interplay between what we see happen—or the film's *syuzhet*, as the Russian formalists named it—and what is actually thought to have occurred in the *fabula*, the world of events ostensibly being revealed on the other side of the camera, is one of the features that gives the film experience its dynamism.

Finally, there is film's thirdness, which is its *signness* or *exoreferentiality*. This is the "orientation toward reality" of a film's images and sounds themselves, insofar as these are taken up by a viewer and related to what that viewer already knows, perceives, or suspects about the world. It is what elicits in us responses like "What do you think he (or she) meant by this?," "*That's* what this is about ...," "This reminds me of X," and "I understand." Spectacle and narrativity are lifeless without exoreference, but too much or too obvious an exoreference—for instance, a clichéd allegorizing on the part of a film—tends to strike viewers with an unwelcome thud. This thirdness, then, is not just the transformational and seemingly open-ended nature of *some* films, as Cubitt's concept of the vector suggests. It is, rather, what emerges as the film opens itself to the world at large, to the profilmic *and* post-filmic world, a world we inhabit and make sense of and into which we incorporate our experience of the things we see and feel (firstness) and follow (secondness) while viewing a film. For any film to generate meaning in a viewer, it must connect with what is already meaningful for that viewer. In this sense, a film affords various possibilities for interpretation; its meaning, however, is never fully predestined. Once it begins to generate thirdness, this production of meanings takes place in the interaction between film and a dynamic world, one that renders the film always open to further interpretation and reinterpretation.

These three dimensions can be thought of as three aesthetic modes of cinematic spectatorship, and each elicits responses in different ways. There is that which strikes us and holds us rapt: the shimmering spectacle of vision and sound that magnetizes our attention as we watch and behold it, transfixed. There is that which draws us in and envelops us within its flow of eventualities, the sequence of events that intrigues us with its possibilities, its virtualities becoming actualities one after another. And there is that which speaks to us, sending signals along vectors that connect with the webs of meaning we bring to the film, the resonances and significances by which we make the film ours. There is the shimmering spectacle, the narrative flow, and the generation and germination of significances. A film that emphasizes the first highlights the *surface* of the images we see, a surface of rippling light and shimmering sound, of objects shown to us or moving rapidly in front of us. Certain genres such as the musical, the blockbuster epic, avant-garde cinema, and erotic or porno-graphic film work more at this level of spectacle. In films in which the natural world is a prominent focus, spectacle may take the form of the sublime—a suspension of the narrative flow in moments of visual splendour evoking feel-ings of awe and wonder. At its broadest, we might conceive of a film's spec-tacularity as including all the immediate sound/image qualities that present themselves to us independently of, or in counterpoint to, the forward trajec-tory of the film's plot or narrative. Over time, of course, any textural modality becomes part of the general film experience as a technique becomes formalized and normalized into a generic convention. The viewers of a Hollywood or Bollywood musical know that when the characters stop their action and begin to sing and dance for an invisible audience, with orchestras sounding suddenly in the background, this is part of what is expected; it is what gives the audience pleasure, even if it advances the plot only minimally or not at all. There are many generic conventions that are recognized as conventions yet give plea-sure both in and of themselves and through that recognition: soundtrack gags, song-and-dance routines, the vividness of colour or the beauty of black-and-white, three-dimensional effects, chase and battle scenes, and so on. Each of these may be interpreted by us, brought into thirdness as we attempt to dissect the reasons why the filmmakers used this technique or whether it "works" in this context or not. But our immediate experience of them is an enjoyment of their *thereness*.

Film's narrativity, in turn, encourages us to see *through* the spectacular (and specular) image, as if through a window, into a world that spreads out before us on the other side of that frame. Like the pleasures of unadorned spectacle—or, rather, cinematic adornment in all its splendour unencumbered by storyline— the pleasures of narrativity are well known by all viewers. Furthermore, they rarely come unadorned by thirdness, that is, by the meaningful "worldness" of recognizable objects, places, and character types. The barest form of filmic secondness might be an abstract film in which simple shapes give rise one to another, so that the viewer can only wonder at the sequential link between one and the next. Mystery films and melodramas make use of a tremendous array of devices, mechanisms of tension and resolution, to emotionally engage viewers and immerse them in the plot's forward movement: we want the good guys to win, the hero to get the girl (or guy), the mystery to be solved. A successfully engaging narrative tends to operate, as Rowe puts it, "on the tension between our anticipation of likely outcomes drawn from genre conventions"—and I would add from life experience—"and the capacity to surprise or frustrate our expectations."[75] Frequently a narrative will take a circular or spiral form, in which an initial equilibrium is disrupted, usually close to the beginning of the film, with much of the film working out the implications of this disruption until we reach an ultimate restoration or new equilibrium. But this form can be rendered complex in so many ways—through narrative breaks, estrangement techniques, multiple diegeses and contradictory narrative perspectives, and even through open-ended and unresolved narratives.

Finally, the category of the sign, the exoreferential at its broadest, would include any reference to the extra-filmic world: to real characters, contemporary or historical, and actual places and events; to everyday life matters or current social and political issues; and to intertextual elements such as stars, auteurs, and other films. Certain traditions of referencing underpin entire genres. For instance, where classical Hollywood films might have referenced the "American dream" or the power of "show business," Soviet films referenced the revolution and its recognizable heroes and villains. In documentaries, the reality-referent is taken as a basic premise, but it can be thin and un-self-reflexive, a simple objectivist or quasi-authentic taking for granted of the film's references to the world, or it can be thickly self-reflexive, incorporating references to the complex or problematic relations between the reality portrayed in a film, the effort involved in making that film, and the complex realities of the extra-filmic world. This reality-referent can also take on ironic, deconstructive, or anti-narrative functions, as in the interruption of the flow of narrative to provide an ironic counterpoint to that narrative, or reference to the filmmaking process and medium, as in Godardian or Brechtian viewer alienation and distanciation techniques.

Each of these categories works alongside and with the others. The difference between spectacle and narrative, for instance, and between surface and depth, is not necessarily predetermined. It is negotiated and changeable over time, just as the difference between the painterly texture and frame of an early modern landscape painting and the three-dimensional world that unfolds within that frame is also a historical product, one that audiences *learn* to read and ultimately take for granted. We know that the brushstrokes of paint demarcating the edge of the *Mona Lisa*'s face are actually located *right next* to the brushstrokes of the field visible in the landscape "behind" her, but we still see her face as "here" before us and the field as "there" in the distance. When looking *into* the film world, a film's texturality is just part of its taken-for-granted background. When something unusual happens—when the projector flutters (an error of the film-screening process), or a character speaks directly to the camera (an intentional effect), or the camera takes on a highly unusual movement—we notice the frame once again.

The difference between the firstness of an oil painting—the imageness and texturality of its thick brushstrokes, its picture frame, and so on—and that of a film is that the latter is always temporal and durational. It includes movement *within* the frame, but also movement between what is in the frame and the world *outside* the frame. It is that temporal dynamism that enables narrative to emerge in cinema in ways that can only be gestured at in static pictures. And with this multiplication of relationships, narrativity, which is the viewer's immersion into the unfolding, diegetic world within the film, and texturality, which is the spectacle of the image itself, can interact in multiple and productive ways. Similarly, the Brechtian techniques that were originally developed to rouse the viewer out of an emotional identification with characters or a submission to the fantasy of what is presented on-screen can, over time, become a source of enjoyment in and of themselves—a kind of pleasurable firstness within third-ness. Or, alternatively, they can become worn-out clichés that we recognize as very much "of their time" (which is why, for some, Godard's early films never age, and for others, his later films seem as immature as his early ones).

These, then, are the three lines by which cinematic experience unfolds. Each has its strengths or powers, but they are mutually strengthening. Spectacle is more meaningful when its images elicit resonant exoreferential mean-ings; narrative has more impact when it is conveyed in powerful, spectacular moments; and exoreferential meanings are left dry and uninteresting if they are not accompanied by compelling narrative elements and enjoyable camerawork, acting, or sound and visual effects. Identification with characters, which is one of the most common ways in which viewers are "taken" by a film, works on all three levels. There is a kind of preconscious level by which viewers are cued to like or to resonate with a character; there is the narrative level, according to which we follow (and evaluate) the things that happen to that character and the ways he or she responds to them; and there is the exoreferential level, which is the way in which we synthesize our own experience of the world with that of the character. Each feeds the others.[76]

Each of these, in all likelihood, also involves a somewhat different kind of cognitive processing on the viewer's part. While neurological correlates of film experiences are difficult to determine and inherently complex, there is a body of evidence from which we can surmise that the three forms of experience I have outlined rely on different arrays of neural capacities. The spectacular dimension, related as it is to Peirce's icon, arises as a response to immediate impressions: images trigger responses based on deeply held, and thus more innate, affective response mechanisms, such as those associated with such ancient parts of the brain as the amygdala and brain stem. Narrative, in turn, involves a form of linear–causal thinking that is central to projective and retrojective cognition—that is, to recalling the past and to projecting oneself and one's world into the future. Recent research suggests that both these forms of narrative or episodic thinking rely on similar neural systems (including the prefrontal cortex, the hippocampus, and the parahippocampal gyrus). Finally, the ability to self-reflexively and creatively synthesize meanings out of multiple sources—from present or recent sensory input to various kinds of memory and imagined possibility—requires a synthetic form of cognition that is likely related to those brain regions and capacities most evident in humans, such as the prefrontal cortex, the cerebellum, "Broca's speech area," and, more important, a high density and complexity of neural networking.[77] In a loose sense, the three dimensions of cinematic experience align well with neuroscientist Paul MacLean's concept of the "triune brain," which consists of a "reptilian complex," a "paleomammalian complex" or "limbic system," and a "neommalian complex" or "neocortex." MacLean viewed these as relatively autonomous sequential developments in the evolution of human brain anatomy, and while his hypothesis has not worn well in its details since it was first developed in the 1960s, it remains suggestive to the model I am proposing. Peirce's triadic phenomenology, in any case, does not require neural correlates in order to remain viable as a logical model. The resonances between one and the other can at least provide a warrant for further neuropsychological research in the directions they point toward.

Scenes, Moments, and Cinematic Impact

What viewers retain most from a film is, in any case, not always divisible into the three categories of spectacle, narrative, and meaning. And it is often not so much the entirety of a film that is remembered as it is its encapsulation or condensation in specific memorable moments. My contention is that it is such condensed "hyper-signaletic" or "resonant moments"—moments in which spectacle, narrative, and meaning are brought together, compactly synthesized in sound/image bits, which may be a scene, a sequence, a series of recurrent motifs or movements, and so on—that best capture the working together of cinema's firstness, secondness, and thirdness. I take the term "signaletic" from Gilles Deleuze, who uses it to refer to the *material* of cinema, "which includes all kinds of modulation features, sensory (visual and sound), kinetic, intensive, affective, rhythmic, tonal, and even verbal (oral and written)."[78] While all cinema is made of such signaletic material, there are differences in its thickness or density, and the moments I will be interested in are those that synthesize, crystallize, and compact together *more* of this material than is the norm. It is these that are retained most powerfully in viewers' affective memories.

To understand such moments, one must take into account the entirety of the film, or at least of the meanings a viewer takes from that film. If there is a central, median-level component that makes up both our experience of films and our experience of everyday life, it is that which is indicated by words like "moment," "scene," and "episode." These can be considered points on a continuum of everyday experience. Recent neuropsychological and philosophical work on memory has established "episodic memory" as one of the distinctly human neurocognitive achievements. It is thought that by around the age of four, children have developed an episodic memory system (or at least an episodic memory capacity) that forms the foundation of their autobiographical sense of self, in addition to providing for the capacity to imagine future scenarios and to navigate across new terrains. One distinctive line of thought, particularly fruitful for an understanding of cinema, is that episodic memory and its relatives rely on the capacity for "scene construction," in which a spatial context serves as the background or setting in which events are perceived as taking place.[79] The process-relational model presented in this book follows this insight into scene construction in its focus on, at one end, the spatial context and setting of an event of experience, and at the other, the action or set of actions constituting that event. But it also takes to heart the "constructionism" implied in the notion of scene construction by understanding the process to be an ongoing and dynamic one, whereby settings and the actions that take place within them—including the actors undertaking those actions—are conceived as active processual constructions, with both ends of the continuum that makes them up—the background and the focal action—emerging out of a vibrant and dynamic middle ground.

To the extent that cinema consists of moments, scenes, or episodes, and that its greatest effects occur in particular, high-impact moments, it is these moments at which the power of cinema becomes distilled into its essence. That essence is *movement*: sound/image movement that is also always *affective* movement.[80] According to a process-relational ontology, cinema in its essence is movement that is, at one and the same time, the movement of thought, of affect, and of image. In his Deleuze-inspired "filmosophy," Daniel Frampton encourages us to follow the thought of a film not by analyzing the filmmaker's intent, or the techniques used to follow through on that intent, and whether they have succeeded, but rather by following the film *as if it is thought itself*, that is, as if the film is thinking and showing us things in self-motivated ways.[81] In this spirit, my discussion of specific films will tend to look for key moments—motifs, patterns, and instances that carry the core affective impulses that a film passes on to its viewers.

In making precisely this point that cinema, for viewers wrapped up in it, is made up not of shots but of moments, Murray Pomerance provides a series of evocative examples. "The cinematic moment has its own organization and architecture," he writes, which "may stand" upon the most singular of cinematic elements:

> Upon an expression of an actor's mouth (John Wayne smiling at Ed Asner in Howard Hawks's *El Dorado* [1963]), a look in the eye (Dorothy Malone malevolently egging on her brother's jealousy from a high window in Douglas Sirk's *Written on the Wind* [1955] or Diane Baker cupidinously watching Sean Connery and "Tippi" Hedren leave for their honeymoon in Hitchcock's *Marnie* [1964]), a tree moving in the wind in the background (as in the Lumières' *Le Repas de bébè* [1895]), the passage of a train (whistling through the station in David Lean's *Brief Encounter* [1945]), the color of an object in the corner of a screen (a view through the doorway of the Hotel de la Gloria in the final shot of Michelangelo Antonioni's *The Passenger* [1945]). It may depend for its power on a long culmination of a character's statements and considerations, a kind of enchainment of increasing probabilities and weights that plays out in a kind of sigh [...]; on the evocation possible when a line of action and intent is played out fully [...]. The moment may endure, as in Charles Foster Kane's dying breath; or may be evanescent, as in the dances of Astaire and Charisse in *The Band Wagon*. While the inherent subjectivity and personality of the received moment make it a slippery subject for rigorous analysis, nevertheless it remains the substance and flesh of our experience of watching films, the reason we wish to watch them again and again, the substrate of their melody, the envelope of their pathos and glory.

Life itself consists of moments, singular becomings stretched end to end but with some attaining a charge and a thickness that makes them endure in their impact across the chain of continuities. "The most important thing about cinema," Pomerance concludes, "is that we are alive with it."[82] And it is this aliveness—in being struck by a cinematic image (firstness), in being rapt and *taken* by the movement of a narrative (secondness), and in the explosive generation of meanings that the combination of images and narratives elicits in us (thirdness)—that the remainder of this book will take as the beating heart of the cinematic experience.

I will not cover all of that experience, but only the parts most relevant to understanding cinema's socio-ecological significance. To better come to grips with this, I will examine how films skillfully mix the three forms of cinematic involvement—spectacle, narrative, and exoreference—along lines that work on expanding the possibilities for film's geomorphism, its biomorphism, and its anthropomorphism. My premise, in this book, is that films can expand viewers' perceptions of *ecological ontology*. This latter term encompasses the ways we understand non-human or more than merely human worlds, with the many differences and overlaps between our phenomenological worlds and other worlds; the relations and interdependencies between these two sets of worlds, human and non-human (which are ultimately one); and the political-ecological systemic relations that entangle these together in historically and culturally variable ways.

The questions motivating my analyses of specific films can be rendered as follows: What does it take for a film to expand viewers' perceptions of ecological ontology? What sorts of firstness, secondness, and thirdness—and what combination of these in hyper-signaletic sound/image moments—move viewers toward an expanded perception of such an ecological ontology, in each of the three registers of the geomorphic, the anthropomorphic, and the animamorphic, and ultimately in all three at once?

Answering these questions is hardly straightforward, and the next three chapters will not address them directly. (A more complete rendering of the model and the questions it raises for film analysis can be found in Appendix 1.) The forthcoming chapters will instead probe the ways in which the three registers of cinema's world-productiveness—its geomorphism, anthropomorphism, and animamorphism—have been developed in a broad range of cinematic works over the last century or so. They will look at how film takes us places, and teaches us to see those places, thereby rendering open a world that is meaningfully laid out for us (Chapter 3); how it presents capacities for action, represented by particular actors or characters, and enables us to affectively and imaginatively experience those capacities (Chapter 4); and how it brings us life itself in its relational dynamism and opens us to different ways of relating to that life (Chapter 5). I will return to a more direct encounter with political-ecological questions in Chapter 6, which will focus on the trope of ecological disaster and, to some extent, its obverse, ecological utopia. That in turn will allow us to hazard some suggestions for how an ecophilosophy of cinema can help us move toward both an ecophilosophical *cinema* and an ecophilosophical *viewing practice*.

3

TERRITORY

The Geomorphology of the Visible

From *Stagecoach* (1939). Directed by John Ford. Credit: United Artists/Photofest.
Shown: Exterior location, Monument Valley, Utah.

Our taverns and our metropolitan streets, our offices and furnished rooms, our
railroad stations and our factories appear to have us locked up hopelessly. Then
came the film and burst this prison world asunder by the dynamite of the tenth of
a second, so that now, in the midst of its far-flung ruins and debris, we calmly and
adventurously go traveling.

Walter Benjamin, "The Work of Art in the
Age of Mechanical Reproduction"[1]

It is almost possible to say that people become the fixed monument around which landscape swirls.... In today's world of computers, film, and television, automobiles, high-speed rail, and airplanes, people sit down and the landscape moves. Crossing the screen faster than a speeding locomotive, able to leap over states of countries in a single bound, television's cars, trucks, and SUVs fragment the spatial continuum of landscape into a mountainous swell of imagery, sights without measure, an oceanic voyage with little hope of landfall.

Mitchell Schwartzer, "The Moving Landscape"[2]

Standing on the bare ground – my head bathed by the blithe air, and uplifted into infinite space – all mean egotism vanishes. I become a transparent eye-ball; I am nothing; I see all ...

Ralph Waldo Emerson, "Nature"[3]

I don't know what it's like when there is no one here, but as soon as humans appear everything begins to move.

Stalker (1979)

FILMS CREATE WORLDS: they lay out a certain set of relations defining what is given, what is possible, who the actors are that enact the possible and make it real, and the nature and character of the background against which their actions take place. This chapter deals with the background and context, the *given* against which, or in front of which, the action happens. It deals with the relations that constitute that background and hold it together. This is the geomorphic dimension of cinema, the territorial ontology that underlies the world of any film. Such an ontology—which is always a sensed or perceived ontology, an implicit understanding about things in general, and therefore about "nature" in the most general sense—can be highly variable. It can take the world to be stable and reliable, or to be unstable, precarious, perplexing, frightening, and even incoherent. It can be simply ours—ours to claim and take and use and transform—or it can be sharply divided between what is ours and what is not ours, territory to be fought over, either with the assurance that truth, or God, or nature itself (progress, evolution, and so forth) is on our side, or without any such assurance.

To understand how such a geographic ontology emerges within a film and how it is territorialized and distributed across the world of that film, we need first to understand how it emerges in life. From this basis we can examine how film impinges on life, building on and complicating it, and then proceed to survey some possibilities for the geomorphism of cinematic worlds. As mentioned previously, the "geomorphy" of cinema worlds is ultimately not extractable from their "anthropomorphy" and their "biomorphy." This chapter, coming first in a sequence of three, lays out a set of themes that will be picked up in different keys in the others; but because these require some ground laying, this will be an extended chapter.

Geomorphism in Life and in Image

In everyday perception, we gain knowledge about how the world is structured by virtue of our ability to move about within it. From our first infant steps, we explore the space around us: the domestic space, the space between us and those we learn to recognize as different from us (mother, father, siblings, neighbours, friends), and eventually the spaces outside the home, in the backyard, the neighbourhood, the schoolyard, and beyond. Piece by piece, step by step, we build up a geography of sites and relations, *scapes* harbouring meanings and affording potential actions and relations.

Our everyday geographies are always already meaningful: here is where we do *this*, there is where we aren't allowed to do *that*; our space ends here, which is where *theirs* begins, but this place here is ours, not (as they claim) theirs. Beginning with our bodily motility, we learn to move around, within, and between places in the authorized ways. We learn to spatialize, to distinguish between inside and outside, public and private, ours and theirs. In time, we expand our space of mobility: we run, learn to manoeuvre a tricycle or bicycle, learn to ride buses and trains and to drive our animal- or fuel-powered vehicles. We learn how to move around the globe or some part of it. We learn that it *is* a globe (or not). Gradually the world fills in for us, the places we first heard about as children becoming places we can visit, places whose existence we can confirm for ourselves directly. And if we learn one day that space is an empty container, a meaningless zone in which material bodies move around, by force of gravity or by cause-and-effect relations, we are learning an interpretation that would strike us as bizarre had we not been prepared for that interpretation over years of learning similar abstractions: about time, space, measurement, calculability, and the universe in general.

Visual media interject themselves into this geomorphism, this territorialization of the everyday, in various ways. Visual representations are, first of all, objects: posters, photos, decorative illustrations, cards, dolls, cartoon characters, images on cereal boxes, outlines of faces or body parts. From an early age we learn that what we see in a photograph or on a television or computer screen may refer to something that is out there somewhere, but also that it need not do that—that it may be fictional or imaginary. As external reference is established as a possibility, the things around us take on more of the character of signs, web-like links connecting us to things we do not see but that we know are or may be "out there." (The Internet's echoing of this architecture is both a recurrence and a massive amplification of something that is mundanely present in all human cultural life.) The effect of visual representations is thus to simultaneously fragment and iconicize the world: they take one piece, one image, from out of its profilmic contexts (literally, those that precede the capturing on film) and enable that piece to circulate and to stand for the original, or for a particular understanding of the original. As this is done repeatedly with fragments of the world, the overall effect is the creation of a world of objects or pictures that stand for places, sites, locations, in ways that highlight certain of their qualities. Usually the qualities highlighted are those that are more easily mobilized, while the contextual, background qualities become lost in translation. A world of proliferating signs becomes a world in which meanings are selected and drawn forward from an ever receding background of potential meanings, virtualities that are always multiplicities. Semiosis becomes ever more multiplied and layered.

Visual images thereby layer a geomorphology onto a world that pre-exists them; or, rather, they participate in the world's proliferating geomorphology. They shape the world into one that extends outward in all directions, from things that are visible and immediately present to those that are distant in time and in space. And even though the moving image may add movement to what it displays, we understand, for the most part, that this movement is one of mobilizable things—people, animals, vehicles, objects—against a background of landscapes that remain relatively stable and unchanging. If we agree that this "geomorphing" is one of the things that cinema does, the question for a socio-ecologically oriented criticism becomes this: What kinds of geomorphologies can a film world take on? How has film altered our perceptions of the non-human world and of our relationship to it, and how *else* can it do that, in ways that have perhaps not yet been tried?

An Initial Typology

There are films that make little or no effort to reproduce the kinds of physical settings that are most familiar from people's everyday experience. Such films, generally avant-garde or experimental in nature, may intend to reproduce something about the experience of visuality: instances of light and shadow visible to the eye, or the feeling of dreaming, falling, or flying (as in some of the mesmerizing non-narrative films of Stan Brakhage). Sometimes, as in abstract and formalist films like Marcel Duchamp's *Anemic cinema* (1926),

Fernand Léger's *Ballet mécanique* (1924), or Tony Conrad's *The Flicker* (1966), the intent is purely visual, visceral, or aesthetic. In others, the film medium is pushed to the extremes of its capacity to disorient conventional spatial orientation. For his three-hour-long *La région centrale* (1971), Michael Snow constructed a special apparatus that allowed his camera to pan, tilt, swoop, swing, roll, and rotate on its own stationary axis in the midst of a subarctic northern Quebec landscape. The result, while disorienting, nevertheless feels strangely *embodying* as well: the film disrupts our normal sense perception and replaces it with a machinic, gravity-defying *seeing*, one that is reminiscent of Ralph Waldo Emerson's famous "transparent eyeball," of a rocky landscape that at times seems like its own Mars-like planet set against a familiar earthly sky.

There are also many films that present a consistent geography, but one intended to represent not something singular but something completely generic. What they portray, to creatively redeploy a term from Gilles Deleuze, is "any-spaces-whatever" (*espaces quel-conque*). They may be an average house in a typical city or suburb, or a regular house on the prairie. But even in selecting *this* house in *this* neighbourhood as the cinematic stand-in for "everyhome," the filmmakers have had to select one of an infinity of options, which in the process associates this option with whatever the film makes of it: normality, ideality, exceptionality, a lingering horror hiding beneath the veneer of every-dayness (as in David Lynch's suburban homes in *Blue Velvet*), or something else.

Most films, however, refer to actually existing places and locations. The narratives they present may be fictional or non-fictional; the *mise en scène* may be naturalistic, striving to eliminate any gap between the world viewed and the world itself, or it may be stylized, theatrical, expressionist, surrealist, poetic, or fantastic. There are many films that refer to places that are merely imagined to be real, places that could be real in a possible future (such as the settled Martian surface in *Total Recall* [1990]), or that offer an alternative present (such as *Batman*'s Gotham City, or the Middle Earth of the *Lord of the Rings* trilogy) or a projected past (as in fictional depictions of the Pleistocene in *Quest for Fire* [1981] or *Clan of the Cave Bear* [1986]). But the places are still intended to be recognizable; they are always places that have, like the ancient Rome of Hollywood toga epics, already been imagined, though each film adds its own folds to those already layered imaginings. And through the ways these places and settings are depicted, they are imbued with further meanings layered over onto whatever pre-existing recognizability they harbour.

All films do a certain work on a landscape: they select images or perspectives of it, whether it is from a studio set or an actual location, and then present these edited together in specific sequences and narratives. By inscribing and contextualizing places, a film turns a set of images from New York City into *New*

York, New York!, a selection of suburban Los Angeles into the land of celluloid fantasies we know as "Hollywood," and other places into "the Wild West," "the Far North," the "Outback," the "borderlands," the "inner city" and "urban jungle," "darkest Africa," "the mysterious East," and "the stormy Caribbean." Walter Benjamin famously argued that the age of mechanical reproduction has led to the disappearance of the aura of the artwork, but the opposite may be the case for photographic and cinematic depictions of places and landscapes. The affective machinery of cinema changes the meaning of those landscapes, imbuing them with an aura that becomes ascribed by viewers to the place itself. It adds to its meanings, consolidating an affective layer that will be there, in our memory and our expectations, if and when we actually travel to that place.

Before we examine this broader cinematic territorialization of the world, let us think about the mechanics by which cinema represents the profilmic world. To start with, film *cauterizes* and *reassembles* reality: it cuts it up into individual, rectangularly framed images, scenes, takes, moments, angles, and impressions and reapportions these into new sequences and combinations. Through sequencing, films reshape time, speeding it up—covering entire lifetimes over the course of a couple of hours (which is a feature common to most forms of storytelling)—or slowing it down in a way that parallels the slower art forms of poetry, ritual, and (slowest of all) painting, which moves at the rate of its own decomposition. Space is also altered; and insofar as everything we see takes place on the screen before us, space is collapsed. Cinema renders time and space more infinitely connectable: back and forth, doubling back in an exchange of references, mirrorings, rotations, and convolutions. It creates a mediated world of infinite connectivity. Neither speech nor writing does that as quickly, efficiently, or powerfully as film. The connections, elaborated through the temporal medium of montage, become *where* film takes us: we follow it where it goes, through recognizing, keeping up, noticing, and piecing together the places we are shown and the relations suggested by their sequenced showing.

Cinema's geomorphism is produced in several distinct ways. Films produce a *segmentation* or *fragmentation* of the world in that we are shown disconnected bits of world—pieces, images, or glimpses that are woven together into a Cubist-like assemblage. It is in this respect that Francesco Casetti calls film "an intrinsically futurist and cubist art, and one in which the cubist and futurist gazes are made seemingly 'natural.'"[4] These fragments appear to us as a form of what Noël Carroll calls "detached display": we see and hear them, but we are not able to orient ourselves toward them in a space that is continuous with our bodies.[5] If we do move, in a movie theatre, the display does not change (except, perhaps, to a miniscule extent in three-dimensional films). Yet this assemblage of sounds and images, far from feeling disjointed, tends to feel *inhabited,* at least once the conventions of the given film genre become recognized by a viewer. Through a perceptual dramatization of space, enacted by action-dramatic relationships such as the shot–reverse shot, the cutaway to something that is being viewed by a character, and other classical film techniques, filmed space takes on a naturalness that feels not fragmented but normal. Film thereby takes pieces of world and fuses them into a synthesis, a newly produced world.

At a broader level, cinema provides for a *thematization of distinct meso-worlds* such as places, landscapes, and regions. Generic or stereotyped portrayals of a place are made auratic, coming to stand in both for the place itself and for a set of meanings associated with it. Imbued with these meanings, the places become iconic, and the images iconographic. In time, specific forms of thematization develop as films come to provide a commentary on the world. We get, for instance, a kind of existentialization of space in the films of modernist auteurs such as Michelangelo Antonioni, Wim Wenders, Theo Angelopoulos, or Bela Tarr: through long takes and "time-images," as Deleuze calls them, these films may comment on landscapes within a broader itinerary that is personal or existential, a comment on human experience in the contemporary world. Another form of thematization would be the kind of *global* space created through the melding together of actions or narratives taking place in different parts of the world, as in Wim Wenders's *Until the End of the World* (1991) or Alejandro González Iñárritu's *Babel* (2006). (Both these forms of territorialization will be discussed at greater length below.)

All of this varies, of course, depending on the style of film and on the expectations and perceptual preparedness of the viewer. Classic Hollywood cinema, through what Noel Burch has called the Institutional Mode of Representation, aimed to smoothen the discrepancies of spectatorship through temporal linearity, narrative cause-and-effect logic, naturalistic or highly conventionalized presentation, an alternation of "objective" and "subjective" point-of-view perspectives, and clear segmentation of scenes, sequences, and episodes, all with the goal of making the viewer a ubiquitous observer immersed within the film rather than one who watches it self-consciously from its outside.[6] The aim was not to challenge the preconceptions viewers have about the world, but to build on a particular set of preconceptions, for instance, about what makes life bearable and what makes America decent.

We could overhastily distinguish between two kinds of films here. The first are those that aim to produce this kind of smooth texture, a taken-for-grantedness that offers entertainment, distraction, and pleasure in the context of a general reassurance that things are as they should be and that they are fine—that the film is to be enjoyed and not to be troubled by, and that whatever troubles and conflicts it displays, by the time the film ends all will have been resolved. Conversely, there are films that present an undercurrent of disturbance, trouble, perhaps even incoherence, without offering a final resolution to reconcile the sense of disturbance or even to brush it under the proverbial carpet. The first kind of film offers reassurance partly through the narrative—there is trouble, but it will be resolved, and all's well that ends well—but also through the general texture of the film. Classic Hollywood films, straight-up comedies, and many of the more entertaining and popular forms of cinema follow this first model. Horror films, psychological thrillers, and many, though certainly not all, art films—David Lynch's *Mulholland Drive* (2001) and Lars von Trier's *Antichrist* (2009) come to mind—tend toward the second variant. But most films fall somewhere between the two poles, and in any case, their valency varies between viewers and changes over time. Of greater interest is not whether a film offers reassurance, but whether, and under what circumstances, that offer is accepted or rejected. Does a film reassure us, for instance, that nature will provide for us or that we need not worry at all about our relationship to it (and threfore to capital, to the mode of production and consumption that characterizes our society)? Does it, like Eisenstein's *Battleship Potemkin* (1925), reassure us that the revolution will happen; or, if it no longer succeeds in providing this reassurance, does it tell us why not?

It is in the slippage between assurances that things of interest happen. This chapter will focus on selected options, especially those that have established influential precedents, in cinema's attempts to ensure some connection or other between viewers and the territory of the given. For the most part, this means we will focus on cinema's production of *landscape* and on the ways in which this production is commingled with human identities. Land, and its visual articulation as land*scape*, are two of the primary "givens" or "groundings" within a film world, but they are not the only ones. Urban, rural, and regional landscape imaginaries differ across national and international contexts, but some of the same tropes can be found underlying all of them: the trope of the journey from home and (usually) back; the conflict between city and country, between civilization and wilderness, or between settled populations and nomads or immigrants; and so on. It is usually only when a local or national cinema tradition, such as the Hollywood Western, becomes disseminated, loved, and emulated worldwide, that questions emerge about its power as a form of cultural imperialism; so it becomes important to understand both what it is that is being disseminated and how it takes on new meanings in new contexts. Here we will barely scrape the surface of the "what" that *it* is, since our goal is to suggest possibilities, not to offer an exhaustive account of each and of their historical fates.

Before considering how cinema remakes the "natural," material world—the world that serves as a background to human action, passion, conflict, and achievement—and how it alters our relationship to it, we should trace our way through the traditions of still imagery that are the ancestors of the "nature" found in the moving image. Those traditions largely emerged in Renaissance and early modern Europe. Our journey in this chapter will take a circular or spiral form: it will circle out from that early modern juncture only to return back to it in the postmodern garb of a more networked, digitally shaped "database" visuality. This journey will take us through the "enframing" of nature to its disassembly into an imagistic organicism; or at least that will be the chapter's underlying theme.

Picturing Nature: Landscape Aesthetics as Socio-Natural Production

Nature, as Raymond Williams put it, is the most complex word in the English language. Its primary meanings include "the essential quality or character *of* something," "the inherent force which directs either the world or human beings or both," and "the material world itself, taken as including or not including human beings."[7] In this concatenation of abstract notions, nature has served as a kind of cultural trump card: when we say that something is natural or unnatural, we generally mean to imply that it is also therefore desirable or undesirable, or at least justifiable or not.

As a categorical stand-in for the non-human and non-artifactual world around us, nature, in Western history, has taken many forms. It has been conceived, literally or metaphorically, as a divinely ordained system of norms and rules, rights, and obligations; a book to be read, interpreted, and studied; a motherly female, nurturing and providing for the needs of her children; a body-like organism whose features mirror those of the human body; a clock-like object or machine, to be studied dispassionately and manipulated for human benefit; a ruthless and harsh kingdom, "red in tooth and claw," from which we humans should distance ourselves through the social contract of civilization; a storehouse of resources; a flourishing web of life; an Edenic Garden that should be set aside in protected areas, to be visited periodically for the replenishment of one's soul; a museum or theme park for curiosity seekers, or an open-air gymnasium for trials of masculinity; a cybernetic system or data bank of circulating information; a spirit or divinity, such as an avenging angel striking back at a humanity that has transgressed its natural order; or a locus for the residence of spirits. Most if not all of these images (using the word loosely) have been embodied in material depictions such as paintings, icons, sculptures, and monuments. Each has featured in narratives, some with the kinds of deep historical roots and broad cultural resonances that qualify them as mythic. Each also suggests specific actions as appropriate in relation to nature: subjugation and domination, classification and management, aesthetic appreciation and contemplation, segregation and protection, reverence and worship, or active defence.[8]

None of these "natures" is absolute and simply given to us; all are interpretations that have been made, produced, and set into motion through human activities. This is not to say that they are *social* constructs and nothing more. They are best considered *co-productions* of human imagination, material practice, and the world's interaction with us. This will be a key point in much of what follows: we live in a world of ideas and meanings, but these meanings are embodied, enabled, carried, and mediated by material objects and practices. We live, also, as bodies amidst other bodies, but these bodies relate to one another by virtue of their experience of one another—that is, through perception, which for humans and at least some other beings also means through interpretation. One way in which Western society has made sense of the world is through the discourse of "nature" and "culture," with the first thought to provide a foundation and matrix for the activities of the second. Not all societies have made this distinction: for some, certain humans were thought to have more in common with certain animals, or gods, or other forces, than with *other* humans.[9] The idea of nature makes sense to us not, or not only, because nature is *really there*, but also because the ways we shape our world *make* it so. Paleolithic hunter-gatherers likely moved around without conceptually dividing the world between the wild and the tame. For agriculturalists, however, this distinction became central and seemingly natural, not because it was built into the structure of the universe but because the world was being actively shaped to keep the wild—predators, competitors for our crops, pests and weeds, nomadic humans—away from the domestic sphere that consisted of *our* crops, *our* animals, *our* town. Ideas of nature became mediated by the things humans did, including by the way they organized the world around them.

Ideas and beliefs are, in this way, shaped by practices and by the technologies and institutions that mediate them. All technologies enhance or alter our capacities to do something or other, and in modernity (as I suggested in Chapter 1), visual technologies have become central to our experience of the world. If, as some have argued, the modern is better thought not as a period of historical time but as a form of experience—one premised on change, progress, and the human domination of nature for humanity's (or at least for some people's) benefit—then modernity's Janus-faced nature is well captured by Karl Marx's suggestion that in capitalist modernity "all that is solid melts into air." Modern vision may have given us a clear picture of the world, but that world itself—a world that had once been experienced as a form of manifest givenness, built on eternal verities, timeless forms of structural relations, a "great chain of being" in which each rock, animal, human, and angel had its recognized place—melts in the face of modernization. Visuality has, in this argument, been part of the process by which the world has been destabilized and mobilized. We live not, as Heidegger put it, in the "age of the world picture," but in the age of the world *motion* picture, a time in which the image and essence of the world have both become *movement*.

Modern visuality provides us with a way of knowing the world and with a form of power over it, a power that tends to shape the world in its image. Visual practices have had a profound impact on how we perceive the natural world. As mentioned already, a key moment in this history was the development during the European Renaissance of single-point, linear pictorial perspective. Perspective was not an idea that dropped from the sky or that spawned in the mind of a single genius; it required a set of conditions to make its emergence and spread possible. These included technical tools and capacities, such as Filippo Brunelleschi's single-hole panel and mirror, Leon Battista Alberti's grid, Albrecht Dürer's perspective apparatuses, and a lens-and-mirrored projection chamber known as the *camera obscura*.[10] Renaissance painters fixed nature's appearance within a *framed view*. Their paintings became windows onto a visible world, which, as John Berger put it, converged onto the single eye in such a way that the visible world was arranged "for the spectator as the universe was once thought to be arranged for God."[11] In the process, the observer and the observed were separated, and the latter immobilized.

Linear perspective continues to shape visuality today and is arguably the predominant form of image composition in mainstream cinema. This is not because it is "true" or "natural," inherent to human experience (which can hardly be the case, given that it was not widespread in other societies before its emergence in Europe). Nor is it because it has been arbitrarily imposed on society by some dominant elite. Like the musical scale, linear perspective is best thought of as a "convention" or even a "composition," constructed out of material, discursive, and semiotic variables, but constructed with sufficient durability that it has been able to spread across a range of cultural boundaries. As Gilberto Perez explains, linear perspective is "motivated by its resemblance to the way we perceive things in life from the particular position in space we occupy at each moment." It is in this sense rooted in embodied experience; but there is no *necessary* reason why a human culture should develop visual objects based on linear perspective. It "won acceptance in the Renaissance,"

Perez argues, "because it expressed the outlook of a confident humanism: from a single viewing point the picture would offer a commanding view of the scene, conveying a sense of the world being revealed, yielding its meaning, to an individual human gaze."[12] Perspective is, in this sense, both accurate *and* a constructed convention. The same can be said of many of the visual devices that cinema makes use of, such as the facial close-up (which directs us to notice the emotional response of a character), the shot and shot–reverse-shot sequence, and the single-focus linear narrative.

Linear perspective comes from a time when optics was a frontier of knowledge and scientific study. Renaissance innovations such as telescopes and cartographic mapping techniques made it possible to navigate oceans, map out and colonize new lands, and control and subdivide territories, carving them up as distinct forms of property. Landscape art, from the sixteenth century on, taught its viewers to appreciate the appearance of land as a *view*, as a perspectival snippet of scenery to be enjoyed by a distanced and (often) elevated onlooker. In this way, visuality emerged out of a more multi-sensorial, sensual and bodily embeddedness to achieve a place of privilege among the senses. This ocularcentrism is related to the nature of the human visual perceptual system. The other senses—sound, smell, touch, and taste—all tend to embed us in a more blurred and immersive sensory surround within which we orient ourselves through motion, interaction (especially in the case of touch), or ingestion (in the case of taste and, in a more attenuated way, smell). Vision, by contrast, allows us, without having to abandon our position, to gain a clear and crisp picture of the outlines of things. It lends itself better to the kind of objectifying and distancing orientation to things that became most useful in the early modern period. Because of these qualities, the visual has been of profound service to science, with its measurement and analysis of the physical world; to the modern state, with its colonial and geopolitical domination over space, territory, and people; and to industrial capitalism, with its drive to commodify things, including labour, land, and nature, so as to profit from their trade.

Landscape art accompanied the rise of the political and economic relations that made it possible to buy and sell land (and to evict those who had previously worked that land). It was used to convey meanings about property, ownership, and status, and it buttressed a new sense of territoriality. Sixteenth-century artists made nature into a pictorial image; then, between the seventeenth and nineteenth centuries, that image was commodified. Over the centuries, a series of English parliamentary acts known as the Enclosures Acts converted land from something held in common to the property of individual landowners. Over the same centuries that landscape became the primary subject of

paintings, agrarian capitalism promoted the idea that land was the possession—and a reflection of the identity—of the gentry who owned it. Landscape
gardening, developed around this same time, reshaped the world into its own
picture, as something to be looked at, walked or drawn through by carriage (if
one had the means), and admired for its appearance. Industrialization, in turn,
created a new discursive polarity between the rapidly growing cities and the
depopulating countryside. Nature became what was "out there" in the country, and certain types of landscape came to represent pastoral, romantic, and
classical ideals. In cities, meanwhile, "nature" became parcelled out into public
parks and gardens and later, in a compromised fashion, in suburbs.

Landscape painting would be used over the course of the eighteenth and
nineteenth centuries to promote specific landscapes as emblems of entire
nations: the countryside as the "heart of England," the Alps as Switzerland's
soul, Karelia as the soul of the Finnish people. Analogously, the Catskills,
the Sierras, and the wide-open semi-desert landscapes of the American
Southwest were the frontier spaces in which Americans ostensibly proved
themselves in the eyes of God and became wedded to the maternal landscape
of their new-found continental homeland. Photography democratized these
views and disseminated them widely. In the late-nineteenth-century United
States, the transcontinental railroad companies—one of that era's fastest-
growing oligopolies—hired photographers and artists to portray the western
landscapes, which would soon become the sacred spaces of the national
territorial imaginary. Eastern tourists would flock to them.[13]

FIGURE 3.1 *The Chasm of the Colorado*, by Thomas Moran, 1873–1874.
Smithsonian American Art Museum, lent by the Department of the Interior Museum.

The affective draw here, of course, was hardly reducible to the spectacle of the monumental (as in Yosemite) or the weird (as in Yellowstone) or to the nationalist and political uses of nature. As less and less of the "purely natural" remained—once its inhabitants, such as peasants and indigenous groups, had been removed—campaigns were launched to protect those last remaining pieces of "wilderness" in the form of what would become nature preserves. In Europe, writers and artists visited and celebrated the Alps and other "unspoiled" areas such as England's Lake District. In the United States, grand and monumental landscapes became part of the national imaginary as distinctively American treasures (and the first national parks), analogous to the cathedrals and built monuments of the Old World. In the hands of Romantic artists and writers such as Thomas Cole, Thomas Moran, Albert Bierstadt, Henry David Thoreau, and John Muir, such nature became "sublime," tinged with the divine.

To understand how our gaze changes a place, consider Thomas Moran's painting "Chasm of the Colorado." This is the kind of place that would have been considered puzzling and unattractive by its first European visitors, just as mountains in Europe were considered by some to be hideous gashes on the Earth's surface, signs that humans had "fallen" by committing Original Sin. Thomas Burnet wrote in 1691 that mountains were "monstrous excrescences of nature," "ruines of a broken World," "wild, vast and indigested heaps of Stones and Earth" resulting from the confusion wrought by humanity, not the smooth order made by God. Such places had to be *made* beautiful, and this was accomplished by Romantic artists and writers. In the United States, railroad companies saw commercial potential in this: they hired artists, photographers, and writers to publicize places like Yosemite and Yellowstone. Historian Frederick Jackson Turner, with his famous frontier thesis of American history, and President Theodore Roosevelt, whose friend John Muir led tours for painter-friends, who visited Yosemite in order to recreate it on canvas, made this beautification part of a nation-building agenda. When Muir was living in the Sierras of California, he described what he considered to be one of the most beautiful places in the world as

> in a high degree picturesque, and in its main features so regular and evenly balanced as almost to appear conventional—one sombre cluster of snow-laden peaks ... the whole surging free into the sky from the head of a magnificent valley, whose lofty walls are beveled way on both sides so as to embrace it all without admitting anything not strictly belonging to it.... Down through the midst, the ... river was seen pouring from its crystal fountains ... then sweeping on through the smooth meadowy levels of the valley.[14]

The visuality in Muir's writing is striking: it is as if he is describing a painting, with the angled walls of the glacial valley framing the swollen river in the painting's middle ground and leading viewers' eyes into background terminating in the towering peaks. Muir was, in fact, describing a scene that he thought would appeal to landscape artists with whom he was in correspondence at the time.

Historian Albert Boime has argued that the Hudson River, Rocky Mountain, and Luminist schools of painters made extensive use of the "magisterial gaze," a wide-frame panoramic view from an elevated position, which constructs land as a scenic vista and spectacle, to be gazed at and admired for its sweeping beauty and to thereby be possessed by its viewer.[15] Photographers like Carleton Watkins mastered this "monarch of all I survey" trope, which framed elements in the fore-, middle- and background to give the three-dimensional effect of looking *through* a landscape. Watkins and others created panoramas, linking large plate negatives to produce a 180-degree, or even 360-degree, view. These became, as Oetterman argues, "both a surrogate for nature and a simulator," "an apparatus for teaching people how to see" nature.[16] By way of contrast to these American landscape artists, Canadian artists—including the canonic nationalist Group of Seven painters—tended to favour views from ground level in which the landscape, instead of inviting the viewer to enter into it and to possess it, appeared to be obstructed by nature itself. There was, here, less eagerness to see what was beyond the obstruction, let alone to possess it. Nature, in the Canadian imagination, is less a place laid open to be surveyed, claimed, and conquered, than a harsh environment in the face of which Canadians huddle together, weaving together a social fabric that makes it possible to survive in a cold, northern locale.[17]

The reproduction of places and landscapes as photographs and paintings made these places accessible and available as icons, auratically heightened pieces of the world "out there." At the same time, as Walter Benjamin argued, any aura that an artwork may have originally imbued in a landscape was diluted as its images came to circulate more and more widely. Photography's apparent veneer of authenticity, its indexical quality (in Peirce's terms), in effect came to hide the loss of context—ecological, social, historical, and geographic—that made those places, or the original places that preceded their photographed images, what they were. Where trains took the masses to nature, photography brought nature to the masses and, in the process, the aura of the original places was transformed or destroyed, even while a new aura was generated around the *image* of nature.[18] As Benjamin wrote: "to pry an object from its shell, to destroy its aura, is the mark of a perception whose 'sense of the universal equality of things' has increased to such a degree that it extracts it even from a unique object by means of reproduction."[19]

By the latter half of the nineteenth century, railways had made it possible for the middle classes to travel to these landscapes and see them from out of the windows of a moving train. Static portrayals of land were supplemented with the dynamic experience of it—a shift noticeable in the atmospheric paintings of Turner, Constable, and others. Railway travel and automobile vision compressed space and speeded up the time it took to traverse it; they enabled a more expansive sense of the landscape as a visual object. It is more than coincidental that the motion picture was popularized at the same time as the private automobile: both make it possible to experience the landscape in motion. Together, the private automobile and the camera rendered everything as potential "scenery" to be viewed and captured through the window of a moving vehicle. Nature became framed as a series of scenic views, lookout points, and picture spots. It became something *out there*, separate from the human realm: outdoors, outside of cities, and especially in the national parks. Some have argued that the framing and sentimentalization of nature leads to disappointment when nature fails to live up to our expectations. Similarly, for young people whose experience of open deserts and national parks is primarily from automobile advertisements, "settings experienced on foot or onsite feel slow, poorly produced, and ironically less real."[20]

The other side of the coin, however, is that the idealized image of a sublime nature has powered the cause of conservation, because it is precisely the tension between the idealized view and the imperfect reality—or the prospect of its imminent destruction—that encourages many to take environmental action. The camera, as Charles Bergman has argued, has been environmentalists' number one tool: nature photography and television documentaries have been "the front line in the environmental battle with the economic forces of exploitation." Environmentalism's dependence on photography includes the Sierra Club's use of the photographs of Ansel Adams, Eliot Porter, and others.[21] In the late 1960s, Greenpeace took to heart Marshall McLuhan's argument about "the medium" being "the message" and produced a series of photographs of environmental activists risking their lives to bear witness on behalf of the new scientific world view of ecology. When, in the late 1960s, earthborne humans were treated to images of the planet from space—a result of the most ambitious technological and military race the world had yet known—it became possible to visualize a single blue-green globe hovering in a black darkness—something that had up to that point been hardly imaginable. Nature, as a consequence, became more than merely what was out there: nature became, once again, *us*, but reflected from a very long distance away.

The past six centuries, then, have witnessed a profound transformation: nature is no longer perceived as a mother or as "God's deputy," but rather as a resource bank or a holistic biophysical system. This transformation has not been linear, nor has it gone without challenge. My point is that underlying cinematic visuality today are archaeological strata in which humans have been *central* and nature has been *ambient*; and as one result of this, nature has taken on the role of property, of aesthetic object, of evolutionary arena, of recreational setting, and more recently of ecological system. When considered as an aesthetic object in itself, the ambient becomes *focal*, and the relations that make it, and those it refers to, become ambient. This is analogous to the ways in which nature takes on a thematic centrality in the literary genre known as "nature writing." I will discuss the relationship between nature writing and nature films in Chapter 5. Here, I will focus especially on the production of an ambient, background *givenness* to the world of the characters and actions that, by and large, make up the focus of traditional cinema.

Anchoring the Filmic World

The classic method of opening a scene or film is through an "establishing shot." This is generally an extreme long shot showing the entire space in which the ensuing action will take place. An establishing shot anchors what is to come, revealing the context and background against which the narrative events will unfold and typically establishing some set of relations between key characters and a geographic or historical setting. When the narrative takes place somewhere specific, the film's initial establishing shots typically show landmarks identifiable with that place: the Eiffel Tower standing for Paris, the Manhattan skyline for New York, and so on. In our terms, an establishing shot creates an objectscape, which is to say that it provides the setting for the subjectscape, since the two are co-emergent. The objectscape, usually made up of material elements recognizable from the extra-filmic world, is thereby connected to that extra-filmic world. We start, therefore, at the outset with a semiotic link: the place we see before us on the screen *is* Paris, or *is* a tropical island (like those to which northerners flock in the winter), or *is* a city-sized spacecraft sailing through interstellar space. So much is given.

What we see of the objectscape, however, is always delimited by the frame of the camera. Here, cinema's inheritance from the Renaissance painters is undeniable. Perspectival representation sets out a contemplative gaze against a viewed and viewable scene (which becomes a "seen"). It is premised on the act of seeing-without-being-seen, a "viewing subject—viewed object" relationship. In comparison to our natural field of vision, what film shows is narrow and circumscribed, monocular rather than bifocal, and incorrigibly rectangular, being an extension of the painterly and photographic frame into time. But this opening up into time is what gives film its power: the frame restricts our view, rendering offscreen everything that does not fit into it (if only temporarily), even while film's temporal openness means we are subjected to a changing stream of moving rectangular images, a stream that allows for a near infinite variability and malleability—now taking us to a bird's eye view, now closing in on a human face, or even on a single teardrop on that face; at one point stationary, at another moving, whether forward, back, side to side, drunkenly or excitedly, or flitting around in a counterpoint of multiperspectival bursts.

The movement inward and outward of the camera, especially with the use of wide-angle and telephoto lenses, makes possible a seeing that is rare or impossible in everyday life. Enlargement of things, as Benjamin argued, "brings to light entirely new structures of matter," while slow motion "discloses quite unknown aspects within" things.[22] Editing makes possible a jumping around from one place to another, resulting in a collision of points of view. The eye is simultaneously liberated of the weight and torpor of the body and tied, as if captured, to the predetermined arrangements forced upon it by the camera's movement (and the editing). One of the cornerstones of the psychoanalytical theorizing spearheaded by the British journal *Screen* in the 1970s was the notion that the viewer identifies with the camera, an identification that results in the voyeuristic pleasure of the gaze that sees but that is itself not seen. For Jean-Louis Baudry and Christian Metz, this provides us with a transcendental subjectivity that, paradoxically, reverts the viewer to a state like that of a childlike "primary narcissism." We are allowed to travel, in our imagination, and the places we travel to and the people we see are, or were, *real* insofar as they were filmed. But they do not see us.

What *sort* of reality is it about these scenes, these physical landscapes, that a film captures? On the surface, film is as realistic as any medium can be. As cognitive film theorist Stephen Prince argues, film is *perceptually* realistic because of the ways it corresponds to our audiovisual experiences of three-dimensional space. It provides a variety of "cues" to "organize the display of light, color, texture, movement, and sound in ways that correspond with the viewer's own understanding of those phenomena in daily life."[23] In this, film is prosaic. According to a common trope, film is to photography as literature is to poetry, with the former of each pair conferring more narrative primacy to human action by virtue of its greater correspondence to the ways we move through the world. The latter, by contrast, presents something more like a vertical snapshot (in depth, in the case of poetry) of the world as it is. The photograph is more poetic, and, as Raymond Bellour has argued, cinema's potential to generate a more pensive form of spectatorship only comes when its movement is stilled through a reversion to the photographic, as in the freeze frame or the workings of *mise en scène*.[24]

P. Adams Sitney insists, however, that cinema, like poetry, has a tremendous capacity for portraying the surface of the world. (Sitney is a historian of experimental film, which is itself often compared to poetry, in contrast to narrative film's prose.) This surface includes weather events such as storms, blizzards, fogs, "the movement of clouds, changes in the intensity of light, the indications of breezes in the vibrations and swaying of flora, and the gradations of rain." Sound cinema, Sitney argues, far from merely giving humans more of a voice in films, "gave the *landscape* a voice: wind, sea, fire, thunder, more often than not artificially produced or doctored for clarity and effect, vitalized landscape images and extended the auditory environment (as did the sounds of birds, animals, traffic, etc.) beyond the visible frame." Speech added another means to call attention to the landscape. In *Fort Apache* (1948), for instance, "a Chicano cavalryman toasts the panning overview of an arroyo in Monument Valley, 'la tiera di mia madre,' at a turning point in the film that marks the domination of the desert by the brutality of the U.S. army."[25]

In a perceptive account of the difference between "setting" and "landscape" in cinema, Martin Lefebvre echoes Bellour's point by arguing that the latter requires the interruption of the narrative by spectacle, and specifically by a contemplative gaze.[26] There is little in cinema that is fully analogous to the 300-year-old tradition of European landscape art, for which landscape is the "primary and independent subject matter of a work." (The exceptions are those experimental films by Michael Snow, David Rimmer, James Benning, Stan Brakhage, Larry Gottheim, Rose Lowder, and others, which consist largely or completely of shots of what can only be called landscape.)[27] But landscape, in Lefebvre's sense, emerges in those moments when a contemplative gaze arises for the viewer.[28] This is generally only momentary, but due to cinema's durational nature—what Lefebvre calls its "doubly temporalized" nature, since it is subjected both to the temporality of the film medium and to that of the spectator's gaze, which depends on the spectator's ability to move back and forth between narrative and spectacular modes of spectation—this perception of a cinematic landscape can be encouraged by specific techniques, such as the long or extreme long shot and the slow pan.[29]

Lefebvre distinguishes between two kinds of cinematic landscapes. There are those that are "intentional," elicited through the filmmaker's citation of a known pictorial landscape. Examples of this include a Van Gogh painting in Vincent Minnelli's *Lust for Life* (1956), a character's reaction to scenery (as in the Marilyn Monroe character's "It's like a dream!" in response to a Nevada vista in John Huston's 1961 *The Misfits*), and the use of landscapes as extra-diegetic leitmotifs or inserts clearly intended to comment in some way on the narrative (as in the camera's lingering on settings absent of humans in the work of high-modernist directors like Antonioni, Angelopoulos, and Wenders, or in the landscape inserts that populate the later films of Godard). Then there are "unintentional" landscapes, where it is the spectator who initiates the bringing of a "landscaping gaze" to something seen on the screen. This distinction, however, presumes that intentionality is entirely that of the filmmaker(s), which is a view that a process-relational approach would wish to complicate. And while Lefebvre suggests that cinematic landscapes are forms of spectacle, it might be more accurate to say that there are more "poetic" or "contemplative" forms of spectacle, and there are more "kinetic" forms of spectacle. Appreciating a landscape view is a matter of interpretation, that is, of thirdness; it is, at least, a bringing into thirdness of the firstness of what we see.[30] Freeze frames, extreme long shots, slow pans, and long takes all make it possible for us to stop and think, but they are always interpreted in the context of the film itself. If they seem unmotivated, they are likely to raise a question like "Why is the filmmaker showing this now?" That an extreme long shot of an outdoor scene is interpreted as a beautiful landscape means that the viewer has picked up the cultural habit of aesthetically appreciating a viewed scene.[31]

If "landscape" is what happens to "setting" once it has been brought in from the margins and made central, then we could posit a continuum between setting and landscape, or setting-as-marginal and setting-as-focal. The opposite of this continuum, an axis running perpendicular to this one, would be a continuum of *action*, populated by the characters who are its agents. Setting, in this sense, is the given, the background, the organization of the world behind and around the active carriers of the narrative. But this setting is never *merely* given, since it is a product of cinema and of the viewer's engagement in the cinematic world. It is always part of a process whereby what appears given has *become* that way. Givenness is enacted; it is a verb for which the noun—an individual, a community, the national state, an empire—acts in a way that *makes* the given *given*. The remainder of this chapter will focus on a series of cinematic instances in which a particular kind of relationship is crystallized between the given world—a world of nature, environment, geography, or objectscape—and the human world. There are many variations on this relationship: for instance, the world as "ours," the world as fixed, or oppressive, and the world as liberating, freeing, an open expanse beyond the *immediately* given. This will not be an exhaustive survey, but my hope is that the variety presented will convey some of the tremendous variability that is possible in cinema. Focusing on films that depict or reflect historical moments when these relations were in flux will be a helpful way of cutting through the myriad of available possibilities.

Staking Claims and Territorializing Identities:
Making the West

There have always been "peoples," groups identifiable by what we now call ethnic, religious, or cultural commonalities, and these have typically emerged in and through relations with specific landscapes and environments. But land is always potentially contested, and each social group that claims it extends that claim through narrative and visual means (and sometimes through force of arms). The idea of a world divided into tightly bounded territories, each encompassing a single group of people and ruled by a unitary governance structure, is, however, a relatively new one. As historian Benedict Anderson has demonstrated, the sovereign nation-state could not have emerged without print media. It was the reproduction and dissemination of historical narratives, newspapers, and educational materials within a national and territorial space that bound together the community of speakers that made up the modern nation. While nation building is complicated, one could simplify the process, without doing too much violence to it, into this equation: *Territory + Narrative + Media = Nation.* (This is a variation on "Geomorphy + Anthropomorphy + Biomorphy = Cosmos," or "Objectivation + Subjectivation + Interperceptual/ Prehensive Relations = World." More prosaically, start with the firstness of the given, add to it the thirdness of the sense made of it and—what is too often forgotten—the secondness of the relations between things, people, events, practices, and technologies that enables that sense to emerge; and what results is a shared world.)

It makes a significant difference which medium is contributing to the mediating variable. Alongside print media, visual media transformed national territory into a visualizable entity. Landscape art, and later photography, helped populate an imagined territory with "scenes" and "settings" by which national histories, with their heroes and narratives, were understood to have taken place. By the middle of the twentieth century, television, through national broadcasting networks, had taken on the role that print media once had. But it was the cinema of the first half of the century that turned landscapes into visual settings for the restaging of national narratives. As they were forming themselves, most nation-states identified certain of their parts as homelands and hearths: the British countryside, the Gaelic-speaking west of Ireland, Austria's Tyrolean Alps, Finland's Karelia, and other perceived cultural heartlands became symbolically imbued with the "souls" of their respective nations.[32] In film, these are the iconic landscapes. The best known and most singly influential example of this process is that rendered by the Hollywood western, the genre most often considered to be the United States' signal contribution to the language of world cinema.

Westerns arose out of the confluence of two developments: cinema's becoming a mass medium—*the* mass medium stitching together the new technological America of the twentieth century—and the aftermath of the closing of the frontier, once Euro-Americans had conquered and settled all the lands from the Atlantic to the Pacific and were proceeding to settle and utilize all that land to its fullest. Western movies were preceded by Western novels, which embodied a mythology emerging out of the insecurities and uncertainties of the nineteenth century: urbanization and industrialization, a massive influx of non-Anglo-Saxon immigrants, struggles for labour power and women's suffrage, along with the white elite's associated fears of the supposedly "feminizing" effects of urban life. The myth of the West grew in the latter decades of the nineteenth century, shaped in and through the novels of James Fenimore Cooper, Owen Wister, Bret Harte, Louis L'Amour, and Zane Grey; the canvasses of Albert Bierstadt, Fredric Remington, and Charles Russell; the photographs of Carleton Watkins and Eadweard Muybridge; the historical writings of Turner and (later President) Theodore Roosevelt; and representative characters such as Buffalo Bill Cody and his Wild West Show. Railway and tourist companies opened up the *actual* West, and photography increased its visibility, stimulating easterners' desire to travel there.

The western movie developed as a retrospective mythology for the American nation, with the settling of the West portrayed as a matter of heroism, drama, and character building. As Turner argued in his frontier thesis, a uniquely American identity was forged out of the encounter between the civilization of settlement and the savagery of the "Wild West." Classic Westerns portrayed this history as an encounter between good and evil, man and nature, law-abiders and outlaws, populists and profiteers, with the struggles between these enacted around a series of further polarities: individual and community, desert wilderness and blooming garden, nature (and natural law) and culture (institutional law), the freedom of open space versus the order of the contained and the settled, the feminine virtues of child rearing and education and the masculine virtues of heroism, justice, and exploration. Born, as André Bazin put it, "of an encounter between a mythology and a means of expression," westerns were about both a place and a way of seeing.[33] The West was ultimately the creation of easterners; it had meaning as long as it could perform the function of its difference, the "there" to the East's "here," which required that it be a place for finding oneself, for trials of masculinity, for a return to nature and innocence, but most of all, for building the nation, in microcosm, from the ground up.

To be such a place, the West had to be visualizable *as* that otherness. As Gary Hausladen has shown, most Westerns have been filmed in southern California (including Lone Pine and Death Valley), southern Utah and northern Arizona (including Monument Valley), New Mexico and southern Arizona, and northern Mexico. Of these, Monument Valley and southern California's Alabama Hills are the most iconic.[34] Places such as Arizona's Monument Valley became fixed in American imaginations as the frontier that shaped the American character. The extreme long shot was central to the western filmmaker's palette, allowing for an exposition of wide-open spaces and grand vistas in unpopulated and minimally vegetated land. The desert of the Southwest, Perez has written, lends itself to the frontier myth "because it is a landscape of inchoation, a world where green seems to be making a beginning ... sublime in its awesome immensity, a sight that dwarfs the beholder and defeats the attempts to contain it; [but] a sublime that allows human beings to inhabit and cultivate it, that offers a field of human possibilities and potential growth: an image of the open frontier."[35]

The Southwest's buttes, mesas, and other natural formations reflect this inchoate formativity: they are architectural monuments that have not yet been shaped into the civilization that they promise and mock by turns. With its "sharp contrasts of light and shadow, ... topographical contrasts of plain and mountain, rocky outcrops and flat deserts, steep bare canyons and forested plateaus," the Southwest exemplifies in visual images the thematic conflict between savagery and civilization.[36] It is, as Jane Tompkins put it, "a land defined by absence: of trees, of greenery, of houses, of the signs of civilization, above all, absence of water and shade." The West was a crucible: "not only a space to be filled," but "a stage on which to perform" and "a territory to master."[37]

If there is a single director who embodies the western, it is John Ford. A pioneer of location shooting and the extreme long shot, Ford is widely acknowledged as having inaugurated the Golden Era of the genre with *Stagecoach* (1939), a film made largely in the panoramic setting of Monument Valley. Ford came back to this landscape in eight other films, though he used it to stand for a multitude of fictional settings, including southern Arizona, southern New Mexico, and Texas. Ed Buscombe notes that Monument Valley has "come to signify Ford, Ford has come to be synonymous with the Western, the Western signifies Hollywood cinema, and Hollywood stands for America. Thus, through a kind of metonymic chain, Monument Valley has come to represent America itself."[38] Ford's framing of the landscape "to exert the maximum contrast between its vast distances and the smallness of the figures that populate it," Buscombe argues, "is a clear echo of nineteenth-century photographic practice." In the western, the action frequently takes the form of a journey and landscape thereby "becomes an obstacle which has to be overcome"; it acts as "a test of the protagonists' characters."[39]

Widely acknowledged as one of the greatest westerns ever made, and named Greatest Western by the American Film Institute in 2008, *The Searchers* (1956) is an indelible instance of Ford's use of landscape. It is about Ethan Edwards (John Wayne), a Civil War veteran obsessed with avenging the burning down of his brother's homestead and the abduction of his two nieces by Comanche Indians. The themes of revenge, racism, miscegenation, and intercultural conflict are not unusual for Ford's westerns; what concerns us here is the way in which the land is fought over by two rival cultures, its status as territory as yet uncertain. In his analysis of Ford's westerns, Peter Wollen describes Ford's world as "governed by a set of oppositions"—"garden versus wilderness, ploughshare versus sabre, settler versus nomad, European versus Indian, civilized versus savage, book versus gun, married versus unmarried, East versus West" (94), but with the "master antinomy" being between wilderness and garden. This dichotomy is in turn "crystallized" in specific "striking images." In *The Searchers*, the opening and closing scenes frame all of this in starkly visual terms. In the first scene, as Richard Hutson describes it, "a hole opens in the center of the screen, a door opening to a view of the buttes and spires of Monument Valley. A woman, in silhouette, steps through the rectangular frame, and looks outward into the valley.... The interior from which she steps is black, conforming to the silhouette and starkly contrasting with the massive expanse and gorgeous color of Monument Valley."[40]

Coming out of her cabin door, the woman recognizes a rider approaching in the distance, framed in turn by two buttes. One by one, her husband and their three children come to greet the husband's brother. At the film's end, the nomadic loner-hero returns once again to the frontier homestead, this time that of the Edwards' neighbours the Jorgensens (the former had been killed, their daughters kidnapped, by Comanches, setting off the revenge quest that takes up most of the film). Carrying the lone remaining daughter in his arms, he deposits her on the porch for the welcoming Jorgensens to take her in. He lingers momentarily in the framed doorway, then turns away and walks into the swirling dust of the desert, back to the wilderness from which he came.

This motif of the doorway separating the homestead, the world of domesticity that is for the most part (in this film) left in darkness, from the colourful, unbounded, and dangerous expanse outside, underlines the ways in which the domestic is a space to be carved out of the wilderness, but also that the process of carving remains always fraught and never complete. At one point in the film, during the funeral for the Edwards, Mrs. Jorgensen states prophetically that "some day, this country's gonna be a fine good place to be. Maybe it needs our bones in the ground before that time can come." Soon afterwards, when the war party finds a Comanche buried beneath a large sandstone rock, Ethan shoots out his eyes, explaining that by "what that Comanche believes," "ain't got no eyes, he can't enter the spirit land. Has to wander forever between the winds." Territory is to be made with the accumulated blood of the ancestors. The irony is that Edwards himself is a wanderer between worlds. He knows the Comanches as well as anyone, speaking their language, but hates them with a vehemence, apparently for killing his mother and later the woman he loved, his brother's wife. He is also incapable of settling. It is as if he is the embodiment of the inchoate landscape of Monument Valley, all raging potential and no territoriality. The West, meanwhile, will belong to those whose ancestors are buried there and whose past will live on to claim it for them in the future. For all its ambiguities, the cinema of John Ford, like that of other classic westerns, replayed this scene endlessly as if to repeatedly claim that landscape for Americans in the twentieth century (even as it rendered it never fully claimable—an ambiguity that was lost in the work of lesser directors).

Dovzhenko's Cinematic Pantheism

A different kind of territoriality is found among those social groups whose history in a place is not in question. The next chapter will explore the encounter between these two kinds, but every part of the world bears evidence today of some conflict between tradition and modernity, between the settled and the new, between the old, rural ways and their capture by the economic grasp of capital. This clash is most ironic when the forces of change come bearing the claims of protection against the very kind of change they embody. Such was the case in the early Soviet Union. When Josef Stalin ascended to power in the mid-1920s, only about 1 percent of Soviet land had been collectivized; the remainder belonged mostly to the peasants who farmed it—about four-fifths of the population. Stalin's strategy of rapid heavy industrialization required that farms produce much larger surpluses that could feed a growing industrial workforce and be exported to pay for imports of heavy machinery. The requisitioning and seizure of grain was resisted by peasants, resulting in decreased production, which Stalin blamed on a vaguely defined class of wealthier landholders called *kulaks*. In December 1929, Stalin announced his intention to liquidate the *kulak* class in an effort to collectivize all farms in the Soviet Union. Over the winter, land allotments were eliminated and combined into collective farms, which were controlled by Communist Party officials and appointees. By late February of 1930, about half of Soviet farmland had been collectivized, and about 70 percent of the farmland in Ukraine, the Soviet Union's breadbasket. By 1936, following another five-year push, and at a cost of several million deaths, about 98 percent of arable land in the Ukrainian Soviet Socialist Republic had been collectivized.[41] A relationship between individuals and land, mediated by subsistence needs and a small-scale market economy, had been replaced by a relationship between a vast bureaucracy and a continent-sized land mass, with the goal of turning the Soviet Union into an agro-industrial powerhouse.

Considered one of the lasting achievements of early Soviet cinema, Alexander Dovzhenko's *Earth* (*Zemlya*, 1930) is a portrait of a Ukrainian village in the midst of this collectivization process. On the surface, it is a film about the appearance of a tractor, the first in the village; it is, as Gilberto Perez describes it, "a tractor movie," but one that rose to the level of "a great film poem."[42] Its poetry concerns not the process of collectivization itself (though that is what Soviet authorities had expected from it), but the cycle of life and of humans living in rhythm with that cycle. It is a paradoxical film that on the one hand is consistent with artists' and intellectuals' overall embrace of the dawning socialist era, but on the other hand portrays this revolution as neither utopian nor tragic, but as displaced into the larger context of natural rhythms and cycles.

The film is framed by two deaths: that of an old man, Semen, and that of his grandson, the revolutionary Vasyl. Neither of these deaths is merely a death; each is set within an ensemble of events. Viewed through twenty-first-century cinematic eyes, the film's montage techniques may seem heavy-handed and readily ascribable to the Soviet milieu. For Eisenstein, Pudovkin, and others, montage was the means by which the image was freed to do the work of the filmmaker. In splicing together one image and the next to produce a new juxtaposition, Soviet filmmakers deployed the fragmentation inherent to the cinematic image in the cause of creating new meanings. In Dovzhenko, however, as Perez argues in a perceptive analysis of the film, the fragmentation of space "helps bring forward the body and individuality of things."[43] The film's first frames include shots of wheatfields stirring in the wind under an open sky; a woman standing, immobile, next to a huge sunflower that sways in the wind; then the sunflower itself, followed by shots of fruits, including apples and melons. Each of these, like a hieratic still life containing and expressing movement and energy, is part of an ensemble, but each is also what it is. Perez writes: "A Dovzhenko close-up wins us over wholly to itself for the time of its projection.... No other filmmaker so excludes from our minds everything not being shown, so leads us to concentrate on what each image contains."[44] Similarly, the film ends, following Vasyl's funeral, with a sequence of hieratic images: wheatfields, apples, and melons under a cleansing and fertilizing spring rain.

Unlike Eisenstein's more didactic form of montage, Dovzhenko creates a lyrical and poetic montage by simultaneously presenting things in their givenness—an apple, for instance, being simply an apple—and retaining a semiotic openness whereby that apple may represent something—life, fertility, wholeness, fruition, abundance, continuity, temptation, and so on—but need not and is not constrained in doing so. Close-ups, Perez argues, are conventionally thought to be synecdoches, where a part stands for the whole: "A doorknob turning stands for a door being opened; a full ashtray means that a stretch of time was anxiously spent." Each of these is a sign that is clear and understandable but also constrained. The thing depicted "is not so important in itself: it recedes in favor of the meaning it carries." With Dovzhenko, however (and this is something that continues in the work of Tarkovsky), "what is there is all that counts, the thing clearly and tangibly in view." In *Earth* "the apples and the wheat are not a mere backdrop for the action, and the people of the Ukrainian village not subordinate to a few main characters: everything that is shown assumes a full importance of its own."[45] Rather than getting lost or absorbed in the movement of the narrative (secondness), these things stand out as singularities, individuations, peaks or plateaux, fully revealed. Things, as Perez puts it, "squarely confronted, show us their full face" and "are held on the screen long enough for our eyes to go beyond the mere appearance and get a grasp of the substance." *Earth* is in this sense not dramatic but "epic in its images" and at the same time is "lyric in the succession of images, in the connections it makes between things."[46]

Immobility in Dovzhenko, as Perez puts it, is the opposite of the inanimate: "it is a moment of life captured, distilled, with the completion of eternity."[47] Dovzhenko's approach here resembles the Eastern Christian tradition of icon painting, where things are meant to be gazed at, not for their beauty and harmony of form (as would a typical viewing of a Renaissance painting), but for their resemblance to what they stand for. In traditional Eastern Christian iconography, they stand for the divine; but in Dovzhenko, they stand for themselves, Platonic ideals of a sort but without transcendent referent. They stand for the immanent energies that radiate or pulsate through them. Dovzhenko continues the tradition of the religious iconographer working in a post-religious world. His images, like those of the later "poetic cinema" master Sergei Paradjanov's *Sayat Nova* (*The Color of Pomegranates*, 1968), are hieratic, almost ceremonial. But there is movement in the ensemble by which these images are brought together, the rhythm of the montage, and in each image itself. As Perez argues, this allows for a cinema that presents the "energies of being," the "intrinsic force that people and things possess."

While it may be disputed whether any film directly exhibits the "energies of being"—the meaning of a film, after all, changes with time and with audience expectations—that cinema *can* do this is a point I will develop below. Another way of making this point is to say, using Heidegger's language, that cinema can "unconceal" the things themselves even as it portrays change unfolding through them, such as in this case the change instantiated by the arrival of the tractor and, by extension, of the revolution. In terms of the triadics of the film experience, there are, first, the images in their singularity: the objects, faces, landscapes, gestures, movements, and energies, with an eruptive force of the virtuality emanating from them. Second, there is the subsumption of the images within the flow of relational events, where happenings necessitate other happenings, and where what is seen is always an indication of movement in the plot or development of the film's story. And third, there is the concatenation of references and potential interpretations, in which our knowledge— about Dovzhenko, the Russian Revolution, collectivization, and the cinematic developments of the time and afterwards—is brought to bear on our experience. In *Earth*, the level of narrative is fairly minimal: an old man dies, a tractor arrives, villagers disagree in their responses to the new artifact and what it represents, a young activist is shot, a funeral is held for him. Yet little happenings are drawn into an overarching sense of things; they are held or borne into a kind of Heideggerian fourfold of earth, sky, mortals, and divinities, an earthbound cyclicality of what Dovzhenko himself called a "biological, pantheistic conception," that subsumes everything yet bestows change with its blessing. In the film's central montage, as Marco Carynnyk describes it, "in the moonlight of a warm summer night, after scenes of plentiful harvest, cattle ruminate, storks nest for the night, and young couples gaze at the dark sky in motionless ecstasy, the hands of the boys on the girls' breasts."[48]

At the time it was released, Dovzhenko's cinematic poetry was not particularly appreciated by Soviet authorities, who would have preferred the film's unity to be granted by the revolution rather than by the village itself, in its embrace with time and change. The film's open-endedness did not suit the regime's needs, which were, if anything, more intently focused on the kind of territorializing, identity-shaping goals that westerns provided for Americans. So *Earth* was denounced as defeatist and counter-revolutionary. Several scenes were excised, including one in which the tractor's radiator is replenished by men urinating from atop the vehicle, another of Vasyl's mother in labour during her son's funeral, and another, near the film's end, in which Vasyl's inconsolable fiancée tears her clothes off and throws herself about in despair.[49] Perez argues that of those characters who "may be called the dissidents to Vasyl's funeral—those who for one reason or another are not participants in the singing," including the *kulak* who murdered him, the priest who is excluded from it, and the grieving father and mother—it is the girlfriend whose "dissidence is undismissible."[50] Dissidence, here, is relative: it is not that the parents and fiancée do not grieve for Vasyl; rather, they do not partake in the celebration of the revolution that Vasyl's death is taken to stand for. The two deaths in the film are, in this sense, "a complex embodiment" of "the large transformation, hurtful and hopeful, that collectivization, and more generally the revolutionary remaking of the world, brought to the land and its people."[51] The film ultimately marks not only a revolution in the Soviet social order, but also a massive transformation in the relationship between that social order and the Earth. Dovzhenko's leap of faith was that earthly cycles would continue, with Communist collectivization being incorporated, through the ritual sacrifice of one of its agents, into the pagan rhythms of the agricultural village.

Nature, Holism, and the Eco-Administrative State

Once the link is severed between a people and its natural context, there is a limited set of responses this severance will tend to evoke. One is the modernist response, which asserts that the link is no longer relevant, since we have the capacity to reshape relations at will, thanks to technology, science, reason, or sheer will. While this can result in a Promethean humanism, of the sort that Stalin's Soviet regime would have approved, it is not necessarily contradicted by an ecological world view: the films of Pare Lorentz (to be discussed next) provide an illustration of how even the strongest ecological critique can be allied with a modernizing sensibility. A second response we might call postmodernist, though it appears in the films of a range of auteurs who are more commonly considered artistic modernists. This response charts the malaise of modernity, seemingly lamenting it but offering little way out except, at best, through adaptation. A third response is counter-modernist in that it seeks to overcome modernity through a retrieval, of one kind or another, of what it has shed. Between these three positions are a range of potential negotiations, which we can examine by focusing on some of the techniques each pursues.

At the time that collectivization, with its goal of rapid and massive industrialization, was in full swing in the Soviet Union, the capitalist juggernaut of Wall Street had come crashing down in the country that was soon to become the Soviet Union's strongest ideological opponent. The Great Depression was in part a result of unhinged capitalism, but, as with the drought that struck the Soviet Union in the late 1920s and early 1930s, the American experience was also a matter of nature responding to human action. Between 1930 and 1936, a series of severe dust storms turned the Great Plains into what became known as the Dust Bowl. Encouraged by the Homestead Act and by the growth of transcontinental railways, waves of ranchers, homesteaders, and settlers and labourers had migrated westward onto the vast plains stretching from Texas up to Canada. Decades of intensive farming without crop rotation, fallow fields, or cover crops, and deep ploughing of the plains topsoil, had displaced the native prairie grasses and made the land vulnerable to drought. After a series of dry years, the soil turned to dust, which was carried away in vast clouds south and east as far as the Atlantic. Millions of acres of farmland became barren and hundreds of thousands of farmers were displaced from their homes—a story made famous in John Steinbeck's *The Grapes of Wrath*.

Franklin Delano Roosevelt's New Deal administration launched a number of programs intended to combat the Dust Bowl and related ecological calamities. These included the Civil Conservation Corps, the Soil Conservation Service, and the Tennessee Valley Authority. In tandem with these, agricultural reform and resource management programs focused on "permanent" agriculture and on the young science of ecology, which had been developing rapidly over the preceding two decades. Alongside these reforms, the New Deal established a number of federally sponsored cultural initiatives; these included funding for populist mural paintings, photographic documentation of Depression-era America, and—for a rare moment in American history—a government-backed film production unit. Having been appointed by Roosevelt as film consultant to the Resettlement Administration, Pare Lorentz produced two documentaries embodying the New Deal philosophy of state-directed ecological intervention. Each of these bears examination as an instance of an eco-nationalist visuality.

Like Dovzhenko's *Earth*, which had made a strong impression on several members of Lorentz's original production unit, *The Plow That Broke the Plains* (1936) foregrounded crisis and change and resolved to bring order to it. The broader frame of *The Plow* is less that of cyclicality, however, and more the biblically rooted one of decline and hoped-for restoration. For Lorentz, the Dust Bowl was explainable in terms of a Puritan narrative of a fall from grace. His panoramic visions established the grasslands as ideally suited to the Midwestern climate; farmers were shown as ignoring ecological realities and, in the process, bringing about ruin. *The Plow* mobilized wide-angle cinematography to present ecological catastrophe as an expression of the sublime. But, as Finis Dunaway argues, this was not the "romantic sublime" of nature as "monumental peaks and towering trees"; rather, it was the "catastrophic sublime" of "nature as a violent, destructive force."[52] The panoramic view of the wide-angle lens makes possible an image of ecology. Lorentz's approach to picturing the world drew on the young science of ecology, with its notions of "climax communities" and a "balance of nature." He utilized Eisensteinian montage techniques, but where Eisenstein had de-emphasized the individual to glorify the collective hero, the masses in action, Lorentz was more interested in an aesthetic of ecological holism.

In *The Plow*, the land itself is the main character. Sketching the history of the Great Plains, the film announces itself, in its opening captions, as "a record of land ... of soil rather than people." Like Dovzhenko's *Earth*, *The Plow* begins with broad, unbounded expanses of grass waving in the wind. The Great Plains, we are told in the narrator's chant-like recitation, are a "treeless, windswept continent of grass.... A country of high winds and sun, without rivers, without streams, with little rain." In place of Dovzhenko's cross-cutting between the human and the natural, here we begin with a natural state of grace and it is human intervention that initiates a long fall from grace. Instead of a single tractor entering the village, as in *Earth*, we see wave after wave of industrial machinery, the frenzied production of agriculture in the 1920s rapidly intercut with shots of the New York stock market and of jazz performance—a montage that, Dunaway writes, "indicts an entire culture of greed and overindulgence, a society that has lost its moral bearings."[53] Ecological calamity follows as dust storms mock the efforts of settlers, turning people into desperate figures fleeing the storms and their homes into piles of dust, wreckage, and abandonment. Having excised a brief epilogue on the work of the Resettlement Administration, Lorentz ends the film with desolate shots of a lone, dead tree in a parched, sand-swept plain.

Responses to this jeremiad, with its stark images of drought and its human figures presented as ciphers thrown about by fate, were sharply polarized. Hollywood blocked the film's commercial distribution, considering it unfair competition from a government agency, but the Resettlement Administration screened it on its own to enthusiastic public response. Critics on the right lambasted the film as government propaganda and as an overly negative portrayal of the farmers and the frontier ethos; eventually they succeeded in banning the film's distribution by federal agencies. Some on the left were also critical, contending that the film dangerously ignored the social realities of capitalism and the responsibility of the landowners and industrialists in bringing about the crisis. The film's overall tone was that "we are all responsible," and its implied solution was a government-led eco-managerialism.

In his follow-up, *The River* (1937), Lorentz continued the ecological strains of *The Plow* while paradoxically portraying the vast dam-building projects of the Tennessee Valley Authority as a new mode of redemptive technological sublime. Much more popularly successful, the film articulated a national vision of progressive conservationist resource management through epic and lyrical visual poetry. Like its predecessor, the film took a massive region of the United States—this time the entire Mississippi basin—as its subject matter, providing an environmental history of it in image and text. It alternates between a celebration of human activities along the river—forests in the north, iron and coal mines in the centre, cotton fields in the south—and a declensionist narrative about the ecological impacts of unplanned human activities: panoramic shots of burnt-out hills and of landscapes rendered treeless. "Black spruce and Norway pine, Douglas fir and Red cedar, Scarlet oak and Shagbark hickory, Hemlock and Aspen," the narrator intones, in one of the Whitmanesque litanies that punctuate the narrative, over panoramic shots of forest. Later, after several "Heads up!" proclamations accompanied by shots of trees coming down, the same litany repeats itself: "Black spruce and Norway pine," this time over shots of charred landscapes. "We built a hundred cities and a thousand towns, but at what a cost!… We cut the top off Wisconsin, and sent it down the river.… We left the mountains and the hills slashed and burned, and moved on." Floods follow: "1903, 1907, 1913, 1916, 1922, 1927, 1936, 1937. Down from Pennsylvania and Ohio, Kentucky and West Virginia, Missouri and Illinois …" proceeds the chorus-like litany of states and of rivers, where earlier we had heard a celebration of their water flowing into and down the Mississippi. This alternation allows Lorentz to combine the jeremiadic sermon against humanity's ecological sins with a celebration of the region's and nation's unity (albeit one represented primarily by white faces).

In contrast to *The Plow*, however, *The River* ends with a celebration of the Tennessee Valley Authority, the New Deal model of administrative conservation planning and utilitarian wisdom: "Where there's water, there's power.… Power for the farmers of the valley. Power for the villages and cities and factories of the Valley.… Power to give a new Tennessee Valley to a new generation. Power enough to make the river work!" *The River*, as Dunaway argues, "converts the sublime terror of ecological catastrophe into the sublime power of the New Deal to use technology to control the natural world," its "panoramic vision crystallizing the New Deal's effort to find spiritual meaning in technology and government planning." The result is "a seamless vision of America as an organic machine, a nation that could avoid catastrophe by engineering a new world of abundance."[54] As storm clouds gathered in Europe, this vision of an organic machine ruled by a benevolent technocracy was enthusiastically received by audiences all around America.

Industry, Existential Landscapes, and the Firstness of Things

What both *The Plow That Broke the Plains* and *The River* ultimately suggest is that nature, the background of human life, is not simply given to us. Its underlying reliability can be shattered, in turn unveiling the cruelty of nature's indifference to human efforts, an indifference that can only be brought under control through human action. In the middle decades of the last century, that action was largely a matter of government management and control. Ecological wisdom today is rarely seen in those terms, especially perhaps when it comes to massive dam projects. Yet more than half a century after Lorentz's films were made, the kind of engineering vision represented by the Tennessee Valley Authority is still being carried out, most conspicuously in contemporary China. The Three Gorges Dam, a massive hydroelectric project on the Yangtze River, was first envisioned by Sun Yat-sen in 1919 and was later rhapsodized in poetry by Mao Zedong in 1956, but it was formally launched only in 1992, with construction beginning two years later. Today, it is the largest engineered structure in the world, built at a cost of some US$24 billion and slated to provide 22,500 megawatts of power (ten times that of the Hoover Dam) once it is fully operational. At least 1.3 million people were displaced or relocated during its construction, and many cities and historical and archaeological treasures have been drowned under water. The social and environmental costs of the project are staggering. Scientists have long predicted an increase in landslides and earthquakes due to the area's geological and seismic instability, a rise in waterborne diseases, and declines in biodiversity resulting from the dam project. Several catastrophic episodes (to which Chinese officials have only grudgingly admitted) have already supported their case.[55]

The impact of the Three Gorges Dam has been documented in several highly original films that neither celebrate nor merely lament it, but that instead attempt to make the instability of such change palpable as only cinema can. These include Zhang Ming's *Rainclouds over Wushan* (a.k.a. *In Expectation / Wushan yunyu*, 1996), Dai Sieje's *Balzac and the Little Chinese Seamstress* (*Ziao caifeng*, 2002), Yan Yu and Li Yifan's documentary *Before the Flood* (2005), Jia Zhang-ke's *Still Life* (*Sanxia haoren*, 2006), Yung Chang's *Up the Yangtze* (2007), and Jennifer Baichwald's documentary about photographer Edward Burtynsky, *Manufactured Landscapes* (2006). *Still Life* sets parallel narratives about a coal miner's and nurse's respective searches for disappeared or estranged spouses against the background of the very real demolition of the ancient city of Fengjie, in preparation for its inundation by the Three Gorges reservoir. The searches end not with happy reunions but with ironic and ambivalent consummations. The quiet strength of the characters contrasts with the sense of foreboding and inevitability associated with the colossal displacements of unfeeling industrial transformation. With its frequently thwarted and drifting narrative threads and its lingering pans across epic tableaux—of fields of rubble, waste, and impending or ongoing demolition, but at the same time of the epic grandeur of the Yangtze valley—*Still Life* has received deserved acclaim.

One ironic counterpoint to the dam to which *Still Life* refers is the volume of luxury cruise ships that have begun cruising the river since the project's beginnings in the 1990s—ships that bear such regal and imperial names as *Queen Victoria, Princess Anne, King of the East, Emperor, Empress*, and *Catherine*. Chinese-Canadian director Yung Chang's *Up the Yangtze* (2007) is a poignant depiction of the dam's impacts that focuses directly on the ironies of such tourism. A narrative documentary (more or less) that follows a Chinese girl who goes to work on one of these "farewell tours" up and down the soon-to-be-flooded river valley, the film plays on its resonances with various reference points: with James Cameron's *Titanic* in the stark class differences that mark the ship's decks, with the local workers on the lower deck and the global tourists on the upper, the intimation being that this is a kind of last journey; with Joseph Conrad's *Heart of Darkness* in its being an upriver trip that seemingly goes nowhere; and with Dennis O'Rourke's documentary *Cannibal Tours* (which I will discuss in Chapter 4), a "reverse ethnography" that is as much about the tourists travelling upriver as it is about what they have come to see. Like many films in the New Chinese Cinema, this Canadian production presents the ironies of a China in which Chinese citizens struggle to master Western languages in order to serve the wealthy tourists, who for their part are providing the revenues that will fully deliver up China to the global economy.

To speak in Daniel Frampton's "filmosophical" terms, the dominant "film-thought" in *Up the Yangtze* encompasses a recurrent set of contrapuntal movements: slow, horizontal movements of the camera and the ship that parallel the movement of the river, counterposed against slow, vertical movements of the camera, of the river's rising water level, and of people moving with their belongings uphill to avoid being flooded. The film begins and ends with scenes that take us (on a ship not shown in the frame) through a series of canal locks onto the river, with the ship's slow movement forward paralleled by the camera's movement back. As the camera moves up the wall of the lock, the wall itself and the ground level at its top move down. Later, on the river, the lateral forward movements of the ship and the camera are implicitly movements back— into time, and into a valley that is gradually being overwhelmed by the dam's inevitable rise. A voice-over opens the film by announcing the filmmaker's trip with his father to the China his father had remembered; "instead we found a brand new China being created." In the closing scene in the canal lock, the ascending/descending motif is carried by the camera and by musical accompaniment, with a descending minor-key ostinato sequence circling around itself as if in an Escher painting until its fade-out. The effect is that we seem trapped in the lock, a lonely roving eye moving slowly within grainy reddish walls, with an eerie green light reflected on one of the side walls and red reflected on the dark water. As the screen fades to black, the slow upscreen movement of the credits echoes this movement, which seems to be overtaking us like rising water.

While this film-thought is perhaps too obviously metaphorical, equating as it does the inexorable rise of the water with the economic changes that are overtaking the lives of the characters, it exemplifies one of the most common tropes illustrating the cultural and economic globalization that has come to dominate the post–Cold War era. A comparison with European modernist filmmakers like Michelangelo Antonioni and Theo Angelopoulos is apt here. In these films, change—whether it is the Fordist industrialization of the 1950s and 1960s or the post-Fordist globalization of the 1980s and 1990s—is depicted as an inevitable and inexorable overcoming of the past. Change, that is, is an enclosure and entrapment within new realities to which individuals can only adapt, by embracing (at best) a kind of dispersed affect of lonely, temporary, and ultimately meaningless and anomic pleasures. Theirs is a cinema of postmodern homelessness.

Jia Zhang-ke's *The World* (*Shijie*, 2004) adheres closely to this tradition. Filmed as Beijing was beginning its preparations for hosting the 2008 Olympic Games, *The World* is about a group of migrant workers at a Beijing theme park that exhibits scale model replicas of landmarks from around the world—the Pyramids, Stonehenge, the Acropolis, the Taj Mahal, the Eiffel Tower, the Tower of London, the World Trade Center's Twin Towers, and others. The theme park is a stand-in for China's all-out plunge into the global economy, its full-speed state-driven "capitalization." The film revolves around the contrast between the glamour and artifice of the characters' paid performances and the lonely resignation of their day-to-day lives, their cramped living quarters, and their understated and often futile efforts at romance and friendship. It is, in effect, about the multiple forms of displacement experienced by the workers, most of whom have moved from the Chinese provinces to labour in this placeless planet-in-miniature where they impersonate Japanese geishas, ancient Egyptians, and black African dancers. As in his *Still Life*, Zhang-ke's characters here are dwarfed by processes over which they have no control. This constitutes a reversal from the Chinese revolutionary and socialist realist films of the 1960s through the 1980s, in which larger-than-life human characters acted to bring about change in the world. As Hongbing Zhang describes them, Zhang-ke's films employ medium and long shots "to keep characters away from the foreground, zooming them out into the broad and distant background, sometimes so far away that they even become indistinguishable from their surroundings."[56] His long takes serve much the same purposes as the audio and video intertextualities of pop music and television that pepper his films, in that they further embed the characters in the larger frame of a globalizing China.

Let us here consider Michelangelo Antonioni's films more closely. Regarded as one of the greatest landscape painters in the cinema, Antonioni is an artist for whom identity and character merge, and on occasion literally disappear, into "the sheer appearance of things—the surface of the world," in Seymour Chatman's lucid phrase.[57] With their elliptical and open-ended narratives, with their long takes and tracking shots that draw attention to rubble-strewn industrial landscapes, modernist architecture, and the stylized interiors that surround their characters, and with his characteristic themes of ennui, alienation, and ambivalence, his films are commonly taken to be about the fragility of emotional life in an industrial, technological world. In *Red Desert* (1964), for instance, palpable and densely atmospheric landscapes—with swaths of fog, huge machinery, clouds of steam and smoke emanating from invisible or backgrounded industrial sources, the sounds of ships' horns and (extra-diegetic) electronic music, and the near-expressionist use of colour in the vividly painted interiors—all seem to echo the ambivalence and anxiety of the painter Giuliana (Monica Vitti) as she makes her life in the industrial port of Ravenna. Matthew Gandy notes an ambivalence in Antonioni's depiction of industrial modernity: on the one hand, his films are most often about the alienating effects on the human psyche of these late modern environments; on the other, his camera embraces the scale and dynamism of what has been called the "industrial landscape sublime."[58] In this embrace, however, is a desire to enable us to *see* the landscapes as the aesthetic objects they are, in a world where the surface of the world is, at once, a firstness, and thus aesthetic, a causal and functional secondness, and a meaning-laden and ethically inflected thirdness.

Rohdie writes that Antonioni's films "pose a subject (only to compromise it), constitute objects (only to dissolve them), propose stories (only to lose them), but, equally, they turn those compromises and losses back towards another solidity," which in the films is "a wandering away from narrative to the surface into which it was dissolved, but in such a way that the surface takes on a fascination, becomes a 'subject' all its own."[59] In *L'avventura* (1960), Anna's disappearance on an unpopulated, volcanic island in the Mediterranean takes the other characters on a search for her, to the point where, for a while, it seems that the only character left is the island and the waves that pound it on all sides. The elemental imagery of water, which we examined in the context of Tarkovsky's *Stalker*, is a recurrent, even obsessive, theme in Antonioni's films of the late 1950s and early 1960s:

> Water, damp, moistness, humidity, rain, drizzle, rivers, the sea, swimming pools, fountains figure in most Antonioni films with their contraries: the desert, dryness, sand, rocks, shimmering heat. A dampness invades all of *Il grido* while the sea dominates much of ... *L'avventura*; ... the damp mist-fog of *Il deserto rosso*; the play of wetness and dryness at the desert house in *Zabriskie Point*, the release and pleasure of the storm at the opening of *Il mistero di Oberwald*, then the morning damp drying on the fields. In *Il grido* wet clings to everything: the air is always damp, the ground muddy, the banks slippery, there is a perpetual drizzle and sometimes an enveloping rain which turns inside into outside—the rain comes into Andreina's small hut by the river, making it dripping, wringing wet—and there is the river itself whose presence is permanent in the film.[60]

The final seven-minute sequence in *L'eclisse* (1962) amounts to what Chatman calls "an establishing shot in reverse, a kind of disestablishing shot" that "accumulates shot after shot of what has until then been only background." The sequence "moves away from the known particular to the unknown general," first showing details that viewers would recall from the earlier meetings of the two protagonists—"the sprinkling system, the nurse pushing the baby carriage, the pile of bricks outside the building under construction, the barrel standing at the corner of the wooden fence"—but eventually dissipating into the randomness and indifference of the suburban buildings and streets that are now noticeably absent of the two lovers, who are like a dream that has faded into the banal reality of the everyday.[61] We are left with the architectural cityscape in its sheer *thereness*, drained of meaning yet available to be seen and felt in itself as it is.

But in cinema, nothing is ever any more purely *there* than anything else we see. Antonioni's landscapes are, as mentioned, a form of firstness—they are the things seen in their shimmering potentiality. But they are also always woven into the sequences that precede and carry them (secondness), and they are always interpreted by us (thirdness). In the case of Antonioni, even the minimal narratives—frequently of dislocated characters and troubled, failing relationships—colour the landscapes so that the *thereness* of the water, the fog, and the suburban cityscape is also a psychologial correlate for the characters and their searches, displacements, and disappearances. It is not only the slowness of his films that makes them difficult for some viewers; it is also the fact that they tend to be about a certain kind of well-heeled but unsatisfied, if not morally vacated, late-modern character type.

This raises the question of whether landscape—the Earth as it appears— can ever only be what it is in itself (as with Martin Lefebvre's "intentional cinematic landscapes"), or whether the very tradition of narrative filmmaking— with its by now ingrown expectation that films are about people doing people-things—makes it impossible to show the earth-world apart from its correlation with human subjectivity. Philosopher Quentin Meillassoux has argued that this kind of "correlationism"—an insistence that we cannot conceive of the world without assuming an already given relationship between the human mind and that world—marks all modern philosophy since Kant, and that it is a limitation on the capacity of thought to deal with the world itself.[62] The next chapter will suggest that this earth-world *can* make itself felt in the diffraction between ecologically different human worlds, while Chapter 5 will argue that it can also make itself felt more directly in the interperceptual dynamism of cinema.

Jennifer Baichwal's *Manufactured Landscapes* is an example of a film that directly addresses the industrial landscape sublime, as represented by the images of acclaimed Canadian photographer Edward Burtynsky. Those images foreground both their aestheticism—which is what immediately strikes most viewers of Burtynsky's ambiguously alluring photographs of railcuts, mines and tailings, quarries, oil fields and refineries, shipyards, and the monumentally scaled Three Gorges Dam construction project—and the social and ecological contexts that make them so troubling. Gerda Cammaer argues that Baichwal's use of cinema's contextualizing capacities—her reversals of scale and focus, her juxtapositions of still and moving images, her zoom-ins and zoom-outs around the actual scenes Burtynsky works to capture in his stills, and the way she follows the details outside the picture frame—allows her film to pursue the ethical questions that are raised only indirectly in Burtynsky's photographs themselves.[63]

Such juxtapositions of modes of cinematic address suggest possibilities that have been pursued most forcefully by experimental filmmakers. Before we look at those, however, let us pick up the Fordian and Dovzhenkian threads— landscape as humanized, or at least as potentially humanizable (through image and through settlement), versus landscape as always already both human and natural—as these work their way into a series of variations on the human–nature relationship.

Post-Westerns, Pantheism, and the Eco-Sublime

To pose John Ford as the director of classic, reassuring westerns, as I may have seemed to suggest above, is to get things more or less wrong. Ford's films were popular and critically acclaimed in his time, but this was because they dealt with popular themes—the settling of America, the quest for justice or for the Promised Land—in compelling ways. Ford is often viewed as a nostalgic conservative, but his politics were closer to a liberal populism. He was, in fact, described by no less radical a filmmaker as (avowed Marxist) Jean-Marie Straub as the "most Brechtian" of directors, whose films lay bare the contradictions at the heart of American politics.[64] And while there was a consistency of themes across Ford's career, there were also significant shifts. One of these was the shift, in Peter Wollen's words, "from an identity between civilized versus savage and European versus Indian to their separation and final reversal, so that in *Cheyenne Autumn* it is the Europeans who are savage, the victims who are the heroes." It was this "richness of the shifting relations between antinomies" that, Wollen argues, made Ford "a great artist."[65]

Westerns have undergone their own evolution, with the appearance in the late 1960s and 1970s of what have been called "revisionist westerns," "post-westerns," and "acid westerns." Films like Peckinpah's *The Wild Bunch* (1967) and *Pat Garrett and Billy the Kid* (1973), Hiller's *Little Big Man* (1970), and Altman's *McCabe and Mrs. Miller* (1971) reverse the valences of the western, in one way or another, as have later gender- and sexuality-questioning westerns like *The Ballad of Little Jo* (1993) and *Brokeback Mountain* (2005). Among the more expansive and ambitious of revisionist westerns was Michael Cimino's *Heaven's Gate* (1980), a film remembered best for its budgetary excesses and box-office failure, which contributed to the financial collapse of its producer, United Artists. Robin Wood had long argued that the critical furor over the film displayed a journalistic groupthink that failed to see beyond the contextual determinants of the moment—Cimino's relatively untested ambitions and United Artists' desire to cash in on the popular, but not necessarily critical, success of his previous film, *The Deer Hunter* (1978). The original version of *Heaven's Gate*, rushed to the screen and clocking in at three hours and forty minutes, was savaged for its narrative incoherence, and Cimino was berated for misusing the blank cheque he had apparently been given by United Artists.[66] To be sure, the film rejects many of the basic principles of classical narrative, but it does this, Wood argues, to reverse "the relationship between foreground (the emotional problems of individuals) and background (the movement of history)," so that the former becomes part of a "grand design." *Heaven's Gate* decentres character development and a logic of action and reaction in favour of a collective hero—the working class of mostly immigrant farmers, men alongside women—and an epic structure of interchangeable set pieces. The film, Wood writes, is like "an immense fresco," each of its building blocks constituting "a separate, lucid, and forceful 'history lesson': about privilege, about poverty, about compromise, about being unprepared, about power, about community, about collective action, about the betrayal of the poor by a rising bourgeoisie, about the destruction of a possible alternative America by the one that is so much with us."[67] I will later discuss collective heroes and parallel, interconnected "network narratives," but what concerns us here is the rhythmic and immersive texture of Cimino's set pieces and the mood-laden, elegiac beauty of his vision of the Western landscape.

A film that pushes this elegiac quality to its greatest degree is Jim Jarmusch's *Dead Man* (1990). This cinematic journey across an American West shares a moody trippiness with acid westerns like *El Topo* (1970), *The Last Movie* (1971), and *Pat Garrett and Billy the Kid* (1973), but it thoroughly deconstructs the genre in its portrayal of a landscape that, as one critic puts it, "America the conqueror has emptied of its natives and turned into a capitalist charnel house."[68] Filmed in a black-and-white self-consciously modelled after the photographs and early ethnographic films of Edward S. Curtis, *Dead Man* is about the companionship between a hapless, on-the-run accountant from Cleveland (played by Johnny Depp), who seeks a job in a Western frontier town called Machine but instead gets involved in a killing, and a William Blake–reciting Native American (Gary Farmer) who had been kidnapped as a child and taken to Britain as an exhibit, but has now returned to the United States. The accountant's name happens to be William Blake, and when the Gary Farmer character, who calls himself Nobody, meets him while travelling to the west coast, he mistakes, or creatively misrecognizes, him as the reincarnated poet whose work he had read and memorized while in England. The film's West is one of ruin and decay, a virtual Land of the Dead featuring abandoned wagons and teepees, skulls and coffins decorating the violent streets of Machine, and Northwest Coastal Indians living out what appear to be their last days as disease and violence threaten to engulf their community. *Dead Man*, as Gregg Rickman puts it, "evades every attempt to affix a positive meaning to its narrative." It "'erases,' inverts, and upends all the various western conventions" through a "series of canceling operations" suggestive of the final lines of Michel Foucault's *The Order of Things*, in which "man" himself is "erased, like a face drawn in sand at the edge of the sea."[69] Unlike Peckinpah and Tarantino, whose post-westerns similarly upend convention, Jarmusch, however, does not romanticize the violence but simply presents it as given, like an inexorable fatal tide.

At the more pastoral end of American landscape cinematography are films that have dealt with the themes of settling the land, building community, and the parallels, commonalities, overlaps, and correspondences between human life and natural cycles. As Jean Mottet shows, the Arcadian dream has been with American cinema since at least the time of D.W. Griffith. In Griffith's 1909 films *The Message* and *The Country Doctor*, this pastoral theme of a settled landscape emerges as "the pathway leading to the river, the low stone wall, the signs of traditional farming, the tree (apparently an elm), the houses that one makes out nestled in the thick vegetation of the facing hillside."[70] There is also a long tradition of populist Hollywood cinema counterposing the dignity of agrarian communities against the corruption of moneyed, and generally urban, interests; and this theme can be found in many variations around the world. In *Green Screen*, David Ingram examines *The Grapes of Wrath* (1940), *The River* (1984), *Country* (1984), and *The Milagro Beanfield War* (1988) as Hollywood instances of this dichotomy.[71] Images of landscape and nature in such films sometimes tend toward a pantheism not unlike that found in Dovzhenko's *Earth*. The term "pantheism" may seem at odds with an American context that more typically draws on Christian ideals, according to which nature is a garden and human–nature harmony is God-given. But the very materiality of cinema emphasizes the *locatedness* of the sacred, its immanence in things, in a way that takes away from the transcendentalizing impulse that would seem more intrinsic to Christianity. This cinematic pantheism is more akin to a Spinozan pantheism, which sees God and nature as one and the same. For Spinoza, there is a shared substance between the human and the natural, the singular and the universal, the local and the cosmic, with nothing above and beyond this substance, or nothing at least that can sustain a position of transcendence above the cyclicality and mutual vulnerability of the natural. Pantheism is a variant of a philosophy of immanence, which makes it a close relative to process-relational thought (though there are differences one could identify, for instance, between the latter's emphasis on change, emergence, and becoming, and the emphasis on repetition and equilibrium that one finds in many forms of pantheism).[72]

With its juxtapositions of human and natural references, pantheism can come close to another tradition of representing nature: the sublime. Unlike the lyrical strains of the pastoral or the classicist beauty of the picturesque, the sublime strikes its viewers more forcefully, confronting them with a sense of their own limits. For nineteenth-century Romantics, the sublime was experienced in encounters with an overpowering and monumental Nature; while for Immanuel Kant, the sublime indicated the limits of representation. Forever inaccessible to the categories of reason, the sublime marked the inherent threshold of our knowledge and signified the cleavage between the conceived and the presentable. As Berleant assesses it, the sublime represents "the capacity of the natural world to act on so monumental a scale as to exceed our powers of framing and control."[73] Theories of the "eco-sublime" have surfaced in recent ecocritical writing; I will examine these more closely in Chapter 6. Images of nature functioning in both sublime and more lyrical modes characterize the films of a number of directors whose work is sometimes labelled "lyric cinema." I have discussed Dovzhenko and will return to Tarkovsky and others within this tradition; here I would like to briefly consider the use of nature imagery in the work of Terrence Malick and in a handful of East Asian films.

Malick's *Days of Heaven* (1978) is a striking example of a revisionist western that leans toward a pantheistic portrayal of nature, even while it questions humanity's presumptive place within the natural order. The story of three working-class Chicagoans—Billy, his lover Abby, and his young sister (and the film's unreliable narrator) Linda—who flee the city after Billy confronts a factory foreman, and whose journey takes them as migrant labourers to a wealthy farmer's land in the wheatfields of Texas, the film contextualizes the traditional western themes of the journey to and settlement of the West within the capitalist economic dynamic where some work and others own, and where the West is what it is only in relation to the industrial East. The film features exquisitely detailed images and sounds of nature: panoramic views of the prairie landscape, a time-lapse shot of growing wheat, close-ups of locusts gnawing on the same wheat, and shots of ponds and rivers, deer, rabbits, partridges, and bison. These feature not simply as metaphors for human activities, but also as a kind of ambiguous commentary, an ironic ecologizing counterpoint that reminds us of the broader contexts surrounding human life. "Placing the human protagonists within the widescreen frame," Ben McCann writes in an analysis of Malick's landscape imagery, "the subsequent dwarfing of their proportions by the natural surroundings is symbolic of their powerlessness against nature; the lack of human perspective and influence within the greater scheme of things." McCann describes the "fetishistic attention to nature's indifferent beauty in the midst of human mayhem" and points to the "dynamic juxtaposition" of images of the natural world, including close-ups and widescreen shots, with point-of-view shots of the characters seeing that world as a means for "cathecting" nature into "both protagonist and spectator."[74]

Malick's strategy is a metaphysical one. He was a Heidegger scholar and translator before becoming a filmmaker. Philosopher Stanley Cavell is, I think, correct in taking Malick's cinematic vision to be about the Heideggerian "illumined, radiant self-manifestation" of things and the associated recognition "that objects participate in the photographic presence of themselves; they participate in the re-creation of themselves on film; they are essential in the making of their appearances." Cavell continues:

> Then if in relation to objects capable of such self-manifestation human beings are reduced in significance, or crushed by the fact of beauty left vacant, perhaps this is because in trying to take dominion over the world, or in aestheticizing it (temptations inherent in the making of film, or of any art), they are refusing their participation with it.[75]

Which is to say that the objects shown are indexically entering into the image, that they leave the marks of their reality upon the image; but also that there is always a tension between the objects themselves, the worldness of the world before (and outside) the image, and the human effort to dominate these objects, manipulate them, and impose our will upon them. Filmmaking is an instance of this wilful imposition on nature, yet it can also be a meditative reflection on the limits, and even the futility, of such imposition. Malick's nature shots, no matter how skilfully arranged and carefully designed—his preferences for natural light and twilight scenes of nature are instances of his cinematographic determination—are also reminders to us that there is a world out there that, while it may serve as a bottomless source of beautiful images, continues its autonomous existence alongside our own and ultimately dwarfs our own by framing our lives with the conditions of our mortality.

This strategy of inserting reminders of the ecology that surrounds and subtends human narratives can be found in other filmmakers, among them Tarkovsky, Werner Herzog, and late-period Godard, and it is a theme I will come back to in the final chapter. It can be found in the forms of "lyrical," "poetic," or "magic realist" cinema developed in Eastern Europe and South America by directors such as Sergei Paradjanov, Yuri Illienko, Juraj Jakubisko, and Glauber Rocha. Perhaps the apotheosis of such pantheistic narrative techniques are such Buddhist- (or Shinto)-inspired East Asian films as Bae Yong-kyun's *Why Has Bodhi-Dharma Left for the East?* (1989), Kim Ki-duk's *Spring, Summer, Fall, Winter ... and Spring* (2003), Shohei Imamura's *The Ballad of Narayama* (1983), and Mitsuo Yanagimachi's *Himatsuri* (*Fire Festival*, 1985).[76] All of these films foreground the cyclical character of human life, inclusive of death, but intersperse their human stories with insistent reminders of non-human nature: shots of waving leaves and running streams, rolling forests and mountain peaks, plants, animals, skies, fire. As in the films of Yasujiro Ozu, there is an alternative landscape sensibility expressed here to that of the Western perspectival gaze: it is as if an East Asian landscape painting, with its human characters dwarfed by their surroundings, were set in gradually unfurling motion—not the kind of heroic, dramatic motion one would find in a Hollywood western, but one percolating with minor significances and perpendicular correspondences. In his analysis of *Why Has Bodhi-Dharma Left for the East?*, Michael Gillespie writes that "everything is flowing. No matter how slowly.... Even stillness flows," with the result that "the attentive viewer begins inextricably to interconnect the relatedness of the characters and the elemental processes that make up the world."[77] Village life in *The Ballad of Narayama*, about an elderly woman whose son, following tradition, takes her up a mountain to face her death, is punctuated by images of snakes, frogs, and moths mating; a snake devouring a mouse, and another giving birth; an eagle snatching a rabbit from out of the clutches of hunters who had shot it; and several scenes of sex—including one of bestiality—intended less to shock than to drive home the point that humans are animals caught, like all, in the cycle of life, death, and reproduction.[78]

None of these quite fits the Western categories of the sublime, the beautiful, or the picturesque, because none of them is premised on the notion of a human observer standing apart from the world being observed. For Imamura and Yong-kyun, as arguably for Malick and Godard, film is not merely meant to be viewed and appreciated. Their films are meant to challenge us toward an involvement with the world of the film, which is made up of the same stuff as the world itself. This, I think, is the difference between these works and the Hollywood films that Pat Brereton argues transform viewers' attitudes toward the natural world. Brereton's case, developed at length in *Hollywood Utopia: Ecology in Contemporary American Cinema*, is worth considering in part because it runs counter to the dominant critical perspective on popular film. Brereton attempts to show how it is that "Hollywood draws on the therapeutic power of raw nature and landscape and that this becomes more ecologically charged and potent when coupled with human agency."[79] This potency comes through the use of cinematic spectacle and the construction of a romantic sublime, for instance, through "extended moments of almost Gothic visual excess," a "kinetic depth effect" created by camera movement across static landscape vistas, and the "transgressive potential and vision of excessive scenography and agency."[80]

Brereton's argument takes in a wide range of films (some of which I will consider later), but he reserves his highest praise for the Steven Spielberg blockbusters *Jurassic Park* (1993) and *Lost World* (1997). In *Jurassic Park*, Brereton claims, the viewer comes to identify with the awestruck observer of spectacular natural phenomena. The film begins with "expert witnesses" regressing "to the awed wonder of children," kneeling in "a reverent posture ... hypnotized by the sublime vision as they gaze into the lake and observe herds of dinosaurs roaming about freely, signaling the collapsing of time and space to produce the ultimate ... nature reserve." Brereton celebrates *Jurassic Park's* transformation of the protagonists' "innocent gaze" during their the descent onto the island that opens the film into a "final ascent" that "registers firsthand experience and ethical knowledge of the primary laws of nature"—that is, the laws according to which interference, or "playing God," with nature results in an unleashing of Frankenstein-like disruptive force.[81] By the end of the 1997 sequel *Lost World*, the protagonist Hammond endorses "an ecological position that supports 'a new policy of non-intervention'" with the island on which the (re-engineered) dinosaurs have staked their ecological claim.[82]

While I sympathize with this argument and find many of Brereton's other examples convincing, his assessment of Spielberg's films underestimates the distinction that Ernst Bloch makes between "abstract" and "concrete" utopias (which Brereton draws on in introducing his argument). In his three-volume magnum opus, *The Principle of Hope*, the early-twentieth-century German Marxist theorist articulated a notion of utopia as a continual reaching forward so as to shape a better future. Utopia, for Bloch, was less a form of speculation about the future than an unleashing of the aspirations and unfulfilled promises of the past.[83] As Hudson puts it, Bloch's utopia "related to the dream of fulfillment, of happiness, of homecoming, which structured the human cultural world because it was given in the dynamic structure of the moment."[84] In other words, the world in its every moment contains an openness to the "not yet," and it is this structural openness that lends an affective immediacy to every hope for positive change toward a better future. Recovering the utopian surplus within human culture is, for Bloch, a matter of wilfully orienting oneself to the future as an open prospect so as to create the conditions for that future to arise. What Bloch called "abstract utopias" are fantastic and compensatory forms of wishful thinking unaccompanied by a will to change things. In contrast, "concrete utopias" both anticipate and *effect* the future. They are a form of "educated hope" that is "born out of and articulates" a "relationship between end and means, passion and reason, aspiration and possibility."[85]

The relationship between mass media entertainment and utopia is complex. Cinematic genres from the musical and adventure-fantasy to experimental film have been called utopian in their portrayal of an abundance and excitement that contrasts with viewers' everyday lives. Hollywood itself has been characterized as a utopian enterprise: in its classic era, some of its leading producers, including many European Jewish émigrés, were guided by a vision of America that emphasized integration, tolerance, hope, and social possibility.[86] In its portrayal of attractive alternatives to local cultural realities, Hollywood film continues to play a utopian role in many parts of the world, for better or worse. In Blochian terms, however, one must distinguish between "abstract," or escapist, utopia and the "concrete" utopia that contributes to positive social change. Critics have pointed out that Spielberg's spectacular portrayals of the natural world celebrate not so much the power of nature as the power of cinema, with its sounds, lights, and spectacular effects and with its godlike creator as an indulgent puppet master behind the screen. For many film theorists, Spielbergian cinema is a kind of Wizard of Oz, to be unmasked by the tools of critical theory.[87] Brereton argues that these critics underestimate cinema's power to affect viewers at a non-rational level and to thereby transform ecological consciousness. Following Bloch's definitions, however, if Spielberg's films were to be such powerful instances of "concrete utopias," they would have to have contributed to revolutionary changes in ecological consciousness.

One could more effectively argue that movie audiences have become not so much ecologically conscious as enthralled by a certain kind of *representation* of nature: nature as a visual spectacle and as a place of beauty and recreation for human visitors—nature, in other words, as *out there*, separate from the mundane lives of city dwellers. The films of Disney Studios have been touted as a powerful source for the re-enchantment of such a nature.[88] But critical opinion remains understandably ambivalent regarding the political or ecological virtues of such portrayals of nature, which sacrifice an understanding of socio-natural systems in the pursuit of narrative, spectacle, and sentimentality. (I will discuss this theme further in Chapter 5.) For *Jurassic Park's* harsher critics, the film's ostensive anti-biotechnology message is undercut by its celebration of cutting-edge technology, including genetic science, robotics, and state-of-the-art digital animation. Following Disney's "theme park model of consumption," the movie, Sarah Franklin argues, is "structured as a ride": it "offers a movie of a theme park which in turn becomes the main attraction of [real-life] theme parks."[89] Premised on the magic of Hollywood spectacle in making possible anything imaginable, the movie became a global brand, with its multibillion-dollar spinoff industry of "dinomania," which Stephen Jay Gould worried might "truly extinguish dinosaurs by turning them from sources of awe into clichés and commodities."[90] The film's "axis" and "central invitation," as Franklin reads it, is "the invitation to 'go behind the scenes'" and "share in the secrets of its own making," thus inviting the audience to celebrate the technologization of life itself, by which the secrets of life are opened up and made available to the human consumer for the cost of admission.[91]

Brereton's and Franklin's divergent positions mirror the long-standing debate over representations of monumental nature that I referred to earlier. Such representations in the art of Thomas Cole, Albert Bierstadt, Carlton Watkins, and others elicited reactions of pleasure and desire that were channelled, by political and economic interests, into the project of colonizing, possessing, and commodifying the continent—but also, later, into the project of conserving land *from* such commodification. To put this in Peircian terms, there is a seething firstness, a generative virtuality or potentiality, within the sublime imagery that Brereton is describing, just as there was for many nineteenth-century Americans within the landscape art of the time. Whether or not this firstness results in an interpretive thirdness that is "concretely utopian" depends on a variety of factors. For one thing, when the firstness is experienced in the context of a thrilling, roller-coaster-like narrative trajectory, as it is in *Jurassic Park*, viewers will tend to become absorbed in that narrative, following it where it leads rather than into too many alternative directions (though of course there is always room for counter-hegemonic readings of films). In other words, the secondness (the narrative dimension) within which the firstness is actualized, and the openings within that secondness toward alternative interpretions, make a difference in enabling alternative vectors toward thirdness.

To understand the ways in which such images generate their powerful affects, we must understand the ability of *moving* images to entice us toward a kind of movement across the surface of the Earth. This movement can be that of colonization and settling, but in our time it is more likely that of travelling, sightseeing, and the desire to experience certain landscapes by moving through them in particular, usually exhilarating, ways. Brereton, following David Bordwell, refers to the "kinetic depth effect" of the camera moving across and through spectacular vistas. David Ingram and others similarly refer to the kinetic thrill of vicariously penetrating a landscape. This movement *across* and *through* things is what distinguishes film from photography. It is what ultimately renders the "tourist gaze," as John Urry called it, *more* than merely a gaze, but really a form of penetrative mobility, a gaze that is embodied within a moving world in which some are able to move farther, and in less encumbered ways, than others. It is what distinguishes Heidegger's "age of the world picture" from our own age of the world *motion* picture.

Kinetic Landscapes, Differential Space, and the Exhilaration of Mobility

The forces of globalization, unlike their depiction in such films as *Up the Yangtze* and *The World*, have not been universally portrayed as oppressive. More often, cinema has celebrated the liberatory potentials of the horizontal movement that spatial displacement makes possible. The ship embarking on new frontiers, the wide-open steppe, the exhilaration of the road—all have enjoined viewers to the pleasures of travel. As suggested above, the western is a paradigmatic model of the journey toward a new community, the journey of settlement proceeding westward across the continent. Journeys are paradigmatic forms of cinema narrative, and as I have argued, all films take their viewers on a journey. But the genre known as the "road movie" does this without any pretences to the contrary. And if travel has always been associated with film and photography, what the road movie adds is the visceral and haptic affects of travel: the feel of the road and the novelties—unfamiliar and exotic people and places, along with the freedom, wanderlust, revelation, spontaneities, possibilities, and uncertainties—that it brings.

By taking characters out of their normal milieux, journeys provide a hinge for novel perspectives and, potentially, for cultural critique. Epic travel narratives and picaresque novels, from Homer's *Odyssey* and Chaucer's *Canterbury Tales* to Cervantes's *Don Quixote* and Voltaire's *Candide*, have traditionally offered variable perspectives on the duality of the domestic/inside and the wild/outside. Some journeys provide their travellers with experiences that, in the end, are reintegrated through the return home; the form of such journeys is A–B–A$_1$. Others provide their travellers with a way out, an escape route, a new becoming, and even perhaps a life of new becomings: A–B–C–X– ... The mixture of "quest to" and "flight from" is always somewhat in play. Some expedition narratives, such as the Bible's *Exodus* and the journey to a Promised Land, and home-founding journeys like that in *The Grapes of Wrath*, can become the settled truths of the next social order. Others, such as tales of bohemian wanderlust (Kerouac's *On the Road*) and upriver (or downriver) journeys to the "heart of darkness," can be cries of rage or joy intended to wake us from our slumbers, or simply to *express*.

As David Laderman describes in his synoptic account of the genre, road movies carry out their cultural critique in various ways: cinematically, through their camerawork, montage, and soundtrack; narratively, through their open-ended, rambling, picaresque plot structures, their unexpected detours and twists; and thematically, as their characters seek out something better and find revelation or redemption in the search. Their frontier iconographies provide for a "vast, open landscape bordered by seductive horizons."[92] Their kineticism—travelling shots of roads and wide-open, moving landscapes, usually accompanied by appropriately paced music—crystallizes the feeling of being on the road, the visceral thrill of high-speed motion, and advertises their vehicles in the process. For all their waving of the flag of freedom, road movies often have conservative subtexts, whether it be through reassertions of traditional gender roles, Orientalist fantasies about the exoticism of other cultures, or imperialist assumptions about the virtues of violence and the sheer *availability* of the world to one's own possessive exploration. Both cars and movies are essential parts of the machinery of assembly-line industrial capitalism. Yet both have become central means of displaying individuality: the car and the motorcycle, cinematically transfigured, have come to represent freedom. "The automobile as icon and driving as action," Laderman writes, "were incorporated in film narratives as early as Biograph's *Runaway Match* (1903) and *The Gentlemen Highwaymen* (1905). The former deploys the car to help a couple elope; the latter uses a car to terrorize a couple."[93]

Like the western, the road movie has undergone historical shifts, but where the western fit more snugly into classical Hollywood narrative forms as they developed, the road movie's popularity has waxed during periods of rebellion and social change. At the very time that the classic western was in rapid decline, the mildly countercultural *Bonnie and Clyde* (1967) and *Easy Rider* (1969) became the new road movie prototypes. Road movies work with the core dialectic of rebellion/conformity, but as with most mainstream films, rebellion is often presented as a titillating image that is destined to be contained within the status quo. But not always: road movies, Laderman notes, are more often made outside the studio system by independent filmmakers, and this combination of their independent origins and the *images* of rebellion they trade in makes road movies more socially transgressive than most films.[94]

If westerns are films about the western American frontier, Dennis Hopper's *Easy Rider* (1969) is the quintessential film about the same landscape once the frontier has been closed and there is nowhere left to go but back. It was filmed as the Vietnam War raged and protests against it grew, during a year when Martin Luther King Jr. and Robert Kennedy were assassinated and when the "silent majority," fed up with the liberations of the 1960s, swept Richard Nixon into power. Despite the naïveté of its politics, however, *Easy Rider* became the countercultural version of a national epic, a *Grapes of Wrath* or *The Searchers* for a generation tired of conformity but, for the most part, only intuitively groping toward an alternative. Intended as a kind of "post-" or "reverse western" with the two heroes riding Harley-Davidsons instead of horses, the film is a document of its times. It portrayed a nation deeply divided, with those divisions geographically territorialized in the film's episodic structure. As small-time drug dealers Wyatt and Billy, whose names echo those of Wyatt Earp and Billy the Kid, set out from the west coast on their Harleys, they pass through a Southwest idealized as a land of enticingly open landscapes, Native Americans and Hispanics, rural communards (the film's hippie commune was modelled after the New Buffalo commune north of Taos, New Mexico), and mysterious but hospitable strangers. The South (from Texas to Florida), on the other hand, as Barbara Klinger puts it, "bears the burden for all of civilization's maladies, including small-town racial prejudice, xenophobia, and the negative effects of modernization, urbanization, and industrial growth," as well as a seething violence that ultimately engulfs the two, leading to the film's apocalyptic climax.[95] Despite its sober assessment of the nation's cultural divide, the film captured the imagination of audiences, making nearly $60 million at the box office, which was almost unheard of at the time for a low-budget film made independently of the Hollywood studios. Its themes—landscapes, outlaws, countercultures, and the freedom of the open road—were quintessentially American, and its combination of music, landscape, and episodic movement across the country helped set off an army of motorcyclists (and hitchhikers) to travel the country, at a time not long after the completion of the nation's interstate highway system.

In *Green Screen,* David Ingram argues that where nineteenth-century landscape art invited viewers to visit the western landscape, the "kinetic landscapes" found in films like *Deliverance* (1972) and *The River Wild* (1994) allow us to penetrate that landscape, providing the vicarious thrill of moving through it at high speeds. *Easy Rider* included several kinetic landscape sequences—picturesque road montages pairing landscape imagery and camera motion with mood-inducing rock and folk songs of the time, including Steppenwolf's "Born to Be Wild" as the two bikers set off into the desert, and The Byrds' "Ballad of Easy Rider" and The Band's "The Weight" as they drive across the Southwest. The latter sequence features a 360-degree travelling-shot pan of Monument Valley, with the men and motorcycles at the centre of the action. The songs are presented as extended moments of spectacle, music-video style well before the emergence of that genre, and with little diegetic sound. These sequencces are excessive to the narrative and are meant to be enjoyed for their scenery, movement, and sound.

In John Boorman's *Deliverance,* the kinetic landscapes encourage a more seemingly conservationist impulse than the road-hunger of *Easy Rider.* Based on the novel by James Dickey, the film tells the story of four middle-aged, suburban Atlanta businessmen on a whitewater canoeing trip down the fictional Cahulawassee River in the forested southern Appalachians of Georgia. The river, we are informed at the outset, is set to be flooded for hydroelectric power and recreation. The four men's quest for an adventure in nature "before it's gone" turns nightmarish following a meeting with local mountain men, whom the film portrays as backward, inbred hillbillies. The film's centrepiece is an attack and rape at gunpoint of one of the four men, Bobby, by two mountaineers on a forested bank of the river. The attack is halted as the adventurers' *de facto* leader, the macho survivalist Lewis (Burt Reynolds), shoots the rapist with an arrow from his hunting bow; this is the first of a series of deaths, injuries, and mishaps to beset the four men's journey. For the remainder of the film, the urbanites struggle, physically and morally, with the river and with the burden of their actions: Should they report the crimes in which they've become implicated, or should they conceal the bodies and play innocent? The surviving men keep their secrets and return to their homes. In the final scene, Ed, the most tormented of the remaining three men (one of whom had died mysteriously), wakes up shaking from a dream of a corpse rising to the surface of the now flooded river.

The film's main dynamic overlays an opposition between city and country, or civilization and wilderness, with a trajectory of decline that is, at once, both that of nature and that of the rural population living in closest proximity to it. The tourists' rite of passage into the wilderness becomes a journey into a rural American "heart of darkness"—an embrace by a nature that is not pure and pristine, that is not a site of the rejuvenation the four men desire, but rather, that is threatening and demonic, a site of terror and brute force that strips them of their civilized veneer.[96] Notwithstanding this chasm between rural and urban *cultures*, however, the film succeeds in mobilizing positive images of wild and seemingly benevolent *nature*. Its scenes of the men "shooting the rapids," filmed with hand-held cameras and edited with quick cuts and jarring transitions, have become canonical in the tropes of environmental adventure filmmaking. *Deliverance* ranked fourth in box office sales for its year and was nominated for the Best Picture and Best Director Oscars. Much of its success can be credited to its cinematography and on-location shooting, especially of the scenes of whitewater paddling, and to the banjo-driven bluegrass music that seems to propel the canoes down the rapids. One of the film's most memorable scenes is a lively and captivating banjo duel between guitar-toting urbanite Drew and an apparently deformed and mentally disabled local albino boy; the song, "Dueling Banjos," played by Eric Weissman and Steve Mandell, became a popular hit. The banjo music is heard throughout the film, and the combination of downriver camera kineticism and *musical* kineticism provides for the movie's most uplifting moments. It is precisely these moments of kinetic harmony—points at which the duelling opposites at the core of the film (urban versus rural, civilized versus wild) are momentarily reconciled—that best capture the movie's utopian affects.

These affects were in turn mobilized into movements to protect such rivers from development *and* to enjoy those rivers once they had been protected, or, if not, then while they lasted. In 1974, partly as a result of the film, the Chattooga River, where much of it was shot, became the first river in the southeast and the second in the nation to be protected by Congress under the Wild and Scenic Rivers Act. (Since then, a further 11,000 miles of 168 rivers have been designated as such.) The film played no small role in catalyzing a whitewater rafting boom in Rabun County, Georgia. Since 1972, some 1.5 million paddlers have gone down the Chattooga (more than thirty of whom died during the journey). Its commercial and private users number close to 100,000 per year, with recreational boating on the river bringing in $2.6 million a year to the local economy. For all that, novelist James Dickey, before his death in 1997, lamented that the Chattooga had been "ruined now by people trying to cash in on it."[97]

The film, then, provides audiences with an ambiguous mixture of potential meanings and affects. Its portrayal of the Appalachian wilderness is deeply ambivalent and troubled. Through Lewis's rants against development, and through the implicit discourse of much of the imagery, the film seems to disapprove of the damming of the Chattooga/Cahulawassee. Yet at the same time, the river's damming is understood to be a way to clean up the defilement and degeneracy that the forest comes to represent in the film.[98] In the words of the cabbie who drives Bobby and Ed back into town in the film's closing minutes: "All this land's gonna be covered with water. Best thing ever happened to this town." The men, no doubt, look forward to its flooding, since it will cover up the bodies of two mountaineers whose deaths they precipitated. In the end, what viewers carry away from the film is up to them: a fear of Appalachian nature, or of its denizens; a desire to protect the river, or to shoot those rapids; or all of the above in various measures, so that the desire to "do the river" becomes a way to conquer one's fear of nature *and* of the men who dwell in it.

Cinematic Tourism, Object Fetishism, and the Global Landscape

If films, as I have been arguing, take us places—or, rather, bring those places to us, delivering them to our eyes, with us never having to leave our seats—this bringing cannot leave those places unaffected. As Dudley Andrew points out, "it was in the service of advertising that several of the first great voyages of cine-matic discovery set off: *Nanook of the North* (1922) was sponsored by a fur com-pany, and *Black Journey* (*La Croisière noire*, 1924) by Citroen."[99] As *Deliverance* demonstrates, seeing a place in film can elicit in viewers a desire to visit that place in reality. Cinematic portrayals can contribute to the popularization and overuse of certain places or to their neglect, to the construction of a certain aura around them or to the dispersion of a pre-existing aura. Its truth-effects, as such, can be educational or not. In this sense, we can study the effects of landscape portrayals in the same way that sociologists study the "media effects" of depictions of violence, pornography, and other human behaviours.

Don Gayton argues that the "indiscriminate" and interchangeable use of "places, landscapes and regions" to stand in for others conveys a sense that place "is a mere commodity, to be traded and substituted at will."[100] Yet one could also argue the opposite: that (to use Gayton's example) the treatment of the town of Nelson, British Columbia, as a proxy for Bainbridge Island in the making of *Snow Falling on Cedars*—or, for that matter, the treatment of any place in the American West to stand in for the mythical West—*elevates* that place. It does this not only by providing jobs and revenue to the local com-munity, but also by valuing that particular landscape for the iconic qualities (in Peirce's sense) it shares with the landscape being referred to. Both places, of course, are being treated as places in quotation marks—as place-images rather than places-in-and-for-themselves. During his road trip to visit the locations of *Easy Rider*, Keith Phipps noted that Las Vegas, New Mexico, where the movie's lead characters were briefly jailed for "parading without a permit," fit his "movie-shaped ideal of what a small town was supposed to look like." "Of course," he writes,

> Las Vegas has an incentive to appear idyllic. If it appears otherwise, filmmakers will need to look elsewhere to find small-town imagery to idealize or subvert in their films. I ended up unsure whether I'd really seen Las Vegas at all, or just some Hollywood idea of small-town authenticity. After admiring a cowgirl painted on the side of a build-ing announcing I'd arrived where "the Great Plains meet the mighty Rockies," I noticed it welcomed me to a town called "Calumet"—Las Vegas' name in *Red Dawn*.

"I could live here," Phipps concludes, "but where would I really be?"[101] But is this saying anything more than that the "sense of place" of a place is always a sense that is determined through what is done there, and through its differences from what is done elsewhere? Gayton's critique of "landscape duplicity" rings true, however, in the example he gives: "When midway through *Romancing the Stone*, the setting changes dramatically from South American canefields and tropical forests to California coastal scrub with no corresponding change in plot, we are expected not to notice or, if we do, not to care." In this and countless other cases, the filmmakers are counting on the audience to be as ecologically illiterate as they themselves are.

Iwashita and Sydney-Smith argue that films' power to shape and influence perceptions and opinions about places may be particularly great when the place is *not* the focus of the film. Propaganda, Mazierska and Walton concur, "is most effective when it is not presented in that guise."[102] Studies of film tourism have shown how portrayals of landscapes in commercially successful movies have led to marked increases in tourist traffic: a 30 percent increase in visitors to New Zealand following the *Lord of the Rings* films, a 40 percent increase to the beaches of the Allied landing in Normandy following *Saving Private Ryan* (even though it was filmed in Ireland), and a 54 percent increase to ten national monuments or national parks within five years of the release of ten selected films including *Thelma and Louise* (Grand Canyon National Park, 1991) and *Close Encounters of the Third Kind* (Devils Tower, Wyoming, 1977).[103] Scotland has become well established as a screen tourism destination in the wake of popular films such as *Braveheart* (1995), *Rob Roy* (1995), and the conservationist "sense of place" film *Local Hero* (1983).[104] The town of Tobermory on the Isle of Mull has seen its tourist traffic increase by around 150,000 a year, in large part because the preschool children's TV program *Balamory* was filmed there—a stunning rise that took the producers as well as the local community by surprise.

All of this underscores the relationship that is central to film's geomorphism—the one between images of places and the places themselves. Film has become an important means for marketing tourist destinations, and as a consequence, many places have set out to attract film companies—to become "film friendly," in industry lingo. But in conditions characterized by huge economic disparities, whatever benefits the tourist revenues bring are more likely to exacerbate existing political differences than to ameliorate them. Rodanthi Tzanelli examined cinematic tourism—specifically, she presented four case studies of the interactions between host and guest communities relating to these productions: *The Beach* in Thailand, the *Lord of the Rings* trilogy in New Zealand, *Captain Corelli's Mandolin* on the Greek island of Kefalonia, and *Dirty Dancing: Havana Nights* in the Caribbean. Her pessimistic conclusion: "Guest countries are left with nothing more than the symbolic capital (the 'island of *Corelli*,' the 'home of Middle Earth') that has been allocated to them from without, stranded between submission to the calls of global capitalism and the need to salvage what they can from from an identity in the process of transformation."[105] Tzanelli also found that of the four cases, New Zealand had come out best: *Lord of the Rings,* a fantasy written by an English writer drawing on North European mythology, became part of New Zealand's heritage, and with strong government support, that country's tourist industry gained a tremendous boost from the immense popularity of the film trilogy.[106] More commonly, however, "forced touristification hardens preexisting ethnic, class and gender structures of inequality."[107] This is in part because the tourist gaze is by its nature a consumptive and colonial gaze; it turns its objects into things meant to represent pre-defined forms of otherness. When that gaze is brought to a community by the gales of global capitalism, the community rarely has the time or leisure to develop policies for how to gaze back in socially and ecologically sustainable ways.

Steven Spielberg's *Close Encounters of the Third Kind* is particularly interesting because it is, in large part, *about* the affective magnetism of a landscape, specifically that of Bear Butte, better known as Devils Tower, in Wyoming. This distinctive "signature landscape" becomes a kind of fetish image for the film's characters, who obsess over it and feel compelled to re-create it, as if captured by an obsessive compulsion—sculpting it in living-room-sized heaps of mashed potatoes, in the case of lead character Roy Neary (Richard Dreyfuss)—until the event that all this frantic activity portends, which is the descent of an alien mothership over the mountain itself, takes place on the landscape of Wyoming. In the year following the film's release, visits to Devils Tower National Monument increased by 74 percent.[108] In my 1990s research on cultural and environmental conflicts over the red rock landscape of Sedona, Arizona, I was intrigued to find a correlation between the stories of those who had moved to this area, compelled by the affective impact of the landscape itself, with its enthralling, cipher-like red rock monuments, and references to the Spielberg film. In this sense, Spielberg's film seems to have caught, and at the same time magnified, a wave of cultural desire to "connect with the earth"—a desire that the burgeoning New Age spiritual movement was to crystallize in places like Sedona (and in more than just that movement's fascination with crystals).[109] Conflicts have arisen among Native American groups, Forest Service rangers, New Agers, and rock-climbing enthusiasts at Devils Tower National Monument, just as they have around Aboriginal sacred rock sites like Uluru (Ayers Rock) in Australia and elsewhere.

There is a duality in this cinematic fetishization of the visible object. There is, in most films, some set of backgrounds against which the foreground action takes place. I have been focusing on the backgrounds on the premise that they never remain purely passive and that their seeming passivity, their givenness, is interactively *produced*. The implication, however—one that I will revisit in Chapter 5—is that there is ultimately only a single landscape within cinema—the landscape *of* cinema itself. A film in its entirety presents a certain "scape" or set of scapes—usually fragmented and multiple, full of juxtapositions and movements, but nevertheless *there* as constantly changing scenery, viewable as a framed view. Parts of this scape—typically its more mobilizable parts, such as people and vehicles—move into the foreground as others recede into the background. One of cinema's most enduring influences on the world relates to its capacity to imbue objects with character, liveliness, allure, and meaning. The objects that advance forward, like those that structure the background, become fetish objects, "commodity fetishes" in Marx's terms—as anyone will recognize who is familiar with TV ads for cars, diamond rings, or brands of soap. The guns in the films of Quentin Tarantino and John Woo, the motorcycles in *Easy Rider* (1969) and in Kenneth Anger's *Scorpio Rising* (1964), the shoes in *The Red Shoes* (1948), the violin in *The Red Violin,* the balloon in *The Red Balloon* (1956) and in the more recent homage to it, *Flight of the Red Balloon* (2008)—all of these are brought to life in ways that still photography can only hint at. These objects take on meanings according to the ways in which they are affectively invested by the characters, the camera, the *mise en scène*, and ultimately by viewers.

For instance, the red balloon in Hou Hsiao-hsien's lyrical and bittersweet *Flight of the Red Balloon* takes on a set of meanings, or perhaps "energies," in and through its drifting alongside the storyline, reappearing periodically and threading a reassuring counterpoint to it, as if it is taking a compassionate, almost angelic curiosity in the lives of the characters. Reviews of the film interpret the balloon variously as a metaphor for beauty, happiness, innocence, imagination, freedom and its elusiveness, fraught intimacy, longing and proximity, perpetually unfulfilled desire, and so on. It is lent affective hues by the piano music that is woven through the disjointed events of the young boy's life and that of his mother, and by the moments of stillness, observation, and wonder during which the boy notices the balloon drifting somewhere outside a window or above a streetscape. In effect, the balloon makes visible the invisible: in the same way that shots of wheatfields swaying in the wind in *Earth* and *Days of Heaven* signal the invisible materiality connecting the separate elements of the seen world, the balloon shows us the movement of air currents that otherwise would not be seen or felt, since film remains an audiovisual medium, not one that can directly transfer the movement of air on skin. Film objects of this sort are more than mere objects. They become carriers of affect, mediators of relations that both *pass on* an energetic quality or charge between humans and things and *represent* that quality itself. They are fusions of firstness (the things, the qualities, the feelings), secondness (the events connected by them), and thirdness (the interpretations and meanings we give them).

In films that explore collective memories and ethnic or community histories, objects may already be carriers of such affect, and they may serve as what Laura Marks calls "recollection-objects": they are fetishes, fossils, and transnational objects that "condense time within themselves" and that carry meanings across space and time even as those meanings change with their altered contexts.[110] Cinematic objects, then, carry worlds with them; and set against the objectscape of a world that is perceivable in a film, they set off affective ripples that move in one direction or another depending on the expectations and capacities of viewers. They may denote the past, tradition, community, possibility, liberation, or something else, and *this* past or *this* liberation is set in relationship to an imagined community of one kind or another—a community that may be steeped in painful memories (such as those of a diasporically dispersed culture) or that may be simply a reservoir of hopes and fantasies (the imagined community of a tourist projection). The differences between such object orientations will be explored in the next chapter.

Enframing the World, or Expanding Perception?

As Dudley Andrew, Antonio Costa, Giuliana Bruno, and others have argued, travel, exploration, and touristic consciousness have been with cinema from its very beginnings. The scenes of international pursuit that characterize Wim Wenders's *Until the End of the World* (1991)—a film that touches down in Venice, Lyon, Paris, Berlin, Lisbon, Moscow, Transiberia, Beijing, Tokyo, San Francisco, and Australia—are not that different in principle from *A Policeman's Tour of the World* (1906), which featured a world tour-chase consisting of tableau shots in Egypt, India, China, Japan, the American West, and New York City. But even if the travel scene, as Bruno argues, is "the primal scene of the motion picture,"[111] the arrival of the first images of the entire Earth from space in the 1960s altered the possibilities for travel in ways we could hardly have imagined beforehand. Stanley Kubrick's *2001, A Space Odyssey* (1968) and Tarkovsky's *Solaris* (1972) played on this new frontier in imaginative and consequential ways: both presented a new form of technological or "outer space" sublime in ways that resonated with the counterculture's search for new *inner* spaces. *2001* was especially notable for its geomorphic displacements and shocks: temporal leaps from an early hominid prehistory to the near technological future; panoramic scenes of space capsules floating in space that dissimulated any sense of verticality or gravity; the use of silence (save for the sound of a lone astronaut's respiration and circulation) to evoke a similar loss of individual bearings in space; and a final, twenty-three-minute "trip sequence" that removed all sense of linear time, as astronaut David Poole was taken through a Stargate and ultimately was reborn as a gigantic human fetus floating in space beside the Earth.[112] Special-effects master Douglas Trumbull, responsible for much of the latter section of *2001*, was later to develop similar techniques in his work on films such as Spielberg's *Close Encounters of the Third Kind* (1977), Robert Wise's *Star Trek: The Motion Picture* (1979), Ridley Scott's *Blade Runner* (1982), Trumbull's own *Silent Running* (1971) and *Brainstorm* (1983), and a series of "special venue" productions shown in theme parks, World's Fair exhibitions, and other large-screen performance spaces.

New cinematic technologies such as those developed by Trumbull have opened up the possibilities for two simultaneous expansions: toward a more global *enframing* of the film world, and toward a more *immersive* cinematic experience of that world. Through widescreen and large-format projection technologies, digital surround sound, stadium-style seating, 3-D projection, and "camera perspectives that swoop, glide, dash and dart through the diegetic action," cinema spaces have turned moviegoing, in Tim Recuber's words, "into a series of technologically induced thrill rides and enveloping simulations."[113] The photographic realism of what is shown is part of this heightened simulatedness, as is the documentary discourse that accompanies many such films. Like virtual reality, today's IMAX and Omnimax film theatres are descendants of the immersive panoramas that have entertained audiences since the late eighteenth century.

In a discussion of cinematic globalism, Martin Roberts distinguishes among three kinds of global films: "the global exploitation film of the *Mondo Cane* variety; the conspicuous cosmopolitanism of the international avant-garde (Wenders, Herzog, Jarmusch, Aki and Mika Kaurismaki, Ottinger); and the coffee-table globalism of *Powaqqatsi* or *Baraka*." The first is a filmic descendant of the carnival peep show. The second exemplifies a "self-consciously nomadic" *flâneurie*, a "detached, sardonic observation of an increasingly transnational world order and the cultural change associated with it." The third follows in the liberal humanist, *Family of Man*-style "One Worldism," a global-panoramic *National Geographic* aestheticization of Otherness.[114] The third of these, while it had many predecessors, was launched as a successful commercial genre with Godfrey Reggio's *Koyaanisqatsi* (1982), which was followed by the same director's *Powaqqatsi* (1988) and *Naqoyqatsi* (2002) and his collaborator Ron Fricke's *Chronos* (1985), *Sacred Site* (1986), *Baraka* (1992), and *Samsara* (2011). The lush cinematography of these films—they feature stunning sequences of computer-controlled time-lapse photography, as well as aerial and tracking shots from urban and (especially) natural settings around the world—and their large budgets, global humanist and mystical, pro-indigenous themes, avoidance of traditional narrative, and reliance on mood-setting music by composers like Philip Glass and Michael Stearns, have deservedly gained them the reputation of being "coffee table films," the cinematic equivalent of "world music."

Baraka exemplifies the paradoxical nature of this genre. Titled after an Arabic and Persian word meaning "blessing," the film takes viewers to 152 locations in twenty-four countries around the world. Many of these are sites associated with spiritual power or significance, such as churches, shrines, monuments, and world heritage sites (the Giza pyramid complex in Egypt, Angkor Wat in Cambodia, and many natural heritage sites). But they also include a coal mine, an air force base, a cigarette factory, a prison complex, Third World *favelas*, and sites of concentration camps and massacres. Like *Koyaanisqatsi*, *Baraka* achieves its power by juxtaposing places associated with sublime beauty and those associated with human misery and technological grandiosity. While there is no narrative, the structuring discourse—at least in the film's dominant interpretation—is one that posits a contrast between what could be called an "organic-harmonious sublime" and an "industrial-cacophanous sublime." The film, however, is open-ended, and one could interpret it as simply being *about* the sublime in all its forms: natural, romantic, technological, industrial, and carceral. The goal, in this sense, is a kind of streaming firstness, a direct and primal experience of otherness, sacredness, and awe, leading presumably to a transcendent mystical insight or *sense*, unobstructed by any elements of secondness, such as narrative, dialogue, or clear causal logic. Because these films provide little information about what they show and no means for a dialogue with those who are shown (in exoticized garb), they end up, as Amy Staples argues, reasserting a colonialist imaginary where the world is ours to see, but where the gaze is exclusively one-way: "we can be everywhere and nowhere at the same time." Or as Sean Cubitt puts it, "the cosmopolitan is at home in the culture of the other, but he does not offer the other the hospitality of his own home."[115] Following Renato Rosaldo's argument about "imperialist nostalgia," Martin Roberts argues that these high-tech, capital-intensive films enable First World audiences "to mourn what capitalism has destroyed while at the same time absolving themselves of any responsibility for it."[116] They are "trip films," but whether we travel them as pilgrims or as mere tourists—that is, whether we are changed in the process or simply consume what we see— and whether we could actually make ourselves vulnerable to the presence of the depicted "other," will depend, inevitably, on us.

There is something that feels oddly complementary between films like *Baraka*, with their quest to intuitively feel out a universal matrix beneath the particulars of cultural traditions, and those like *The Matrix* (1999), which posit a universal Real beneath the details of the Imaginary but which also suggest that the Real has been taken over by some parasitic, demiurgic cohort of god-like impostors. In both cases, reality is supposed to underlie appearances, but in the latter case the reality presents evidence of its takeover by a radical Otherness, such that we must battle to recover it in the purity and innocence of its origins. Both present variations on a neo-Gnostic ontology. In *The Matrix* this is a Gnostic dualism of struggle between forces of delusion and forces of insight, while in *Baraka* this is a Gnostic intuitivism, whereby insight is gained through contemplation of what is given to our vision. Humanity is being redefined here in its global relationship to Otherness and to Sameness (which makes these films more of a topic for the next chapter). At the same time, the audience for such films—and other cosmopolitan products such as *Crouching Tiger, Hidden Dragon* (2000) and *Babel* (2006)—is being redefined as an ever more global one.

The primary goal of *The Matrix*, however, is arguably to sell tickets, while the goal of *Baraka* and others like it may well be to affect their viewers, even to *transform* them, by framing the world differently than what we are used to. Their mode of spectacle is slower and more deliberate. Their methods are those of experimental cinema, albeit somewhat tamed by their glossy packaging.[117] Much of this chapter has focused on the "framing" of the world in cinema, a framing that generally follows the long-standing tradition of linear perspective, with its assumed single observer viewing and appreciating a scene from a distance. Appreciating landscape in itself, rather than in its relationship with people (as in the pantheist materialism of Dovzhenko) or as a reflection of the psychological and narrative dimensions of a film, involves a particular spectatorial gaze at the world. I have referred to the Heideggerian critique of modernity as a form of visual and cognitive "enframing" of the world, but I have also suggested that this is probably not all that goes on when we look at the world. When the world is perceived as an object of beauty, it is an object of beauty *for us*, and therefore one that we might wish to possess as such. But it is also an object of the beauty that is *the world's*. It may be possible, in other words, to see beauty without wanting to possess it. In the same way, it may be possible to travel through the world without necessarily wanting to *order* it for ourselves in the process. Travelling may be tourism (of the consumptive kind), but it may also be celebration, service, devotion, or encounter with something different and interesting in itself.

Visual media, however, can enhance our perception of the world beyond that of unmediated, direct perception, allowing us to see visual qualities, details, and patterns that would otherwise be unavailable to us. Such is the case when we watch time-lapse or slow-motion photography. Time-lapse photography allows us to see formal patterns in the unfolding of a flower and its movement in relation to the sun, or the rhapsody of a landscape, city, or planet over the course of a day as compressed into a few minutes (as in David Rimmer's seven-and-a-half-minute-long *Landscape* [1969]). Slow-motion photography allows us to see the coordinated movement of the limbs of an animal or human as it moves (as in Eadweard Muybridge's early stop-motion studies of locomotion). In *The Garden in the Machine*, experimental film theorist Scott MacDonald argues that the real potentials for cinematic expression of nature and of ecology lie with the avant-garde. Similar arguments have been made before, by Gene Youngblood, P. Adams Sitney, and filmmakers like Stan Brakhage and Maya Deren, but MacDonald's is the most synoptic effort to bring an ecological argument to the world of experimental film.[118] His primary focus is on films that challenge our viewing habits and that "retrain" our perceptions of natural (and human) processes.[119] They do this through long takes, extended durational formats, unusual montage and editing techniques, manipulation of focus and exposure, superimpositions, unusual camera movements, the use of silence and natural sound, and the foregrounding of subjects—places, landscapes, rivers, changing seasons, and everyday visual and sensory occurrences—that usually serve only as backdrop in mainstream cinema.

Rooted in the structural cinema movement of the 1960s and 1970s, the films of James Benning provide a good example of a landscape-scaled approach to such a non-narrative cinema. Benning has made a series of films focused on the American West, including a trilogy of films about California. Each of the latter is a feature-length film made up almost entirely of two-and-a-half-minute-long, tripod-mounted outdoor shots, utilizing only natural, diegetic sound. Benning's films eliminate all the features of conventional narrative cinema, such as human characters and storylines, point-of-view shots, and the rest. They provide only a lengthy series of languidly paced and unadorned landscape images, which together make up an ambiguous narrative of environmental change. The films focus on land use activities, from forestry and mining to military uses. Benning's earlier, Utah-based film *Deseret* (1995) included a spoken series of environmentally focused texts about Utah taken from news stories in the *New York Times*. Another of his films, *13 Lakes* (2004), consists entirely of ten-minute-long static takes of thirteen different lakes across the United States, with the rectangular image divided at the horizon line into earth/water and sky, and no "action" *per se* except what occurs during the filming: "the slow drift of cumulus clouds, raindrops falling on a tranquil mere, or a brisk wind sweeping across the surface of the water."[120]

For Benning, as for many of the other filmmakers celebrated by MacDonald, the medium—in this case, a series of slow and deliberate visual meditations crafted in ways antithetical to Hollywood film—is closely inter-twined with the message, which here is the changing human relationship to nature. "Ultimately," as MacDonald puts it, Benning's "unusual cinematic structures ... *are* his fundamental argument. So long as we follow the Hollywood model and continue to repress the complex realities of geography and history on the assumption that there are no real alternatives, we will not find our way out of the dilemmas that face us."[121] Other structurally oriented experimental filmmakers such as Michael Snow, Hollis Frampton, David Rimmer, and Chantal Akerman have similarly attempted to do away with narrative in order to focus exclusively on the camera's gaze and the way it captures the world (and, by extension, the ways the world eludes it).

Pushing further from the perspectival realism that has been canonized in mainstream narrative cinema, we come to the work of avant-garde filmmakers like Stan Brakhage. Perhaps the best-known and most prolific of cinematic experimentalists, Brakhage made more than 400 16mm and 8mm films, most of them silent, in a career spanning almost half a century. Brakhage's writings on cinema articulate a model of the film artist as an artisan-craftsman working with the very building blocks of perception. His goal was the anti-narrative cinematic goal of deconstructing the imperial gaze and recovering a more originary form of perception, an innocent gaze that would recover the world's sensual materiality at its most immediate. In the opening paragraph of his manifesto "Metaphors on Vision," he wrote:

> Imagine an eye unruled by man-made laws of perspective, an eye unprejudiced by compositional logic, an eye which does not respond to the name of everything but which must know each object encountered in life through an adventure of perception.... Imagine a world alive with incomprehensible objects and shimmering with an endless variety of movement and innumerable gradations of color. Imagine a world before the "beginning was the word."[122]

Cinema, for Brakhage, was about the act of seeing and its connection to the elemental foundations of life—birth, death, sex, beauty—as well as about the basic materiality of the film medium, which encompasses light and colour emulsion in all their physicality. In some of his films he worked directly with the film stock itself, scratching, painting, and taping objects to the celluloid in order to emphasize the materiality of the medium and the qualities of its capture of light. For *Dog Star Man* (1962–64) and *Song 14* (1966, 1980), he grew mould on the filmstrip. In his two-and-a-half-minute film *The Garden of Earthly Delights* (1981)—a bioregional "locavore" film well before that movement was conceived—he painstakingly assembled collage-like arrangements of montane-zone vegetation, including seeds, flowers, leaves, and blades of grass from nearby his Colorado home, directly onto the 35mm filmstrip. The end result, when viewed, is a flickering kaleidoscope of colour by which viewers are drawn into the very act of seeing the light of projected "nature," not from the panoramic distance of a "magisterial gaze," but from the intimacy of being caught in the middle of nature itself, as if we were in the midst of the teeming, animated intensity of living process.

Instead of merely recording the world, Brakhage celebrated the camera's capacity to produce a virtually unlimited vision. Writing presciently in 1963, Brakhage urged us to "[c]onsider this prodigy," the camera,

> for its virtually untapped talents, viewpoints it possesses more readily recognizable as visually non-human yet within the realm of the humanly imaginable. I am speaking of its speed for receptivity which can slow the fastest motion for detailed study, or its ability to create a continuity for time compression, increasing the slowest motion to a comprehensibility. I am praising its cyclopean penetration of haze, its infra-red visual ability in darkness, its just developed 360 degree view, its prismatic revelation of rainbows, its zooming potential for exploding space and its telephotic compression of same to flatten perspective, its micro- and macroscopic revelations. I am marveling at its Schlaeran self capable of representing heat waves and the most invisible air pressures, and appraising its other still camera developments which may grow into motion, its rendering visible the illumination of bodily heat, its transformation of ultraviolets to human cognizance, its penetrating X-ray. I am dreaming of the mystery camera capable of graphically representing the form of an object after it's been removed from the photographic scene, etc. The "absolute realism" of the motion picture is unrealized, therefore potential, magic.[123]

What Brakhage is calling for here is as materialist a vision as any, because it is fully engaged with the medium *as* a medium, in a world that is all about mediation, relationship, contact, and sensory experience. A related variant of experimental film that highlights the material ecologies of the medium (including its very objectness), but that also accentuates its social and perceptual ecologies, is the collage or found-footage film. Images of the decay of film are the focus of Bill Morrison's *Decasia* (2003), which consists solely of excerpts of old films whose nitrate stock has deteriorated to the point where the images have become abstract. Collage films such as Bruce Connor's *A Movie* (1958) and Craig Baldwin's *Tribulation 99* (1991) satirize conventional representation while commenting on the mediaticity of our image-saturated era.

Such unusual styles necessarily require work from their audiences, especially when cinema's enjoyable secondness, the narrative, is decentred or even eliminated altogether from the viewing experience. As the insistent Italian producer in Jean-Luc Godard's *Passion* (1982) keeps reminding the director of the film-within-the-film, a recreation of classical paintings in cinema, what viewers want is *"La storia! La storia!"* The difficulty of seeing some of the films MacDonald celebrates—a difficulty mitigated only when filmmakers make their work available online—is compounded when the experience is restricted to highly controlled settings. Benning, for instance, is committed to showing the California trilogy as a single, extended event. Despite their inaccessibility to broad audiences, however, experimental filmmakers have been influential in the development of mainstream cinema. Techniques developed by Brakhage, Godard, Kenneth Anger, Maya Deren, Gregory Markopoulos, Jean Cocteau, and others—from hand-held camera movement and high-speed cutting and editing techniques to direct address of the audience and even writing directly onto the film—can today be found in mainstream films, television series, music videos, and even commercials.

Rather than account for all such variations in filmmaking practice, I will conclude this chapter with a reading of a single film that incorporates numerous experimental techniques into a feature-film adaptation of Shakespeare's *The Tempest*. Both the original play and Peter Greenaway's adaptation raise issues that are relevant to the next chapter, but here we can prefigure some of those arguments by focusing on the ways in which the film works explicitly to deconstruct the kind of gaze that the Western pictorial tradition has passed on to its most powerful descendant, cinema. Before turning to Greenaway's *Prospero's Books* (1991), I will briefly discuss a documentary that brings together several of the themes we have covered in this chapter—cinema as seeing, the landscape gaze, the ecological sublime, and the journey from here to there as a form of spatial territorialization—in a way that reminds us that cinematic geomorphism is never entirely separate from the geomorphology of the world as it already exists. If Peter Mettler's *Picture of Light* (1994) instances the ways in which technology facilitates a form of seeing that is always selective but nevertheless revealing, Greenaway's film extends the technology of cinema into a form of seeing that is multi-perspectival, self-reflexive, deconstructive, and at the same time highly embodied, material, and performative. It is these elements that I will focus on in the chapters to come.

"Burn But His Books": Deconstructing the Gaze from Both Ends

Much has been written about the cinematic gaze: the ways in which it enframes a world for us, conditioning a certain way of looking at things and, henceforth, of treating them; the ways it revives an infantile, voyeuristic narcissism; and even the ways it looks *at* us, monitoring our every movement so that we perform in the knowledge or suspicion that we ourselves are being watched (or so a more paranoid reading of certain film-theoretical texts might suggest). Whatever the gaze is, it is never one-way, for there is never a gaze without an object, which means, in a process-relational view, that where there is subjectivation, there is always objectivation. The gaze, mediated as it is, serves as medium for an exchange. If our gaze has too often been imperial (as the next chapter will argue), deconstructing that gaze from one end alone is hardly possible. Eyes see and are seen. Bodies present themselves and are presented to. What the intervention of the cinematic apparatus does is mediate the relationship such that certain capacities are heightened at one end while others are diminished. What happens at the other end depends both on the apparatus and on how it is used.

Austrian-Canadian director Peter Mettler's *Picture of Light* is a film that plays out many of the themes of this chapter. It is a journey, undertaken by rail and motor vehicle, to a place that is *elsewhere*, far from the metropolitan centre from which the voyagers set out (Toronto). The travellers' goal is the goal of all cinema reduced to its bare essence: to capture light. Specifically, the film documents Mettler's film crew's expedition to film the Northern Lights, *aurora borealis*, at a place where they are most visible and seemingly alive, in the vicinity of Churchill, Manitoba, the northernmost station on the rail line. The film enacts what it posits: that the image is central to our world; that it is also a phantom—a "material ghost" as Perez would call it—and that the best we can hope for with cinema is to run after such a ghost.[124] If film only captures sight and sound, how, then, can it capture cold, how can it capture the essence of the North? This perennial Canadian question is answered in three related ways in the film. The first is through time and speed, and especially through a slowing down of both: the time that it takes the crew to arrive at its destination, to settle in and await the night when the lights will be at their peak, and a certain languor that drifts into the film, not unlike the snow that gradually fills a hotel room after a casually demonstrative rifle shot opens a hole in its thin wall. The second is through image: water dropping from the bottom of a stalled train vaporizes in mid-air; colour drains out of the image, the lens filling with fog from the coldness. And the third is through sound and voice-over. Sounds become muffled, as if heard through the thick hood of a parka or the sound of swimming underwater. Or at other times, with the characters surrounded by snow, sounds are deadened, with no reflecting surfaces to echo them back and provide a sense of landscape. A self-reflexive, ruminative voice-over drifts into the soundtrack like thoughts separated by vast gaps of space, repeating themselves at times to make sure they have said what they thought they had said. When, finally, the Northern Lights are given full reign by the camera, they are shot at slow speed and optically printed to stretch time, and we are told that they are like thoughts swirling in our minds, and like ghosts dancing.

If Mettler's film begins as a fairly conventional documentary and sets out to do something that filmmakers have tried to do from the beginnings of cinema—to capture a picture of light—*Prospero's Books* begins at cinema's other end, or its many ends, where it interfaces with its predecessors— theatre, dance, painting, and, as the title suggests, books—and where it flows into its destined descendants in the world of convergent, digital new media. Its subject is Shakespeare's last published play, a story often taken to summarize Shakespeare's oeuvre and to simultaneously capture a moment at the inauguration of transatlantic modernity—written on the cusp of the European discovery and colonization of the New World and inspired, in part, by documented encounters between European explorers and New World "savages." In this respect, *Prospero's Books* situates itself at both ends of the modernity I have been describing in this chapter. I take this argument in part from Paula Willoquet-Maricondi, who presents Greenaway's project in this film as a challenge to a triad of practices that "became fundamental to the establishment of modernity in the seventeenth century": "the hegemonic role of vision, the rise of transcendental reason, and the concomitant Cartesian subject's colonization and mastery of the world."[125]

This is a film, then, about power, and specifically about the power of vision, of art, of writing and language—in a word, the power of mediation, which is of course the essence of Peircian thirdness. This power is the kind that brings things together, suturing one thing and another in their encounter, and that also sets them in relationship to each other, which has all too often meant in a relationship of uneven power, of stratification. To examine the film in light of this onto-political concern, I will highlight three of its central characteristics: its self-reflexivity, especially in relation to this power-embeddedness of the media that make it up; its processuality, performativity, and enactment, which is where it comes into full congruence with a process-relational onto-logical project; and its materiality, which places into question the traditions of separating mind from body, spirit from matter, art from nature, organism from mechanism, imagined from real—all dualities that have become entrenched in the centuries that separate Shakespeare from us.

"Prospero's power," writes Willoquet-Maricondi, "is his ability to abstract; his most powerful tool of control is language—specifically, written language, which introduces a sense of order and linearity to the world that replaces the cyclical rhythm of nature and the fluidity of the spoken word."[126] Prospero orders the world by summoning it into being and by imposing a structure onto it. His method for mastering his world is to separate himself from it. His books—twenty-four of them, which the play only mentions (without provid-ing a number) but which become the centrepiece of the film—embody the knowledge that supplies his power over the island and its inhabitants: they document, quantify, measure, and classify the world, and in doing so they are Prospero's means for managing it. The books are library and archive, atlas and universal cartography.

The film, however, brings the books to life: their contents literally spill out of them, taking on a liveliness that far exceeds the literal text. "When the atlas is opened," the narrator says of Book 5, "the maps bubble with pitch. Avalanches of hot, loose gravel and molten sand fall out of the book to scorch the library floor." In James Tweedie's account, the film presents "an extended meditation on the relationship between the mystical authority of the book and the hybridizing act of reading and writing."[127] As if to accentuate this open-endedness, the final scenes have Caliban—who had earlier instructed Stephano and Trinculo, in their coup plotting, to "Burn but his books" for "without them He's but a sot"—surfacing to snatch the last two books out of the clutches of the water to which Prospero has decreed them. These two books, the folio collection of Shakespeare's plays and a slimmer, separate book referred to as "Prospero's unfinished The Tempest," are, of course, the two that have actually survived. Their future, by implication, is being left in the hands of their readers.

The film, however, is excessive in nearly every way: scenographically, iconographically, acoustically, sensorially, referentially. It is, as Tweedie puts it, "carnal, hyperkinetic, hybrid, and all of Prospero's worst fears realized before us." In its baroqueness of vision, the film emulates the forms of knowledge that it satirizes, with their obsessive compulsion to ordering and taxonomic encyclopedism, but it pushes that emulation to a point of intensity where it begins to come apart under its own weight. .Prospero, we must remember, is a magician, living in a time when magic was considered a science of the observation, interpretation, and manipulation of the correspondences between things—people, animals, plants, medicines, gemstones, musical tones, elemental humours, and stars.[128] In his project of successfully enrolling the island's denizens to do his bidding, Prospero is both their overlord and their manager, a successful natural magician who lives in harmony with those (like Ariel) that would harmonize, but who must rule over the unruly elements (such as Caliban and Sycorax) that would not.

The film is played like a grand masque, a spectacular courtly entertainment choreographed to please its patron (in this case, Prospero himself), featuring music and dance, elaborate stage design, architectural framing and costuming. In this the film, like Prospero's own conjuring of the world of the island (and the masque within the original play, a kind of world within a world), is a demonstration of the "world making" that I have ascribed to all cinema. But in Greenaway's hands the world that is produced here is a visually sumptuous and highly referential, self-deconstructing text that uses high-definition graphics and computer technology to layer spoken and written text, film and graphic imagery, music and sound, dance-like choreography, dramatic action, and densely stylized, architecturally and videographically framed tableaux. It is a world of multiple framings, mirrors, layers, and correspondences, interweaving a thick textuality with an elemental materiality, by way of intercuts, overlaps, insets, script overlays, windowed screens, and a complex audio mix.

With its foregrounding of its own framedness—including an emphasis on colonnades, draperies, mirrors, and graphic video framing devices—the film enacts what it aims to disassemble, which is the visual-textual enframing of the world and the colonial staging of its imperial subjects, aestheticized, eroticized, and classified. Its antidote to this legacy is a "'playful gaze' of multiple reflections, superimpositions, and metaframings of images."[129] The film's sets are largely static and dioramic, its camera movement dominated by still shots and long, slow tracking shots across *tableaux vivants* rich with architectural and art-historical allusion: "The bathhouse abuts an interior lifted from the Alhambra, Miranda's bedroom is reached by descending the Arcoli Steps on the Capitoline, and Ferdinand wanders through a Breughel cornfield with pyramids in the background. The costume of the characters apes outfits from paintings by Rembrandt, Vermeer, and Antonello da Messian. Thus," concludes Ryan Trimm, "in progressing from one architectural or artistic allusion to the next, the film offers a spin on 'moving pictures.'"[130]

Greenaway here is deconstructing 500 years of linear perspective while retaining an epic, multilayered form of narrative at the film's centre. This deconstruction, however, leaves us with much more than a dematerialized textuality. In staging its central conflict—that between the magician and ruler, Prospero, and Caliban, his conquered slave—the film may seem to overly privilege Prospero by giving him (John Gielgud) all the vocal parts and thereby ventriloquizing the other characters. But the film is deeply, richly material, elemental, and carnal. It gives Caliban a presence that is visceral and transgressive. His body, Douglas Keesey writes,

> exhibits grace under pressure, a lithe writhing and sinewy torment. The Saint Vitus' dance Caliban performs under Prospero's tortures, the choreography of jerks and spasms of one whose life has been made a hell on earth, offers physical evidence of blighted potential and an injured soul. Beyond this, the muscular uprising with which Caliban attempts to lift himself from this prison of a sewer rock, and the extravagant leaps and pirouettes he exhibits at the thought of freedom from Prospero, show a physical exuberance and a longing for liberty that are hard to mistake for mere lewdness and vagrancy.[131]

Just as Caliban flaunts his nakedness through contortions and bodily taunts, half or completely naked bodies fill many of the images in the film (something that Greenaway was criticized for by many American critics). The four traditional elements—earth, water, fire, and air (or at least wind)—are everywhere in evidence. The very first image, one that returns at the end, is a series of drops of water seemingly splashing onto the screen. From the outset, as Tweedie's description of the opening scenes makes clear, this elementality is central:

> The long horizontal tracking shot that accompanies the opening credits surveys a group of figures with an allegorical relationship to water, the subject of Prospero's first book. Noah, Moses in the bulrushes, Leda and the Swan, and Icarus all make cameo appearances as the visuals virtually exhaust the connotative capacity of the word *water*, made visible and audible in the rhythmic dripping that begins and ends the film. Add to this the visual pun on "making water" as Ariel urinates and Prospero calls forth a storm, the toy galleon and countless other nautical references, the waves and waterfalls, the bathhouse supplied with "large, exotic shells and a basin and brushes, sponges and towels," and the visual images begin to reflect some of the complexity of the word.[132]

Greenaway, who is well aware of film's capacities as a "material ghost," a refracted, dis- and re-assembled replica of the real things of the world, deconstructs not to leave us drifting in textual space but to leave us vibrating with the material *thingness* of what is there in front of us. To bring all this back to the topic of film's geomorphism: *where*, in the end, does this film *take place*? Trimm, taking up Rodowick's Deleuzianism, posits its space as an "any-space-whatever"—that is, all indeterminate potential, an unplottable space of the cell and the soundstage, "a soundstage at once no place and everywhere in its possible transformations."[133] But this neglects to recognize that not *every* any-space is *any* anyspace, at least not any-space-*whatever*. *Prospero's Books* takes place in a time-space of the cusp, an in-between space, a space of contact and encounter between textuality and performance, between Europe and its outside, between art and nature, cinema and the world. Prospero moves through the sets, from tableau to tableau, but without ever really arriving anywhere. This space is a layered space, its layers sometimes kept separate and sometimes overlapping or fused together: there is Prospero's study, which is in a sense the centre of things; there is a smattering of scenes in more or less distinct places—the cornfield, the swamp, below the surface of the water, though all of these are distinctly stylized, sometimes in ironic miniature; and there are the books, which come to life across the other visual spaces, but also in the vocal layers of the film. But most of all, there is the studio set, which functions as a large organic machine, an animated factory of bodies and mechanical parts, through which the camera moves in slow horizontal tracks. It is here, in the factory—the central production site of modernity, but here in its double aspect as organic-mechanical construction site and as imagistic and imaginal production workshop, the centre from which images are produced and disseminated—that *Prospero's Books* most literally takes place. Here is Jonathan Beller's "cinematic mode of production," turned to the deconstructive ends of staging modernity's own unravelling.

In his mid-century classic *The Machine in the Garden*, American literary critic Leo Marx argued that Shakespeare's *Tempest*, with its dialectical reconciliation of "America as hideous wilderness" and "America as paradise regained," presented a kind of prologue to all American literature, a template for the hopeful vision of a "symbolic middle landscape" created through the improvement of nature by art and learning.[134] Marx took Caliban to be a stand-in for the "untrammeled wildness or cannibalism at the heart of nature,"[135] a view that has since been challenged, if not upended, by a generation of postcolonial theorists. But if, as Marx's interpretation might suggest, the apotheosis of Western cinematic visuality was to become the classical western, with its redemptive journey toward a wilderness out of whose clutches Americans have forged a bright "city on the hill," then one could argue that *Prospero's Books* amounts to a deconstruction of the entire metaphysic of classical cinema. In the film's final scene, Ariel, released by Prospero from his place in the latter's artificial hierarchy, runs in delight until he jumps out of the frame, with only his two-dimensional silhouette remaining. Greenaway's parting image can be taken to suggest that we ourselves can be freed from our own imaginal hierarchies and dualities—freed, then, to imagine things altogether differently.

To fully grasp the shift indicated in a film like *Prospero's Books*, it is necessary to appreciate the ways that classical narrative modes have evolved in recent years. Greenaway's film is merely one example of a trend that has become undeniable—a shift from a classical realist aesthetic, with its Bazinian assumption that film gives us access to the world, the film screen being in effect a window onto the world of the film, toward what some have called an aesthetic of the "archive" or "database."[136] Eleftheria Thanouli convincingly argues that this shift is a broader one from a classical to a "post-classical" cinema.[137] Rooted in institutional and technological developments of the past forty years, post-classical cinema opts for a "hypermediated realism" for which the screen itself is a "windowed world," no longer primarily a photographic space but a graphic space, one that has substituted the "invisibility" and seamlessness of the classical film world with a more discontinuous and opaque visual surface that prioritizes the graphic and painterly qualities of the image. This is pursued through an array of strategies, which include fast cutting rates, the use of extreme lens lengths, close framings, free-ranging camera movements, spatial montages, extreme shallow focus, and clustered images (such as the split-screens, back projections, and miniatures that are ever-present in *Prospero's Books*). Post-classical cinema's approach to time, as suggested by Deleuze's writings on the time-image, is much more open, flexible, and non-linear than that of classical cinema. Its geomorphism, to put it in our terms, is no longer that of a world that is *there for us*, given as an objective reality (at least within the as-if framework of cinematic narrative). It has instead become a world of mediation, explicitly avowing its own practice in mediating a world that is always already mediated.

Few theorists would argue that a post-classical paradigm—or a postmodern one, for those who prefer that term—has already replaced the classical one. The latter is arguably still dominant, or perhaps it has been incorporated into a more fluid model that features both classical and post-classical elements.[138] The geomorphic implications of post-classical cinema, in any case, remain unclear and are likely to remain highly variable from one film to another. What post-classical methods point to, however, is what this chapter has been developing an argument for: that the *given* is never *merely* given—it is always produced. Its production, however, is complex and laborious, involving not only the crafting of representations about the world, but also the manifold productive labours of many material-semiotic actors—labours by which worlds of affective and perceptual practice are crafted, cinematically and experientially.

Like the world itself, cinema is given shape by embodied beings interacting in a more-than-human world. All of us—indeed, all things that could be said to act—participate in that interaction, in our own ways and in our own times. This "all," as suggested by the *Pan* of the pantheists, and by the spirits and sprites of Prospero's enchanted isle, is shaped into foregrounds and backgrounds for active beings like us *because* this is the way that action happens: I perceive or pursue an object, which is a figure against a background, an emergent clip carved out from a receding objectscape. It—or what it, in its next moment, has become—perceives and pursues me. Each prehension is an asymmetrical vector, the form and feel of which becomes its concrescence, its subject–superject, which then becomes available as data for the next arising of subjectivity, the next prehension.

The meeting of the perceivers and pursuers takes us into the world of the subjects, which, for humans, is the world of the anthropomorphed; but the general dynamism of that interperceptivity is broader and more expansive than that. These twin themes of cinema's anthropomorphism and its biomorphism will be the themes, respectively, of the next two chapters.

4

ENCOUNTER

First Contact, Utopia, and the Becoming of Another

From *Nanook of the North* (1992). Directed by Robert J. Flaherty. Credit: Robert J. Flaherty.

For Kant, the world emerges from the subject; for the philosophy of organism, the subject emerges from the world.

A. N. Whitehead, *Process and Reality*[1]

Made it, ma! Top of the world!

"Cody" Jarrett, White Heat (1949)

[A] person is not absolutely an individual. His thoughts are what he is 'saying to himself,' that is, is saying to that other self that is just coming into life in the flow of time.

C. S. Peirce[2]

Films stand sill, but their subjects move on. [...] Even as a film is being shot, its subjects are in transition, moving toward a future that the film cannot contain.

David MacDougall, *Transcultural Cinema*[3]

I HAVE ARGUED THAT CINEMA'S WORLD-MAKING CAPACITY is distinguishable into three registers: the geomorphic, the biomorphic, and the anthropomorphic, with the second being a vibrant middle-ground in which the first and the third are actively separated from each other. Because of this mediating dynamism of the second term, I will address it last. It is this interperceptual dynamism that brings us closest to the essence of cinema; it is what makes the cinematic experience distinct and is therefore the point of there being such a thing as cinema at all. This dynamism, as with all processes of mediation, is characterized by a tugging in two directions, toward the object and toward the subject; or toward the figure that, in acting, asserts its transcendence over and against the ground, and by that very movement, toward the ground without which any measure of that action is impossible. In any single moment of experience there is a perceived object or set of objects, and there is an emergent subject. In the formation of a world—which is something we take to be *real* in order to *dwell* in it—the "objective" becomes condensed into a set of taken-for-granted features and characteristics of the given world, and the "subjective" becomes condensed into a set of possibilities for actors or agents to performatively enact. The previous chapter dealt with the first term in this set, or at least with some of the ways in which such an objective world is laid out by cinema, which always means laid out for us, its observers, dwellers, users, and admirers. The present chapter will deal with the second, the subjective.

Subjectivity is part of every moment of being, of perception, and of action, and it is always emergent in relation to objectivity. Anthropomorphism, in the way I am using the term, has to do with a certain shaping, or scaping, of subjectivity across the face of the world—a certain recognizing of the capacity for first-person action. It is a kind of *ethnomorphism* as well, insofar as subjectivation is always part of shared relationality and always harbours an internality of experience that can only be understood "from the inside," in the way that an ethnographer comes to understand the inside of another cultural world by participating in and interpreting it. "Anthropomorphism" is named here for the human, the *anthropos*, because it points to a capacity that we—modern, cinema-dwelling humans—take to be central to our nature: the freedom to act wilfully and to thereby bring about change. This should not imply that humans set the standard for all things, that we are life's pinnacle of evolutionary achievement. Rather, it is that we set our own standards, within limits negotiated with the world; and that these standards have something to do with our subjectivity, that is, with our capacity to respond to what is given in our experience. (Cinema is, in this regard, primarily a human activity.) Similarly, it is not to imply that we *know* what a human is capable of. As A.N. Whitehead put it, "the life of a human being receives its worth, its importance, from the way in which unrealized ideals shape its purposes and tinge its actions."[4] The realization of ideals is the actualization of potentials, but the potentials are never fully determinable in advance, nor are they fully determining. Anthropomorphism, in the sense I am using the term, is not ultimately about the becoming of things we *recognize* as human or human-like. It is about subjectivation, self-making, which is a process as open-ended as any. It is a form of *subjectomorphism*, of becoming, though not a becoming of anything predetermined. Just as the horizon for anthropomorphism recedes from us as we move forward, so does the horizon for any subjectivating entity—the canomorphic horizon for a dog, the delphimorphic for a dolphin, the electromorphic for an electron. In cinema, this subjectomorphism is about cinema's distribution of these possibilities across the social field, between individuals and socially defined groups and categories.

There is, however, a process that each human—each becoming-human, to speak in processual terms—takes up from the outset. From the moment we come spilling out of the womb, if not earlier, we begin to simultaneously identify and differentiate. Ejected from the warm comfort of the uterine environment, we are flung into the world that William James famously called a "blooming, buzzing confusion." But once we feel the warmth of a mother's body, see the curve of her breast and the gaze of her face (or the faces of others), we are comforted again. This is, of course, an "automatic" response. Even if it is only an outline of eyes and the smiling curve of a mouth, we recognize a friendly face when we see one. And over time, we gain the ability to test out these faces, to see which ones respond to us and which do not; which are reliable and which carry on an internal life of their own, kindred but mysterious; and, ultimately, which are considered appropriate relational others and which are not. As we come to identify a thread of continuity in our experience, we learn to differentiate: between that unnamed body we come to know as our own and the others we come to know as mother, father, siblings, and strangers. This differentiation is accomplished through tactility, movement, sound, sight, and eventually language, whereby it is extended to social group classifications, which open up tremendous possibilities for variation. This differentiation of the subjective is what ultimately gives rise to the categories by which we distinguish the social world into genders, clans, moieties, classes, races, nations, or whatever categories it comes to take on. This is anthropomorphism writ large.

Visual media enter into this anthropomorphism as part of a general proliferation and intensification of semiosis. Images are *iconic* in that they resemble specific things, individuals, or character types. (Perhaps the basic icon, recognizable by every human infant, is a smiling face.) They are also *indexical*, being indications that those people and things *were actually there* when this photograph was taken or this drawing was drawn (which is what gives photo-portraits their haunted quality). And they are *symbolic* to the extent that they take on other connotations. Moving images are all the more indicative of activity, and therefore of agency. Through their focus on facial expression, gesture, and movement, films display a refinement and precision of expressive detail in a person's taking up a stance in the world and acting on that stance. There are many means by which anthropomorphism is embedded within a film. For instance, films conventionally tend to alternate perspectives that we recognize as objective—seeing people in medium-shot, as if we were invisible observers standing several feet away—with those we recognize as subjective, shot and shown to us from the point of view of a character in the film. Presentations of such points of view are accomplished through camera perspective, angle, and movement, with facial close-ups typically revealing internal states and emotions and medium shots showing action; through voice-over narration and orientation within the sound field; through following the line of narrative concerning a certain person or group; and so on.

Classical Hollywood narratives are typically about the ways in which characters meet and respond to problems, obstacles, and issues. Actions give rise to reactions through chains of events in which agency is embedded in what the main characters do. In Deleuzian terms, the cinema of the "movement-image" is one in which the representation of life is "oriented by and toward action," with time "measur[ing] the movements of an acting subject."[5] This is epitomized by the "action-image," where narrative structure is provided by the unbroken sensory-motor continuity of the main characters and actions: we move from a Situation through an Action (or set of actions) to a Changed Situation (S-A-S_1). At the core of this is the protagonist's ability to act decisively in whatever situations he or she encounters. Agency is primarily that of the central characters, who are the characters with which viewers most identify. We learn to recognize a character's internal states, and we come to align with them (or against them, if they are not sympathetic) to one degree or another. We learn to take our own place, as observers within the cinematic field. There are countless variations on these basic principles: melodrama and tragedy acquire their force from the inability of the main characters to act appropriately, or to alter the circumstances that close in around them, while comedy commonly works with the humorous incongruence between intended actions and unintended outcomes. Documentaries, meanwhile, traditionally focus their narratives on key individuals and the events in which they are involved.[6]

But films can also question the distribution among the various actors of the agencies they portray, and they can be about the possibility of alternative forms of agency. Even Hollywood has a long tradition of social critique, in which individuals, with whom viewers are encouraged to identify, are set against powerful social forces of tradition—for instance, of racial or other social stereotypes and the interests vested in maintaining them. In what Deleuze calls the "time-image," the movement of the film, rather than being centred on the actions of the protagonists, becomes focused on the direct experience of time, on multiple causalities, and on the possibility of reflection, of commentary on the state of things, and of liberation or respite from the cause–effect logic of everyday activity. This can be accomplished through alternative narrative modes—reflexive, unreliable, multiple, or non-linear ones—and through disjunctive editing involving temporal and narrative discontinuities (jump cuts, for instance), distanciation or alienation effects, and the "MTV aesthetic" of rapid cutting and exhilarating camera movements. In documentaries, where subjects may not be as central as the "objective eye" of the (invisible but authoritative) filmmaker, especially when accompanied by a traditional "voice of God"–style omniscient narrator or by talking-head "expert witnesses," non-traditional modes of filmmaking—self-reflexive, participatory, and collaborative—have rendered the agency of the filmmakers more visible.

In fact, a moment's thought ought to make it clear that this category of the anthropomorphic is what films tend to be primarily *about*. Films present stories about heroes and villains, outsiders and insiders, tragic and comic figures, the righteous taking on the corrupt, rebels striking out (with or without a cause) against tradition. There are films about individuals finding new capacities for action, contemplation, or beauty; about those facing devastating losses and tragic circumstances; and about those fated to repeat the same errors eternally. Sometimes films are about collective actors—gangs, networks, conspiracies, social movements. Some films portray openings toward the unimaginable and fantastic—characters who walk into the minds or dreams of others (as in Christopher Nolan's *Inception*), or who travel through time, and even change their gender in the process (as in Sally Potter's *Orlando*), who explore strange new worlds, meet their makers, confront death and laugh in its face, or merely observe history from the sidelines (as in Hal Ashby's *Being There* or Robert Zemeckis's *Forrest Gump*). There are working-class heroes and heroic collectives (as in John Sayles' *Matewan* and *Men with Guns*, Bernardo Bertolucci's *1900*, Michael Cimino's *Heaven's Gate*, and Robert Redford's *Milagro Beanfield War*), and villanous collectives as well—groups that are manifestly depicted as inferior, evil, or savage. And there are conspiracies that seem to encompass nearly everyone, as in *The Matrix*, *Dark City*, and *The Parallax View*. There are also films in which the filmmaker him or herself, reflecting on the practice of filmmaking (as in *8½*, *Day for Night*, or any of numerous films by Godard), expands our understanding of what film itself is capable of. And, of course, there is the conflation of film characters with the stars who are acting them, with the result, over time, that the star—say, John Wayne, Clint Eastwood, Julia Roberts, or Sean Penn—becomes a living idol who represents a particular way of being, a particular crystallization of anthropomorphic possibility that fans of that star come to desire and emulate.

The Ethnographic Paradigm

Placing this category of the anthropomorphic into a trichotomy alongside the geomorphic and the biomorphic is intended in part to demote it from its traditional place at the centre (of cinema and of life) to a place at one end of a continuum. My interest in this book is not to cover all of cinema, of course, but only enough to provide insights into its relation to the socio-ecological. So this chapter's focus will be on films that provide variations on the human capacity to act in relation to the ecological world. That world, for starters, can be taken to be the geomorphic world examined in the previous chapter. But human divergence from that world is complicated by the various markers of human difference: gender, race, social class, cultural group, sexual orientation, religious affiliation, and so on. All of these have been used as markers of closeness or distance from "nature." And nature itself, as we have seen, does not offer much firm ground—it is a produced, or socio-ecologically co-produced, category, a "mobile army of metaphors," as Nietzsche put it. This means that we will, in effect, be swimming in movable currents here. But even an army has its tanks, its bodies, and its familiarity with territories (or lack of it); even currents are produced by observable relations; and even metaphors, as Peirce insisted, are grounded in firstness. This exercise, then, is intended to provide us with a mobile yet operatively useful hinge from which to examine the relations among human becomings as they variably diverge from what is given.

Modernity has been premised on the metaphor of advancement, civilization, and progress from a state "closer to nature"—more in its thrall—to a state that has overcome or transcended nature. At its extreme, modernity embodies a Promethean impulse: the belief that the world is one's oyster, there for us to break open and do with as we will. But the modern has included its own self-critique, in the form of those who reverse the valences of this model of nature, arguing that we ought to look back, nostalgically, to those who still live "in harmony with nature." The best-known recent incarnation of this form of socio-natural critique is James Cameron's *Avatar* (which I discuss in Chapter 6), in which the marine Jake Sully must determine his path between the devil-take-all Prometheanism represented by Colonel Quaritch and the holistic living-in-harmony-with-nature of the indigenous Na'vi.

The boundaries around agency become most explicit in films that display a normative individual or collective agent—such as a group that represents modern Western society—encountering a non-normative, heterogeneous, other agent-group. We might call this encounter the "ethnographic" dimension of cinema, in that it contrasts two radically different cultures and provides for some kind of translation between them. Ethnography, in the sense that the word is used by anthropologists, involves such translation, but it also requires substantial investment of time in order to learn the ways of the other culture, which involves becoming an insider to some degree. Among visual anthropologists, Jay Ruby has staked out the strictest position with regard to what qualifies as "ethnographic film." For him, this term refers only to films made by anthropologically trained individuals using ethnographic field methods, with the goal of contributing to the anthropological project of understanding culture and its varieties. My use of the term is not so strict; if anything, it comes closer to the position of Bill Nichols, for whom ethnographic film is "extra-institutional" film that accepts "as a primary task the representation, or self-representation, of one culture for another." Even more broadly, I would follow anthropologist Sol Worth's suggestion that *all* films are ethnographic, being "records of culture—as objects and events which can be studied in the context of the culture within which they were used." Traditionally, as Fatimah Tobing Rony notes, ethnographic cinema described "a relationship between a spectator posited as Western, white, and urbanized" and a culturally encoded and exoticized other, "a subject people portrayed as being somewhere nearer to the beginning on the spectrum of human evolution."[7] But while such stereotypes endure, anthropologists have tried to free themselves from them over the past several decades, and it is this freeing that I will do my best to follow.

There is, in this sense, an ethnographic or at least quasi-ethnographic dimension to be found in any film to the degree that there is a contrast portrayed between two or more "cultures." But as my scare quotes are meant to suggest, even the word "culture" is problematic, for it suggests a bounded group of people or a singular and definable possession of such a group. Identifying such distinct cultures is difficult in a rapidly changing, globally interconnected world. A process-relational view complicates the effort by insisting that culture is always dynamic, mutable, relational, and processual and that it is always thickly intertwined and enactively embedded in a bio-ecological milieu. Nevertheless, there are stabilities that can be identified at the meso-level of human collective activities, which, following actor-network theory, we could call "nature-cultures" or "socio-natures." These are socio-ecological ensembles or networks that are distinguishable in terms of their local and global extension, their temporal scale, and their distinctive patternings of organic, social, and technological elements. As Bruno Latour argues, all nature-cultures "simultaneously construct humans, divinities and nonhumans" and all "sort out what will bear signs and what will not…. In constituting their collectives, some mobilize ancestors, lions, fixed stars, and the coagulated blood of sacrifice; in constructing ours, we mobilize genetics, zoology, cosmology and haematology."[8] Latour's point is not to argue that one way is better than another, but only that all do the same sort of thing: all *sort* and *compose* the world through the material, technical, and discursive processes by which they enact relations and construct their socio-natural collectives. Because of their differences, however, interactions between different networks are not necessarily symmetrical in their impacts. Arturo Escobar refers to three distinct "regimes of nature" marking the contemporary world—three "articulations" of "the historical and the biological," which he names "organic nature," "capitalist nature," and "technonature." The first of these is more deeply embedded in local ecosystems, while the latter two (which are more difficult to tease apart today) are drawn extensively into global capital flows and are intensively dependent on the extraction and use of petrochemical resources. While this primary difference between the organic and (in its contemporary convergence) the technocapitalist may be broadly overdrawn, and while it can easily play into morally charged preconceptions about the modern and the pre-modern, it remains a useful framework for articulating socio-ecological differences.[9]

The "ethnographic" dimension of such socio-ecological contrasts can be explicit within films; or, more commonly, it can be implied, where the contrast is between the culture *portrayed* and the invisible culture tacitly *assumed* by the filmmaker and audience. In his discussion of Luis Buñuel's *Land Without Bread* (*Las Hurdes*, 1932), Gilberto Perez distinguishes four kinds of relationships between the "us" and the "them" of such implicit cultural comparisons: (1) the "humanitarian film," the implied formula for which is "we're OK, they're not OK"; (2) the "usual travelogue," which "takes a rather condescending interest in the exotic (we're OK, they may be OK)"; (3) "the more serious anthropological film," which "tells us that the traditions and practices of another culture are as good as our own (we're OK, they're OK) or even superior (they're OK, we may not be OK)"; and (4) the rare film like *Land Without Bread*, which "presses us to the realization that the trouble with them is but an aggravated case of our own trouble: they're not OK and neither are we."[10] His reference to *Land Without Bread* is instructive. Produced before there was even a recognizable genre of ethnographic documentary, this film, which announced itself as "a filmed essay in human geography," might be thought of as the first "mockumentary" because of its parody of colonialist ethnography. Its sneering condescension and denial of humanist commonality made *Land Without Bread* as shocking, in some ways, as Dalí's and Buñuel's famous sliced eyeball in *Un chien andalou* (1929), and its freak show exhibitionism presaged later films like *Mondo Cane*, except that the latter neglected the social critique—Perez's "and neither are we"—that Buñuel included as a matter of course.

In what follows, I discuss a variety of approaches to this ethnographically presented socio-ecological difference. As I have been emphasizing, the cinema experience constitutes a kind of journey, and journeys—which typically take characters and viewers from a "here" to an "elsewhere"—are paradigmatic of cinema. The first half of this chapter emphasizes the metaphor of "contact" or "first contact" across cultural boundaries. Moments of contact are moments of firstness—that is, first encounters with something or someone that necessarily initiate processes of interpretation: "Who or what is this? And to what extent are they like us?" In their most traditional and ethnocentric forms of expression, such contact films follow what E. Ann Kaplan calls an "imperial gaze," a method of representing cultural otherness as simultaneously deficient, closer to nature, and subject to visual objectification and control by the mastering Western eye. Yet there are alternatives to these stereotypical representations. My analysis will range widely: from proto-ethnographic films like *Nanook of the North* and *Chang*; their commercial and spectacular hybrid progeny, exemplified by blockbusters like *King Kong* and *Jurassic Park*; and journeys "upstream" to a mythical time of origins (as in *Apocalypse Now*); to explicitly ethnographic films, mockumentaries, and counter-ethnographies; disputably post-colonial revisionings of original encounters between Europeans and indigenous populations (such as Werner Herzog's *Aguirre, the Wrath of God* and Terence Malick's *The New World*); fictional depictions of hypothetical societies (as in *The Wicker Man* and, in a later chapter, *Avatar*); and indigenous productions such as *Atanarjuat* and *Ten Canoes*. In the final part of the chapter, I return to questions of the depictions of action and choice in film, because the capacity to act is the essence of filmic anthropomorphism. Action can be individual or collective, and it occurs in response to conditions that provoke, induce, evoke, or set the possibilities for it. In a later chapter I will return to the specific kinds of ecological conditions that our world faces as a context for environmental action today, but the concluding section of this chapter will begin to explore relations between individual and collective action, particularly as seen in socio-ecological "network narratives" such as Alain Tanner's *Jonah Who Will Be 25 in the Year 2000* (1975).

Nanook/Allakariallak and the Two-Way Gaze

In the introduction to her critical analysis of ethnographic strategies in popular film, Fatimah Tobing Rony writes that "we turn to the movies to find images of ourselves and find ourselves reflected in the eyes of others." Unfortunately, the cinema gaze has tended to reproduce and, through its mediating power, to intensify the differences that are already present in society. Rony draws on W.E.B. Du Bois and Frantz Fanon to articulate a notion of "double consciousness" by which a person of colour identifies both with the "savages" onscreen and with "the explorer, the bringer of civilization, the white man who carries truth to savages—an all-white truth." The "native" is even more "othered," she writes, than the "Negro groom" in that he or she is "represented as trapped in some deep frozen past, inarticulate, not yet evolved," "landscaped as part of the jungle mise-en-scene, or viewed as the faithful Man Friday to a white Robinson Crusoe, or perhaps romanticized as the Noble Savage struggling to survive in the wild."[11] This denial of coevalness, as Johannes Fabian has called it, temporalizes cultural difference so that "we" are presumed to be living in the present, capable of a full subjectivity, while "they" always and evermore belong to the past.[12]

The previous chapter dealt with cinematic travel in terms of how it produces a geography of spatially differentiated places. Here our concern is with how the mapping of cultural difference onto that spatial differentiation produces an "anthropology" of differentiated peoples. Travel can be explicit and diegetic, occurring within the film (as in *King Kong*), or it can be implied, which is what it is in most documentaries about exotic locales. Whether implicit or explicit, travel produces a displacement from the centre, where the filmmakers and presumed viewers come from. It is underwritten by the authority of the filmmakers' having "been there" and seen the things they describe and depict. But it also brings with it an assortment of proverbial baggage, conjuring associations, in Bill Nichols's words, "with spiritual quests, voyages of self-discovery, and tests of prowess, with the pilgrimage and the odyssey, as well as with the expansionist dreams of empire, discovery, and conquest. Movement and travel participate in the construction of an imaginary geography that maps the world required to support the sense of self for whom this world is staged."[13] In a discussion of early cinema's "ability to 'fly' spectators around the globe," Shohat and Stam note that the "spatially-mobilized visuality" of "the I/eye of empire spiraled outward around the globe, creating a visceral, kinetic sense of imperial travel and conquest, transforming European spectators into armchair conquistadors, affirming their sense of power while turning the colonies into spectacle for the metropole's voyeuristic gaze."[14]

From the early 1900s until the emergence of sound cinema in the late 1920s, which moved the vast majority of film production into studios, countless short films were made with travel motifs. Travelogues, *documentaires romancés*, expedition and safari films (like Cherry Kearton's *Roosevelt in Africa* [1910]), and scientific research films intended to establish then-current evolutionary theories about the "races"—all "offered up the world as an 'archive' of human variation," as Rony puts it.[15] Martin and Osa Johnson's *Simba, The King of Beasts, a Sage of the African Veldt* (1928) epitomized the safari film genre, in which heroic filmmakers penetrated the world's wildernesses to "hunt" and display the exotic specimens they collected. *Simba's* opening titles call the film "the high mark of attainment in the cinematographic recording of adventures in Africa—the classic land of mystery, thrills and darksome savage drama through all the days of history." The film continues: "This dramatic record of sheer reality comes to you as a presentation of the true Africa, largely without the invading presence of the white man, made at a cost of tireless patience, endless courage, privation and perils, thirst and fevers on 15,000 miles of wild safaris." Produced under the auspices of the American Museum of Natural History, the film displays, in Catherine Russell's words, "a reflexivity that serves to champion the camera as a device of penetration, ethnography, aestheticization, and industrialization." Intertitles such as "Here was the age-old story of Man emerging from savagery" position the Africans lower on the Darwinian hierarchy, "earlier" in time, "a halfway point between men and animals," with the whites cast as colonial protectors of the Africans.[16]

Other films, such as those of Edward S. Curtis, mythologized the "vanishing Indian." These were the cinematic equivalent of "salvage ethnography," in that they were efforts to record what could be recorded of cultures before they disappeared forever. At one end, as with Curtis and Robert Flaherty, such ethnography assumed a certain nobility, authenticity, and elegiac beauty among the peoples it portrayed. At another, as Rony argues, it aimed to establish the inherent pathology or unsustainability of ostensibly primitive ways of life. Curtis's *In the Land of the Headhunters* (1914) involved extensive reconstructions of historical native costumes, dances, and material artifacts; to all of this, Curtis added a melodramatic storyline of romance, headhunting, and evil sorcery.[17] Flaherty's films, including *Nanook of the North* (1922), *Moana* (1926), *Tabu* (1930), and *Man of Aran* (1934), reconstructed and enacted other cultures ostensibly closer to nature—Inuit in Arctic northern Quebec, Samoan islanders in the South Pacific (in both *Moana* and *Tabu*), and Aran islanders off the coast of Ireland—with the goal of portraying a kind of universalized Family of Man at its primal best. Flaherty's proclaimed intent was to show "the former majesty and character of these people, while it is still possible—before the white man has destroyed not only their character, but the people as well."[18] In contrast to Curtis's melodramas, however, Flaherty's narratives were explicitly dramas of survival, structured on the man-versus-nature duality. This brought them into the realm of liberal humanism but still left the individual characters and performers as little more than exemplary types.

Flaherty's *Nanook of the North*, however, was groundbreaking. Immensely popular around the world upon its release, it led to a phenomenon of "Nanookmania," which included ice cream bars in Germany and the United States named after its main character, the Inuit protagonist Nanook, and even a Broadway song inspired by him.[19] It ultimately served to establish the genres of documentary and ethnographic film, though it fit neither model particularly well. Nanook's scenes were staged for the camera; the family portrayed was in fact a group of actors selected for their photogenic qualities; and unlike Flaherty's Inuit, the actual Quebec Inuit wore Western clothes and lived in western-style buildings, were familiar with guns, outboard motors, and gramophones, and were part of a fur-trading cash economy. Flaherty spent months living with the Inuit before making *Nanook*, so the film can still be considered the first to incorporate the participatory observation ideal that was popularized the same year by Bronislaw Malinowski in his now-classic *Argonauts of the Western Pacific* (1922). Faye Ginsburg documents that Inuit community members worked with Flaherty "as technicians, camera operators, film developers, and production consultants."[20] They "performed for the camera, reviewed and criticized their performance and were able to offer suggestions for additional scenes in the film."[21] Rony argues that an Inuit landscape aesthetic, located in the "extremely beautiful, long takes of the snowy landscape," a land that ultimately "takes over as a protagonist," crept into the film as well, despite Flaherty's avowed goal of depicting the universal oppositon of "man *versus* nature."[22]

The film establishes its apparent authenticity through the traditional ethnographic "double movement" by which the ethnographer, Flaherty, is presented as having "been there" among the Inuit; at the same time, most signs of white contact are erased. There are exceptions, such as a scene of Nanook's family visiting a trading post. One of the film's most famous scenes typifies this presentation of "first" (or nearly first) "contact" between the indigenous and the modern, in that it works as a moment of cross-cultural firstness. This is the scene of Nanook repeatedly biting into a gramophone record, as if he is trying to taste it so as to find out what it is. Seemingly a sign of his ignorance of modern technology, Nanook's apparent childlikeness appealed to the film's viewers. Rony refers to Nanook's enigmatic smile, which, rather like the Mona Lisa's, intrigued audiences, since smiling at the camera was unusual at the time. Nanook's popularity emerged in part because of the way in which the Inuit protagonist was humanized through the camera. At the outset, after the film introduces us to the harsh northern landscape and to "the most cheerful people in all the world—the fearless, lovable, happy-go-lucky Eskimo," we meet a "great hunter famous through all Ungava—Nanook, the Bear," who is immediately shown in close-up, hooded in fur and looking tranquilly out, then down, and up again, for several seconds. Over the course of the film his lined and weathered face, Rony argues, "becomes a landscape" that is surveyed, examined, and penetrated. The film's last shot shows him sleeping in the igloo; for Rony, this "sleeping body of Nanook, like a corpse, represents the triumph of salvage ethnography: he is captured forever on film, both alive and dead, his death and life to be replayed every time the film is screened."[23]

Rony argues that this cinematic "salvage ethnography" is tantamount to an "ethnographic taxidermy," the product of a "hunt for images" of the disappearing native that would display the successful outcome of the hunt while making the dead appear as close to living as possible.[24] Like the wilderness preservation ethic that had become enshrined in the monumental national parks of the American West, "taxidermic" ethnographies aimed to preserve what they could of a dying culture, for the benefit of posterity. The analogy with wilderness preservation is instructive: the point in both cases is to re-create something presumed to be authentic, whole, and essentially static in nature, the product of evolutionary processes perhaps, but no longer evolving or evolvable. From a process-relational perspective, such "climax communities," whether natural or cultural, have met their end and can only be museumized. Presenting either nature or cultures in their ethnographic present, as if they are timelessly given as such, renders the ethnographic observer *outside* what is being observed and obfuscates the relational processes and interactions that make the preserved artifact possible in the first place. The result is a static diorama: an object to be gazed at through the eye of science, colonial power, romantic nostalgia, or sensationalist spectacle.

Rony's argument is cogent, yet I would wish to make the more general point that all cinema is by its nature taxidermic: it renders alive something that is essentially not alive, not because it lacks movement (which it does not) but because it is only light and sound, lacking the capacity to initiate change once the cinematic elements are drawn together into an edited and assembled product. Cinema can be made open-ended—for instance, in open-form digital films with multiple storylines from which viewers can select their own. But it cannot be made into a living, self-perpetuating organism. Rony's critique, therefore, can be applied to all cinema. Films *do* come alive, however, when they are encountered by viewers, and here is where *Nanook* has maintained a liveliness over the decades. In a poignant verdict on the audiences that have been most fascinated by *Nanook*, Rony points out that "until the 1970s, no one bothered to ask members of the Inuit community in which the film was made for their opinions of the film. Only then was it learned that the name of the actor who played Nanook was Allakariallak" and that this man died, seemingly of hunger, two years after the film was made.[25] In the 1980s, French filmmaker Claude Massot returned to the village of Inukjiak and the Belcher Islands to shoot a documentary called *Nanook Revisited* (1988) in which locals, including descendants of one of the Inuit fathered by Flaherty, recall the making and staging of scenes of the film, laugh uproariously at the seal-hunting scene, and lament its inaccuracies. In contrast to Westerners, who viewed the film as a work of cinematic art, the Inuit were more interested in it as a document of those who acted in it, because, as the local television station manager pointed out, "these pictures and the still shots are the only pictures of that time in this region."[26]

Films like *Nanook*, then, not only depict cultural encounters but also enact them. Faye Ginsburg points to the positive effects of the Nanook legacy on Inuit communities: in particular, the film inspired young Inuit, such as Peter Pitseolak and Zacharias Kunuk (who will be discussed later), to become photographers and filmmakers themselves.[27] Given the inherent differences in audience expectations and understandings between the culturally "othered" community and the presumed domestic viewing audience, the actions of the indigenous actors can diverge radically in the meanings they generate. Discussing Nanook's enigmatic smile, Michelle Raheja writes that "Nanook's response might register one thing to his non-Inuit audience and another to members of an Inuit community who recognize the cultural code of his smile."[28] Tony Hillerman's novel *Sacred Clowns* presents an entertaining example of what Michael Real calls an audience's "co-authorship" of a cinematic text, in this case John Ford's late western *Cheyenne Autumn* (1964). This was Ford's effort to present Native Americans as sympathetic victims of racist government policies. Yet the Navaho who flock to the annual showing of the film at the Gallup, New Mexico, drive-in read much more into it than anything Ford could have possibly intended. Cast to play the film's Cheyenne Indians—parts of the film were shot in Monument Valley, which lies within traditional Navaho lands—the Navaho actors "speak Navajo, dress like Navajo, conduct Navajo ceremonies, are in Navajo country, and are Navajo." More than that, when the film's Cheyenne leaders speak sombrely, ostensibly about treaties and the needs of their community, what their actual Navaho speech refers to, according to Hillerman, is "earthy and humorous irrelevanc[ies]," for example, about "the size of the colonel's penis"—which sends the Navaho drive-in audience into peals of laughter and horn honking. Real refers to this as "oppositional semiotics," which is "*planted by the actors* and read appreciatively by the Gallup-area Navajos."[29]

Rony's point about Nanook's humanization through what we might call the "landscaping" of his face raises other issues connected to cinema epistemology. If the classic tool of cinematic geomorphism is the extreme long shot (and, to some extent, the long-take tracking shot), that of anthropomorphism is the facial close-up and, to some extent, the medium action shot. But closing up on an indigenous character's face entails a cinematic encounter that can take on very different meanings in non-Western cultural contexts. In the late 1960s, Sol Worth and John Adair gave cameras to Navaho youths to see whether the films they made would mirror Western conventions or reflect a more animist sensibility. Rony recounts that at one point, Worth was watching one of the Navaho filming her grandfather as he painted in sand. Frustrated with the young filmmaker's reluctance to pull in for a close-up of her grandfather, Worth grabbed the camera from her. Rony reads this as an indication of the violence inherent in the difference between Western filmmaking and an indigenous sensibility of restraint and respect for personal and social space. In part, what is at stake here is the importance of defining "what is photographable" and how the camera should operate in a social context that has pre-defined measures of appropriate and inappropriate behaviour. The films of Hopi filmmaker Victor Masayesva Jr. reflect a reticence that "denies the audience the sense of visual power inherent in seeing and consuming everything."[30] Rony celebrates "third eye strategies" such as open or concealed resistance, the recontextualization of archival footage (such as Flaherty's or Curtis's), parody (as in the carnivalesque performances of Coco Fusco and Guillermo Gómez-Peña), and culturally defined restraint in the representations of certain subjects and acts. Another example of a form of "concealed resistance" is that of the Navaho dancers in Edward S. Curtis's photographs, who apparently performed sacred dance backwards so as not to violate their sacredness. Such methods, which I will return to later in this chapter, amount to the demand for a kind of "sovereignty over one's image."[31]

Setting aside the innovations and ambiguities surrounding the depictions of indigenous people in *Nanook*, the film, as mentioned, also depicts a certain relationship between the Inuit and their northern landscape. It does this through the development of a style, praised by Andre Bazin, of long takes, depth-of-field cinematography, and on-location storytelling using non-actors as actors. Siegfried Kracauer called Flaherty a filmmaker of the "flow of life," which he characterized as a cinematic motif that "occupies a unique position" in that it "corresponds to a basic affinity of film," being "in a manner of speaking ... an emanation of the medium itself."[32] Dean Duncan expands on this by arguing that *Nanook* innovated in two areas that have remained integral to the documentary tradition: "process and duration—the detailed representation of how everyday things are done (burning moss for fuel, covering a kayak, negotiating ice floes, hunting, and caring for children) and how long the doing takes."[33] In his own notes on the making of the film, Flaherty recounted many of the difficulties of filming and development in the cold geography, difficulties that no doubt lent authority to his own explorer-discoverer persona but that also accentuated the material processes that shaped the aesthetic of the film. In the "film washing," for instance,

> three barrels of water for every hundred feet was required. The water hole, then eight feet of ice, had to be kept open all winter long and water clotted with particles of ice had to be taken, a barrel at a time, from a distance of more than a quarter of a mile away. When I mention that over 50,000 feet of film was developed over the winter with no assistance save from my Eskimo and at the slow rate of eight hundred feet a day one can understand somewhat the amount of time and labor involved.[34]

King Kong's Imperial Gaze: From Ethnographic to Cinematic Spectacle

If *Nanook* had redeeming ethnographic qualities, other films that followed it took its combination of narrative and travel motifs and turned them to commercially more spectacular uses. Two filmmakers who began their moviemaking careers as quasi-ethnographic adventurers influenced by Flaherty, U.S. Air Force pilot Merian C. Cooper and army cameraman Ernest B. Schoedsack, were to almost single-handedly transform popular cinema as we know it. In films like *Grass: A Nation's Battle for Life* (1925) and *Chang: A Drama of the Wilderness* (1927), Cooper and Schoedsack used real locations, real non-actors, and fairly authentic scenarios to depict the ways of life of remote peoples and places. In *Grass*, the filmmakers, together with news reporter Marguerite Harrison, are introduced as valiant explorers who "sought and found the Forgotten People," the Bakhtiaris, who are called "our brothers still living in the cradle of the race." *Chang*, filmed in a remote area of Siam (Thailand), involved Cooper and Schoedsack spending months studying natives and animals to determine the best ways of filming them, while making their story up on the fly (and later through editing and intertitling). Animals would often be trapped, then released and photographed. Three crew members were bitten by pythons; Schoedsack had recurrent malaria and sunstroke and often worked while having a high fever. Here, as in Flaherty's films, there is a journey to a place that is posed as the West's Other: it is primitive, not modern; wild, not civilized.

The methods and skills they honed in making these ostensibly ethnographic films were put to commercial use in their 1933 blockbuster, *King Kong*. One of the first big-budget sound films, *King Kong* was a massive success when it came out, netting $2 million in the midst of the Great Depression and setting off a long chain of sequels. The film was a prototype for the Hollywood special-effects spectacle. With its journey format—the film is about a moviemaking expedition to Sumatra with the goal of capturing the monstrous creature who rules over the primitive tribespeople of the island and bringing him back to New York for the sake of entertainment—*King Kong* helped establish the self-celebratory model of American popular cinema.

Let us examine the ways in which the film's anthropomorphism maps onto its geomorphism. In classical fashion, the film depicts a journey from "here" (New York City) to "there" (Skull Island, a "lost world" somewhere in the East Asian South Pacific) and back again. The film crew, rather like anthropologists, set out from the most advanced centre of metropolitan Euro-American civilization to the outer boundaries of humanity, where apparently pre-modern savages still live in a state of nature, or more precisely a state of enslavement to nature, locked in an cruelly intimate contract with the wild. The islanders are ruled by the massive apelike creature they have named "Kong," and their natural contract, as Michel Serres might call it,[35] requires them to sacrifice virgins to keep the creature at bay. The film's images were striking for its time:

> the fog over the sea, black birds lying everywhere, from a distance the dull rhythm of drums, and then, looking, the coastal line and towering above it, the massive cliffs in the form of a skull.... The devouring, gleaming depth of the jungle; the immense gate in that enormous wall made of tree trunks, which separates the world of the natives, of humans, from the rest of the island. [And later] Kong's cavernous lair, almost ceremoniously situated at the highest point above the expansive sea; vapors rise, as in the cave of Delphi, from the rifts in the rocks.[36]

The Western visitors—a film crew equipped with just enough firepower for the job—conquer the primal beast and bring him back to New York City as an exhibition spectacle for the masses (not unusual for the time). The beast breaks away and wreaks havoc, threatening the very symbol of American civilization, the Empire State Building. (The parallel with the 9/11 terrorists aiming for the Twin Towers is not merely coincidental. By 2001 this pattern of targeting a society's most conspicuous architectural constructions was deeply grooved.) The best military technology is used to take Kong down. At the same time, the whole story is given a Hollywood twist by making it about the beauty of a white woman, Ann Darrow / Fay Wray. "It wasn't the airplanes," director Carl Denham (Robert Armstrong) says. "It was beauty killed the beast." So the story becomes ostensibly a universal one, about the power of beauty to tame the wildest beast—and, by extension, about the power of the camera gaze, which bestows glamour on woman, as represented by Fay Wray, and which delivers us all from the evil that lurks in the dark, restless heart of our own nature.

The "here" of white America is thus equated with doing, with looking, and with pursuit—with active agency—while the "there" of Skull Island / Kong is the done-to, the looked-at, and the pursued. Civilized white humanity is at one end of a continuum, with white males, led by the camera-wielding filmmaker and expedition leader, Carl Denham, in the most active role. It is Denham who initiates the trip, who guides it successfully to its destination, who conquers the beast and brings him back, and who, in the end, shoots him down. The white woman, Ann Darrow, is a mediating figure, passive and closer to nature than the camera-wielding white men, but active insofar as she provides the lure for capturing the attention of the beast, Kong. The dark-skinned men of the island are closer to nature and caught within its grip, and the dark-skinned women—most notably the sacrificial virgin—are lowest on the totem pole. (In between the white woman and the dark-skinned men is Charlie, the Chinese cook, whose character and body language position him as deferential, comical, and feminized.) The women, in both cases, embody "to-be-looked-at-ness," which is used to attract and placate, or capture, the wild beast. Between humanity and nature there is a literal wall, a boundary that separates and pro-tects primitive humanity from the wild. Once wild nature has been conquered and subdued, there will presumably be nothing left to fear and no more need for a wall of protection. All will have been (violently) rendered visible to the gaze of cinematic spectacle.[37]

The role of the creature Kong in all this could be left for the next chapter, but it is appropriate to discuss it here, since he is the creature that defines humanity, the ultimate Other whose opposition to "us" holds in place the entire continuum—white men, white women, black men, black women, animals, Kong. The beast, however, seemingly cannot be allowed to coexist alongside modernity *as* the wild beast; nor can this other humanity that lives in contract with him (the Skull Islanders) be left alone to coexist with him. The wall between Kong and us must be penetrated, and he must be tamed, his wildness harnessed for the needs of commodity capitalism: he must become spectacle. When it becomes clear that he cannot be controlled, he must be killed. This basic storyline opens up all manner of Freudian, Jungian, post-colonial, feminist, and even Christian interpretations: Kong as Christ figure; as scapegoat and sacrifice to expiate our guilt as partakers of the original sin of knowledge; as the sin of visual consumption; as the genocide and extermination of the Native; and so on. (The unasked questions throughout the film could be: What happened to the original inhabitants of North America, and of the island of Manhattan specifically? Why do "we" have to go so far to find the remnants of wild nature? And what will happen once those remnants are gone?) Kong, however, evokes our sympathy, while the dinosaurs who are his enemies on the wild side of the island do not. This is because Kong is presented as innocent: attempting to make contact with us, he is in the position of the wild beast *wanting to become human*; that is, in the position of our domesticates. If he has to be destroyed it is because he transgresses the natural order and threatens us. He is too powerful; only when he is defanged and declawed can he be allowed into our society, as pet and as spectacle.

The film thus reflects the colonialist and social evolutionary assumptions that were the common sense of the day in the United States, assumptions that equated "civilization" and "progress" with distance from wild nature. White men, on this scale, were farthest along that path of progress, women and non-white men somewhere in the middle, closer to nature, and nature itself something to be feared and conquered. What is new in this colonialist storyline is that it has been turned into a means for staging entertainment. The metaphorics of light and the dynamics of seeing are central to this transformation. In this caricatured version of the Englightenment narrative, the filmmakers bring the "light" of the camera's gaze to the previously unexposed "heart of darkness." One of cinema's unique features is that it generates emotional involvement through its capacity to track glances from one person to another and from a person to a scene. It generates meaning by showing meaning being made *visually*. The camera, and Carl Denham (the cameraman in the film), look at Ann Darrow; we look at Darrow/Wray and admire her; she gazes back, objectified for us as an object of beauty. She, we, and later the audience at the theatre in New York City (within the film), look at Kong. Darrow, in fact, has been trained to look at Kong in just the right way, registering shock, horror, and fascination through the gaze we see on her face, both in the audition and practice run and in the later actual encounter with the beast. By the end of the film, Kong is returning her and our gazes, looking longingly, wanting to be accepted by her (and, vicariously, by us). So there are the lookers (the white filmmakers, the New York audience, Ann Darrow in relationship to Kong, and us all along) and the looked at (Ann Darrow, Kong, and the non-whites throughout the film). Looking becomes spectacle, which is also an enactment of power relations. When Denham says that "seeing is believing," we can take this to be the moment at which the power of the "seeing industries"—the entertainment media that show us the world, framing it for us in particular ways—establishes itself as uniquely powerful. Fay Wray / Ann Darrow is, in the process, made the object of a multiple gaze: that of the camera-narrator, of the sailors and male characters within the film, of Kong, and of us, so that the film's "subject of enunciation"—as Nils Elliott puts it—"circulates among all these figures."[38] In the end, all eyes are on the prize, the object of the spectacle, King Kong—and on Fay Wray, the female object of the male gaze. In the process, as the camera has been brought to the viewable Other (woman, jungle), we, the viewers, have learned how to look and how to see through the colonizing, spectacular gaze.

King Kong is thus a film about film, a spectacle about spectacle, and therefore a film about how the world has been transformed from one of actual colonization and violent conflict to one of spectacles for passive viewing audiences. Film is equated to, and transcends, colonial adventurism (going to Skull Island and taking what we want) and military domination (taking Kong down with fighter planes). At the same time, King Kong celebrates cinema's capacity to give us both the spectacle of power (Kong) and that of beauty (Darrow/Wray). This is all, as E. Ann Kaplan argues, a fairly precise exemplification of the imperial gaze, which sees everything but is itself not seen. "The gaze of the colonialist," she writes, "refuses to acknowledge its own power and privilege: it unconsciously represses knowledge of power hierarchies and its need to dominate, to control." Like the male gaze, the colonial gaze objectifies "mutual subject-to-subject recognition" even while refusing it. But there is "always the threat of being toppled," which leads to an undercurrent of anxiety and injects the Self–Other relationship with a frisson of excitement.[39]

I am saying little here that is not already standard knowledge among post-colonial and anti-racist cultural theorists. As a sign of its times, King Kong captured the relationship between America—especially as represented by the movie and broadcasting industries centred in Los Angeles and New York City, the equation between the two being cemented into place around this time—and the rest of the world, which came to be portrayed more and more by Hollywood to Euro-American audiences and, ultimately, to the rest of the world. In this way, the world was refracted back on itself through the prism of the American entertainment industry. *King Kong* is, notwithstanding, for the millions of people who have watched it, fabulous entertainment.

Around the time it was made, with the advent of sound cinema, film production moved onto studio sets and away from on-location shooting, and as a result, cultural otherness came to be portrayed in even more stereotypical forms by Hollywood cinema. As Jay Ruby puts it: "For forty years"—that is, until the rise of portable cameras and sound equipment in the 1960s—"movie audiences learned about the exotic Other through back-lot Tarzan films employing African Americans as natives and cowboy and Indian movies using Mexican Americans as Native Americans."[40]

If Otherness is defined by cultural codes that are organized with the aid of gender and race categories, some variation of such a reading should apply to the vast majority of films depicting Otherness, including horror and science fiction films portraying hostile life forms, vampires, viruses, and the like. Such films, viewed critically and contextually, raise the question of what *kinds* of monsters a given society produces, and *why* those kinds: What do they tell us about how we imagine ourselves and those who are different from us? Early Cold War aliens—those depicted in 1950s movies like *Invasion of the Body Snatchers* (1956)—threatened our sense of individuality (through the takeover of our minds) and of collective security. But during that same era, subcultural and utopian aliens, such as the redemptive, messianic Klaatu from *The Day the Earth Stood Still* (1951), provided a counter-current to this, posing liberal-universalist critiques of the dominant Cold War mindset. When the Cold War ended, the friendlier aliens of the 1980s, such as *ET* (1982), were replaced by the paranoia of *The X-Files*, at a time when trust in government had fallen to an all-time low in the United States. Much has been and could be written about these shifts and their relationship to changing socio-political currents and global developments.[41] (Chapter 6 will touch on these themes.) My intent in mentioning them here is only to point to another genre in which otherness and difference have been portrayed.

Beyond Hollywood, which has fostered both dominant and alternative cinematic currents, a variety of distinct national cinemas, with their own traditions of identity and difference, have developed over the past century. If *King Kong* exemplifies what we might call the *imperial-spectacular gaze structure*, elements of that structure have been appropriated by filmmakers beyond the confines of Hollywood for other ends and subjected to internal and external critiques. I will return later to the broader question of "best practices" for ethnographic filmmaking, including for the depiction of cultural difference in fiction films. In the next section, I focus on a few exemplary approaches within popular and fine art filmmaking practices for portraying moments of contact across radical cultural (and cultural–natural) difference.

Upriver Journeys, Hearts of Darkness, and Contact Zones

The moment of contact between "us" and "them" is such a recurrent theme in popular cinema that it verges on an obsession. Every human society develops narrative and/or imagistic modes for distinguishing its collective identity from the identities of contrasting others. Over the past several centuries, however, as Western society has expanded around the world through colonization and political and economic domination, "uncontacted" societies have become more and more rare. So fascination with moments of "first contact" have taken on a higher currency. This becomes clear on those occasions when some organization or media outlet announces the "discovery" of, or a rare photographic contact with, "one of the last uncontacted tribes." In May 2008, and again in 2010 (!), Survival International used those words to describe a group living near the Brazil–Peru border.[42]

The tradition of Western explorers penetrating the dark remainders of the non-civilized world extends from the Spanish conquistadors to popular depictions in the tales of Tarzan, in works of literary fiction like Joseph Conrad's *Heart of Darkness*, and—more perhaps by the absence of the "others" than by their presence—in such recent television fare as *Survivor* and *Lost*. Francis Ford Coppola's *Apocalypse Now* (1979) is among the better-known reimaginings of the "heart of darkness" trope. It is an upriver journey, with the geomorphic trajectory implicitly equated both with a movement *within*—to the dark heart that allegedly represents something about the condition of the human soul—and with a movement *back*, to a past that is generally imagined to have been left behind during civilization's ascent. Coppola's film drew on the director's readings of mythographic texts such as James G. Frazer's *The Golden Bough* (which is featured in a scene at the compound of Colonel Kurtz) to make a statement that was seemingly about the horrors of war, and the Vietnam War in particular, but more broadly about human nature. An armchair anthropologist, Frazer had documented rites and traditions from around the world, ostensibly correlating myths and practices of the sacrifice of "divine kings" and "scapegoats" with the early religions of agriculturally based societies. The film plays out this kind of myth, with Kurtz (Marlon Brando), an American colonel gone rogue and leading his own cult-like compound in the Cambodian jungle, being killed by his would-be replacement, Willard (Martin Sheen), who is the movie's protagonist. Like its model, Conrad's novella *Heart of Darkness*, *Apocalypse Now* finds in the rainforest a savagery that is powerful, frightening, and primal. The jungle here is no longer simply a place for demonstrating one's manhood, as it was for Edgar Rice Burroughs's *Tarzan*. If anything, it is a place where manhood itself is revealed to be tragic and horrible: "The horror," Kurtz intones in the film's closing moments, "the horror."

Coppola's film was modelled in part on Werner Herzog's *Aguirre: The Wrath of God* (1972), about a Spanish conquistador leading an ill-fated expedition down the Amazon toward what he believed to be the fabled city of El Dorado. Here is another myth that the Western mind associates with the jungle: the idea that there are riches, a City of Gold, to be discovered within. While the journey depicted is literally a journey *down* river, with its narrative of the Europeans being overcome by the rainforest, it is consistent with the metaphorics of upriver journeys. Herzog intended *Aguirre* to be a film about how Europeans saw this very foreign environment when they first entered it. It is a film about seeing, but where *King Kong* replicates the colonial gaze—the gaze by which we see the land to be tamed spread out before us, and can then map and colonize it—*Aguirre* deconstructs that gaze. Instead of showing us the jungle as a place to be mapped, tamed, and conquered, Herzog shows it as a place where the travellers' coordinates no longer hold, where nothing is as it seems. As Lutz Koepnick puts it, Herzog's "jungle rejects any attempt to be read, mastered, or even represented."[43]

In *Aguirre*, Koepnick writes, "Herzog literally stages colonialism's struggle with its own invention of South America as mere nature."[44] In contrast to the privileged vista points of the monarch-of-all-I-survey scene, Herzog begins the film with a spectacular aerial shot that depicts the Spaniards descending precariously, through clouds and fog, down a steep Andean mountain and into the jungle. As they descend, they seem to lose all bearings; animals and objects fall along the way. Herzog, Koepnick writes, "draws the spectator into this stumbling of the colonial power, forces the viewer to partake of the very loss of perspective and sublime eyesight the Spaniards suffer amid the mud and the chaotic heaps of leaves. Dirt and water on the eye of the camera emphasize this threatening lack of vision."[45] Afterwards, with few exceptions, all that we see takes place on or along the river from the perspective of the Spaniards, who look out onto a jungle they can make little sense of. Gradually they lose the markers of their civilized identities: "The cannons, the might of paper and ink," Sharman recounts, "and the horse, three symbols of European power and superiority, are one after the other claimed by the jungle."[46] The linearity of the journey is offset and overtaken increasingly by images of circularity. The wild-eyed conquistador Aguirre is the living embodiment of the will to mastery—the drive to colonize, conquer, and claim for oneself an entire new world, a world of heretofore unknown and unclaimed lands, subjects, and prizes—but his project fails utterly. In the end, he is reduced (even in evolutionary terms, it would seem) to stumbling around on a dilapidated raft littered with dead bodies, accompanied only by hundreds of little monkeys. No prize is waiting for him at the end of this journey; as the African slave Okello intones, there is "no ship ... no forest ... no arrow." Nothing has been gained, no inkling of understanding, let alone control, of this world. The circle closes in on the raft, just as the camera circles around it in the final shot. The victor, if there is one, is nature and its cycle/circle of death.

Herzog's films are never as easy to read as they may seem at first, and it has been argued that his effort to depict the failure of Aguirre's mission—and, by extension, of the European Enlightenment project—is torn by ambiguity and complicity. Many of Herzog's films focus on individuals whose drive to make a mark on the world is obsessive and extreme. In both his documentaries and his feature films—*The Flying Doctors of East Africa* (1969), *Land of Silence and Darkness* (1971), *The Great Ecstasy of the Sculptor Steiner* (1974), *La Soufrière* (1977), *Aguirre* (1972), *Grizzly Man* (2005), and others—Herzog seeks out those who push beyond the human and against the boundaries of hard, material reality. Les Blank's documentary *Burden of Dreams* (1982), shot during the filming of *Fitzcarraldo* (1982), shows Herzog to be very much akin to these obsessive characters. Yet while the projects presented, such as Aguirre's to found a new civilization built of gold, characteristically fail, his focus on their efforts can be taken as a celebration of their superhuman drive, as sublime in its depiction of the heights they reach, but also as ironic in its understanding of the inevitable failure to sustain such heights. I will discuss Herzog's own ideas about nature in Chapter 5, but here it should be noted that this criticism of his work as complicit with what it critiques is one that could be applied, in various ways, to many films made by white, Western (European, North American, or Australian) auteurs depicting the conflict between the West and indigenous Others. Such films include Peter Weir's *The Last Wave* (1977), Nicholas Roeg's *Walkabout* (1971), Herzog's later film *Where the Green Ants Dream* (1984), and others in the vein of *The Mission* (1986), *At Play in the Fields of the Lord* (1991), and *Dances With Wolves* (1990). Another kind of "imperialist nostalgia," as Renato Rosaldo has called it, is in evidence in films like *Heat and Dust* (1983), *Passage to India* (1984), *Out of Africa* (1985), and *The Gods Must Be Crazy* (1981)—all films that, according to Rosaldo, display a nostalgia for "traditional" colonized cultures that conceals the brutality of domination through its pose of "innocent yearning."[47] Much of this problematic reiterates, in modified form, some of the issues that have been already addressed in relation to the imperial gaze. Even so, it is important to recognize the progress that some white filmmakers have made in their efforts to engage with indigenous communities in their re-envisionings of such "first contact" scenarios.

Terrence Malick's *The New World* (2005) is an example of a film marked by the director's keen desire to "get it right," even as the story itself seems to militate against this possibility. The film is about the 1607 encounter between English colonists and indigenous "naturals" on the Virginia coast and the events that ensue: the building of the colony of Jamestown, the romance between Captain John Smith and Pocahontas, and the latter's later life in England. A film of epic scope and dramatic visceral impact, it fared less well at the box office than Malick's earlier films partly due to its arty cerebrality, and perhaps because the Pocahontas–John Smith love story, now largely debunked by historians, has been cinematically exhausted for contemporary audiences. Malick's efforts at historical and representational accuracy, however, were notable. The film's time-consuming and arduous seventeen-week production involved the building of a replica of the Jamestown fort less than ten miles from the original setting, using only wood from local forests; the painstaking reconstruction by linguistic anthropologist Blair Rudes of a defunct proto-Algonkian language, and the subsequent learning of that language by the Native American actors; a meticulous attention to detail and historical accuracy in the costumes, props, and body painting and tattooing; and Malick's insistence on shooting with available natural light and hand-held cameras and Steadicams rather than complex lighting and sophisticated camera set-ups. In a well-researched assessment of the film's portrayal of Pocahontas and her people, indigenous historian Steve Pavlik notes some criticisms, particularly of the love story narrative (by historians) and the overdoing of Native costuming, body painting, and movement (by Native critics). But he judges the film positively on all other counts, including its efforts to consult with and engage local Native American tribes and tribal members, as well as historians and anthropologists; to portray historical details with rare accuracy (with the exception of the love story); to reconstruct the extinct Virginian Algonquian language in a way that will assist in its revitalization; to "portray the religion and spirituality of the Powhatan people in a non-exploitive and non-condescending manner"; and to provide a dignified and respectful representation of Pocahontas.[48]

At its heart, however, the film is about the same themes that Malick has insisted on more and more over the course of his filmmaking career—themes that amount to what Ron Mottram describes as "an Edenic yearning to recapture a lost wholeness of being, an idyllic state of integration with the natural and good both within and without ourselves."[49] The disparity between the everyday and this state of wholeness and integration is, in *The New World*, mapped onto the difference between the English settlers and the Powhatan. The Jamestown colony, as Eric Repphun describes it, "is all dirt, mud and confusion. The men spend their time squabbling over the minutia of English law and digging for gold while they slowly starve." Their settlement is often framed as images of confinement, "from the inside of buildings looking out"; its inhabitants clomp around in heavy armour and wool, shivering in the winter and staring strangely into space.[50] The Powhatans, by contrast, are fully at ease in their world, moving lithely and with the dexterity of animals through grass, trees, and water and delighting in their own company and that of the natural world. The contrast between the two peoples is absolute (if not quite as stark as the one between the rival groups in James Cameron's *Avatar*). Yet there is a risk in this strategy, one that is captured in Ed Buscombe's argument that while the film "throws into sharp relief how threadbare are the claims of the English to represent civilization," ultimately "Malick's view of the Indians as part of the natural world militates against any real possibility of understanding them as inhabiting a separate and different culture. The Indians," he concludes, "merely represent an idealized escape from civilization, not an alternative form of it." Buscombe seems to be arguing that the Indians have not been humanized *enough*—that in our terms, they are not *anthropomorphic* enough but instead have been folded over into the natural world—naturalized, biomorphed. Pocahontas, he argues, remains unknowable in a way that isn't the case for (say) John Smith; and cultural transfer between them is "wholly one way." When the Powhatans are shown speaking their own language (which there is plenty of), we are given subtitled translations only when narratively important information is being conveyed to us. At other times, there are no subtitles, which has the effect of rendering the Indians "even more unknowable, at times simply a part of the natural world, at other times a culture which is impenetrable."[51] A few critics have gone further than this: Leo Killsback, in *Wicazo Sa Review*, writes that "it was a shame to see the Powhatan kingdom ... depicted as less than human in this twenty-first-century movie. The random movements of the Powhatan people were akin to those of monkeys.... They lacked any sophistication or anything human."

I am not sure that the unidirectionality of agency that Buscombe ascribes to the film is at all clear, and I hesitate to speculate what Killsback considers sophisticated humanity (though it is clear that he dislikes the choreography of acclaimed Apache/Ute actor, dancer, and choreographer Raoul Trujillo). We do, however, get extended sequences of Powhatan living their lives and engaging in conversations, games, food gathering, and warfare, and of John Smith's forays into their cultural world as he learns their customs and language. We also follow Pocahontas/Rebecca to England, a part of the Pocahontas story that most renditions rarely pursue in as much depth as here. It may be that she remains more or less "unknowable" to most viewers, though it would take some audience research to establish whether viewer identification was greater with Smith (or anyone else in the film) than with her. Malick's goal, however, is not to generate viewer identification with a *character* so much as identification with a *condition*: the human condition, and the modern condition more specifically. The Native American alternative to that condition was, of course, demolished through the brutal historical circumstances that the film portrays well enough. Yet Native Americans survive and, moreover, act in movies today. As with the Maori warrior rituals portrayed in *Whale Rider* (2002), there is a certain stylization of indigenous performativity in *The New World*—of bodies, gestures, movements, and so on—that risks overemphasizing the differences between "us" and "them." But these are vibrant performativities, aimed not only at exhibiting otherness to a generically white/Western public, but also at exhibiting culture and tradition to diverse audiences, including those of indigenous descendants themselves. Some of the criticisms directed at filmmakers like Malick come close to being criticisms of such films for not being what they are not—that is, for not being films about contemporary Native Americans, or about "the Native American perspective" on historical events. The making of *The New World*, however, *was* in part about contemporary Native Americans, and here Malick deserves credit.

In terms of the four variations on the portrayal of cultural difference described by Gilberto Perez, Malick's falls into the third category: "they're OK, we may not be OK." His goal, however, is not so much to present two different cultures *per se* but rather to throw us into the situation of having to grapple with the conditions of their difference—which, for Malick, are also the conditions of our perhaps "fallen" humanity. The fourth strategy—"they're not OK and neither are we"—may well describe what Herzog and Coppola strove to present in *Aguirre* and *Apocalypse Now*, though neither of them was fully committed to such a strategy. *Aguirre* is more about the impossibility of knowing the other; there is ultimately only the Western colonial gaze, which, when deconstructed, leaves us floating in circles, like Aguirre's raft in the film's closing image. *Apocalypse Now*, on the other hand, may depict war as hell, but its only alternative—Kurtz's army of crazed jungle dwellers—is even more hellish than the world Willard returns to in the end.

A film that, if rather perversely, does equal justice to the two sides of an ontological divide by portraying both as ethically lacking, is Robin Hardy and Anthony Shaffer's *The Wicker Man* (1973)—which, ironically, also demonstrates how the life of a film can rapidly escape its makers' intent. With its quirky, even campy, mixture of horror, mystery thriller, faux-ethnography, and musical, *The Wicker Man* takes an original approach to a universal theme, that of the lone traveller journeying into a foreign cultural world and being shocked by what he finds there. Ads for the film announced: "They do things differently on Summerisle." Based on David Pinner's novel *The Ritual*, the film is about a police officer and devout Christian, Sergeant Howie, who travels from the Scottish mainland to a remote Hebridean island called Summerisle to investigate the reported disappearance of a young girl, Rowan Morrison. On the island, he discovers a populace that lives by a pre-Christian Pagan religion that had been revived at the behest of the island's lord in the mid-1800s. In his attempt to unravel the mystery of the girl, Howie is drawn into a web of intrigue until it is revealed—to viewers and to Howie—that he has been summoned, in effect, by the islanders to become the human sacrifice that will restore the fertility of the island for the year to come. In a community-wide ceremony on a cliff overlooking the sea, Howie is dragged screaming into a huge wicker statue of a man. The wicker man is ignited as the rhythmically swaying islanders sing the Middle English folk-round "Sumer is Icumen In" while the terrified Howie shouts out lines from Christian psalms and prayers.

While not a portrait of an indigenous society, the film depicts a society that has, in effect, gone "back to nature" to such an extent that Sergeant Howie's arrival is an odd form of "first contact." Like *Apocalypse Now*, *The Wicker Man* is steeped in the quasi-anthropological writings of James G. Frazer; the difference is that where Frazer's primitive society takes on rather negative connotations in Coppola's film, here it is depicted as life-affirming, playful, and a generally viable alternative to modern-day Britain. Considering that this was a low-budget B-movie in a light horror genre, the filmmakers took their ethnographic mission surprisingly seriously.[52] In an ironic nod to the ethnographic genre, the film opens with a caption thanking the people of Summerisle for allowing "privileged insight into their religious practices." Both Hardy and Shaffer ostensibly spent months researching Frazer's twelve-volume compendium of folklore and beliefs, *The Golden Bough*, as well as extant practices of what seemed to be old traditions still found scattered around the British Isles, alongside a smattering of modern Druidic and Wiccan lore. The particular practices portrayed in the film—amulets and charms, fertility rituals and sex magic, folk songs and maypole dances, May Day processions and festivities—resemble neither ancient British nor contemporary Wiccan or Druidic Paganism in any real sense; however, they are presented as a form of Paganism reconstituted in the nineteenth century, and as such, they are reasonably accurate insofar as they reproduce a Victorian-era understanding— such as would have been available to Frazer—of what the ancient Celtic peoples might have practised.[53] As the filmmakers attest, "the whole series of ceremonies and details that we show have happened at different times and places in Britain and Western Europe. What we did was to bring them all together in one particular place and time."[54]

Plagued initially by distribution problems, including a disastrous initial release and managerial interference that resulted in severe edits (there are now several different-length versions available), the film began to accrue recognition only gradually.[55] Today it has a strong cult following and has spawned a number of documentaries, fan publications, and appreciation societies, as well as an annual Wicker Man music and arts festival (held in Kirkcudbrightshire, Scotland, since 2002), an academic conference (in 2003), a critically derided 2006 Hollywood remake, and a 2011 sequel by Hardy called *The Wicker Tree*. Related to the issues discussed earlier of geomorphism and tourism, Galloway, where the film was shot, and to a lesser extent the Scottish Western Isles, where the action ostensibly takes place, have seen a marked growth in tourism inspired by the film.[56] Part of the film's attraction for its fans is in the subtlety, sophistication, and humour of its portrayal of the conflict between two alternative cultures. The film unfolds as a kind of debate between Howie's Christianity and the islanders' Paganism. In a conversation between Howie and the island's magistrate and landowner, the charismatic Lord Summerisle (Christopher Lee), Howie objects to the sight of naked girls jumping over a bonfire in hopes of supernatural impregnation; to this, Summerisle retorts that Jesus was "the son of a virgin, impregnated, I believe, by a ghost." In the end, Howie's sacrifice as a "willing, king-like virgin fool"—his chaste bachelorhood is established in the film's opening minutes, his office as sergeant and representative of the law makes him king-like, and he dons the garb of Punch, the Fool, in the May Day procession—clearly calls to mind the sacrifice of Jesus on the cross, though whether Howie is a sacrificial scapegoat, a Christian martyr, or a mere victim of unusual beliefs, is left an open question. The film's polysemic nature—its ambiguity and elasticity of meaning, excessive ethnographic detail, inconsistency with generic conventions, and lack of narrative closure—is what makes it possible for both Pagan and Christian viewers to interpret it sympathetically.[57] As Fry argues: "Those who share Howie's values can take comfort in his martyrdom and the dignity with which he faces death, while Pagans of all sorts and those sympathetic to New Age ideas and unsympathetic to Christian values can see his death as merited and symbolic of the demise of what he represents."[58] Kingsley points out that the film "never at any time takes sides, not once tells the audience what it ought to be thinking or feeling; it shows courage in its handling of religious belief, revealing to us its glories, and its dangers, too. And it never loses its sense of humour, not even at the end."[59]

Here we see the discrepancy between the authors' intent and the audience's reception of the film. Both director Hardy and scriptwriter Shaffer have referred in interviews to the "incipient fascism" of religious cults, and the final scenes can be taken as depicting this in graphic form.[60] According to the filmmakers, the film portrays both Christianity and Pagan religion as social constructs that function in ways that "keep [...] people in the thrall of superstition."[61] Despite this intent, however, Pagans and Neo-Pagans have responded to the film positively over the years. Steven Sutcliffe notes a "gradual 'Paganisation' of the film," a reclamation of it by avowedly Pagan audiences, who are a significant proportion of the film's cult following. Pagan audiences have commented favourably on the film's sympathetic portrayal of Pagan virtues and values, its sensitively detailed recreation of seasonal rituals, music, and other practices, and especially its presentation of Paganism as valid and normative—which is a reversal of tradition, in that the film depicts Christianity as an interloper on the home turf of Paganism, rather than the latter being "a transgressive, exotic practice" against the background normativity of Christianity.[62]

Of the films discussed in the book so far, *The Wicker Man* is arguably the most utopian in its construction of a fully formed alternative society. As with Boorman's *Deliverance*, much of this affectively utopian character is carried by the music, which includes original songs by Paul Giovanni, adaptations of thoroughly researched traditional songs and folk ballads, which are sung with verve and often feature frankly sexual lyrics, and incidental music played on traditional instruments, mostly by students recruited so that the music would sound under-rehearsed. The music does more than simply provide atmosphere. With its wide range of moods and its frequently diegetic function (i.e., where it is part of the on-screen action), it contributes much to the coherence of the narrative and of the island's Pagan culture. The film also follows the tradition of portraying Britain's Western Isles as liminal edges and "cultural fringes in the Anglo-British imagination," as places that hold "lingering residues of Gaelic culture and the fabled 'Isles of Paradise' and 'Isles of The Dead' of Celtic mythology."[63] Popular interest in "Celtic spirituality" and "Celtic music" have both increased markedly over the past three decades, and *The Wicker Man*, despite its horror film trappings, resonates with many neo-pagans today all the more for this reason. Pagan audiences have therefore tended to forgive its inaccuracies—including its portrayal of human sacrifice as central to their culture—in favour of enjoying and celebrating the insider perspective the film provides. Nichols, in his "Neo-Pagan Filmography," calls it "the most loving portrayal of a Pagan society ever committed to film."[64] That Sergeant Howie's sacrifice does not fatally offend the film's fans tells us one of three things: they may accept it as part of the generic horror film package, and therefore as a superficial addition to an otherwise valuable film; they may even, as both Sutcliffe and Fry argue,[65] get a certain pleasure from it; or they may actually accept that an occasional sacrifice may be warranted to maintain the cosmic order.[66] Insofar as the latter is the case (and there has been little audience research done that would prove or disprove it), it may be a sign of the success of the cultural relativism promoted by the film's quasi-ethnographic strategy, which itself can be taken as a kind of utopian impulse.[67]

Ethnography Beyond First Contact

The last half-century has seen much progress among anthropologists toward an understanding of ethnography as a collaborative venture. The introduction of highly portable synchronous-sound cameras around 1960 led to two loosely distinguishable traditions among those using film to document other cultures. In France, anthropologist Jean Rouch developed a highly reflexive style of collaborative and multivocal ethnography that incorporated the filmmaker directly into the diegetic space of the film. Among Rouch's notable works were a series of so-called "ethnographic science fiction films" including *Jaguar* (1965), *Petit à Petit* (1968), *Cocorico, Monsieur Poulet* (1983), and *Madame l'Eau* (1992). In the United States, Robert Gardner and John Marshall, influenced by the "direct cinema" documentary movement, steered toward a "purer" and less interactive approach. Their idea was to film as much as possible in order to capture the flow of reality in the fleeting moments when the camera was no longer perceived as intruding into the cultural setting being filmed. The camera, in this sense, blends into reality to the fullest extent possible, with the result that what comes out of the camera is a kind of omniscient, and at the same time immanent, "eye of God," a seeing that is everywhere at once within the action.

The observational cinema ideal, as developed by Marshall, Gardner, Timothy Asch, David MacDougall, and others, emphasizes long, uninterrupted takes, synchronized sound, slow pacing, and the delivery of context-rich detail about the people portrayed. Karl Heider describes this ideal in terms of its "ethnographicness," which is attained through a holistic attention to "whole bodies," "whole actions and interactions," and "whole people," that is, with actions deeply contextualized within their cultural and interpersonal settings; through a preference for natural, synchronous sound and the incorporation of local voices; and through a self-reflexive acknowledgment of the ethnographer's presence.[68] Ethnographic filmmakers like David and Judith MacDougall have shifted somewhat, over the years, from their original observationalist ideals toward a more participatory form of cinema, conceived as "a record of the meeting between filmmaker and that society."[69] In *Transcultural Cinema*, David MacDougall draws a contrast between two kinds of reflexivity: "external reflexivity," by which a filmmaker seeks, in Ruby's words, to "make people aware of point of view, ideology, author biography, and anything else deemed relevant to an understanding of the film,"[70] a "metacommunication" that "frames the frame" but leaves the positivist subject–object duality intact; and, on the other hand, a "deep reflexivity" that contextualizes what it shows internally, creating a sufficiently complex encounter with its subjects that it can hold up well against a plurality of readings, including by the subjects themselves.[71]

The MacDougalls' approach can be seen as a synthesis of Rouch's self-reflexively engaged style and Heider's more withdrawn but holistically ethnographic ideal. These can in turn be compared to styles of feature filmmaking that aim to present non-Western or non-mainstream cultural contexts. In the next part of this chapter, I focus on films that can be taken as representative of three distinct modes of cultural representation. The first of these is a holistic mode that attempts through stylistic choices (narrative, framing, character structure, and so on) to give more authentic voice to a context intentionally depicted as different from a mainstream, Western one. The primary examples here will be Julie Dash's *Daughters of the Dust* (1991), a film that has been called a "a foreign film from the U.S." and "third cinema in the 'first' world,"[72] and Zacharias Kunuk's Inuit–Canadian production *Atanarjuat* (*The Fast Runner*, 2001). I will contextualize these with reference to Teshome Gabriel's articulation of a "Third World film aesthetic." The second mode to be discussed is a self-reflexive and deconstructive one, exemplified by Rouch's one-time collaborator Chris Marker, especially his *Sans Soleil* (*Sunless*, 1983), and, in a more deconstructive vein, by the counter-ethnographic "mockumentaries" and satirical collage films of Ken Feingold, Bruce Conner, Craig Baldwin, and others. Finally, following a discussion of "green identities" in popular films, I will discuss Alain Tanner's *Jonah Who Will Be 25 in the Year 2000* (1975) as an example of a film that exemplifies something like the kind of "deep reflexivity" referred to by David MacDougall but brought into a fictional narrative about politics, hope, and the possibility for social and cultural change.

Cinematic Holism, Auto-Ethnography, and Visual Sovereignty

Over the past half century, ethnographic subjects have expanded well beyond anything capturable by the early anthropological penchant for isolated and "primitive" tribal groups. In a world more global, mobile, and culturally hybridized than ever before, relations between ourselves and others, "us" and "them," are necessarily more complex and interesting than any depictions of "first contact" can provide.[73] Because of their social position of being primary caregivers in culturally uprooted worlds, non-Western women migrants are perhaps the class of individuals in whose lives the tenuous hybridity of this kind of global nomadism is most keenly felt. In *Looking for the Other: Feminism, Film, and the Imperial Gaze*, E. Ann Kaplan examines a series of films by women about women who travel from one place—often a home that has been rendered uninhabitable in one way or another—to a diasporic new home that is also never quite a home: Claire Denis' *Chocolat* (1988), Mira Nair's *Mississippi Masala* (1992), Pratibha Parmar and Alice Walker's transnational collaboration *Warrior Marks* (1993), and the films of Trinh T. Min-ha, Julie Dash, and others.[74] With similar intent, Laura Marks, in *The Skin of the Film*, theorizes an "intercultural cinema" that uses experimental means to "represent the experience of living between two or more cultural regimes of knowledge," a cinema that, in Marks's terms, produces a haptic or tactile visuality that renders the "intercultural" experience more palpable than cinema has conventionally done.[75]

One of the films that both Kaplan and Marks dwell on at length, Julie Dash's *Daughters of the Dust* (1991), can be taken as a paradigmatic example of the interplay between specific kinds of geomorphism and anthropomorphism to produce an alternative set of possibilities for socio-ecological representation. As I discussed in the previous chapter, collective identities have traditionally developed in and through relations between land and place; territory plus narrative plus media, I suggested, equals nation. In practice, the process of people's identities commingling with land has always been dynamic and in flux, though for some people it has sometimes been more dynamic than for others. Scholars of land use and economic geography have identified a variety of regimes of collective land and property management. At one end of a continuum is an "open access" system, where a given piece of land or set of resources belongs to no one in particular and is, therefore, available to anyone. Following Deleuze and Guattari, we can call this a deterritorialized system.[76] Open-access regimes have long been considered unsustainable, since they are thought to lead inevitably to a "tragedy of the commons," where land resources are depleted through overuse by unmanaged users. At the other end—or, rather, at a series of other possible ends—are divergent forms of territorialized relations ranging from the communal to the feudal to the capitalist. Western modernity has followed a certain historical trajectory in the course of which land use relations have moved from the more communal and/or feudal to the capitalist. A turning point in this development was the land enclosures of the early modern period. Over the course of several hundred years, from roughly the fourteenth to the nineteenth centuries, the British Parliament passed a series of laws known as Enclosures Acts, according to which land that had been held in common or subject to complex negotiations over who had which kind of access to it, became privately held by a rising class of landowners. Land was, in effect, privatized and rendered into a commodity that could be bought and sold in the marketplace. Peasants who had previously been able to subsist on the fruits of the land were now left without access to it; they were evicted, which forced them to relocate to newly established factory towns and cities.

Daughters of the Dust does not refer specifically to this macro-history of property relations; however, the broad background against which the film's events take place is the history of land use relations among African-American former slaves on the Sea Islands of Georgia and the Carolinas. The film takes place over the course of a single day in 1902, a Sunday on which the children and descendants of Nana Peazant gather to bid goodbye to their mother/grand-mother and elder, while others grapple with the dilemma of whether to stay on the island with Nana or move to the mainland and its seeming opportunities. The Peazants are Gullahs, descendants of African-American slaves who had managed to preserve more of their African cultural heritage by virtue of their strong concentration in geography and in origin (they came from related West African tribes), and by regaining the land abandoned by their slave masters in the wake of the Civil War—land they were allowed to purchase. The Gullahs profited from the Port Royal Experiment, a project intended to turn former slaves into citizens and property owners. By the 1890s, three-quarters of the land in Beaufort County, South Carolina, was owned by African Americans, and the Emancipation Proclamation and the Thirteenth, Fourteenth, and Fifteenth Amendments have allowed the Peazant family to choose between remaining on the island or moving to the mainland. The film's central dilemma is thus a choice between tradition and modernity, between island Afroculture and mainland Euroculture. There are other dilemmas and tensions in the film: one is between "new" religions (Christianity and Islam) and Nana's traditional, syncretic ancestral practices; another is whether or not to participate in the anti-lynching campaign that is developing at the time. But these play a second-ary role to the main point of debate between the Peazants.

In a perceptive analysis of the film, ecocritic Jhan Hochman examines how it interrogates and revisions the ways in which the human relationship to land is mediated by the organization of labour, leisure, and community structure. Hochman explores three ways in which people "belong to land: through photography, through belief (myth/religion), and through dwelling (leisure, labor, and social organization)."[77] The first of these is represented by Mr. Snead, a photographer who accompanies Viola to the island and who, in the end, chooses to remain on it. Snead is the only one who can see—in the viewfinder of his camera—the film's ghost-narrator, the unborn child of Eula, and Hochman interprets this as Snead's becoming "a figure in nature's own camera."[78] The second way, that of belief, is represented cinematically through the film's reference to the legend of the Ibo walking across the sea to West Africa. It is embodied in the character of Nana Peazant, who, for Hochman, holds to an "African stewardship ethic" centred on the perception of obligations to ancestors as well as to descendants, all of them cradled "in a time that owns all things."[79] The third way, that of dwelling, is embodied in the leisure activities that feature prominently throughout the film, such as walking, sitting in trees, and telling stories; in the non-alienated labour of blacksmithing, dye making, rice husking, farming, gathering Spanish moss, and preparing food; and in the social organization portrayed in the film, which is communal and based on extended families.[80]

The film is thus a fictionalized recreation of a decisive historical moment for the Gullahs, a moment that director Julie Dash spent a decade researching, and its primary appeal has predictably been with African-American women, for whom the character of Nana Peazant would be a readily recognizable role model. One need recall that it took 230 years for a black man, a (part) African-American, to become president of the United States and for a woman to be considered a potential president; it will take longer for an African-American woman to be considered for either role. *Daughters* is in part about healing the legacy of that double oppression: as African-American feminist critic bell hooks (Gloria Watkins) wrote about the film, *Daughters* includes "images of us as we've never seen ourselves on the screen before."[81] Its cinematography is lyrical and impressionistic, featuring a preponderance of wide-angle and deep-focus shots. In line with a more holistic ideal, the film's narrative is non-linear and multi-layered, with multiple points of view and cross-cutting between shots creating a sense of simultaneity rather than linearity, of community rather than individuality, of complexity rather than simplicity. Instead of presenting a single option as better than others, the film in its narrative interplay offers a layered dialogue of positions and voices weaving themselves into one another. The film is ostensibly narrated by the unborn daughter of a young married couple, Eli and Eula; Eula had been raped by a white man (and probably the former slave owner). The film's narrative movement, however, is not linear and progressive, but circular and regenerative, with a focus on the web of collective relations and of stories within stories, connecting past to present to future, rather than on the accomplishments of singular characters.

This circularity is very different from the kind of circularity I described in connection to Herzog's *Aguirre: The Wrath of God*. There, circularity was disorienting; it took away the bearings of linear progression in order to leave us, like its characters, feeling adrift in a hostile and human-unfriendly world.

For Dash and for many Third Worldist filmmakers such as Trinh Minh-Ha and Ousmane Sembene, circularity reflects a participatory sense of being "at home in the world." *Daughters of the Dust* presents a model where the world *is* us (to the extent that we can identify with its characters), where we *are* the world, and where the relationship between the two is mediated by narrative, memory, and ritual and commemorative practice. Geomorphism is married here to anthropomorphism, with tension brought about through the decision point faced by the characters—in this case, whether to stay or leave the island. This decision point is simultaneously individual and collective, and the characters' particular answers to the dilemma are less important than the film's evocation of what the decision point feels like, in a world where being-at-home is distinctly possible, even quite tangible, yet where the future remains open to collective action.

In all these respects, *Daughters of the Dust* has much more in common with African storytelling traditions than with conventional cinema narratives. Indeed, Dash has stated that she "wanted the audience to feel as if it was looking at a foreign film."[82] In this respect the film falls into the category described by Teshome Gabriel's influential 1985 article "Towards a Critical Theory of Third World Films."[83] Gabriel was referring specifically to the work of such filmmakers as Brazil's Glauber Rocha, Senegal's Ousmane Sembene, and Bolivia's Jorge Sanjinés. In the work of these directors, Gabriel argues, techniques are foregrounded that in mainstream Western cinema would be considered "cinematic excess" but "which in the Third World context seem only too natural." He explains that this is because "Third World films grow from folk tradition where communication is a slow-paced phenomenon and time is not rushed but has its own pace," while Western culture "is based on the value of 'time'—time is art, time is money, time is most everything else. If time drags in a film, spectators grow bored and impatient." The two different styles are also rooted in cultural contexts that are dominated, in one case, by artificial objects and environments, and in the other, by more or less natural environments. As Gabriel puts it, "the slow, leisurely pacing approximates the viewer's sense of time and rhythm of life," and "the preponderance of wide-angle shots of longer duration deal with a viewer's sense of community and how people fit in nature." The technique of cross-cutting between seemingly simultaneous actions "shows simultaneity rather than the building of suspense." Gabriel accounts for the minimal use of close-up shots by pointing out that "the isolation of an individual, in tight close-up shots, seems unnatural to the Third World film-maker because (i) it calls attention to itself; (ii) it eliminates social considerations; and (iii) it diminishes spatial integrity."[84] The panning shot is used more in such films—often in place of cuts—since they help maintain the integrity of space and time. The Third World aesthetic makes more effective use of silence and more frequent use of direct address to the audience. Also, it varies its camera angles in such a way as to emphasize social or political dynamics in which narrative authority is differently distributed than it is in modern social settings. (There is commonly, for instance, a deference to elders and even to the historical continuity stretching from long-dead ancestors to unborn future generations.) Its main characters constitute a different kind of heroic individual: "wish-fulfillment through identification is not the films' primary objective," Gabriel writes. Rather, "it is the importance of collective engagement and action that matters. The individual 'hero' in the Third World context does not make history, he/she only serves historical necessities."[85]

Gabriel's Third Worldist ideal has not exactly conquered cinema screens around the world—some have criticized it for fostering an elitist art form that will never appeal to the masses. What interests us, however, is its ultimate goal, which is consistent with the kind of holistic ethnographic ideal that Heider, MacDougall (especially in his earlier work), and other ethnographic filmmakers have defended for the cultural or ethnographic documentary genre. With more Third World and indigenous filmmakers taking up the camera, a multitude of variations have emerged that mix some of the techniques described here with other, more mainstream cinema techniques. From a socio-ecological perspective on film, the emergence of indigenous cinema is one of the most promising developments of recent years. From the early work of Flaherty, in which indigenous individuals served as unrecognized collaborators, to the more explicitly collaborative work of Rouch, MacDougall, and others, we have come to the situation where indigenous production groups are making films and television programs themselves. This is the case, for instance, with government-sponsored programs in Australia and Canada, such as the publicly supported and indigenously controlled Aboriginal Peoples Television Network, on air since 1999; the Inuit production group Igloolik Isuma; Warlpiri low-power television in Australia (created by Eric Michaels working with local activists); Vincent Carelli's Video in the Villages project and Terry Turner's Kayapo projects in South America; and the work of individual indigenous filmmakers such as Zacharias Kunuk (Inuit), Alanis Obomsawin (Abenaki), Victor Masayesva, Jr. (Hopi), Barry Barclay and Merata Mita (both Maori), Rachel Perkins and Tracey Moffatt (Australian Aboriginal), and others.[86] Successful feature films, such as Nils Gaup's (Sami) *Pathfinder* (Norway, 1987), Lee Tamahori's (Maori) *Once Were Warriors* (Maori/New Zealand, 1995), Chris Eyre's (Cheyenne/Arapaho) *Smoke Signals* (USA, 1998), Ivan Sen's (Gamilaroi/Australian) *Beneath Clouds* (2001), Phillip Noyce's *Rabbit-Proof Fence* (Australia, 2002), Niki Caro's *Whale Rider* (New Zealand, 2003), Zacharias Kunuk's *Atanarjuat:*

The Fast Runner (Canada, 2002), and Rolf de Heer and Peter Djigirr's *Ten Canoes* (Australia, 2006), show varying degrees of collaboration between white and indigenous filmmakers and artists. While many of these films deal with issues specific to aboriginal communities today or in the recent past, including the painful legacy of indigenous–settler relations, *Atanarjuat* and *Ten Canoes* focus exclusively on indigenous communities in the times before European contact. The films blend Western cinematic techniques with many of those identified by Gabriel as Third World techniques, such as long takes, extensive use of silence, unusual framing and camera angles, and indigenous storytelling techniques.

Ultimately, a cinematic anthropomorphism that has as its goal the articulation of fundamental socio-ecological difference probably needs to go well beyond a comparativist ethnographic conception, in which one culture is pitted against another. As Michelle Raheja argues, it should embrace what she calls "visual sovereignty." (One could add narrative and auditory sovereignty to this conception as well.) Discourses of sovereignty predate European colonization and can be found, in some form or other, wherever there is a cultural group articulating its own uniqueness, that is, wherever there is a subjective "we" emerging as a figure from out of a ground of relational conditionalities. Any "we" is ultimately a relative and conditional term, fated to pass away in time as do all things, but as a point of articulation it draws together a variety of material and symbolic forms: narratives, performances, memories, texts, symbolic objects, and in today's world, visual media such as films.

Raheja argues that *Atanarjuat* is a particularly good example of a film that articulates indigenous visual sovereignty. The first feature-length dramatic film written, produced, and acted by Inuit, *Atanarjuat* is, on the surface, a cinematic version of a myth, a legendary narrative that in the past would have been told primarily through oral means. In today's economy of cinematic capitalism, the film stages several forms of visual and media politics. It peoples, or territorializes, a particular geographic space, that of the Canadian Far North, and in the process reinscribes indigenous epistemologies onto a (post)modern medium. Its cast is all-Inuit: they speak Inuktitut (with English subtitles), wear traditional garb, and perform ostensibly traditional acts. The film pays close attention to the quotidian actions of hunting, gathering, and food preparation, to the materiality of feet crunching through the snow, and to the quality of light on rocks, snow, ice, water, and various mixtures and permutations of these elements. The film was created through a collaborative and participatory, community-based process that included pre-screenings for community members and elders. The social and material ecologies of its production are also settings for the articulation of a sovereigntist politics. The making of the film provided economic opportunity, and its success brought $1.5 million into a local economy suffering from a 60 percent unemployment rate. (Igloolik Isuma Inc. and Arnait Video Productions, both funded in part by the Canadian federal government, have already produced more than twenty documentary, experimental, and dramatic feature films.)[87]

Raheja argues that the film reinscribes cultural difference as a site of fluid and adaptive regeneration, for instance, by inverting "what non-Inuit might consider 'aberrant' cultural practices—interacting with supernatural powers, eating raw meat, and engaging in a polygamous, sometimes violent trade in women, for example—through humor and the strategic use of ethnographic film conventions."[88] The filmmakers were clearly well aware of the multiple audiences the film would reach, sometimes making ironic reference to these intercultural contexts. In the film's final scene, Raheja writes,

> as the credits roll and Kumagla's *ajaja* song is still heard, camera sleds pulled by actors and the crew film a naked Atanarjuat running on the ice, Oki walks along the beach in hip waders and a motorcycle jacket listening to headphones, and actors out of costume wave to the camera from a modern boat. These shots, like Nanook's smile, poke fun at the spectator, forcing the viewer (who has the patience to sit through to the film's end) to imagine *Atanarjuat* as a narrative film produced by a vibrant contemporary Inuit community, not a documentary on the mythic past or footage from a bygone era.[89]

One could argue that by altogether avoiding the history of indigenous/settler relations, films like *Atanarjuat* and *Ten Canoes* risk courting old stereotypes of the indigenous as primitive. In their broader ecologies, however, they present vibrant indigenous communities confronting issues of identity, heritage, and survival through modern as well as traditional means. While *Atanarjuat's* story takes place well before European colonization, it metaphorically plays out the dynamics of colonial–indigenous relations: it is about an outsider, a shaman from the North, whose effect on an Inuit community is disastrous, and the ways in which the community struggles to purge itself of the damaging effects of the malevolent forces that his arrival has triggered. It bears resonant affinities with some of the magic-realist cinema of Latin America and, even more so, with the poetic cinema that burgeoned in Communist Eastern Europe in the 1960s (such as Sergei Paradzhanov's *Shadows of Forgotten Ancestors*, the 1964 film that launched the Ukrainian Poetic Cinema movement). These films are not explicitly ethnographic by our definition; they do not stage encounters between two cultural groups divergently situated in relation to nature. But they are implicitly "ethno-differential" and culturally sovereigntist: they are about other ways of living that are not defined in reference to contemporary industrial capitalism. They are, of course, products of industrial cinema, and any attempt to deny that by overemphasizing the poetic vision of the artist or the collective vision of the community could be criticized as a form of Orientalism. But at the same time, such films recapture the power of industrial cinema for other purposes. (In the case of Paradzhanov, his was a similar sovereigntist effort to revitalize the distinct cultures of at least four different peoples: Ukrainian Hutsul in *Shadows of Forgotten Ancestors*, Armenian in *Sayat Nova*, Georgian in *The Legend of Suram Fortress*, and Azeri in *Ashik Kerib*.)

From the Deconstruction of Filmic Reality to Its Reflexive Reconstruction

One thing that has remained in the background of my discussion so far is the difference between documentary and fictional cinema. All films, I have argued, make use of the same primary material: they are constituted by image–sound sequences that have a Peircian firstness or primordiality about them, a secondness woven into their narrative sequentiality, and a thirdness that emerges as they produce meanings in viewers and audiences. The meanings that arise from films vary depending on audience expectations of what the films are about. With documentaries this "aboutness" is generally different from that of fictional feature films. But most documentarians today acknowledge that the distinction between the two forms is not a *natural* one; rather, at least in part if not in whole, it is a *produced* one. As with the history of linear perspective, detailed in Chapter 3, audiences have learned to recognize the documentary aesthetic *as* an aesthetic, so that when its characteristics—hand-held cameras, grainy images, on-the-fly interviews with subjects caught in a newsworthy situation, and so on—appear in a fiction film such as *District 9* (2009) or *Children of Men* (2006), this is recognized as an artistic choice that lends a particular kind of feel—an urgency, in these two cases—to the events depicted.

Contemporary documentary aesthetics are rooted in the *cinéma vérité* and direct cinema movements of the 1950s and 1960s, which took advantage of newly portable cameras and sound equipment to present the flow of reality as it unfolds in the presence of the camera. Concurrent with the development of *cinéma vérité* techniques in France was the development of *vérité*-styled, self-reflexive interventions into fictional worlds by filmmakers such as Jean Rouch, Chris Marker, and Jean-Luc Godard. Godard became the most famous to use Brechtian film techniques—"alienation" or "distanciation" devices that break the flow of the narrative and the coherence of the filmic world by directly addressing the viewer. One finds the full palette of such techniques in Godard's films of the 1960s and 1970s: jump cuts and temporal discontinuities, deliberate mixing and breaking of genre conventions, characters directly addressing the camera or commenting on the roles they are playing, juxtaposition of unrelated images and sounds, anti-naturalistic lighting and set design, visible signs of the film's production (such as cameras, microphones, and production notes), the inclusion of documentary footage and other references to actual historical events, the use of multiple screens, textual intertitles, spoken or whispered voice-overs, multiple formats (such as video, photographic stills, and animated or digitally manipulated imagery), an overflow of intertextual quotations, and so on. Such techniques are intended, at least in part, to shift the object of the camera's gaze from the narrated scene to the filmmaker, the audience, and the political situation presumed to be shared between them. They are meant to puncture the conventionally presumed barrier between the world on the other side of the screen—the illusion of an actual world *over there*—and this world in which we sit and watch. They are intended to break through as direct communications by the filmmakers into *our* worlds. At the same time, while they may rupture the escapist pleasures of narrative entertainment, such techniques can, and often have, become vehicles for viewer pleasure. When done well, they can be highly enjoyable to watch, their thirdness contributing to the firstness of the viewing experience and even to a kind of meta-level secondness, where the narrative is no longer just that which proceeds in the diegetic world of the film, but also that which unfolds between filmmaker and audience: Godard having fun with us, playfully (or annoyingly) jostling with our expectations, and so on.

Godard's films, like those of cinematic essayists Chris Marker and Haroun Farocki, became a style of cinema clearly positioned between the more direct address of first-person documentary and the fictional world-creation of the feature film. For our purposes, it is worth tracing two of the ways in which such blurring of the fiction/reality divide has proceeded. The first of these pushes self-reflexivity and illusion-breaking techniques to their deconstructive extremes, which occurs in such genres as the "reverse ethnography," the "mockumentary," and the found-footage film. The second maintains the filmmaker as a central presence in the film, the result being first-person, subjective-essay-styled films that blend the open-endedness of essayistic writing with the film medium's ability to capture and display "evidence" of the world—the sights and sounds captured on camera—even as they prompt us to question what exactly that evidence is evidence *of*. Let us consider each of these in turn.

In the context of ethnographic depictions, self-reflexive deconstructions of the documentary realist (and cinematic-illusionist) aesthetic, when pushed to their extreme, result in what have been variously labelled "anti-documentaries," "mockumentaries," "counter-ethnographies," and "reverse ethnographies." The term "mockumentary" customarily refers to films that are clearly intended to be "fake" documentaries: films like *This Is Spinal Tap* (1984) or *A Mighty Wind* (1993), which playfully satirize a phenomenon (in these cases, the heavy metal "hair band" and the aged and overbearing folk musician set) for the sake, primarily, of entertainment. Within the ethnographic genre, however, films such as Dennis O'Rourke's *Cannibal Tours*, Ken Feingold's *Un chien delicieux*, Craig Baldwin's *O No Coronado!*, and in some ways Luis Buñuel's *Land Without Bread* provide reversals of a sort intended to elicit a potentially uncomfortable recognition of our complicity with what the films depict. O'Rourke's *Cannibal Tours* (1978) follows a small luxury cruise ship carrying European and North American tourists up the Sepik River in Papua New Guinea toward an imagined "heart of darkness" where cannibals, now tamed, are supposed to dwell. Filmmakers have long been visiting Papua New Guinea to make ethnographic-styled films about the tribespeople encountering Westerners and dealing with the changes that "contact" has brought their ways of life. O'Rourke's film mixes footage and interviews of the tourists with that of the villagers, who pragmatically sell their wares while commenting on the tourists and performing the roles the tourists expect of them—or refusing to do so. In effect, it becomes a film about the inadequacy of tourist stereotypes of the Other. The filmmaker incorporates his own presence through his responses to the interview subjects and through various other means—for example, his image is shown reflected in windows. In this way, viewers are reminded of the constructed nature of the film. At the same time, the film both participates in and debunks the tourist gaze by presenting the "cannibals" themselves as self-reflexive commentators on these us–them encounters and by contextualizing them within a history of relations between Westerners and New Guineans.

Like the Aboriginal-made *Babakiueria* (1988; the title is a play on the term "barbecue area") and Jean Rouch's *Petit à petit* (*Little by Little*, 1969), which included an African protagonist "doing anthropology" among Parisians, measuring their skulls and interrogating them about their folk cultures, Ken Feingold's *Un chien délicieux* (1991) takes this kind of encounter to a different extreme. Over the footage of a wizened old man speaking in front of his hut, intercut a few times with a single photograph of four Parisians around a kitchen table, the film gives us, in what seems to be voice-over translation, the narrative of this elderly Burmese man's journey to Paris in the 1940s to live among Surrealist artists and anthropologists and to work at a museum directed by Michel Leiris. Taken at face value, the film is a simple reverse ethnography, an account of a Burmese villager's visit to Paris, including his perceptive commentaries about

Parisian life and about the artists and intellectuals centred on the company of André Breton and Leiris. The man finds it bizarre, for instance, how Parisians dote on their dogs, a fact he contrasts with his home community's use of dogs as food. While his Surrealist friends pride themselves on their ability to explore and break taboos, the man's suggestion that they all cook a dog as a celebratory meal before his departure for home does not initially garner their enthusiasm. But he convinces them to find a dog, roast it, and consume it with him. The film's single photograph allegedly depicts Breton and others around a kitchen table, at which they have just consumed the dog. At this point in the film, the man suggests to the filmmaker (whom we do not see, since he has been behind the camera all along) that because he is leaving the man's village soon, perhaps they should do the same for him. "You should film the way we prepare it, because I think it would be useful for your American people to know how to do it," he says. "You'll see, it's very delicious.... You should make it like a step-by-step guide, you know? Like one of those TV cooking programs." The remainder of the film presents a graphic depiction of the clubbing, skinning, and roasting of a dog, in sync-sound with no voice-over.

All of this can be taken as a simple, if intentionally provocative, reverse ethnography, as a lesson in the cultural relativity of what is valued in different societies—except that the only three indications that the man is actually saying what we've seemingly heard him say are (1) the photograph, though we cannot be sure what it is a photograph of (though someone familiar with Breton would recognize that he is in the picture), (2) the fact that the French-accented voice-over occurs simultaneously over the footage of the man speaking, while he is poking his bamboo stick in the ground, and (3) the killing and roasting of the dog, which seemingly corresponds to the man's story. In actual fact, the voice-over narration was written by Ken Feingold, and when audiences have found that it does not correspond with what the old man is saying, some have become angry with the filmmaker, feeling that they have been exploited and deceived.[90] Feingold's intent is to make us question the veracity of the "truth-effect" of voice-over translation, and to carry this out, he sneakily draws us into believing what will turn out to be false. At the same time, the graphic depiction of the dog roast is "documentary reality," not, as is customary, smoothened out through editing and self-censorship, but displayed through the ethnographic method of a long, uncut, observational take.

Like other counter-ethnographies, Feingold's film places into question the reality of what film shows us. In effect, it puts quotation marks around what we see and hear, but without providing sufficient information for us to assess its truth value. If documentary evidence, as traditionally defined, is the faithful depiction or recollection of whatever event appears to be captured by the camera, films like Feingold's suggest to us that there is no such thing as *pure* documentary evidence, because the veracity of any piece of footage can only be established outside the film itself: in interviews with the director and others, in investigations of the original scene and its filming, and elsewhere. Film, however, does present evidence of *some* sort to us, and as long as viewers restrict themselves to an awareness of exactly what that is—scenes of an elderly man in front of a hut, a French-accented voice providing commentary that appears to run alongside the man's foreign-language speech, a photograph of people around a table, and footage showing the killing and roasting of a dog— then a film has nevertheless *shown us things*. How we fill in the gaps between those things to constitute a coherent narrative fabric is up to us.

The first-person essayistic films of Godard, Marker, Farocki, Jean-Pierre Gorin, Trinh Minh-Ha, Chantal Akerman, Kidlat Tahimik, Agnès Varda, Su Friedrich, Aleksandr Sokurov, Ross McElwee, Rea Tajiri, and others merely make this same point more explicit. They are, in a sense, more honest about what they present, which is a statement—poetic, confessional, polemical, or dialogical—of an author to his or her audience. Anthropomorphism in such films cannot be understood apart from the persona of the author, and therefore apart from film's capacity to speak as an *authored* form of communication. Yet the speech can be muted, complex, veiled, playful, uncertain of itself, or insistently certain (as in the muckraking political films of Michael Moore). An essay film's mode of address to us, its viewers, incorporates us into its anthropomorphic orbit insofar as we are asked to participate in its act of responding to the world. As Laura Rascaroli writes in one of the most rigorous analyses of the genre, the structure of the essay film is "that of a constant interpellation; each spectator, as an individual and not as a member of an anonymous, collective audience, is called upon to engage in a dialogical relationship with the enunciator, hence to become active, intellectually and emotionally, and interact with the text." In the best of such films, problems and questions are raised but not answered. Implicit in the essay structure is "the tentative assumption of a certain unity of the human experience, which allows two subjects to meet and communicate on the basis of such a shared experience," with the two determining and shaping one another.[91] This mutual shaping is, of course, not done within the text, but within the larger world that the text is spoken into.

All films, of course, *take place* within, and *speak* within, a communicative world that extends far beyond themselves; this is part of what it means to speak of the "ecologies" of moving images. Experimental film screenings at small venues for audiences of filmmakers and film students are one way in which films rely on a shared world to even be seen in the first place. But even a film as popular as *Avatar* or *Titanic* is a communication within the dialogue between "James Cameron" and the world. Essay films, however, are manifestly *about* the communication between filmmaker and audience; they stage this communication, performatively enacting it in a way that communicates something about the nature of filmic communication. They are meta-communicative, with part of their communication being the assertion, implied or explicitly stated, that communication is a form of action in the world.

In Marker's and Godard's more ambitious efforts, all of history—or all of cinema, as in Godard's *Histoire(s) du Cinema* (1988–98)—becomes both subject matter and material medium by which the filmmaker organizes a certain relationship to that subject matter. Many films in this genre—Alain Resnais's *Night and Fog* (*Nuit et brouillard*, 1955), for instance, as well as Resnais and Chris Marker's *Statues Also Die* (*Les statues meures aussi*, 1953)—deal with images and memories connected to events of collective or political trauma. Others, like Agnès Varda's *The Gleaners and I* (*Les glaneuses et la glaneuse*, 2000), connect the process of capturing and reusing images of the world with the process of finding, collecting, making, and reusing food and material objects. The latter film is among the finest meditations ever made on the ecologies of objects, including those of images (moving or otherwise). In its reuse of images, it shares a certain quality with found-footage films such as Chris Baldwin's *Tribulation 99* (1991), a collage of found footage from science fiction and monster flicks set to a tongue-in-cheek narrative of paranoid voice-over apocalypticism, and with the same filmmaker's *O No Coronado!* (1992), which hilariously re-creates the bumbling travels of the Spanish explorer Coronado through the southern United States, also using mainly found footage. The difference, however, is that Varda's directorial presence is more *reliable*, more ethically positioned with respect to what she shows and tells us: this is me interacting with people who glean the leftovers from already harvested French farms. Baldwin's use is a reuse that requires no moral bond, since it is a mere reuse of images. Varda's use implicates the filmmaker herself in the scenes and situations she captures, vitalizes, and makes available to us through her presence.

The film that has been hailed most often as epitomizing the essayistic genre is Chris Marker's *Sunless* (*Sans Soleil*, 1982). *Sunless* is a hybrid film: it is a global travelogue of footage shot in Iceland, Guinea-Bissau, Japan, the Cape Verde Islands, San Francisco, Hong Kong, the Île-de-France, and elsewhere, linked by a voice-over narration read by a woman retelling the contents of letters she has received from a male filmmaker named Sandor Krasna; it is also a poetic and philosophical meditation on time, place, memory, history, revolutionary politics, image, cinema, and representation; and it is an experimental montage featuring an image synthesizer that creates denaturalized images that Marker/

Krasna (or perhaps Krasna's Japanese filmmaker friend), in homage to Tarkovsky, calls "the Zone." As Catherine Lupton puts it, the film "enacts a process of sorting things out and linking them together, while continually addressing itself to the nature and function of this process."[92] The film is, in this sense, about how we, both as individuals and as social collectives, remember and how we forget. Its images (of happiness and melancholy delights), historical moments (of revolutions, of disasters), and scattered glances (of the women of Djibouti, or of the cats of Tokyo) all take place in a kind of extra-temporal zone—a space outside of time and space, or perhaps a space that is always *next to* the time and space of life but that remains somehow apart from it. It thereby offers us a reflective distance on our own lives and on the histories that embed them.

Marker's metaphorical Zone is, in this sense, like the organic machine of *Prospero's Books*, except that here we are not in the construction site, where the world's images are produced and from which they are disseminated, but rather in an observation tower hovering somewhere above the worldly fray. Here we sit with the narrative presence of Marker himself, a presence that beckons us to *think along with him*. The essay film traffics in the metaphysics of presence, and even if we know that the filmmaking moment is long past, its images and sounds reach out to us as always already *addressed*—to us, to others before us, and to those who may come after us. Films like *Sunless*, Godard's *Histoire(s) du Cinema*, and Varda's *The Beaches of Agnes* (*Les plages d'Agnès*, 2008) are about the opening into thirdness; they ask us to share in a subjectivation that is open-ended, a thirdness that is always in the process of being made. In this they urge us to subjectivate with them, to go wherever that "with" may end up taking us.

Green Identities: Images of Choice, Hope, Struggle, and Community

I have argued that cross-cultural encounters are an obvious way for films to present "anthropomorphic difference" and that "visually sovereigntist" indigenous productions and first-person essay films, each in their own way, can provide methods for either projecting (in the first case) or commenting on (in the second) cultural or socio-ecological difference, even if they do not depict such difference directly. Socio-ecological difference can also be depicted in culturally more homogeneous circumstances, at least if such difference is defined in terms of options for environmental action. Action is the primary subject matter of cinema: films depict actions, and narrative films depict characters facing circumstances and taking actions in response. This is, as I have said, at the core of filmic anthropomorphism, and it is time to examine it more directly.

The actions taken by characters are generally only as interesting as the characters themselves. That is, whether actions are interesting depends on whether the characters who perform them are fleshed out into believable, suitably complex characters and played with conviction by well-chosen actors. Alternatively, actions are as interesting as the events portrayed. Action in and of itself may captivate: we may enjoy watching a car chase because our senses enjoy the thrill of movement as we imagine—and participate in—the feeling of being in that speeding vehicle (without the possibility of death or even vehicular damage). But such scenes will not generate much interest over time unless their meanings—their exoreferentialities—bring our attention back to them repeatedly. Yet there is a sense in which action itself can be more or less convincing, and more or less admirable. Gilles Deleuze attempted to get at this in his brief but widely cited discussion of the relationship between a character and *choice*, and of the "mode of existence of the one who chooses." Deleuze distinguishes between four kinds of film character:

> The formidable man of good or the devout person (he for whom there is no question of choosing), the uncertain or indifferent (he who does not know how to, or is unable to choose), the terrible man of evil (he who chooses a first time, but can then no longer choose ...), finally the man of choice or belief (he who chooses choice or reiterates it): this is a cinema of modes of existence, of confrontation of these modes, and of their relation to an outside on which both the world and the ego depend.

This is, he continues, "not simply a question of a film-content: it is cinema-form ... which is capable of revealing to us this higher determination of thought, choice, this point deeper than any link with the world."[93] D.N. Rodowick and Ronald Bogue expand on these as four modes of life: "the 'white' men of moral absolutes," who are ideologues or true believers, "for whom the answers are already given and there is nothing to choose"; the "grey men of uncertainty or vacillation," who "lack the capacity to choose or who never know enough to be able to choose"; "creatures of evil and the blackness of drives," who "make a single choice that commits them to an inevitable and unavoidable sequence of actions that afford no further choice"; and "those who choose to choose, those who affirm a life of continuous choosing." The last are those, favoured by Deleuze, who "affirm the possible," leaping "beyond rational and ethical certainties into an open Whole, their leap being an act of trust in possibilities beyond their present comprehension." Choosing to choose is a "way of living in this world" informed by "a belief in the possibilities of this world."[94]

Whatever we may think of Deleuze's preferences—and my suspicion is that philosophical existentialists (which is what Deleuze himself was, once we scrape off his thickly layered ontological and metaphysical preoccupations) would agree with him, while others may not—what this passage helps elucidate is cinema's particular ability to depict the act of choosing. Cinema, being a medium that shows us characters in the midst of action, can reveal what choosing looks like: the agony of decision, the torment of uncertainty, the ecstasy of carrying through with a motivated action. Certain forms of effort and attainment lend themselves to cinematic depiction: the boxer (*Rocky*), the ski jumper (Herzog's *The Ecstasy of Woodcarver Steiner*), the football star, the decisive hero of one kind or another. Choosing for them becomes a kind of determination to pursue one's choice irrespective of the difficulties it brings. The most popular films depicting environmental action feature this kind of melodramatic hero, as in the crusading lawyers, muckraking journalists, or devoted activists of *Erin Brockovich* (2000), *Silkwood* (1983), *A Civil Action* (1996), *On Deadly Ground* (1994), *The China Syndrome* (1979), and *Gorillas in the Mist* (1978). To the extent that taking action is a matter of choosing and not merely of circumstances conspiring together to produce effects, cinematic depictions of such moments of choosing hold great potential for eliciting, in viewers, an understanding of the capacity to act.

Deleuze was an enemy of clichés, and environmentally themed narrative films have unfortunately abounded with clichés. In his synoptic overview of environmental politics in popular film, David Ingram summarizes the virtues and pitfalls of popular melodrama, which tends "to construct environmental issues as individualized, Manichean conflicts between one-dimensional villains and heroes," typically simplifying "the complex, often ambiguous allocation of blame and responsibility in such matters" into pat and glib formulas.[95] On the other hand, citing Richard Slotkin, Ingram suggests that even while simplifying issues, popular fictions can "dramatize ideological contradictions and work out possible resolutions to them"—for example, when images of protest serve as signifiers and reminders that collective dissent is possible.[96] Evaluating depictions of environmental heroism and villainy in terms of their value for spreading environmental messages and affects is analogous to those Marxist, feminist, or anti-racist cultural critiques that judge images of class, gender, or race based on whether they portray specific groups in a positive or negative light. Such analyses often tend toward the banal but can be insightful when they are sensitive to the complex tensions found in such representations and to social and ecological realities. Andrew Light's analysis of the portrayal of Chico

Mendes in *The Burning Season* (1994) is a rich discussion of identity politics and of the moral motivations that underpin competing identities.[97] Films like Silkwood, about nuclear whistleblower Karen *Silkwood* (who was killed), and *Erin Brockovich*, about the California toxic pollution whistleblower (who lived to tell her tale), elicit responses—particularly from female audience members—that draw energy from their portrayals of admirable, risk-taking heroines.

Yet environmentalism, by its very nature, tends to be a collective rather than an individual form of action. A film like the documentary *No Impact Man* (2009), about journalist and blogger Colin Beavan, who decides to minimize his environmental impact over the course of a year, depicts an individual taking on the daunting task of changing the world, but leaves too many questions unanswered about the wisdom of such individualism. Environmental problems are problems in the relationship between a social group and its environment. They are *collective* matters, and successfully addressing them requires collective mobilization and action. Cinema history contains many images of collective action. Well known examples of such action include the depictions of stereotypically unified class collectivities in Soviet socialist realist propaganda—such as in Eisenstein's *Battleship Potemkin*, which while not "socialist realist" nevertheless helped shape the genre—and in later Third World liberationist films, such as Gillo Pontecorvo's *The Battle of Algiers* (1966). Such strategies are not likely to work well in a context, such as today's North America, where individualism runs rampant and class consciousness is practically nonexistent. Traditionally, the "buddy film" has offered a more open-ended narrative form insofar as it tends to allow competing attitudes and ideas to be bounced off each other in dialectical fashion.

What *may* lend itself more to ecological thinking is the kind of non-linear, ensemble, or "network" narrative that has become popular over the past few decades. Network narratives consist of lines of individual narratives that converge and diverge in ways that highlight both the causal links and the indeterminacies of the connections that make events possible.[98] I will reserve my discussion of network narratives and their chaotic indeterminacies for the final chapter. Here, however, it is important to point out the centrality of "character ensembles" for films that depict environmental conflict and community. The best of such films—the dialogic ensemble films of John Sayles (*Matewan*, *Limbo*, *City of Hope*, *Lone Star*, *Sunshine State*), Robert Redford's *The Milagro Beanfield War* (1988), Bill Forsyth's *Local Hero* (1983), and others in this vein— tend to be place-centred. They are about the relations that constitute a certain town, city, or locale.

Among the more critically successful of such films—notable for its depiction of the network connections among a suite of characters, the hope their convergence makes palpable, and the harsh, unfriendly reality that hope finds itself facing—is a film that exemplifies the third mode I referred to earlier: the self-reflexive, Brechtian style of narrative. Yet it breaks out of the restrictions of that style by offering a lyrical optimism alongside its political critique. This is Swiss director Alain Tanner's *Jonah Who Will Be 25 in the Year 2000* (1976). Called by its director "a dramatic tragicomedy in political science fiction," the film concerns the legacy of the "events of '68"—the student–worker uprising in France, with its social and political experimentation, factory and university occupations, worker–farmer cooperatives, independent news agencies, and relation to allied movements elsewhere—on eight characters living in or near the Swiss city of Geneva, near the French border. Dreamers, philosophers, out- casts, and realists, each of them, as Stam puts it, is "trying, in diverse ways, to free themselves from the institutional and societal chains that oppress them": one through radical and unorthodox teaching methods in his history classes, another through tantric sex and periodic trips to India, a third through organic gardening, a fourth through undercharging pensioners at a supermarket, a fifth through foiling a malicious development scheme, and so on.[99] These charac- ters struggle to stay true to their ideals, but their tactics, for the most part, end up failing them in the long run. But through a series of events, the eight characters come to meet, live, or work at an organic farm outside the city, which becomes the site of a spontaneous and understated sort of quasi-utopian communal experiment. It, too, ultimately fails, and in the end they go back to their individual (or family) lives.

Those lives, however, are portrayed with humour, charm, and lyricism. Co-written by director Alain Tanner and English writer John Berger, the neo- Marxist art critic and novelist, the film uses an episodic and non-linear struc- ture and Brechtian distanciation techniques to engage viewers intellectually in the lives and thoughts of its characters. Following Brecht's "epic theatre" model, it consists of "a sequence of scenes closed in on themselves in order the better to reply to each other," as Tanner puts it.[100] These are constituted by "shot-sequences"—relatively long, uninterrupted, and somewhat autonomous segments, punctuated by sparse and pointillistic musical interludes, skits, and songs, moments of guerilla theatre, and occasional black-and-white scenes that function as momentary utopian thought-bubbles portraying what a character is imagining. This structure loosely follows a network narrative, made up of multiple, overlapping, and sometimes intersecting narratives. In this case, the narrative strands converge only to come apart again. But like much of what happens in the film's finer narrative threads, it is a kind of failed convergence, a utopia deferred, one that is imbued with positive, or at least bittersweet, affect, so that the "almost" becomes a Blochian "not yet"—a critical utopianism that highlights the conditions that make the characters' dreams seem presently unreachable, but worthy and attainable in a possible future.

This critical utopianism, or "counterpoint of hope and realism" as Berger calls it, is introduced at the film's outset when, against the backdrop of the statue of Geneva's most famous citizen, Jean-Jacques Rousseau, an off-camera voice quotes Rousseau decrying civilized man's enslavement by institutions. In a Rousseauian vein, the film suggests that humans are convivial by nature but that this nature has become constrained and misshapen by unjust political, educational, and economic institutions. The film's title is a reference to the child born to one of the film's couples, named after the biblical Jonah who was saved by a whale. In a memorable scene, the characters paint a mural of themselves in vivid colours on a wall bordering the farm. In the film's final scenes, preceded by the caption "A Day in 1980" (five years after the preceding scenes), the five-year-old Jonah is seen alone marking graffiti on the same wall. This image can be taken to mean that art remains as a material carrier of the characters' temporarily suspended utopian aspirations and that the child, born of the belly of the whale and of the utopian moment of their communal experiment, remains to pick up where the others left off. The film is, like this image, a fable; it is, as Richard Porton calls it, a "pedagogical exercise" that "without excessive heavyhandedness" struggles "to endorse, and by implication teach, concerted resistance during a period when radical hopes were waning."[101] Reactions to the film have remained largely positive, at least on the political left. Writing in *Dissent* magazine nearly thirty years after its release, Joanne Barkan noted that the hopes and desires portrayed in it are those that still animate the democratic left: "dignity in work, education for democratic citizenship, environmental stewardship of the planet, non-material fulfillment."[102]

The effects of such films depend, of course, on their audiences. For a traditional environmental melodrama, the (environmentalist) hope may be that audience members will identify with the individual hero who takes on an environmental challenge and acts to change the world for the better. By contrast, in films like *Jonah* the hope is that audiences will identify less with individual characters than with the collective hopes and dreams they embody. There are moments in such network narratives that crystallize certain feelings of possibility—the openness of the world to change. *Daughters of the Dust* presents this sort of extended moment, albeit one that may only feel that way for its intended primary audience, which is African-American women. (Whether it does for others will depend on many factors, including the capacity of viewers to step out of their own life experiences and identify with those of others.) *Heaven's Gate*, though it was a box office disaster, was precisely about the collective possibilities, squelched as they were, of a moment in time. In a similarly non-linear, slow-motion kind of way, *Jonah* presents such a moment of possibility, although with so little gain to show for its characters, it may seem that it is not hopeful enough. Perhaps the imagination of the political Left remains too encumbered with its own failures, or too conscious of the monolithic potency of its opposite—the capitalism that is everywhere in evidence around it.

Films depicting individual rather than collective possibilities may ultimately seem more believable. Heroic individuals overcoming great odds still make for some of the most successful and critically lauded storylines, from the *Star Wars* films to the *Lord of the Rings* trilogy, from *Million Dollar Baby* (2004) to *Slumdog Millionnaire* (2008) to *Precious: Based on the Novel "Push" by Sapphire* (2008). Even when they fail to overcome those odds, as in the greatest tragedies, the appeal in part is that we can relive not only the vanishing of those possibilities, but the counterfactual imagination of how things could have happened *otherwise*.

This feeling that action is possible and that it is within our grasp is constitutive of the feeling that we can *become*—become genuinely human, for the first time perhaps, or become something else we can only dream of. This is film's anthropomorphic promise, its capacity to open the world for us so that the world becomes open to change. Between our relationship to the world, depicted geomorphically in cinema, and our capacity to act in and through it (perceived as film's anthropomorphism), there is a field of connections and relations that normally remains relatively stable, but that films can also render open, vital, and alive. This, the focus of the next chapter, is film's biomorphism.

5

ANIMA MORALIA
Journeys across Frontiers

From *Grizzly Man* (2005). Directed by Werner Herzog. Credit: Lions Gate Films/ Photofest. Shown: Timothy Treadwell with grizzly bear.

[The] world does nothing but signify. To be a world is to effervesce with an excess of signification. That this should be so is the product of an apparent contradiction: the world communicates because it is not whole.

Sean Cubitt, *EcoMedia*[1]

Cinema is a sensuous object, but it also comes – and becomes – before us a sensing and sensual subject and, in the address of the eye, allows us to see what seems a visual impossibility: that we are at once subject and object, the seer and the seen.

[. . .] the cinema provides us with a philosophical model that gives us concrete and empirical insight into and makes objectively visible the reversible, dialectical, and social nature of our own subjective vision.

Vivian Sobchack, *The Address of the Eye*[2]

There is no manifestation of life which does not contain in a rudimentary state – latent or potential – the essential characters of most other manifestations. [. . .] [T]here is not a single property of vegetable life that is not found, in some degree, in certain animals; not a single characteristic feature of the animal that has not been seen in certain species at certain moments in the vegetable world.

Henri Bergson, *Creative Evolution*[3]

Animal images in art, religion, and dreams are not merely depictions *of* animals. Animal images are also showing us images *as* animals, living beings that prowl and growl and must be nourished; the imagination, a great animal, a dragon under whose heaven we breathe its fire.

James Hillman, *Egalitarian Typologies versus the Perception of the Unique*[4]

They're here!

Poltergeist (1982)

EXPANDING ON A NOTE in Maurice Merleau-Ponty's late writings, film phenomenologist Vivian Sobchack writes that "more than any other medium of human communication, the moving picture makes itself sensuously and sensibly manifest as the *expression of experience by experience*. A film is an act of seeing that makes itself seen, an act of hearing that makes itself heard, an act of physical and reflective movement that makes itself reflexively felt and understood." Cinema, she continues, "transposes, without completely transforming, those modes of being alive and consciously embodied in the world that count for each of us as *direct* experience." Cinema "uses *modes of embodied existence* (seeing, hearing, physical and reflective movement) as the vehicle, the 'stuff,' the substance of its language."[5]

Sobchack focuses much of her analysis of cinema on the relationship between the viewer and the viewed, which is more complex in the case of film than one may initially think. Cinema, in her assessment, is not only a viewed object but also a viewing subject. It is bi-directional in that it *selects views* of the world to show us, its viewers. While this relationship between the viewer—the abstract "us" or the concrete me, you, and others—and the "viewed view," or the film, will be an important part of what I examine in this chapter, my main focus will be on the film-world itself. Specifically, it will be on the biomorphic dynamism of film-worlds—that is, on the animate forms that specific film-worlds present to us. In any such world, the things viewed can also be "viewed view(er)s," and the heard objects can be expressive, speaking or sounding subjects. As we witness the play of relations between viewers and viewed, hearers and heard—the relations that constitute the liveliness of what is shown to us in a film—we, the final viewers, become engaged in that dynamism, because we recognize it as more or less the same kind of dynamism as that of the world that precedes the film. If film is "the expression of experience by experience," it *moves* us because we recognize it *as* experience. And if the universe is "experience all the way down," as process-relational philosophy asserts, then film can also be a medium for communicating the experientiality that is part of all living form.

In its focus on the play between a film's anthropomorphism, its geomorphism, and its biomorphism, this chapter builds on the previous two. The three morphogenetic registers are ultimately inseparable, since the former two emerge out of the dynamism making up the third: they are temporary resting points at either end of an interactive shuttle. The two ends of the shuttle are those of action and conditionality, figure and ground, the anthropomorphic and the geomorphic, and it is between them that our experience of a film-world unfolds. This chapter, like the previous two, will proceed from a general exploration of biomorphism to a specific examination of certain of the forms it takes: in this case, the forms it takes in nature and wildlife documentaries, in animation (especially Disney) and horror films, and in films that explore and sometimes blur the boundaries between humans and non-human animals. This blurring of the boundaries is something that unfolds in our experience of a film, and this chapter will explore some of the ways we are drawn in along film's vectors—the movements being offered us, which we accept or resist either as we choose or—perhaps as often as not—choicelessly and unreflectively.

The chapter, then, is most concerned with movement: the movement of things on the screen before us; the movement of what is seen, heard, and done between the subjects and objects of a film, and between the subjects and objects of the film-viewing experience; and the movement of our own cognitive and affective involvement in and out of a film-world. It is movement that enables the blurring or breaking of boundaries, and movement of a different kind that erects those boundaries in the first place, framing what is doable and allowable in one place but not in another, for one type of thing but not for another. The movement is sensory and perceptual; it is part of what Whitehead calls "prehension"—that is, the taking into account of something by an emergent subject. But, following a process-relational account, that subject does not emerge once and for all. It emerges moment to moment, its subjectivity circulating back and forth between it and the other things with which it interacts; and those things, too, are always active within this interperceptual circulation.

Together, all of this movement makes up the biomorphism, or the becoming-aliveness, of all three levels of our study: the film-world, the film-experience, and the relationship between film and the extra-filmic world. As such, it takes cinema as both *depicting* the animate and as *being* animate, and it assumes that in the movement of this animacy is a vast space for ethical action (this space will be explored in still greater depth in the book's final chapter). The chapter title plays on the ethical dimension of this animacy: it recalls Theodor Adorno's reflections on morality in a post-Auschwitz world, *Minima Moralia*, just as that volume recalled Aristotle's *Magna Moralia*.[6] But it frames this tangle with morality within relations that are constituted by the sensual embrace of things that are alive and vibrant and that are only sometimes human and sometimes not. It takes us, then, in the direction of an ethics of the image—and of the imaging—that moves through and across very different kinds of bodies in a universe that is open, alive, and unpredictable.

Pointing, Seeing, Gazing

Children start pointing at things sometime between eight and fifteen months of age. To do this intentionally, they need first to understand how to look where their caregiver is looking, that is, how to follow their mother's gaze. The term in physics for this following of a line, including a line of sight, is "vector."[7] This skill, for children, is both spatial and intersubjective in its perception of an intention in the other's gaze. Following the gaze means gazing in the direction of another's gaze and thereby triangulating between oneself, another, and a third that is the gazed-at and on which intended meanings converge. This is a form of Peircian thirdness: in the interaction between child and mother (a secondness) and between each of them and an object (additional secondnesses), a meaningful relationship (thirdness) is formed.

Seeing is rather distinct from the other senses. When we hear, what we hear is locatable in the world around us, but its impression on us is immersive; it seems to fill the space around us. When we add the olfactory, tactile, and kinesthetic senses, we get a world that is more like William James's "blooming, buzzing confusion" than it is the clearly delineated world of sight. Sounds and voices blend into a chorus, a harmony, a counterpoint, a cacophony. Smells confuse the distinction between what is me and what is you. With sight, however, it is clear to me where my flesh ends and where yours begins and that the space between them is empty until and unless we touch.

Even so, seeing you, I recognize (if your eyes are open) that you may see me and that you may see my seeing you. But if you have no eyes by which to see, or no eyes that I know of—if you are an object of my gaze but not a subject in your own right—then the seeing is one way. If you are, say, a wall, a rock, a photograph, or a film, then you do not see me—unless we extend the relational ecology to include not only the film but its maker, distributor, and seller, as well as the views that it depicts and that I may wish to seek out and visit (or carefully avoid) after seeing. At this point things get complicated. As Susan Sontag argued in *On Photography*: "In teaching us a new visual code, photographs alter and enlarge our notions of what is worth looking at and what we have a right to observe. They are a grammar and, even more importantly, an ethics of seeing. Finally, the most grandiose result of the photographic enterprise is to give us the sense that we can hold the whole world in our heads—as an anthology of images."[8] Chapter 3 explored some of the ways in which films have become a way for us to "hold the whole world in our heads"—though I would say in our bodies as well—and a means by which we transmit *values* about how to do this.

But if we hold the world, or some partial and edited version of it, in our heads and bodies, we humans are not the only ones who do that. Anything that retains a memory of an earlier event can be said to *model* the world via images. That is how living things evolve: by learning, creatively adapting, and passing on those adaptations from one generation to the next. In a process-relational view, every "actual occasion" involves a taking account of the world—of what is experienced—and a responding to it, with the "taking account" altering what is passed on to the next moment through the means available for that (which may be genetic, epigenetic, cultural, or some other means). Images amplify our ability to "hold the world" and to thereby take account of it *differently*. They extend, accentuate, shape, distort, and fragment that world and rework its features into new and meaningful arrays. And to the extent that the images themselves consist of other imaging entities, things that respond to other things, the imaging gaze is always interactive.

In contrast to the dominant visuality that I described at the outset of this book—that of the self-contained, monocular Cartesian observer—what I am suggesting here is that *looks always circulate*. In *Looking West*, John Dorst argued that dominant modes of Western visuality are, in our time, being supplemented and even supplanted by a "circulating look," a mode of visuality in which lines of sight are multiplied, visual mastery is rendered uncertain, objects become elusive and deceptive, and the apparatus of looking is acknowledged as constitutive of the act of seeing. This visuality of the circulating look is, he suggests, an effect of the postmodernization of capitalism, that is, of capital's extension into new modes of consumption, in which the accumulation of goods and capital "is inseparable from the ceaseless desire to mark semiotic differences and to engage in the endlessly renewable display of identity."[9] But it is also a recognition that other sets of eyes have entered the network of exchange set up by competing gazes. Dorst refers to the example of Devils Tower, or Bear Butte, the unusually shaped rock monument in Wyoming that is famous for being the landing site of the alien mothership in Steven Spielberg's *Close Encounters of the Third Kind*. At the *real* Devils Tower, the circulating gaze now officially includes the eyes of Native Americans, whose claims on the monument have been recognized by the National Park Service, which manages the site.[10]

This circulation of gazes has, in a sense, long been part of mainstream cinema. It is found in conventions like the "shot–reverse shot," whereby we see something from the perspective of one character, and then we see the same thing from the perspective of another. The two mix and blend into a perception of a seamless whole, the scene as it ostensibly "really is." But cinema today often involves a more complex array of perspectival shots and points of view, with many variables—camera angle and placement, shutter speed, depth of field, lens magnification, camera movement, the mixing of analog and digital formats, and so on—interacting to create a dynamic ensemble of affectively imbued views. Some of these views may be recognized as "point of view shots," fragments of the world seen from a particular character's first-person perspective. Others are clearly intended as third-person, "objective" views. Many shots are something in between the two, as in a moving camera that we might recognize (if we stop to think about it) as hand-held by, or resting on the shoulder of, an individual who is moving through a scene, but that also gives us a sense of mobile subjectivity within a scene that is assumed to be objectively there.

Nature and wildlife films have characteristically tended toward a third-person perspective, with a "voice of God" narrator typically adding to this sense of omniscient objectivity. Sometimes such films introduce a first-person perspective, such as that of the narrator (say, David Attenborough) or of a scientific observer or interview subject, whose quest for a particular animal or natural phenomenon viewers are elicited to follow. There are films, however, that present what may approximate the point of view of a *non-human* subject: a bird's-eye view, or even a narrative expressing something like the perspective of an animal (as in the French-language version of *March of the Penguins*, which I will discuss below). These rarely consider the actual perceptual capacities of non-human animals, such as the echolocation abilities of birds or bats, which would be difficult or impossible to reproduce audiovisually. However, techniques such as microphotography and X-ray, infrared, or thermal photography do allow for a much-expanded capacity to "see" things that we normally would not be able to see and thus extend our optical capacities into the ranges of animals that perceive what we, when technologically unaided, do not.

In the world of ecological exchanges, then, a "circulating gaze" need not be restricted to that of two-eyed bipeds like us. Any gaze is a particular form of trained observation, a regulated mode or style of prehension. Recall that for Whitehead, prehension is the basic relational act. It is the grasping of one thing, or many things, by another, where the grasped is a concresced and objectified occasion available as data to the other, and the grasping is the subjective form of the prehension itself in the creative synthesis of its becoming. Each such synthesis results in a (however slightly) altered world. At the mesocosmic level at which we humans consciously dwell, there is enough regularity among the societies of actual occasions for us to be able to perceive stable objects: I, you, this animal, that film, this country, that decade, these lives. But at its core, each prehension is a creative act, a relay or vector along which the world itself unfolds, continually generating the next set of affordances for further prehensions.

If a child's pointing at something is a skilled, learned procedure for manifesting Peircian thirdness, then the full spectrum of prehensive activities that make up the human and non-human worlds makes for a universe overflowing with thirdness. This flow requires embodiment: it is a flow that occurs through the interperceptual dynamism of sensory or prehensive contact, coupled with the interiority, the subject-making (and *Umwelt*-making) by which that contact becomes an exchange and an experiential event. Film funnels the options of this ceaseless relay into two main perceptual channels—the visual and the auditory, which are the dominant features of the human sensory apparatus. But with a world that is in motion, and a medium (cinema) that is made of motion, the world has a way of slipping through even into these restricted channels.

One of the promises of the cinematic medium is the enhancement of perception to include things that the unaided eye and ear cannot perceive. As it happens, this enhancement of perception has been entangled with the animate since the beginnings of cinema.

Animating the Image, Imaging the Animate

The use of film to reveal what happens *in nature* that cannot otherwise be *naturally observed* by humans goes back to the origins of cinematic media. The cinema, Paul Sheehan notes, "is born with the movement of animals—a horse jumping, a seagull in flight, some fish swimming in a tank, a cat licking its paws and drinking from a bowl."[11] In the early films and pre-cinematic moving images of Eadweard Muybridge, scientist and "chronophotographer" Étienne-Jules Marey, August and Louis Lumière, and Thomas Edison, it was these animals and others that embodied the very kineticism that the moving image was intended to capture. With the aid of multiple cameras and a projection instrument he called a zoopraxiscope, Muybridge demonstrated, through his motion picture studies of galloping horses, that all four horse's hooves were in the air at once, thus settling a popular debate at the time. Marey in turn settled the mystery of how a cat manages to land on its feet when dropped from a height.

Early motion picture technology arrested motion in order to reveal how it worked; it made motion tangible and decipherable to an extent that had not been previously possible. For these early filmmakers, animal motility served to underwrite the cinematic medium, lending evidential support to its reality claims. Akira Lippit draws out the logic of this to argue that "cinema *is* an animal, animality a form of technology, technology an aspect of life. A life forged in the radical reanimation of the conditions of vitality as such."[12] When an animal is killed in a film—as in the infamous example of Thomas Edison's sixty-second film *Electrocuting an Elephant* (1903), which was intended to make the case against the alternating current (AC) electrical system that rivalled his own direct current (DC)—the animal's death, Lippit argues, is transfigured into a kind of eternal life of its own: the film "transfers the anima of the animal, its life, into a phantom archive, preserving the movement that leaves the elephant in the technology of animation" (which turns out to be a kind of technological re-reanimation of a dying pachiderm, in this case).[13] "The animal survives its death as a film, as another form of animal, captured by the technologies of animation."[14]

At the same time, cinematic animals resist being fully drawn into the narratives and fantasies the medium makes available. Non-human animals, as we know, are not actors, at least not to the same degree as human performers. They may be made to do certain things—cajoled into or trained for the task—but in this they are not reducible to the performative labour required by the film industry. Because animals "thwart the techniques of manipulation and control that are the chief operating principles of feature-film production," they are one of the clearest ways in which "reality" intervenes in the making of a film.[15] Sheehan argues that in breaking through the "falsely protective aura of the image, the aura that rules out the accidental and the unintentional," animals bring "a kind of indeterminate *otherness* into the frame."[16] Whatever attempts are made to have the animals perform some lesson, analogy, or metaphor for humans, "the recalcitrant actuality of animal being inevitably stymies all attempts at complete anthropomorphosis."[17]

But it is not just non-human animals that do this: it is children, landscapes, environmental conditions, and even human actors to the extent that they elude the intentions of the filmmakers and even of themselves. It is, in fact, the world and all its actants that stymie film's intended outcomes with their "recalcitrant actuality." Once an image or sound is there in the film, its range of potential meanings opens up to the interpretive inventiveness of its viewers, and to the degree that the filmmakers had intended *specific* meanings (as opposed to any that may arise for their viewers), this range will always be larger than that which had been intended. There is a "more than what was intended" both at the point of origin, in the firstness of the images and sounds taken from the profilmic world, and at the point of reception, which is the thirdness that continues generating other thirdnesses as it ricochets from one viewing and interpretive context to another.

The process by which images and meanings are produced as they ricochet between (emergent) selfhood and (emergent) otherness, however, is one that is crystallized in the cinematic animal precisely because the animal shares more or less the same sensory equipment we do—eyes and ears, for instance. However, we do not know to what extent, if any, they share or transcend the *interpretive* capacities we ascribe to ourselves. In other words, when we see an animal in a film, we know, or suspect, that animal to be a *real* animal, not an actor. When that animal returns our gaze, even as we hold a camera facing toward them, we do not know what they make of us. Jonathan Burt, in *Animals in Film*, insightfully dissects the ways in which the "image of the animal's eye" signals "the significant participation of the animal in the visual field."[18] In a film like Robert Redford's *The Horse Whisperer* (1998), Burt writes, the gaze of the screen animal "marks the point of contact across the species": "the central link between horse and human throughout the film is the look as exemplifying the frequent shots of the horse's eye."[19] Paul Sheehan expands on this notion to make a case for the disruptive role of animals in the films of Werner Herzog. Animals are a prominent motif in Herzog's films: the rats that take over the northern European town in *Nosferatu* (1979), the monkeys that besiege the raft in the closing minutes of *Aguirre: The Wrath of God* (1972), the dancing chicken of *Stroszek* (1976), the cats in *Woyzeck* (1979) and *Heart of Glass* (1976), the bears in *Grizzly Man* (2005), a film I will examine closely later in this chapter, and so on. Sheehan argues that they serve as "indicators of the stubbornly materialistic background world upon which Herzog mounts his visionary quests" and that, in the process, they "delineate the boundaries of [Herzog's] dreaming and temper its rhetorical excesses."[20]

Animals in these cases bound the human world by presenting what is outside and beyond it, greater (or lesser) than it. They do this more directly than do plants or other entities because they are recognizably closer to us in their capacities yet still separated by a gulf whose width we cannot really measure. Animals displayed in a film can, of course, serve a multitude of functions, each of which plays out a spectrum of effects. They can simply happen to be there, as in documentary footage that captures a passing dog or seagull without intending to do so. They can be intentional commentaries on the humans—symbols, metaphors, allegories, and the like. They can be simple stand-ins for those humans: animals like Mickey Mouse who are less mouse than story personae, little people representing something people-like in the guise of something less people-like. Or they can be themselves, either generically (Lassie as the template for "good, smart dog") or actually (as in a film about the gorilla Koko or Nim Chimpsky, the chimpanzee featured in *Project Nim*).

Like Muybridge's horses and Marey's cats, however, insects, plants, and other life forms can also be "re-perceived" and "transcoded" through the image-altering capacities of the moving image. Time-lapse photography, as in Paul Moss and Thelma Schnee's *Power of Plants* (1949), has often been used to show plants growing through rocks, metals, and other obstacles. The use of cinema to provide a window onto the lives of other organisms and of largely unhumanized ecosystems is epitomized by the films of Jean Painlevé (from 1928's *La Pieuvre/Devilfish* to 1945's *Le Vampire/The Vampire*, to 1972's *Acera, ou Le bal des sorcières / Acera, or the Witch's Dance*, about acera mollusks) as well as by the Walt Disney Studio's True-Life Adventures series, beginning with *Seal Island* (1948), *Beaver Valley* (1950), and *Nature's Half Acre* (1951), and culminating in commercial breakthroughs like *The Living Desert* (1953) and *The Vanishing Prairie* (1954). What meaning emerges from these windows onto other lives depends on the shape of the window, but also on the cultural context and the viewers: Disney's films have tended to be seen as conservative in their effects, whereas Painlevé's films accentuated those very features of their chosen organisms that posed some challenge to conventional assumptions and values—about sex, gender, reproduction, and social dynamics.[21]

More recent films like Claude Nuridsany and Marie Pérennou's *Microcosmos* (1996) take full advantage of developments in microphotography to present the worlds of insects as they have rarely been seen before: ants in a metropolis-like anthill tending to a colony of aphids, a dung beetle struggling like Sisyphus to push its ball over barriers along the ground, and so on. While we enjoy these scenes because of their anthropomorphism (in the traditional sense of the word), our affective involvement with them is at the level of bodily indices: we understand what it *feels* like to move a certain way, or to make repeated efforts in the face of large obstacles. Here we are crossing a boundary toward accessing a different subjectivity from ours, but we maintain the umbilical cord of our imaginary embodiment as we cross it.

There are boundaries that separate us from the more or less known—animals, plants, insects, matter. But there are also boundaries that are continually being pushed open by technological innovations and by the imagination that accompanies them. Experimental filmmakers from Dziga Vertov to Stan Brakhage have explored film's potential to produce new subjective perceptions of the world, so as to allow viewers to become "an eye outside the eye," in Jean Epstein's words.[22] Theorists from Epstein and Vertov to Brakhage and Deleuze have probed and celebrated this ability of the camera eye to become a new, technological eye that would see the world unencumbered by the human form. Yet every eye is an eye, a point that draws into itself the world that surrounds it, and a perspective on the images that an eye can perceive. Even the most technological eyes have tended to be understood in terms familiar to us from something that is already there "in nature"—for instance, from insects, those models of "swarming, distributed intelligence" that, Jussi Parikka argues, have served as a source of potent metaphors for a century and a half of media theory.[23] The eye through which cinema sees the world is both human, because it is modelled on our seeing of the world, and unhuman, because it is its own, an eye whose capacities we can explore and push to its own limits.

"One of cinema's greatest powers," wrote Jean Epstein, "is its animism. Objects have their attitudes. Trees gesticulate."[24] This use of cinema to reveal the liveliness and instability of things that otherwise appear stable and inert to us—to render *lively* those things that a camera captures—brings to fruition cinema's promise to act as a form of "nature writing." The emphasis here is on the active *writing*, with the camera as *stylo*, as pen, in Alexandre Astruc's Vertovian phrase. When examining what a cinematic "nature writing" might be, it is important to consider both the genre that comes closest to that literary genre—nature and wildlife film—and the animation genre that literally writes the inanimate into animate form. First, then, how do so-called nature and wildlife films present the world, and what is the "nature" and the "wildlife" they present?

Writing, Seeing, and Faking Nature

The tradition of nature and wildlife films is many decades old. The precursors, tributaries, and subgenres of these films include any and all of the following: animal *actualités* (which were among the earliest films made), hunting and safari films, animal adventure stories, scientific-educational films, "blue chip" documentaries (from Disney's "True-Life Adventures" to today's glitzy spectacles such as the *Planet Earth* television miniseries), outdoor and sporting documentaries, action-adventure series (featuring such intrepid explorers as Jacques Cousteau, Steve Irwin, and Jeff Corwin), conservation films, and animal welfare films. Critical analysis of the genre, however, has been slow in coming. Only in the past two decades have critical histories of wildlife film been written. For the most part, those histories have shown that while such films may promise a kind of documentary realism in their portrayals of nature, what they actually offer is much closer to a particular, and distorted, *idea* of nature than to the thing itself. In the most incisive and detailed critique of the genre, *Wildlife Films*, Derek Bousé argues that wildlife/wilderness/natural-history films and television present an image of nature that is "molded to fit the medium," whose "market-driven, formulaic emphasis on dramatic narrative and ever-present danger" results in a natural world full of "movement, action, and dynamism," but one in which decontextualized subjects, especially those of "charismatic mega-fauna," dwell in visually magnificent settings well outside human history or the vagaries and complexities of social and scientific practice. As a result of conditioning by television documentaries, Bousé suggests, visitors to national parks commonly complain "that the animals don't seem to *do* anything; they just lie there."[25]

Many elements of the medium, including the use of telephoto and tele-scopic lenses to bring distant objects closer, and of remote and simulated sounds to perpetuate the illusion of being there, as well as the seamless insertion of stock images and of technical effects such as slow or speeded-up motion, and even the use of trained animals to simulate wild ones, ostensibly bring viewers a sense of unmediated reality based in an epistemology of documentary realism. As Bousé and others demonstrate, however, they do these things in deceptive ways, conveying a perception of nature that is very different from that which can actually be found "in nature." (This is aside from the sometimes horrific abuses that have accompanied the making of animal and wildlife films, which Bousé documents with unflagging rigour.) In nature documentaries, Karla Armbruster argues, viewers are commonly encouraged to identify with an omniscient narrator and all-seeing camera; this ensures an "innocence of involvement in the forces affecting the natural world" even while allowing a penetration of that world's most inaccessible reaches.[26] When this is coupled with the ideological tendencies imposed by the political economy of documentary production, what we get is a situation in which, as Bill McKibben describes it, "the upshot of a nature education by television is a deep fondness for certain species and a deep lack of understanding of systems, or of the policies that destroy those systems."[27]

In *Reel Nature*, Gregg Mitman examines the tensions between wildlife film-makers' ostensible mandate of scientific accuracy and the commercial imperative that has sustained the industry. He details controversies over the staging of scenes—including claims of nature being "faked"—in such documentaries as the television series *Wild America* (1982–96), and the ways in which the voyeuristic portrayal of wild animals objectifies them and naturalizes a view of animals as being "there for us." Assessing the relationship between nature/wildlife films and changing American ideas of wilderness and of other forms of social categorization (race, class, gender), Mitman argues that Walt Disney's sentimental portrayal of animals "sanctified the universal 'natural' family as a cornerstone of the American way of life."[28] Ultimately, he writes, Disney's "framing of nature as entertainment reinforced a tourist and recreational economy that places a much greater demand on the very areas that conservationists [are] trying to protect from the influx of people and the values of consumer society."[29] Along similar lines, Scott MacDonald argues that while Disney's True-Life Adventures "may have created in their first audiences a greater awareness of the natural environment," it was "an awareness qualified by a deep complacency," with the natural world being valued "precisely to the degree it can be understood to reflect and confirm the ideology of contemporary American middle-class family life."[30]

At their best, these critiques by Bousé, Mitman, MacDonald, Armbruster, McKibben, Alex Wilson, Cynthia Chris, and others contextualize the genre of nature and wildlife documentaries in order to show not only that they do not present pure nature at all, but also that they *do* reveal the changing assumptions that people bring to "nature." Yet once it is understood that nature films are *not* nature, we are still left with the question of what they are and what *nature* is. This makes things difficult, for the assumption that there is a *pure nature*, one we can objectively access, carries a heavy epistemological price tag. Faking nature, after all, can only be done if there is a *real* nature "out there" that can somehow be brought "in here"—into the film. But this very idea that nature is "out there" and not "in here" requires a dualistic separation of *reality* from its *representation* that a process-relational perspective disputes.[31] If, on the other hand, we take Henri Bergson's arguments to heart, we have to admit (even against Bergson's own conclusions about the medium) that cinema is literally a form of "nature writing," or at least of "nature imaging." It, like the world itself, consists of images in movement. Film is, in this sense, as much *nature naturing*—nature being its own animate form of liveliness—as is anything.

But let us look closer at the charge that wildlife documentarians present a "faked nature." It would surprise many viewers to find out how much of what passes for wildlife documentary is actually constructed in the editing studio from shots that are barely related to their final uses. Even a series as widely lauded as *Planet Earth* (2006) is hardly what it, at first blush, seems. According to its executive producer, only about 30 percent of the rushes for this phenomenally successful international co-production were shot at normal 24-frame-per-second speed. The remainder were shot in "slow motion," though only slow enough (for instance, at 45 frames per second) to make the movement of animals more "beautiful," not slow enough to appear obviously "unnatural."[32] Similarly, as *Planet Earth*'s original narrator, Sir David Attenborough, once commented in another context, "When you're filming with a long-focus lens, you can't record the real sounds; many of those horrible bone-crunching noises are actually done by a man in a studio, carefully crunching bones in front of a microphone."[33]

This discrepancy between what viewers see and hear in a nature film and what they *think* they see and hear is important to understand and account for. But it doesn't follow that the nature portrayed is necessarily a nature *faked*. Or it does follow, but only if we agree to uphold the dichotomy of a nature "out there" and a non-nature "in here." The "nature" presented by nature documentaries is almost always a nature that is "out there": a nature populated by animals engaged in the "struggle for life" or something of the sort. And that struggle happens to be faster, more violent, and more exciting than any scenes we would see if we were to film a random moment of the natural world—if nature could be captured from behind, as it were, caught in the act of being exactly what it is. This nature "out there," however, already includes what we have made of it, insofar as it is already pre-interpreted *as* "nature," which means it is no longer a random moment of the natural world *worlding*. As I argued in Chapter 3, definitions of nature—as the non-human world, or as the pre-linguistic, pre-cultural, pre-technological world of biotic processes, laws, and forms, or as the ambient background and essential bedrock over and against which the human adventure arises as an exceptional and transcendent force—are all cultural and historical productions. They are relationally mediated by what people do and how they live on the Earth, but they are not universals. The faking of nature, then, can only mean the faking of a *particular* nature, that is, the presentation of something as if it were something else. In this sense, the distortions of a nature documentary can be judged as faked if they are intended to represent things that they are not. But do viewers *believe* that what they see is actually nature as it would be out there, beyond the camera's grasp? This is what we are not sure about, and it is the crux of the "faked nature" problem.

It is Bousé who presents the most sustained critique of nature films' shortcomings in delivering *real* nature. Yet his argument relies on the same dichotomy of a nature "out there"—most readily found in the "wilderness"—and a culture "in here," among us humans. He begins his first chapter, "The Problem of Images," with a claim that already assumes a great deal about nature. "Anyone who spends time outdoors," he writes, "has probably realized that most *real* experiences of the natural world, away from cities and development, tend to be experiences of serenity and quietude. This is what has accounted for most notions of nature's regenerative and spiritually redemptive power." He continues: "Yet stillness and silence have almost no place in wildlife film, or in film and television generally," which are about "movement, action, and dynamism" while "nature is generally not."[34] Bousé is assuming here not only that *real* nature is "away from cities and development" but also that it is not a place where humans live or work at all. It is a place, rather, for "experiences of serenity and quietude." Yet this concept of nature is one that emerged only with the rise of a class of citizens who *could* retreat to a nature purified of its wilder denizens, be they human (such as the commoners, whose rights to land were taken away through Enlosures Acts and other land grabs) or non-human (wolves, wild animals, weeds, and so on). With its assumption that nature is a place for "serenity and quietude" because it is so *for us*, this concept of nature is not only anthropocentric, but also *classist*, since nature has hardly been that for most people throughout history, who had to work, often hard, for subsistence *in* nature.

Another line of attack in Bousé's arsenal is the criterion of temporal realism. Comparing "the purposes of film and television" with the "realities of nature," he asks us to "consider the example of African lions, who often spend up to twenty hours a day at rest. In a one-hour (fifty-two-minute) wildlife film for television this would amount to about forty-two minutes of relative inactivity—true to nature, perhaps, but anathema to distributors, broadcasters, and advertisers."[35] What Bousé doesn't mention is that by this criterion of a temporally "proportional" representation of reality, as he calls it—or what we might call a "random slice of nature"—edited films would have to be replaced with twenty-four-hour static surveillance camera videos, and storytelling itself would have to be replaced by mere sitting around watching things happen of their own accord. Not allowing the temporal compression made possible by narrative editing would mean not allowing drama, characters, story, or artistry. If such a criterion were imposed, all that would remain in place would be the dichotomy between the watchers (us), safely ensconced on one side of the screen, and the watched (the lions) in their secure captivity on the other side.

Bousé's standard for critiquing nature documentary, then, is a realism that aims to faithfully represent a certain world as it is, a god's-eye view that would neither affect nor be affected by the reality it reproduces. To be fair, this is more or less the same goal as that of some of the ethnographic and observational filmmakers I discussed in the previous chapter, who attempted to present the reality of a foreign cultural event by providing as much context, and as little manipulation, as possible. This goal is laudable and can serve useful pedagogical purposes. But it does not follow that it is "closer to reality" than any other kind of filmmaking. Bousé contrasts wildlife films with "avant-garde films, music videos, and advertisements," which "may all start from no reality at all, and stay there," and with "Hollywood films," which "may start with only surface reality, and penetrate no deeper." Wildlife films, he argues, "have reality as their foundation and starting point, yet typically proceed through a series of artificial formal interventions, as well as fictionalized, dramatic narratives."[36]

This sort of parsing out results in an impoverished view of reality, one that a process-relational perspective rejects in principle. One could argue, as Werner Herzog has often done, that it is the film that attempts to portray exactly what happened as it happened—"just the facts, ma'am"—that remains on the *surface* of reality, probing no deeper than appearances.[37] Reality, in a process-relational view, is thick with meaning, intention, feeling, desire, expectation, anticipation, and narrative; it is seething with thirdness. Exoreferentiality is always there, as an array of potentials that actualize in the encounter between the image and the viewer. Its referents are "external" whether they refer directly to real or historical events; or to images, ideas, or concepts known from other images and films—and thus bearing an already mediated relationship to "real events"—or even to entirely new images and ideas. Mediation is, after all, part of the reality being mediated by image technologies. Following Peirce, mediation goes "all the way down," even if unmediated firstness arises at every relational moment.

The best filmmakers, whether of fictional or documentary works, realize this. Capturing this "always mediatedness" may mean, for instance, presenting a diversity of perspectives on an event or phenomenon. This strategy reaches its apogee in films like Jean Epstein's *The Three-Sided Mirror* (1927) and Akira Kurosawa's *Rashomon* (1950). The latter film juxtaposes multiple witnesses' perspectives on a crime, presenting them all as variously self-serving and subjective, with the "truth" being elusive and ultimately undecidable. Subjective perspective reaches a different kind of extreme in Julian Schnabel's *The Diving Bell and the Butterfly* (2007), which presents the world through the eyes of a man who has been almost totally paralyzed following an accident. Only his left eye remains under his control (at first), and most of the film's early moments are filmed as if through the man's left eye, complete with blinks. A more extreme example of subjective perspective might be Derk Jarman's *Blue* (1993), which presents a narratively and musically rich soundtrack accompanied by a blue screen, a reference to the blindness accompanying the severe AIDS that afflicted the director at the time. (It was the last film he made before his death.) With documentary films, there may be primary documents that are presented as unmediated—say, a piece of footage such as Abraham Zapruder's famous clip of the John F. Kennedy assassination—but the meaning of the footage is never self-evident without a context of shared cultural assumptions. And there always remain a welter of questions by which filmmakers decide how to represent multiple perspectives fairly and without obvious bias. This may mean, for instance, finding the experts who could address the rival perspectives on a topic and "allowing" them to speak, with viewers being given the opportunity to arrive at their own conclusions. More recently, the way to present the mediatedness of what is shown has been through self-reflexive techniques, such as those discussed in the previous chapter.

Self-reflexiveness rarely features in nature documentaries, and when it does, it tends to take the form of celebrating the prowess of the filmmakers themselves—which makes recent films like *Planet Earth* little different in this respect from the work of early film explorers like Cooper and Schoedsack, Martin and Osa Johnson, or Robert Flaherty. But where nature documentaries do contribute to the perception of multiple perspectives is in the presentation of *non-human* perspectives. The view that is available through a film camera is not, and never will be, identical to the view available through the eyes of another organism, but efforts to produce *something like* the latter view can be helpful in conveying something of the difference between a human and another creature. If nature documentaries fail to meet the criteria proposed by realist critics, most of the films I will focus on in the remainder of this chapter largely fail them as well. Yet many of these films have brought natural phenomena—animal lives, insect perceptions, biological cycles, biospheric events—to viewers in ways that have made them newly accessible, or that have confounded viewer expectations while expanding their capacities for understanding and empathizing with species quite different from our own.

Making Nature: Inter-Natural Coproductions

The best-known examples of such films are the blue-chip documentaries: big-budget, state-of-the-art productions such as those narrated by today's granddaddy of the genre, Sir David Attenborough. Attenborough's list of accomplishments includes several television miniseries, including *Life on Earth* (1979), *The Private Life of Plants* (1995), *The Life of Birds* (1998), *The Life of Mammals* (2002), *Life in the Undergrowth* (2005), *The Blue Planet* (2002), and *Planet Earth* (2006).[38] The eleven-part series *Planet Earth*, an international co-production involving the BBC, the U.S.-based Discovery Channel, Japan's NHK, and the Canadian Broadcasting Corporation, took five years and some $25 million to produce, making it the most expensive documentary series made to date. It was also the first to be shot entirely in high-definition. Its producers claim that it was the "most watched cable event of all time," reaching more than 65 million viewers.[39] Many of its sequences were produced with a Cineflex HD Heli-Gimbal camera, originally engineered for military purposes, which provides gyro-stabilized shots from a 360-degree rotational platform mounted beneath a helicopter. This highly manoeuvrable "eye in the sky" allows for shots, such as those of predator packs hunting prey animals in national parks, that could hardly have been obtained previously.

Much of *Planet Earth* follows the traditional nature documentary formula, with nature here being largely about three things: eating, being eaten, and the stunning visual beauty of it all. Humans are not shown as part of the food web; instead, we are the largely invisible spectators, encouraged to sit back while an omniscient narrator, and orchestral music, guide us along. At the series' outset, Attenborough's voice informs us that the series will "take [us] to the last wildernesses," echoing the taxidermic mode of early cinematic explorer-travellers like Flaherty, Cooper and Schoedsack, and the Johnsons. Richard Beck goes so far as to call *Planet Earth* the "terminal vision" of this exploratory impulse. But if it is terminal, it is so only for the moment: as Scott MacDonald reminds us, with neither scientific research nor cinematic technology standing still in their development, nature films that seem state-of-the-art at one point soon come to seem outdated, their strategies appearing "educational to one generation, but hopelessly corny to the next."[40]

Beck argues, more probingly, that the series "calibrates its moral universe" by granting "moral approval to attractive events," thereby equating ethics with aesthetics.[41] Its slow-motion and time-lapse photography, and its "shots of all kinds, at all speeds ... filled with colors of an almost otherworldly intensity," depict the humanly "uninhabited areas of the earth ... in such a way as to block the formation of intellectual or conceptual links between them and the political and economic processes that continue to accelerate their degradation."[42] Beck's concern here is valid, but it is worth pointing out that the original eleven-part series was followed by three additional episodes, titled *Planet Earth: The Future*, which provided a forcefully argued conservationist message. Alas, the follow-up episodes were not screened during the series' original run on Discovery Channel. As well, each of the series' episodes included a final segment in which some aspect of the series' production was exhibited in an exciting "watch how we did it" mode. Nils Lindahl Elliot argues, correctly, that this new formula—presenting a segment on the "making of" the given episode—represents not a genuinely "reflexive" mode of representation, which would acknowledge the effects and interests behind the production, but merely an "interactive" one that invites viewers "to join the filmmakers in celebrating their own technological prowess and ingenuity."[43] Even these segments, however, were not screened during Discovery Channel's American premiere, though all of them were shown together in a follow-up titled *Planet Earth: The Filmmakers' Story*.

Yet there can be little doubt that enjoyment of the series, at least for some viewers, correlates with a heightened appreciation of the beauty and diversity of the Earth's ecological systems. Over 80 percent of its nearly 3,000 Amazon.com reviewers, as of the present writing, have given the series a full five stars, and many of the most highly rated reviews mention not only the "breathtaking beauty," "mesmerizing visuals," and variations on these themes, but also the "new appreciation" it gives "for the wonder that surrounds us."[44] Similarly, its 16,500 user votes on the Internet Movie Database have given it a near-perfect rating of 9.7 out of 10.[45] In an insightful analysis of Attenborough's previous BBC venture, *The Blue Planet*—an analysis that can be extended to *Planet Earth*—Sean Cubitt examined the ways the series employed high-end production and post-production technologies as well as skilful soundtrack and montage techniques to convey a sense of joy and wonder in the "subjectless creativity" of the blue planet. For Cubitt, there is a tension between the intrinsic-value ethic represented here and the scientific and technological mastery required to deliver it. Yet he argues that the series presents "a mode of looking that encourages the world's unmotivated upsurge to well up into us, clasp itself to us, merge with the salt water in our veins." He notes a "reluctance" in the series "to prize the individual or even the species above the ecosystem as a whole," such that it is "the ocean as a whole" that "looks back, feels us as surely as we feel it."[46]

This notion that the ocean "looks back" and "feels us" is a troubling one. Even Vivian Sobchack's phenomenological investigation of the "viewed view" was about the viewing that is done by the film—which means *in* and *through* the camera lens and mediated by all the translations the image must undergo as it moves from the original act of filming to the final act of being viewed. To assert that the world (or the ocean) looks back at us is to assert that the world can see us seeing it. When a deep-sea submersible descends into depths rarely visited by humans—or, remotely controlled, beyond such depths—the ocean, or at least certain of its constituents, feels and responds to this human intrusion. At least some oceanic inhabitants notice the strange craft, swim toward or away from its light, gaze at it curiously. This reiteratres Francesco Cassetti's point that the camera is always "inevitably implicated in what is being filmed. In chasing things, [it] shares their destiny. In exchange, it cannot hide its presence."[47] Cubitt's point is that there is sensing and communicating going on that is at least two-way, if not multi-directional: "What the amazing, awesome, marvellous, wonderful sights and sounds of *The Blue Planet* indicate throughout is that techne is the only route through which we now can sense the world, most especially that part of the world's conversations which are not conducted in wavelengths we can hear, see or otherwise apprehend."[48] Human technological mediations facilitate an exchange of percepts and interpretants in environments that not so long ago were mute within human discourse. *Planet Earth's* and *Blue Planet's* fans celebrate this extension of human ingenuity and communicativity *and* the aesthetic nature of the response that is captured in the films. For them, the "making of" scenes are important because they help us understand and appreciate how the filmmakers did it; they, in effect, celebrate the expansion of the human colonization of the world through technology. But in a world where communication is multi-directional and multi-channel, the colonization of the oceans by camera-equipped humans is, arguably, also a colonization *of humans by the ocean*. It is one way by which each is clasped, reciprocally, by the other.

One of the most remarkable nature documentaries in terms of the efforts made by its makers to provide audiences with a global view of a non-human world, and to do so not merely by *reproducing* what is seen but by actually *producing* it through interaction with the animals in question, is *Winged Migration* (2001). This French production, directed by Jacques Cluzaud, Michel Debats, and Jacques Perrin, took four years of work, employing some five hundred people including twelve airplane pilots, three film directors, fifteen camera operators, and six teams working full-time and making more than three hundred trips to all the continents. The result is a sweeping global tour showcasing the migrations of dozens of bird species, from bald eagles and Canada geese to Asian great cranes, Arctic gulls, and Antarctic penguins. Cameras, Lisa Uddin writes, "move continuously between visual scales, from the intimate close-ups of White Storks embracing, to the panoramas of Sandhill Cranes flying at sunset, to the aerial-cum-satellite cinematography of an Arctic tern's movement across the earth's curvature." But what the film keeps coming back to is the recurrent scene, the hyper-signaletic moment, "of birds flying in single, group and mass formations."[49] The film takes on a rhythm of being in particular places—lakes and ponds, fields where a farm machine has ploughed, recognizable cityscapes or iconic landscapes, which include Monument Valley, New

York City with its Statue of Liberty, and others—followed by the uplift and flight free of any such identifiable backgrounds, soaring high above boundaries in what for these winged flyers is their natural milieu. In these scenes of flight, the film's geomorphism encompasses the entire Earth. Uddin interprets this as a primal scene of mobility, with the birds serving as "powerful archetypes of the bourgeois tourist" in a world of global capitalist circulation. But this is perhaps overinterpreting, or at least favouring one interpretation from among many.[50] The birds can, for instance, equally be seen as refugees, whose continued movements depend on their not being noticed by the human systems that check and control movement on the surface of the Earth. The film presents, in any case, a more embodied variation of the globality that has for decades been represented in photographs of the entire Earth. Its embodiment is of two kinds: an *avi-optical* embodiment, whereby we can gain what Jennifer Fay calls an "avifaunal perspective," a sense of what the world looks like to a bird flying over long distances;[51] and an *aerial* embodiment, to do more with what it feels like to fly *as* a bird and *alongside* birds.

It is this flying-alongside that makes the film especially intriguing. The full extent of this "alongside" is only revealed in *The Making of Winged Migration*, a companion video that accompanied the film on its DVD release. (The proliferation of such accompanying materials is one of the ways in which cinema is opening, self-reflexively at times, to its multiple social, material, and perceptual contexts.)[52] It turns out that the production of *Winged Migration* required the production—or at least the cultivation—of birds that would tolerate flying in the presence of the noisy, camera-equipped light aircraft that filmed them. Many of these birds were raised, from birth, to be part of such a human–avian–machine collective: they were "imprinted" on human "mothers"—crew members and graduate students hired to raise them—and trained to run and fly in interactive proximity with people and with technology. The latter included remote-controlled aircraft, paragliders, hot air balloons, and two-seater ultralight aircraft built expressly for the film, in addition to trucks, motorcycles, motorboats, remote-controlled all-terrain robots, and a French Navy warship. Among the species raised from birth and "imprinted" on staff members were some, such as storks and pelicans, that had never been successfully treated this way before. The result, then, was the creation of new hybrids consisting of people, machines, and birds, for which the classifications "wild" and "tame" are no longer adequate.

For all the respect shown to the birds by their human partners, some had to be crated and shipped to the places where they would be filmed. The multiple contradictions here, and the many ways in which boundaries between birds (wild?) and humans (tame?) were crossed and recrossed in the production of this film, make it an object that raises questions that can hardly be answered in a singular manner. For Fay, the film "gestures to the *longue durée* of migration which exceeds the life and death of any single bird, and which may well exceed the life and death of human kind." It acknowledges "the world and history we share with birds in which they flicker in and out of perception"—a world where, as the film shows, a hunter shoots a bird and another bird gets mired in what appears to be petrochemical sludge (though it isn't really that, *ergo* it is staged or "faked"). But it also points to the "otherwise hidden domain" where we discover "the way that we, like [the birds], are animals."[53] This sense of shared animality is perhaps a more radical interpretation of the film, one that a typical viewer may or may not assume. Responses to the film are, consequently, an arena for the voicing of many tones in the contemporary thinking through of human–animal relations.[54]

Animation, Plasmaticness, and Disney

Thinking about the cinematic animal can hardly be done without thinking about animated cinema. In *The Cinema Effect*, Sean Cubitt associates the early history of animation with Peircian thirdness and with the "vector," which takes us "from being to becoming, from the inertial division of subject, object, and world to the mobile relationships between them" and to the perpetual enactment of beginnings and the possibility of the image "becoming otherwise than it is."[55] While my own understanding of cinematic thirdness diverges somewhat from Cubitt's, his account of animation, as evidenced in the paradigmatic early films of Émile Cohl, is useful for how it points to the qualities of metamorphosis and transmutation that the genre has at its core. If the moving image can be drawn or painted or photographed frame by frame, or even drawn directly onto film frames, with no need for it to be found in the "real world" first, what is to stop it from doing anything we might imagine it doing? In films like Cohl's *Fantasmagorie*, the transmutation of Cohl's animated figures presents viewers with a "double presence of the screen image as at once object and image," with the line appearing to us "simultaneously as the drawn/written and as the act of drawing/writing, as iconic sign and as the incomplete, infinite process of signifying."[56]

In *EcoMedia*, Cubitt builds on this idea by drawing attention to the relationship between animal cartoons and the drawing of animals more generally—a practice we know goes back more than 30,000 years to the caves of Chauvet in southern France—as well as to the drawings, or at least the markings of territory, *by* animals. For an animal marking or "drawing" its territory, Cubitt argues, "a drawing is a technique that gives gesture, an arrangement of matter, meaning." Human drawing is distinguished from animal marking by its organization of the drawing "in space and time" such that "it attains the status of an object, something discrete, separable from the physical mark, and significant because it distinguishes the physical from the dimensional properties."[57] In turn, machine drawing, such as computer-generated imagery (CGI), which simultaneously organizes and produces information "out of the ordering of dimensions," eliminates the *gesture* of drawing. Its result is that knowledge of physical things becomes replaced by "knowledge as array, as data, as statistics of performances and behaviors atomised and particulate, freed of the continuity that objects have in Kant's logic of dimensions."[58] Classical animation techniques thus preserve gesture while permitting "trans-species identification" of the sort that a photographic image, with its "evidence of alienness, would not allow."[59] This transmutability across boundaries of species, objects, and bodies becomes especially pronounced in the long-standing tradition of avant-garde and surrealistic animation that stretches from Émile Cohl, Max and Dave Fleischer, Wladyslaw Starewicz, and Norman McLaren to Walerian Borowczyk, Jan Svankmajer, the Quay Brothers, Hiyao Miyazaki, and Tim Burton.

Examining the more popular animations of Walt Disney, however, is instructive insofar as the Disney Studios have probed and prodded at the human–animal boundary for decades while managing to reach many millions of viewers around the world. The core of Disney animation, like the core of fairy tales, is metamorphosis: a pumpkin is turned into a stagecoach, sparkles in the air coalesce into a fairy godmother, a ragged maid (Cinderella) is transformed into a wealthy princess, mice turn into horses, princes into beasts, a goat into a phonograph, and a princess into a witch. A puppet (Pinocchio) comes to life. Russian filmmaker and theorist Sergei Eisenstein admired what he called the "plasmaticness" in Disney's animated animals. In Ian Christie's words, this referred to "the infinite flexibility of figures, their interchangeability with natural objects, and ability to collapse and reanimate at will."[60] But he lamented that Disney did not extend this lively metamorphism to the backgrounds surrounding the figures. According to Eisenstein, Disney ignored the "unlimited possibilities for landscape elements ... to live and pulsate." "The possibility of transformation," as Daniel Morgan argues, "is directed towards the individuals, while the background—hence, the underlying conditions—remains unchanged."[61] In terms of our framework, the foreground/background distinction keeps in place the conventional difference between subjectivity and objectivity: "we" develop while the world does not.

While this contrasts with the more fully plasmatic work of animators like Hayao Miyazaki and Jan Svankmejer, an examination of the backgrounds of Disney feature films nevertheless reveals the remarkable power of animation to refigure viewers' perceptions of objectscapes as well as subjectscapes. Disney's animation often employed a multiplaned camera, so that the background, middle ground, and foreground appeared to move at different speeds, thereby replicating the human perception of spatial depth and movement. This mixture of realism and plasmaticness was an especially potent combination.

Disney has often been criticized for shaping the cultural landscape in profoundly conservative directions. Ecocritics have critiqued Disney portrayals of nature for presenting a sentimentalized and distorted view of animal lives and ecological realities and for projecting middle-class American values—or, in some interpretations, racist, classist, and hierarchic or even neo-monarchist values—onto the natural world.[62] Counterposed to these views, however, is the less commonly voiced argument that Disney was one of the forces shaping the American "liberal" culture that exploded in the 1960s, with its "be true to yourself" individualism and its powerful environmentalist sentiments.[63] Disney's innovations included the use of wild nature as a setting for extended animated features, as in *Snow White* (1937), *Fantasia* (1940), *Bambi* (1942), and *Sleeping Beauty* (1959); a preoccupation with a question that is central to children's imaginations, "What is the meaning of home?;" and a dual foundation in the pastoral aesthetic that articulates, in David Whitley's words, "an expression of innate sympathy between all living things" at the same time as it seeks an escape or retreat from the stresses and hypocrisies of urban-industrial life.[64] All of this makes for an interesting and multivalent mix.

It would be an unusual child who grew up in North America in the middle or latter decades of the twentieth century and did not come to learn the Disney formula first-hand. In the True-Life Adventures nature documentaries, as Scott MacDonald describes, "we are sutured into the Disney vision by the continual presence of the narrator; by the music, which is carefully and continuously synched with the action so as to create particular, interpretive cinematic moods; and by the film's visual and textual framing of the 'adventures' of the animals." The films produce animal characters intended "to lure children, mothers, and fathers into emotional identification." As in any Hollywood melodrama, "we enjoy the pleasure of gazing at the private lives of characters we can identify with, and we share the characters' gazes at each other."[65] All of these elements—with the exception only (though not always) of the all-knowing narrator—are present in the animated films, but all the more so. Animal characters speak in the films, but long after the movie is over, they continue to do so through the various pop-cultural forms and product lines that have emerged from the movies over decades of successful merchandising, marketing, and theming by the Disney corporation, and that have been willingly consumed and supported by millions of enthusiastic fans.

While its original run encountered a lukewarm wartime reception, Disney's *Bambi* (1942) has proved to be one of the most resilient and successful films ever produced by Disney Studios. It was, in retrospect, a breakthrough in animated nature films, and it is currently the third largest grossing movie in history. The film has proven controversial, however, having been accused of turning Americans against hunting.[66] *Bambi* depicted its lead animals with the exaggerated heads and eyes, reduced muzzles, and hyper-expressive faces that made them appear cute, like human infants. At the same time, the movie set a new standard for animated naturalistic realism.[67] Yet the film can hardly be called ecologically realistic: all the denizens of its well-ordered forest commonwealth live friendly, happy, playful, and talkative lives (up to a point, at least). From the first scene on, the film draws viewers into a natural world that is modelled on the national parks of the American West, especially Yosemite.[68] But unlike the 1929 Felix Salten novel on which it is based, there is little predation or death, and there is no place for humans in nature. Tension in the film comes, famously, only from the presence of "man," who remains an unseen invader of the forest, setting fires or killing animals, seemingly indiscriminately.

That man-generated tension is what produced determined opposition to the film from the American hunting lobby even before it was released. Hunters have taken it to be an anti-hunting screed, perhaps singularly responsible for a rise in anti-hunting sentiments across the United States. Ralph Lutts argued exactly this in a classic 1992 article; Matt Cartmill's history of attitudes toward hunting calls the film "the most powerful piece of anti-hunting propaganda ever produced."[69] Lutts argued that the "scene with the single greatest impact on the public was the death of Bambi's mother."[70] Others have taken this to be the most terrifying scene in any children's movie—even though the killing occurs off-screen, with the human hunter never being visible. There is no doubt that the film's popular success, and the power of this particular scene, both rely on the way the film builds sympathy for the lovable, vulnerable fawn, whose mother nurtures and cares for him (while the father is distant, aloof, and uncommunicative). Arguments like these are supported by an often cited correlation between the film's release and the public squashing of Aldo Leopold's 1943 proposal for an antlerless deer season to control the Wisconsin deer herd.[71] After studying the correlation trends between *Bambi* releases and re-releases and a host of other sociological factors, however, A. Waller Hastings has concluded that no clear correlation can be found between hunting attitudes and releases of the film—indeed, he notes, the image of hunters was already in tatters by the time *Bambi* came along. What changed American attitudes toward hunting, according to Hastings, was the large-scale demographic shift from rural to urban areas over the first half of the twentieth century.[72]

In his sophisticated study *The Idea of Nature in Disney Animation*, David Whitley argues that whatever the film's actual impact on attitudes toward hunting, *Bambi* laid the "emotional groundwork" for a generation of environmentalists.[73] Its stark juxtaposition of the romance, love, and beauty of the forest with the harsh realities of human predation of animals remained a powerful motivator for many children who grew up in the middle of the last century. The film has been criticized from all angles: for not being realistic, or more precisely for being both too realistic and not realistic enough, with its sanitized and idealized picture of static nature; for, as Lutts puts it, "motivat[ing]" but "not educating"—"It may stimulate action," he writes, "but not understanding"; and for simply being such an obvious point of departure for eco-sentimentalism. *Bambi*, as Una Chaudhuri puts it, "is a site of the wild tamed, named, and commodified." Against all this, Whitley argues on behalf of what I am calling the film's biomorphism.[74] In his analysis, it is the animals' gaze that directs viewers' responses to the world that surrounds those animals: "The apprehensive, surveying gaze of the grazing deer gives way to focused awareness solely of features to be navigated around in the flight path; thence to taking in the comforting detail of a familiar environment experienced in safety; and, finally, to the transformed world, dimly glimpsed through grief, for which the falling snow provides a compelling visual metaphor." There is, Whitley argues, more going on in the film than "a set of distorted paradigms of the way the natural world around us operates" or "a displacement of human loss onto animal forms. The animal figures are also teaching children how to look at significant detail in the world around them and to integrate these perceptions within their whole emotional response." He continues: "The 'facts' may be distorted but the process of engagement and the sensitivity to nature that the film encourages have a capacity to connect with viewers in more fundamental ways."[75] And while the fire sequence toward the film's end results in a charred landscape with blackened stumps and scorched earth, Whitley argues that there is sufficient ambiguity at the end to allow for a reading of fire—and therefore of humans—as being both destructive and renewing. Friend Owl's oak tree still stands undamaged, and new spring flowers and vegetation are seen sprouting.[76]

The effects of films like these can hardly be studied without recourse to ethnographic methods. Much of the rest of this chapter will delve into audience responses to recent films about the human–animal boundary. Before proceeding to these films, however, it is worth spending a few moments on the topic of seeing as it is encountered in the genre in which otherness is presented in its most dramatic form: the horror film.

Boundary Traffic: Seeing, Being Seen, and the Horror of Crossing Over

In the previous chapter, I discussed *King Kong* as a paradigm case of a particular way of seeing, the imperial-spectacular gaze, which is a way of transmitting "seeingness" between bodies—between Carl Denham, Ann Darrow, King Kong, ourselves, and so on. Darrow (Fay Wray) is made the object of multiple gazes—those of the camera-narrator, of the camera within the film, of sailors and male characters within the story, of Kong, and of us, its actual audience—so that the film's "subject of enunciation … circulates among all these figures."[77] In Donna Haraway's perceptive account of its primate politics, *King Kong* also stages the "drama of the touch," the troubling touch across the species boundary, which takes on a frisson of excitement even as we, or Ann, shy away from it.[78]

King Kong is a monster movie that by today's standards is not particularly monstrous. Yet our seeing this particular monster is analogous to our seeing *any* monster, or anything else for that matter: it is all in the perspective. The promontory vantage point from which we gaze down over a landscape, say in a classic Western, gives us a sense of distance as well as a sense that "here it is, spread out for us to make our own." The perspective of travelling through a landscape, especially in a high-speed vehicle, gives us a sense of being able to penetrate mysteries, explore new worlds, discover what is there for us if we make the effort. The sense, on the other hand, of being seen by some unknown force we cannot see, and of being hunted as prey, taken from behind, penetrated, as in Ridley Scott's *Alien* (1979), is quite the opposite of the imperial gaze. There is no safety here, and none is intended: there is pure violation, though it is a violation only in the imagined body (and the audiovisual body), not the actual, complete, life-or-death body. The audience members anticipate this feeling of utter vulnerability because that is what they have come for: to be momentarily terrified by something that ultimately will have no power over them, because it is only a movie. This has been one of the arguments in the long debate over the virtues, or disvirtues, of horror films: they are a way of taming the wild, or of keeping a certain wildness within us temporarily satisfied but ultimately at bay.

Horror films operate on this tension between the seen and the unseen, the horror of seeing and the dread of not seeing (but being seen). And there are the accompanying fears of what not seeing might lead to—attack, death, mutilation, deformity, exposure of the body in all its vulnerability and creaturely materiality, and the takeover of what we know to be *human, like us,* by the inhuman, the abject, the dead, the undead.[79] Films have long played on our fears of some sort of nature. In some cases it is a human nature, though a particularly *inhuman* human nature, but in others it is a completely alien nature. Whichever is the case, that nature has spun out of our control or simply intends to unravel that control—examples are alien invasion films, monstrous insect or animal films, zombie films, slasher films, occult horror films, exploding-head films, sadistic thrillers, and so on. Some of these, like the Korean eco-thriller *The Host* (2006) and the animal-horror mystery *Wolfen* (1981), are clearly intended to depict our relationship with nature as having gone awry. Others are more subtle but provide clues to such a reading for those who look for them. Hitchcock's *The Birds* (1963), for instance, was inspired by a 1961 report of seabirds attacking people and divebombing windows near Santa Cruz, behaviour that was ascribed by biologists to a toxin (domoic acid) found in the fish the birds had been eating. The film occludes any directly ecological reading in favour of an attack on the scopophilic pleasure of seeing itself. As it drifts from romantic comedy to avian horror tale, its references to seeing—birds repeatedly attack the eyes of their victims, and the phrases "I see" and "cover your eyes!" are often heard—are coupled with a growing association of the birds with the female characters. The arrival of Melanie (Tippie Hedren), the love interest for the San Francisco lawyer visiting his mother, in the coastal town of Bodega Bay is what sets off the bird attacks. Both she, "in her tense and affected stance, head cocked self-consciously on one side," as Robin Wood puts it, and Mitch's mother, overbearing in a somewhat equine way, are birdlike.[80] Most horror films, though, leave themselves open to interpretation and to transmogrification in our dreams and nightmares: *Invasion of the Body Snatchers* (1956), *Night of the Living Dead* (1968), *The Texas Chainsaw Massacre* (1974), *Halloween* (1978), *Alien* (1979), *Aliens* (1986), *Scanners* (1981), *Saw* (2004), and so many others. What is horrifying in all of these is the agential power that bursts through the social boundaries we have set for such power. It is unhuman, inhuman, anti-human, or simply ahuman, and when it invades the human realm—the social body or, especially, the material body—it comes to seem utterly demonic.

King Kong encourages us to sympathize with the beast; other monster films tend to offer less sympathy. But monsters are never merely monsters, or not for very long. In 1933, *King Kong* may have captured something of the relationship between "us" and the otherness of the primeval jungle, at least to the extent that the depiction of the latter seemed *real* (i.e., indexical, in Peirce's terms) or at least *realistic* (i.e., iconic or symbolic-representational). To many viewers it may not have done that even then, but today it surely captures, at best, only an indication of how far the goalposts of realism have shifted in the intervening decades. One can hardly watch the original *King Kong* today without noticing how dated it is, how unscary its jungle is, and how silly, campy, or offensive its tribal characters appear to us now. (All of that is only part of the reason why it has begged for updates, such as Peter Jackson's 2005 remake.) What it does capture, however, is something of the *mediatedness* of our relation to the firstness of any conceivable primeval jungle. It shows us that the relationship between spectacle (which means our own voyeurism) and reality is mediated, with the mediation being both potentially fallible (because the beast might escape and threaten us all) and utterly infallible (because it's only a movie), and indeed both at once. It builds tension around the boundary between us and the untamed other, making it more alluring and magnetically charged even as it reveals the magnetism to be artificially produced.

King Kong, as Casetti argues, stages the scene of cinematic production from the raw materials of a material world: a real beast must be found and captured, the natives must be placated, and so on, before the filmmaking adventurers can bring back the prize for the spectacle-hungry masses. It shows that this relationship between reality and spectacle requires a coercive exploitation of the former to create the latter, with all the emotional investments this spectacle constitutes for us. The beast's rebellion is nature's own resistance to this exploitation. His exploitation constitutes the sacrifice that allows civilized spectacle to emerge as victorious. But whether the beast is Kong (and thus a mediated representation of our relationship to some evolutionary and/or colonial Other) or Ridley Scott's monstrous alien in *Alien* (and thus a mediated representation of our relationship to some more cosmic other), the cinematic beast has always been a kind of admission that there is an *outside* to the safe and bounded human world and that that outside must be expoited, tamed, yet still feared for it to have the kind of charge for us that we wish it to have. These struggles with the beasts of our imagination are boundary skirmishes that energize the boundary itself, adding to its weightedness, power, magnetism, and excitement.

Stacy Alaimo's eco-feminist analysis of monster movies provides a generally negative assessment of the genre. Movies like *The Beast* (1975), *The Island of Doctor Moreau* (1977), *DNA* (1997), *Congo* (1995), and *Mimic* (1997), Alaimo concludes, articulate a "vertical semiotics" that polices the boundary between humans and nature by reasserting the hierarchy between the two. This is often done through the use of visual metaphors involving clearly demarcated underground/overground worlds; through technological flight that elevates humans above biological threats; and so on. The point is that the monsters are things that we fear, but by watching them on the screen—and seeing them ultimately conquered—we overcome them, even if we do not necessarily over-come our fear of what they stand for. Alaimo contrasts these monster films, which provide for an ultimate human victory over the Other, with films like *Habitat* (1997) and *Safe* (1995), which "dramatize the impossibility of demar-cating protected places" and provide no transcendence or reassurance.[81] At the same time, she recognizes that despite the reassuring closures of films in which humans are ultimately shown as transcending the monstrous nature that threatens them, "in the muddled middles of these films" viewers may be able to "experience a kind of corporeal identification with" the monstrous and hybrid creatures portrayed. She concludes: "Perhaps the horrific but pleasur-able sense of the 'melting of corporeal boundaries' ... can catalyze some sort of resistance to the desire to demarcate, discipline and eradicate monstrous natures."[82] In this tentative suggestion, Alaimo approximates the argument made famous by Deleuze and Guattari, according to whom certain represen-tations of animals and monsters afford the possibility of an experiential or affective "becoming-animal," a resistant "line of flight" away from modernity's dichotomous understanding of the human and toward a closer intimacy or embrace of animal others.[83]

Becoming-animal is a movement along the lines of the therianthropic or theriomorphic—that is, the depiction of humans as animals or as incorporat-ing animal characteristics—with the difference that this movement is proces-sual, an *actual* becoming, and not merely representational.[84] The flipside of the therianthropic is the anthropomorphic rendering of animals, and both tenden-cies have a long and respectable pedigree. Animals have served as symbols, models, and allegorical mirrors for humans for millenia.[85] In Christian Europe, non-human animals have long been popular and convenient figures for dem-onstrating moral lessons and modelling human behaviour; this can be seen in medieval bestiaries, religious illustrations, saintly narratives, folk tales, and popular rituals.[86] John Berger, in his widely cited essay "Why Look at Animals," argued that visual depictions of animals have multiplied as humans have displaced themselves from direct interaction with real animals, and that these representations have characteristically sentimentalized animals and, in the process, narrowed down our understanding of what animals are. Many theorists have argued that humans typically define what it is to be "human" in contradistinction to "the animal," commonly positing some trait or other as a distinguishing feature of humanity that thereby becomes a privileging marker by which humans can claim a separate and superior ontological status.[87] This ongoing negotiation of "the human" as opposed to "the animal," with the intention of propping up the first over the second, is what Italian philosopher Giorgio Agamben has referred to as "the anthropological machine."[88]

If animal representations in art and literature contribute to social constructions of the human, depictions of the relationship between humans and animals contribute to the social constructions of both. In what remains of this chapter, I will examine a range of "becomings-animal," and of negotiations occurring at the human–animal boundary, to assess how each side of this boundary is made to mirror or resonate with the other, but also what promise these becomings harbour for those who cross the line and actually *become other*, if not quite becoming parrot, bear, horse, or wolf. I will work in steps, beginning with a gentle, even conservative, form of *analogical* human–animal relation, and proceed to more radical forms. My interest is in drawing a preliminary map of how the boundaries at which human–animal relations arise are affectively charged, that is, how they become imbued with valences—positive, negative, or ambivalent—as well as with affective potencies. This typically involves processes of othering—that is, the establishing of a distance between the human and the animal, or between the human or civilized norm and those people who are closer to nature or who veer too close to crossing the line, who become-animal—and the valorization of one side over the other in this oppositional dyad. I will attend to the cinematic and ethnographic strategies by which this process occurs.

The actual effects of film can hardly be measured without talking to those most affected by them, and since film's effects are to a large degree *affects*, which percolate and spread according to an always mysterious rhythm, any ethnographic methodology here will have to be longitudinal, consisting of studies that follow viewers' relations with cinematic images, ideas, and rhythms over time. Reception studies of critical and audience interpretations of films (such as Cynthia Erb's *Tracking King Kong*) have tended to focus on print commentaries about films, but the Internet has made the responses of fans and of "average" viewers much more available to scholars today.[89] While this book is primarily theoretical in intent, the reception of films constitutes an important terrain for evaluating whether the book's arguments ring true or not, and some of the readings that follow extend my analysis precisely in such a direction.

Animal by Analogy: Penguins and Family Values

Luc Jaquet's *March of the Penguins* (2005) features as its lead actors a colony of Emperor penguins in Adélie Land, Antarctica. Filmed over the course of a year, it portrays the annual drama of the penguins journeying between their ancestral breeding grounds, which protect them from harsh winds and provide solid pack ice throughout the year, and the open ocean where they hunt. As summer turns to winter, freezing ice sets this area farther and farther away from the open ocean, and the penguins, monogamous within each breeding season, take turns by gender in journeying to the ocean to fish for krill and other food. After the females transfer their single eggs to their male partners for protection from the cold, the males huddle together for warmth—thousands of them are seen huddling in a black-and-white mass, each cradling a single egg beneath its white fur—while the females waddle and slide in an arduous trek of some sixty miles to and back from the open ocean. Once the chicks have hatched and the females have returned to feed them, the males take their turn journeying. The timing of the entire cycle is portrayed as exquisite yet precarious: the females, it seems, have returned not a day too soon as the half-starved males have supplied tiny amounts of regurgitated food to their chicks to tide them over while they have waited. By the end of the film, the spring thaw has brought the ice margin much closer to the breeding grounds and the adult penguins and young can go to the water freely, with the youngsters taking their first dives into the ocean. After that they are on their own, until the cycle begins again at the end of the following summer.

The filmmakers' strategy largely follows blue-chip wildlife film conventions, while updating these with state-of-the-art techniques. French nature documentaries have often followed what by American standards are unconventional narrative methods. *Microcosmos* and *Winged Migration* both included very little narration. The original version of *March of the Penguins*, titled *La marche de l'empereur*, was even more unusual, with its poetic rendition of an anthropomorphized penguin point of view—what Kasic calls a "first person, non-human plural" form of narration. But the film's North American distributors, National Geographic, altered this to a more conventional, omniscient "voice of God" narration for the English-language version.[90] In the film, stunning cinematography captures the penguin colony in epic grandeur. Images of penguins in action are set against spectacularly stark Antarctic landscapes and melded together with a narrative documenting the travails of the annual drama— "tenderness, separation, reunion, and, if successful, new life." This is recounted (in the English-language version) in narrator Morgan Freeman's lightly playful, compassionate baritone, and propelled by a current of lightly orchestral programmatic music. Drama comes in the form of winter storms, predators such as leopard seals and petrels, and occasional indications that not all penguins or eggs live to survive the yearly round. Only as the final credits roll do we see the film crew itself amid the penguins, with inquisitive penguins assembling around the cameras. What seems a heroic journey for the penguins is, by implication, paralleled by the efforts of the film crew to capture this tale in sub-zero temperatures and bring it to audiences for the first time. The film's resounding popularity can be attributed, at least in part, to this novelty, an opening onto a largely unknown (to most viewers) world, conveyed with storybook simplicity by characters whose cuteness can hardly be denied. *March of the Penguins* revels in a "soft-core anthropomorphism" and carries an environmental message that is, at best, implicit. Any viewer aware of global warming will surmise that its impact on the Emperor penguins' delicately timed annual cycle will likely be dramatic, yet the fact that this cycle has gone on for "millions of years," as the narrator tells us, may also lead a viewer to think that it can continue indefinitely as shown. (In fact, global warming, already proceeding more rapidly at the poles, appears to be having variable effects on different penguin populations.)

At the time of the film's release, work was already proceeding on another penguin-starred film, an animated musical featuring stunning CGI graphics and overlaying realistic images of penguins over the movements of human dancers. *Happy Feet* (2006) features a soundtrack of popular music of the past sixty years and an overt environmental subtext that blames human activities for the overfishing and pollution that have endangered the waters that penguins depend on for survival. The film tells the tale of Mumble, a hapless but sympathetic penguin born with an inability to restrain his feet from dancing. Penguin society is portrayed as dominated by a council of tribal elders who uphold rigid community morals to maintain order. Mumble, however, born of an Elvis-like father and Marilyn Monroesque mother, will not be restrained. He sets off on a journey to find the cause of the decline in the fish his colony feeds on. Along the way, singing and dancing as he goes, he meets and befriends a group of Hispanic-sounding male penguins, attends to a revival meeting–style celebration led by the womanizing, fortune-telling guru Lovelace, and encounters elephant seals, killer whales, and deep-sea trawlers. Mumble gets captured by one of the latter and taken to the penguin exhibit of a marine park, but ultimately his and his cohorts' tap-dancing routines convince their human captors to mobilize and pass a ban on Antarctic fishing. The tap-dancing penguin outcast thus, in "following his bliss," as the late Joseph Campbell might have put it, becomes a hero, an interspecies environmental emissary and a saviour to his race.

Both *March of the Penguins* and *Happy Feet* met with tremendous box office success. *Happy Feet* was the top-grossing movie after its release and made it into the top 100 all-time films in worldwide box office receipts, while *March of the Penguins* became the second highest grossing documentary of all time.[91] Each also attracted widespread attention for its environmental and social subtexts.[92] Conservative pundits, such as American talk radio host Michael Medved, lauded *March* for its affirmation of "traditional values" such as marital fidelity, steadfast parenting, selflessness, and personal sacrifice.[93] Some conservative Christians claimed that the film made a good case for "intelligent design." When reports began circulating about the Christian Right's embrace of the film, liberal bloggers recalled the case of Roy and Silo, a same-sex penguin couple at New York's Central Park Zoo, which had adopted and raised a penguin chick together. The *New York Times* editorialized, in response, that "anthropomorphism, like after-shave, is best used sparingly."[94] The appearance of *Happy Feet* came as a salve to those who professed befuddlement at the "family values" embrace of *March of the Penguins*, and as an irritant to those behind that embrace. Environmental and animal rights groups applauded *Happy Feet's* conservationist message. The Tuscon-based Center for Biological Diversity timed a request to the EPA for listing a dozen penguin species as endangered to coincide with the release of the film.[95] Fox News anchor Neil Cavuto, on the other hand, decried the film's "far-left" message and called it an "animated *Inconvenient Truth*," and Michael Medved claimed that this "most disturbing" film contains a "bizarre anti-religious bias" and a pro-homosexuality subtext.[96]

Analyzing *March's* uptake by Evangelical Christians as an allegory for humans and, at the same time, as providing evidential support for the creationist theory of "Intelligent Design," Rebecca Wexler has argued that the filmmakers unknowingly made this interpretation possible. They did so by underlining their own scientific credentials while unreflexively mixing images of penguins with "scientific potential"—specifically, those that reflect an "invisible, third person," observational perspective—with point-of-view shots that elided the difference between human and penguin perception. Wexler argues, further, that the point-of-view shots obtained by cameras attached to a penguin swimming underwater may "transmit scientific perspectives" because they are an actual technique used by penguin biologists. But this assumes that an image obtained through a scientific technique can in and of itself be "scientific"—which it cannot. Science is more than a collection of empirical data. To be scientific, any datum—an observed behaviour, an object found "in the field," a gathered statistic, an image or film sequence—must be embedded in a theoretical matrix of assumptions, hypotheses, and interpretive discourses; it is these which render it interpretable.[97] Wexler aptly criticizes "secular and scientific media" observers for imbuing *March of the Penguins* "with an implied objectivity" in the same way that Evangelical Christians did. But she fails to acknowledge that without additional extra-cinematic support, *no* film can embody "scientific truth."[98] Furthermore, the very tradition of censoring anthropomorphism out of accounts of animals has been critiqued by numerous observers as a methodological weakness, since it presumes that there are no commonalities between humans and other animals—which is a scientifically untenable assumption.[99]

To gauge the ways in which Christian viewers engaged with these two films in the aftermath of their popular runs, I examined a variety of online conversations debating their merits. Many prominent Christian film review sites gave both films relatively positive reviews, while favouring *March of the Penguins* and expressing caveats about the sexual themes in *Happy Feet*.[100] The most prominent Evangelical Christian Web forum devoted to discussing popular films, Christian Spotlight on Entertainment, demonstrated strong divergences among Evangelical Christians on the virtues and vices of the latter film. Part of an influential organizational and online network, Christian Spotlight on Entertainment includes detailed reviews as well as viewer ratings and comments on hundreds of popular films. Ratings consist of a "moral rating," which ranges from "excellent!" to "extremely offensive," and a "moviemaking quality" rating of between 1 and 5 stars. In addition, viewers make an overall assessment: "positive," "negative," or "neutral." The site divides viewer comments into general ones and those by "young people" (under eighteen).

The site's reviewers gave *March of the Penguins* an average "moral rating" of "better than average" and a star level of 4. Both adult and young viewer comments were strongly positive. The film was lauded for its portrayal of the alleged family values of the Emperor penguins—their tender and devoted care-giving of their young, their monogamous commitments (even though these were seasonal and not lifelong), their bravery in the face of the harsh environment—as well as for the production qualities and the filmmakers' dedication in making the film. Several noted the film's congruence with a "creationist" perspective; only one viewer protested against the implied evolutionary reference to the "millions of years" in which penguins have lived in Antarctica. Some criticized the film's anthropomorphism (for instance, the narrator's suggestion that the penguin behaviour constituted "love") or debated the issue of monogamy, with some recognizing that the monogamy was serial and temporary and that this did not represent a model for human pair bonding.[101]

Happy Feet, by contrast, garnered overwhelmingly negative responses from the website's adult viewers (34 negative, 9 positive, 5 neutral) but significantly more ambiguous responses from teenagers (6 positive, 2 negative, 5 neutral). Both groups tended to see the exceptional animation and enjoyable music in positive terms, and many agreed that the sexual innuendoes and violence made the film inappropriate for young viewers. However, many adult viewers charged the film with promoting "humanism," a "liberal" or "left-wing" agenda of "political correctness," radically environmentalist or pro-animal rights views, "sexual permissiveness," individualism, and, for some, pro-evolution, pro-homosexuality, and "peacenik" or pro-UN "one-worldist" sentiments. Adult viewers commonly noted an "anti-Christian" message in the film, seen in the mocking representations of the Elders of the High Council and in the donation-seeking and womanizing "evangelist" Lovelace. Some expressed disappointment or anger at having been misled, "deceived," or "conned" by previews that had presented the film as innocent family entertainment. Others derided the film as a "thinly-veiled, anti-Christian screed," as a "scathing attack against fundamentalists" that "has stepped the fight against Christianity in movies to the next level," or as a film in which "the knives of criticism and the poison of propaganda are cleverly hidden behind the cute feathery gloves of adorable creatures, and thus much more dangerous and ominous than a direct assault."

Reactions among young viewers differed significantly from those of adults and were particularly distinguished by the teens' sophistication with regard to media effects. In contrast to the frequent adult criticisms of the film's portrayal of religious elders, younger viewers tended to agree with those portrayals, seeing them as representing not all Christians but only "stuffy" traditionalists. Some young viewers defended the language and sexual innuendoes, noting that these were hardly different from what was commonly found "in any public school or street in the country." In many cases, young viewers were responding directly to the negative views expressed by adult critics. One seventeen-year-old argued that "What I'm REALLY upset about is the way people have looked at this film, and not just this film either.... Sometimes parents can try and focus on the bad things about a movie and not focus on the good. Many have complained that the sea lion was portrayed too ferociously, well hate to break it to you but ... THAT'S THE WAY THEY REALLY ARE ... YELLOW TEETH, SCARY FACE and all." This divergence between teen and adult opinions shows that Christian viewers actively used the film's imagery to delineate their views from those of other Christians and to shape the discourse about film and about social mores within the Evangelical community. While the sample is small, this divergence may point to a broader division that had been noted in media discussions about the support base of 2008 U.S. Republican presidential candidate Mike Huckabee, whose combination of social conservatism, economic and foreign affairs populism, and concern for the environment and social justice garnered more support among young and working-class Christians than among established conservative Christian organizations.[102] The volume of responses to *Happy Feet* (in comparison with *March*) also suggests that viewers were responding not only to the film but also to previous viewers' responses; in other words, this was a self-generating discussion that revealed fractures within the website's readership.

What is evident, however, is that the responses almost universally focused on the meanings of these animal representations for human social and ethical behaviour, not for any human obligations to penguins or to the natural world. There were a handful of exceptions, but by and large the penguins were used within this interpretive community as symbols and models that reflected either forms of social behaviour appropriate to humans or the creator's "intelligent design." While Evangelical viewers might naturally gravitate toward a more anthropocentric perspective, the films themselves facilitate this kind of reading. *March* portrays the penguin colony as living in its own self-contained world, the boundaries of which are marked by a challenging environment and by external threats such as harsh storms and predators. Humans are absent, or rather, present only implicitly as observers; our mode of participation is a photographic and touristic one. As an animated fantasy, *Happy Feet* is more obviously an anthropomorphic parable. The divergence within its animal world is between penguin tradition and nonconformist dancing penguins, but the movie complicates this framework by bringing the penguins into contact with a human world that is the penguins' real external boundary threat. While *March* does not explicitly deal with the human–animal boundary at all, *Happy Feet* simultaneously mobilizes and reasserts that boundary. It does this, first, by showing how humans have transgressed a previously established boundary (i.e., industrial practices are endangering the ecosystems on which penguins depend for their survival), and then by having the penguin hero learn to communicate with humans (by dancing in the aquarium) in order to convince them that penguins should be allowed to continue their lives unmolested by humans, or at least that penguins deserve moral consideration. In this sense, the film becomes a kind of *Animal Liberation* for children—they are like us, they suffer, they dance—and audience responses clearly show an agreement or disagreement with this agenda.[103] But ultimately the film remains an animation feature in which the penguins are portrayed anthropomorphically for entertainment's sake, with the environmental message subordinated to the delight of sharing an enjoyable fantasy. Humans and animals, in these films, become each other only by analogy, and ultimately the boundary remains little changed from how it was before the film came along.

Individual Crossings: Bittner's Birds, Treadwell's Bears

Wild Parrots of Telegraph Hill (2005) and *Grizzly Man* (2005) present more complex cases of human–animal boundary relations. Each activates and energizes this boundary by portraying boundary activity as forcefully motivated and affectively engaging. Both Mark Bittner, a homeless drifter who befriends a colony of parrots living above the streets of San Francisco, and "grizzly man" Timothy Treadwell *want* to communicate with their animal subjects. In Bittner's case, the stakes for this communication are comparatively low; in Treadwell's case, they are higher and ultimately lead to his and his girlfriend's deaths at the hands of an Alaskan brown bear.

Director Judy Irving's *Wild Parrots of Telegraph Hill* documents the evolving friendship between the rootless, bearded and ponytailed, middle-aged former street musician and self-proclaimed "dharma bum," Mark Bittner, and a flock of parrots in San Francisco. While caretaking a home in the Telegraph Hill neighbourhood, Bittner begins observing several dozen parrots, and comes to feed and name them, noting his observations in a running diary. Over time he becomes an amateur parrot behaviourist, skilled enough to make useful contributions to the ornithological knowledge base about these exotic species (primarily cherry-headed conures, also known as red-masked parakeets, with occasional blue-crowned conures, mitred conures, and hybrids). The film portrays Bittner as a quirky and likeable, bohemian Saint Francis (as he is called by another character in the film) and allows viewers to share in his discoveries about the likeable parrots. In the process, we get to know the parrots and their idiosyncratic personalities: cool and curmudgeonly Connor, feather-plucking Scraperella, indoorsy and music-loving but Jekyll-and-Hydeish Mingus, and others.

Where *March of the Penguins* was a fairly traditional zöo-ethnography about a foreign (avian) culture, in that its subjects are portrayed as having lived this way "for millions of years" and the filmmakers are not seen intervening in their subjects' lives, *Wild Parrots* is clearly *about* the intervention of a human in the lives of the parakeet and vice versa. That is, it is about interspecies communication and translation and the mutual enrichment that results from it. This is, in effect, a tale of global migration: several North American and European cities have established wild parrot populations, and it is generally agreed that these are escaped or released "refugees" from the human trade in exotic pets or zoo animals. Like human migrants (and unlike the birds in *Winged Migration*), they are exiled foreigners making a home in a new land. Bittner's role is a friendly and supportive one, which makes the film neither a form of "salvage ethnography" where what is being documented is a "dying culture," nor a form of domestication for the purpose of spectacle, as is the case with zoo animals and with nineteenth- and early-twentieth-century exhibitions of "primitive" humans. *Wild Parrots* shows a gentle transgression, by its lead character, of the boundary between human and non-human—a boundary that is already destabilized at the outset. The urban environment, after all, includes many non-natives, not least among them the humans, and the parrots are merely seeking to find their coexistence within it. With its sensitive exploration of Bittner's story, the film embraces and supports, with visual evidence, the anthropomorphism he defends as (at times) reasonable. The birds are shown to be distinct characters with rich emotional lives, but they can be cruel to one another, and there are the predatory hawks circling overhead to ensure that their lives do not lack danger. Bittner presents his unfolding interest in the birds as a solitary position caught between the "parrot industry," which sees them as "escaped merchandise," and the organized ornithological community, which expresses indifference, since as non-natives they are "as bad as starlings." The latter "ecocentric" view is mentioned on another occasion, when a city official relates the suggestion by a small minority of "environmentalist and conservationist types" that the non-native parrots be removed and that they be experimented on instead, but these views are presented as unpopular and given short shrift in the film. At the same time, the film's visual imagery—picturesque shots of the colourful birds amidst similarly colourful foliage, shots of children looking up longingly toward city trees in which the birds are perched, and so on—glorifies and sentimentalizes the birds as well as their saintly feeder and companion. This is not inconsistent with the biocentric sentiments that Bittner voices toward the end of the film ("all life is one whole"), but the question of appropriate intervention into nature is not addressed in great depth in the film.

The trajectory of the story, in fact, takes viewers along a surprising path. When Bittner is forced to move out of the neighbourhood, he resigns himself to the fact that they are their own birds and that his life is with the human world. By the film's end, Bittner has cut his hair—he had previously stated that he would do that only if he got a girlfriend—and paired up with the filmmaker, Judy Irving. In the background, then, as the film has probed Bittner's relationship with the parrots, another relationship—and another boundary-crossing intervention, that between filmmaker and subject—has been unfolding, something the film acknowledges only in its final sequence. In the film's real-world aftermath, the two married, and Bittner continued to write and advocate on behalf of the parrots. His subsequent writing has shown an evolving ethical engagement with the issues raised by the book and the film. Bittner's desire to write a book had been triggered by a 1998 bill introduced into the California State Legislature mandating the eradication of all non-native species. While the bill died quickly, the USDA had previously targeted other urban parrot populations for elimination, and when Irving approached him about a possible film, Bittner agreed that this might be a good way of creating "a protective glow around the birds." As he admits, however, "fame is a double-edged sword," and in a later essay Bittner explored the tension between paying too little and too much attention, where the first can lead to allowing senseless eradications (such as those suggested by the ecological nativists) and the second risks developing dependency in the birds on their human feeders, making it easier for them to be captured or to pass on diseases.[104]

Irving's and Bittner's film popularized a relatively small population of parrots, and Bittner has since gone to some lengths to defend his role and to set out the parameters of involvement with what is essentially a wild species of urban bird. As a result of the attention paid to the parrots by a growing group of human feeders in a local park, he eventually took up the position that the latter group's activities were threatening the welfare of the birds. Paradoxically, the man best known for feeding parrots was moved to working for the passage of a city ordinance prohibiting the feeding of wild parrots in San Francisco's city parks. In the process, Bittner engaged in vigorous and deeply personalized debates with the park feeders, both in person and in online forums, with the latter eventually rejecting his entreaties and resorting to character assassination of the man many had earlier seen as an ally and model, the "Saint Francis of Telegraph Hill." In the end, Bittner sided with allies in the wildlife conservation and animal rescue communities against the park feeders and petitioning tourists and passersby, who enjoy interacting with the growing population of birds (by this point numbering a couple of hundred). The City Board of Supervisors voted 10 to 1 in favour of a ban, expanding a previous ordinance to include the feeding of parrots in city parks.[105]

This debate over the role of humans vis-à-vis parrots is not explored very explicitly in the film, since many of these issues unfolded after its release. What the film does make clear is that Bittner spent many months—sometimes standing still "for hours," as a neighbour put it—building a relationship of trust with the birds. His authority as their human representative, a position he came to accept, did not arise out of any obvious desire to speak on their behalf, but rather out of a thoroughly reasoned and long-term commitment to their welfare as *wild* birds, that is, as birds who would not become dependent on his feeding. This lack of dependence is, at least, a point he makes repeatedly in the film, and even more so in his later writings, when he argues that his feedings are only occasional and that they eventually ceased altogether.

A more contentious case of one individual's long-term commitment to the supposed welfare of a wild animal population is that of Timothy Treadwell, subject of Werner Herzog's *Grizzly Man*. Just as Bittner had "found himself" in his interactions with the parrots, Treadwell (*née* Dexter) found his own spiritual mission in the wilds of Alaska living, over thirteen summers, among or in very close proximity to the grizzly bears of Katmai National Park. Treadwell was co-founder, with one-time girlfriend Jewel Palovak, of the organization Grizzly People, formed ostensibly to protect bears in the wild. Thanks to the videos he made over several summers in Alaska, his appearances on talk shows with David Letterman and Tom Snyder, his talks at schools around the country, and his book (co-authored with Palovak), *Among Grizzlies*, Treadwell became something of a wildlife celebrity. Then, in early October of 2003, the remains of the bodies of Treadwell and Amie Huguenard were found in the stomach of a brown bear.

Grizzly Man takes the structure of an autopsy or detective story, with the question being not "whodunit?" but *why* did this happen? How did Treadwell get to the point where it *could* happen? Herzog has a plenty of evidence to work with, for Treadwell had left behind more than a hundred hours of his own video footage. One of the main strengths of the film is that Herzog allows many answers to be presented regarding the film's central question before he consolidates his own response. Interviews with individuals who knew Treadwell in a range of circumstances—his Grizzly People co-founder and one-time lover Jewel, other former co-workers and friends, park rangers, the pilot who flew him to his campsite, his parents, an actor friend, a medical examiner—present divergent perspectives. Treadwell is shown to be a complex character. An aspiring, if failed, actor, a former alcoholic and drug addict, a committed activist, and now a central character in his own digital videos shot with the bears in Alaska, he seems by turns playful, nervous, whiny, risk taking, obsessive, grandiose, paranoid, and utterly committed to his cause, though the exact nature of that cause is left somewhat unclear. He claims it is to guard and protect the grizzlies, though others, including park rangers, claim they are already protected: there are 35,000 bears in Alaska, 3,000 of them on Kodiak Island, and all the land in question is a federal reserve on which very little poaching has been documented (including by Treadwell).[106] Yet Treadwell proclaims to the camera, in repeated takes at the end of one summer: "I came, I served, I protected, and I studied, and I promise I'll be back." He freely admits that the animals have given his life meaning—"I had no life, now I have a life"—and that he, "Timothy Treadwell, the kind warrior," would "die for them." The government and park authorities become Treadwell's perceived enemies: he rants against their supposed indifference to wildlife and their "schemes" to prevent him from protecting the bears from poachers. But Treadwell's words are, in some instances, belied by the evidence of his own video footage. His denunciations of poachers are substantiated, we are told, by a single instance of a "close encounter with intruders," who leave behind a note etched in a log—"Hi Timothy. See you in 2001"—and a happy face sign, which Treadwell characteristically interprets with dark foreboding, though viewers have little reason to take it that way.

Like Timothy's other interlocutors, director Herzog "steps in, in his defence," his persona being that of a filmmaker commenting on how Treadwell used the camera "methodically" as a tool to get his message across, "often repeating takes fifteen times." This point of cinematographic commonality becomes an opening for Herzog to explore his deeper concern, which has to do with the power and beauty of nature—something Herzog suggests Treadwell captured incidentally rather than intentionally. Herzog notes how some of Treadwell's shots of nature, despite his own "action movie" intents, maintain "a strange beauty," the images developing "their own life, their own mysterious stardom." He refers to Alaskan glaciers as a "landscape in turmoil" and a "metaphor of [Treadwell's] soul." While Treadwell was clearly focused on the bears, the foxes with whom he had developed a seemingly friendly and playful relationship became co-stars of his own films. And throughout the film, flies buzzing around Treadwell, or around Herzog's interview subjects, or simply milling around the camera and even bumping into it, remind us of the often annoying or uncomfortable presence of nature in a landscape commonly romanticized as America's "last wild place."

As it progresses, the film becomes an intellectual duel between two views of nature, Treadwell's (as Herzog presents it) and Herzog's (or at least the one presented by Herzog as his own). Where Native people, as we are told by an Alutiiq native (who is also an anthropologist), had respected "the line between bear and human" for "seven thousand years," Treadwell, Herzog tells us, sought a "primordial encounter" but "crossed an invisible borderline." Treadwell was trying to show the world that bears are misunderstood, that they are wonderful creatures not to be feared, and that they deserve to be revered, but his helicopter pilot acquaintance voices the view that Treadwell acted as if he "was working with people wearing bear costumes" and that he thought they would "bond as children of the universe." This theme of anthropomorphism and sentimentalization becomes a running debate. Herzog, finally, states his own view of the universe: "I believe the common denominator of the universe is not harmony, but chaos, hostility, and murder." Later, as we look into the eyes of the bear that may have killed Treadwell and Huguenard, Herzog intones: "What haunts me is that in all the faces of all the bears that Treadwell ever filmed, I discover no kinship, no understanding, no mercy. I see only the overwhelming indifference of nature. To me there is no such thing as a secret world of the bears, and this blank stare speaks only of a half-bored interest in food."

Our own look into the bear's gaze at us (via Treadwell's camera) thus comes pre-interpreted by Herzog, and many commentators have argued that as a result the film offers a biased view of Treadwell: Treadwell as seen, and as already judged, by Herzog.[107] But visual evidence, particularly the gaze of an animal, reaches deeper into the affective reception of viewers than does its textual accompaniment, especially when that accompaniment is as contested and multi-voiced as it is in this film.[108] While Herzog pits his view against Treadwell's, the film remains irreducible to their two voices. Herzog's sympathetic engagement with Treadwell's efforts and his expressed admiration for his filmmaking cut against the grain of this disputative structure. So do the other views presented; the film works, in this sense, as a heteroglossic dialogue among different positions. At the film's close, as folk singer Don Edwards intones "and Treadwell is gone.... Damned old coyotes and me," Treadwell is seen walking away into nature, leaving a touching ambiguity: Herzog seems to have made a good case that Treadwell was a paranoid and self-obsessed neurotic, yet his subject's effort to go to the edge is sensitively memorialized as he becomes one with the nature portrayed in the filmic image. The edge, then, can be an opening onto madness or onto nature, or both. The film is left open, with some texts, sounds, and images suggesting one thing, others another.

In the end, the film gets taken up by audiences according to their own interpretive predilections. This can be seen in the prolific debates generated by the film on environmental websites, listservs, and blogs. One such debate unfolded on a site hosted by the National Resources Defense Council (NRDC) Action Fund following an 18 October 2005 posting by Louisa Willcox, a biologist, friend of Treadwell's, and director of the NRDC's Wild Bears Project. Willcox praised Treadwell's dedication to bear conservation, which encompassed "the problems of poaching, habitat loss, [his critique of] the careless behavior that lead [sic] to bears getting hooked on garbage and dying unnecessarily," as well as his "fearlessness" and "selfless commitment to the education of children." She acknowledged that he broke rules—including those specifying the distance to be kept between humans and bears in Katmai National Park—and other norms of the bear management world, especially the one against anthropomorphism, but also the implicit one that outsiders should not tell Alaskans how to manage their resources. At the same time, she situated Treadwell's findings and claims (noting that he "was perhaps the first to record the lives of so many generations of individual bears in such detail") within an emerging "school of thought among experts" that people can live "in closer proximity to bears without weapons, if they know what they are doing."[109]

The discussion that followed Willcox's post continued over several months, eliciting some 160 posts from more than a hundred participants before the weblog closed in late 2006.[110] The views expressed showed a dramatic divergence. Many attacked Treadwell's character and characterized him as a mentally ill, narcissistic, and self-obsessed "failed actor" whose sentimentalization of bears and attempts to live in close proximity to them did more harm than good. A strong minority of respondents expressed admiration for Treadwell, portraying him as an inspiring example of heroic and passionate dedication to the cause of animals and wilderness. The NRDC blog only sporadically debated the virtues of the film; most of the discussion it generated concerned Treadwell—his character, actions, and ambiguous legacy. Knowing Treadwell personally was often presented as a kind of accreditation or badge of authenticity; those who knew him were much more positive about him, while those who only knew him from the film tended to distrust him. The value of wilderness was emphasized repeatedly ("Let the wild remain wild!" "Leave the bears alone!"), and this often developed into an argument against Treadwell's methods, which were seen as endangering the bears by desensitizing them to human presence. A striking feature of the debate was the extent to which comments reiterated views stated by various characters in the film: that Treadwell's quest was religious; that he should be honoured "for protecting bears" and for "living in wild nature"; that he "wanted to be a bear" or "desired to get into their world" but that "the reality is that we never can"; that "he crossed the boundary" that indigenous Alaskans had lived with for seven thousand years; that he did it all to make money; and so on. In this sense, it is clear that the film set up a certain range of positions and that these positions were taken up by viewers within the debates that followed.

In response to the ferocity of some of Treadwell's critics, a group of his defenders set up an independent online forum, the Yahoo group TimothyTreadwell_Paths, as a "safe haven" for those who wanted to discuss his legacy and influence "without being judged by the people that did not like him."[111] The site continued for several years and amassed several thousand posts, some of them pertaining to Treadwell and others to bear-related conservation issues. Among the posted comments were observations by fellow activists, wildlife biologists, bear guides, and even hunters. A moving eulogy by Paul Watson, former Greenpeace activist and founder of the anti-whaling group Sea Shepherd International, unabashedly defended his departed friend.[112] "For thirteen years," Watson wrote, Treadwell "did what no other human being had ever done—he walked amongst the great bears, listened to them and spoke to them. He walked through the wilderness without a gun, armed with courage, a vision, and a camera. In so doing he walked into another dimension and saw things from a singularly unique perspective." He succeeded, in other words, in becoming-animal to an extent that others have not. Frank Baele, a California schoolteacher and former Katmai national park ranger,[113] similarly wrote that

> Herzog didn't get it right. Timothy didn't have a death wish, he had a life wish. Timothy lived his life to the fullest. Think of it, he experienced moments of looking into a grizzly's eyes (some were huge) at really close range daily and then used all his senses to figure out each bear's personality and the appropriate behavior he should take to stay

alive for 13 summers…. He educated thousands of students about bears [and] often did this for no fee.

Many of the forum's comments took the tone of personal confessionals, heartfelt defences of "Timmy," or criticisms of his critics, including Herzog. A frequent contributor argued that "part of [Treadwell's] filming himself was out of sheer lonliness [sic] and boredom." He continued: "Herzog, here … I am trying not to lose my temper, hold on … people HAVE GOT TO REALIZE that the footage in Grizzly Man was spliced and edited together to show the man spiraling [out of control]."[114] Another questioned whether Treadwell's footage "REALLY contain[s] a meticulous depiction of the disintegration of his personality" or if this was the strategy chosen by Herzog to create a character consistent with his other films.[115] Interviews with Herzog were posted and discussed, with some commenting that the fifteen to twenty hours he watched (by Herzog's own account) of the hundred or so hours of video footage was inadequate as a basis for making a judgment of Treadwell's character. (Herzog employed four apprentices to search the remaining footage for particular kinds of material.) These accounts of Treadwell conflicted with Herzog's and others' claims that Treadwell "filmed everything" because he "planned a big movie with him as the rock star Prince Valiant."[116]

Among the most interesting contributions to online discussions of Treadwell were those written by viewing guides such as Charlie Russell, Kevin Sanders, and John Rogers.[117] Russell, an Alberta-based naturalist, author, and photographer, noted the tension between viewing guides and hunters, a tension that has grown since bear viewing "has become a bigger part of the Alaskan economy than hunting them." Hunters, Russell asserted, "understandably feel threatened about this trend because many photographs show bears and people mingling together peacefully. This has made killing grizzly bears for sport look more like murder than an act of bravery. Hunters desperately needed Timothy's blunder to put the danger back into bear encounters." Russell and the others contested the perception that Treadwell didn't know what he was doing: "The fact that Timothy spent an incredible 35000 hours, spanning 13 years, living with the bears in Katmai National Park, without any previous mishap, escapes people completely…. Most people now see him only the way Herzog skillfully wanted his audience to see him; as an idiot who continually 'crossed nature's line,' what ever that means." According to Russell, the main line that Treadwell crossed, and "the one thing that upsets people the most about Timothy, to the point of loathing him," was "that he talked to bears in a kind way." This was crossing the human–animal boundary in a way that in Alaska is considered "unforgivably stupid."[118] Rogers acknowledged that

Treadwell had developed "an exceptional understanding of bears" and that "his bear etiquette was impeccable," but he also noted disapprovingly (as did the others) that Treadwell's precautionary electric fence and pepper spray, which others use as a matter of course in bear country, came to seem unnecessary to him so that he stopped using them, with eventually fatal results.[119]

A point of recurrent disagreement among Treadwell's commentators emerges around the basic question of what the deaths of Treadwell and Huguenard *mean*. Do they demonstrate that he was lucky, naive, stupid, or a "nutcase" for thirteen summers and that he finally got his due? Or do they prove that he was careful and smart all that time but made a single, fatal mistake—which was, staying on too long into the autumn, a season when bears were busy fattening up for the winter and when competition among them was growing more intense? Both views get aired in the film, but those who take the latter position in online debates tend to question the video evidence as presented in the film more than do those who take the former position. In this sense, the film raises the same question as any documentary about a subject of disputed significance—whether and to what extent the film accurately depicts its real-life subject. The existence of reams of video footage shot by Treadwell himself—much of it seemingly "live" and personal in nature—contributes to a tendency among viewers to accept what they see as authentic and to conclude, for instance, that what we are seeing is Treadwell's personality deteriorating. On generic websites such as Amazon.com, most of the film's online reviews laud the film itself, but they also tend to note Treadwell's character flaws. Many of these reviews speculate about his mental health; some even insist it was deteriorating. Rarely, though, do these reviews suggest that the film was edited so as to highlight that deterioration.

What may be more interesting for us, however, is the role that Treadwell's *own* editing of his life—that is, the role of the camera in *his* film-in-the-making—played in shaping what was to become *Grizzly Man*. Treadwell, as Sanders put it, "filmed everything" to the extent that the camera became "an extension of his body."[120] While cameras have been used in this way before, the emergence of portable digital video coupled with the rise of a reality-TV aesthetic has made it all the more possible not only for film to be an extension of one's body, but also for the body to become an extension of the camera, that is, for one's actions to become a kind of projection of the narrative that one imagines the camera itself calling for. *Grizzly Man* and the debate that followed it suggest to us what happens when one's video footage goes astray, when the pieces of one's film-in-the-making get diverted from their intended purposes and begin to make their way into other films. Herzog's film is hardly the final product of Treadwell's life: books, magazine articles, online discussions, video spoofs, and even an (apparently faked) "real death audio" have been produced and are in print or online circulation.[121] Both the film and the film-within-the-film have been inserted into a larger circulation of moving imagery in which both Treadwell and Herzog are characters shaped by those who write and speak about them. Herzog's relationship to his characters is, in this sense, pertinent; so when he remarks that "I argue [with Treadwell] like I argue with my brothers, *and I love them*," it should not be surprising that this love for his characters echoes the love that Treadwell so clearly expresses for his bears.[122] In the digital era, then, we might suggest that the boundary between human and animal turns into a movable set of emotionally activated lines that are reflected, refracted, and doubled over in the relationships between filmmakers and their subjects, and between each of these and their audiences.

Sheer Becomings: One or Several Types of Packs

While *Grizzly Man* prowls around the boundary between human and bear, sniffing it out from a variety of boom and camera angles, it is in Treadwell's own persona, as captured by his own camera, that we are able to follow his own animal becoming. As Neimanis observes, this is visible in the ways he moves among the bears:

> He lumbers, keeping his head low and his eyes unchallenging (most often hidden by black-lensed sunglasses). He intuits his rank alongside the submissive grizzlies, deferring authority to the more dominant and aggressive bears in the group. At the same time we can observe his sense that these movements also have to express (or at least feign) confidence and assurance, as Treadwell knows that evident fear and total submission will result in attack. Among the bears, his posture and his gait accustom themselves to the grassy plain, the maze of trees and the sandy flats that comprise the home of the bears. His affective molecularity is also called out in response to the animal emotions in which he becomes entangled—we see this for example in his heart-felt affinity with the dogged determination of Mickey the bear, who loses a tussle with Sergeant Brown.[123]

Treadwell's "motor and affective connections to the foxes" are shown in his "mischievous antics and sprinting movements, stubborn and vaguely childish pouts, and playful yet also stroppy mannerisms."[124] Treadwell's animal becomings extend to his quest to "remain hidden from the authorities, from the people that would harm me, from people who would seek me out as a story" and instead to "be a spirit in the wilderness."[125] Treadwell would seem, in his own account at least, to be seeking a "becoming-imperceptible," which for Deleuze and Guattari is the teleological end point of all becomings, such that after his death a friend can remark that "he finally figured out a way to live here forever." At the same time, his obsessive video documentation of his behaviour asserts a desire to become heroic—which raises the question of whether the intertwining of moving-image media with non-human becomings may shift those becomings into a different register, toward a becoming all the more *perceptible*.

At the farthest end of the scale of becomings-animal, we leap off into a no man's land where viewers follow the lure of the Other to its ultimate extreme. Tales of vampires, werewolves, and berserkers have circulated for centuries, and fans of more recent films portraying these creaturely transformations occasionally let themselves slip into the stream of such a becoming, with results that fall outside the conventions of morally or legally sanctioned behaviour. The notorious Central Park Jogger case of 1989, which resulted in the conviction of five New York City teenagers for allegedly raping and murdering a woman, popularized the term "wilding" for a form of gang violence linked to city parks and natural areas. The teenagers, who later claimed that their confessions had been coerced from them by police, were eventually released when DNA evidence demonstrated a convicted rapist and murderer's sole guilt in the case. But the term is still encountered in politicians' calls for stronger policing and for harsher sentences against violent criminals. It has become a trope within the formulation of a boundary whose transgression is associated with deviant, delinquent, and perhaps mentally unstable forms of masculine aggression.

That a becoming-animal might also mean a becoming-predator is something that writers of gothic literature have always known and celebrated, but this is only one option among many. As Deleuze and Guattari put it, becomings-animal are of another "power, since their reality resides not in an animal one *imitates* or to which one *corresponds* but in themselves, in that which suddenly sweeps us up and makes us become—a proximity, an indiscernibility that extracts a shared element from the animal far more effectively than any domestication, utilization, or imitation could: 'the Beast.'"[126] Becoming-animal, as Patricia Pisters puts it, is "not based on resemblance or affiliation but on alliance, symbiosis, affection, and infection."[127] It is, in Astrida Neimanis's words, "communicative and contagious, working according to a logic of infection, whereby human molecularity and animal molecularity collide in each others's [sic] zones of proximity."[128] If the human is itself an active organization of intensive forces, speeds, movements, and affects, and is always in a state of becoming-other, any becoming-animal is simply a reordering via an opening toward something of another that happens to be animal. Neimanis writes that "'to emit a molecular dog' means to access some mode of our molecular embodiment—a growling hunger within our viscerality, a dejected whimper in our affectivity, even if such growls or whimpers are never actually emitted."[129] We "become animal," Alphonso Lingis suggests, as "our legs plod with elephantine torpor," or "as our hands swing with penguin vivacity, our fingers drum with nuthatch insistence."[130] Movies are, of course, one means by which such visceral contagion spreads. A catalogue of cinematic becomings-animal would range across a wide spectrum, from the vampiric and lycanthropic (Murnau's *Nosferatu, Eine Symphonie des Grauens*, 1922; Browning's *Dracula*, 1931; *The Wolf Man*, 1941; Herzog's *Nosferatu, the Vampire*, 1979; *An American Werewolf in London*, 1981; *The Howling*, 1981; Coppola's *Bram Stoker's Dracula*, 1992; and Mick Nichols's *Wolf*, 1994) to films with more ambiguous and unusual bodily renderings, as in Alan Parker's *Birdy* (1984), David Cronenberg's *The Fly* (1986), and Apichatpong Weerasethakul's *Tropical Malady* (2004), in which a tender gay romance becomes transmogrified into a folkloric tale of a soldier's encounter with a ghostly shaman-tiger.

Even the more classical horror film transformations can be presented in such a way that the transgressions blend a critique of societal norms with an aestheticization of otherness. An example is Michael Wadleigh's *Wolfen* (1981), a metaphysical mystery-horror fantasy whose pioneering use of point-of-view action shots and thermal photography (later used to similar ends in *Predator* [1987]) offered audiences something of what it feels like to run with wolves. The film interleaves a narrative featuring a police investigation into a series of savage murders in abandoned areas of New York City with Native American tales of werewolf-like shape-shifters. It suggests that the landscape rightfully belongs both to the Wolfen and to its original human inhabitants, whose contemporary representatives feature as construction workers working on the city's skyscrapers and bridges. Feeling cornered in what is left of their hunting grounds, the Wolfen selectively target dying homeless people—human society's unwanted—as well as a few property tycoons attempting to infringe on their territory. In the film's closing shots, as a pack runs gracefully through an abandoned South Bronx landscape and the old church that is at its centre—not unlike the Room at the center of Tarkovsky's Zone—a voice-over intones: "In arrogance, man knows nothing of what exists. There exists on Earth such as we dare not imagine. Life as certain as our death. Life that will prey on us as we prey on this Earth."

A different sort of becoming-animal is found in Neil Jordan's gothic horror-fantasy *The Company of Wolves* (1984). Based on a screenplay by Angela Carter in which several fairy tales, centred on "Little Red Riding Hood," are given a post-Freudian feminist reworking, the film is a visually sumptuous presentation of a Chinese-box-like series of nested narratives that play out as the dreams of a pubescent girl, Rosaleen.[131] Transformations between people and wolves abound: a pack of wolves devours Rosaleen's spiteful older sister; her grandmother warns her of men who are "hairy on the inside" and whose "eyebrows meet in the middle"; a man who had disappeared, supposedly the victim of marauding wolves, returns some years later to his since-remarried wife and turns into a wolf upon discovering her new children; another man, having taken a lotion from the Prince of Darkness, sprouts hair all over his body; wedding guests transform into wolves; a she-wolf transforms into a feral child; a huntsman, having beaten Rosaleen in a race to her grandmother's home (and then devoured the grandmother), turns into a wolf upon being shot by Rosaleen, but when the villagers arrive and try to kill it, Rosaleen herself has become a wolf; and, finally, when Rosaleen has woken up from her dreams, her bedroom is invaded by a *real* pack of wolves. As she screams, her own voice calmly recites the final voice-over: "Little girls this seems to say, Never stop upon your way. Never trust a stranger friend, No one knows how it will end. As you're pretty so be wise, Wolves may lurk in every guise. Now, as then, 'tis simple truth, Sweetest tongue has sharpest tooth." Keith Hopper argues that the film's multiple endings—"firstly, when Rosaleen shows her compassion for the wounded wolf and becomes a wolf herself; secondly, when the wolves break through her bedroom window into the 'real' world; and, finally, when Rosaleen calmly recites a more lyrical version of Perrault's traditional moral over the credits"—work to decentre any possibility of comforting narrative certainty.[132] Rosaleen's final choice to run with the wolves is taken by some, including feminist film theorist Laura Mulvey, as her acceptance "not so much" of "the bestiality of *men*" as of her "now recognized, but unrepressed sexuality."[133] As Rosaleen's mother puts it in the film, "If there's a beast in men it meets its match in women too."

If sexuality is always lurking in the background of such therianthropic becomings as are found in the werewolf and vampire genres—and Jordan's/Carter's and Weerasethakul's variations show that it is—the matter of actual human–animal sexuality, or bestiality, is a frontier that few films have crossed. Robinson Devor's *Zoo* (2007) is an exception to that rule. The film is a documentary (in some sense of the term) about a secretive community of male zoophiles, or "zoos," who conversed online and gathered periodically at a rural farm outside Seattle to practise and sometimes videotape bestiality. Following the death of one of the participants, Kenneth Pinyan (played by Adam McLain), from internal bleeding resulting from a perforated colon after a sexual encounter with an Arabian stallion, the case became a luridly reported tabloid news sensation and resulted in the criminalization of bestiality in the state of Washington. The film's disarmingly contemplative aestheticization of its taboo-ridden subculture was harshly criticized for its apparent sympathy with its subject community. In contrast to other media reports, the film portrayed the events allusively, employing re-enactments, stylized and dreamlike cinematography, and audio testimonies of the dead man's zoophile companions, whose voices were presented without authorial comment and granted a status on a level with the comments of animal rescuers, police, and others.

An issue that arose in the film's aftermath was that of the horses' consent to the activities, which Devor believed were consensual.[134] But as Robert McKay observed in a lucid analysis of the film, Devor omitted explicit images of bestial activities for fear that the film would not be distributed. As a result it is not clear whether the film leaves a gap that makes it less possible, or less imaginable, for audiences to engage with the film ethically, or whether in fact, as Devor claims, the film is better able to do this because it avoids sensational depictions of what would otherwise be tainted as bestiality porn.[135] The issue of horse consent is one that our society has few tools for dealing with; it is also muddied by the apparent training of the horses to act sexually with humans. At what point does training become collaboration, be it scientific (as in most scientific experimentation), aesthetic (as in *Winged Migration*), or sexual and recreational (as in *Zoo*)? And at what point does it *cease* being collaboration? How are we to know that the animals are willing participants in something, even when it is a shared, companionable activity? In her work on companion species, Donna Haraway offers some suggestions for the kinds of questions we might ask our alter-species collaborators, beyond the Benthamite question of whether the animals are suffering: How do animals play, and work, and how do we do so with them? How do we arrange our contact zones for such "naturalcultural" entanglements with mutual regard for each others' capacities, needs, and desires?[136]

At the very least, such questions require *zöo-ethnographic* intervention—a rigorous exploration of what these things look and feel like from within the *animal* worlds—and this is something that *Zoo* made little effort to incorporate. The film, however, raises questions about the dynamics of opticality that bring us back to the central concerns of this chapter. When we watch apparently illicit becomings-animal through what seems to be the point of view of a human participant, are we seeing it—and *can* we see it—as would a horse? A horse-man or wolf-woman? Or is there an entire culture and history of human assumptions and affects watching over our shoulders with us: an entourage of interloping voices and eyes carrying taboos and proscriptions, illicit desires, moral standards, and secret histories on their backs? What do we bring with us when we enter the dark zone of cinematic encounter?

Here it is worth coming back to Andrei Tarkovsky's *Stalker* for insights into this murky zone. As was evident in my earlier discussion of the film, its title is somewhat of a misnomer, since the Stalker is not one who actually stalks an animal or another human being. He is not a hunter; if anything, he is more hunted, a *becoming-hunted*. He may be stalking *something*, but it is not clear what that is, and he is probably at least as much *stalked* by that something, a something that is imperceptible but felt through the ellipses in the landscape-space of the film-world. The Stalker's journey into the Zone is a journey into a world that stalks him, just as the planet Solaris haunts and stalks its orbiting visitors in Tarkovsky's *Solaris*. Those astronauts become-Solaris by a movement into the affective texture of the virtual forces that constitute them, their lives and memories, their bodies and psyches. In the same sense, Timothy Treadwell's journey is into a Zone that contains his fears and desires as much as it contains the actual bears that remain unknowable, not only to Treadwell but to us. Kenneth Pinyan's journey into zoophilia was also a journey into a Zone of dreams and longings, but also of the unknown—but real—otherness of stallions. In watching films about (and featuring) these zoomorphic adventurers, our journeys follow theirs to a degree we have some control over—which means that some of us follow them farther than others—into a Zone made up of the convergence of *their* worlds, *our* worlds, and *another* world in which neither of us can tread safely and surely. It is these *other* worlds that remain unknowable, unpredictable, and quite real. They are the Zones where cinema opens up to landscapes of radical otherness.

Boundary Strategies: Ethics of the Contact Zone

In each of the films examined in the second half of this chapter—from *March of the Penguins* to *Zoo*—there is some exchange between humans and (other) animals. *March* is overtly about penguins, but its resonance with audiences is ascribable not only to their resemblances to us, but also to the filmmakers' outstanding efforts to capture them on film for us. The relationship between the humans and the animals is, however, a matter mostly of analogy and of observation. As in a traditional ethnography, the filmmakers observe but appear not to alter what they see; theirs is a scientistic and touristic mode of participation that we, the viewers, enjoy vicariously.[137] Capitalizing on the popularity of the Antarctic avians following the success of *March*, *Happy Feet* added an environmental as well as a satirical cultural-political message to the proliferating thirdness surrounding cinematic penguins. Some audiences agreed with that message and enjoyed the film all the more; others disagreed and bemoaned its cultural "agenda." In essence, both films pursued what was primarily a strategy of *analogy* or *similarity*. The penguins portrayed are likable: they are objects of our empathy because they remind us of ourselves. This can be a matter of anthropomorphic projection—as it is with the dancing penguins—or a matter of objective biological kinship, which would account for our understanding of the difficulties faced by penguins in caring for their young and in struggling to survive in a harsh environment. The human–animal boundary in *Happy Feet* works its way into the picture both in the human incursions into the penguin world and in Mumble's communication across the boundary, but these are easily understood to be normal features of the Disney-like world of anthropomorphic animated cinema.

The birds who star in *Wild Parrots* are anthropomorphized; we relate to them because of the human qualities that are projected onto, or reflected by, their behaviour. They are made more sympathetic by their cuteness, which means (in part) by their resemblance to human infants. Yet a large part of that film's affective draw comes from the sympathetic portrait of Mark Bittner. He is the centre of attention, a human who has made moves toward becoming-other—becoming-parrot—or at least he is reaching out across the human–parrot boundary and being altered in the process. This, then, is an engaged, post-traditional ethnography, where the ethnographer is both Mark Bittner and filmmaker Judy Irving lurking in the background (and us, vicariously taken along for the journey); where Mark represents the special human crossing over into the jungle of parrotdom even while being presented as an average bloke, a homeless guy who lucked out and found his niche serendipitously through a zen kind of non-doing; where both ethnographers—Bittner by his gradual but dramatic change of life, Irving by her own unfolding relationship with him—are changed in the process; and where the ostensible subjects of the ethnography, the tribe of San Franciscan parrots, are already post-traditional to start with, refugee migrants carving out a fragile place for themselves in a foreign land. The boundary is a place of encounter, a contact zone, and the contact is charged with meaning, affect, and possibility.

With *Grizzly Man* we have a human subject who is not necessarily sympathetic, and animal subjects that are not at all anthropomorphized—at least not successfully, though Treadwell tries hard to do this for us, while Herzog (who has the last word) disavows that effort. Yet this is a dramatic story that struck a sharp chord with audiences. Dealing with the "autopsy" of a dramatic and grisly/grizzly death, the film risks becoming what Herzog called a "snuff film," but he carefully decided not to show us the death (which could have been reconstructed for the camera) nor to play the soundtrack from Treadwell's camera, which was running as Treadwell was being fatally attacked. Instead, Herzog shows us himself listening over headphones to the soundtrack of the attack and telling Jewel Palovak, Treadwell's partner and "widow," that she should never play this recording for anyone. In this way Herzog craftily preserves his own claim to being a dignified and respectful filmmaker and, at the same time, reinforces his onscreen persona as gatekeeper and guide, whom we are presumably to trust with his selection of what's worthy of inclusion and what isn't.

Yet this boundary between showing death and only hinting at it, like the boundary that Treadwell crossed with the bears, is affectively energized—made compelling—through the very process by which the satisfaction of boundary crossing is deferred. The entire film, as Jeong and Andrew have noted, is haunted by Treadwell's spectre, since we know all along that we are watching the electronic ghost of a man who was mauled by a bear.[138] (Indeed, in its opening minutes Treadwell is seen saying, "I can smell death all over my fingers"—a thought that remains with us throughout the film.) In its many reflective and refractive mirrorings between Treadwell as he portrays himself, Treadwell as recounted by others, Treadwell as Herzog relates to him, and so on, the film is a kind of *postmodern salvage ethnography*: postmodern in its reflexive ironies, conveyed with nods and winks; and a salvage film in that it is salvaging remains from a heap of leftover video footage; but also a salvage ethnography in that it wants to resuscitate the remains of the dying breed—the romantic and half-mad pursuer of wild dreams—by which it remains fascinated. It is part auto-ethnography (Treadwell's) and part autopsy, a film that doesn't seem sure whether it is celebrating or mocking its subject, raising up or kicking sand on the corpse at its centre, whose putrid remains are mentioned repeatedly but never shown. It is a film that in the end leaves divergent interpretive possibilities open to its audience. Because the film follows Treadwell to the human–animal boundary, shows him crossing it, and at the same time distances us—or at least the filmmaker-playing-himself—from the crossing, the boundary becomes a highly charged one that attracts and repels in more or less equal measure.

Then there are films like *Wolfen*, *The Company of Wolves*, *Zoo*, *The Fly*, and *Tropical Malady*, which stage variations on the crossing of the boundary, but perhaps with less of a secure foothold for viewers to remain on *this side* of it. (Another in this vein is Carroll Ballard's *Never Cry Wolf* [1983], a Canadian feature about a government wildlife scientist who lives in the wild alongside wolves and eats mice to prove to himself that large carnivores can do that rather than overhunt caribou, and that climaxes with the scientist running naked alongside caribou with the wolves in pursuit.) I say "perhaps" because these are all "just movies," and once they are over we can treat them like we do dreams, stories, or anything else from which we can gain the distance of daylight and "objectivity." With horror films or documentaries, we have at our disposal the convenient retreat to questions elicited by the genres. Was this a good film? Were we sufficiently scared (for the moment) by the monsters, appropriately convinced by the characterizations and narrative connections? Was the documentary a fair representation of the actual events? Genre-defying films, or those, like *Zoo*, that cut too close to the bone, attempt to scramble some of the paths by which we can beat a retreat to such interpretive safety. In all cases, however, even while the retreat is easily accessible, there are affective vectors we can travel on and with while watching—movements we can follow, garments we can try on for size, feelings we can taste—and these leave behind a residue, a trail of resonating strings within our biomorphic makeup.

The various strategies pursued in these films with respect to the portrayal of the human–other boundary can be mapped along two sets of axes. The first of these is that of *similarity versus difference*, that is, whether the entities on either side of the boundary, humans and animals (or monsters), are perceived as essentially similar or as essentially different. The second I will call *system versus flux*, which refers to whether the human–other boundary is stable, unstable, or non-existent. In the case of the latter axis, there are three possibilities. The boundary can be assumed to exist and be left untouched; I will call this *system*, since it presumes a certain stable ordering of relations. The boundary can be rendered unstable by being approached and crossed, or it can be energized through an ambivalent dynamic, as in *Grizzly Man*, *Wolfen*, and *The Company of Wolves*; I will call this *kinesis*, since it allows for movement across the boundary or change in the placement of the boundary markers. Or the boundary can be cast aside altogether, which I will call *flux* or *anti-system*. These two axes can be mapped against each other, resulting in six possibilities. See table 5.1.

TABLE 5.1   Strategies for Negotiating the Human–Unhuman Boundary

	(a) System	(b) Kinesis	(c) Anti-system / flux
1. Similarity	representation, resemblance, correspondence, imitation, analogy	moral extensionism	animism, Levinasian ethics
2. Difference	otherness, hostile wilderness	romanticism, sublime; becoming-animal	Derridean ethics

1a. System/similarity. Animals are perceived to be akin to humans, but as a reflection, model, symbol, analogy, correspondence, or partial equation. The portrayal of similarity, reflection, or correspondence involves a representational movement across the boundary, but the boundary remains in place and the terms on either side are not understood as movable or changeable. All static forms of cosmology fall into this tradition. These include the medieval notion of a Great Chain of Being, Renaissance ways of ordering the world according to resemblance and correspondence (as described, for instance, in Michel Foucault's *The Order of Things*), modern evolutionary family trees that represent similarity and difference according to genealogy, and popular representations of "Disnified" animals. Many media depictions of animal heroes fall largely into this category: television animals like Flipper and Lassie are loved in large part because their behaviour resembles human (or childlike) "good behaviour" more than we would normally expect, but these are the exceptional animals that prove the rule that animals are not and never will be quite human. They serve as lessons for our good behaviour and to inculcate qualities of loving and caring in us.

2a. System/difference. Animals or the wild are considered fundamentally Other to humanity, the two making up a duality, the poles of which must be kept at a safe distance from each other. The creation of walls by agricultural societies to keep out their "savage" hunter–gatherer neighbours—as expressed, perhaps, in the ancient Sumerian *Epic of Gilgamesh*—and the long heritage of walling off otherness, by literal or cultural means, fall into this tradition. For many ecocritics, this is the dominant orientation in industrial society; it is the epitome of human anthropocentrism and species chauvinism. Yet in practice it has often been meliorated by a recognition that there are "good" animals and "bad" animals—those we domesticate and interact with, and those we keep at bay. System-as-similarity (1a) can coexist with system-as-difference (2a), with animals being seen as corresponding to humans up to a point, but as ultimately different in that they are lower on the hierarchy of valued entities.

1b. Kinesis/similarity. Animals and humans are considered fundamentally similar in crucial respects, and on this basis change in their status is made or advocated. An example of this would be the moral extensionism advocated by animal rights philosophers like Peter Singer and Tom Regan, who would extend the category of morally considerable subjects to animals because they share relevant characteristics with humans, such as the capacity for suffering (Singer) and the fact that animals, like humans, are "subjects of a life" (Regan). The reverse movement would be the ascription of the category of animality to certain humans. Movement here can be considered teleologically preordained, ethically justified, or simply a morally neutral possibility.

2b. Kinesis/difference. Movement across the boundary is considered possible and, for some, laudatory. This is best exemplified by the Romantic tradition that sees nature and wilderness as domains of truth, sublime power, and authenticity. Humans are urged to move in this direction, but it is recognized that this will be an elite or solitary practice, as seen, for instance, in the efforts of Romantics from Ruskin and Wordsworth to Goethe and John Muir to explore these lofty heights. Shamanic and neo-shamanistic practices would seem to fall into this category as well, as would Deleuze and Guattari's seeming advocacy of becoming-animal.

3a & 3b. Flux/similarity and *flux/difference.* There is considered to be no fixed boundary, only a shared ground of encounter that makes relationality, reciprocity, or responsibility possible. Systemless understandings of commonality or of difference (with the distinction between the two being one of emphasis) might include animist sensibilities, according to which all things are ensouled or animated by spirit; the Franciscan ideal of service to living beings (without the anthropocentric baggage that often comes with it); or the philosophies of Emmanuel Levinas and Jacques Derrida, with the former tending toward similarity and an ethic of responsiveness based on the face of the Other, and the latter tending toward a view of difference and an ethic of obligation "without why." Perhaps more commonly, there are a range of positions that would embrace an animality on some heterodox philosophical grounds, whether Darwinian (or Social Darwinist), or Nietzschean, or that of one of the subcultures that periodically arise to reject social conformities and value systems (as in certain occult, Satanic, and Black Metal undergrounds).[139]

Films and other cultural products can follow one or more of these strategies—which are strategies not necessarily in being consciously pursued as such, but only insofar as the representation of human–animal relations will always participate in the maintenance, or dismantling, of boundaries in one way or another. Often the strategies pursued within a text may conflict with those evident in the format, genre, or broader contexts surrounding the text. *March of the Penguins* falls mainly into the first two categories (1a and 1b): by portraying another species in a sympathetic way, it makes a gesture toward greater inclusion of the moral community, but the system of differences remains in place. *Happy Feet* portrays boundary crossing occuring from both sides—human incursions into the world of the penguins, and successful penguin communication across the boundary in response—and thus it partakes of the "animal rights" strategy (1b). But the film's generic location as an animated CGI feature domesticates the radical potentials that might be found in such boundary crossings. *Grizzly Man* conveys both *similarity* and *difference*: Herzog's cautionary language against Treadwell's boundary crossing suggests the system-enforcing conservatism of categories 1a and 2a, but his own attraction to the boundary and to those who cross it (2b) speaks in their favour. The film suggests that Wild Nature as a powerful and attractive Other is a place we shudder in the face of, glance at in fear and trembling, yet keep returning to in fascination. A synthesis of these positions is the tradition of recognizing certain people as specialists in this domain: shamans (who are feared but also sought after for the power they wield), or "holy fools" (as in the Russian figure of the *iurodivii*) who are allowed to act crazily because it is recognized that they are closer to God and beatific in some sense, even if their actions are otherwise incomprehensible. Both Bittner and Treadwell draw from this tradition, and Herzog has made a career of staking out such characters, who are drawn to cross the boundary between the human and inhuman, civilization and madness.[140] Tarkovsky's Stalker is such a holy fool, and his attraction to the boundary represented by the Zone, coupled with a certain incomprehensibility surrounding what the Zone is and what it means, makes that film a particularly good instance of 2b (kinesis–difference) and the twin categories of the Anti-System or Flux.

Films, in the end, rarely take up a single coherent position on the continuum of human–animal relations. Rather, filmic representations of human–animal relations construct certain forms of similarity and difference, which viewers then take up in their own responses by moving along or projecting themselves within the space between the human and the animal, affectively or cognitively taking up positions, shifting positions, and approaching the boundary by identifying with a character (like Bittner, Treadwell, Rosaleen, or the Stalker) or by retracting when faced with the prospect of its crossing. What occurs while viewing a film may be later revisited, amplified, or modified in the context of further interpretation, conversation, and unconscious modification (as in the work that dreams do upon us). Films both generate and contribute to extra-filmic debates by providing material for the positions taken up in those debates.

The possibilities of the film medium are more thoroughly exploited when films make available *multiple* positions on such challenging questions as the human–animal relationship, and when tensions are set up between these positions, which viewers can then mediate for themselves. The debates over *March of the Penguins* and *Happy Feet* have been more concerned with whether penguins offer a model for human behaviour than with whether humans should change their behaviour in relation to penguins. This, I think, is because these films do not afford a broad multiplicity of affectively engaged positions—possible stances that viewers can take up on the human–animal relationship issue, supported by strongly portrayed visual and discursive statements within the film's structure of image, text, and sound—to raise this issue to a matter of great contention. While *Happy Feet* does concern itself with the impact of human activities on penguins, the nature of the animated animal adventure genre is such that audiences can easily opt for judging the film based on its entertainment value and its "childworthiness." Similarly, *Wild Parrots of Telegraph Hill* does not offer the range of well-supported positions on Bittner's relationship with the parrots, the city's policies regarding parrots, and so on, that would make the film a matter of contention to the same extent as *Grizzly Man*. However, *Wild Parrots* has played this kind of role for those directly affected by it, particularly local bird feeders whose interest in urban parrots was triggered by seeing the film, and those, like Bittner, who have taken a stance against public feeding of the birds in city parks.

Of the films discussed here, it is *Grizzly Man* that has generated the most discussion and debate about the nature of the human–animal boundary. This is in part because it is a documentary about a real person—and unlike *Zoo*, a documentary that did quite well theatrically. It is also, however, because the film presents a range of views of the character, who is depicted as having crossed or transgressed this boundary, and because these views are well supported by visual and textual "evidence." Not all of this evidentiary material takes a form that viewers consciously use. Some of it works on a precognitive affective level, striking chords in viewers depending on their affective predilections. *Grizzly Man* is arguably the film among these that follows the most heteroglossic or dialogical form, with the stance taken by the director—or, rather, by the character played by Werner Herzog *as himself* in the film—as only one voice and position (if an obviously strong one) on the human–animal relational nexus. It is, in this sense, less easily digestible than the other films. The film's composite, inherently contradictory, and even somewhat putrid body, with its whiffs of Treadwell's ghost hovering in the air as we watch, offers an inherent resistance, a material recalcitrance, to any simple reconciliation of positions.

It is this recalcitrance to unanimity or uniformity, coupled with effective use of cinema's capacity for narrative tension and visual spectacle, that makes a film like *Grizzly Man* a better generator than most of productive discussion around such contentious issues as the appropriate relationship between humans and other animals. A film's transgression of genre conventions—which in the case of *Grizzly Man* is less clear than in some of Herzog's other "documentaries" (such as *Lessons of Darkness*, which I will discuss in the next chapter)—can add to this recalcitrance.

Animals, in any case, are "good to think with," as Claude Lévi-Strauss put it, because they are in between the sense we have of ourselves (humans) and the sense we have of the world as a movable feast of relations and processes. The ways that film encourages us to think with animals—by virtue of the material and interperceptive bodies of those films themselves—can make a difference in how and what we think. This thinking, which is always also a feeling, is part of what makes films and us biomorphically *telic and kinetic*. It is what makes us alive, taking on new forms with every movement our bodymind takes as it watches, hears, ripples along with, and follows the lures and openings afforded by a film world unveiled in the act of cinematic spectatorship.

6
•◆•

TERRA AND TRAUMA
The Geopolitics of the Real

From *Lessons of Darkness* (1992). Directed by
Werner Herzog. Credit: Canal+/Première.

Postmodernism is what you have when the modernization process is complete and
nature is gone for good.

Fredric Jameson, *Postmodernism, or,*
the Cultural Logic of Late Capitalism[1]

I believe that without recognizing it we have already stepped over the threshold of such a change: that we are at the end of nature.

Bill McKibben[2]

This was once a forest, before it was covered with oil. Everything that looks like water is in actuality oil. Ponds and lakes are spread out all over the land. The oil is treacherous because it reflects the sky. The oil is trying to disguise itself as water.

Werner Herzog, *Lessons of Darkness* (1991)

Our survival on this planet is not only threatened by environmental damage but by a degeneration in the fabric of social solidarity and in the modes of psychical life, which must literally be reinvented. The refoundation of politics will have to pass through the aesthetic and analytical dimensions implied in the three ecologies—the environment, the socius and the psyche. We cannot conceive of solutions to the poisoning of the atmosphere and to global warming due to the greenhouse effect, or to the problem of population control, without a mutation of mentality, without promoting a new art of living in society. [. . .] The only acceptable finality of human activity is the production of a subjectivity that is auto-enriching its relation to the world in a continuous fashion.

Félix Guattari, *Chaosmosis: An Ethico-Aesthetic Paradigm*[3]

IT IS TIME TO RECAPITULATE the argument made so far. The universe, I have argued, is best thought of as a concatenation of events or moments of experience. In the specific experience of watching a film, we, its viewers, are drawn into the world of that film. We are taken on a journey into a particular film-world. Over the course of the moments that constitute our experience of the film, we selectively take up the lures and affordances the film presents to us. These lures consist of three types: those that are simply there before us; those that are there by virtue of their relations with those that preceded them; and those that are there by virtue of all that we bring to them. We are drawn into film-worlds through a triadic process: first, through an affective vibration alongside its immediate, spectacular texture; second, through a "sliding into" the sequentiality of its forward movement, its character as "one thing happening after another," which generates connections between events and therefore a kind of primary meaningfulness; and third, through a complex, productive, cognitive and emotional engagement with what we are watching, an engagement that generates meanings and affects according to the resemblances, references, and other connections made between the film and the world outside the film. Such exoreferential meanings and affects are generated in all viewers of any given film, and they in turn contribute to the rearrangement of the perceptual ecologies of the larger world. In their making, distribution, and consumption, films also rearrange the material and social ecologies of that world, but it is the perceptual work of film that constitutes its most distinctive and generative function.

Film-worlds, like all worlds, are held together along a series of dimensional variables, of which three have concerned us here: the anthropomorphic, the geomorphic, and the biomorphic. These three echo the structure of experience in general, insofar as every moment of experience can be distinguished into three elements: a subjectivating pole, an objectivating pole, and a relationship between the two. The first of these is the subjectivity that prehends or takes account of things in its environment in a way that constitutes its particular experience of that environment. It is the active doing, which is the active making of a self, a subject, a becoming-*as* and a becoming-*to*. For humans, this is the anthropomorphic, the becoming that defines us in terms of its own end point (which always remains open). The second pole is the object or set of objects that is prehended, the becoming-*for* insofar as an object, once constituted as such, is always an object for a subject; this always consists of objectified remnants, as it were, left over from previous moments of subjectivation. This is the geomorphic. The first, then, is the experience seen from its inside, the experience of the experiencer; the second is the thing experienced as seen from its outside, the objects of the world that are "out there" in our vicinity. The third element is the relationship between these two, the mechanics of the process of dipolar becoming. It is the particular form taken by the prehension, proceeding as it does along visual, auditory, olfactory, kinesthetic, conceptual, and other lines of access. This access proceeds in turn through an active relational movement or interchange between the subject and the object, with that movement circulating among things so that the subject of one moment becomes the object of the next, and so on and so forth, in a continual relay of interperceptivity and interagency.

As one moment is followed by another and another, there is a cumulative buildup, a habituation, by which subjectivation and objectivation come to take on a certain consistency, which is the constitution of our familiar everyday worlds. For human subjects, this might mean that certain things—for instance, walls, dollars, atoms, stars—are taken to be mere objects laid out in a particular manner for us, while others—other people, certain animals, gods—may be taken to be subjects rather like us, demanding a more reciprocal form of relationship. The point in all of this is that these forms of objectivity and subjectivity—the particular kinds of objectscapes and subjectscapes that become our worlds—are not predetermined. They are produced in the interactions themselves, secreted through action—which includes perception, and which arises at any and every moment that experience happens. We humans, then, are not the only ones who act—far from it. But with our shared cultural worlds, with our technologies for dramatically rearranging the ecologies of the more-than-human universe, our relationship to the *extra*-human has become an issue for us. Examining how moving images have contributed to that relationship is therefore imperative at this time in history. And one way in which they can contribute is by enabling us to think through that relationship more deeply and with greater emotional engagement.

This final chapter will take up this theme of the relationship between humans and the non-human world as a moment of fraughtness, of challenge and uncertainty, of fear and trepidation for us film-viewing humans. Even a casual follower of environmental news is aware that humanity today is collectively taxing the planet in ways that are unprecedented in our history. Ecosystems are being disrupted, resources are being exhausted while those that remain are being fought over, and species that took millennia to emerge are disappearing at rates unseen since before humanity's emergence on this planet. While this news invites a variety of interpretations—some of which deny that it is news, or that it is real or urgent—a background awareness of present or future ecological calamities is arguably one of the persistent and widely shared psychological facts of our time. This awareness is fuelled by imagery: by photos and images of the Earth seen from space, of fires burning in the Amazon, of floods and hurricanes, of drought and famine, of oil spills and toxic chemical releases, of polar bears stranded on Arctic ice floes and islands of plastic spiralling in the middle of the Pacific ocean, and of signs warning us to keep out of certain places or refrain from using certain objects. The possibility of a broad-based ecological collapse is easily visualized because we have already seen it, in films ranging from those that directly depict eco-collapse or its aftermath, such as *The Day After Tomorrow*, the *Mad Max* series, *Waterworld*, *The Road,* and *WALL-E*, to those that merely hint at the possibility or that thematize it within the conventions of horror, science fiction, or animated fantasy.

I will examine several such films in this chapter, contextualizing them within a discussion of geopolitics, trauma, psychoanalysis, and the ethics of the image. This chapter will recapitulate themes from the previous three, with a twist: geomorphism here will generally mean a grasping toward the *global* of the Earth as a whole, and an Earth that is under threat; anthropomorphism will tend toward being a thought about *all humanity*, or about connections across and beyond human social boundaries; and biomorphism will become the *ecological milieu* that binds the two together. Each of these dimensions raises questions for socio-ecological analysis. Geomorphism raises questions of belonging and ownership, questions of the relationship between subjects and the objectscapes portrayed. In a context in which liberal-capitalist property relations dominate, the most common form of this geomorphic question is "Whose is it?" or "To whom does it belong?" There are objects, and we wish to know which property-owning subjects they are assigned to. In a different context, however, such as that of indigenous property relations, the geomorphic question might take an opposite form: not "Whose is *it?*" but "Who is *its?*" or "Who belongs to *it?*" In other words, the relationship of object to subject should not be taken for granted: the idea that objects *belong to subjects* is a modern Western construct, and it may be helpful, if not necessary, to reverse our terms so that subjects are considered as belonging to objects as well.

Anthropomorphism, in turn, is about the distribution of the capacity to act and the recognition of this capacity in formal procedures. It raises questions of politics: *Who* can do *what?* Who counts as an agent? Whose capacities are constrained, and in what ways? What sorts of people or entities are at the heart of the action, capable of *doing*, and which ones are peripheral or, more to the point, disabled and incapable of action by virtue of their positioning with respect to the subject at hand, which in this case is the trauma of real or imagined ecological collapse? Biomorphism, finally, is about action, or interaction, itself—not that of subjects or objects, but of the immanent movement of things themselves, which are always in process of becoming and of exchanging the properties of seeing and being seen, taking and being taken, prehending and being prehended. Biomorphism is therefore about the ethics immanent to the specific interactions that constitute the world, moment to moment. The question raised by a film's biomorphism is this: What sorts of relations are unfolding here? How, and in what direction, are they moving? How am I moving, flowing, working, crafting, performing, with and alongside them? In the situations we are examining in this chapter, this means how does the movement proceed and how is it contained, constrained, and incapacitated? I have argued that film's worlds *move* because the world they take from, capturing and rearranging bits and pieces of it, also moves. They change, transmit change, and *are* change. In change is crisis, opportunity, and creative transformation. Change in the world negotiates points of crisis, but change in the film world, like change in literary and artistic worlds of all kinds, compacts and crystallizes moments of crisis. That is, after all, what makes these worlds compelling. Among the crises lived in the world at large is that which is unfolding between humans and the extra-human world today, and it is this crisis—which for many is a kind of half-recognized sense of impending trauma—that will be in question in this chapter.

Whole earth imagery has become ubiquitous since the Apollo and Sputnik missions, and strains of cinematic eco-globalism can be seen in the science fiction genre and in art-house non-narrative features such as *Baraka* and

Koyaanisqatsi (discussed in Chapter 3). Most such films include portents of the fraught eco-human relationship. Less obvious appearances of eco-trauma can be inferred from films that depict social dislocation against a backdrop of environmental "strange weather." I will examine a handful of such films here that refer indirectly, as I argue, to the "traumatic kernel" of ecopolitics in a way that films such as *The Day After Tomorrow* cannot do. This is because the latter aim at evoking eco-trauma directly, whereas trauma, being the sort of thing that it is, may be better dealt with through indirection. That said, certain popular examples such as *Twelve Monkeys, Children of Men*, and *Avatar* point to the possibility of a highly resonant depiction of global trauma in its many-layered complexity. Of these, I will focus most closely on *Avatar*, though I will discuss a broader array of strategies of socio-ecological representation found in films such as *Fast Food Nation, Darwin's Nightmare, The Cove*, and *Lessons of Darkness*.

Any discussion of trauma must sooner or later come to grips with psy-choanalytic film theory, especially, given its currency in recent years, in the variant espoused by prolific Lacanian psychoanalyst and philosopher Slavoj Žižek. In later sections of this chapter, I argue that what psychoanalysis reads as *psyche*, and what Žižek alternately reads as the Real or as subjectivity, can also be read, through a kind of eco-Deleuzo-Heideggerian, process-relational detour, as *earth*—that is, as the set of material and bodily metabolisms and inter-corporeal relationalities that underpin the psyche and serve as its mate-rial "undergrowth of enjoyment." The chapter concludes with an attempt to synthesize the insights of a process-relational perspective toward an aesthetic, an ethic, and an "ecologic"—a triadic philosophy of the eco-imaginary as it unfolds through popular and avant-garde filmmaking in our contemporary context. I end by discussing Terrence Malick's *The Tree of Life* and Lars von Trier's *Melancholia* as two especially acute depictions of an insightful and provocative eco-imaginary. In the context of an ecophilosophical viewing practice, these two films constitute worthy examples of ecophilosophical cinema. The traumas they depict are not explicitly ecological in the conventional sense; but in the expansive, multi-ecological sense of the word entertained in this book, they are particularly potent presentations of what cinema, 120 years after its emergence, has come to in our time.

Trauma and the Imagination of Disaster

Traumatic moments are as close as our experience gets us to the shock of pure firstness. When the car I am driving begins to skid off an icy road, I have little time to think what to do. Instead I experience the sensations we associate with the emotion called fear, as my body kicks into gear, adrenaline rushing through it, increasing my heart rate and blood flow and heightening my perception of the relevant sensory stimuli. My foot may initially press hard on the brake, at least until a kind of narrative secondness kicks in, which allows me to think: the car is skidding, and I should turn the wheel in the direction of the skid. This secondary, "rational circuit of fear," as neuropsychologist Joseph LeDoux calls it, is slower to arise than the "primitive circuit of fear," but it is more helpful in situations—such as driving fast cars—that our bodies have not been prepared for over the course of biological evolution.[4] At this point in my response I am still caught in the flow of the moment: the shock of the skid, the rush of adrenaline, the immediate cognitive response of steering into the skid, which I have learned through practice. As the car safely steers back onto the road, I can relax my muscles, note the altered state of my body, and begin to think more freely, more laterally and self-reflexively—more in line with Peirce's thirdness—and I begin to appreciate what has happened and how fortunate I am to have survived a brush with death.

This sequence of firstness–secondness–thirdness is not quite as pat in real life as the above description of a near-accident makes it sound. For one thing, any event as such is already a second, in Peirce's terms: it is an encounter of force and resistance between two entities. But in our experience of this event, the force striking us is initially new and unassimilated, so our experience of it consists of the firstness of what strikes us. For another thing, the encounter is never *entirely* new, for it comes to us—that is, to our awareness of it—filtered through the perceptual apparatus of our brains and bodies. It could happen, for instance, that in the midst of skidding I am flooded with a bodily memory of a previous experience, such as that of falling to the ground while playing hockey as a child. This memory doesn't come to me as *meaning* (thirdness) so much as it is a sensation in the body that is mixed into the firstness of my initial perception of the skid. But it indicates how the meaning of previous experiences is already sedimented into the pre-reflexive immediate response to a particular stimulus—in this case, the loss of control of my car. And if I do not successfully steer out of the skid, then my body will feel the impact of collision less as a pain than as a convulsive shock that floods my entire awareness. The pain comes second, as I realize that I have been in an accident and am now "in pain." Thus while pain is a bodily response, it is not necessarily mere firstness. It may be that as well, but it could be caused largely by the recognition that *this* is pain that I am feeling, and that it is *I* who am in pain.

It is the aftershocks of a violently disruptive event and the ways they continue to register for a survivor or observer that are the focus of most work in contemporary trauma studies.[5] The paradigm case in trauma studies is the

Jewish Holocaust, the Shoah, which Shoshana Felman and Dori Laub consider "an event without witness," not only because the perpetrators destroyed much of the evidence of what they did, but also because the victims had no appropriate frame of reference to account for it at the time.[6] Examining trauma more broadly, Roger Luckhurst defines it as "the piercing or breach of a border that puts inside and outside into a strange communication," that "violently opens passageways between systems that were once discrete, making unforeseen connections that distress or confound." Trauma is "worryingly transmissible" through verbal or visual testimony that moves others to overwhelming sympathy and through a more directly affective transfer of bodily symptoms.[7] Being neither assimilable into memory nor forgettable, trauma haunts, re-emerging in the form of flashbacks, nightmares, hallucinations, and phobias. If it brings us close to pure firstness, it never gets us there, because in the interpretation of something as traumatic there is always an oscillation between firstness (the shock of some remembered encounter), secondness (the encounter itself, with its indexical marks and traces), and thirdness, which is the field within which the oscillation continues for those trying to make sense of it.

Observers have noted the emergence of a "traumatological aesthetic" in contemporary literature and of a more generalized "culture of trauma," especially in post-9/11 America, where discussion of all manner of traumas has saturated the hum of talk radio, celebrity media, popular bestsellers, and grass-roots pressure groups, even working its way up into government inquiries and medical task forces.[8] Janet Walker notes the growth of a "trauma cinema" since the 1980s and 1990s, which she characterizes as stylistically non-realist, as typified by "non-linearity, fragmentation, nonsynchronous sound, repetition, rapid editing and strange angles," and as approaching the past "through an unusual admixture of emotional affect, metonymic symbolism and cinematic flashbacks."[9] Within this category, Walker includes such films as *Apocalypse Now* (1979), *Platoon* (1986), *JFK* (1991), *Thunderheart* (1992), and the Yugoslav war film *Before the Rain* (1994), but also Errol Morris's documentaries *The Thin Blue Line* (1987) and *Mr. Death* (1999) and women's experimental autobiographical documentaries, including Michelle Citron's *Daughter Rite* (1980), Lynn Hershman's *Confessions of a Camelum* (1985) and *First Person Plural* (1990), Lise Yasui's *Family Gathering* (1988), and Rea Tajin's *History and Memory* (1991).

But if paradigmatic Holocaust films like Claude Lanzmann's documentary *Shoah* (1985) are about the "witnessing of a catastrophe"[10]—a catastrophe that is understood to have happened and to have left a gaping wound in the world—films of *ecological* trauma are about the witnessing of a catastrophe that has not yet occurred. Or it has occurred in isolated instances—Bhopal,

Chernobyl, Fukushima, hurricanes Katrina and Sandy—of a much broader, slower, and more cataclysmic unfolding that may or may not ever transpire in its full form. Ecological catastrophe is a trauma whose perpetrators and victims are ill defined and whose historians and archivists—usually environmental scientists and activists—carry a credibility that is always open to question. It is typically the kind of trauma that E. Ann Kaplan classifies as "mediatized," spread via images and scientific discourses rather than from direct experience and face-to-face accounts.[11] One might consider it a form of "postmodern trauma"—a term sometimes reserved for accounts of questionable events like alien abductions and "satanic ritual abuse," whose memories emerge and fester in an epistemological wilderness where the reality of the cause is uncertain and fraught with contradiction. Such trauma is arguably *hyper*-real in its having occurred countless times already, not in life but in the media (tabloid newspapers, books, movies).[12] The cinematic prefiguration of trauma was in part what elicited controversy in the wake of the events of 11 September 2001, when critics like Jean Baudrillard, Paul Virilio, and Slavoj Žižek argued in various ways that we were already more familiar with the events from their cinematic antecedents than from any contact we might have with anyone directly affected by the airplanes overtaken on that morning.[13]

Awareness of the traumatic possibility of ecological collapse—the potential falling away of the conditions that make our collective lives possible and bearable on this earth—does not normally strike anyone with the impact of a car accident or an airplane crash. Such awareness, for those who carry it, gathers slowly, accumulating evidence like clouds rolling in the background of our awareness, until something tips us over the edge, taking us out of the familiar phase-space of our everyday awareness of the world into a less familiar one that recognizes its utter insecurity and vulnerability. Sometimes, however, such tipping-point events can be direct and vicious. The sensation, for instance, of an earthquake suddenly shifting the ground beneath one's feet contains trauma in its firstness. This is the trauma of the immediate sensation that unsettles, disturbs, or throttles us, eliciting a panic reaction or a fight-or-flight response in our bodies. Once we recognize that this sensation of shock, horror, bewilderment, numbness, or fear is traceable to the sudden movement of the ground beneath our feet, we experience the secondness—the causal connectedness—of the traumatic moment. It is only later, when we have conceptualized the trauma into a particular representation, a hook onto which we can hang our response—"this is the Big One," "I remember the devastating earthquake that shook this city in 1954," or, in other contexts, the marks of other remembered events such as Auschwitz, Hiroshima, Chernobyl, or Fukushima, the simple names of which trigger sets of associated responses—it is only then that we have trauma in its thirdness. This may be trauma tamed and contained, but it is also trauma retained and kept vibrating.

Watching such events unfold on a screen primes our response to disaster should it occur in life, but it also risks the overexposure that leads to "psychic numbing." If trauma narratives and cultures, as some critics contend, are in part produced by the very media that mediate them, then it makes it all the more important to know what the effects of such productions are. Allen Meek argues that trauma "has been enlisted in the quest for authentic experience and historical anchorage in an age of spatio-temporal dislocation" and that it is a result of "a compulsive repetition of the image" that cannot be located because of its (the image's) nature as groundless, placeless, and decontextual-ized.[14] To the extent that images of eco-trauma are mediatized and vicarious forms of experience, eco-theorists would want to know whether they result in anything more than what Kaplan calls "empty empathy"—empathy "that does not result in pro-social behavior." As Kaplan puts it, catastrophe images focusing on the pain of others who are strange to us, and with whom we share no socio-political context in which we might effectively respond, have the tendency to fragment our response-ability. "Each catastrophe image cancels out or interferes with the impact of the prior image."[15]

How, then, should we think about the history of ecological disaster in cinema? Disaster has been a prominent leitmotif in film for a long time, though its history has its ebbs and flows. The 1970s were a particularly productive time for disaster films (including eco-disaster films, such as *Soylent Green* and *Silent Running*), and the 1990s and 2000s have, to some degree, followed suit.[16] Disaster can be addressed directly, as in fictional disaster films or in sensationalist or eco-advocacy documentaries; or it can hover as a possibility in the background. And some direct images can be more direct than others. *The Day After Tomorrow* offers a direct image of what a sudden cooling of the Earth might feel like; it is iconic (in Peirce's sense), providing pictures, photographs, and sounds of disaster. *Titanic*, on the other hand, while also iconic in providing a direct image of a historical shipping disaster, also carries an indirect image of disaster in general—the hubris of modern technological pride, for which the *Titanic* story has become a symbol. The post-apocalyptic genre, which includes such films as the Australian *Mad Max* series, *Waterworld* (1995), *28 Days Later* (2002), *Time of the Wolf* (2003), *I Am Legend* (2007), and *The Road* (2009), provide images of the *post*-disaster, images that have an indexical relationship, a relationship of secondness, to the disaster presumed to have occurred. Films that include footage of actual disasters (documentaries or otherwise) bear an indexical relationship to those disasters as well.

The rise of eco-documentaries was dramatic in the first decade of the twenty-first century. Alongside more overtly political films such as those of Michael Moore (*Fahrenheit 9/11, Sicko*) have been a series of environmental documentaries on topics ranging from global warming (*An Inconvenient Truth, The Age of Stupid*), to energy (*Who Killed the Electric Car?, The End of Suburbia, A Crude Awakening*), to food production and consumption (*Super Size Me, King Corn, Food, Inc.*, and the fictionalized version of the journalistic expose *Fast Food Nation*), to the environmental crisis in its totality (Leonardo DiCaprio's *The Eleventh Hour*).

How do such films affect viewers' perceptions of the ecological issues they depict? The impacts of films are often distinguished into the cognitive and the affective.[17] We can learn things from a film when that film presents facts about the world that are not widely known. This is a primary goal of many documentaries, but it is also at least a secondary goal of many fiction films that draw attention to events, personalities, or situations that the filmmakers feel are inadequately understood. Films are arguably more effective, however, in getting us to *feel* something about a person, event, topic, or phenomenon. And it is this affective dimension that complicates our understanding of "the facts" in that it orients and motivates us in a particular way toward those facts. We are more likely, for instance, to accept the reality of anthropogenic climate change if we accept certain implicit metanarratives of contemporary environmentalism—that humans have overshot the traditional limits on their ability to affect the world; or that capitalism, industrialism, patriarchy, Christianity, or some other social force has unmoored us from the natural order, destabilizing the cosmos in the process. If, on the other hand, we reject these premises, we will be more motivated to reject scientific findings that such an unmooring has occurred. This motivated orientation to "facts" is rooted less in what we think and more in how we feel—that is, in the stance we have taken with regard to certain expressive images and ideas, certain ways of speaking, certain social movements and sensibilities.[18]

With *An Inconvenient Truth* (2006), the Al Gore vehicle for enlightening viewers about anthropogenic climate change, the issue of how *facts* were combined with *affects* was germinal to the film's impact. The film centres on a PowerPoint presentation by Gore of his argument that global warming is real. But its success hinges less on its presentation of facts than on the context that surrounds the film. This was Al Gore—he who was "once the next president of the United States of America"—in his moment in the sun, his full "coming out" as a committed spokesperson for a cause that was finding a recharged audience in the waning years of the George W. Bush presidency. The film combines argumentation with narrative and powerful imagery. In Aristotelian terms, its rhetoric combines *logos* (reasoned argumentation) with *ethos* (establishing the author's credibility) and *pathos* (appealing to viewers' emotions). To perform the latter, it situates images of nature associated with a nostalgically tinted past—scenes from Gore's rural childhood home and images of the Earth seen from space—within the narrative of a present in crisis and of a future that is in our hands to shape but that we must act on quickly if we are to shape it adequately. As Murray and Heumann argue, the film mobilized "environmental nostalgia," evoking viewers' "eco-memories" through its juxtaposition of Gore's narrative of personal reckoning with images we all recognize—both the personal ones that remind us of our own places of childhood comfort and the collective ones that remind us about where we might have been when we watched the moon landings.[19] But as this description already tells us ("where *we* might have *been*"), such eco-memories are pegged most directly to a particular generational slice of North Americans. Their effectiveness for other audiences is less certain than for the liberal baby boomers who constitute Gore's first line of political support.[20]

Research on the impacts of *An Inconvenient Truth* and of the fictional global warming film *The Day After Tomorrow* confirm that the effects of films are not especially predictable, but that when viewed in context of the broader ecology of debate around an issue—in these cases involving environmentalists, political conservatives, industry leaders, and legislators—such films can generate significant spikes of media and public attention. Responses to the Gore film among American viewers were typically divided along partisan political lines. But the film was a spectacular commercial success, appealing not only to Democrats but also to independent voters and helping generate the strongest consensus about climate change that the country had seen in years. In the wake of the so-called Climategate crisis, however, during which media attention was redirected to the alleged improprieties of climate scientists, views about the veracity of Gore's arguments underwent a downturn in public opinion.[21]

Audience studies of *The Day After Tomorrow* (2004) were equally interesting.[22] This Roland Emmerich blockbuster depicts rapid global warming, which precipitates a shutdown of the Gulf Stream current, resulting in the almost immediate onset of an ice age. The film was derided by many of its scientific and environmental critics, who saw it as hyperbolic, a disaster film that pulped and mangled the science of climate change in order to draw crowds into theatres. But the film succeeded at that: it grossed nearly half a billion dollars worldwide in its first month, and 70 percent of its adult viewers, according to one study, rated it as good or excellent, with only 13 percent considering it poor or terrible.[23] Several studies of viewer responses, carried out in the United States, Britain, Germany, and Japan, have pointed to a heightened degree of concern among its viewers about climate change and its impacts. Two nationally representative American surveys, directed by Anthony Leiserowitz, showed the film to have had "a significant impact on the climate change risk perceptions, conceptual models, behavioral intentions, policy priorities, and even voting intentions of moviegoers." It "led moviegoers to have higher levels of concern and worry about global warming, to estimate various impacts on the United States as more likely, and to shift their conceptual understanding of the climate system toward a threshold model"; it also encouraged them "to engage in personal, political, and social action to address climate change and to elevate global warming as a national priority."[24]

Not surprisingly, however, studies have not necessarily shown an increase in viewers' abilities to distinguish science *fact* from dramatized science *fiction*.[25] While environmental advocates highlighted the film's science, conservative critics focused on its obvious exaggerations, and journalists were attracted to the drama of the conflict between the two positions. A study of 300 to 400 moviegoers, which included focus groups held about a month after viewing, found that viewers were generally well aware of the low (or nonexistent) scientific credibility of Hollywood films for communicating science, but that the film's special effects nevertheless "aided the visualization of scientific data and information for some and, for many participants, the force of this imagery was sufficient to heighten their concern about the potential impacts of climate change after seeing the film."[26] Another study, however, compared a group exposed to scientific literature on the causes and potential impacts of abrupt climate change with a group exposed only to the film (and a third control group), and found that those exposed only to the film were more likely to treat climate change as a more *distant* threat in location and in time. This underscores a growing body of communication theory which suggests that "negative" and "catastrophic depictions of climate change impacts *depersonalize* the problem for the public."[27]

Movies alone are rarely, if ever, enough to convince the unconvinced about a controversial subject. In this case it seems that Democratic voters in the United States were more likely to watch the film than Republicans (although most viewers saw it not out of political conviction, but simply because it was a widely promoted blockbuster).[28] What such movies do, however, is generate interest and debate. When accompanied by media exposure and advocacy on behalf of its topic, films such as these can serve as "dramatic focusing events" or "teachable moments" and as "windows of opportunity" for building discourse coalitions around climate change.[29] The building of such coalitions does not occur within a homogeneous mass called "the public." As Leiserowitz noted, "the 'U.S. public' is in fact many publics—a plurality of different groups and interpretive communities, each predisposed to attend to certain risks and issues and to discount or ignore others."[30] This is particularly significant when trauma cinema is being discussed. If the cinema of eco-trauma, like other forms of trauma culture, produces "new subjects" (as Kaplan puts it) and gives rise to "trauma cultures," then studying the *affects* of eco-cinema has to involve study of the subcultures for whom these depictions resonate most strongly.[31] I will come back to this in my discussion of James Cameron's *Avatar*. But first, let us examine how eco-trauma is depicted as a figure in the background of the "normal" fabric of everyday life.

Strange Weather, Network Narratives, and the Traumatic Event

Many films are not centrally about a disaster yet contain the whiff of disaster or some collective trauma in their background. Interpreting what is going on in the background of a film is not that different from interpreting what goes on in the background of one's mind—something that psychoanalysis has been trying to do for more than a century. Films, however, are collective products, and it makes sense to study their resonance with an eye for what it says about something collective and social. In *The Geopolitical Aesthetic*, neo-Marxist cultural theorist Fredric Jameson proposes the term "geopolitical unconscious" to designate what he later described as the thesis that "all thinking today is *also*, whatever else it is, an attempt to think the world system as such."[32] Cultural texts, for Jameson, can therefore be read as forms of "political fantasy which in contradictory fashion articulate ... both the actual and potential social relations which constitute individuals within a specific political economy."[33] Culture, in this reading, "conflates ontology with geography and endlessly processes images of the unmappable system" of advanced industrial capitalism.[34] Accordingly, the historical evolution of capitalism, which has been marked by discontinuous bursts in its power to penetrate and colonize heretofore uncommodified spaces, generates its own social spaces and artistic responses. At a highly generalized level, these, in Jameson's analysis, have included realism, modernism, and now postmodernism. The originality of Jameson's postmodernism thesis, elaborated in his celebrated *Postmodernism, or the Cultural Logic of Late Capitalism*,[35] lies in his reading of various products of culture as heralding, reflecting, and responding to the latest stage in the development of capitalism—the shift in the second half of the twentieth century to a post-Fordist, media-saturated, transnational form of capitalism, in the course of which the modernization process has made its way around the globe and commodification has been extended—albeit unevenly—to all levels of social and biological life.

From a socio-ecological perspective, however, Jameson's premise needs some thickening. This is because the world system is not just a political-economic one, in which social relations and psychic realities are predominantly shaped by the uneven economics of global capitalism; it is also a political-*ecological* one. It is one in which the warp and woof of uneven development and global inequality are directly related to the ways in which advanced industrial capitalism both commodifies and thoroughly transforms the natural world and our relationship with it. Jameson's postmodernism thesis can be taken as an instance of an idea that caught on *because* it resonated with broader political-ecological shifts. In his *Postmodernism* book (and in the article on which it was based), Jameson called postmodernism what we have "when the modernization process is complete and nature is gone for good."[36] Just a year earlier, journalist Bill McKibben had written a book titled *The End of Nature*, in which he lamented that with the appearance of the "ozone hole"—evidence of an impending global extinction crisis, and new data confirming potentially catastrophic anthropogenic climate change, nature—at least as we used to know it—had "ended."[37]

Jameson's and McKibben's pronouncements about nature's demise, each dating from the early 1990s and each becoming a bestseller in its genre, provide an apt historical conjuncture for us to grapple with the political contexts of the eco-imaginary. Expanding on Jameson's idea, we could say that the contemporary world system can hardly be thought about without reference to the totality (until recently unthinkable) of the ecological system that sustains and interpenetrates with the political-economic system.[38] Recognition of humanity's large-scale impact on the environment dates as far back as the 1960s with the publication of such books as Rachel Carson's *Silent Spring*, Barry Commoner's *The Closing Circle*, and Paul Ehrlich's *Population Bomb*, but the idea that humans are reshaping and altering the very foundations of something called "the global ecology" did not really come to widespread popular attention until the late 1980s. In particular, the idea of global warming delivered a shock to public thinking about the environment. On a swelteringly hot day in late June 1988, James Hansen, director of the Goddard Institute for Space Studies, testified before a U.S. Congressional Committee that he could state "with 99% confidence" that a long-term climate warming trend was occurring. He added that he was virtually certain that the "greenhouse effect" was its cause. While Hansen's statements were not always accurately reported, their front-page coverage in newspapers and on radio and television talk shows was unprecedented. Later that year, *Time* magazine named the Earth "Planet of the Year" in place of its customary "Man of the Year." Planetary nature, then, had emerged as an actor on the global stage at the same time as Jameson and McKibben were writing its epitaph.

The late 1980s and early 1990s saw the creation of the Intercontinental Panel on Climate Change, the release of the Brundtland Commission Report *Our Common Future*, the popularization of the term "sustainable development," and the high-profile international mega-event in Rio de Janeiro that came to be known as the Earth Summit. These were followed, in 1993, by the election of an American president whose running mate had written an environmentalist manifesto, *Earth in the Balance*, the title of which was meant to suggest how precariously poised we all are on the cusp of dramatic if not catastrophic change. In the more rarefied world of North American academe, this feverish five- or six-year period saw the second major wave of environmental studies program creation.[39] Coming as it did at the end of the Reagan–Thatcher–Mulroney era, and competing with the collapse of the Soviet Union and the impending rush of globalization, it was somewhat remarkable that global ecology became such a hot topic. Yet by the middle of the decade, it had been all but eclipsed by the economic rush of post–Cold War Clinton-era globalization. A question that has not been answered decisively enough is why and how this disappearance of the issue came about.

It is in the midst of this disappearance, in the mid- to late 1990s, that we find a spate of films about social relations that include portents of ecological disaster in their backgrounds—films in which nature, in an unruly and threatening guise, returns to disrupt the everyday texture of human social life. These were not films about anything particularly environmental; in fact, they focused almost entirely on the social world. Yet that *almost* is the operative word; it is what allows us to take these films as barometers for the "strange weather"—as Andrew Ross has called it—that lurks in their backgrounds.[40] Robert Altman's loose cinematic adaptation of Raymond Carver's *Short Cuts* (1993) opens with images of helicopters, looking like giant bugs against the night skies, spraying entire Los Angeles neighbourhoods with insecticide against medflies and their larvae, the terror of the California fruit industry. Over the course of the film's first fourteen minutes, while we are being introduced to the eight or nine overlapping narratives that make up the film's polyphonic patchwork quilt, the helicopters continue to do their thing, with a television commentator editorializing about the spraying, comparing it to other "wars" that have been waged in recent memory—against Iraq, against terrorists, against drugs, and so on. (Its list of wars would have hardly changed a decade later, only lengthened.) But the war on the medfly is a war against something that is simply *there*, against an intrusion of nature that has disrupted the wheels of industry and the workings of the social fabric. Some two hours and a handful of deaths, suicides, and marital breakups later, the film comes to a close, as incongruously as it began, with a 7.4-magnitude earthquake rumbling across the Greater Los Angeles area. Just as the tremor begins, one of the characters explodes in a mindless rage and murders a cyclist with a rock blow to the head, while rocks begin to fall from a cliff behind them. The local news reports the girl's death as the earthquake's single fatality, while a weather expert muses aloud about how wonderful it is to live in LA. These allusions to nature's disruptive force frame the panoramic set of stories that make up the film's loosely connected, non-linear narrative.

With its swirling juxtaposition of interpersonal and emotional predicaments, *Short Cuts* served as an obvious model for Paul Thomas Anderson's equally epic, equally decentred 1999 film *Magnolia*. Both films are textbook examples of the network narrative, which weaves several distinct subnarratives together into a loosely connected patchwork. Like Altman, Anderson punctuated his stories with references to weather, including actual weather reports, a lot of rainfall, and at least three characters saying "it's raining cats and dogs" at different points in the film. In the film's climax, Anderson upped the ante a notch higher than Altman had. An earthquake would have been too obvious and derivative (for a film in and about Southern California), so *Magnolia* concludes with a biblically proportioned rain of frogs pounding on windshields, splattering onto wet roads, and plopping into spotlit San Fernando Valley swimming pools. The film makes explicit what other films to be examined here leave more implicit; but throughout its three hours, the social landscape is the central actor. As for the frogs, Anderson explains that "as far back as the Romans, people have been able to judge the health of a society by the health of its frogs: the health of a frog, the vibe of a frog, the texture of the frog, its looks, how much wetness is on it, everything. The frogs," he continues, "are a barometer for who we are as a people. We're polluting ourselves, we're killing ourselves, and the frogs are telling us so, because they're all getting sick and deformed."[41]

In both these films, acts of real or Hollywood *nature* interrupt the narrative, serving as a kind of Freudian uncanny or Lacanian Real, as excessive remainders that invade the representational frame, jarring and dislocating the social worlds portrayed even while remaining outside those relations and in some ways fundamentally unassimilable by them. These are events that simply happen, out of nowhere. Their effects on the lives of the characters are ones that, for the most part, cannot be resisted (the exception is the medfly infestation, though here it is the spraying of the insecticide that is more invasive and irresistible). More than anything else that happens in these films, these acts of unruly nature unify the otherwise disparate stories by putting the characters "in the same boat" in relation to them.[42] I suggest that these uncanny visitations of nature displace, threaten, and solidify a certain post–Cold War but pre-9/11 reimagination of *community*, setting off strange rumblings at levels ranging from that of the family unit to that of the global human ecumene. But let me develop this thesis with a few more examples.

Unruly visitations of a vaguely threatening ecology do not appear only in films set in or near Los Angeles. (And in a certain obvious sense, both *Short Cuts* and *Magnolia* are more about California—specifically Los Angeles, if not self-referentially mostly about Hollywood—than about anything else.)[43] The 1990s were a particularly fruitful decade for what we might call the "post-nuclear" genre of filmmaking: I use this word in a double sense, where the nucleus that had been decentred (if not exploded) was that of the bomb—the technological threat that held together the bipolar geopolitics of the Cold War world—but also that of the patriarchal family and the traditionally ordered set of social relations for which it served as the formative, cellular kernel. The West's nuclear adversary having disappeared, and the terrorist threat not yet having arisen, these films took place mostly in a safely middle-class North American world, one in which global reference points are obscured or nonexistent and in which family and interpersonal relations are central. Films like *Short Cuts*, *Magnolia*, Ang Lee's *The Ice Storm* (1997), Atom Egoyan's *The Sweet Hereafter* (1997), and Sam Mendes's *American Beauty* (1999) work out the tensions inherent in the nuclear family by portraying the underbelly of a certain mainly suburban idyll, its fabric torn asunder by the centrifugal forces underlying its smooth but emotionally paralyzed exterior. And almost without exception in these films, natural disasters, or accidents caused by "nature," serve as the framing signifiers within which their post-catastrophic aftermaths unfold.

In Ang Lee's evocation of middle-class, exurban 1973 Connecticut, a deadly but chillingly beautiful ice storm, during which a boy dies by electrocution from a fallen power line, serves as a metaphor for the "big chill" that followed the overindulgence and socially and politically fragmenting fallout of the sixties: messy affairs, spouse-swapping parties, toxic discontent, and chronic miscommunication among adults, children, and everyone concerned. Snow and ice are responsible for another collective trauma, in *The Sweet Hereafter*, when a school bus skids off a road and tumbles down into a lake, killing most of the children on board. The film charts the painful unravellings of familial (and incestuous) ties that follow. And in *American Beauty*, the single moment of calm epiphany within the figurative storm of social and familial dysfunctionality occurs when the lead character's daughter watches an extended fragment of a silent video made by the neighbour's spookily self-possessed son, in which an empty plastic bag whirls about in a delirious windblown dance. Set against the parallel currents of family turbulence and the droning white noise of media culture, these appearances of disorderly, uncanny nature—or, in Mendes's film, even the barest cypher of nature, the invisible wind allusively gestured to by the performance of an inanimate piece of trash—invoke an alternative, unhuman order, one whose very incommensurability sets up a jarring moral counter-oscillation to the social realities portrayed. Yet like the "airborne toxic event" in Don DeLillo's paradigmatically postmodern novel White Noise, these unnatural appearances of nature seem more like allusions to a scrambling of the boundaries presumed to exist between nature and humanity, a scrambling in which we ourselves are implicated.[44] Like the threat of global warming, they hover, with a kind of reptilian stare, on the horizon of collective consciousness. In a traditionally Jamesonian geopolitical reading, these nuclear family tensions would be more than mere family tensions; they would be read, rather, as conflations/reflections/refractions of the tensions inherent in the bipolar Cold War nuclear system and the military-industrial economy that underpinned it. But a political-ecological rendering suggests that something larger may be askew.

There is an interesting parallel here between the post-Reaganite, post–Cold War 1990s and the post-civil-rights, counterculture 1970s. For the liberal left, both were decades that offered breathing room, either from the struggles of the 1960s or from the conservative onslaught of the Reagan era. The left may not have been on the ascendant, but on some level, *cultural* liberalism had become integrated into the mainstream. In the 1970s this seemed fresh and new, but it was tempered by the recognition (on the left) that the antiwar left had failed to galvanize the nation (in the case of the United States) and that the generation portrayed in The Big Chill (1983) was satisfied to take the partial gains of the sixties and integrate them into the liberal-capitalist consensus of the time, thus opting for short-term fulfillment over any long-term systemic change. In the 1990s, an analogous recognition on the left may have been that the *global* left had failed—the Soviet Union had collapsed and now there was little desire on the part of the masses to critique the seemingly victorious capitalist system. Yet in the mainstream, it was the decade of Reaganism, with its wars on "welfare mothers" and other public scapegoats, that could be forgotten; and with Bill Clinton's ascendancy to the presidency, liberal Americans could feel confident that "one of us," at least in a cultural sense, was now at the helm of the nation.

The Sublime and the Real

Reading these appearances of nature as signifiers of some out-of-kilter global eco-social system, or of a psychic guilt that "we" (humanity) feel for our treatment of nature, risks both essentializing the human and making too much out of cinematic details that could be explained more simply. Ice storms, unstoppable rains, and other acts of nature punctuating a film narrative are forms of what literary critics used to call "pathetic fallacy," the creative misattribution of human characteristics to natural objects, or the use of nature to express human psychological states. In this understanding, an earthquake or ice storm is not *about* the earthquake or ice storm at all. To this charge, an ecocritic would respond that a river may be just a river and that a textual ice storm may in fact be *about ice* as well, not simply a comment on human miscommunication. In other words, the signifier could in fact also be pointing back at a natural signified, not only at a human one.

In any case, *Short Cuts* and *Magnolia* are arguably about California more than anything else (with California itself being a signifier of the promise and future of America and the West), and Ang Lee's *Ice Storm* is about the 1970s, and all three films are about social or familial relations more than they are about political or ecological systems. But Jameson's model of wide-angle, big-picture interpretation nudges us to read such things for their resonance at deeper and more disparate levels. His geopolitical unconscious is unconscious, after all, and for a species that has become the world's dominant, it seems reasonable to think of the unconscious as global or becoming so. *Magnolia's* rain of frogs and *Short Cuts'* medflies and earthquake can be references to Biblical pestilences and apocalypses, but they are also about those things that happen of their own accord, those weird, freaky acts of nature that Californians, as much as anyone, live with a persistent, low-level and generally unacknowledged fear of. There is an indication, a kind of promise, in these films of something *beyond* the state of incessant motion, the frenzied desires and clashing emotions, insecurities, miscommunications, and roiling chaos of these characters' personal and interpersonal lives—a something around which, or in relation to which, the vortex of everyday life turns without ever being able to face squarely, something unrepresentable except as it breaks through in such spurious, random acts of (seemingly violent) nature. In a Lacanian reading, these things represent the Real—the excessive, excluded, and incommensurate remainder of reality, which resists symbolic capture and always threatens to return and intrude, revealing the essential fragility of the nuclear bonds that make up the social. They constitute tears in the fabric of social meanings—the fabric into which we are incorporated as we become social and linguistic beings—which point to the gap at the centre of human identity, the inassimilable outside, yet which simultaneously offer what Slavoj Žižek calls an "undergrowth of enjoyment."[45] To an ecocritic, Žižek's suggestive phrase evokes a verticality to desire, whereby the genital "bush" and the "lower" animal realms, subsisting beneath the civilized self, provide an obscure enjoyment even as they provoke anxiety and elicit repression, denial, or sublimation into other, presumably "higher" forms of expression.[46]

The vertical semiotics of "sublimation" and the "sublime" warrant further examination here. The discourse of the sublime, already discussed in Chapter 3, is often invoked in discussions of visual depictions of nature, and it is one that has been resurrected within the torrent of writing on postmodern culture. At the same time, Freud's notion of sublimation suggests a skeptical stance toward anything that warrants being raised to the level of a genuinely transcendent sublime. As figured by Kant, Burke, and others, the sublime was that which confronts us with the limitations of our representations but also of our ability to control the world. For Burke and the nineteenth-century Romantics, the sublime was experienced in encounters with an overpowering and monumental Nature. Inspiring awe and astonishment, pleasure alongside pain, it was marked by a radical ambivalence in which the desire to be inundated by the sublime coexisted with a fear of being annihilated by it. For Kant, the sublime took on a form more to do with the limits of representation: forever inaccessible to the categories of reason, it marked the inherent threshold of our knowledge and signified the cleavage between the conceived and the presentable. For both Kant and Burke, the sublime represented the "incommensurability between Nature and the human."[47]

In advanced industrial capitalism, nature has been effectively tamed and eclipsed and the sublime has taken other forms: the technological sublime, which marvels in the grandiose and monumental works of an alienating technology;[48] the apocalyptic or nuclear sublime, represented by Auschwitz, Hiroshima, and Alamagordo;[49] and the everyday sublime alluded to in Surrealist art and in Freud's notion of the uncanny—that is, the "sense of strangeness confronting us in familiarity" and "the excessive material presence of the object."[50] The sublime has been resuscitated in postmodernist and post-structuralist writing as an indeterminate, ineffable alterity that hovers over human attempts at comprehension—think here of Lacan's Real, Derrida's *différance*, Kristeva's *signifiance*, Baudrillard's inhuman system of objects, and Lyotard's and Jameson's differently inflected renditions of the postmodern sublime. Lyotard returned to the theme repeatedly, presenting the sublime as an excess of indeterminacy that invades and dislocates the effort to create meaning.[51] Manifesting the unresolved tension between presentability and unpresentability, the sublime "allows the unpresentable to become perceptible" through allusion.[52] Nicoletta Pireddu reads this postmodern retrieval of the sublime paradoxically both as an impossibility—or the recognition of an impossibility, that of reversing time—and as "an attempt to reconstruct a 'beyond' of any kind," a new hope for overstepping the limitations of the postmodern condition.[53] It is a "longing for stimuli, even in the form of 'shock,' that might reawaken responses that have been 'numbed' by overhabituation."[54]

For Jameson, technology now serves as a source of the sublime: it mesmerizes and fascinates, holding out the promise of a representational shorthand for grasping the global network of power and control. But the repressed, for Jameson, is not a capital-n Nature forgotten or ravaged by technology; rather, it is historicity, the ability to make narrative sense of the whole system. The information-saturated postmodern media universe, with its ubiquitous eye in the sky of satellite surveillance, confers a paranoid modality on postmodern life, and Jameson reads the high-tech paranoia of the cyberpunk and conspiracy genres more generally as "degraded" attempts "to think the impossible totality of the contemporary world system."[55] His readings of conspiracy films in *The Geopolitical Aesthetic* show a prescient sense for the decade of the *X-Files*, a series that appeared a year after that book was published. *X-Files* is perhaps the best example of the argument I have been making: as a political fantasy about the labyrinthine workings of an unmappable and highly secretive system of global domination, it makes a tight fit with Jameson's argument; but the role of nature throughout the series—as unexplainable goo coming from the ground, as uncanny biological hybrid, as mysterious residue or side effect of creepy shadow-government experiments, as both alien and very deep inside us, in our brains and bodies—is a telling indicator of how ecology at every level had gotten woven into the paranoid fantasies of power and powerlessness in premillennial America. The show could also be read as a serial compendium of the kinds of "monstrous natures" noted by Stacy Alaimo, who argues that while some of these entail a form of "border work" that attempts to elevate humanity onto a transcendent perch above and superior to the natural world, others provide a space for reimagining our corporeal identification with the animal, the organic, and the messily and monstrously hybrid.[56]

In the libidinal and imaginal economy of emergent globality—the globalization that constituted the principal sign of the world system throughout the 1990s—these viral and monstrous excrescences could be taken as reminders that sociality, however orderly or unruly, is always contaminated by an unencompassable foreign element. But the repressed other is not historicity, as Jameson argues, but something more like the recognition of our complicity with the ecological crisis—arguably the hidden collective trauma of postmodernity—and with the (ontologically and epistemologically) colonial incursions with which this crisis is historically bound. Cartesian dualism had repressed the entire network of biological interdependencies and corporeal confraternities that shape and structure our material existence; now these erupt fitfully at a time when collective responsibility for eco-social collapse beckons at our consciousness. It is not that such sentiments haven't erupted fitfully throughout the modern era—in Gothic tales and horror stories from

Mary Shelley to Kafka to the films of David Cronenberg—but that their eruption during the millennial 1990s has taken particular forms associated with
technological experimentation and political conspiracy. At the same time, in
the body politic of North American culture, those same sentiments can be
taken as indicators of liberal guilt driven inward onto the socially conservative
terrain of the late Clinton years: that is, the terrain of moral character as against
moral ambiguity, of chastity and its desecration, and so on. Recall that these
filmmakers (Altman, Egoyan, Anderson, Lee, et al.) are upfront or implicit
social liberals; but in the temporal bubble of the Clinton 1990s, they somehow
felt compelled to examine the moral sloppiness of the middle- and upper-class
America that surrounded them on all sides.

The Eco-Imaginary in Post-9/11 Culture

But let me return to my main thesis here, which is that representations of
connectedness (or lack of it), of communication and miscommunication, of
the threads that tie together the most elemental, cellular level of social life
(the family), can be read as saying something about the most global level, that
which we are calling "political ecology"—at least when they are framed by disruptive acts of nature, which, like flashes of lightning, throw those social facts
into stark visibility. This thesis has something to do with the embryonic field
of ecopsychology, particularly with Theodore Roszak's underdeveloped but
evocative conception of an "ecological unconscious." Roszak calls this unconscious "the core of the mind," representing the "record of cosmic evolution."
The goal of ecopsychology, as he puts it, "is to awaken the inherent sense of
environmental reciprocity that lies within" that unconscious.[57] Roszak's notion
assumes a quasi-Jungian essentialism about the mind that we need not swallow;[58] it is enough to make the historical argument that global ecology and a
skewed relationship between humanity and the Earth had become thinkable
ideas, socio-psychological facts, by the late 1980s, and that by the mid-1990s
these facts had undergone a kind of repression, with opinion polls showing
that the environment had fallen off the public radar, displaced by the economy
or by moral and cultural politics.

These cinematic moments can be read, to use Andrew Ross's term (see
Chapter 2), as "images of ecology," with the difference that the images examined here are not quite conscious or intended as such; they require a kind
of psychoanalytic retrieval for their ecological significance to be drawn out.[59]
They are similar to the genre of horror film, which portrays monstrous natures
dressed as threatening biological phenomena or as human–natural hybrids.
But while the latter have been richly explored for their articulations of gender,

race, class, and nature,[60] these more recent and "latent" and "decentred" appearances of uncanny nature have not been much analyzed by critics. They provide a contrast to the consciously environmental messages of *The Day After Tomorrow* and its eco-dystopian predecessors such as *Silent Running*, *Soylent Green*, the *Mad Max* series, and *Waterworld*. The spectacle of disaster is what the latter genre of films is about, so the characters tend to be poorly developed, the storylines predictable, and the environmental messages both easier to refute, as they inevitably fall short of the science they gesture toward, and more easily tamed into the predigested discourse of polarized left–right politics. The unconscious eruptions, storms, quakes, and freezes in the "indirect disaster" films we have been discussing are not so easily tamed. They remain unassimilable, hovering uneasily at the edges of our awareness. Or at least that is the promise: the art of such films, Slavoj Žižek suggests, lies in "the paradox of anamorphosis: if you look at the thing too directly ... you don't see it. You can see it in an oblique way only if it remains in the background."[61] In the case he is describing, which is the film *Children of Men* (2006), "it" is "the oppressive social dimension," but I think this argument also applies to the socio-ecological dimension. A Jamesonian ecocritic might ask: How is it that such irruptions appear, and where and when do they cluster in popular culture and media? How do they resonate with, supplement, or disrupt the social worlds portrayed? Is there a way we can retrieve the wild, untamed core, the kernel or undergrowth of enjoyment in these representations, to keep a certain wildness in play through times in which the ecological or eco-geopolitical unconscious seems *especially* unconscious?

Since the 1990s, at any rate, the eco-imaginary has flared up again to the point that we need not seek such indirect manifestations of it. We have had rapid global climate change depicted in *The Day After Tomorrow*, the complete (and literal) trashing of the Earth in *WALL-E,* and the vicious attempt to trash another pristine, Earth-like planet in *Avatar*. And there have been numerous features that leave the ecological option open amidst an array of mysterious causes of societal decline. In *Children of Men*, it is an infertility pandemic; in *12 Monkeys* (1995), *I Am Legend* (2007), and *28 Days Later* (2002), it is a virus, perhaps genetically engineered. While the causality remains murky in such cinematic treatments, audiences are likely to know (exoreferentially) that, among other things, environmental toxins, including endocrine-system-disrupting chemicals, might have such consequences as depicted in *Children of Men*. Other films, like *Syriana* (2005) and *There Will Be Blood* (2007), more clearly portray the dark political ecology of resource capitalism, either in its current global form (*Syriana*) or in its historical emergence (*Blood*).

Continuing our interest in the formal dimensions of films that are about
global relations, we find a persistence and even a growth in fragmented and
multilinear narratives. (These have been part of a broader growth of alternative
narratives that include "database narratives," "forking paths" narratives,
multiple-draft narratives, modular narratives, puzzle films, and the like.)[62]
The kind of fragmentation that was once the province of experimental auteurs
like Alain Resnais now appears in popular features like *Pulp Fiction* (1994),
Traffic (2000), and *Crash* (2004) and in Guillermo Arriaga and Alejandro
Gonzalez Iñárritu's trilogy, each film more popular than the last: *Amores Perros*
(2000), *21 Grams* (2003), and *Babel* (2006). With its multiple story lines of
global connections and *missed* connections, *Babel* insists on being taken as
a metaphor for the transnational links between those best poised to travel
the world freely (usually American tourists) and those who remain in their
places (such as the film's Algerian boys) or who travel only for work (such
as the Mexican maid) while remaining socially and emotionally moored to
their home worlds and their class identifications.[63] Many of these films involve
twisted and sometimes even reversed temporalities, following the trend of the
multilinear or hyperlink narrative. The latter is more typical in films exploring
the nature of memory, identity, and consciousness, such as *Memento* (2001),
Mulholland Drive (2001), *Eternal Sunshine of the Spotless Mind* (2004), *Happy
Endings* (2005), and *Premonition* (2007). Such films give viewers the sense that
memory is not something directly related to a retrievable past and that the
future is hardly a logical outcome of the present. In films like *Syriana* (2005),
The Constant Gardener (2005), and *The Good Shepherd* (2006), such disorienting
multilinearity is combined with an exploration of the textures and flows of
global security and resource conflicts.

In some films, however, it is not so much the narrative as it is the
filmic texture that is multilinear and hyperlinked. *Children of Men*, Alfonso
Cuaron's radicalization of P.D. James's dystopian novel, is notable for its
dense entanglement of ecological and social themes: power differentials
and inequities between classes and races lead to the unjust distribution of
environmental "goods" and "bads"—an issue to which environmental justice
advocates have long drawn attention. The film makes all of this believable
both in its futuristic context (the action occurs in 2027) and in the context of
the world from which its imagery is taken. That world is today's mediascape,
with its wars (Iraq, Palestine, Bosnia, Somalia, Afghanistan, and so on) and
security apparatuses: border walls, detainment centres, refugee camps,
religious profilers, and obsession with keeping terrorists off airplanes. All
of these things are combined with a Tarkovskian attention to landscape,

especially in the film's stunning long takes, which emphasize the environment surrounding the characters in the same way that *Blade Runner* did some twenty years earlier. Comparing *Children of Men* with the more conventionally post-apocalyptic zombie film *I Am Legend*, Kirk Boyle lauds the way the "disaster-capitalism complex" is critically engaged in the former film's "yoking together" of images of "globalization, immigration, inequity, environmental degradation, permanent states of emergency, politics of fear, surveillance society, terrorism, and ghettoes."[64]

Political Ecologies in Multiple Dimensions

There are also films that present ecological issues directly yet take on board some of the lessons of the aesthetic of indirection described earlier. There are several ways this might be done. Richard Linklater's *Fast Food Nation* (2006) provides one model. A feature-film dramatization of a non-fiction book by Eric Schlosser, the muckraking investigative bestseller *Fast Food Nation: The Dark Side of the All-American Meal*, the film mixes documentary fact with a fictional ensemble drama of parallel and semi-convergent stories centred on a hamburger chain called Mickey's. Much of the film takes place in and around the fictional, prototypical American town of Cody, Colorado. Like other network narratives, *Fast Food Nation* tells several overlapping and connected stories, which radiate "like spokes from the hub of a central theme," as A.O. Scott puts it. Its characters include minimum wage workers at a fast food restaurant, Mexican immigrants working at a meat-packing plant, cattle ranchers, and a Mickey's marketing executive who visits the town to look into reports of contaminated food.[65] Some network films connect their spokes through a central traumatic event (in the case of *The Sweet Hereafter*, Gonzalez Iñárritu's *21 Grams* [2003], and Paul Haggis's *Crash* [2004]), it is a fatal traffic accident); others, like *Short Cuts* and *Magnolia*, proceed in a more decentred fashion. In the case of *Fast Food Nation*, the event is actually a dark secret at the heart of the industrial food system—that, as several characters suggest in one way or another, we literally and figuratively "eat shit." That secret is then connected to the related dark secrets of cross-border immigration and capitalist exploita-tion.[66] The film's mixed reception tells us either that its ambitions overran its modest budget, or that the complex interconnections between industrial food production, racism, sexism, and capitalist globalization are not easy to depict in a single film without a certain degree of preachiness and overextension. Or perhaps it tells us both.

Another film that aims to disclose such interconnections, this time in the guise of a *cinéma verité*–styled documentary exposé, is Hubert Sauper's

Darwin's Nightmare (2004). At the centre of this film's nightmarish trip into a socio-ecological hell is the Nile perch, a fish that was introduced to Lake Victoria in Africa sometime in the 1950s or 1960s and that has resulted in the near extinction of more than 200 of the lake's indigenous fish species. But it is not the fish itself that Sauper is interested in. Rather, it is the global trade in Nile perch, which links in a multitude of ways the fishermen of Tanzania; other local people (including fume-sniffing children, orphaned by war or by AIDS), who survive, in part, by scavenging the discarded and maggoty remains of the fish; the Eastern European airplane pilots who fly the processed fish fillets to Europe and who, it is strongly hinted, sometimes fly arms into African combat zones; the prostitutes who serve the pilots (including one who is killed by a client during the making of the film); and the African and European bureaucrats and processing plant owners, who insist on maintaining business as usual through it all. Like a detective quietly analyzing a crime scene, Sauper's camera teases its way into the lives of the local fishermen, homeless villagers and prostitutes, Russian and Ukrainian pilots, and others eking out a living (or not) on the sidelines of the transnational export fishing industry. Two million Europeans, Sauper suggests, eat Nile perch every day, while a similar number starve from famine in Tanzania and its surrounding region. As he states in an interview accompanying the DVD, it was Sauper's own revolt at this fact that he wanted to viscerally transmit to the viewer.

Darwin's Nightmare won numerous international awards and was nominated for the Best Documentary Oscar. In France, the film inspired a movement that succeeded in removing the Nile perch from many supermarket shelves.[67] But the film also had its critics, including the Tanzanian government, African environmental and NGO representatives, and development studies scholars, who derided its bleak depiction of an industry that had brought great benefits to the country.[68] The film's success led Tanzanian President Jakaya Kikwete to devote an entire nationwide monthly address to criticizing it, and apparently led to threats of deportation being issued to journalists interviewed in the film.[69] In their defence, it could be argued that Kikwete and his forerunners had contributed to the growth of a Tanzanian middle class, that they had worked vigorously to negotiate peace in the region, and that they welcomed refugees from neighbouring countries. None of that is shown in Sauper's bleak portrayal of what the film's website calls "The Heart of Darkness." This raises the related issue of Sauper's orientalizing gaze at the horror of Africa: *Darwin's Nightmare* presents shocking images of rotting, maggot-swarmed fish carcasses, street children fighting over snatches of food and surrounded by mounds of garbage, a legless child, a woman visibly weakened by famine and AIDS (we are told), and similar scenes assembled to predictable effect. Sauper's seeming proximity to his subjects lends the kind of ethnographic credibility that most documentarians crave. Some, like A.O. Scott, see in this an "ethical vision" with an apocalyptic tenderness that rivals that of William Blake.[70] Documentary theorist B. Ruby Rich notes that Sauper offers "a reciprocity of vision that returns the gaze, repays respect in kind, and recognizes that even African villagers can be world-class experts on their own society, life, and fate."[71] African responses have been generally more critical than this. Olivier Barlet has argued astutely that this sort of shocking imagery, rather than mobilizing people to do anything about what they are shown, elicits guilt and resignation. The film, he says, fails to provide a space for reflection in which viewers can arrive at their own relationship to the images.[72]

One of the lessons that comes from viewing such films is that they never, on their own, provide sufficient information for us to evaluate their factual validity. More research is always needed. The question here is more complicated than whether, or to what extent, film can bring to viewers a better understanding of such complex phenomena as globalization and the socio-ecological collapse wrought by political, economic, and ecological forces working in lethal unison. The critiques of *Darwin's Nightmare* combine the kinds of criticisms we have seen of the "inaccuracies" in *An Inconvenient Truth* and *The Day After Tomorrow* with those of the "racism" of films like *The Cove* (2009). The latter is Louie Psihoyos's documentary about Western environmental activists' efforts to document and thereby prevent an annual "dolphin slaughter" at the Japanese port of Taiji. *The Cove* reflects a dual rhetorical strategy. On the one hand, the film sets up an emotional frame for appreciating the activists' efforts by focusing on the transformation of its lead character, Rick O'Barry, from trainer of the television dolphin star Flipper to passionate activist on behalf of cetaceans. As it proceeds, however, it becomes an eco-thriller, complete with suspenseful and ominous music and fast camera movements, about courageous activists using stealth-camera guerrilla techniques—"camouflage, stuntmen, hydrophones, unmanned drones, and 'military-grade' hi-def and nightvision cameras"—to capture footage of the kill.[73] The activists apparently believe in the indexical power of the image: if audiences see the primal scene of slaughter for themselves, they will surely act to end the practice. But they show little effort to interact with Japanese environmental activists (of whom there are many), and the film ends up falling into a stereotypical depiction of its Japanese subjects, becoming, in Ilan Kapoor's words, "a case of (mostly) 'white men saving cute dolphins from yellow men.'"[74] Though a success in the West—the film won the Academy Award for Best Documentary—*The Cove* has proven divisive and controversial in Japan.

Each of these films—*Fast Food Nation, Darwin's Nightmare,* and *The Cove*—confronts the problem of how to present the raw, emotionally impacting firstness of contemporary socio-ecological horrors in ways that will elicit not only the secondness of audience involvement in the film's narrative but also the thirdness of curiosity about the horrors portrayed, and ultimately a deepened understanding and capacity to act in response to them. The filmmakers' goals include the instrumental one of bringing about change, and at least the two documentaries (*The Cove* and *Darwin's Nightmare*) have had a measurable impact on the issues they depict. Both, however, show the centrality of two issues we have been exploring: that of documentary truthfulness, and that of the ethical relationship to the subjects of the Western filmmaker's gaze.

Both these issues arise in full force in Werner Herzog's *Lessons of Darkness* (1992), a film that represents a very different strategy for depicting socio-ecological horrors. I have already discussed some of the ambiguities of Herzog's filmmaking style: his penchant for blurring the difference between fact and fiction, his romantic and often obsessive attraction to extreme personalities and landscapes—extremes both anthropomorphic and geomorphic. *Lessons of Darkness* is composed of documentary images of the burning oil fields of Kuwait in the wake of the First Gulf War. But Herzog has little interest in helping us understand why the war occurred and who should be held responsible for its results. Instead he presents us the images themselves in all their power, clothed only in the quasi–science-fictional, apocalyptic garb of his occasional voice-over narration and subtitles: "a planet in our solar system," "A Capital City," "The War," "After the Battle," "Finds from Torture Chambers," "Satan's National Park," "And a Smoke Arose Like a Smoke from a Furnace," and "I am so tired from sighing; Lord, let it be night." The result is an apocalyptic yet also ironic vision of a hell on earth that is visually sublime but politically intangible. Herzog himself has called the film "a requiem for a planet that we ourselves have destroyed."[75] Like an extraterrestrial visitor to the post-apocalypse, Herzog is vulnerable here to the same critiques that followers of deep ecology have faced for years: that by identifying the perpetrators of the ecological crisis with an all-embracing "us," we lose the political precision necessary for under-standing how it came about, who has benefited from it, who has suffered most, and how to challenge the institutional actors responsible for it.

Yet Herzog's artistic decisions can be defended on the grounds that we *know* about the war already. Viewers at the time had already seen the video-game-like images that characterized American media coverage of the war, and they were likely to already have well-formed opinions about the justifications for the war. With its "stubborn refusal to contextualize itself," as Nadia Bozak puts it, the film intended to present the images *differently*. Bozak writes that in contrast to the frenzy of cable television coverage of the war, *Lessons of Darkness* "slows down and even fossilizes the events of the war, turning fire-fighting machinery into dinosaurs, abandoned weaponry into ancient bones."[76] Such aestheticization had long been Herzog's response to the political violence of the world. In a 1979 interview, he stated that "we live in a society that has *no* adequate images anymore" and that "if we do not find adequate images and an adequate language for our civilization with which to express them, we will die out like the dinosaurs." Referring to the environmental issues of the time, he continued: "We have already recognized that problems like the energy shortage or the overpopulation of the world are great dangers for our society and for our kind of civilization, but I think that it has not been understood widely enough that we absolutely *need* new images."[77] If this was true in the 1970s, one would presume it to be no less true in the 1990s, and perhaps much more so in the second decade of the twenty-first century.

But how new are Herzog's images? Are they not simply a reiteration of well-known Western tropes: apocalypse, humanity's decline, and the futility of hope, all set to a soundtrack of Wagner, Mahler, Prokofiev, Verdi, Schubert, Grieg, and Arvo Pärt? Several of Herzog's other films, including *Fata Morgana* (1971), *La Soufrière* (1977), about the anticipated eruption in 1976 of an active volcano on the island of Guadeloupe, and *Wild Blue Yonder* (2005), share with *Lessons of Darkness* a tone of tender and lyrical, apocalyptic beauty, a resignation in the face of what appears to be humanity's passing, and a feeling of waiting or homeless wandering, as if something momentous is about to occur, or has already occurred, or both. With their kinetic landscape shots—taken from helicopters, moving vehicles, or underwater cameras—of landscapes largely empty of humans, they seem like archaeological digs through abandoned cities, devastated ones, or worlds without human contact at all, yet brimming with signs of its demise. Like *Lessons of Darkness*, *La Soufrière* blurs several sets of lines: between documentary and fiction, between observation and performative enactment (Herzog's own persona being ever-present, which in this case includes taking his crew up to the caldera to poke their camera inside the steaming volcano, as if to dare nature to scald them with smoke and ash), and between the hilarious and the deadly serious. The film highlights the barbed existential irony that when, in 1902, the inhabitants of neighbouring Martinique were preparing to leave before an anticipated volcanic eruption, their governor persuaded them to stay; 30,000 died. Now, seventy-five years later, the inhabitants left—except for the few that Herzog's crew finds and interviews, and of course, Herzog himself, who is attracted to the volcano like a moth to the flame. And the volcano balked.

Of all the filmmakers we have examined, Herzog is the one who most obsessively pursues the sublime, which in his hands becomes simultaneously an ecological, apocalyptic, and ironic sublime. So many of Herzog's films are about what we might call The ~~Event~~, a crossed-out sublime moment that we witness only through its "before" and its "after," its ominous, rumbling premonitions, and its decisive yet perplexing and ambiguous aftermath. Unlike the kind of transcendent event celebrated by philosopher Alain Badiou (modelled after Pauline Christianity's messianic event), which ruptures the ontological fabric to create a new condition for subjectivity, Herzog's is not a historical event.[78] It is not the kind of lightning streak that marks history with the shadow of its exposure, such as May '68 (for Badiou), the Revolution (whether Russian, French, American, or another one), or Jesus's Passion and Resurrection. Herzog's ~~Event~~ is one before which humanity pales into insignificance, even if our creative capacity to reach out to that ~~Event~~ is, for him, worth celebrating. It is, in this sense, a most direct answer to the filmmaker's existential question: Why film at all? What, if anything, is worthy of being turned into a film event? And, therefore, where should film take us, into what world, what Zone, and with what capacities to transform us?

If there is a single question this book asks of any film, it is this: *What is the Zone into which this film takes us?* For process-relational thinking, the *what* necessarily translates into a *how*: How are we taken into it, and how does that Zone feel to us when we are in it? What psychic and emotional imprints does it leave upon us, and how do those circulate in the world after we have left its immediate cognitive-affective field? The films I have been examining take viewers into a Zone in which we are confronted with an event, a catastrophe, or some kind of compelling emergency—the looming climate crisis, the tragedy of global socio-ecological breakdown, or (as in *Fast Food Nation*) the hidden truth about what, in William Burroughs's potent phrase, is "on the end of every fork."[79] In Herzog's version, this event requires little adumbration, while at the other extreme, as in Linklater's film, the pieces of the puzzle need a couple of hours of narrative elaboration for their connections to be made tangible.

The filmic Zone is, in one sense, merely a single pole of the dipolar relational fabric of a dynamic film-world. It is the "there" that contrasts to the "here," the "other" as contrasted to the "us." At the same time, however, the Zone is the entire relational field uniting the two ends, and it is important to remember that the "here" and the "us" are also cinematic constructs, depicted or implied, without which their polar opposites could not exist. For this reason the *real* filmic Zone is the field of their mutual resonance and mutual opposition, the dialectical dynamic between the *here* and the *there*. If the Zone in *Lessons of Darkness* is one of apocalyptic trauma—populated by oil fields that, in Herzog's characterization, pretend to be the sky (by reflecting it), and by instruments of torture and victims of war rendered mute by its psychological impact—it is also a Zone into which we bring ourselves as we follow the camera. We bring our responses—to Herzog's narrative persona, to the strains of Wagner's *Parsifal* and other music—with us as we journey.

Movement into the Zone of a film, then, is something that is negotiated by each viewer and by distinct viewing communities. Each such negotiation transpires within a field of possibilities marked by prior expectations, sensibilities, and affective potencies that are not fully actualized until well after the film's viewing. It takes time for a film's elements—its images, sounds, narratives, and exoreferential resonances and evocations—to make their way into thirdness. A film in which this movement into thirdness can be glimpsed particularly clearly, because it was so widely viewed and so thoroughly discussed, is James Cameron's blockbuster spectacle, *Avatar* (2009).

Avatar's Eco-Apocalyptic Zone

By many measures the most successful film ever made, seen by more viewers around the world than any other film in history, *Avatar* offers perhaps the best case study of the collective traversing of an eco-apocalyptic Zone by cinema audiences.[80] At once eco-utopian and dystopian, the film brings together a combination of geomorphic and anthropomorphic effects familiar by now from previous chapters. It depicts the "ethnographic" contact between a society much like ours—a mining company exploiting the resources of a foreign land, in this case the planet Pandora, a lush, vegetated moon in the Alpha Centauri star system—and a tradition-bound indigenous society called the Na'vi. The latter are presented as radically other: they are blue-skinned and ten feet tall, and they live in a state of harmony with Pandoran "nature"—an attitude that clearly eludes the planet's human invaders. The human colony is engaged in scientific efforts to communicate with the Na'vi and learn about their world; soon, however, these biological and anthropological efforts are trumped by the imperative to mine the ore of the mineral unsubtly named "unobtanium," which happens to be found in greatest abundance beneath the sacred trees of the Na'vi. Former marine Jake Sully is brought in to replace his deceased brother in a genetic engineering program that produces human–Na'vi hybrids to communicate and interact with the indigenous inhabitants. When Sully is rescued by the Na'vi princess, Neytiri, and is granted the opportunity to learn Na'vi ways directly, he gradually "goes native." When the mining colony, with its private security army SecFor, launches a war to take control of the resources protected by the Na'vi, Sully and a few other compatriots are forced to take sides. They join the Na'vi and help enlist a sweeping coalition of species to fight back and force the human army off the planet.

Two aspects of the film make it especially interesting from a process-relational perspective: first, its success as sheer spectacle, especially in its biomorphic generation of a captivating alien world; and second, its exoreferential productivity. Let us examine each of these in turn. The sheer spectacle of *Avatar* is what elicited the greatest interest in the early stages of the film's reception.[81] The film is spectacular on multiple fronts: in its immersive 3-D effects, CGI, and advanced motion-capture technology; in the thrills-and-chills of its lengthy, high-tech, rapid-fire battle scenes; and, of greatest interest for an ecocritical reading, in its scintillating portrayal of the biotic life of Pandora, perhaps the most seductive and alluring vision of another planet ever presented in cinema. *Avatar* was Cameron's long-time dream film, one that he had first thought of making in the 1970s but began to write only in the early 1990s, and he intended it to push the technology of computer graphics, motion capture, and 3-D cinema to levels heretofore unseen. Both *Avatar* and Cameron's previous blockbuster, *Titanic*, reflect their director's love of deep-sea diving: the former in the many submersible scenes of the *Titanic* wreck, the latter in the way the world of Pandora comes alive in bioluminescent splendour. As one online commenter and scuba diver put it, there is "no other ecological encounter which is so alien to our physiology, and so decentering. When one dives there is a kind of avatarship experience of suspension." The diving features, he argued, can easily be recognized

> when Sully first playfully and childishly smacks luminescence to stimulate it. A junior diver is the one that touches everything (often killing it to some degree). But it is not the portrayal of diving that Cameron was after.... It was the kinesthetic transferral, the displace-ment, the suspension, the alien drift, the wobbly wonder that bombards a diver, no matter how experienced. When every single living thing in an environment is physiologically superior to you. When every single living thing is aesthetically more beautiful. When your own suspension is technological and precarious before what can only be called a *witnessing*. The effect is ecological.[82]

The novelty of the 3-D experience is underscored by the film's repeated emphasis on seeing, from the recurrent shots of Sully's eyes and the first-person shots of his avatar's view of the Na'vi and their world, to the frequently repeated Na'vi greeting "I see you," intended as an acknowledgment of empathetic understanding of another. Sully is a fairly typical Hollywood action hero. He is disadvantaged to start with, being a disabled survivor of warfare, marginalized and ridiculed in multiple contexts: among the mercenaries sent to Pandora to defend the human colony, the scientists of the avatar program, and the Na'vi themselves. But he triumphs over adversity to become the sixth in a succession of Na'vi spiritual leaders known as Toruk Macto, with the ability to tame the birdlike creature known by that name and to unite the Na'vi clans. Following Sully's trajectory can be a particularly immersive experience for viewers. In a study of the film's capacity for eliciting viewer empathies, Lisa Sideris notes that studies with virtual body transfers show a strong sense of ownership and identification with one's avatar body well after one has "returned" to one's own body.[83] Sully's transformation and "empathic education," Sideris demonstrates, remains "imperfect and incomplete," inasmuch as it shows him cutting corners and reverting, on many occasions, to the "jarhead" mentality that supposedly characterized his identity as a marine.[84] This leaves the film open to critiques that it exhibits the very colonial assertiveness it is attempting to curtail. It is, in this sense, a flawed and compromised version of the sorts of empathic tracts that have characterized the environmental movement, from Aldo Leopold's poignant account of the "fierce green fire" in a dying wolf's eyes to Rachel Carson's efforts to "think myself into the role of an animal that lives in the sea."[85] How viewers *follow* Sully in their identifications thus becomes one of the points at which viewer responses begin to diverge.

In its luxurious depiction of the Pandoran world, which takes up much of the film's first half, viewers have the option of enjoying this world, finding it beautiful, compelling, and attractive; of failing to enjoy it, remaining unmoved or even finding it frightening or unattractive (it is, after all, full of horrific creatures); or of moving between these two extremes—for instance, being won over by its beauty in the same way that Sully is apparently won over. With its 3-D graphics and its immersive camera work and character movement (both real and animated/simulated), the film elicits a strong sensation of movement into a biomorphically rich and strange world. But the filmic spectacle of the Pandoran biosphere is upstaged in the film's second half by the spectacle of war between the Na'vi, with their coalition of animal allies, and the high-tech military machine. Here the film recalls Cameron's work on the *Terminator* series. Viewers have the option of enjoying the spectacle and the bodily sensations of warfare—hunting and being hunted, shooting and being shot at, flying mounted on strange birds, and the jarring sensation of sudden attack, all in extremely rapidly edited jolts—or enjoying their identification with one side or the other. Or they can enjoy the implicit message that "war is hell," thereby identifying with the underdogs, yet perhaps also appreciating that there may be times when we must take up arms to defend ourselves. Or, finally, they can reject all of these forms of enjoyment—which may account for the critical responses of those who disliked the film.

To understand how viewers come to align with one of these responses, we need to examine more closely how the narrative structures these options for us. In its narrativity, the film is not very original. It is a traditional linear narrative of an encounter and conflict between two cultures, one that takes the side of the underdogs but insists on the hero being a renegade member of the overdog (white, human) group. This hero is a traditional masculine point of identification: it is his struggles that we follow, and in the end he triumphs, "gets the girl," and even becomes a messiah. Geomorphically, there is a "here" and a "there": the mining colony represents the industrial-capitalist Earth we all know, while the alien world of the Pandoran Na'vi is the Zone we ourselves enter, explore, take pleasure in, and, arguably, come to dominate. In this metaphorical meeting between West and non-West, it is the West that is expanded by taking on something of its Other through a transmission that ultimately depends on the technology of the transfer—the avatarship of Jake Sully. Critic Robert Hyland is not alone in reading all of this as a "colonial control narrative" in which the white male ex-marine masters and subordinates a series of others: starting with his own alien avatar body and extending to the Pandoran terrain, Na'vi language and culture, various beasts—which he literally penetrates to force them to do his bidding—the Na'vi princess, and finally the entire Na'vi people.[86]

At the same time, there is no denying that the conflict is between two radically different cultures and ways of life and that the Na'vi, with or without Jake Sully, present an imagined alternative to the society that is dominant on *our* planet. What makes the film interesting in this respect is the way it lays its structuring oppositions onto one another, opening itself up to a range of exoreferential analogies and allegorical interpretations. It is these that were the focus of the second stage of the public debate over the film once the attention to the 3-D and CGI subsided. Allegory is a classic instance of exoreferentiality: a case of something in the film standing in for something else in the real world. Among the allegorical interpretations that have been made of *Avatar* are the following: the human takeover of the planet as an allegory of rampant resource extraction, neo-colonialism, rainforest destruction, U.S. militarism, the global military-industrial complex, the Iraq Wars, the "War on Terror," and/ or the genocide of indigenous peoples; the relationship between the humans and the Na'vi as a form of anthropological encounter, of "cultural understanding through immersion," of cultural imperialism, and of the "white messiah complex"; the destruction of Hometree as a metaphor for the 9/11 attacks; and Pandora as an allegorical representation of the Gaia hypothesis, of the Internet, and of cinema itself.[87] Let us look at a few of these more closely.

One of the ways in which American audiences grappled with the film was through the lens of the decades-long "culture wars" between the liberal left and the conservative right. Read as a liberal-environmentalist credo, the film became a lightning rod for right-wing critics, who lambasted both its superficiality and its thinly disguised attack on corporate militarism, which the critics found "anti-American."[88] Its depiction of Na'vi religion triggered right-wing critiques of its animism, pantheism, paganism, eco-religiosity, and New Age "hippie spiritualism."[89] Critics on the left, meanwhile, divided themselves between those celebrating the film's anti-corporate, anti-militarist, anti-imperialist, pro-indigenous, and ecological sentiments, and those critiquing its contradictions and ironies. Political theorist and media critic James Der Derian called it "the best anti-war film since *Dr. Strangelove*," a film that "spectacularly … repudiates the utility of war" and that "manages to entertain and to critique, to revel in the pleasures and to expose the pathologies of the military–industrial complex within a wholly new media-entertainment matrix."[90] Others derided the film's racism. Slavoj Žižek lambasted its suggestion that "a paraplegic outcast from earth is good enough to get the hand of a beautiful local princess, and to help the natives win the decisive battle" and that "the only choice the aborigines have is to be saved by the human beings or to be destroyed by them"—that is, "they can choose to be the victim of imperialist reality, or to play their allotted role in the white man's fantasy."[91] In other words, the Na'vi can either be real and lose (to "imperialist reality"), or be fake, a "white man's fantasy," and win. Yet one could counter-argue that critics like Žižek have stacked the deck. Couldn't losing (getting crushed by the imperialist machine) be just as fake, since it is only a movie, and as we know, the real people at the other end of the imperialist wars of our time—Afghanistan comes to mind—have not so clearly lost? And couldn't winning (with the help of a few white humans, but against the vast majority of them) be equally real if one's victory inspires people around the planet to rise up against their resource-robbing oppressors? A film is not only what happens between the dimming and the turning back up of the lights. It is also what happens in our discussions, dreams, and lives as we work with the images, sounds, and symbols it makes available to us. In this sense, the judgments of critics may be too hasty.

In an analysis that takes in Cameron's entire oeuvre, Lacanian theorist Todd McGowan argued that the film pits a Spielbergian "paternal" ideology, which convinces us that the social order is solidly founded in the patriarchal authority represented by Colonel Quaritch, against the eco-maternalism of

Eywa, the mother-goddess of the Na'vi. The latter represents an ideology of wholeness and plenitude as well as the "sense of belonging to a transcendent network of significance." Cameron is far from alone among contemporary filmmakers in questioning patriarchy in favour of an ecological or maternalist holism. In McGowan's reading, however, there is a productive tension between the maternal as plenitude, visible in the Na'vi belief that Eywa "does not take sides" but "protects the balance of life," and the maternal as itself divided: Eywa does, in the end, take sides and get drawn into the political. Yet the final struggle between Sully and Quaritch, McGowan writes, "has all the trappings of Hollywood's ideological denouement," in which "the psychology of the villain takes center stage": Quaritch's "individual homicidal psychosis trumps the villainy of the structural evil and allows the spectator to personalize evil."[92]

McGowan's neo-Lacanian argument runs against the prevailing tenor of pro-ecological views expressed about the film. Many other observers simply assumed—and fan accounts typically supported this assumption—that the maternal Eywa triumphed in the film and that this ought to be celebrated.[93] From another perspective, however, all of these messages are undercut by the implicit message that it is technology and Hollywood magic—the Image Industry—that enchants, seduces, and delivers us from evil. The tension between the film's ostensibly critical message and its technological wizardry recalls the debate discussed earlier with regard to *Jurassic Park*. As ecopsychologist Renee Lertzman put it, "while the film purports to be proenvironmental—'Enter the world,' the tagline says—the psychic message delivered by the story is about leaving the world.... Don the glasses and leave our world of plastic cups and sticky soda, and drift among the trees and exotic species likely to be endangered on our own planet."[94] And more than in most fantasies, what that psychic message is about is new life, perhaps eternal life, through the New Age sciences of neuro-energetics, gene splicing, and virtual reality. Jake Sully the Na'vi avatar (not the marine) is, after all, a zombie and a drone: his body is a remote-controlled, genetically engineered robot that comes to life, echoing the fantasy of a hyper-capitalist American dream of remaking oneself as someone else entirely.

This fantasy underlying the avatar theme is the crux of social ecologist Max Cafard's lengthy and searing indictment of the film. Cafard calls *Avatar* "the most important film in history," unsurpassed "in showing the ways in which ideology turns things into their precise opposite."[95] Its explicit message "that civilization is oppressive and destructive and that we should break with it, smash its power, and go to live in egalitarian, ecological communities instead," and its delivery of this message using the most sophisticated affective technologies in history, conspire to blind viewers to the fact that the film's "ability to inspire any active opposition to war and imperialism is nil."[96] Instead it offers "pseudo-subversive images," commodified forms of dissent that provide only imaginary substitutes for action. The minimal actions it inspires—such as the "Home Tree Initiative," which 20th Century Fox developed in partnership with the Earth Day Network to plant a million trees in 2010 by signing up adopt-a-tree "warriors of the earth"—have borne little fruit. Cafard caustically notes that the initiative had managed to enlist only 290,000 "adoptive tree parents" by the end of the year; one could argue, however, that this is not bad, for what it's worth.[97] The film's "most powerful ideological message" and "final truth," in Cafard's reading, is the message that only "the Drone," the "latest product of the drive for technological domination ... from a distance," "can save us."[98] The Drone, he writes, "reveals the *telos* of superpower military-industrial technology." While "the dominated can be more intensely terrorized," the dominators are rendered less and less vulnerable (though fantasies of vulnerability paradoxically increase as tolerance of risk declines).[99] Along related lines, Caleb Crain attacks the movie's "moral corruptness," arguing that its anti-imperialism and anti-corporatism are red herrings planted to distract us from "the movie's more serious ideological work: convincing you to love your simulation—convincing you to surrender your queasiness." On Pandora, he writes, the Na'vi are "digital natives" and "all the creatures have been equipped by a benevolent nature with USB ports in their ponytails."[100] At the very least, it is reasonable to agree that the film navigates a tension between technophilia and technophobia and that this tension plays itself out between its overt "symbolic" message (in a Lacanian sense) and its implicit "imaginary" or "real" function.

The theme of encounter between colonialists and indigenous people made the film particularly interesting to cultural anthropologists and to non-Westerners. One anthropologist, writing on the environmental anthropology listserv E-ANTH, characterized the film as "like a giant anthropological piñata," while others noted the resemblance between the film's "avatars" and the real-world "human terrain avatars" of the U.S. military's occupation of Iraq.[101] That anthropology has long been deeply implicated in militarism and colonialism is reflected in the film's depiction of scientist Grace Augustine and her human–Na'vi avatar project. Yet many on the same listserv reported audiences as far apart as Brazil and Malaysia leaving theatres energized and mobilized for discussing issues of imperialism, globalization, capitalism, and struggles over control of resources. The film's pro-mining humans, one anthropologist suggested, are recognized as the same faces as those of private security companies at extractive mines around the world, at a time when human rights abuses at such mines are up to an all-time high.[102]

Avatar's popularity gave it currency among media-savvy environmental and indigenous activists as widely dispersed as South America, Palestine, and South and East Asia. It encouraged activists in the occupied Palestinian village of Bil'in to paint themselves blue in a protest march that resulted in the Israeli army tear-gassing and sound-bombing them.[103] Footage of the incident juxtaposed with clips from *Avatar* circulated on YouTube. Bolivia's indigenous president, Evo Morales, praised the film as an "inspiration in the fight against capitalism."[104] In Ecuador, members of various indigenous groups were impressed by the parallels between the Na'vi predicament and their own struggles against mining corporations and corporate or governmental military proxies. A little digging reveals that this meeting of indigenous people and movie screens, as reported in the media and disseminated widely on websites, was arranged by Lynne Twist of the Pachamama Alliance after she read a blog-post suggesting that very thing.[105] Proceeds from the film have gone to fund reforestation projects in South America, and in India a tribal group appealed to James Cameron to help them stop the open-pit mining of a mountain by (the perversely named) Vedanta Resources.[106] In China, even while the film was breaking box office records and the government was moving to restrict it to a small number of 3-D screens—presumably because of its (counter)revolutionary potential—tourist operators were promoting the Huangshan and Zhiangjiajie mountains as models for the "hanging mountains" of Pandora.[107]

Environmentalists' responses echoed this mixture of activist and pragmatic sentiments and motivations. Writing on the Mother Nature Network blog, Harold Linde called *Avatar* "without a doubt the most epic piece of environmental advocacy ever captured on celluloid," one that hits "all the important environmental talking-points—virgin rain forests threatened by wanton exploitation, indigenous peoples who have much to teach the developed world, a planet which functions as a collective, interconnected Gaia-istic organism, and evil corporate interests that are trying to destroy it all."[108] James Cameron encouraged these readings, calling Pandora "an evocation of the world we used to have ... before we started to pave it and build malls, and shopping centers."[109] Others, noting the attention being paid to the film, looked for real-world analogues among indigenous peoples fighting off corporate exploitation in the Peruvian Andes, Malaysian Borneo, the Ecuadoran rainforest, the Indian Himalayas, and elsewhere.[110]

North American indigenous responses were not so much positive as pragmatic, and many were prefaced by low expectations that Hollywood could possibly reflect their perspective. In a nuanced account, Cherokee professor Daniel Heath Justice acknowledged the film's value for drawing attention to indigenous issues but took it to task for its simplistic narrative and its distancing of the audience "from any complicity with these evils on our world" and thereby making "real and lasting change" all the less likely. Audiences can identify with cartoon heroes but "are exempted from the hard work that actually accompanies the struggles for decolonization, social and environmental justice, and peace."[111] On the other hand, an extensive mixed-methods study of responses to the film among Native and non-Native Hawaiians found that the "vast majority" of those surveyed "were able to identify moral messages from the film months after viewing it," that they retained "pro-'environment' messages," including "of the importance of humans connecting to the land," and that they "readily identified the connection between Hawaii's history and *Avatar's* plotline." Indigenous Hawaiians, in particular, "identified and related to messages" concerning the film's animist spiritual sensibilities and "the need to respect culture."[112]

But it is *Avatar's* uptake by its most active fans—especially those who have gathered in new online communities based directly on it—that highlights its most telling *affective* impacts. Media reports in early January began to note a phenomenon that came to be called "post-Pandoran depression." This was a malady apparently suffered by those for whom the real world of Earth seemed lacklustre compared to the alluring world of the Na'vi.[113] Discussions of this "depression" first emerged on the website Avatar-Forums.com under threads with titles like "ways to cope with the depression of the dream of Pandora being intangible." The number of posts on that topic eventually surpassed 3,000.[114] Examining the discussion, one finds a combination of eco-despair— the response, according to ecopsychologists, that many people feel when they come to recognize the extent of the ecological crisis—and something more like Virtual Reality withdrawal. *Avatar* is a movie and not the kind of VR environment that is repeatedly visited by gamers, yet in its 3-D version it comes close to being as immersive as VR, and thus the withdrawal symptoms are hidden or subsumed into the seemingly more real ecological reality check. The film's "wilderness sublime" is made real, if not hyper-real, through the intensity of its cinematic portrayal. And the equally intense depiction of the viciousness of the colonizers' land grab, the assault on people and nature, and the accompanying Trail of Tears–like dispersal of the Na'vi, is hardly mitigated by the reprieve they seem to gain at the film's end—a reprieve that anyone who knows history understands can only be temporary at best, or wishful thinking at worst. What awaits our inevitable return to Earth, then, can be doubly disappointing.

Help was on its way, however, for those suffering from the malady. It came in the form of video games, soundtracks, growing online communities, and even dictionaries and biological and social-history field guides to Pandora.[115] The Web forums Avatar-forums.com and Naviblue.com grew to several thousand members each, and within a year of the film's release close to a million posts had been published on some 30,000 separate topics.[116] Many "depression" sufferers sought to reimmerse themselves in the fictional *Avatar* world—for instance, by listening to the film's soundtrack, painting Pandoran landscapes, writing *Avatar* sequels, spending time on the *Avatar* Web forum, and viewing the film repeatedly. Others, however, showed strong spiritual or political leanings, with some producing conversion narratives recounting forms of newfound activism on behalf of real-world communities whose plight resembled that of the fictional Na'vi.[117] According to at least one study, spiritual themes among fans showed a strong selectivity in favour of a focus on the film's ecological, pantheistic, and animistic themes and away from a concern with the film's violence and apparent technophilia.[118]

Gauging the level of activism triggered by *Avatar* in light of critiques like Cafard's, for whom its capacity for contributing to activism is nil, is not an easy task. The film is a hybrid of pop culture and radical critique that has set in motion a series of material, social, and perceptual-affective currents around the world. It presents various forms of cinematic excess—spectacle beyond what the narrative seems to warrant—including in its luxurious depiction of the Pandoran world, but also in its rather conventional cinematic glorification of war. Its exoreferentialities offer audiences many openings for interpretation, and viewers tend to follow the ones to which they are most responsive. If there is a single coherent message, it is arguably something to do with the seemingly insatiable human craving for possessible objects, represented in the film by the quest for unobtanium. Yet even children could swap in the things most desired on Earth: oil, diamonds, toys, eternal life. The film's response to this craving is contradictory, however. The text suggests that the answer would be to develop a culture that satisfies itself with what is in its midst (in the Na'vi life-world of Pandora), not elsewhere (on the distant planet Pandora). Its message appears to be the Buddhist–Lacanian one that craving for objects that are actually ungraspable inevitably leads to suffering. Yet such a message, as Cafard writes, is "contradicted by the film itself as a technologically utopian project, and by its plot elements that involve either explicit or mystified technological liberation." In the end, he writes, "the film ironically affirms precisely the same project that it negates."[119] As Lertzman notes, "it is not only the minerals on Pandora that are 'UnObtainium' but the idealized image of nature before the Fall itself: the fantasy of returning to the Garden that continues to plague most of us with any form of environmental consciousness."[120] If the Pandoran world becomes an elsewhere that is more attractive than our own lives in *this* world—as appears to be the case for at least some of those afflicted by "post-Pandoran depression"—then we have simply replaced one set of fantasies for another.

But this, in the end, is the basis of *all* cinematic power: moving images draw us into them, and their allure captivates us, in much the same way that *Stalker's* Zone and the alien planet in *Solaris* draw their ambivalent beholders into their gravitational fields. In the case of *Avatar*, the Zone is a shimmering, vibrant, 3-D environment, a world of movement in which sensory delight and wonder seem rediscoverable. But it is also a place of technical wizardry and messianic violence, where the complexities of the world's political ecologies have been rendered as black-and-white caricatures. *Avatar* has presented opportunities for activists to stake their own cases in a new set of image-frames, but its potential to deepen audiences' engagement with the elusive materialities of the world's real ecologies may be more limited than its fans would like. At the same time, fandom, once triggered, sets off on its own trajectories, which in this case may include those that turn viewers into radical activists. Few blockbuster films do this, so the ones that might are worth paying attention to.

Toward a Peircian Synthesis: Aesthetics, Ethics, and Ecologics of the Image-Event

So far, this chapter has explored various forms of cinematically depicted ecological trauma. We have moved from the obvious—films like *The Day After Tomorrow* and *An Inconvenient Truth*—to the uncertain, hesitant, quixotic, and poetic (*Short Cuts*, *Lessons of Darkness*). With *Avatar*, we have returned to the rather obvious. Insofar as the real world includes the capacity for actual ecological trauma, we are left with the question of whether cinematic depictions contribute to our ability to avert or confront the real thing if and when it happens, and if so, how. To the extent that ecological collapse is already in our midst, the question becomes how we might witness it: Is it sheer spectacle, to be consumed for its thrill, or is it something we might actively become involved in resisting, mitigating, or transforming?

In their discussions of traumatic imagery, E. Ann Kaplan, Dori Laub, and others have referred to the possibility of "ethical witnessing," a form of observation that mobilizes the consciousness of large communities by enabling one to "take in and respond to the traumatic *situation*," a situation that extends beyond the film and that provides the film's fulcrum for meaning—that is, the original firstness to the secondness of the filmmaking and the thirdness of its reception by viewers.[121] If images, as Kaplan writes, "can be 'an invitation to pay attention, to reflect, to learn, to examine the rationalization for mass suffering offered by established powers,' then they are ethical."[122] Images that revive our "belief in this world," as Deleuze called it, would thus be images that revive our ability to take *this* world seriously, acting so as to move in the direction by which our own ethical predilections find satisfaction.

But the ethics of ecological witnessing are complicated by the fact that ecology provides no clear ethical position for its observers. If ecology is merely a description of how things work—how organisms adapt to and interact with their environments, and how the fabric of living matter churns onward, adaptively reconstituting itself in the wake of whatever internally or externally generated disequilibria might arise—then an ecological ethic consists of nothing more than a dispassionate striving to understand these things. This is science: learning for the sake of understanding. Environmental and ecological ethicists rarely remain satisfied with such a position: almost all work hard to develop guidelines for action that will *improve* things or at least meliorate the worst consequences of human actions. But improve them in what direction, and for whom?

These issues have troubled and divided ecophilosophers for decades. Some have responded with an "enlightened anthropocentrism," arguing that humans need to act in ways that will ultimately suit us best and that protecting natural systems, for instance, will do that. Others have responded biocentrically, playing down human needs in favour of some more general systemic needs of "nature," such as species diversity, ecosystem stability, "ecological integrity," and so on. Still others have developed variations of a social-ecological ethic, such as eco-feminism, eco-Marxism, eco-anarchism, ecological democracy, conservative or libertarian environmentalism, and so on; or an action-based pragmatism that would meet a variety of social and ecological needs without privileging any overarching set of ontological or foundational principles; or a virtue ethic that would focus on developing our own capacities for ethical action without presuming to calculate the ends of that action.[123]

A process-relational ethic shares much with several of these and leaves no one off the hook. It focuses on how we are engaged in the production of our own worlds and those of others, such that the matter becomes a pragmatic one of finding satisfaction in actions, but also an open-ended one that is sensitive to how those actions reverberate in the world. It is here that Peirce's triadic formulation of process can be particularly helpful. As Peircian scholars have acknowledged, drawing out an aesthetic and an ethic from Peircian phenomenology is tricky, given that Peirce himself, for all the many thousands of pages he wrote during his prolific (yet largely unpublished) life, rarely attempted it. In fact, he sometimes admitted ignorance both of aesthetic and of ethical theory, even as they fit into important places within his philo-sophical system. But let me propose a few pointers in the direction of a Peircian eco-ethico-aesthetics.

In his mature later writings, Peirce took aesthetics and ethics to be two of the three "normative sciences," the third being logic, and the three corresponding, respectively, to the Beautiful, the Good, and the True. The normative sciences as a whole form the second division of philosophy. The first division, phenomenology (or phaneroscopy), inquires into phenomena as they *appear*, that is, in their firstness; the third, metaphysics, into reality as it *really is*, in its thirdness. The normative sciences examine phenomena in their secondness, that is, in the ways they act upon us and we in turn can act upon them. Secondness is characterized by encounter, effort, and resistance. Thus aesthetics, ethics, and logic all deal with the effort to act in ways that are consonant with valued beliefs, rules, or principles, but in circumstances that may resist that effort. They are not for mere contemplation; rather, they are to be put to use. They concern the art of living, which, for Peirce, means the art of cultivating habits that allow us to appreciate and manifest the beautiful or admirable, the just and virtuous in our relationships with others, and the truthful in our understanding of the world.[124]

Habits play an important role in Peirce's philosophy in that they are tendencies that are within the realm of human self-control. It is through the cultivation of new habits that we can modify our behaviour in coordination with our beliefs, so as to test whether those beliefs ought to be accepted or rejected. (One might say that this is how we come to "in-habit" a belief.) Aesthetic habits concern firstness, the "quality of feeling" of a phenomenon; so aesthetics involves the cultivation of "habits of feeling" that allow us to appreciate the "admirable."[125] Ethical habits concern secondness, or reaction and relation, such that ethics, for Peirce, relate to "the deliberate formation of habits of *action* consistent with the ethical ideal" and with the "deliberately adopted aim."[126] Logical habits concern thirdness, or mediated representation, pattern, and law. The goal of logic is to discover the "habits of inference that lead to knowledge, including positive knowledge" (supposing there is a reality to a given phenomenon), and "to such semblance of knowledge as phenomena permit (supposing there is no perfect reality)."[127] While logic is about truth and falsity, and ethics is about "wise and foolish conduct," aesthetics is about "attractive and repulsive ideas" and more generally about "expressiveness."[128] Given their relationship to firstness, secondness, and thirdness, there is for Peirce an order to the three normative sciences: aesthetics precedes and underpins ethics, and both in turn inform logic, which encompasses all three. Following this sequence of logical priorities, we may speak of there being *three* aesthetics (of firstness, secondness, and thirdness), *two* ethics (of secondness and thirdness), and *one* logic (of thirdness); or, alternatively, of an aesthetics that concerns firsts, an ethico-aesthetics that concerns seconds, and a logico-ethico-aesthetics that concerns thirds.

An aesthetics of firstness, then, is not just about our perception and appreciation or evaluation of things that appear to us, such as art or physical appearance. It is also about our comportment toward those appearances. It is about the ways in which we *allow* things to appear to us and the ways we cultivate the appearance of things to us. This aesthetic of appearances, or of firstness, concerns perceiving and cultivating something like the beauty in things, or cultivating, rather, our capacity for perceiving the appearances and arisings—the firstness—of the world. "Beauty" is a risky term to use here, since it is culturally variable. Peirce found the term inadequate, preferring the Greek terms *kalos* and *agamai,* since they accommodated the unbeautiful within their scope, and Peirce acknowledged that aesthetic goodness is hardly encompassable within our own perception of what is pleasant or not.[129] Observation, on the other hand, is commonly thought to be mechanical, not dependent on cultural categories, but simply related to accuracy regarding the phenomenon being observed. But work by cultural anthropologists and by historians of science and technology has shown that observation and accuracy are also culturally variable. In a world of relational processes, where things always arise in a relational context, aesthetic perception would involve perception of the thing itself against and in relation to its background—a perception of the wholeness of what appears in its arising and passing, which means an observation of something that is emerging into being (firstness), into interactivity (secondness), and into meaning (thirdness).

An ethico-aesthetics of secondness is about cultivating ways of responding to others so as to sympathetically recognize *their* positioning in their interactions with us. If ethics is the cultivation of skilful action in response to others, and if self and other are perceived as dynamically interactive forms arising out of patterned relational dynamics, then ethics becomes a matter not of rules and injunctions, but of motivated action amidst encounter. An *aesthetic* of process-relational *ethics* would be a cultivation of empathic relations, relations amidst subjectal arisings that we know arise independently of us yet are, in some sense, analogous to our own subjectivation.

Finally, there is a logico-ethico-aesthetics of thirdness. Informed by the aesthetic (inhabited feelings and percepts) and the ethical (inhabited action), logic becomes something different from the rule-based form of reasoning, which is thought to be counterposed against the failings of illogic. It is, rather, more akin to what we might call *eco*logic, a skilful understanding of relational emergence (appearance), interaction, and generality. An ethico-aesthetics of ecology involves recognizing and cultivating the vitality of the systemic connections that sustain a whole. In its non-dual, processual form, this is the cultivation of skilful understanding that emanates as *praxis*, since it enfolds action and perception within itself.

Each of these aesthetics—of appearances, of relations, and of ecology—is a selective response to a broader array of possibilities that encompass beauty alongside ugliness, good alongside evil (or justice alongside injustice), and systemic cohesion alongside disorder and collapse. Such an aesthetic, being attentive to these options and acknowledging their viability even as one opts for one of them over another, recognizes that chaos or injustice, for instance, are not necessarily "bads." One may arrive at the conclusion, in given circumstances, that it is right to cultivate the beauty and truthfulness of the chaotic, or the ugliness of justice. Such a logico-ethico-aesthetics, in other words, is not prescriptive in advance of a particular situation. It is a method of movement through a situation that recognizes the dependence of thirdness (logic, ecology, regularity) on secondness (ethics, action, actuality), and of both on firstness (appearance, aesthetics, potential).[130]

This triadic conception, however, allows us to cover a lot of ground. It proposes that there is a continuity between phenomena, action, and truth. Each in this sequence is a development dependent to some extent on the ones previous to it, and one that always emerges out of a complex world, with the move between them not determined or predictable in advance. Each plays a role in the art of living; but there are many arts of living. The arts of democracy, for instance, combine the ethico-aesthetics of secondness (empathic relationality and "inhabited action") with the logico-ethico-aesthetic of thirdness (of ecology, that is, how things fit together, at least in the organization of a social order). With respect to art, one finds variable modalities. The sublime, for instance, might be thought of as an oscillation between firstness (the sheer irruption of things, and the aesthetic of their appearances) and thirdness (the recognition of systemic and ecological patterns), whereby we are confronted by something that is much greater than ourselves. If the ecological whole is thought of, following a Heideggerian conception, as the pleromatic earth that subsists beneath and always withdraws from the worlds in which we live, then the sublime is about that ungraspable vastness breaking into our caricatured preconceptions of it, becoming momentarily visible, sensible, or at least intuitable. Yet its means of breaking in is through the firstness of chance occurrence. This, it seems to me, is what Herzog may be aiming for in his perambulations around the landscape of an unknown cataclysmic ~~Event~~, and the function of the weather events in *Short Cuts* or *Magnolia*. By contrast, the beautiful is something more purely appreciable in its sheer firstness, without reference to any order or pattern; while the picturesque could be defined as what is appreciable in the relation of its parts, that is, a kind of thirdness tamed by the absence of firstness.[131]

To the extent that each of these three aesthetics (aesthetics of firstness, ethico-aesthetics of secondness, and logico-ethico-aesthetics of thirdness) is a matter of cultivation, they would seem to apply most closely to the "receiving" end of the cinematic event, as a set of guidelines for film spectatorship. But insofar as we have an impact on the making of films, either directly as film-makers, or indirectly as audiences and policy shapers, we can also affect the kinds of films that are made, which means that we can affect the firstness of the films themselves and of the worlds they open up for viewers. Our experience as viewers of films includes two aspects: an immediate one, which involves our habits and comportment toward films as we watch them—habits of attention, response, appreciation, critical interpretation, and so on; and a more extended one, which involves our habits as interpreters and public conversants about the films in the broader contexts in which they exist, including contexts of genre, technology, culture, politics, and history.

Like most books on film theory and criticism, this one aims to contribute to the larger project of such critical viewing and interpretive practice. It should, however, give us some guidelines for evaluating whether and to what extent a film is *good*. What kinds of films may "revive our belief in this world" and encourage the kinds of ecological "ethical witnessing" suggested by my readings of Kaplan, Laub, Deleuze, and others?

Toward the "Good Film"

I proposed, at the end of Chapter 2, that a good film, from a process-relational, socio-ecological perspective, is one that expands viewers' perceptions of "ecological ontology." Such an expansion is a historical task: it is something that we might agree is useful at a time when the changing relations between humans and the extra-human world—which also means in the intra-societal relations (of nation, race, class, gender, and so on) that mark and shape those broader relations—have become fraught and difficult. An ecological ontology is one that understands the material, social, and perceptual domains of our lives in process-relational terms, such that any object, be it a film or an automobile depicted in a film, can be understood as an event arising out of a certain concatenation of processes, with after-effects and implications for other processes.

What sorts of films have the potential to expand viewers' socio-ecological perceptions and understandings? Films, I have acknowledged, are limited in their capacity to convey knowledge about socio-ecological issues. But they can bring attention to those issues, or, more subtly, they can affectively orient viewers to such issues or to the images, representations, and arguments in which those issues are registered and conveyed. Generalizing from suggestions made in this book so far, I would propose that the best films, from this perspective, are *affectively generative*, specifically in their capacity to elicit a heightened perception of or orientation toward the socio-ecological, but that they are *not monological*. They generate interpretive "buzz," eliciting contrasting interpretations or stances toward an issue even as they encourage an impulse to reconcile those conflicts by thinking about, exploring, debating, or pursuing something related to the set of socio-ecological themes in question. To do this, they are likely to work at each of the Peircian levels: they engage viewers in the immediacy of the spectacle, exciting or unsettling them so as to render them more open to the worlds they present; and they provide the kind of narrative impetus that elicits interest in a given film's development, while also allowing the narrative elements and exoreferentialities multiple openings for interpretive elaboration. The Zone, in such a film, is a place that buzzes with affect and meaning, but a meaning that always remains somewhat wild.

There is an unresolved, and perhaps unresolvable, tension between two of the criteria I am suggesting here. On the one hand, I have proposed an *instrumental* criterion: that a good film generates a certain kind of effect in encouraging or facilitating a deepened socio-ecological and eco-ontological perception and understanding. One could conclude from this that certain films have certain effects and that those that have an eco-ontologically beneficial effect are better than those that do not. On the other hand, I have also argued on behalf of films that are open-ended and capable of generating multiple readings. In Chapter 1, I noted a preference for films that are "more open and dialogical" in that they make available "a broader range of positions with respect to the main vectors of affective engagement the film sets into motion." Throughout I have been implicitly preferring certain films, such as *Stalker* and *Grizzly Man*, that have shown a broad range of interpretations among viewers and that remain somewhat "wild" in their meaning-making potential.

Judging the interpretive openness of a film is not the same as observing the range of interpretations that have actually arisen from it. Most films fail, in one degree or another, to elicit the precise responses their makers intend in their audiences. One could argue that every film, owing to the complexity of the medium, harbours an excess that eludes the intended project of the filmmakers.[132] Once a film is finished, however, it becomes possible to speak of its *own* intent, separate from that of its makers and corresponding only to the inherent qualities and characteristics of the film in its final form. This is what Daniel Frampton means when he speaks of the film as "issuing from itself" and "becom[ing] the creator of its own world."[133] On the other hand, there are films that may well be intended by their makers to elicit contradictory or incongruous emotions, affects, and responses. Carl Plantinga calls this quality in a film its "affective counterpoint." Such counterpoint can be motivated by an intent to generate irony or some other complex cognitive or emotional response. Plantinga's examplar here is Terrence Malick's *The Thin Red Line* (1998), which, he argues, develops a "structure of feeling" that is "designed to offer the spectator an experience of rumination and questioning, and to offer an experience of the differing ways one can think of the world in light of its exquisite beauty, on the one hand, and jarring violence and ugliness, on the other hand."[134] Judging by the wide range of responses to Malick's film *and* by the fact that many (though not all) critics judge it to be quite good, *The Thin Red Line* would appear to be relatively successful in this regard. Yet production of such "affective counterpoint" is arguably a unified goal, not a contradictory one, though its unification may occur on a level beyond conventional generic expectations.

A preference for cinematic and interpretive openness translates, in some measure, into a preference for films and narratives that provoke thought and discussion. The latter is essential to a thriving democracy, so we might consider this to be a *democratic* or *pluralistic* criterion for good films. A process-relational understanding of the universe presumes that a creative pluralism and open-endedness is central to any and *all* activity and that it is also a *good* (by definition), so we could also consider this an *ontological* criterion. That said, any suggestion that the universe *is* such and such (pluralistic, open-ended, processual) and that this is *good* is an instance of what Hume called the naturalistic fallacy. There is nothing inherent in the state of things that necessitates that this state is good and should be promoted and conserved. By the same token, when the state of things is said to be open and changing, there is no necessary reason why *greater* or *faster* change should be better than *less* or *slower* change. All such arguments, on their own, remain suspect unless some other, contextually specific reasons can be offered for why pluralism, openness, and so on, are good things.

Fortunately, such contextually specific reasons are available to us. The context in which a process-relational ecophilosophy of the cinema makes most sense—and the form and argument of this book is intended to suggest this—is the context in which the relationship between humans and the more-than-human Earth has become fraught and problematic. To the extent that we can agree that humanity faces an ecological crisis today and that we require creative thinking (and feeling) to respond to this crisis, the political and ontological arguments suggested above have validity. Some have argued that the current state of socio-ecological affairs requires not a democratic or pluralistic resolution, which takes time and energy to carry out, but some kind of imposed "eco-authoritarian" solution.[135] I will not rehearse the arguments on behalf of either of these positions here, except to say that there is a fundamental political choice facing environmental thinkers and activists and that my process-relational perspective, consistent with the work of Whitehead, Peirce, James, Dewey, Deleuze, Connolly, and others, supports a democratic rather than an authoritarian and imposed solution. Creativity is seen by all of these thinkers as ontologically *and* culturally-contextually significant for humans to take account of and develop. The instrumental criterion on socio-ecological effectiveness is thus, at the very least, to be balanced against, if not subordinated to, the political and ontological criteria of pluralism, creativity, and freedom.[136]

There is, however, a spectrum of possibilities for cinematic communication, as there is for any form of communication, and one could argue that each of the different styles, intents, and effects of films has its potential usefulness. The new field of "neurocinematics," while still embryonic in its achievements, provides a useful insight into the differences between cinematic styles. The field's founding figures, Uri Hasson and his colleagues at New York University, have conducted fMRI scans of the brain activity of multiple viewers using segments or episodes of different kinds of film material, from tightly struc-tured classical narratives by Alfred Hitchcock (a television episode of *Alfred Hitchcock Presents*) and Sergio Leone (a segment from *The Good, The Bad and The Ugly* [1966]) to less structured television material (the semi-improvised comedy *Curb Your Enthusiasm*) to unedited video footage from a surveillance camera in Washington Square Park. The results, measured as "inter-subject correlation" of activation in the frontal cortex, visual and auditory systems, and other brain regions, showed provocative results. By far the highest similarity of brain response across all viewers—65 percent—was for the Hitchcock epi-sode, with 45 percent for *The Good, The Bad and the Ugly*, 18 percent for *Curb Your Enthusiasm*, and only 5 percent for the park footage. The authors propose a continuum of film according to the level of control aimed for and attained, with real life at one end, propaganda at the other, and documentaries, art films, and classic Hollywood running between them from the less controlled to the more controlled end.[137]

The implication here is that certain kinds of film, whatever their goals, achieve greater control over viewer response than others. It is not that such control is a good thing, or that all filmmakers should aim for the highest level of control. There are many filmmakers who aim to create more open-ended and "difficult" films, and there is no doubt that some viewers gain pleasure from such "reduced control." No one would argue that the unstructured park footage constitutes good cinema, but many have argued that films like Tarkovsky's *Stalker*, Tarr's *Werkmeister Harmonies*, Lynch's *Mulholland Drive*, and Malick's *Thin Red Line* do. So the point is not that open-endedness is a virtue in itself. At some level, however, most arguments on behalf of the value of "difficult films" rely, to some degree, on the agreement in response among critically informed or "prepared" viewers. It should come as no surprise, for instance, that many of the art films I have discussed achieve high ratings on websites, like Rotten Tomatoes and MetaCritic, that compile and quantify the reviews of professional film critics. The difference, in this case, is a matter of spectatorship, and since there is a wide variation in spectators, one could argue that there ought to be a wide variation in film styles. An argument on behalf of *better* spectatorship, however, necessarily presumes that we can improve the ways we watch and make sense of films. Before pursuing this matter further, let us briefly contrast two of the films we have examined so far, *Avatar* and *Stalker*.

For all the generativity of its spectacle and the many allegorical interpretations it enables, *Avatar* remains tied to a singular and linear narrative arc. It is, in this sense, more "controlling" of audience responses. The two sides that are pitted against each other in this narrative, humans versus Na'vi, only harden over the course of the film, and only a singular movement between them—the good guys crossing over to join the underdogs—is fully actualized. The film can be taken as an allegory of one thing or another, but it will almost always be an allegory with good guys and bad guys. It is, in this sense, a film with a great deal of cinematic excess—spectacular effects of one kind of another—but little of that excess escapes the film's "central conflict."[138] The film's narrative conflict is ostensibly between the Na'vi and their oppressors, but it is more appropriate to think of the film as having a *unified central axis* that requires the conflict between the two sides to shield us from asking the questions the film is not prepared to raise: such as, *what if the two sides, the techno-industrial and the romantic-reactionary, are really two arms of the same one-eyed monster?* And while the film can be taken to represent real-world issues, such as the travails of indigenous peoples around the world, in this it will generally either energize a viewer's already existing sentiments about that issue, or trigger a defensive resistance.

Stalker, on the other hand, is a far less monological film. Interpretations of it vary more widely than do those of *Avatar*, without any clear agreement over which characters are good or bad, right or wrong, or what the Zone is meant to represent. At the same time, one could hardly deny that many viewers find viewing it difficult and unpleasant. Its affective generativity is constrained by the limited culture of viewership that can tolerate and appreciate such slow and indirect films. My use of the film is a rather specific use, dependent on an interpretation that is somewhat consistent with other critics' interpretations and that relies on a detailed exploration of the historical background of the film's making and its reception. Nevertheless, viewers can easily find things to disagree with in my reading of it. I chose *Stalker* as a paradigm case for my interpretive model for a particular reason: because its Zone is a compelling metaphor for the terrain within which cinematic subjectivity emerges. I have suggested that this terrain can be taken to be an unrepresentable void of sorts—a gap (in Lacanian terms), an open, cognizant emptiness (in Buddhist terms), or a ceaseless differentiation (which would fit both Deleuzian and Derridean philosophical frameworks), but which nevertheless dynamically affects and interacts with the representable subject. All this, of course, takes place by means of representation—of the representable *and* the unrepresentable. Tarkovsky takes us to the point where we can not only ask, "What is the Zone?" or "What is Solaris?," but also where we can understand that to say anything more precise and concrete than what the film's images themselves say would be tricky and ultimately contestable. Just as the Stalker guides his followers slowly and carefully through the unpredictable and unknowable terrain of the Zone, I am suggesting that the filmmaker (or production collective) is a stalker in this sense as well. Or, rather, that the film itself is like this: it guides viewers by means of the cinematic elements of image and sound—objects, colour, earth, water, the discarded but resonant remnants of things, and so on. All of these are given time to reveal themselves in their imagistic essence, even if that essence remains ultimately elusive.

While there are many features of a film like *Stalker* that one could focus on in making a case for open-ended narratives and interpretive effort or "difficulty," the matter of time—the film's slowness—is one that may be particularly useful for us to consider insofar as it correlates in interesting ways with the perception of what I am calling "ecological ontology." There are those who argue that slowness and indirection have an inherent virtue in cinema; the recent "contemporary contemplative cinema" movement takes such an argument as its core tenet, and for many of its followers *Stalker* is undeniably a virtuous film.[139] As the palette of film's technical possibilities has expanded, however—to include, for instance, extremely long takes and ever wider screens, high-speed editing and frenetic camera movement, 3-D animation and CGI graphics, and much more—so has the range of cinematic styles one finds in popular and art cinemas. Debates over "slow cinema" versus "intensified continuity," "post-continuity," and the "MTV aesthetic" attest to the fact that techniques intended to generate a certain effect can develop into distinct and full-fledged styles, fashions, genres, and audience taste cultures.[140] That said, cinematic time bears some relationship to ecological time. Ecology, after all, is about the enfoldment of objects or processes within other processes, all of which unfold according to their own durations. Often these durations are longer and relatively imperceptible from the perspective of human activities, which is why they are easy to ignore. Let us explore this issue of cinematic time in greater depth.

Ecology, Time, and the Image

One of the central insights of the ecological sciences is that everything comes from somewhere and goes somewhere—everything is in motion between one state of matter-energy and another. When we treat something merely as a resource bank or waste disposal site, a source or a sink, a "from" or an "away to," we relegate a subset of the systemically interrelated circulatory network that constitutes an object's socio-ecological system to a shadowy "outside," hoping to forestall its return by a kind of freezing of time or bounding of space. We make a cut in time (and in space), but this cut is artificial and ultimately unsustainable; the Real will always return in one form or another. This is precisely where an ecological ontology becomes most congruent with Buddhist ontology and strongly resonant with psychoanalysis. In a Buddhist understanding, there are no inherently self-existent things; there are only relational processes within which what we perceive as "objects" and "selves" codependently arise, always changing, and are destined to pass from their current state into another, and another. Time does not stand still, and as our society induces progressively quicker rates of change on and in the world, it also intensifies its efforts to stave off the changes it sets in motion. We try to freeze property lines, national boundaries, and personal and group identities, to stop the aging of our bodies, to squeeze out as much productivity as we can from a dwindling resource base, and we aim to do all that without facing the inevitable consequences—collapsing ecosystems, population movements, and the like—that these efforts set into motion.[141]

As an art form of time, cinema can help us arrive at a more adequate understanding of the nature of time. Gilles Deleuze argued that the production and dissemination of a direct image of time in postwar cinema not only has expanded our capacity to conceive of our own and the world's temporality, but also has expanded our capacities for *ethically inhabiting time*. This means that it has expanded our capacity for thinking, feeling, and affectively being with others, for generating productive syntheses in the differential fabric of the world, and thereby for *becoming*. In Deleuze's account, which is strongly indebted to Bergson's philosophy of duration and organicity, there are moments within films that give us a feel for the way in which a moment—any and every moment—is riven with possibilities, torn through by variable durations and temporal rhythms: how a moment is a qualitative multiplicity, a confluence of intersecting relational processes, each of which opens up to worlds of possibility, even as most of these close and pass away with each action taken. Moving-image media, by Deleuze's standard, hold great potential for enhancing our ability to understand and visualize the relationship between the world and ourselves in our common nature *as* time, duration, becoming, and change.

Time-lapse photography—such as a sequence showing the unfolding of a flower speeded up so that it appears to move in the same way that a human moves—is perhaps too obvious an example of cinema's creative reimagination of time. Tarkovsky's long, slow takes of landscapes in decay and decomposition are another. Take, for instance, the "dream sequence" of *Stalker* that I described in Chapter 1, in which the downward-facing camera pans over the course of two minutes across a pool of water containing objects that are being reclaimed by the elements: rusted coins, a syringe, parts of a watch, and so on. Like all of Tarkovsky's long takes, this one has been taken to be about the "pressure of time" running through the shots.[142] *Stalker* as a whole can be said to be about the time it takes to arrive at the yawning gap, the dark void and open wound at the centre of the self, which is represented by the Room at the centre of the film's Zone. Michelangelo Antonioni's shots of landscapes in which characters are noticeable by their absence—emptied landscapes, in effect—similarly stage time as a process of disappearance, where the cinematic event comes after a person or process has gone offstage. Long takes and lingering cameras in the films of Bela Tarr, Chantal Akerman, Abbas Kiarostami, Aleksandr Sokurov, Carlos Reygadas, Lisandro Alonso, Gus Van Sant, and Albert Serra play a role somewhat analogous to this, if different in each instance.

But the slowness of thought and memory depicted in such scenes is only one option for the time-image. Cinematically imaged time can also be mercurially swift, or recursive; it can consist of multiple rhythms and counterpoints, coexistent "sheets of past" unfolding in parallel, at different speeds, meshing together, converging and diverging and spinning by one another, overlapping in thick and thin streams of duration and relational motion. The identity of a person, a place, an idea, can crystallize in moments where past (memory) and present converge onto an open future; but it can also seethe with tension or be torn asunder. What Deleuze calls the "crystal-image" is a moment that simultaneously looks *forward* to the not-yet and *back* to a past that sets the conditions for it. It is a forking bifurcation point pregnant with possibilities and at the same time caught in the momentum of time's flow(s), a "point of indiscernibility" between the *actual* of perception and the *virtual* of recollection, an image that "makes visible" the "hidden ground of time, that is, its differentiation" or "splitting" into "two flows, that of presents which pass and that of pasts which are preserved."[143] Time, for Deleuze, "consists of this split, and it is this," a "gushing of time as dividing in two," that "we see in the crystal."[144] If time itself *is* this tornness, then in a world of qualitative multiplicities ceaselessly generating new possibilities, the times and destinies of things are multiple. Understanding one's own possibilities— how subjectivity congeals under pressure, how it opens and escapes its own frames—is part of the project whereby seven billion humans can come to a more workable accommodation with one another and with the other life forms with which we share the Earth. To the extent that moving-image media can generate viscerally felt images of the *times of things*—things in production and in decay, in differentiation and in synthesis, things making up the unfolding materiality of the world, of identity and of relationality (in all their narratively spun forms), and the swift, dark flow of their vanishing—to that extent cinema is a powerful tool for ecophilosophy.

I referred earlier to the form of spectatorship that would be most conducive to a process-relational eco-ethico-aesthetics. Let me spell out a few more contours of such a cinema spectatorship in light of this understanding of the moving image. It is, first and foremost, a viewing practice that is attentive to the ways in which moving images *move* us, in their firstness, secondness, and thirdness. This movement can be taken as an opening of ourselves to the contingency and openness, and at the same time to the determining nature, of the moments we witness in cinema. What a subject does in one moment shapes, to some extent, the possibilities of the moments that follow. If we, viewers who *cannot* act in the film we are watching, can be made to feel the *possibility* of action of a subject in the film, a possibility that is always a multiplicity of possibilities, even as we watch those possibilities pass and be replaced by a series of determinations—actualizations of one possibility and not of others— then we can be made to feel the way in which time is a simultaneous arrival and passing of the possible *and* an opening up to new possibility. This is how we turn a moment of film into a Deleuzian crystal.

Film, as we have seen, is episodic; it is made up of moments or events, with some of these being more memorable and impactful than others. In Chapter 2, I referred to such moments as "hyper-signaletic," the implication being that they contain a thickness or density of the sort of sound-image material that results in spectatorial affect, narrative engagement, and the proliferation of exoreferential meanings. Now we can define these more accurately as thicker not in the *content* of the image (or sound-image), but in the relation that continually unfolds between the film and the viewer. This relationship will be different for different viewers, yet it depends on material that is shared. The resonance of a moment of cinema depends on its firstness (the image itself), its secondness (the narrative sequence), and its thirdness (its exoreferentialities), but all of these are only firsts, seconds, and thirds in relation to a perceiver. This means that the image is always both an image-*of* and an image-*for*. The moment of imaging is always relational.

One of the interpretive traditions that has explored the power of images most deeply is the one that arises from the psychological work of Carl Gustav Jung. Jung's own writings are often considered too mystical and essentialist for understanding the intricacies of historically specific cultural contexts. This criticism may apply to Jung's notion of a collective unconscious, when that is taken to be an unchanging reservoir of archetypal images that underlies all human psychic experience. Setting aside the collective unconscious, however, Jungian psychology offers a potent understanding of the image, one that has been developed especially powerfully in the "archetypal psychology" of James Hillman. While its debt to Jung is central, archetypal psychology is, in Hillman's hands, also derivative from a longer-standing Neoplatonic philosophical heritage that focuses on the power of the image. One of the leading modern interpreters of this heritage, French religious scholar Henry Corbin, coined the term *mundus imaginalis*, or the "imaginal," for the world of images, which he considered to be intermediate between the material and the ideal worlds.[145] Following Corbin, the foundational datum for Hillman's archetypal psychology is the *image*, which is conceived not as a representation of something *else* but as irreducible and autochthonous, "psyche itself in its imaginative visibility."[146] The source of images, for Hillman, is "the self-generative activity of the soul itself," with "soul" being a term for the "*tertium* between the perspectives of body (matter, nature, empirics) and of mind (spirit, logic, idea)." Soul, in Hillman's definition, is "the perspective *between* others and from which others may be viewed," "a perspective rather than a substance, a viewpoint toward things rather than a thing itself."[147] This makes it very much akin to the mental-perceptual mediating dynamic between subjectivation and objectivation that is at the centre of reality conceived as relational process.[148]

The image, in Hillman's account, is not only something seen but also a *way* of seeing, and soul is the way of seeing that "deepens" events into experiences.[149] It is, in this sense, a way of perceiving that allows the fruition of secondness (an event) into thirdness (meaningful recognition). Archetypal or mythic images are not images that "ground" or "compensate" for some lack or deficiency, as in traditional psychoanalysis. Rather, they enable and open up: they are "images of intelligibility" that disclose "the plot of things, the way in which the world appears and we are in its images."[150] Humans, in this account, are not mere viewers of images; rather, we *dwell* in images. The human is "a sense-enjoying, image-making creature," an animal "in an ecological field that affords imagistic intelligibility." Our task is not merely to see and respond to things, but to see "the face of the Gods in things." This requires an active imagination and an "aesthetic culture," and it calls for a "polytheistic psychology" appropriate to the kind of pluralistic universe proposed, among others, by William James.[151] The method of archetypal psychology is a "giving over to the images and cultivating them for their sake."[152] Images, according to Hillman, make a "moral claim" upon their subjects, and the appropriate response to this claim is metaphorical, poetic, and imaginative, a method of "sticking to the image" so that the image can "release and refine further imagining."[153] This releasing is a releasing *into the image*, which, since it is a moving image, always means *into a world that takes one somewhere else*. In and through that movement one becomes other. Where a more conservative Jungian interpretation, then, might consider archetypal images to be those things that keep us tethered to an underlying substrate of meanings, the one I am proposing is one that keeps us tethered only to the ongoing creative becoming of the universe.[154]

This notion of cultivating images *for the sake of* the images themselves is not the kind of thing one hears from Peirce, for whom semiosis is ultimately moving in the direction of greater reasonableness. For Hillman, by contrast, the movement often seems to be away from reasonableness toward something more mysterious and unfathomable. Yet the movement, for both, is in the direction of an openness, and to the extent that Peirce's reason remains grounded in ethics and, ultimately, aesthetics, the implication is that reason itself is the fruition of the very possibilities found in ethics and aesthetics. If the image is understood in a process-relational sense *as movement*, or, more precisely, as a particular constellation of possibilities for movement, as a fragment of time that looks simultaneously backward and forward to its past and future virtualities, then every image ought to be seen as a *living and moving* image. Jungian and archetypal psychology most commonly deal with images from dreams and myths, but the source of images need not distract us from the practice of seeing images as containing affective and semiotic capacities, vectors along which we can move if we open up to them.

The ultimate cinematic image, then, is an image that moves powerfully, reshaping the vectors for movement in its wake. Images of eco-trauma, such as those examined in this chapter, are part of a broader constellation of images whereby the relations between humanity and a larger cosmos are imaged, encountered, and set into motion. Let us recap some of the ways in which we have seen films lay out the times and spaces of things in ways that set into motion sets of relations between humans and land or territory. This can serve as a backdrop to the larger matter of the human–universe relation, which I will delve into in the final section of this chapter.

One of the ways in which the triadic model developed in this book can help us consider the cinematic presentation of the "times of things" is by offering a key by which we might differentiate such times. As with all things process-relational, where nothing is what it is on its own (for very long) without becoming or at least exchanging properties with its opposite, *timing* is always also *spacing*. But there are many ways by which the spacing of time, and the timing of space, can occur. Slowing things down, for instance, can be a means of gaining distance from someone (in order to escape their grip) or from one's own actions (so as to get some perspective), but it can also be a way of becoming more intimate (with oneself or another) or of extending one's control over another (as in the slowing down of violence to render it torturous). Speeding things up can be a way of taking flight (toward freedom), but also a way of intensifying an interaction (a conflict, a love affair). A film's geomorphism, anthropomorphism, and biomorphism tend to create a complex layering of such times and spaces.

In Chapter 3, we considered different variations on the relationship between land and "us." In the shift from the inchoateness of its origins to the settledness of the classic western's American West was a land that was perpetually *becoming ours*; in Dovzhenko's *Earth*, a land that was *already us*; in Pare Lorentz's *The River*, a land that was *for us*, to be managed wisely; in *Easy Rider*, a land *for us to encounter and experience*; and in Antonioni's existential landscapes or the Three Gorges of *Up the Yangtze* and *Still Life*, a land *becoming* or *already other*. Each of these implies one or more timings: the slowness but divinely ordained unfolding by which the West becomes "ours," the circularity of Dovzhenko's village (and of the Revolution), the speed by which we pass through a (slower) landscape in *Easy Rider*, or the aimless languor by which we move through it in, say, Wim Wenders's more leisurely road movie *Kings of the Road* (1976). All of this gets more complicated when we consider the alternative anthropomorphisms discussed in Chapter 4: Nanook's Inuit, as opposed to the film's presumed viewers; the nature-enslaved tribals of *King Kong*, as opposed to their camera- and weapon-wielding visitors from New York City; the slow-food bohemian radicals of *Jonah Who Will Be 25 in the Year 2000*, as opposed to the implied but only occasionally depicted capitalists. And there are the implied alternatives of Chapter 3: the Indians in classic westerns, or the traditional lives displaced by the Three Gorges Dam or by Antonioni's industrial landscapes (whose time is that of the disappearing, decadent or noble, past); the lives of the people whose landscapes are being passed through by the bikers in *Easy Rider*; and so on. With the biomorphic, we get similar differences. There is, for instance, the "eternal time" of nature in *March of the Penguins*, or the eternal "eating and being eaten" of bear time in *Grizzly Man*, which is counterposed to human time, at least as these are articulated by Herzog-as-played-by-Herzog. And there is the way in which the becoming-wolf of Rosaleen in *The Company of Wolves* or of the shape-shifters in *Wolfen* involves taking on a different temporality and spatiality, one that roams smoothly across the striated territorialities of country and city, day and night, human and wolf.

Each of these involves a way of moving (biomorphism), a territorialization that relates movement to space (geomorphism), and a differentiation among humans moving and spacing *differently* (anthropomorphism). Movement, spacing, and differentiation are, in this sense, elements of any moving sound-image presented to us when we view a film. A moving image is an image we can enter and move with, because it is always already an image of motion, a biomorphic image, and it typically affords variable possibilities (temporal and spatial ones) for such movement. How we actually move with it is a function of our own decisive form of involvement with the image. Each biomorphic image, however, is also an anthropomorphic and a geomorphic image, insofar as the morphology that takes shape in and through it includes a figure and a ground, a subject-world and an object-world, though these continue to change shape as the movement proceeds.

Ecophilosophical Cinema: Moving Images on a Moving Planet

If we live in an age of the world motion picture, we also live at a time when the picture of our world *is* a picture of motion. One variation of that world picture is the picture of the Earth from space. Most people are likely to think of this image as a static one: it is commonly seen as a still photograph, perhaps as an image on a poster or T-shirt, or a logo or backdrop to television news programs. In this, it recalls Heidegger's "world picture," which presents the world as a representation that is fully rendered in front of us and made subject to our instrumental demands. But we might think of this image as "static" in a different and more lively sense. For those who lived through the collective moment when images of the Earth from space became available, the memory of those images is likely to be imbued with the static of an errant and finicky radio contact between an earthly base (Ground Control in Houston, Texas) and a series of humanoid images moving on a distant moon that had suddenly come "one step" closer. Television was the collective medium of that historical moment, and the sound of that encounter reminds us that static, and therefore stasis, are always already aflutter with movement and discharge that escapes the resolution required to keep a moving image in its place.[155]

No matter how still an image is, it is always already moving, just as is the light that it captures in its movement from the object rendered visible. In the case of the image of the Earth from space, this light would have travelled a distance of more than 30,000 kilometres from the surface of a moving planet to an artificial satellite moving in orbit around it. This image would be "moving" in a few other senses as well. The first such image to have been widely disseminated was *Earthrise*, photographed by William Anders aboard the Apollo 8 mission in December 1968.[156] It and a photograph taken almost four years later, known as *Blue Marble*, are among the most widely distributed images in history. The latter is notable for the fact that it shows the entire surface of the Earth lit up, the former for the spectacle of a partially visible Earth rising over the lit surface of a lifeless (except for its visitors) moon. The period between 1968 and 1972 provided the only opportunities to date for a human being to see the full orb of the Earth (or one side of it, rather), and only the last of these, Apollo 17, orbited far enough away from the Earth that it allowed a person to view the whole planet in sunlight. All the images made after 1972 that show the entire surface of one side of the Earth are not single-exposure photographs, but composite, computer-aided digital images.[157] Yet all of these were preceded by others ancestral to them: globe-shaped maps from as early as the 1600s, planetary globes used as emblems and logos for universal exhibitions and world's fairs, for missionary organizations, newspaper and media organizations, airlines and art museums, on covers of science fiction books and magazines, and in movie studio logos (most notably for Universal Studios). And they in turn have evolved into new and composite forms. Among the most complex, lively, and interactive of these is Google Earth, that "virtual 3D globe patched together from satellite imagery, aerial photos, and Geographic Information System (GIS) data" that, in Stefan Helmreich's words, has become a "personal and personalizable Earth, a quintessentially contemporary computational object, an app."[158]

These images move, then, in their evolution and in their circulation. Their capacity to affectively move their viewers is also well known. All of these movements are related to the more general kind of movement described by Peirce's categorization of things into their firstness, secondness, and thirdness. By definition, these are connected by the movement between them, a movement that proceeds unceasingly. Today's images of the entire Earth are iconic, indexical, and symbolic all at once. In their resemblance to the Earth—a resemblance they helped create since we had not seen it before them, though we had imagined, and imaged, it—they are *icons*. As products of photographic technologies, and of the military space race between the two superpowers that carved up the global polity between each other for half a century, they are *indices*. And as multivalent signs that elicit so many different responses among viewers today—awe, wonder, sadness, beauty, fear, boredom (because we have seen it used too often for too mundane ends), trepidation, and even disgust (for what we have done to it, or for even being up there where, as one of my students put it, "we don't belong")—they are *symbols* that continue to open up to new iterations and interpretations.[159] Each such image harkens back (or forward) to the firstness of the "first contact" across that sky, when a certain humanity, in looking back upon itself suddenly viewed differently, became a *subject*. This was a moment that some alive today lived through, while others have only inherited it in mediated forms, but it has remained one of the powerful images in which the Earth's worldness has been disclosed to us in the decades following the 1960s. Whole Earth iconography, in Benjamin Lazier's words, has "sedimented" itself "into the mental architecture of the West" such that "for the foreseeable future, environment will be inflected by planet, cityscape by globe, and skyline by space—not the 'space of experience' but the void." Lazier notes that the "lived experiences of earthliness and worldliness," as Heidegger and Hannah Arendt had imagined them, "are available, if they are available, only against the background of this new dispensation."[160] And even if this image has become habituated, having come to signify technological achievement, global telecommunications, commerce, tourism, and much else, it has also served as the basis for a host of further developments (such as Google Earth) to the point that there is no going back from it, no withdrawing of it from our collective consciousness. There is always only a movement forward.

There is a famous image of Buzz Aldrin on the moon, photographed in 1969 by his Apollo 11 spacemate Neil Armstrong, that has a haunting quality that relates to this future-directed openness of the moving image. What haunts me in it is that the image on his helmet is a mirror image of the space around him. The helmet image suggests that there is nothing behind the mask, inside that cavernous helmet, save for an infinite and infinitely reflective blackness. This blackness is the void of space, a void from out of which *we* somehow emerge and yet into which we are ultimately consigned to disappear. The "we" here is not just humans, who have taken those steps on the moon (or watched them being taken). It is all the forms of subjectivation arising through relational process, the process of making a self in the midst of gaining and losing access to otherness, moment to moment. This is the place of the withdrawing earth, where an astronaut's planting of a flag will make no difference because the dark depth will overcome it; a place where Elton John's "Rocket Man" burns up his fuel alone (as the lyrics go), and where David Bowie's Major Tom ("Space Oddity") loses his signal from Ground Control, his circuit going dead over and over. If Apollo and other space missions brought us the Earth as picture, as a planet captured by technology, visualizable as an entity that our experts can map, measure, quantify, and manage—yet a planet in all its boundaryless, post-nationalist glory—then the movement on the image of that picture includes the full and undisclosed potential of walking on a moon, and in a universe, neither of which is necessarily hospitable to us. That potential includes the moonwalks of Armstrong, Aldrin, and other astronauts, as well as the interpretive moonwalks of Marcel Marceau, James Brown, David Bowie, and Michael Jackson, all of whom gave us the moon as dance floor. It includes conspiracy theories about the lunar landing as a hoax, and imagined alternative histories in which another nation may have reached the moon first, in which other planets have been successfully colonized, or in

FIGURE 6.1 Astronaut Edwin E. Aldrin Jr., lunar module pilot, walks on the surface of the moon near the leg of the Lunar Module (LM) *Eagle* during the Apollo II extravehicular activity (EVA). Astronaut Neil A. Armstrong, commander, took the photograph with a 70mm lunar surface camera. Photo and caption courtesy of NASA.

which our own extinction renders all other possibilities (for us) moot. (More on extinction in a moment.)

The moon, like the stars, is a kind of early ancestor to cinema—a moving image that is open to a perceiver's interpretation. Its apparent movement around the sky and its rhythm of waxing and waning, seemingly coordinated with the female menstrual cycle (though science tells us it is the other way around), and its different appearances under different conditions, with faint blemishes from huge surface formations, hold up a certain kind of mirror that for centuries encouraged humans to imagine not only what it was, but who we ourselves were. When the Apollo astronauts reached it, we were able to look down and see ourselves again, differently. But the moon itself remains largely unmapped (for most of us), a Zone as mysterious as the one traversed by Tarkovsky's stalkers. The fact that it remains tidally locked with the Earth, one side of it visible and the other always facing away from us, makes that other side seem all the more shadowy. More to the point, the movement that has allowed us to take photographs and measurements of the Earth from above is also the movement that allows us to calculate the effects of our own activities down below. As increasing numbers of scientists and others are recognizing that human activities are setting off significant changes in the climate and ecological systems of this planet, the realization may dawn that a zone of *earthly* uncertainty stretches out before us into the future. How do we walk into that zone, a zone of possibility that will always be haunted by the shadow of our own finitude? As we walk into that blackness, there is always ever only the movement forward.

Two recent films grapple with an understanding of the crystalline nature of time, in Deleuze's sense, while providing images powerful enough to affect, in some small way, our experience of the forward movement of life on this planet. These films appeared on the cinematic horizon together: both were first screened at the Cannes Film Festival in 2011, and both enthralled many critics with their successes, their excesses, and their contrasts. Terrence Malick's *The Tree of Life* (2011), as I read it, presents a cinematic image intended to *move us toward movement*, while Lars von Trier's *Melancholia* (2011) presents an image intended to help us reach a kind of resigned or defiantly resistant stasis in a universe that moves so powerfully that it can and will destroy us. Both, however, are philosophical films, by which I mean not films *about* philosophy, but films that in themselves constitute a highly original form of film-philosophy. Both are *eco*philosophical films in that they theorize, in interesting ways, the relationship between human life and earthly and cosmic nature. They do this not with logical or deductive reasoning, but with cinematic reasoning, which means with the tools of the specifically cinematic movement of image, thought, and affect.[161]

Both films are about troubled human characters and their relationships with others, in particular with familial others. They are in this respect continuous with the films discussed earlier in reference to the "strange weather" of the 1990s. Both films, however, render their familial reference points at once foreign and cosmic. With its star-studded cast and the critical attention that greeted it, *The Tree of Life* played to large audiences even if it did not do particularly well at the box office. For a widely released film, it is unusual for its heady mix of experimental and non-narrative techniques with an elliptical but recognizable narrative. Malick's familiar preoccupations are pursued here on a broader canvas than ever. The film is, as one critic put it, "a family chamber drama" staged "on a cosmic scale."[162] Its narrative core is an exquisitely realized period piece about growing up in suburban Waco, Texas, in the 1950s (which coincides with Malick's own autobiographical generalities). But this is wrapped in a thickly painted overlay of cosmic reference points, narrative voice-overs, extra-diegetic classical music, and poetic nature imagery. Where Malick's earlier films embedded their human story lines in a world whose contours extended beyond the human—to animals, insects, and the changing of the seasons—here that background encompasses the entire evolutionary movement of life, from the Big Bang onwards.

What seemingly holds the narrative together is the present-day perspective of the main character, Jack O'Brien (Sean Penn), who is looking back on his childhood. But this basic outline is never certain: the voice-overs and first-person perspectives are attributable to different characters, the locations (such as the 1950s O'Brien family home) appear to change over time without clear rhyme or reason, and the narrative ellipses render everything ambiguous. The result is what Plantinga called "affective incongruity," or, as Jim Emerson put it, that "those who've written about it can't even agree on what they've actually seen."[163] Its early scenes of family life, punctuated by images of sunflowers, waterfalls, figures swinging from trees, and the sound of Tavener's "Funeral Canticle," are followed by a cosmic "creation" or "evolution" sequence in which colourful swirling gases and stellar nebulae, dinosaurs, planets, and an asteroid on a collision course with Earth are accompanied by classical requiems and by Jessica Chastain's voice-over questions. The latter are seemingly addressed alternately to a creator and to a child: "Where were you? ... Who are we to you? ... Answer me," and later, "Life of my life ... I search for you ... My hope ... My child." The scenes of growing up—boys playing with hoses and sprinklers, climbing trees, sneakily throwing grasshoppers down shirts, lobbing balls up on the roof, creeping into a female neighbour's vacant home and stealing her negligee from a bedroom drawer, then embarrassedly sending it floating down the river—are exuberant in their movement, both of the camera and of bodies, and in a general unpredictable fluidity of perspectives, words, and visual and bodily expressions. The evolution sequence, on the other hand, has become notorious for its apparent disproportionality and its CGI dinosaurs, and the significance of the similarly ambiguous late scenes in which Jack O'Brien encounters long-dead family members on a dune-swept seashore remain open to a religious reading that some viewers find cloying, others simply indecipherable. If filmmaking were intended to create the perfectly proportioned object, critics' laments about the latter two sequences in particular would lead to a decisive rejection of this film's artistry.

An implicit argument of this book, however, has been that cinema is not about perfection, nor about attainment of any kind. It is about movement, extension, and the ongoing process by which feeling and meaning are generated by this movement. *The Tree of Life* extends itself like a flowering vine groping toward the sun, its titular tree being less of an achivement than a continually unfolding branch, a *rhizome* in Deleuze and Guattari's sense. As Kent Jones puts it, the film "doesn't move forward but pulses, like a massive organism, and its beginning and end point are the same: a ball of primal energy in the blackness, ready to generate more theophanies." It comes not in isolated images but "in bursts of attentively covered emotion and energy," recalling the instants, the signaletic moments, that swirl within our own episodic memories of childhood, but following a rhythm, "the film's signature action" as Jones puts it, "of dilation and contraction, optically, formally, and thematically."[164] To a greater extent than almost any mainstream film director today, Malick, who is known for his tight control over the filmmaking process, seemingly allows things to flow here of their own accord. If anything, the film is *about* that flow: of images, fragments, glimpses, memories, feelings, and dreams; the flow of emotionality in its thickness and its tensility; the flow of thought in its many voices and in the questions that punctuate its quest for sense (especially Jack O'Brien's / Sean Penn's, but also that of the other characters); the flow of connections, felt and probed but never rendered exact, between past and present, cause and complex effect, moments of loss and the haunting abysses they leave behind; and the flow of cinematic light and sound, of music (several requiems among them), and of the camera eye (under Emmanuel Lubezki's deft direction), which is almost ceaseless in its elliptical motion in and around, toward and away from, the people and things that populate this unsettled world. In his comparison of the film with newer-generation fare by Nolan, Aronofsky, Fincher, and other directors, Roger Denson notes that

> By contrast, in its mimicry of life and nature, *Tree of Life* dissolves narrative—at least linguistic narrative—to its most visually fluid state,

allowing iconography to flow into swirling eddies of pictorial flux, not merely convergences of information, but projections of life that despite their conceptual and simulated forms seem perfectly in keeping with our experience. *Tree of Life* is less a narration than it is a pictorial genesis, evolution, and lineage of timeless primordiality to the present-day personal. We witness a succession of conceptual streams of thought flow through one another on a variety of physical levels, see theoretical manifolds converging, all as if before the formation of language. It's *Tree of Life*'s perpetual flux and tensions, even more than the relentless beauty of the montage and action, that keep *Tree of Life* vibrant and provocative.[165]

The film is, in this sense, about the movement from random creativity (or Peircian firstness) to bruising actuality (or secondness) to realization (or thirdness). It is about the process of asking questions (through the film's many off-screen voices) and awaiting their answers, about the frustration that builds when the questions and the still seething traumas underlying them are met with silence, and about, even so, allowing the arrival of those answers—as the kinds of strangers who enter through the back door of the childhood home that keeps being set ablaze in one's memory.

One of those questions, voiced as a statement in the film's first minutes by Jack's mother (Jessica Chastain), is about there being "two ways through life: the way of nature, and the way of grace." Normally when a filmmaker dangles a heavy-handed trope like this in front of the audience in a film's opening minutes, the audience can be reasonably certain that the line will convey what the film is about. Most reviewers take "nature" to be represented by Jack's self-possessed, hypocritical, and occasionally abusive father (Brad Pitt), and "grace" by his selfless mother (Chastain). But with Malick, things are rarely so simple. All of his films include voice-over narrations, sometimes by multiple voices, and sometimes (as in *The Thin Red Line*) by voices whose characters are not clearly identifiable. These textual fragments rarely weave themselves into a singular and coherent commentary. Instead, they clatter and clash against one another, revealing ellipses in the space between them and resulting in what Bakhtin called heteroglossia—a polyphonic text in which meaning emerges in and through the tensions, diffractions, and refractions between the individual lines spoken and the narrative strands, emotional tones, and rhythms of the images and sounds that follow. Nature is opposed to grace only in the sense that life is made of tensions that always "wrestle within me," as Jack's voice puts it (this being Peirce's secondness), and that seek, and sometimes fleetingly achieve, reconciliation (meaning, thirdness). All of life is such relational process:

"nature" is its arising as qualities and the wrestling between them when they are actualized; "grace" is the dawning meaningfulness that emerges within the Open, the gap between one line and another, one image and another, one effort and another. Grace, meaning, thirdness, is out of our hands, yet strangely sensed if those hands remain poised to receive it. But it emerges out of a kernel that is traumatic at its core. In *The Tree of Life*, the tornness at the heart of the family, like the nature–grace tornness at the heart of the human condition, is a gap, a question mark seemingly branded on our foreheads that forces us to seek meaning. (Sean Penn's character, at times, seems indeed to be little more than a prototypically branded forehead.)

Jeff Reichert's words are pertinent as we make sense of this film, which comes some twelve decades after the first moving-image pictures were produced: "While watching the film, remember that its unutterably complex, meaning-making cavalcade of images evolved from a single shot of a train pulling into a station captured over a century earlier."[166] This trajectory leading from the Lumières' "Train Pulling into a Station" (*L'arrivée d'un train en gare de La Ciotat,* 1985) to *The Tree of Life*—as one point shooting out from the centre of the branching tree of cinema—is, I would suggest, just as "interesting to contemplate" as the "tangled bank" that Darwin famously contemplated in his account of evolution in *The Origin of Species*. Darwin's closing words seem apt in considering this trajectory:

> There is grandeur in this view of life, with its several powers, having been originally breathed [by the Creator] into a few forms or into one; and that, whilst this planet has gone cycling on according to the fixed law of gravity, from so simple a beginning endless forms most beautiful and most wonderful have been, and are being, evolved.[167]

What makes the movement from the Lumières to films like *The Tree of Life* so interesting to contemplate is the openness by which this cinematic evolution has proceeded. This is an openness that a process-relational perspective tells us is built into the very structure of the universe, in its movement from possibility to actuality to generality, from the virtual to the actual to the ceaselessly meaning-making.

Like *The Tree of Life*, von Trier's *Melancholia* follows an unusual and non-linear narrative arc. It begins with an eight-minute overture of gothically dreamlike, imagistic tableaux scored to the Prelude from Wagner's *Tristan und Isolde*. In Wagnerian fashion, slow-motion images provide leitmotifs to the rest of the film: a blond woman (Kirsten Dunst) stands on an improbably large, stately lawn in a wedding dress, birds fall from the sky around her, a brunette clutches her son, a horse melts into the earth as if drawn down by invisible weights, the blonde's feet get entangled in tree roots as she moves through a wooded glade, bolts of electricity discharge upwards from her hands to the sky, and a massive blue planet slowly approaches and then quietly collides into the Earth.[168] The rest of the film is divided between two parts, each titled after one of the sisters who are the film's main characters. The first half, "Justine," presents the ill-fated wedding reception of the titular character and a likeable but vapid groom, taking place at the ostentatious country-club home of her sister Claire (Charlotte Gainsbourg) and wealthy brother-in-law John (Kiefer Sutherland), as a black comedy of empty pomp and ceremony gone crazily awry. The second half, "Claire," presents the return of the single, and now chronically depressed, Justine to Claire and John's home for rehabilitation. Meanwhile, we find out that the mysterious "rogue planet" Melancholia is soon to veer by the Earth in what astronomers claim will be a "fly-by." Searching on the Internet in defiance of her husband's warnings, Claire learns that others hypothesize that the "fly-by" will initiate a "dance of death," with the two planets exercising each other's gravitational fields into a slingshot orbit that will result in a head-on collision.

The film focuses on the psychological interplay between the seemingly reasonable but increasingly agitated Claire, who fears for herself and her loved ones, and the severely depressed and at times almost catatonic Justine, who gradually becomes the stronger of the two in her resolute acceptance of their fate. The two sisters constitute the film's primary dynamic, which is mirrored by the relationship between the Earth and its murderous twin planet. Justine, whose name suggests Justice and who is called "Auntie Steelbreaker" by her nephew Leo (the only human character in the film with whom she seems to have much of an emotional connection), tries but cannot hold it together for her wedding. Yet even in her chronically debilitated depressive state, she is depicted as possibly clairvoyant, sensing that Melancholia will in fact destroy the Earth and that there is nothing to fear or regret about that. Claire, on the other hand, whose name suggests clarity (though Justine sometimes calls her "Clay"), presents a strength and solidity in facing worldly norms, but ultimately weakness or simple incapacity when facing the abyss of total destruction. To put it in Deleuzian terms, Claire believes in the world deeply (at least the social world) and is afraid for it when it appears to be threatened by this menacingly foreign planet killer. Justine, on the other hand, takes this intruder to be a saving grace.

By the standards of traditional narrative and emotional realism, *Melancholia*, as its critics point out, fails in some significant ways. Scientifically, of course, there is little realism in proposing the existence of a planet that has "hidden behind the sun" all this time and that suddenly comes hurtling out toward the Earth. But as a psychological metaphor, the planet Melancholia could hardly have been given a more aesthetically potent treatment. The success of the film lies in the impact of its images and in the dialogue between responses to the meaning of those images, especially to the image of utter annihilation. The blue planet Melancholia is a mesmerizing metaphor for a kind of double to the known world, a hidden, deadly intruder that is destined to be the bringer of total extinction. But where a Buddhist or Lacanian reading of extinction as the shadow of reality could have sufficed, von Trier insists on insinuating a Gnostic dualist thread whereby, in Justine's words, "life on earth is evil" and *deserves* to be destroyed. In response to the threat and to Claire's inability to accept it, Justine comforts Claire's son Leo by building a protective "magic cave" out of wooden sticks to shelter the remaining trio—Leo, Claire, and herself—from the impending doom. As in Tarkovsky's (and Soderbergh's) *Solaris*, the final consummation is both an ecstatic release and a crushing annihilation, and the image of a planet colliding into the Earth is mesmerizing in its simple beauty. As in *Solaris*, the planetary double is the instrument of seduction and destruction as well as of realization: it tears down illusions, renders them impotent, and swallows us in its embrace. *Melancholia* is, if anything, a more stark, direct, and atheistic version of this embrace. It is a direct hit that leaves nothing behind. Its Zone is utter annihilation, leaving behind little but a dry laugh echoing in the vacancy of space. Yet despite the bleak nihilism of its seeming message, it is quite possible to leave the theatre, as critic J. Hoberman did, feeling "light, rejuvenated and unconscionably happy."[169]

The two films that lurk most conspicuously behind both *The Tree of Life* and *Melancholia* are Kubrick's *2001, A Space Odyssey* (more frequently discussed by critics in this context) and Tarkovsky's *Solaris*. The latter is about a planet that also acts as a double to the Earth, tearing down psychological illusions but ultimately swallowing those who orbit it—rather like the extraterrestrial space (and the computer HAL) that swallows, or attempts to swallow, the astronauts who venture into it in Kubrick's film. Malick seemingly opts for the affirmation of life, while von Trier opts for its negation. Either film could be taken in either direction by a viewer, but each presents a preferred reading based on the resonant images that linger. In the case of *Solaris*, the images that linger are likely to include those of astronaut Kelvin's rustic home on Earth, and of his ghostly wife, because these resonate with other Tarkovskian images and are thus more legible to viewers of his films. In the case of *Tree of Life*, it is the affirmative images—of nature, of love, of seasonal change, and so on—that tend to linger, again in part because of resonances with its director's oeuvre. In the case of *Melancholia*, which is von Trier's first film after the manically aggressive

Antichrist (a film made in the depths of the filmmaker's own depression), the partner planet represents a destroyer of worlds, pure and compelling in its awful beauty. *Tree of Life*'s movement is a reaching out, a moving forward into meaning while recognizing that we make that meaning in a kind of partnership with the universe. *Melancholia*'s movement is a collapsing inward: while meaning may be sought out in the negation of the Earth by Melancholia—for instance, in Justine's belief that life on Earth is evil or in her creation of the imagined magic cave—that meaning, even if beautiful, is understood to be futile, a magic cave that is little more than a trick of the mind.

Both of these graspings toward meaning—Malick's tree and von Trier's magic cave—can be taken as the power of the imagination and, by extension, of cinema. In Malick's case they affirm the power of ontogeny, the creative impulse that continues to generate life and meaning despite our trials, errors, missteps, and misapprehensions. The latter constitute the trauma of the open relational gaps that our lives fill in with meaning: "mother, father, always you wrestle within me." In von Trier's case, imagination and cinema affirm a passionate and deliberate yet futile movement against eschatology, the end and collapse of things.[170] The gaps here will finally overcome any relationality; the Real, in a Lacanian sense, will destroy the Symbolic and the Imaginary, even if the latter, like the magic cave, may make things interesting in the time it has left. Both films, in the end, leave behind searing images that, judging by the responses of online reviews, unsettle and haunt, leaving behind an oscillating charge that seeks resolution in framing one's own relationship with the meaning, future, and potential end of life. The image of the blue planet Melancholia appearing and slowly growing over the horizon of the Earth, overtaking it in its inevitable growth, becomes a kind of post-human response to the shots of the Earth from the Moon with which I opened this section. Von Trier seems to want us to think the aftermath of humanity and of a human-centred Earth. Seeing this killer of planets—not in the frenetic guise of a Hollywood action-packed adventure, but in the slow and deliberate grace of its arrival—makes extinction thinkable and affectively imaginable in a way that only cinema can. It is as simple and as powerful a strike at the anthropocentric world view as has ever been cinematically conceived.

While neither *The Tree of Life* nor *Melancholia*, nor for that matter *Stalker* or *Solaris*, directly depict an ecological catastrophe—all are too personal and non-confessionally spiritual to deal with the immediacy of a politicized topic such as that—each provides a flow of images that renders real the relations among transient subjectivity, anthropomorphosis, and the larger ecologies of the Earth and universe. *Stalker* (and, in some ways, *Solaris*) presents us with a downward-looking view, as in the Stalker's dreaming—of what we don't know, or perhaps it is dreamless sleep—as the camera pans across objects and processes redolent of their own elusive temporalities. *The Tree of Life* presents a view that seems to be arching its head upward, toward a universal light that is visible through the branches of a tree, but always arching in a circuitous manner, becoming diverted and then again continuing its upward, forward thrust. With *Melancholia*, the little traumas of life are subsumed into a singularly high-impact, planeticidal event, with the result that the gaze becomes a gaze neither upward toward an open future, nor downward toward a grounded materiality; rather, it is inward into the traumatic abyss of extinction. Together, these films might be seen as presenting affectively charged moving-images of distinctly different interpretations of the relations among humans, the Earth, and the universe.

All of these films, like many others discussed in the preceding pages, remind us that the cinema experience is, at its best, a journey into a Zone in which we risk being transformed, irreparably, through an encounter with another that transcends us, an inassimilable core of contingency that grounds all possibility. This "another" can be corralled into a religious interpretation as divine, as some of Malick's and Tarkovsky's viewers have done with their films, or, ironically, as demonic (as with von Trier's *Antichrist*). But to the extent that each of these views comes pre-interpreted, neither is faithful to the thing itself. The thing, following Žižek and Lacan, is what we might simply call the Real. But if it is the Real that grounds all possibility, then it is also that Real that grounds the possibility of life as it has evolved on this planet, and whatever may have preceded it and evolved alongside it elsewhere, and of the subjectivity that continues to emerge in our own potential for decisive action. This subjectivity is continuous with nature, not radically opposed to it, but its continuity follows its own rules, not ours, though we may participate in their making.

The Tree of Life gestures at this continuity between the cosmic process and our own openness and finitude, and renders undecidable its valence— as basically good, as ultimately traumatic, or as prickly and paradoxical. The film's approach recalls Peirce's evolutionary optimism, even if it recognizes the fraughtness of such an optimism—the "war at the heart of nature," in the words of the lead character in Malick's earlier *The Thin Red Line*. *Melancholia*, on the other hand, suggests a radical discontinuity and finitude. In this it is more consistent with Žižek's psychoanalytic pessimism. In Žižek's assessment of today's ecological threat, he suggests that we ought to "accept that, at the level of possibilities, our future is doomed, the catastrophe will take place, it is our destiny—and, then, on the background of this acceptance, we should mobilize ourselves to perform the act that will change destiny itself by inserting a new possibility into the past."[171] This recognition of catastrophe is not one that, for Žižek, constitutes an acceptance that humans have transgressed the natural order. On the contrary, he argues that there *is* no nature to transgress, or to turn to for solutions. We should instead recognize "the utter groundlessness of our existence: there is no firm foundation, a place of retreat, on which one can safely count. 'Nature doesn't exist': 'nature' qua the domain of balanced reproduction, of organic deployment into which humanity intervenes with its *hubris*, brutally throwing off the rails its circular motion, is man's fantasy."[172] Our destiny is ours to create, even if there is virtue in accepting the final impotence of our creativity. The two films thus represent different assessments of nature, of ourselves, and of the future. Between them lies a spectrum of possibilities that has perhaps become stretched particularly wide at this point in cinema history. Each, in its way, can be considered ecophilosophical insofar as it raises deep questions about the relationship between humans and nature and generates affective images of possibilities that are perhaps best imaged as *moving* images. And to the extent that we, as viewers, rise to meet them in this capacity for movement and mobilization, so our viewing practices become ecophilosophical as well. They are, like *Stalker*, very differently poised instances of what an ecophilosophical cinema might look like. But such a cinema requires an ecophilosophical viewer to take them in the direction of an ecophilosophical thirdness.

Every finished film is, in the end, a complex fabric of kindling waiting for a viewer to light it. How it will burn in the minds and lives of its viewers is a great unknown. Filmmakers try to predict and control for the factors surrounding its burning. They are, after all, responsible for producing the mix of affordances that will greet the viewers upon the lighting of the match (the unspooling of the reel, the rolling of the tape, the scanning and reading of the disk, the clicking of the play button). But those affordances, being affordances for affect and interpretation, are always already outside their control. Some filmmakers know this and willingly relinquish control over those elements. Or they craft a mixture of total control and maximum release, an opening up to the flow of how those elements come together at the scene of production and/ or in the editing room. Malick is one director who has seemingly arrived at a mixture of control and release; Tarkovsky was perhaps another. (Evaluating von Trier is a more complicated task, which I will not attempt here.) In doing so, they are working to craft a worthy experience from the elements that make up our age of the world motion picture. But they are also working to release us, and themselves, from the claustrophobic sense of our subsumption within a sea of images—the sense with which this book's exploration of the moving image began.

In and through the image, they seek release from the image. And that release, in a process-relational view, is the moment within every moment in which reality is ultimately real. It is the moment of openness, the leap from the firstness of possibility to the secondness of actualization, and from the secondness of encounter to the thirdness of its arrival at meaning. These two leaps are a single leap insofar as they occur through decisive action, the action by which we feelingly take account of and respond to what we encounter. The "we" that we arrive at is the Open, the field of unmapped possibility, and cinema is one of the more powerful vehicles by which we might get there.

AFTERWORD

Digital Futures in a Biosemiotic World

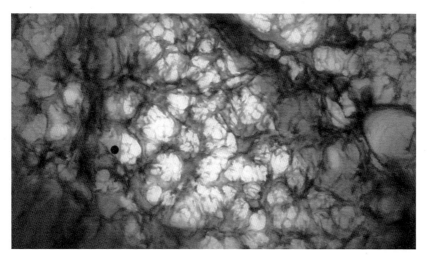

From *The Tree of Life* (2011). Directed by Terrence Malick. Credit: River Road
Entertainment/Fox Studios.

According to the feeling-imbued philosophy of a pluralistic universe, to care about
the diversity of humanity writ large is to take a step toward caring about the larger
world that courses through and around us. It is to care about litter in motion in the
creativity of a cockroach, the fecundity of rainforests, lava flows, swimming DNA,
the sonority of the human voice, turbulent water flows, and the human body-
brain-culture network. Above all, it is to care about that delicate balance between
creativity and stability that enables nature and civilizations to change while maintaining themselves. To appreciate the element of energetic uncertainty circulating
through the world is to cultivate cautious solicitude for the world.

William Connolly, Pluralism[1]

What action can still be meaningfully accomplished in the new "world space" of endless circulation and modulation? What cinematic image of achievement can still be generated, in a world where all is time, where "time is money," where money is the "most internal presupposition" of cinema, and where money always implies, as in Marx's formula M–C–M, "the impossibility of an equivalence ... tricked, dissymmetrical exchange" [...]?

Steven Shaviro, *Post-Cinematic Affect*[2]

The modern fact is that we no longer believe in this world. [...] Restoring our belief in the world – this is the power of modern cinema . . .

Gille Deleuze, *Cinema 2*[3]

AS I WRITE, A VIDEO SHOT by a Chinese security camera showing a two-year-old girl being hit and run over by a truck, followed by several passersby ignoring her, has been circulating across television and computer screens around the world for a few days. Watching the video, I feel myself descend, rapidly, into a pit of momentary emotional despair, as I imagine that the victim could just as well have been my son. I know nothing of the context: who the girl was, who her parents were, who were the drivers of the vans and the bicycles that passed her by, nor even what kind of life goes on in that distant city. But I know the event shown actually happened, and I also know that it elicited a round of anguished soul searching, blame seeking, and recriminations among Chinese citizens. The video is short, no longer than the original reels of the Lumières, and just as silent. It has become a live and mobile moment, a moving episode, an event that captures and transmits an intensity of feeling. Every time it is viewed, the moving image transposes itself into a particular state of feeling, for someone, and then into meaning.

Most of this book has described films that are extended in time and in space, containing moments like this one tied end to end with others to create a journey of sorts, lasting from several minutes to a few hours. That journey is singular and bounded, with viewers moving from a here to a there, and sometimes back again, over the time it takes to be viewed. Taken collectively, however, cinema presents a universe whose outer circumference is always expanding. That circumference is not bounded at all; it is open, because there are always new films to be made, new kinds of films being made, and new sense to be made of them. The expanding circumference marks the expansive imagination of cinematic humans and of a cinematic Earth.

But even within that circumference, not all the dots that connect together to shape it are singular, bounded units like the ones I have been describing.

More and more of them are fluid bursts—more like bacteria that share genetic information across boundaries, or rhizomes that connect with others in ever-widening webs, than like sedentary organisms that take root and bear fruit in a single plot of soil. The very shape of films, and of the film-viewing experience, is no longer what it used to be. Today it is no more likely that one will watch a two-hour film straight through than it is that one will watch and rewatch favourite clips, seek them out on YouTube, stop watching part-way through to change the channel or eject the disk and come back to it midstream some time later. And films today are part of a rapidly diversifying landscape of moving images, a landscape in which the basic reference points of movie watching have been blurred and disassembled. DVDs and Internet resources provide multiple entry points for viewing a single film—which, with its "director's cuts," alternative versions, and various add-ons, isn't always as singular as films used to be.[4] What television did when it created a constant stream of filmic presentations has been multiplied to a point of no return. Cable television provides a staged running commentary about the world and key events of the day, and the growing availability of international programming among satellite and cable providers allows for a sampling of multiple takes on these events. YouTube and its siblings provide an ever-expanding archive of cinematic material uploaded, downloaded, re-edited, cross-referenced, spoofed, and endlessly commented upon. The one-to-many model of theatrical movie releases is being replaced by a many-to-many model of distributed computing and file sharing. And the growth of interactive media, from multiuser video games to increasingly lifelike virtual worlds, has opened up the viewing experience to radical reorganization in the midst of its very flow.

Until recently, film theory had been premised on the assumption that the live-action cinematographic "recording of reality" was the essence, or at least the default option, of cinema. Film required a photographic process—the mechanical recording of images through the registration of reflected light onto a photosensitive chemical surface. But the digital revolution has thrown this assumption into question to the point that some now maintain the opposite: that animation, or the graphic manipulation of images, is now the default option of cinematic media, and that the mimetic representation of reality is, at best, the exception that proves the new rule. Some have claimed that mimetic representation is in its death throes and that the era of cinema—moving images captured on film emulsion and projected onto two-dimensional, rectangular screens in front of large audiences—is over. Others argue that it is merely film that is coming to its end; cinema, the *kinematic* or moving arts, will continue in new forms.

This debate over the continuity or discontinuity of the digital present from the cinematic past will continue for some time. Cinema, or the moving image, is no longer wedded to photorealist indexicality, but such indexicality remains a viable option, one that continues to underlie many people's reception of cinema, if not necessarily its production. For even if, in D.N. Rodowick's words, "all that was chemical and photographic is disappearing into the electronic and digital," much of what is digital remains oriented toward fulfilling viewers' apparent desire for photographic or perceptual realism and "depictive credibility."[5] Cinema's stamp remains imprinted on emergent media forms. In one of the most influential accounts of such media, Lev Manovich perceptively noted the "general trend in modern society toward presenting more and more information in the form of time-based audiovisual moving image sequences, rather than as text." "A hundred years after cinema's birth," he continues, "cinematic ways of seeing the world, of structuring time, of narrating a story, of linking one experience to the next, have become the basic means by which computer users access and interact with all cultural data."[6] Cinematic codes that have come to shape online interfaces, computer games, virtual worlds, and other media forms, include one-point linear perspective (which, as I argued in Chapter 3, is inherited from Western painting), the conventions of the mobile camera and the rectangular window-like framing of represented reality (of which the same can be said), cinematographic and editing conventions, and much else. In this respect, cinema "has found a new life as the toolbox of the computer user." Its aesthetic strategies—its "means of perception, of connecting space and time, of representing human memory, thinking, and emotion"—have become the "basic organizational principles of computer software."[7]

- The argument about cinematographic indexicality, drawing as it does on a basic Peircian principle, deserves further consideration. A cinematic image, whatever else it may be, bears some relationship to a profilmic world, a world to which it refers by virtue of its having been connected to it through the capture of light (for instance) onto photochemical emulsion. In Manovich's words, "cinema is the art of the index; it is an attempt to make art out of a footprint," which is the footprint of the reality that was stamped onto the photographic medium in its transformation into a projectible film.[8] As Niels Niessen argues, however, an index, for Peirce, is more than a mere relation to a profilmic referent. It is that relationship as it is perceived by a viewer; it is, in other words, a sign *to an interpretant*. And the relationship between an image and its profilmic referent is never fully given in the image itself. It is always mediated by other elements, such as the screened or printed representation, the sound accompanying it, the context in which it is appearing, and the spectator's prior knowledge and expectations about the process by which the image has come to be what it is. Most or all of these variables remain in place in digital cinema, even if the expectations themselves are changing.[9]

But with changing expectations come novel possibilities. Rodowick notes that while digital cinema retains much of the viewerly and representational impetus that predated it, it gives rise to new potentialities that we, novelty seekers, are bound to pursue. The shift from photographic process to digital process, with its basis in numerical manipulation and data synthesis, sampling, and sequencing, contains profound openings that have yet to be followed to their limits. The digital image, Rodowick writes, "is more and more responsive to our imaginative intentions, and less and less anchored to the prior existence of things and people." Cinema, he predicts, "will increasingly become the art of synthesizing imaginary worlds, numerical worlds in which the sight of physical reality becomes increasingly scarce."[10] Cinematic space and time are being altered in the process, as is our involvement with that space and time. Roderick Coover notes, for instance, that "what works in streaming and in new media are short works; they are works accompanied by text; they are works from different people contributing to a common space; they are fragmented; they are multiply linked."[11] More generally, digital video eliminates the intensive productive labour involved in filmmaking, which also means the magic and ritual of the old filmmaking process, in favour of a light and spontaneous *caméra-stylo*, a "camera-pen" that can capture reality effortlessly anywhere. For instance, multiple hand-held cameras can provide multiple points of view on an event as it happens, in places where setting up a film shoot would have been impossible until recently. Yet digital video paradoxically also provides the possibility of total control of the image. It brings us, at the same time, much *closer* to reality and much *further away* from it than cinema ever could.[12]

Francesco Cassetti's criteria for the cinematic are worth returning to here. The cinema, for Cassetti, is a circulation or "vacillation" between "the image-artifice" and the "image-imprint," between "having a grasp on the world, having too much of it, and not having any left at all."[13] It is, in his comprehensive analysis, an ever-inventive negotiation and synthesis between a series of five forces and counterforces, which happen to be among the great contradictory "demands of modernity": the oppositions between fragment and totality, subjectivity and objectivity, human and machine, excitement and order, and immersion and detachment:

> The world offers itself only in fragments but the desire for totality continues to press. Reality is always filtered by someone's perception, but this does not exonerate us from distinguishing between

> perceptions and facts. The machine offers us a gaze that is extraordi-
> narily sharp, but humans want to continue to feel in some way a part
> of it. Sensory excitement makes us feel alive and present, but we also
> must not lose control of our surroundings or ourselves. Spectator and
> performance are, by now, one and the same, but it is often necessary
> to establish distance.[14]

Cinema, Cassetti claims, was the eye of the twentieth century. Today, it is no longer effecting the same mediations, which have been entrusted to other media: to television, the Internet, the cellphone, the palm-held device, and others, with the result that the emblem of our more "liquid" age has become "the slippery morphing image."[15]

How, then, do we move into a world of slippery, morphing images? And is their slipperiness a guarantee of their deceptiveness, or could it somehow bring us *closer* to a reality that is also slippery and morphing? To answer these questions, we ought to understand how this cinematic world is part of a larger set of shifting constellations. In *Post Cinematic Affect*, Steven Shaviro takes up the quasi-Jamesonian task of mapping how this slippery morphing image reflects and heralds a changing geopolitical condition, as well the opportunities it presents for resistance to that condition. Shaviro describes the contemporary condition as a world of neoliberal, networked, and hyperflexible capitalism, a "world of crises and convulsions" that is "ruthlessly organized" around the relentless and singular logic of commodification and capital accumulation. In this world of "modulation, digitisation, financialization, and media transduction," we have shifted from disciplinary forms of governmentality, in which individuals were moulded into subjects according to relatively fixed parameters spanning a series of disciplinary and organizational spaces, to a flexible society of ongoing, never-resting and never-sated *modulation*, where continuous recombination is a basic necessity for keeping up with the twists and turns of ever-unfolding hyper-capitalism.[16] There is, in other words, nothing solid left beneath our feet: just as the global financial system sloshes around like a drunken gambler on a storm-tossed ship, so do jobs, careers, personal and collective identities, corporate and national marketing strategies, and values all shift and mutate to keep up with the flow of a fluid and elusive reality.

One set of aesthetic possibilities for dealing with this condition is that which Shaviro, following Benjamin Noys, calls "accelerationism," or the extreme use of the new capacities within the new cinematic mode of production to squeeze out new possibilities for liberation. Shaviro seeks to identify the "aesthetic poignancy of post cinematic media," media that assume that "the only way out is the way through"—*through* a world without transcendence, and through an exacerbation or radicalization of capitalism "to the point of collapse," as Noys puts it.[17] In films like Olivier Assayas's *Boarding Gate* (2007), Richard Kelly's *Southland Tales* (2006), Mark Neveldine and Brian Taylor's *Gamer* (2009), and the Grace Jones / Nick Hooker music video "Corporate Cannibal" (2008), Shaviro finds an aesthetically productive and useful exploration of "the contours of the prison we find ourselves in." "Corporate Cannibal" provides a good entry point into Shaviro's argument. In it, Grace Jones plays herself as an endless modulator of her own image, an image that "swells and contracts, bends and fractures, twists, warps and contorts and flows from one shape to another," all the while projecting a certain style, a certain "singularity" of "Grace Jones" as celebrity icon, a "long string of Jones's reinventions of herself." Jones is the transgressive "posthuman" who, unlike Madonna, who "puts on and takes off personas as if they were clothes," cannot retreat into the anonymity of the unmarked (because white) artist. Jones, a black woman, is already marked to start with and is therefore playing "for keeps," devouring "whatever she encounters, converting it into more image, more electronic signal," and "track[ing] and embrac[ing] the transmutations of capital" as she goes. Jones in this sense represents "the chronic condition of our hypermodernity," a hypermodernity that we, or most of us, cannot escape.[18]

Shaviro points out that in this video there is no longer a reliable relation between figure and ground, or between stillness and movement, a pre-existing "structure of space" *within* which things happen. In my terms, there is no longer any frame keeping the geomorphic or objectal separate from the anthropomorphic or subjectal. There is only continual modulation free of any stable parameters. This argument recalls Sean Cubitt's analysis of Émile Cohl's *Fantasmagorie* (1908), which I recounted in Chapter 2, with the difference that Cohl's line drawing maintained a distance between the drawer and the drawn, artist (Cohl) and performance (the film), while Jones's persona, in Shaviro's reading, comes fully wrapped without remainder in her ever-changing masks. The corporate cannibal played by Grace Jones can be read as a form of excessive parody, a "taking on" of the role in both senses of the word—as a form of mimicry, an act, and as a semi-threatening response, an "I know you're out there and I know your game" to the corporate cannibals who do populate the world. But it is as much an expression of the reality of a cannibalistic capitalism as is that capitalism itself.

In my discussion in Chapter 2 of Jonathan Beller's neo-Marxist analysis of the "cinematic mode of production," I suggested that cinema and capitalism are historically and technologically correlated with each other, and that therefore the twists and turns of the latter find their counterpart in the former, but that reducing one to the other risks missing the alternative possibilities offered by cultural tools for reworking the world. In this book's analysis of cinema as a world-making enterprise, and of our experience of cinema as one that is open to the movement of thought and affect, I have tried to suggest that there are many ways in which we might work with cinema to remake the world. The question underlying the debate over the digital can be phrased this way: Is the "slippery morphing image" just the latest variation of the kinetic image, or is it something new and different altogether? "Cinema" and "kinesis" share roots in the same Greek words for movement (*kinēin*, to move; *kinēma*, *kinesis*, movement; *kinētikos*, moving), which suggests that the cinematic is and always will be the *moving*. It will always be inherent to a world of image–reality– affect, a world that is in motion and that moves those who partake of and constitute it. The morphing image, on the other hand—from the Greek root *morphē*, form, shape—is an image that takes shape and brings form, then takes shape again and brings new form. "Movement," in our conventional way of thinking it, suggests that there is something that moves, that goes from point A to point B but remains unchanged in its essence. In contrast, "morphing," or form taking, more clearly indicates the immanent nature of movement that a process-relational perspective insists on. Something takes form *and that form is what it is*; its new form is what it has *become*.

Worlds take forms: they geomorph, biomorph, and anthromorph. We move into and with them, and although we may not become them, since we remain distinct forms ourselves, we are changed in the process. The kinetic and the cinematic are in this sense essentially morphic, form-taking, and shape-shifting. Cinema is a form of morphogenesis, a form of becoming. If this was less evident fifty years ago, it is becoming more evident today—as it was at the beginning of cinema. Manovich argues that as live-action footage, in digital cinema, is digitized into pixels, it becomes just another source for digital images, another graphic, "raw material for further compositing, animating and morphing."[19] At the same time, editing and special effects become collapsed into the same category of "image processing." The physical reality that, if Kracauer had his way, would be redeemed by cinema appears more elastic today than it did in Kracauer's time, but this is not necessarily the "melting into air" of "all that is solid" that Karl Marx spoke of. Manovich argues that live-action, narrative cinema will one day come to be seen as merely an episode, "an isolated accident in the history of visual representation." Such a history will have brought the moving image back full circle from its earliest forms as animated drawing or painting, through its heyday as live-action narrative representation, to its newly rediscovered form as animated image-interface. "*Born from animation*," he emphasizes, "*cinema pushed animation to its periphery, only in the end to become one particular case of animation.*"[20] Animation and morphogenesis, in this view, have always been with us; now we have the tools to creatively extend them into new forms of worlding.

If the hyper-capitalist condition shows a preference for the "slippery morphing image," then Manovich's argument suggests that this may not be entirely reducible to the history of capitalism. One might envision ways of working with that image to undercut its teleological drive (as Shaviro's examples arguably do), but also ways of working against that image, refusing its imperatives, or cutting against them in creative ways. For instance, "slow cinema," like the slow food movement, may constitute one way of refusing the insatiable imperatives of capitalist modulation. As its critics point out, it may be a way that appeals primarily to a "bourgeois bohemian" connoisseurial class of cinephiles, an aesthetic for those with the time and ability to luxuriate in the pleasures of art films. But slowness offers its own powers of morphing, especially when used judiciously in combination with other narrative and aesthetic modes.

Each of the preceding four chapters has discussed ways in which new geomorphisms, anthropomorphisms, and biomorphisms are being explored in contemporary cinema. *Prospero's Books* was an early example of the influence of the digital "database aesthetic" on film practice. Made in 1991, it presciently depicted a world of morphic interfaces and hyperlinks, yet a world that, as I argued, reflexively comments on the very process of cinematic production and of the artistic imagination in general. Cinema, in that world, is not a window onto *another* world, but rather a matrix of interfaces into virtual worlds that interpenetrate with ours. *Jonah Who Will Be 25 in the Year 2000* was an example of an ensemble or network narrative premised on the hope embodied in the present moment for change to a system that seemed all too solid, but that offered bubbles of breathing space in which alternatives might be imagined and enacted. Other network narratives, such as *Short Cuts* and *Magnolia*, situate the viewer in relation not to a specific character but to a set of eco-social situations in which we are, by extension, all enmeshed. Anthropomorphosis, in these cases, is problematic and troublesome, but it is wedded to the troublesome nature of earthly existence. Films like *Darwin's Nightmare*, *Lessons of Darkness*, *The Tree of Life*, and *Melancholia* all offer images of movement, which means forms of biomorphism—vectors of movement we can follow and morph into as we travel with them. Images, in any case, do many things and work on many levels; they are not reducible to their political-economic functions. People find unpredictable ways to work with them for meeting their needs, and those needs are not likely to be restricted to the imperative to succeed, or even just survive, in a hyper-mobile capitalist economy.

The inclusion of a music video among Steven Shaviro's four case studies is indicative of the general trend that I have been referring to, where the boundaries between different forms of cinema are blurring and recombining. Music videos are no different in principle from other cinematic works; one could even argue that they crystallize all that I have been saying about the moving image. They pack in, often with utmost intensity, the *movingness* of the audiovisual image: the affective spectacle of a particular set of motions, speeds, sounds, glimpses, gazes, sensations, feelings; the cutting together of one thing into another, sutured by rhythm and song, to create some sense of a narrative arc, or at least of movement or tension between the kinds of structuring dualities that make narrative possible; and the semiotic openness by which what would normally stand on its own—a song or musical piece—becomes overlaid by and adjoined to other things entirely. One might argue that music videos *reduce* the interpretive openness of a piece of music by locking it into a series of visual and narrative reference points. But every such reduction is also a transformation that creates new possibilities for interpretation. In any case, the images of a music video, propelled by its music, are intended to stay with viewers, and because most music videos are under five minutes in length, those images are carefully chosen, with little digression from their basic sense. Their exoreferentiality may be focused almost entirely on the production of the artist's persona, such that we might be expected to say little beyond, "This is the best thing she"—Lady Gaga, Grace Jones, Rihanna, or whoever—"has done yet!" But this artist's persona is always implicated in broader cultural relations, within which fan responses find their meanings and chart their affective paths through the world. At their most effective, music videos elicit a deeply affective charge, a *frisson* or wave intended to carry a viewer somewhere, both over the satisfactory burst of duration that constitutes the video itself and well beyond it afterward. Much the same could be said of any videos that "go viral" on the Internet, whether they are "found" or "spontaneous" videos—as, for instance, the surveillance video of the Chinese girl run over by the truck, or the many videos one can find online of the massed movement of starling formations or of bizarre animal encounters—or carefully produced "documentary" videos, such as the 2008 viral video *Where the Hell Is Matt?*, which featured a man from Connecticut dancing awkwardly on location in forty-two different countries.

In his imprecisely titled essay "Twenty-Five Reasons Why It's All Over," Wheeler Winston Dixon provides twenty-four reasons why the cinema "as we knew it" is dead; then, for his twenty-fifth point, he concludes, "And yet, despite all this, the cinema will live forever." "The classics of the past," he writes, "will continue to haunt us, informing our collective consciousness of mid-to-late-twentieth-century culture." "Film 'as we know it' has always been dying and is always being reborn. What we are witnessing now is neither more nor less than the dawn of a new grammar, a new technological delivery and production system, with a new series of plots, tropes, iconic conventions, and stars." The cinema, however, "will always continue to build on, and carry forward, the past."[21] This is, of course, what Alfred North Whitehead argues about all forms of experience. All things, indeed, are always becoming, building on and carrying forward the past into new registers, new dimensions, new vectors of transmission on which future worlds are borne. Cinema, if we keep its definition loose enough to indicate the mediated transmission of any and all moving images, is with us to stay. Once it has established itself in the world, we can never unlearn it, since we now know that it has always been with us: as potential, as firstness, in the seething dynamism of interperceptual relationality, and over the last hundred and some years as a techno-material, social, and perceptual reality. A nuclear Armageddon might eliminate its expression for a while, but even that thought bears the irony that the only reason we can imagine it is because we have seen it already—in cinema.

If I can claim to have been moved by Lars von Trier's image, in *Melancholia*, of a massive blue planet closing in on the Earth and finally decimating it, this is to say that I have *moved along with* that image and have in some sense lived and experienced it. Having been so moved, and having given that image the power to transform me, I am no longer in the place where I began. This collision, or at least my response to it, has become a cognitive and affective virtuality for me, an imaginal reality, something I can feel for and about because I have practised this feeling while, and after, watching it. I have moved along a vector that has made that set of possibilities mine. This does not mean that such a planetary collision has become any more likely than it ever was. But it does mean that I am now more prepared to respond to it, were it to ever arise. This preparation is not *mere* imagination, as if what I have lived in my imagination is unreal. It is an exercise of *real* imagination, which means the development of a kind of muscle that poises me for an engaged responsiveness to a certain present or future possibility.

The cinematic is an exercise in such virtuality. Cinema is not unique in this: storytelling, literature, theatre, and performative arts in general harbour similar capacities. But cinema is distinctive in its fusion of visual and sound images in temporally sequenced forms, and these, for the most part, will continue in digital worlds. Our capacity for making sense of a quickening and hyper-modulating world remains a skill we can cultivate, both through a better ability to deal with speed and the loss of bearings—as perhaps comes more easily to those who have grown up with digital media—and through more traditional viewerly disciplines, such as the maintenance of self-reflexivity while watching, the appreciation of sounds and images with a connoisseurial delight for details, and the bringing of a broad palette of cultivated knowledge and memory to bear on the viewing situation. Being better *informed* viewers means being better able to take things away from the viewing.

Like Steven Shaviro, Jonathan Beller, Fredric Jameson, and other critical theorists, I have tried in this book to contextualize cinema in a larger set of societal developments, on the principle that a good viewer is one who is capable of cognitively mapping one's experience within the larger world of political-economic determinants. To their analytical predilections, I have injected an ecological sensibility that I believe must be central to the critical task today. Cinema is, after all, a product of a certain political ecology: an outcome of industrialization, in both its capitalist and state socialist forms. The changes that cinema is undergoing today are part of what some call post-industrialization, but what is more precisely the post-Fordist globalization of that same political ecology. Cinematic technologies are part and parcel of a world that has become faster, more mobile and fluid, and more tightly integrated—economically, politically, and culturally—even as its gaps and critical fissures have become intensified and globalized. Cinema will continue to help us *think and feel* these changes, and in its best forms it will do this in ways that help us shape their direction as well.

Cinema, as I have argued and as Nadia Bozak delineates in her recent book *The Cinematic Footprint: Lights, Camera, Natural Resources*, is a thoroughly ecological process.[22] It has always depended on a powerful combination of at least two forms of solar energy: the capture of reflected solar light itself, and the indirect products of that energy that have been stored and compounded over millennia in the form of fossil fuels and their photochemical derivatives. Cinema is a form of captured, organized, and released light–heat–energy–movement. If the universe is made up of a kind of moving–morphing image–substance–stuff, as we might today reconceive Bergson's notion of the image, then cinema is a vehicle for reorganizing that stuff. All life on this planet is the product of one or another permutation of the interaction between energy (light and heat) originating from the sun and the surface of the Earth that it strikes. The sundry permutations of that relationship—some of which are hinted at in films like Terrence Malick's *Tree of Life*, Jennifer Baichwal's *Manufactured Landscapes*, and the celebratory light experiments of Stan Brakhage—are the evolved permutations of a single, endlessly differentiating process. Cinema arose alongside the industrialization of material production—that is, alongside the unleashing of productive capacities that had been stored on or beneath the surface of this planet for millennia. Digitalization is simply the latest phase of the development of the bio-socio-technical apparatus that has undergirded industrialization. It builds on earlier phases, and in this sense today's and tomorrow's digital world cannot exist without the infrastructure of petrochemical industrial civilization. But tomorrow's world may, if the right decisions are made today, be able to develop the material, social, and perceptual infrastructure of a *post*-carbon, *post*-fossil-fuelled society.

Delineating what such a society may look like is a task for future volumes. It will, no doubt, include new geomorphisms, biomorphisms, anthropomorphisms, and (we can be sure) post-anthropomorphisms. I have outlined an ecophilosophy that assumes these to be always open and in process, and my hope is that the contours of their history spelled out here can help us think and feel our way toward new and more beautiful and satisfying forms. There will, in any case, be further cinematic developments to speak of, if there are any human developments to speak of at all. As older cinematic technologies and practices are subsumed within newly emergent ones, the forms and possibilities of expression open up and rearrange themselves. And as that occurs, we ourselves are opened up and rearranged. There is nothing to fear from this, as long as we remember that we are linked to the earthly and universal firstnesses that continue to generate the possibilities for arrangements of any kind: the causal secondnesses and the interpretive thirdnesses that arrange and disclose our worlds for us, to us, and through us.

For all its shifts, then, cinema will live on. The historical trajectory of moving sound-image works, viewed by audiences sometime after their creation, continues to pulse forward and to generate new shoots spreading into new times and spaces. In this, cinema is more like Darwin's ever-changing and ever-expanding bush, unpredictable in its emergent folds and outgrowths, than like any Social Darwinist's vision of a line of ascent culminating with us (whoever that "us" may be). Debates over the essence of cinema, and claims of its looming end, have appeared and reappeared continually since its origins, marking every significant technological cinematic development, from montage and sound to colour, widescreen, and portable cameras, to the proliferation of kindred media like television, video, and interactive digital formats.[23] While its centrality to our mediated world may fade into the undergrowth, cinema will continue as a world-constituting force that we travel with, or into (for periods of time), engaging ourselves cognitively and affectively with what it presents to us. And that experience will contribute to the reconstitution of our material, social, and perceptual ecologies and identities. If these are reconstituting themselves all the more quickly and forcefully, then perhaps the least we can say about cinema is that *it is movement*, and that when movement becomes as pervasive as it has become, the task for a philosophy of cinema also changes.

In place of the old philosophic task of making sense of a relatively stable world—or, at least, a world in which instability was produced against the background of a stable nature—we now have the task of helping ourselves *move with a moving world*, in the best, most ethically defensible, and most interesting ways possible. The world's motion is a forward motion, because that is the only motion that time allows—though cinema enables a motion back and forth and all around, as long as these, too, are always ever forward. And to the extent that moving images are an important site of opening within which the forward motion of the world can be engaged, both ethically and aesthetically—and not merely stilled or resisted—then the art of the moving image becomes a key point for our ethical and aesthetic practice as points of subjective agency within the process-relational unfolding of the universe.

One of the images I have pursued in this book is that of cinema as a *stalker* of the world. Vilém Flusser put it this way: "If one observes the movements of a human being in possession of a camera ... the impression given is of someone lying in wait. This is the ancient act of stalking which goes back to the paleolithic hunter in the tundra."[24] With my repeated reference to Tarkovsky's film *Stalker* I intended, in part, to suggest that the stalking is not all just one way, or at least not only in the direction Flusser intends. Tarkovsky's Stalker is himself, in many ways, the stalked. He is haunted by the Zone, by its ambiguous allure, its lore, its promise of possibilities for change and newness in the world. The Stalker's quest is no doubt a quest for redemption, but with its cinematic materialism (as Žižek called it) the redemption it points to is both a redemption of humanity, a redeemed anthropomorphosis, and a Kracauerian redemption of physical reality. Cinema's stalking of the world has created many worlds that stalk *us* if and when we allow them to, and since the "we" who subject ourselves to these cinema-worlds are changed by them, neither we nor cinema remain the same. Redemption is, in this sense, a mutual project for subjects-in-the-making in a shared and interactive, processual and biomorphic cosmos. We who open ourselves ecophilosophically to the best potentials of an ecophilosophical cinema will perhaps be those most *stalked* by the Earth and the cosmos. Such is an adequate task for an ecophilosophy of the cinema.

A process-relational understanding of cinema highlights the insistence that we live in a communicative world, a world of relations always in process between subjects-in-the-making and objects-given-to-that-making. For a subject to be made, there must be semiosis. The universe is brimming with the making of meaning; it is a biosemiotic cosmos. And among the meanings that are made for creatures like us are meanings of worldness, in which possibilities for future worlds are entertained, thought and felt, played and worked with, responded to and realized. Cinema is the making of worlds and the taking on of those worlds, in limited ways but in ways that allow us to change the shared worlds we create together. Its possibilities, as such, are endless.

APPENDIX
Doing Process-Relational Media Analysis

The process-relational model follows a film through three concurrent and parallel life cycles, or three *ecologies*: the material, the social, and the perceptual. The model can be pictured as in Figure A1.

In this model, the focus is on perceptual ecologies, because that is where film's main distinctiveness lies. The film experience—the experience of viewers watching and interpreting a film—is a key moment in film's impact on perceptual ecologies. It consists of the process of viewers entering into a film-world (which is anthropomorphic, biomorphic, and geomorphic) through encountering filmic firstness (sound-image spectacle), secondness (narrativity), and thirdness (exoreferentiality). The effects of the film experience continue after the viewing of a film as its images, sounds, feelings/affects, and meanings percolate into the lives and worlds of viewers.

FIGURE A1   The Process-Relational Model

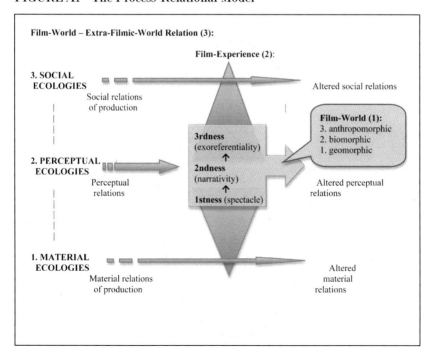

Questions that a process-relational analysis of films might ask include the following. (Note that the word "film" can be substituted with other terms, such as "television program," "video," "genre," "artwork," etc., as appropriate for one's analysis.)

1. The Film World

- **Geomorphism**: How does the film present the objectivity of the world and of things? How does it depict place, space, and territory (e.g., as stable or unstable, conflictual, negotiated, clearly belonging to one group or another)? How does it portray differences between the various kinds of space: between here(ness) and there(ness), home(ness) and away(ness), "our" world and "their"/other worlds?
- *Place and landscape*: How is non-human nature, including specific places and landscapes, portrayed? How does this correspond to what you know of these places and landscapes?
- *Relationship*: How is the relationship between people and the non-human landscape portrayed, and how is it differentiated among various social groups? (Recall the variations examined in Chapter 3: land as us; land as *for* us; land as *becoming* us; land as encounter/experience; land as other; etc.)

- **Biomorphism**: What sorts of relational processes are depicted in the film? How does the film depict aliveness as well as sensorial interactions (seeing, hearing, feeling, etc.) between different kinds of things?
- *Animals, wildlife, non-human agency*: How are non-human animals and life forms portrayed, and what, if any, differences are there in how the various forms of life shown in the film are portrayed?
- *Relationship*: How is the relationship between people and animals or other non-human life forms portrayed? What kinds of tensions (if any) arise at the boundaries between humans and other forms of agency? How are these tensions mediated or developed over the course of the film? For instance, are there boundary crossers, and how is their boundary crossing portrayed?

- **Anthropomorphism**: What sorts of human (or human-like) actors or agents people this film? Who are the main subjects or active agents in the film, and how is their subjectivity or agency expressed, enabled, and constrained? How are obstacles dealt with, problems solved, obligations met, changes produced, ideas conceived?
- *Cultural difference*: What capacities for action are portrayed, and how are they distributed among different actors? If there is a contrast between two radically dissimilar social groups, what, in the film's depiction, are the differences and similarities between them? (Recall the variations examined

in Chapter 4: "we're okay, they're okay"; "we're okay, they're not okay"; "they're okay, we're not okay"; "neither we nor they are okay.") How are these differences mediated or developed over the course of the film?

- *Power*: How are power relations and political agency represented? Are certain people/groups shown to be passive and others active, and, if so, is this presented in a critical light or does it appear natural, unquestioned, and unchangeable? What dilemmas or problems are the characters faced with, and are the underlying structural causes highlighted or are these left unquestioned or unaddressed?
- *Identities*: How are the following represented:
  - Gender and gender relations?
  - Race and race relations?
  - Socio-economic class?
  - Ethnicity and cultural identity?
  - Sexuality and sexual orientation?
  - Normalcy and deviance?
  - What, among humans, is represented as "natural" and/or "unnatural"?

2. The Film Experience

- **Firstness** (spectacle): What kinds of audiovisual elements and combinations present themselves in this film? How do they appear? What are the recurrent images, sounds, or image–sound combinations that repeat at key moments and "stay with you" the longest? What moments elicit strong affective responses, and how do they do that?
- *Mood and sensibility*: How do you feel while and after viewing the film? How do other viewers/audiences feel? What is it about the sounds, images, juxtapositions, rhythms, actions depicted, and so on, that generates these feelings? What "resonant images" does the film leave you with?
- *Genre*: Does the film clearly fall into a particular style or genre? How does it vary generic conventions so as to play off your expectations?

- **Secondness** (narrativity): How are viewers drawn into the story within the film-world?
- *Narrative form*: What kind of story is told? What happens, and to whom? How is the story told? What is the structure of the narrative—that is, how could its "skeleton" be portrayed? (A common narrative structure follows the form A–B–A₁: Equilibrium → Disruption by the appearance of an opposing force or problem → Search/quest addressing the conflict → Restoration of a previous or new equilibrium.) Is the narrative linear-singular, linear-multiple, network, non-linear, etc.?

- *Discursive structure*: What are the oppositions that structure the narrative—for example, how do basic dualisms (good/bad, male/female, white/black, rich/poor, cowboy/Indian, etc.) map onto each other—which "goes with" which? How do these unfold over the course of the film?
- *Identity*: Which characters, images, personae, do you identify, empathize with, and cheer for? Which ones do you feel a desire for or an aversion toward? How does this vary for other viewers? What subject positions are offered to the reader/viewer? What subject positions are not offered?

- **Thirdness** (exoreferentiality):
- *Socio-historical references*: What is this film about? What historical events are depicted or referred to, and how does their depiction compare with what you know about these events? Is the film commenting on current social phenomena? Which ones, and how?
- *Intertextual codes and discourses*: Does the film share a specific set of images, textual tropes, generic conventions, or socio-historical reference points with a certain set of other films (with a genre, type of film, etc.)? How, if at all, does it *vary* these tropes and conventions? Why do you think it does this? How is it similar/different in relation to other works by the same author(s), to similar images in different media, and so on?
- *Reception history*: How has the film been received, interpreted, used, and otherwise appropriated into people's lives? How has its reception changed over time, and how do these changes relate to social, political, or economic developments? Has the film been economically successful? Artistically successful? With whom has it been most popular, or unpopular? What has its appeal and resonance been for specific audiences (e.g., fan groups, youth subcultures, political movements)? How has it been used to shape subjectivities and identities?

- **Hyper-signaletic moments**: Which are the moments that crystallize the film's principal meanings most completely? How do they do that? Through what combinations of firstness, secondness, and thirdness?

3. The Film-World—Real-World Relation

- **Material ecologies**: What material and technological processes occurred to make this film possible? What direct and indirect impacts, including ecosystemic impacts, occurred as a result of its production, distribution, and consumption? Are there any significant differences between the production of this film and the production of most other films?

- **Social ecologies**: What are the significant social, cultural, and/or political-economic contexts in which the film was produced? Who produced it, how was it produced, and for whom or to what end?

  What socio-structural constraints were placed on the film's production? In other words, what were the economic determinants of production (money, technology, socially organized forms of human labour)? And what was the production context (e.g., the Hollywood film industry, the international film festival circuit, the capitalist "free market," a national or culturally specific niche market)? How have these factors shaped or constrained the message conveyed within the object? For example, how does the narrative reflect broader ideological and political-economic realities?

- *Audience*: Who are the intended audiences, and what seems to be assumed about them and their expectations?

  How has the film been marketed, distributed, and exhibited? Is it part of a larger industry, genre, or product package? How is it constrained and channelled by its distribution and marketing arrangements? How, if in any way, does the film alter or challenge such relations?

- **Perceptual ecologies**: What constraints and possibilities are inherent in the particular style, genre, or type of film, and how does the film vary, work within, or challenge those constraints? What are its operative, generic (to do with genre), formal, and/or technical codes, and how does the film work with them? These techniques and codes may include basic narrative styles or genre forms (e.g., the western, the musical, the gangster comedy, the science fiction film), acting styles, camerawork (e.g., colour versus black-and-white, camera positioning and movement, composition styles, lighting techniques), *mise en scène* (composition of elements within the frame), montage (editing), sound and music, and so on.

- *Context*: In what contexts is the film generally shown, and how does it fit into those contexts? Are there apparent contradictions between its overt message and these contexts (e.g., between a magazine article and the ads surrounding it, between a TV program and the commercials that disrupt it)? How do audiences work out these contradictions?

  And see the questions above under "The Film World" and "The Film Experience."

NOTES

Notes to Preface

1   Note that I have reversed the second and third Peircian terms here, since it is the life-world that is the existential, dynamic "secondness" of a film-world, while the subject-world is that which emerges as meaningful subjectivity at the end of the film's meaning-making process. The reasons for this shift will become clear as these categories are developed in the book.

2   Gilles Deleuze, *Cinema 2: The Time-Image*, trans. H. Tomlinson and R. Galeta (Minneapolis: University of Minnesota Press, 2007), 172.

3   Siegfried Kracauer, *Theory of Film: The Redemption of Physical Reality* (New Brunswick, NJ: Princeton University Press, 1997).

Notes to Chapter 1

1   Francesco Casetti, *Eye of the Century: Film, Experience, Modernity,* tr. E. Larkin (Columbia Unviersity Press, 2008, orig. 2005), 192–93.

2   Raúl Ruiz, *Poetics of Cinema 1: Miscellanies*, tr. B. Holmes (Paris: Éditions Dis Voir, 1995), 114.

3   Ron Burnett, *How Images Think* (Cambridge: MIT Press, 2005), xxii.

4   Heidegger's argument is made in "The Age of the World Picture," in *The Question Concerning Technology*, trans. and ed. William Lovitt (New York: Harper and Row, 1977). On the origins of single-point perspective, see Erwin Panofsky, *Perspective as Symbolic Form* (Cambridge, MA: MIT Press, 1991); and Hubert Damisch, *The Origin of Perspective,* trans. John Goodman (Cambridge, MA: MIT Press, 1994). On the hegemony of the visual within modernity, see Martin Jay, "Scopic Regimes of Modernity," in *Modernity and Identity,* ed. Scott Lash and Jonathan Friedman (Oxford: Blackwell, 1992); Jay, *Downcast Eyes: The Denigration of Vision in Twentieth-Century French Thought* (Berkeley: University of California Press, 1993); David Michael Levin, ed., *Modernity and the Hegemony of Vision* (Berkeley: University of California Press, 1993); and Jonathan Crary, *On Vision and Modernity: Techniques of the Observer in the Nineteenth Century* (Cambridge, MA: MIT Press, 1992). The general argument that modern society, since the print revolution, has been a visually dominated culture was articulated with particular force by Marshall McLuhan and Walter Ong; see McLuhan's *The Gutenberg Galaxy: The Making of Typographic Man* (Toronto: University of Toronto Press, 1962) and *Understanding*

Media: The Extensions of Man (Cambridge, MA: MIT Press, 1994[1964]); and Ong's *Orality and Literacy: The Technologizing of the World* (London: Routledge, 1982). Their work has more recently been subjected to substantial critique; see Mark M. Smith, *Sensing the Past: Seeing, Hearing, Smelling, Tasting, and Touching in History* (Berkeley: University of California Press, 2007). On the magisterial gaze, see Albert Boime, *The Magisterial Gaze: Manifest Destiny and American Landscape Painting, c. 1830–1865* (Washington: Smithsonian Institution Scholarly Press, 1991). Laura Mulvey's classic 1975 essay of feminist cinema critique, "Visual Pleasure and Narrative Cinema," can be found, alongside responses to her critics, in Mulvey, *Visual and Other Pleasures* (London: Macmillan, 1989).

5   W.J.T. Mitchell, *What Do Pictures Want? The Lives and Loves of Images* (Chicago: University of Chicago Press, 2005); James Elkins, *The Object Stares Back: On the Nature of Seeing* (New York: Simon and Schuster, 1996); *idem, Pictures and Tears: A History of People Who Have Cried in Front of Paintings* (New York: Routledge, 2001); Bruno Latour and Peter Weibel, eds., *Iconoclash: Beyond the Image Wars in Science, Religion, and Art* (Cambridge, MA: MIT Press, 2002). The work of theorists such as Henri Bergson, Gilles Deleuze, Maurice Merleau-Ponty, Alfonso Lingis, William Connolly, Jane Bennett, Brian Massumi, Michael Taussig, Eve Sedgwick, and Gillian Rose points in various ways to this dimension of affective relationality between the seer and the seen. Psychoanalytic theorists of film have also highlighted the ways in which film "interpellates" us into its own ideologically organized subject positions; we are, in this way, rendered passive in the face of film's activity on us. Critical analysis of advertising has often pointed to the power of images to manufacture desires; see, for example, John Berger, *Ways of Seeing* (London: Penguin, 1972); and Sut Jhally, *The Codes of Advertising: Fetishism and the Political Economy of Meaning in the Consumer Society* (New York: Routledge, 1990, 2d ed.). Some theorists argue that digital culture is responsible for our sense of being overwhelmed and inundated by "liquid images"; see, for example, Luciana Parinia and Tiziana Terranova, "A Matter of Affect: Digital Images and the Cybernetic Re-Wiring of Vision," *Parallax* 7, no. 4 (2001): 122–27.

6   Guy Debord, *The Society of the Spectacle,* trans. Ken Knabb (Detroit: Black and Red, 1973); Jean Baudrillard, *Simulation and Simulacra,* trans. Sheila Faria Glaser (Ann Arbor: University of Michigan Press, 1994); Jonathan Beller, *The Cinematic Mode of Production: Attention Economy and the Society of the Spectacle* (Hanover: University Press of New England, 2006).

7   "Media ecology" has become a popular rubric for considering some of the interrelations that I will be examining in this book. Matthew Fuller, in *Media Ecologies: Materialist Energies in Art and Technoculture* (Cambridge, MA: MIT Press, 2005), identifies at least three long-applied usages of the term, not one of which quite captures what I'm intending here. Fuller's own usage, which draws on Félix Guattari and Gregory Bateson (among others), does at times come quite close to covering the full range I will be discussing (though my focus on cinema is more limited than his, which is on the media in general). I particularly like his decision to use the word "ecology" for its expressive capacity for indicating "the massive and dynamic interrelation of processes and objects, beings and things, patterns and matter" (2).

8   While I use the terms "cinema" and "film" more or less interchangeably in this book, I understand "cinema," with its Greek roots (*kinema, kinein, kinesis,* meaning "movement" or "motion"), to be the broader category, equivalent to "moving image media" and inclusive of traditional celluloid-based photographic cinema, animated cinema, electronic cinema (television), and digital cinema. Film, on the other hand, literally suggests the celluloid medium. Those cinema/media scholars who speak today of the "end of cinema" tend to define it less broadly than I do. David Norman Rodowick, for instance, in *The Virtual Life of Film* (Cambridge, MA: Harvard University Press, 2007), writes: "By 'cinema' I mean the projection of a photographically recorded filmstrip in a theatrical setting" (26). I examine debates about cinema's "end" in this book's afterword.

9   David Bordwell, *Narration in the Fiction Film* (Madison: University of Wisconsin Press, 1985), 110; *idem,* "Convention, Construction, and Cinematic Vision," in *Post-Theory: Reconstructing Film Studies,* ed. David Bordwell and Noel Carroll (Madison: University of Wisconsin Press, 1996), 87–107.

10 Giorgio Agamben, *The Open: Man and Animal,* trans. Kevin Attell (Stanford: Stanford University Press, 2004).

11 The mystical traditions that are closest to the perspective of this book are those of Mahayana Buddhism, notably the Chan and Zen traditions of China and Japan and the Dzogchen and Vajrayana traditions of Tibet. The resonance with these and others will not be explored much in this book, though I will occasionally refer to Buddhist perspectives. They will be explored in a forthcoming volume I am writing on process-relational philosophical themes.

12 Steven Dillon, *The Solaris Effect: Art and Artifice in Contemporary American Film* (Austin: University of Texas Press, 2006).

13 Dillon, *The Solaris Effect:* "There is photographic" (8); "copy, a reproduction" (10); "built out of desire" (16).

14 Slavoj Žižek, "The Thing from Inner Space," in *Sexuation,* ed. Renata Salecl (Durham, NC: Duke University Press, 2000), 248–50. This essay also appears in *Mainview,* September 1999, http://www.lacan.com/zizekthing.htm.

15 James Quandt, "The Poetry of Apocalypse," *Cinematheque Ontario,* http://www.ucalgary.ca/~tstronds/nostalghia.com/TheTopics/Quandt_Essay.html.

16 Robert Bird, *Andrei Tarkovsky: Elements of Cinema* (London: Reaktion Books, 2008), 163.

17 For instance, on the way the soundtrack in *Stalker* renders "reality" ambiguous, see Stefan Smith, "The Edge of Perception: Sound in Tarkovsky's *Stalker," The Soundtrack* 1, no. 1 (2007): 41–52.

18 Bird, *Andrei Tarkovsky,* 168. Kovacs and Szilagyi are cited in Vida Johnson and Graham Petrie's *The Films of Andrei Tarkovsky: A Visual Fugue* (Bloomington: Indiana University Press, 1994), 142–43.

19 Jim Rossignol, "Worlds from the Zone," *The Escapist,* 22 Ma 207 http://www.escapistmagazine.com/articles/view/issues/issue_98/544-Worlds-from-The-Zone; GSC Game World, "Stalker: Clear Sky," 2009, http://cs.stalker-game.com.

20 Jane I. Dawson, *Eco-Nationalism: Anti-Nuclear Activism and National Identity in Russia, Lithuania, and Ukraine* (Durham, NC: Duke University Press, 1996).

21   Bird, among others, suggests that Tarkovsky may have invented the problem as a pretext for correcting what he thought were the film's defects; see Bird, *Andrei Tarkovsky,*.

22   The deaths of crew members have led to some speculation, including inevitable (for their time) theories of poisoning by the KGB. The film's sound designer, Vladimir Sharun, is among those convinced that the chemical plant was to blame. See Stas Tyrkin, "In *Stalker* Tarkovsky foretold Chernobyl," *Komsomolskaya Pravda*, 23 March 2001, available at Nostalghia.com, http://people.ucalgary.ca/~tstronds/nostalghia.com/TheTopics/Stalker/sharun.html.

23   For a related theorization, see Daniel Yacavone, "Towards a Theory of Film Worlds," *Film-Philosophy* 12, no. 2 (2008): 83–108; and Christopher S. Yates, "A Phenomenological Aesthetic of Cinematic 'Worlds,'" *Contemporary Aesthetics* 4 (2006), http://www.contempaesthetics.org/newvolume/pages/article.php?articleID=394.

24   John Mullarkey, *Refractions of Reality: Philosophy and the Moving Image* (Basingstoke: Palgrave Macmillan, 2009), xv.

25   Only in the final stages of writing did I come across Laura Marks's reworking of Deleuzian and Peircian themes to make this very same point. Drawing on a Bergsonian notion of the image (which I explicate in Chapter 2), she refers to "the Earth" as "that from which all images emerge and to which they all return." Images, she writes, come from the larger "universe of images," "infinitely vaster than the small amounts of information and images" we draw from it, and "virtual to their actual." "The universe of images is amorphous, unarticulated and imperceptible as such," leaving no trace "unless they are 'captured' as information or image. The universe of images contains all possible images in a virtual state, and certain images arise from it, becoming actual." Laura Marks, "Information, Secrets, and Enigmas: An Enfolding-Unfolding Aesthetics for Cinema," *Screen* 50, no. 1 (2009): 86–98 at 94 and 88.

Notes to Chapter 2

1   Alfred North Whitehead, *Adventures of Ideas* (New York: Free Press, 1967, orig. 1933), 197.

2   Edgar Morin, *Cinema, or the Imaginary Man,* Minneapolis: University of Minnesota Press, 2005 (1956), 156.

3   Brian Massumi, *Semblance and Event: Activist Philosophy and the Occurrent Arts* (Cambridge: MIT Press, 2011), 28.

4   Andrew Ross, *The Chicago Gangster Theory of Life: Nature's Debt to Society* (London: Verso, 1994), 171.

5   Ibid., 172.

6   Félix Guattari, *The Three Ecologies,* trans. Ian Pindar and Paul Sutton (London: Athlone Press, 2000).

7   This use of the term "mental" is intended also to resonate with the notion of a "mental environment," as promoted by "culture jammers" such as the Vancouver-based *Adbusters* magazine, which labels itself the "Journal of the Mental Environment."

8   Bruno Latour, *We Have Never Been Modern,* trans. Catherine Porter (Cambridge, MA: Harvard University Press, 1993).

9   Guattari, *The Three Ecologies.* On Bateson, see his *Steps to an Ecology of Mind* (Chicago: University of Chicago Press, 1972) and *Mind and Nature: A Necessary Unity* (New York: E.P. Dutton, 1979); and Peter Harries Jones, *A Recursive Vision: Ecological Understanding and Gregory Bateson* (Toronto: University of Toronto Press, 1995). On the Peirce–Bateson connection, see Jesper Hoffmeyer, ed., *A Legacy for Living Systems: Gregory Bateson as Precursor to Biosemiotics* (Springer Science, 2008), especially the chapter by Søren Brier, "Bateson and Peirce on the Pattern That Connects and the Sacred," 227–55.

10   My use of the term "intersubjective" falls into a long tradition associated with phenomenological philosophy and the phenomenological social sciences. "Interobjective" is used less frequently, though one finds it used in more or less the same way I am using it in works of actor–network theory and (more commonly) in the "integral theory" of Ken Wilber and his followers. See, for instance, Sean Esbjörn-Hargens and Michael E. Zimmerman, eds., *Integral Ecology: Uniting Multiple Perspectives on the Natural World* (Boston: Shambhala/Integral Books, 2009).

11   Maurice Merleau-Ponty, *The Visible and the Invisible* (Evanston: Northwestern University Press, 1968). On the relationship between Merleau-Ponty's late ontology and Whiteheadian process philosophy, see William S. Hamrick and Jan van der Veken, *Nature and Logos: A Whiteheadian Key to Merleau-Ponty's Fundamental Thought* (Albany: SUNY Press, 2011).

12   Jane Bennett and William Connolly, "Contesting Nature/Culture: The Creative Character of Thinking," *Journal of Nietzche Studies* 24 (2002): 148–63 at 159–60. On the "affective turn" in social theory, see Teresa Brennan, *The Transmission of Affect* (Ithaca: Cornell University Press, 2004); Patricia Clough with Jean Halley, eds., *The Affective Turn: Theorizing the Social* (Durham: Duke University Press, 2007); Patricia Clough, "The Affective Turn: Political Economy, Biomedia, and Bodies," *Theory, Culture, Society* 25, no. 1 (2008): 1–22; William Connolly, *Neuropolitics: Thinking, Culture, Speed* (Minneapolis: University of Minnesota Press, 2002); Brian Massumi, *Parables for the Virtual: Movement, Affect, Sensation* (Durham: Duke University Press, 2002); Nigel Thrift, *Non-Representational Theory: Space, Politics, Affect* (London: Routledge, 2008); and Melissa Gregg and Gregory Seigworth, *The Affect Theory Reader* (Durham: Duke University Press, 2010).

13   There are points of connection between these approaches, especially Cubitt's and my own, and the "ecological" film theory of Joseph Anderson and Barbara Fisher Anderson; see J.D. Anderson, *The Reality of Illusion: An Ecological Approach to Cognitive Film Theory* (Carbondale: Southern Illinois University Press, 1996); and Anderson and Anderson, *Moving Image Theory: Ecological Considerations* (Carbondale: Southern Illinois University Press, 2007). But the latter is grounded in a more restrictive understanding of perception and cognition than Cubitt's and mine. Based in James Gibson's theory of direct perception, the Andersons' work is oriented toward identifying ways in which film viewing is undergirded by the reciprocal relationship between a perceiver and her immediate environment. The

experience of film viewing, however, is both densely cultural and highly artificial, and a thoroughly ecological interpretation of film should recognize the many layers of relationship between viewers, the film medium (as it has historically developed), the culture within which film objects exist as viewable objects, and the many "realities" being referred to in the worlds portrayed by film. Many useful insights have emerged from cognitive film studies more generally, some of which I will refer to in this book. Historically, much cognitive work has, for my purposes, overemphasized mental representations and puzzle solving at the expense of the emotional and affective dimensions of film spectatorship. This has, thankfully, been changing in recent years; see, for example, Greg Smith, *Film Structure and the Emotion System* (New York: Cambridge University Press, 2003); Carl Plantinga and Greg Smith, *Passionate Views: Film, Cognition, and Emotion* (Baltimore: Johns Hopkins University Press, 1999); and Torben Grodal, *Embodied Visions: Evolution, Emotion, Culture, and Film* (New York: Oxford University Press, 2009). Within cognitive science more generally, the subtradition with which my work bears the strongest relationship is the "enactive cognitivism" of Varela, Thompson, Rosch, and others, and the so-called "4E" (embodied, embedded, extended, enactive cognition) tradition that has grown from it. See Francesco Varela, Evan Thompson, and Eleanor Rosch, *The Embodied Mind: Cognitive Science and Human Experience* (Cambridge, MA: MIT Press, 1992); and *Phenomenology and the Cognitive Sciences* 9, no. 4 (2010), Special Issue on 4E Cognition. According to these theorists, it is the interaction or "structural coupling" of agents and their environments that brings forth the "worlds" in which we live. Even the latter form of cognitivism can be broadened with a more flexible account of agency and interaction, as suggested, for instance, by the post-Deleuzian and neo-Whiteheadian work of current process-relational thinkers; see, for example, John Protevi, *Political Affect: Connecting the Social and the Somatic* (Minneapolis: University of Minnesota Press, 2009).

14   Henri Bergson, *Matter and Memory*, trans. Nancy Margaret Paul and W. Scott Palmer (New York: Zone Books, 1991).

15   Jonathan Beller, *The Cinematic Mode of Production: Attention Economy and the Society of the Spectacle* (Hanover, NH: University Press of New England, 2006).

16   On the plurality of production contexts, see, for instance, Emanuel Levy, *Cinema of Outsiders: The Rise of American Independent Film* (New York: NYU Press, 1999); Peter Biskind, *Down and Dirty Pictures: Miramax, Sundance, and the Rise of Independent Film* (New York: Simon and Schuster, 2004); and Anne Jäckel, *European Film Industries* (London: British Film Institute, 2003). And witness the rise to international prominence of such non-Hollywood international co-productions as *Slumdog Millionnaire*, with its sweep of the Academy Awards in 2009.

17   Stuart Hall, "Encoding/Decoding," in *Culture, Media, Language: Working Papers in Cultural Studies, 1972–79.* ed. Centre for Contemporary Cultural Studies (London: Hutchinson, 1980), 128–38 at 136.

18   Ecocriticism is the school of critical cultural theory rooted in environmental and ecological currents of thought. If the main lessons of environmentalism are, to put it in its most pithy and often-heard phrases, that "everything is connected to everything else" and that "everything comes from somewhere and goes

somewhere," then this interest in the "metabolism" by which human activities are intertwined with nature finds a natural ally in Marxism's interest in modes of production. For a version of this argument, see Lance Newman, "Marxism and Environment," *ISLE* 9, no. 2 (2002): 1–25.

19 My article "Green Film Criticism and Its Futures" had provided a summary of ecocritical approaches to film as of 2007. See "Green Film Criticism and Its Futures," *Interdisciplinary Studies in Literature and Environment* 15, no. 2 (2008): 1–28. Since then, the number of ecocritical film (or "ecomedia studies") texts has grown exponentially. Among the best in the genre are David Ingram, *Green Screen: Environmentalism and Hollywood Cinema* (Exeter: University of Exeter Press, 2004); Pat Brereton, *Hollywood Utopia: Ecology in Contemporary American Cinema* (Bristol: Intellect Books, 2005); Sean Cubitt, *EcoMedia* (Amsterdam: Rodopi, 2005); Joe Heumann and Robin Murray, *Ecology and Popular Film: Cinema on the Edge* (New York: SUNY Press, 2008); idem, *That's All, Folks? Ecocritical Readings of America's Animated Futures* (Lincoln: University of Nebraska Press, 2011); idem, *Gunfight at the Eco-Corral: Western Cinema and the Environment* (Norman: University of Oklahoma Press, 2012); Nadia Bozak, *The Cinematic Footprint: Lights, Camera, Natural Resources* (New Brunswick, NJ: Rutgers University Press, 2012); and various anthologies such as Deborah Carmichael, ed., *The Landscape of Hollywood Westerns* (Salt Lake City: University of Utah Press, 2006); Paula Willoquet, ed., *Framing the World: Explorations in Ecocriticism and Film* (Charlottesville: University of Virginia Press, 2010); and Sean Cubitt, Salma Monani, and Steven Rust, eds., *Ecocinema Theory and Practice* (London: Routledge, 2012).

20 Cited in Ingram, *Green Screen,* 21.

21 Ibid., 124.

22 See Melissa Felder and Associates, *Green Practices Manual: Environmental Options for the Film-Based Industries: Expanded 2009 Guide* (Toronto: Green Screen Toronto and Project Partners, 2009), available from http://www.planetinfocus.org/green-screen -publications, accessed December 2011; and UCLA Institute of the Environment, *Sustainability in the Motion Picture Industry* (Sacramento: California Integrated Waste Management Board, 2006). Bozak's *The Cinematic Fooprint* is the first book I have seen that assesses a wide range of films from a theoretically sophisticated material-ecological perspective. The book came out too late for me to incorporate many of its insights into this book. For a similarly eco-materialist perspective on media in general, see Richard Maxwell and Toby Miller's *The Greening of Media* (New York: Oxford University Press, 2012).

23 See Chapter 1 of Bozak, *The Cinematic Footprint,* for an insightful discussion of the movement toward "carbon neutrality" in filmmaking.

24 Scott MacDonald, *The Garden in the Machine: A Field Guide to Films About Place* (Berkeley: University of California Press, 1002), xxiv. See also Paolo Cherchi Usai, *The Death of Cinema: History, Cultural Memory, and the Digital Dark Age* (London: British Film Institute, 2001).

25 Dudley Andrew, "An Atlas of World Cinema," in *Remapping World Cinema: Identity, Culture, and Politics in Film,* ed. Stephanie Dennison and Song Hwee Lim (London: Wallflower Press, 2006), 19–29. While it is a little dated now, Robert Stam and

Ella Shohat's *Unthinking Eurocentrism: Multiculturalism and the Media* (London: Routledge, 1994) remains, to my mind, the best single overview of the global "social ecology" of cinema production, consumption, and representation.

26   Cubitt, *EcoMedia*, 118, 145.

27   Other philosophers who could be mentioned here include Gabriel Tarde, Wilmon Sheldon, Wilfrid Sellars, Cornelius Castoriadis, Michel Serres, Richard Neville, Robert Corrington, John Deely, Manuel DeLanda, John Protevi, Freya Mathews, and Karen Barad; the Japanese "Kyoto School," including Nishida Kitaro and Keiji Nishitani; a wide range of Western and Near Eastern artists, writers, and mystics, such as Jelaluddin Rumi; many of the European Romantics and American Transcendentalists (Goethe, Coleridge, Emerson, Muir); and a variety of African and indigenous philosophies around the world. Process-relational views are related to certain forms of panpsychism; see David Skrbina, *Panpsychism in the West* (Cambridge, MA: MIT Press, 2005). They are also deeply influential in recent "post-constructivist" and "non-representational" scholarship in the social and cognitive sciences, including actor–network theory (Bruno Latour, Michel Callon, John Law), enactive cognitivism (Francesco Varela, Evan Thompson), developmental biology (Susan Oyama), ethology and biosemiotics (Jakob von Uexküll, Thomas Sebeok, Jesper Hoffmeyer), relational and non-representational geography (David Harvey, Doreen Massey, Nigel Thrift, Sarah Whatmore, Steve Hinchliffe), and the speculations of theoretical physicists and biologists such as David Bohm, Ilya Prigogine, and Stuart Kauffman.

28   For general accounts of process-relational themes, see Nicholas Rescher, *Process Metaphysics: An Introduction to Process Philosophy* (Albany: SUNY Press, 1996); Nicholas Rescher, *Process Philosophy: A Survey of Basic Issues* (Pittsburgh: University of Pittsburgh Press, 2000); Douglas Browning and William T. Myers, *Philosophers of Process* (New York: Fordham University Press, 1998); and David Ray Griffin, *Founders of Constructive Postmodern Philosophy: Peirce, James, Bergson, Whitehead, and Hartshorne* (Albany: SUNY Press, 1993). For examples of the evolving dialogue among the different positions within process-relational theory, see Keith Robinson, ed., *Deleuze, Whitehead, Bergson: Rhizomatic Connections* (Basingstoke: Palgrave Macmillan, 2008); Catherine Keller and Anne Daniell, eds., *Process and Difference: Between Cosmological and Poststructuralist Postmodernisms* (Albany: SUNY Press, 2002); Steven Shaviro, *Without Criteria: Kant, Whitehead, Deleuze, and Aesthetics* (Cambridge, MA: MIT Press, 2009); Anne Fairchild Pomeroy, *Marx and Whitehead: Process, Dialectics, and the Critique of Capitalism* (Albany: SUNY Press, 2004); Michel Weber, ed., *After Whitehead: Rescher on Process Metaphysics* (Frankfurt: Ontos, 2004); Roland Faber and Andrea M. Stephenson, eds., *Secrets of Becoming: Negotiating Whitehead, Deleuze, and Butler* (New York: Fordham University Press, 2011); Isabelle Stengers, *Thinking with Whitehead: A Free and Wild Creation of Concepts* (Cambridge, MA: Harvard University Press, 2011); and William Connolly, *A World of Becoming* (Durham: Duke University Press, 2011). Comparative studies of process philosophy and Buddhism include Steve Odin, *Process Metaphysics and Hua-yen Buddhism: A Critical Study of Cumulative Penetration vs. Interpenetration* (Albany: SUNY Press, 1984); and Peter P. Kakol, *Emptiness and Becoming: Integrating*

Madhyamika Buddhism and Process Philosophy (*Emerging Perceptions in Buddhist Studies,* vol. 22; Delhi: D.K. Printworld, 2009).

29   Brier, "Bateson and Peirce on the Pattern That Connects and the Sacred," 239.

30   Whitehead's metaphysical system is the one most commonly referred to as "process-relational." See his magnum opus, *Process and Reality: Corrected Edition,* ed. David Ray Griffin and Donald W. Sherburne (New York: Free Press, [1933]1978), as well as the later *Adventures of Ideas* (New York: Free Press, [1933]1967), esp. Part III; and *Modes of Thought* (New York: Free Press, [1928]1938). For a useful, if rather simplified, introduction to his thought, see C. Robert Mesle, *Process-Relational Philosophy: An Introduction to Alfred North Whitehead* (West Conshohocken: Templeton Foundation Press, 2008). For more detailed exegeses, see Michel Weber, *Whitehead's Pancreativism: The Basics* (Rutgers: Trasaction Books, 2006); and Isabelle Stengers, *Thinking with Whitehead: A Free and Wild Creation of Concepts* (Cambridge, MA: Harvard University Press, 2011).

31   At times Whitehead suggests that subjects and objects are co-arising, co-implicated, and simultaneously emergent. At other times, however, he speaks of a "vector relation," an "object-to-subject structure of human experience" (see "Objects and Subjects," in *Adventures of Ideas,* 144), such that objects *precede* the subject, which constitutes itself in response to the objectivity of what precedes it: "Each occasion has its physical inheritance and its mental reaction which drives it on to its self-completion" (146). This tension can be seen as part and parcel of the same process: once a prehension is satisfied, it becomes an object for the next prehension. At the same time, a prehension responds not only to its *own* prior moment (to the extent that there is continuity), but also to other moments in its immediate environment. In principle, however, one could also say that previous subjectivities give rise to (what become) objectivities. To simplify matters, I will speak of subjectivity and objectivity as co-arising. See also Michael Halewood, "A.N. Whitehead, Information, and Social Theory," *Theory, Culture, Society* 22, no. 6 (2005): 73–94 at 75.

32   The "wilfull acts" of an amoeba are described in Lynn Margulis and Dorian Sagan, *What Is Life?* (London: Weidenfeld and Nicolson, 1995), 184.

33   Whether a particular object—say, a rock, a thought, an air bubble, a sentence, or a nation—is "real" or nor will depend on whether it involves this active becoming, this "taking account"—which may not be evident to one who is outside that thing. We see other things as objects of our own concrescent becoming. But this is not to say that what is an "object" for us may not be either a subject for itself or, perhaps more likely, part of some larger "real" entity, or else made up of smaller "real" entities.

34   Karen Barad, *Meeting the Universe Halfway: Quantum Physics and the Entanglement of Matter and Meaning* (Durham, NC: Duke University Press, 2007).

35   Whitehead, "Objects and Subjects," in *Adventures of Ideas,* 131, 130.

36   Peirce, "Man's Glassy Essence," *The Monist* 3 (1892): 1–22 at 21. The differences between Whiteheadian and Peircian metaphysics, while significant, are beyond the scope of this book. For comparative insights, see the respective chapters on the two philosophers in Charles Hartshorne, *Creativity in American Philosophy*

(Albany: SUNY Press, 1984); Sandra Rosenthal, "Contemporary Process Metaphysics and Diverse Intuitions of Time: Can the Gab Be Bridged?," *Journal of Speculative Philosophy* 12, no. 4 (1998): 271–88; Robert C. Neville, "Whitehead and Pragmatism," in *Whitehead's Philosophy: Points of Connection*, ed. Janusz A. Polanowski and Donald W. Sherburne (Albany: SUNY Press, 2004), 19–39; and the writings of Robert S. Corrington. I have written about the differences between Peirce, Whitehead, and Hartshorne on my blog, *Immanence* (see http://blog .uvm.edu/aivakhiv/2010/06/09/peirce-whitehead-hartshorne-process-relational -ontology), and will be expanding on this in a forthcoming book.

37   See Edward S. Reed, *Encountering the World: Toward an Ecological Psychology* (New York: Oxford University Press, 1996).

38   See especially Isabelle Stengers, *Cosmopolitics I,* trans. R. Bononno (Minneapolis: University of Minnesota Press, 2010); and *idem, Cosmopolitics II*, trans. R. Bononno (Minneapolis: University of Minnesota Press).

39   In a sense, Whitehead's dyad of emergent subjectivity and encountered objectivity can be taken as the actual occasion described "from the inside," while Peirce's triad of representamen–object–interpretant is the same moment described "from the outside," with an emphasis on its connection or grounding within relations that remain outside the perceptual dyad. Both Peirce and Whitehead eliminate any permanent distinction between subjects and objects, or mind and matter, refocusing instead on the *evental process* of actual occasions (Whitehead) and signs (Peirce). Every actual occasion is a sign relation—that is, an active, feeling-based prehension of something that is rooted—iconically, indexically, symbolically, or through some combination of these—beyond the immediately perceivable situation.

40   An accessible introduction to biosemiotics is Jesper Hoffmeyer, *Signs of Meaning in the Universe,* trans. Barbara Haveland (Bloomington: Indiana University Press, 1996). Literary scholar Wendy Wheeler's *The Whole Creature: Complexity, Biosemiotics, and the Evolution of Culture* (London: Laurence and Wishart, 2006) ambitiously relates the field both to cultural studies and to the ecological problematic.

41   This is a complicated point that I will not be able to explore in depth here. Peircians generally emphasize the triadicity of things, whereas other processual philosophers do not. Hartshorne, who has gone perhaps as far as any philosopher in synthesizing Peircian and Whiteheadian approaches, collapses the triad into an active dyad that continually unfolds between "relatives" and "absolutes," such that reality is "a cumulative process of 'inclusive transcendence' whereby relatives become absolutes sublated within more inclusive relatives (e.g. subjects become objects of subsequent subjects)"; see Peter Kakol, *Emptiness and Becoming: Integrating Madhyamika Buddhism and Process Philosophy* (Delhi: D.K. Printworld, 2009), 55. To my mind, this also collapses the distinction between Peirce's firstness, with its relationship to qualities that are *virtually* present but not *actual* in the unfolding structure of the universe, and thirdness, with its sense of a universe in which habituation and generalization grow and extend, even as they are continually being multiplied and disrupted by chance (emanating from firstness) and by the active agency of semiotic beings. Articulating the metaphysical stakes of this philosophical divergence would take us beyond what is needed for my reading of cinema.

42   Sean Cubitt, *The Cinema Effect* (Cambridge: MIT Press, 2005), 5–6.

43   Alexander Kluge, cited in Lucia Nagib, "Towards a Postive Definition of World Cinema," in *Remapping World Cinema: Identity, Culture, and Politics in Film*, ed. Stephanie Dennison and Song Hwee Lim (London: Wallflower Press, 2006), 30–37 at 34.

44   Wendy Wheeler, "Postscript on Biosemiotics: Reading Beyond Words—and Ecocriticism," *New Formations* 64 (2008): 137–54 at 144. There is debate among Peirce scholars over whether or not semiosis is supposed to encompass everything, or what, if anything, eludes it. In other words, are there objects that do not enter into semiosis, and how would we know about them?

45   Stanley Cavell, *The World Viewed: Reflections on the Ontology of Film*, enlarged ed. (Cambridge, MA: Harvard University Press, 1979), xvi.

46   See, for instance, Peter Wollen, *Signs and Meanings in the Cinema*, 3rd ed. (Bloomington: Indiana University Press, 1972); Kaja Silverman, *The Subject of Semiotics* (New York: Oxford University Press, 1983); Teresa De Lauretis, *Alice Doesn't: Feminism, Semiotics, Cinema* (Bloomington: Indiana University Press, 1984); and Laura Marks, *Touch: Sensuous Theory and Multisensory Media* (Minneapolis: University of Minnesota Press, 2002).

47   floyd merrell, *Peirce, Signs, and Meaning* (Toronto: University of Toronto Press, 1997), xi.

48   Martin Schwab, "Escape from the Image: Deleuze's Image-Ontology," in *The Brain Is the Screen: Deleuze and the Philosophy of Cinema*, ed. Gregory Flaxman (Minneapolis: University of Minnesota Press, 2000), 109–39 at 112.

49   Peirce, "The Principles of Phenomenology: The Categories in Detail," Chapter 2 in *Collected Papers of Charles Sanders Peirce*, vol. 1, ed. Charles Hartshorne and Paul Weiss (Cambridge, MA: Harvard University Press, 1931–58), 148–80.

50   Charles Peirce, *Collected Papers* 5.44, quoted in Nils Lindahl Elliot, *Mediating Nature* (London: Routledge, 2006), 248. *Haecceity*, a term Peirce took from Medieval philosopher Duns Scotus, has more recently been popularized by Deleuze and Guattari. Peirce sometimes describes *secondness* as the haecceity of an actual event or encountered object; in this sense, firstness *precedes* haecceity. In the context of our experience of a film image, however, it makes sense to describe filmic firstness as haecceity.

51   Charles Peirce, "The Principles of Phenomenology: The Categories in Detail," in *Collected Papers*, I:150.

52   Cubitt, *EcoMedia*, 49.

53   Cubitt, *The Cinema Effect*, 66; Garrett Stewart, *Framed Time: Toward a Postfilmic Cinema* (Chicago: University of Chicago Press, 2007), 10–11. I should mention that the influence of Cubitt's analyses of film, both in *The Cinema Effect* and in his shorter book *EcoMedia*, on my own understanding of Peirce's applicability to film studies has been profound.

54   Cubitt, *The Cinema Effect*, 66, 71, 66.

55   Ibid., 66–67.

56   Ibid., 50–51.

57   Ibid., 67.

58   Ibid., 70.

59   Ibid., 71–72.

60   Ibid., 73.

61   Ibid., 76.

62   Ibid., 360.

63   Deleuze, *Cinema 1: The Movement-Image*, trans. Hugh Tomlinson and Barbara Habberjam (London: Continuum, 1992), 198.

64   Francesco Casetti, *Eye of the Century: Film, Experience, Modernity*, trans. Erin Larkin and Jennifer Pranolo (New York: Columbia University Press, 2008), 68.

65   Johannes Ehrat's *Cinema and Semiotic: Peirce and Film Aesthetics, Narration, and Representation* (Toronto: University of Toronto Press, 2005) presents the most ambitious, thorough, and challenging application of Peircian semiotics to cinema, to date. While Ehrat's general understanding of cinema as Sign process (and most specifically Iconic Sign process) is one that bears obvious similarities to my approach, the details of how it is to be applied in cinema remain somewhat oblique in his lengthy tome. I have chosen, in any case, to simplify Peirce in order to create an easily graspable model that maps usefully onto the other ideas drawn on here, such as those of Whitehead. Critical discussion of how faithful my approach is to Peirce's "pragmaticism" will have to await another occasion.

66   Peirce's triadics make my point here much more crisply than would any combination of Whitehead's terms. In any event, there is no exact correlation between Peirce's categories and Whitehead's system, but a good case has been made (by Steans and Hartshorne, among others) that Peircian firstness is closest to Whitehead's notion of "eternal objects" (and to Deleuze's "virtual"), secondness to Whitehead's basic notion of "prehension," and thirdness to Whitehead's "symbolic reference" (or, more generally, "mentality"). Symbolic reference is itself an integrative interplay between "perception in the mode of presentational immediacy," or the "bare sight" of what is there, and "perception in the mode of causal efficacy," or perception taking into account memory and the past and "constituted by its feeling-tones." Alternatively (though this would be a more difficult case to make), firstness may be taken as analogous to presentational immediacy, and secondness to causal efficacy, while thirdness constitutes the mediation and synthesis of the two. On the first set of correlations, see Jaime Nubiola, "Peirce and Whitehead," in *Handbook of Whiteheadian Process Thought*, vol. 2, ed. Michel Weber (Frankfurt: Ontos Verlag, 2008), 481–87.

67   Laura Mulvey, "Visual Pleasure and Narrative Cinema," *Screen* 16, no. 3 (1975): 6–18, is probably the most cited article in the history of film theory.

68   Bart Testa, "Review-Essay: *The Cinema of Attractions Reloaded*," *Canadian Journal of Film Studies* 16, no. 2 (2007): 119–26.

69   Wanda Strauven, "Introduction to an Attractive Concept," in *The Cinema of Attractions Reloaded*, ed. Strauven (Amsterdam: Amsterdam University Press, 2006), 11–27 at 18.

70   Tom Gunning, "An Aesthetic of Astonishment: Early Film and the (In)credulous Spectator," in *Viewing Positions: Ways of Seeing Film*, ed. Linda Williams (New Brunswick, NJ: Rutgers University Press, 1995), 114–33.

71 Martin Lefebvre suggests these terms in "Between Setting and Landscape in the Cinema," in *Landscape and Film*, ed. Lefebvre (London: Routledge, 2006), 19–60 at 29.

72 Tom Gunning, "The Cinema of Attraction: Early Film, Its Spectator, and the Avant-Garde," in *Film and Theory: An Anthology,* ed. Robert Stam and Toby Miller (Oxford: Blackwell, 2000), 229–35 at 232.

73 See, for example, Christian Metz, *Film Language: A Semiotics of the Cinema,* trans. Michael Taylor (Chicago: University of Chicago Press, 1974), 116.

74 Todd McGowan, *The Real Gaze: Film Theory after Lacan* (Albany: SUNY Press, 2007), 72.

75 Allan Rowe, "Film Form and Narrative," in *Introduction to Film Studies,* 2nd ed., ed. Jill Nelmes (London: Routledge, 1999), 91–128 at 117.

76 This argument runs parallel to Peter Wollen's claim that "the aesthetic richness of the cinema springs from the fact that it comprises all three dimensions of the [Peircian] sign: indexical, iconic and symbolic," and that it is "only by considering the interaction of the three different dimensions of the cinema that we can understand its aesthetic effect." Wollen, *Signs and Meanings in the Cinema* (London: British Film Institute [1969]1997), 141. I have simply expanded Wollen's claim to include the more primary categorical underpinnings of Peirce's three types of sign.

77 On the relationship between memory and projective imagination, see Daniel Schacter, Donna Addis, and Randy Buckner, "Remembering the Past to Imagine the Future: The Prospective Brain," *Nature Reviews Neuroscience* 8 (2007): 657–61. And on the differences and similarities between human and other animal brains, see Ursula Dicke and Gerhard Roth, "Intelligence Evolved," *Scientific American Mind* 19, no. 4 (August–September 2008), 70–77. The point of the latter article is not that human brains are more advanced than others (which has been the traditional and dominant view for a long time). Human brains share with those of other mammals many of the features mentioned, including numbers of neurons (with whales and elephants), but the "Broca's speech area," responsible for language, appears fairly unique. The difference between the latter two forms of cognitive response, analogous to my "narrativity" and "exoreferentiality," is perhaps the trickiest to establish according to neural correlates. My response to this challenge, which is necessarily tentative, is that the former, at its most basic, involves a close following of events but not much self-reflexivity, whereas the latter involves a more holistic and synthetic form of thought that, at its most advanced, is highly self-reflexive and creative.

78 Gilles Deleuze, *Cinema 2: The Time-Image,* trans. Hugh Tomlinson and Robert Galeta (Minneapolis: University of Minnesota Press, 2007), 28.

79 On scene construction, see Demis Hassabis and Eleanor Maguire, "Deconstructing Episodic Memory with Construction," *TRENDS in Cognitive Sciences* 11, no. 7 (2007): 299–306; and idem, "The Construction System of the Brain," *Philosophical Transactions of the Royal Society B* 364 (2009): 1264–71. On episodic memory, see Mark Wheeler, Donald Stuss, and Endel Tulving, "Toward a Theory of Episodic Memory: The Frontal Lobes and Autonoetic Consciousness," *Psychological Bulletin*

121 (1997): 331–54; Tulving, "Episodic Memory: From Mind to Brain," *Annual Review of Psychology* 53 (2002): 1–25; and John Sutton, "Memory," *Stanford Encyclopedia of Philosophy*.

80   Douglas Kellner uses the terms "resonant images" and "paleosymbolic scenes" for those affect-charged images and sequences that remain with viewers, often working at an unconscious level to shape behaviour and style and to move us to "later thought and action." See Kellner, *Media Culture: Cultural Studies, Identity and Politics Between the Modern and the Postmodern* (New York: Routledge, 1995), 107.

81   Daniel Frampton, *Filmosophy* (London: Wallflower Press, 2006).

82   Murray Pomerance, *The Horse Who Drank the Sky: Film Experience Beyond Narrative and Theory* (New Brunswick, NJ: Rutgers University Press, 2008), 7–8.

Notes to Chapter 3

1   Walter Benjamin, "The Work of Art in the Age of Mechanical Reproduction," in *Illuminations,* ed. Hannah Arendt, trans. Harry Zohn (New York: Schocken Books, 1969, orig. 1936), 268.

2   Mitchell Schwarzer, "The Moving Landscape," in *Monuments and Memory, Made and Unmade,* ed. Robert S. Nelson and Margaret Olin (Chicago: University of Chicago Press, 2004), 84–86.

3   Ralph Waldo Emerson, "Nature," in *Nature: Addresses and Lectures* (Philadelphia: David McKay Publisher, n.d., orig. 1836), 14.

4   Francesco Casetti, *Eye of the Century: Film, Experience, Modernity,* trans. Erin Larkin with Jennifer Pranolo (New York: Columbia University Press, 2008), 36.

5   Noël Carroll, *Theorizing the Moving Image* (Cambridge: Cambridge University Press, 1996), 63.

6   See Noël Burch, *Life to Those Shadows* (Berkeley: University of California Press, 1990).

7   Raymond Williams, *Keywords: A Vocabulary of Culture and Society* (London: Taylor and Francis, 1976), 184.

8   I have written about these concepts of nature at greater length elsewhere. See, for instance, my *Claiming Sacred Ground: Pilgrims and Politics in Glastonbury and Sedona* (Bloomington: Indiana University Press, 2001), 36–38. See also Kate Soper, *What Is Nature?* (Oxford: Blackwell, 1996); and Raymond Williams's classic article "Ideas of Nature," in *Problems in Materialism and Culture* (London: Verso, 1980), 67–85.

9   The category "human" is itself really only a few hundred years old in the West. See, for example, Philippe Descola and Gísli Pálsson, eds., *Nature and Society: Anthropological Perspectives* (London: Routledge, 1996); Michel Foucault, *The Order of Things* (New York: Vintage Books, 1973); and Stephen Horigan, *Nature and Culture in Western Discourses* (New York: Routledge, 1988).

10   This story is told in many places; see, for instance, Nils Lindahl Elliot, *Mediating Nature* (London: Routledge, 2006), 58ff.; Martin Jay, "Scopic Regimes of Modernity," in *Modernity and Identity,* ed. Scott Lash and Jonathan Friedman (Oxford: Blackwell, 1992), 178–95; Jonathan Crary, *Techniques of the Observer* (Cambridge, MA: MIT Press, 1990); Susan R. Bordo, *The Flight to Objectivity: Essays*

on *Cartesianism and Culture* (Albany: SUNY Press, 1987); and David Michael Levin, ed., *Modernity and the Hegemony of Vision* (Berkeley: University of California Press, 1993). Elliot's *Mediating Nature* is the most impressive attempt I have seen to apply a Peircian semiotic lens to the history of environmental imagery and thought. I have benefited from his outline of Peircian concepts and drawn liberally, in this section, from his historical overview of changing concepts of nature.

11   John Berger, *Ways of Seeing* (London: BBC and Penguin, 1972), 16.

12   Gilberto Perez, *The Material Ghost: Films and Their Medium* (Baltimore: Johns Hopkins University Press, 2000), 23–24.

13   This was especially the case with the places that were to become national parks. As Alfred Runte puts it, "as masterpieces of nature, the parks set the standard for artworks that the railroads hoped would attract both settlers and tourists to the romantic West." Runte, *Trains of Discovery: Western Railroads and the National Parks* (Niwot: Roberts Rinehart, 1994), 12.

14   John Muir, *The Mountains of California* (New York: The Century, 1907), 49.

15   Albert Boime, *The Magisterial Gaze: Manifest Destiny and American Landscape Painting, c. 1830–1865* (Washington: Smithsonian Institution Press, 1991).

16   Stephen Oetterman, *The Panorama: History of a Mass Medium* (Cambridge, MA: Zone Books, 1997); cited in Elliot, *Mediating Nature,* 261. In contrast to Watkins's and others' "invitational" landscape photography, Joel Snyder makes the case that Timothy H. O'Sullivan's (more or less contemporary) photographs of the American West were singularly "counterinvitational" and "antipicturesque" (though sometimes "sublime"): "They repeatedly deny what Watkins's photographs characteristically confirm, namely, the possibility of comfortable habitation, of an agreeable relation of humans to the natural landscape. They portray a bleak, inhospitable land, a godforsaken, anesthetizing landscape." See Snyder, "Territorial Photography," in *Landscape and Power,* ed. W.J.T. Mitchell (Chicago: University of Chicago Press, 1994), 175–201 at 189.

17   This argument was made most forcefully by Gaile McGregor in *The Wacousta Syndrome: Explorations in the Canadian Langscape* (Toronto: University of Toronto Press, 1985). To be fair, it has been both widely praised and widely critiqued in the Canadian context. See, for example, Susan Glickman, *The Picturesque and the Sublime: A Poetics of the Canadian Landscape* (Montreal and Kingston: McGill–Queen's University Press, 1998), 55ff.

18   Elliot, *Mediating Nature,* 148.

19   Benjamin, "The Work of Art," 223.

20   Schwarzer, "The Moving Landscape," 97.

21   Charles Bergman, "'The Curious Peach': Nature and the Language of Desire," in *Green Culture: Environmental Rhetoric in Contemporary America,* ed. Carl Herndl and Stuart Brown (Madison: University of Wisconsin Press, 1996), 281–305 at 295. And see Finis Dunaway, *Natural Visions: The Power of Images in American Environmental Reform* (Chicago: University of Chicago Press, 2005).

22   Walter Benjamin, "The Work of Art in the Age of Its Technological Reproducibility: Third Version," in *Selected Writings,* vol. IV. *1938–1940* (Cambridge, MA: Belknap Press, 2003), 265.

23   Stephen Prince, "True Lies: Perceptual Realism, Digital Images, and Film Theory," in *Film Theory and Criticism*, 6th ed., ed. Leo Braudy and Marshall Cohen (New York: Oxford University Press, 2004), 270–82 at 277.

24   Raymond Bellour, "The Pensive Spectator," trans. Lynne Kirby, *Wide Angle* 9, no. 1 (1987): 6–10.

25   P. Adams Sitney, "Landscape in the Cinema: The Rhythms of the World and the Camera," in *Landscape, Natural Beauty, and the Arts*, ed. Salim Kemal and Ivan Gaskell (New York: Cambridge University Press, 1993), 103–26 at 113, 106, 110.

26   Martin Lefebvre, "Between Setting and Landscape in the Cinema," in *Landscape and Film*, ed. Lefebvre (London: Routledge, 2006), 19–60.

27   For an account of such experimental films, see Scott MacDonald, *The Garden in the Machine: A Field Guide to Independent Films about Place* (Berkeley: University of California Press, 2001).

28   Lefebvre, "Between Setting and Landscape," 23.

29   Ibid., 29.

30   Lefebvre implies as much when he concludes that landscape "manifests itself in an interpretive gaze" (ibid., 51).

31   This is not to deny that certain kinds of landscape views, as evolutionary psychologists would argue, might not be considered pleasing in many, if not most, cultural contexts (with variability according to whether the context is, for instance, that of a rainforest or a desert). But without the cultural embodiment of such a landscape aesthetic—for instance, without the language for a concept such as "beautiful"—it would be impossible to communicate anything about such recognition. Culture either *enables* the appreciation of specific landscape aesthetics, or it fails to do that.

32   On the relationship between globalization processes and changing notions of place and heritage, see, for example, Gregory Ashworth, Brian Graham, and John Tunbridge, *Pluralising Pasts: Heritage, Identity, and Place in Multicultural Societies* (London: Pluto Press, 2007); Graham, Ashworth, and Tunbridge, *A Geography of Heritage: Power, Culture, and Economy* (London: Arnold, 2000); Geoffrey Hosking and George Schopflin, eds., *Myths and Nationhood* (New York: Routledge, 1997); Tim Edensor, *National Identity, Material Culture, and Everyday Life* (New York: Berg, 2002); and Barbara Bender and Margot Winer, eds., *Contested Landscapes: Movement, Exile, and Place* (Oxford: Berg, 2001).

33   André Bazin, *What Is Cinema?* vol. 2, 2nd ed., selected and trans. Hugh Gray (Berkeley: University of California Press, 2005), 142.

34   Gary Hausladen, "Where the Cowboy Rides Away: Mythic Places for Western Film," in *Western Places, American Myths*, ed. Hausladen (Reno: University of Nevada Press, 2006), 296–318.

35   Gilberto Perez, *The Material Ghost: Films and Their Medium* (Baltimore: Johns Hopkins University Press, 2000), 242.

36   John Cawelti, *The Six-Gun Mystique Sequel* (Bowling Green: Popular Press, 1999), 24.

37   Jane Tomkins, *West of Everything: The Inner Life of Westerns* (New York: Oxford University Press, 1992), 71, 74.

38   Ed Buscombe, "Inventing Monument Valley: Nineteenth Century Landscape Photography and the Western Film," in *The Western Reader,* ed. Jim Kitses and Gregg Rickman (New York: Limelight Editions, 1998), 115–30 at 120. "Metonymy" refers to the figure of speech in which a single attribute of something is used to stand for the whole thing. For an ecocritical reading of Monument Valley's depiction in Ford's *Stagecoach*, see Deborah Carmichael, "The Living Presence of Monument Valley in John Ford's *Stagecoach* (1939)," in *The Landscape of Hollywood Westerns: Ecocriticism in an American Film Genre,* ed. Deborah Carmichael (Salt Lake City: University of Utah Press, 2006), 212–26.

39   Buscombe, "Inventing Monument Valley," 125–26, 127.

40   Richard Hutson, "Sermons in Stone: Monument Valley in *The Searchers*," in *The Searchers: Essays and Reflections on John Ford's Classic Western*, ed. Eckstein and Peter Lehman (Detroit: Wayne State University Press, 2004), 93–108 at 93.

41   The policies of forced collectivization and dekulakization, with their direct results including the sacrifice of five to eight million people in Ukraine in 1932–33 alone, are amply documented by historians. See, for instance, Robert Conquest, *The Harvest of Sorrow: Soviet Collectivization and the Terror-Famine* (New York: Oxford University Press, 1986); and Oksana Procyk, Leonid Heretz, and James Mace, *Famine in the Soviet Ukraine: 1932–33* (Cambridge, MA: Harvard University Press, 1986). As a result of official denunciations, including Demian Bedny's attacks calling Dovzhenko a "pantheist, biologist, Spinozist and bourgeois nationalist," the filmmaker was henceforth given Siberian projects and condemned to years of internal exile. Many in the Ukrainian cultural renaissance of the 1920s were less fortunate: deported and/or murdered during the 1930s, the generation eventually became known as the "Executed Renaissance." See Ray Uzwyshyn, "Philosophy, Iconology, Collectivization: *Earth* (1930)," http://uwf.edu/ruzwyshyn/dovzhenko/Earth.htm, part of the visual essay *Between Ukrainian Cinema and Modernism: Alexander Dovzhenko's Silent Trilogy* (Pensacola: University of West Florida, n.d., http://uwf.edu/ruzwyshyn/dovzhenko/Introduction.htm, accessed 27 July 2010, adapted from Uzwyshyn's doctoral dissertation by the same title, New York University, 2000). On Soviet collectivization policies and practices more generally, see Peter Kenze, *A History of the Soviet Union from the Beginning to the End*, 2nd ed. (Cambridge: Cambridge University Press, 2006). On Ukraine specifically, see Paul Robert Magocsi, *A History of Ukraine* (Toronto: University of Toronto Press, 1996), 554ff.

42   Gilberto Perez, *The Material Ghost: Films and Their Medium* (Baltimore: Johns Hopkins University Press, 2000), 163.

43   Ibid., 167.

44   Ibid., 168.

45   Ibid., 168–69.

46   Ibid., 171, 170.

47   Ibid., 180.

48   The Dovzhenko quote as well as the subsequent lines are from Marco Carynnyk, "Introduction," in *Alexander Dovzhenko: The Poet as Filmmaker: Selected Writings,* ed. Carynnyk (Cambridge, MA: MIT Press, 1973), viii.

49   Ibid., liii.

50   Perez, *Material Ghost,* 190.

51   Ibid., 164.

52   Finis Dunaway, *Natural Visions: The Power of Images in American Environmental Reform* (Chicago: University of Chicago Press), xix.

53   Ibid., 49.

54   Ibid., 78, 85, 86.

55   Mara Hvistendahl, "China's Three Gorges Dam: An Environmental Catastrophe?," *Scientific American,* 25 March 2008, http://www.scientificamerican.com/article.cfm?id=chinas-three-gorges-dam-disaster, accessed 5 July 2010.

56   Hongbing Zhang, "Ruins and Grassroots: Jia Zhangke's Cinematic Discontents in the Age of Globalization," in *Chinese Ecocinema: In the Age of Environmental Challenge,* ed. Sheldon H. Lu and Jiayan Mi (Hong Kong: Hong Kong University Press, 2009), 129–53.

57   Seymour Chatman, *Antonioni, or, the Surface of the World* (Berkeley: University of California Press, 1985), 2.

58   Matthew Gandy, "Landscapes of Deliquescence in Michelangelo Antonioni's *Red Desert,*" *Transactions of the Institute of British Geographers* 28 (2003): 218–37. The term "industrial landscape sublime" is used in reference to the photography of Ed Burtynsky by Mark Haworth-Booth in "Edward Burtynsky: Traditions and Affinities," in *Manufactured Landscapes: The Photographs of Edward Burtynsky,* ed. Lori Pauli (Ottawa: National Gallery of Canada and Yale University Press, 2003), 34–39.

59   Sam Rohdie, *Antonioni* (London: British Film Institute, 1990), 3.

60   Ibid., 98–99.

61   Chatman, *Antonioni,* 80, 81, 82.

62   Quentin Meillassoux, *After Finitude: An Essay on the Necessity of Contingency* (London: Continuum, 2009).

63   Gerda Cammaer, "Edward Burtynsky's *Manufactured Landscapes*: The Ethics and Aesthetics of Creating Moving Still Images and Stilling Moving Images of Ecological Disasters," *Environmental Communication* 3, no. 1 (2009): 121–30.

64   Barton Byg, *Landscapes of Resistance: The German Films of Danièle Huillet and Jean-Marie Straub* (Berkeley: University of California Press, 1995), 41.

65   Peter Wollen, *Signs and Meaning in the Cinema* (London: Secker and Warburg, 1969), 94–96, 102.

66   Robin Wood argues that this was a kind of journalistic mob reaction, fuelled in part by their own "liberal anxiety" about *The Deer Hunter's* "allegedly right-wing position"—a view Wood cautiously and judiciously declines. See Wood, *Hollywood from Vietnam to Reagan ... and Beyond* (New York: Columbia University Press, 2003), 270–98. Almost alone among North American critics, Wood calls the film "among the supreme achievements of the Hollywood cinema" (317).

67   Ibid., 303.

68   Kent Jones, "Dead Man," *Cineaste* 22, no. 2 (1996): 45–46 at 45.

69   Gregg Rickman, "The Western under Erasure: *Dead Man,*" in *The Western Reader,* ed. Jim Kitses and Gregg Rickman (New York: Limelight, 1998), 381–404 at 396; Foucault quoted at 401.

70   Jean Mottet, "Toward a Genealogy of the American Landscape: Notes on Landscapes in D.W. Griffith," in *Landscape and Film*, ed. Martin Lefebvre (London: Routledge, 2006), 61–90.

71   David Ingram, *Green Screen: Environmentalism and Hollywood Cinema* (Exeter: University of Exeter Press, 2000).

72   On pantheism, see Michael Levine, *Pantheism: A Non-Theistic Concept of Deity* (London: Routledge, 1994). On the differences between a process-relational account and a more pantheistic one, see Steve Odin, *Process Philosophy and Hua-Yen Buddhism: A Critical Study of Cumulative Penetration vs. Interpenetration* (Albany: SUNY Press, 1982).

73   Arnold Berleant, *The Aesthetics of Environment* (Philadelphia: Temple University Press, 1992), 234.

74   Ben McCann, "Enjoying the Scenery: Landscape and the Fetishisation of Nature in *Badlands* and *Days of Heaven*," in *The Cinema of Terrence Malick: Poetic Visions of America,* 2nd ed., ed. Hannah Patterson (New York: Wallflower Press, 2007), 77–87; "fetishistic attention" at 78; other quotes at 81.

75   Stanley Cavell, *The World Viewed: Reflections on the Ontology of Film*, enlarged ed. (Cambridge. MA: Harvard University Press, 1979), xv–xvi.

76   Several critics have noted that *Spring Summer Fall Winter ... and Spring* is the most uncharacteristically muted of Kim Ki-Duk's controversial (and often violent) oeuvre, and some have questioned its ostensive Buddhism. I would particularly recommend Hyunjun Min's analysis of the film in Deleuzian terms as "an assemblage of haecceities" (117) or "nonhuman becomings" (127); see Min, *Kim Ki-Duk and the Cinema of Sensations,* Ph.D. diss., University of Maryland, 2008.

77   Michael Gillespie, "Picturing the Way in Bae Young-kyun's *Why Has Bodhidharma Left for the East?*," *Journal of Religion and Film* 1, no. 1 (1997), accessed 14 July 2010, http://www.unomaha.edu/jrf/gillespi.htm, para. 29. See also Meghan Brinson, "Engaging Zenamatography: *Why Has Bodhidharma Left for the East?*," *Chrestomathy: Annual Review of Undergraduate Research at the College of Charleston* 3 (2004): 26–39.

78   Other films that could be included in a loosely "Buddhist" genre include *Passage to India* (1994); Im Kwon-Taek's *Mandala* (1981) and *Come Come Come Upward* (1989); and Jeong Ji-Young's *Beyond the Mountain* (1991) and *Travellers and Magicians* (1993).

79   Pat Brereton, *Hollywood Utopia: Ecology in Contemporary American Cinema* (Bristol: Intellect Books, 2005), 38.

80   Ibid., 14, 41, 213.

81   Ibid., 77–78.

82   Ibid., 80.

83   Ernst Bloch, *The Principle of Hope,* trans. Neville Plaice, Stephen Plaice, and Paul Knight, 3 vols. (Cambridge, MA: MIT Press, 1986/1959).

84   Wayne Hudson, *The Reform of Utopia* (Burlington: Ashgate, 2003), 21.

85   Ruth Levitas, "Educated Hope: Ernst Bloch on Abstract and Concrete Utopia," in *Not Yet: Reconsidering Ernst Bloch,* ed. Jamie Owen Daniel and Tom Moylan (London: Verso, 1997), 65–79 at 73.

86   See Wheeler Winston Dixon, *Visions of Paradise: Images of Eden in the Cinema* (New Brunswick, NJ: Rutgers University Press, 2006); Eugen Doyen, "Utopia and Apocalypse—The Cultural Role of Hollywood Cinema," unpublished ms., 1996 (originally retrieved from Internet; no longer available); Richard Dyer, "Entertainment and Utopia," in *Genre: The Musical: A Reader,* ed. Rick Altman (London: Routledge and Kegan Paul, 1981), 175–89; Caryl Flinn, *Strains of Utopia: Gender, Nostalgia, and Hollywood Film Music* (New Brunswick: Princeton University Press, 1992); and Christine Geraghty, *Women and Soap Opera* (Cambridge: Polity, 1991).

87   For critiques of Steven Spielberg's cinema, see Alex Cholodenko, "'Objects in Mirror Are Closer Than They Appear': The Virtual Reality of *Jurassic Park* and Jean Baudrillard," *Journal of Baudrillard Studies* 2, no. 1 (2005), http://www.ubishops.ca/baudrillardstudies/vol2_1/cholodenko.htm; Sarah Franklin, "Life Itself: Global Nature and the Genetic Imaginary," in *Global Nature, Global Culture,* ed. Sarah Franklin, Celia Lury, and Jackie Stacey (London: Sage, 2000), 188–227; Robert P. Kolker, *A Cinema of Loneliness: Penn, Stone, Kubrick, Scorsese, Spielberg, Altman* (New York: Oxford University Press, 2000); Mark J. Lacy, "Cinema and Ecopolitics: Existence in the Jurassic Park," *Millennium—Journal of International Studies* 30 (2001): 635–45; Michael Ryan and Douglas Kellner, *Camera Politica: The Politics and Ideology of Contemporary Hollywood Film* (Bloomington: Indiana University Press, 1988); and Wood, *Hollywood from Vietnam to Reagan.*

88   See Douglas Brode, *From Walt to Woodstock: How Disney Created the Counterculture* (Austin: University of Texas Press, 2004); and David Whitley, *The Idea of Nature in Disney Animation* (Burlington: Ashgate, 2008).

89   Franklin, "Life Itself," 202–3.

90   Ibid., 212.

91   Ibid., 216.

92   David Laderman, *Driving Visions: Exploring the Road Movie* (Austin: University of Texas Press, 2002), 14.

93   Ibid., 3.

94   Ibid., 36ff.

95   Barbara Klinger, "The Road to Dystopia: Landscaping the Nation in *Easy Rider,*" in *The Road Movie Book,* ed. Steven Cohan and Ina Rae Hark (New York: Routledge, 1997), 179–203 at 192. See also Elaine Bapis, "*Easy Rider* (1969): Landscaping the Modern Western," in *The Landscape of Hollywood Westerns: Ecocriticism in an American Film Genre,* ed. Deborah Carmichael (Salt Lake City: University of Utah Press, 2006), 157–81.

96   In this sense, the film follows in the tradition of Joseph Conrad's *Heart of Darkness* and Francis Ford Coppola's *Apocalypse Now,* with wild nature becoming the site of human degradation, a kind of apocalypse of the soul, and with white fears projected onto a racially stereotyped "other." As critics have pointed out, *Deliverance* portrayed its locals as "stereotypical mountain hicks—toothless, imbecilic, unwashed"; see David Bell, "Anti-Idyll: Rural Horror," in *Contested Countryside Cultures: Otherness, Marginalisation, and Rurality,* ed. Paul Cloke and Jo Little (London: Routledge, 1997), 94–108 at 102. At the time, this portrayal

was protested by local audiences and denounced by Appalachian scholars; see Jerry Williamson, *Hillbillyland: What the Movies Did to the Mountains and What the Mountains Did to the Movies* (Chapel Hill: University of North Carolina Press, 1995), 158. As John Lane shows in *Chattooga: Descending into the Myth of Deliverance River* (Athens: University of Georgia Press, 2004), it still manifests as resentment in Rabun County, Georgia, where much of the film was shot.

97 Lane, *Chattooga*, 5, 9; American Rivers / National Park Service, *Use and Economic Importance of the Wild and Scenic Chattooga River: Final Report*, Roger Moore and Christos Siderelis, principal investigators (American Rivers Inc. and Park Planning and Special Studies, and Rivers, Trails and Conservation Assistance Programs of the National Park Service, 2003, http://www.americanwhitewater .org/content/Document/fetch/documentid/271/.raw), 8; Dickey quoted in Lane, *Chattooga*, 9.

98 Jhan Hochman, *Green Cultural Studies: Nature in Film, Novel, and Theory* (Moscow: University of Idaho Press, 1998), 71ff.

99 Dudley Andrew, *What Cinema Is!* (Oxford: Wiley-Blackwell, 2010), xviii.

100 Don Gayton, "In Film, Out of Place," *Alternatives* 24, no. 4 (1998): 8–9 at 8.

101 Keith Phipps, "The *Easy Rider* Road Trip," *Slate*, 16 November 2009, http://www .slate.com/id/2233176/entry/2233171, accessed 10 July 2010, 4 (of 5).

102 Chieko Iwashita, "Media Representation of the UK as a Destination for Japanese Tourists: Popular Culture and Tourism," Susan Sydney-Smith, "Changing Places: Touring the British Crime Film," and Eva Mazierska and John K. Walton, "Tourism and the Moving Image," all in *Tourist Studies* 6, no. 1 (2006). Quote: 5–11 at 10.

103 Roger Riley, Dwayne Baker, and Carlton S. Van Doren, "Movie Induced Tourism," *Annals of Tourism Research* 25, no. 4 (1998): 915–36; Agustin Gámir Orueta and Carlos Manuel Valdés, "Cinema and Geography: Geographic Space, Landscape and Territory in the film industry," University Carlos III of Madrid, Department of Humanities: Geography, Contemporary History, and Art, 2009, http://hdl.handle .net/10016/3608, accessed December 2011.

104 On *Braveheart,* see Tim Edensor, "Reading *Braveheart*: Representing and Contesting Scottish Identity," *Scottish Affairs* 21 (1997): 135–58.

105 Rodanthi Tzanelli, *The Cinematic Tourist: Explorations in Globalization, Culture, and Resistance* (New York: Routledge, 2007), 149.

106 See Chapter 3, "'National Elf Services,'" in Tzanelli, *The Cinematic Tourist,* 57–82.

107 Ibid., 144.

108 Sue Beeton, *Film-Induced Tourism* (Buffalo: Channel View Publications, 2005), 22.

109 See Adrian Ivakhiv, *Claiming Sacred Ground: Pilgrims and Politics at Glastonbury and Sedona* (Bloomington: Indiana University Press, 2001); and idem, "Seeing Red and Hearing Voices in Red Rock Country," in *Deterritorialisations: Revisioning Landscapes and Politics,* ed. Mark Dorrian and Gillian Rose (London: Black Dog, 2003), 296–308.

110 Laura Marks, *The Skin of the Film: Intercultural Cinema, Embodiment, and the Senses* (Durham, NC: Duke University Press, 2000), 77.

111 Giordana Bruno, *Atlas of Emotion: Journeys in Art, Architecture, and Film* (New York: Verso, 2002), 67.

112 See Annette Michelson, "Bodies in Space: Film as 'Carnal Knowledge,'" *Artforum* 7, no. 6 (1969): 54–63; Scott Bukatman, "The Artificial Infinite: On Special Effects and the Sublime," in *Alien Zone II: The Spaces of Science Fiction Cinema,* ed. Annette Kuhn (London: Verso, 1999), 249–75.

113 Tim Recuber, "Immersion Cinema: The Rationalization and Reenchantment of Cinematic Space," *Space and Culture* 10, no. 3 (2007): 315–30, 323, 316.

114 Martin Roberts, "*Baraka:* World Cinema and the Global Culture Industry," *Cinema Journal* 37, no. 3 (1998): 62–82 at 66–67.

115 Amy Staples, "Mondo Meditations," *American Anthropologist* 96 (1994): 662–68 at 667; Sean Cubitt, *The Cinema Effect* (Cambridge, MA: MIT Press, 2005), 338.

116 Roberts, "*Baraka,*" 69.

117 See Anahid Kassabian's argument in "Would You Like Some World Music with Your Latte?: Starbucks, Putumayo, and Distributed Tourism," *Twentieth Century Music* 1, no. 2 (2004): 209–23.

118 See P. Adams Sitney, *Visionary Film: The American Avant-Garde, 1943–2000,* 3rd ed. (New York: Oxford University Press, 2002); Gene Youngblood, *Expanded Cinema* (New York: E.P. Dutton, 1970); Stan Brakhage, *Essential Brakhage: Selected Writings on Filmmaking,* ed. by Bruce McPherson (New York: Documentext/McPherson and Co., 2001); and Maya Deren, *Essential Deren: Collected Writings on Film* (New York: Documentext, 2005).

119 Scott MacDonald, "Toward an Eco-Cinema," *Interdisciplinary Studies in Literature and Environment* 11, no. 2 (2004): 107–32.

120 Michael J. Anderson, "James Benning's Art of Landscape: Ontological, Pedagogical, Sacrilegious," *Senses of Cinema* (2005), accessed 16 July 2010, at http://sensesofcinema.com/2005/36/james_benning-2/.

121 Scott MacDonald, *The Garden in the Machine: A Field Guide to Independent Films About Place* (Berkeley: University of California Press, 2001), 349; emphasis in original.

122 Stan Brakhage, "From *Metaphors on Vision,*" in *Film Theory and Criticism: Introductory Readings,* 6th ed., ed. Leo Braudy and Marshall Cohen (New York: Oxford University Press), 199–205 at 199.

123 Ibid., 199.

124 Perez, *Material Ghost.*

125 Paula Willoquet-Maricondi, "*Prospero's Books,* Postmodernism, and the Reenchantment of the World," in *Peter Greenaway's Postmodernist/Poststructuralist Cinema,* ed. Willoquet-Maricondi and Mary Alemany-Galway (Lanham: Scarecrow Press, 2008), 177–202 at 178.

126 Paula Willoquet-Maricondi, "Aime *Cesaire's A Tempest* and Peter Greenaway's *Prospero's Books* as Ecological Rereadings and Rewritings of Shakespeare's *The Tempest,*" in *Reading the Earth: New Directions in the Study of Literature and Environment,* ed. Michael Branch et al. (Moscow: University of Idaho Press, 1998), 209–24 at 215.

127 James Tweedie, "Caliban's Books: The Hybrid Text in Peter Greenaway's *Prospero's Books,*" *Cinema Journal* 40, no. 1 (2000): 104–26 at 107.

128 On the Elizabethan world picture, see Frances A. Yates, *The Occult Philosophy in the Elizabethan Age* (London: Routledge and Kegan Paul, 1979).

129 Willoquet-Maricondi, "*Prospero's Books*," 182.

130 Ryan Trimm, "*Moving Pictures, Still Lives*: Staging National Tableaux and Text in *Prospero's Books*," *Cinema Journal* 46, no. 3 (2007): 25–53 at 38.

131 Douglas Keesey, *The Films of Peter Greenaway: Sex, Death, and Provocation* (London: McFarland and Company, 2006), 107.

132 Tweedie, "Caliban's Books," 107.

133 Trimm, "Moving Pictures, Still Lives," 35.

134 Leo Marx, "Shakespeare's American Fable," in *The Machine in the Garden: Technology and the Pastoral Ideal in America* (New York: Oxford University Press, 1964), 34–72.

135 Ibid., 69.

136 See, for instance, Viktorija Vesna Bulajić, ed., *Database Aesthetics: Art in the Age of Information Overflow* (Minneapolis: University of Minnesota Press, 2007); Janine Marchessault and Susan Lord, eds., *Fluid Screens, Expanded Cinema* (Toronto: University of Toronto Press, 2007); and Thomas Elsaesser, "The Mind-Game Film," in *Puzzle Films: Complex Storytelling in Contemporary Cinema,* ed. Warren Buckland (Oxford: Wiley-Blackwell, 2009), 13–41.

137 Eleftheria Thanouli, *Post-Classical Cinema: An International Poetics of Film Narrative* (London: Wallflower Press, 2009).

138 The term "post-classical" has been used and debated for some time now; it frequently is taken to refer to popular films with more fragmented plots, a high level of "knowing," playful allusiveness to other films, styles, and media, and related features. See Peter Kramer, "Post-Classical Hollywood," in *The Oxford Guide to Film Studies,* ed. John Hill and Pamela Church Gibson (Oxford: Oxford University Press, 1998), 289–309; Thomas Elsaesser, "Classical/Post-Classical Narrative," in *Studying Contemporary American Film: A Guide to Movie Analysis,* ed. Thomas Elsaesser and Warren Buckland (London: Arnold, 2002), 26–79; and David Bordwell, *The Way Hollywood Tells It: Story and Style in Modern Movies* (Berkeley: University of California Press, 2006). It is rivalled by other terms that focus on specific stylistic changes; for instance, Steven Shaviro makes a strong case for a "post-continuity" cinema. See Shaviro, *Post Cinematic Affect* (Ropley, UK: zerO books, 2010).

Notes to Chapter 4

1 Alfred North Whitehead, *Process and Reality*, Corrected Edition, ed. D.R. Griffin and D.W. Sherburne (New York: Simon and Schuster, 2010, orig. 1929), 88.

2 Charles Sanders Peirce, *1934–1935 Collected Papers of Charles Sanders Peirce,* Volumes 5 and 6, ed. C. Hartshorne and P. Weiss (Cambridge, Massachusetts: The Belknap Press of Harvard University Press, 1934; orig. in *The Monist*, 1905), 5.423.

3 David MacDougall, *Transcultural Cinema* (Princeton, NJ: Princeton University Press, 1998), 33.

4 Alfred North Whitehead, *Modes of Thought* (New York: Free Press, [1938]1966).

5 Paola Marrati, *Gilles Deleuze: Cinema and Philosophy* (Baltimore: Johns Hopkins University Press, 2008), xii.

6 Deleuze's account of the movement-image is *Cinema 1: The Movement-Image*, trans. Hugh Tomlinson and Barbara Habberjam (Minneapolis: University of Minnesota

Press, 1986). Another widely accepted overview of classical Hollywood cinema style is found in David Bordwell, Janet Staiger, and Kristin Thompson, *The Classical Hollywood Cinema: Film Style and Mode of Production to 1960* (New York: Routledge, 1985).

7   See Jay Ruby, *Picturing Culture: Explorations in Film and Anthropology* (Chicago: University of Chicago Press, 2000); Bill Nichols, "The Ethnographer's Tale," in *Blurred Boundaries: Questions of Meaning in Contemporary Culture* (Bloomington: Indiana University Press, 1994), 66; Sol Worth, *Studying Visual Communication*, ed. and intro. by Larry Gross (Philadelphia: University of Pennsylvania Press, 1981), 191; and Fatimah Tobing Rony, *The Third Eye: Race, Cinema, and Ethnographic Spectacle* (Durham, NC: Duke University Press, 1996), 8.

8   Bruno Latour, *We Have Never Been Modern*, trans. C. Porter (Cambridge, MA: Harvard University Press, 1993), 106.

9   Arturo Escobar, "After Nature: Steps to an Antiessentialist Political Ecology," *Current Anthropology* 40, no. 1 (1999): 1–30. I have written at greater length on this topic in "Toward a Multicultural Ecology," *Organization and Environment* 15, no. 4 (2002): 289–309.

10   Gilberto Perez, *The Material Ghost: Films and Their Medium* (Baltimore: Johns Hopkins University Press, 2000), 45.

11   Rony, *The Third Eye*, 5.

12   Johannes Fabian, *Time and the Other: How Anthropology Makes Its Object* (New York: Columbia University Press, 1983).

13   Bill Nichols, *Blurred Boundaries: Questions of Meaning in Contemporary Culture* (Bloomington: Indiana University Press, 1994), 68–69.

14   Ella Shohat and Robert Stam, *Unthinking Eurocentrism: Multiculturalism and the Media* (New York: Routledge, 1994), 104.

15   Rony, *The Third Eye*, 85.

16   Catherine Russell, *Experimental Ethnography: The Work of Film in the Age of Video* (Durham: Duke University Press, 1999), 141, 145.

17   Curtis, the famous photographer, later changed the name of his film to the more palatable *In the Land of the War Canoes: A Drama of Kwakiutl Life in the Northwest*. The restored version, a surviving 1972 print, was edited by Bill Holm and features new original music and dialogue by Kwakiutl (Kwakwaka'wakw) community members, many of whom consider the film important not only for its visual record of their relatives who were actors in the film, but also because of its interpretation of a Kwakiutl story. See also Anne Makepeace, *Coming to Light: Edward S. Curtis and the North American Indians* (coproduction of Anne Makepeace and WNET, 2000), a documentary that discusses Kwakiutl involvement in the production of *In the Land of the Headhunters*; and Pauline Wakeman, "Becoming Documentary: Edward Curtis' *In the Land of the Headhunters* and the Politics of Archival Reconstruction," *Canadian Review of American Studies* 36, no. 3 (2006): 293–309.

18   Cited in Ruby, *Picturing Culture*, 89.

19   Asen Balikci, "Anthropology, Film, and the Arctic Peoples," *Anthropology Today* 5, no. 2 (1989): 7; Laurel Smith, "Chips of the Old Ice Block: *Nanook of the North* and the Relocation of Cultural Identity," in *Engaging Film: Geographies of Mobility and*

Identity, ed. Tim Cresswell et al. (Lanham, MD: Rowman and Littlefield, 2002), 94–122 at 112; Erik Barnouw, *Documentary: A History of the Non-Fiction Film* (Oxford: Oxford University Press, 1983), 43.

20   Faye Ginsburg, "Screen Memories: Resignifying the Traditional in Indigenous Media," in *Media Worlds: Anthropology on New Terrain*, ed. Faye Ginsburg, Lila Abu-Lughod, and Brian Larkin (Berkeley: University of California Press, 2002), 39–57 at 39.

21   Ruby, *Picturing Culture*, 88.

22   Rony, *The Third Eye*, 115.

23   Ibid., 115.

24   Ibid., 100ff.

25   Ibid., 104.

26   Ibid., 124.

27   Ginsburg, "Screen Memories," 39. For more on the history of Inuit Tapirisat (the Inuit Brotherhood in Canada) and early Inuit interventions into satellite broadcasting service, see Laila Sorenson, "The Inuit Broadcasting Corporation and Nunavut," in *Nunavut: Inuit Regain Control of Their Land and Their Lives*, ed. Jens Dahl, Jack Hicks, and Peter Jull (Copenhagen: International Working Group for Indigenous Affairs, 2000); Lorna Roth, *Something New in the Air: The Story of First Peoples Television Broadcasting in Canada* (Montreal and Kingston: McGill–Queen's University Press, 2005); and Faye Ginsburg and Lorna Roth, "First Peoples' Television," in *Television Studies*, ed. Toby Miller (London: British Film Institute, 2002), 130–31.

28   Michelle H. Raheja, "Reading Nanook's Smile: Visual Sovereignty, Indigenous Revisions of Ethnography, and *Atanarjuat (The Fast Runner)*," *American Quarterly* 59, no. 4 (2007): 1159–85 at 1160.

29   Michael Real, *Exploring Media Culture: A Guide* (London: Sage, 1996), 270–71; Tony Hillerman, *Sacred Clowns* (Demco Media, 1994), 120–21.

30   Rony, *The Third Eye*, 212–13.

31   Ibid., 216.

32   Siegfried Kracauer, *Theory of Film: The Redemption of Physical Reality* (New York: Oxford University Press, 1960), 73.

33   Dean W. Duncan, *Nanook of the North*, Criterion Collection notes, http://www.criterion .com/current/posts/42-nanook-of-the-north, accessed 3 August 2010.

34   Robert J. Flaherty, "How I Filmed 'Nanook of the North,'" *World's Work*, October 1922, 632–40, .

35   Michel Serres, *The Natural Contract*, trans. Elizabeth MacArthur and William Paulson (Ann Arbor: University of Michigan Press, 1995).

36   Helmut Färber, "*King Kong*: One More Interpretation, or What Cinema Tells about Itself," *Discourse* 22, no. 2 (2000): 104–26 at 112.

37   My reading here is indebted to Rony's in Chapter 6 of The *Third Eye*, as well as to Färber's "*King Kong*," Robert Torry's "'You Can't Look Away': Spectacle and Transgression in *King Kong*," *Arizona Quarterly* 49, no. 4 (1993): 61–77; and others.

38   Nils Lindahl Elliot, *Mediating Nature: Environmentalism and Modern Culture* (London: Routledge, 2006), 189–90.

39   E. Ann Kaplan, *Looking for the Other: Feminism, Film, and the Imperial Gaze* (New York: Routledge, 1997), 78–79.

40   Ruby, *Picturing Culture*, 10.

41   See, for instance, Robin Wood, *Hollywood from Vietnam to Reagan ... and Beyond,* exp. and rev. ed. (New York: Columbia University Press, 2003); Michael Ryan and Douglas Kellner, *Camera Politica: The Politics and Ideology of Contemporary Hollywood Film* (Bloomington: Indiana University Press, 1988); and Ella Shohat and Robert Stam, *Unthinking Eurocentrism: Multiculturalism and the Media* (New York: Routledge, 1994).

42   See Survival International, "Uncontacted Tribe Photographed Near Brazil–Peru Border," http://www.survivalinternational.org/news/3340, 29 May 2008, accessed 31 August 2010. Survival International keeps track of more than a hundred groups that "choose to reject contact with outsiders" (see http://www.survivalinternational .org/uncontactedtribes). But the photograph of the "uncontacted tribe" in question made a rather dramatic media and online impact, as if this was indeed the last tribe to have been "discovered" by Westerners.

43   Lutz Koepnick, "Colonial Forestry: Sylvan Politics in Werner Herzog's *Aguirre* and *Fitzcarraldo,*" *New German Critique* 60 (1993): 133–59 at 136.

44   Ibid., 139.

45   Ibid., 145.

46   Gundula Sharman, "The Jungle Strikes Back: European Defeat at the Hands of the South American Landscape in the Films of Werner Herzog," *Journal of Transatlantic Studies* 2, no. 1 (2004): 96–109 at 100.

47   Renato Rosaldo, "Imperialist Nostalgia," *Representations* 26 (1989): 107–22 at 108.

48   Steve Pavlik, "Searching for Pocahontas: The Portrayal of an Indigenous Icon in Terrence Malick's *The New World,*" 2009, http://blogs.nwic.edu/pavlik/ files/2009/05/pavlik-the_new_world_review.pdf, accessed 1 July 2010, 22ff. (quote at 25). On the mixed Native American reception of the film, see Lise Balk King, "Writer Director Terrence Malick delivers visual poetry in story of Pocahantas," *Native Voice* 5, no. 1 (18–31 January 2006), B1; Jenifer Hemmingsen, "Not Much New in 'The New World,'" *Indian Country Today* 25, no. 31 (11 January 2006), B1; and Sandra Hale Schulman, "A Maverick Filmmaker Envisions a Dream of Native America," *News from Indian Country* 20, no. 1 (9 January 2006), 16.

49   Ron Mottram, "All Things Shining: The Struggle for Wholeness, Redemption, and Transcendence in the Films of Terrence Malick," in *The Cinema of Terrence Malick,* ed. Hannah Patterson, 2nd ed. (London: Wallflower Press, 2007), 14–26 at 15.

50   Eric Repphun, "Look Out Through My Eyes: The Enchantments of Terrence Malick," in *Eternal Sunshine of the Academic Mind: Essays on Religion and Film,* ed. Christopher Hartney (University of Sydney, Studies in Religion, 2009), 13–24 at 22.

51   Edward Buscombe, "What's New in *The New World?* Edward Buscombe on an Extended DVD Version of Terrence Malick's 2005 Retelling of the Pocahontas Story," *Film Quarterly* 62, no. 3 (2009): 35–40 at 39.

52   Donald V.L. Macleod, "Anthropological Investigations: An Innocent Exploration of *The Wicker Man* culture," in *The Quest for the Wicker Man,* ed. Benjamin Franks et al. (Edinburgh: Luath Press, 2006).

53 Frazer's *The Golden Bough* was based on the now outmoded conception of "cultural survivals," whereby any "superstitious" practices were thought of as inheritances from long ago, destined to be lost as humanity progressed to a more enlightened understanding of the world. His understanding of the practice of human sacrifice was also notably different from what is portrayed in the film. On the debate over the film's portrayal of pagan religion, see Mikel J. Koven, *Film, Folklore, and Urban Legends* (Lanham, MD: Rowman and Littleleld / Scarecrow Press, 2008); Richard Sermon, "The Wicker Man, May Day, and the Reinvention of Beltane," 26–431 and other essays in Franks et al., eds., *The Quest for the Wicker Man: History, Folklore, and Pagan Perspectives* (Edinburgh: Luath Press, 2006); and Jonathan Murray, Lesley Stevenson, Stephen Harper, and Benjamin Franks, eds., *Constructing the Wicker Man* (Glasgow: Crichton Publications, 2005). For an authoritative account of British folk beliefs and practices, including those connected to Beltane, see Ronald Hutton, *The Stations of the Sun: A History of the Ritual Year in Britain* (Oxford: Oxford University Press, 1996).

54 David Bartholomew, "The Wicker Man," *Cinefantastique* 6, no. 3 ([1977]2008), http://www.wicker-man.com/articles/cinefantastique_TWM_article_1977.pdf, 7.

55 Elizabeth Kingsley presents a thorough account of its distribution history in "'The Wicker Man (1973),' and You Call Yourself a Scientist!," posted 14 May, http://www.aycyas.com/wickerman73.htm. See also Melanie J. Wright, "The Wicker Man," in *Religion and Film: An Introduction* (London: I.B. Tauris, 2007), 79–106. The horror, fantasy, and science fiction magazine *Cinefantastique* devoted an issue to it in 1977, describing it as "the *Citizen Kane* of Horror Movies," and several versions came into distribution as the production company underwent permutations and ownership of the film changed hands more than once.

56 Lesley Stevenson, "Sightseeing in Summerisle: Film Tourism and *The Wicker Man*," in Murray et al., *Constructing the Wicker Man*, 107–22; Wright, "The Wicker Man."

57 Wright, "The Wicker Man," 101ff.

58 Carrol L. Fry, *Cinema of the Occult: New Age, Satanism, Wicca, and Spiritualism in Film* (Cranbury: Rosemont / Associated University Presses, 2008), 183.

59 Kingsley, "'The Wicker Man (1973)," 183.

60 Franks et al., *The Quest for the Wicker Man*, 57.

61 Bartholomew, "The Wicker Man," 9.

62 Steven J. Sutcliffe, "Religion in *The Wicker Man*: Context and Representation," in Murray et al., *Constructing the Wicker Man*, 37–56 at 51; Judith Higginbottom, "'Do as Thou Wilt': Contemporary Paganism and *The Wicker Man*," in Franks et al., *The Quest for the Wicker Man*, 126–36 at 128, 131. See also Fry, *Cinema of the Occult*; and Mike Nichols, "Neo-Pagan Filmography," revised 2 May 1997, http://www.sacred-texts.com/bos/bos115.htm, accessed December 9, 2013.

63 Philip Hayward, "Western Edges: *Evil Aliens* and Island Otherness in British Cinema," *Shima: International Journal of Research into Island Cultures* 1, no. 2 (2007): 91–92, http://shimajournal.org/issues/v1n2/i.%20Hayward%20Shima%20v1n2.pdf.

64 Nichols, "Neo-Pagan Filmography."

65 It has also been argued that the "symbolism of burning a 'Christian copper'" carried resonances for youthful audiences both in the post-1968 years and in the

1980s, especially after Britain's "New Age traveller" subculture, disproportionately represented in the country's sizeable Pagan community, suffered massive injuries at the hands of police following the 1986 "Battle of the Beanfield." The latter was a now-legendary standoff between squadrons of armed police and several hundred unarmed revellers ("hippies," as they were called in the press at the time) attending Summer Solstice festivities at Stonehenge. See Sutcliffe, "Religion in *The Wicker Man*," 40; Ivakhiv, *Claiming Sacred Ground*, 88ff.

66   The question of human sacrifice is a complex one. As Howie finds out, the crops had failed the previous year on Summerisle, for the first time in more than a century, so resorting to a human sacrifice would not have been the norm. Yet one can argue that it is the exception that proves the rule that, ultimately, human life is part of a calculus of reciprocal relations between humans and their gods, and if the latter require sacrifice, then the former better provide. In any case, research shows that human sacrifice was not uncommon among agrarian and imperial societies; see, for example, Jan M. Bremmer, ed., *The Strange World of Human Sacrifice* (Leuven: Peeters, 2007). Tom Brass, moreover, argues that *The Wicker Man* embodies a version of the "agrarian myth" that uses religious belief to prop up the landlordism of the island's power structure, which is headed, after all, by Lord Summerisle. See Brass, "Nymphs, Shepherds, and Vampires: The Agrarian Myth on Film," *Dialectical Anthropology* 25 (2000): 205–37. All of this is forgiven by many contemporary Pagans, for the reasons given above.

67   The film's influence can be surmised in the growth of festivals and other events incorporating the burning of wicker figures; these include the Burning Man Festival in Nevada, which attracts some 40,000 people every year; the Wicker Man festival in Scotland; and explicitly Pagan festivals and rituals specifically incorporating imagery from the film. See Peg Aloi, "'And with Thee Fade Away into the Forest Dim': Neopastoralism and Romantic Renascence in the Ritual Literature of Modern Witchcraft," in *New Versions of Pastoral: Post-Romantic, Modern, and Contemporary Responses to the Tradition,* ed. David James and Philip Tew (Cranbury: Rosemont / Associated University Presses, 2009), 58–79; Walter W. Arthen, "The Wicker Man: A Ritual of Transformation," *FireHeart* 1 (1997), EarthSpirit Web, last updated 26 June 2009, http://www.earthspirit.com/fireheart/fhwkman.html; and Sarah M. Pike, *Earthly Bodies, Magical Selves: Contemporary Pagans and the Search for Community* (Berkeley: University of California Press, 2001). According to Aloi's research, *The Wicker Man* played a role in the development of the Provider Cycle, a set of rituals developed by Michael DesRosiers, founder of the Order of Ganymede, a Pagan group in Boston, in the 1970s (71–72). The film's music has also been widely influential within the Pagan musical subculture, even though the soundtrack was only released commercially in 2002, circulating until that time only in unofficial bootleg form. Documenting the film's influence on a wide range of musicians, particularly within the neofolk, "wyrd folk" ("psych folk"), dark-wave, and goth genres, Pagan blogger and journalist Jason Pitzl-Waters writes that "it is hard to over-state the influence the Wicker Man soundtrack had on Pagan and occult-themed music"; see Pitzl-Waters, "Musical Influence of The

Wicker Man Soundtrack" and "The Wicker Man Soundtrack," in *A Darker Shade of Pagan*, 20 and 22 June http://www.adarkershadeofpagan.com/labels/The%20 Wicker%20Man.html.

68 Karl Heider, *Ethnographic Film*, rev. ed. (Austin: University of Texas Press, 2006).

69 In Keith Beattie, *Documentary Screens: Non-Fiction Film and Television* (New York: Rowman and Littlefield, 2004), 52. ˙

70 In David MacDougall, *Transcultural Cinema*, ed. and intro. Lucien Taylor (Princeton, NJ: Princeton University Press, 1998), 88.

71 Ibid., 88ff.

72 April Biccum, "Third Cinema in the 'First' World: *Eve's Bayou* and *Daughters of the Dust*," *CineAction* 49 (1999): 60–65.

73 That said, Bob Connolly's and Robin Anderson's 1983 film *First Contact* presents an intelligent overview of such depictions in cinematic encounters featuring indigenous New Guineans.

74 E. Ann Kaplan, *Looking for the Other: Feminism, Film, and the Imperial Gaze* (London: Routledge, 1997).

75 Laura Marks, *The Skin of the Film* (London: Duke University Press, 2000), 1.

76 See Gilles Deleuze and Félix Guattari, *A Thousand Plateaus* (Minneapolis: University of Minnesota Press, 1987).

77 Jhan Hochman, *Green Cultural Studies: Nature in Film, Novel, and Theory* (Moscow: University of Idaho Press, 1998), 142.

78 Ibid., 144.

79 Ibid., 147–48.

80 Ibid., 151.

81 In Julie Dash, with Toni Cade Bambara and bell hooks, *Daughters of the Dust: The Making of an African American Woman's Film* (New York: New Press, 1992), 40.

82 In Joel R. Brewer, "Repositioning: Center and Margin in Julie Dash's 'Daughters of the Dust'," *African American Review* 29, no. 1 (1995): 5.

83 Teshome Gabriel, "Towards a Critical Theory of Third World Films," in *Questions of Third Cinema*, ed. Jim Pines and Paul Willemen (London: British Film Institute, 1994), 30–51.

84 Gabriel, "Towards a Critical Theory," 44–45.

85 Ibid., 48.

86 See Pamela Wilson and Michelle Stewart, eds., *Global Indigenous Media: Culture, Poetics, Politics* (Durham, NC: Duke University Press, 2008).

87 See Raheja, "Reading Nanook's Smile," 1159–85.

88 Ibid., 1168.

89 Ibid., 1179.

90 I am basing this in part on my observations from screening the film in class, but also from accounts elsewhere. See Allen Feldman, "Faux Documentary and the Memory of Realism," *American Anthropologist* 100, no. 2 (1998): 494–502 at 501; Ken Feingold, Coco Fusco, and Steve Gallagher, "Trouble in Truthsville," *Felix* 1, no. 2 (1992): 48–49, 128–131; and Laura U. Marks, "Suspicious Truths: Flaherty 1991," *Afterimage* 19, no. 3 (1991): 4, 21.

91   Laura Rascaroli, *The Personal Camera: Subjective Cinema and the Essay Film* (London: Wallflower Press, 2009), 35. See also Timothy Corrigan, *The Essay Film: From Montaigne, after Marker* (New York: Oxford University Press, 2011).

92   Catherine Lupton, *Chris Marker: Memories of the Future* (London: Reaktion Books, 2005), 154.

93   Deleuze, *Cinema 2: The Time-Image,* 177–78.

94   First parts of the first three "modes" (the "white," "grey," and "evil"): D.N. Rodowick, "The World, Time," in *Afterimages of Gilles Deleuze's Film Philosophy*, ed. D.N. Rodowick (Minneapolis: University of Minnesota Press, 2010), 97–114 at 105. Latter parts and other quotes: Ronald Bogue, "To Choose to Choose—to Believe in This World," in *Afterimages of Gilles Deleuze's Film Philosophy*, ed. D.N. Rodowick (Minneapolis: University of Minnesota Press, 2010), 115–33 at 121. Final quotes ("way of living," "a belief"): Bogue, "To Choose," 129.

95   Ingram, *Green Screen*, 2.

96   Ibid., 4.

97   Andrew Light, *Reel Arguments: Film, Philosophy, and Social Criticism* (Boulder, CO: Westview, 2003).

98   On network narratives, see David Bordwell, "Mutual Friends and Chronologies of Chance," in *Poetics of Cinema* (New York: Routledge, 2008), 189–250.

99   Robert Stam, "The Subversive Charm of Alain Tanner," *Jump Cut* 15, no. 1 (1977): 5–7, 1.

100 Alain Tanner, "Interview with Alain Tanner," in *Jonah Who Will Be 25 in the Year 2000: Screenplay by John Berger and Alain Tanner,* trans. Michael Palmer (Berkeley: North Atlantic Books, 1983), 165–74 at 170.

101 Richard Porton, *Film and the Anarchist Imagination* (London: Verso, 1999), 194.

102 Joanne Barkan, "Jonah after the Year 2000," *Dissent* (Winter 2004): 105–9 at 108.

Notes to Chapter 5

1   Sean Cubitt, *EcoMedia* (Amsterdam: Rodopi, 2005), 118.

2   Vivian C. Sobchack, *The Address of the Eye: A Phenomenology of Film Experience* (New Brunswick, NJ: Princeton University Press, 1992), 309.

3   Henri Bergson, *Creative Evolution,* trans. Arthur Mitchell (New York: Dover, 1998, orig. 1907), 106.

4   James Hillman, *Egalitarian Typologies Versus the Perception of the Unique,* Eranos Lectures Series 4 (Dallas: Spring Publications, 1986), 55.

5   Vivian Sobchack, *The Address of the Eye: A Phenomenology of Film Experience* (Princeton, NJ: Princeton University Press, 1992), 3–4. Emphasis in original, with the exception of the phrase "expression of experience by experience."

6   Theodor Adorno, *Minima Moralia: Reflections from Damaged Life* (London: Verso, 2010).

7   Jesper Hoffmeyer, *Signs of Meaning in the Universe*, trans. Barbara Haviland (Bloomington: Indiana University Press, 1996), 103.

8   Susan Sontag, *On Photography* (New York: Picador, 1977), 3.

9　John Dorst, *Looking West* (Philadelphia: University of Pennsylvania Press, 1999), 111.

10　I have argued this point at greater length in Ivakhiv, "Seeing Red and Hearing Voices in Red Rock Country," in *Deterritorialisations: Revisioning Landscapes and Politics*, ed. Mark Dorrian and Gillian Rose (London: Black Dog, 2003), 296–308.

11　Paul Sheehan, "Against the Image: Herzog and the Troubling Politics of the Screen Animal," *SubStance* 37, no. 3 (2008): 117–36 at 119.

12　Akira Mizuta Lippit, "The Death of an Animal," *Film Quarterly* 56, no. 1 (2002): 20; emphasis added.

13　Ibid., 13.

14　Ibid., 19.

15　Sheehan, "Against the Image," 121.

16　Ibid., 122.

17　Ibid., 123.

18　Jonathan Burt, *Animals in Film* (London: Reaktion Books, 2002), 71.

19　Ibid., 56, 54.

20　Sheehan, "Against the Image," 129.

21　This is Scott MacDonald's argument in "Up Close and Political: Three Short Ruminations on Ideology in the Nature Film," *Film Quarterly* 59, no. 3 (2006): 4–21 at 10.

22　Quoted in Jussi Parikka, *Insect Media: An Archaeology of Animals and Technology* (Minneapolis: University of Minnesota Press, 2010), 236n36.

23　Ibid., xxxv.

24　Jean Epstein, "Le cinématographe *Vue de l'Etna*," reprinted in *Écrits sur le cinéma* I:132–52 (1974), at 134. Cited in Francesco Cassetti, *Eye of the Century: Film, Experience, Modernity* (New York: Columbia University Press, 2008), 141–2.

25　Derek Bousé, *Wildlife Films* (Philadelphia: University of Pennsylvania Press, 2000), "molded ...," 4; "market-driven ...," 5; "movement ...," 4; "that the animals ...," 6.

26　Karla Armbruster, "Creating the World We Must Save: The Paradox of Television Nature Programs," in *Writing the Environment: Ecocriticism and Literature*, ed. Richard Kerridge and Neil Sammels (London: Zed, 1998), 218–38 at 232.

27　McKibben, *The Age of Missing Information*, 79.

28　Gregg Mitman, *Reel Nature: America's Romance with Wildlife on Film* (Cambridge, MA: Harvard University Press, 1999), 11.

29　Ibid., 130–31.

30　MacDonald, "Up Close and Political," 8.

31　John Law deconstructs this inside/outside dichotomy in the context of social-scientific efforts to reproduce reality. See Law, *After Method: Mess in Social Science Research* (London: Routledge, 2004).

32　Peter Lee-Wright, *The Documentary Handbook* (London: Routledge, 2010), 364.

33　In Bousé, *Wildlife Films*, 32.

34　Ibid., 4.

35　Ibid., 6–7.

36　Ibid., 14.

37   This is Werner Herzog's critique of *cinema vérité* documentary, which he says "reaches a merely superficial truth, the truth of accountants." He opposes this to "poetic, ecstatic truth." His "ecstatic truth," however, may not be the same as mine or someone else's, and while his films resonate deeply with certain audiences, they can be analytically contextualized in ways that highlight their own silences and elisions. See Herzog, "The Minnesota Declaration: Truth and Fact in Documentary Cinema," in *Herzog on Herzog*, ed. Paul Cronin (London: Faber and Faber, 2002), 301.

38   Bousé argues that blue-chip wildlife documentaries are characterized by visual splendour underpinned by high production values and by a focus on "charismatic mega-fauna," a dramatic storyline, and a general absence of science, politics, historical reference points, and people—or, as he puts it, "at least, *white* people." The result is what cameraman Stephen Mills calls a "period-piece fantasy of the natural world." Bousé, *Wildlife Films*, 14–15.

39   Discovery Communications, "Discovery Channel's Planet Earth the Most Watched Cable Event, Reaching over 65 Million Viewers: Series Breaks Records across Multimedia Platforms," May 1, 2007, http://corporate.discovery.com/discovery-news/discovery-channels-planet-earth-most-watched-cable, accessed October 6, 2011. Its success is incontrovertible. "Warner Home Video has shipped more than three million copies of the five-DVD Planet Earth boxed set since its release in April of 2007, according to Williams in *The New York Times*, more than any other documentary ever." Richard Beck, "Costing Planet Earth," *Film Quarterly* 13, no. 3 (2009): 63–66 at 66.

40   MacDonald, "Up Close and Political," 6.

41   Beck, "Costing Planet Earth," 64.

42   Ibid., 65.

43   Nils Lindahl Elliot, "Showing to Save? A Critique of Natural History Documentaries on Television," http://cmcee.wordpress.com/2008/02/01/showing-to-save-a-critique-of-natural-history-documentaries-part-1, accessed December 2011.

44   Amazon.com website for *Planet Earth: The Complete Series* [HD DVD]: Customer reviews (ranked by "most helpful"), http://www.amazon.ca/product-reviews/B000MR9D5E/ref=cm_cr_dp_see_all_top?ie=UTF8&showViewpoints=1&sortBy=bySubmissionDateDescending, accessed September 27, 2012.

45   IMDb, *Planet Earth* (TV series 2006), http://www.imdb.com/title/tt0795176, accessed September 23, 2012.

46   Sean Cubitt, *EcoMedia* (Amsterdam: Rodopi, 2005), 59.

47   Casetti, *Eye of the Century*, 143.

48   Cubitt, *Ecomedia*, 59.

49   Lisa Uddin, "Bird-Watching: Global–Natural Worlds and the Popular Reception of *Winged Migration*," *Reconstruction* 7, no. 2 (2007): paras. 7–8, http://reconstruction.eserver.org/072/uddin.shtml.

50   Ibid., para. 20.

51   Jennifer Fay, "Seeing/Loving Animals: Andre Bazin's Posthumanism," *Journal of Visual Culture* 7, no. 1 (2008): 41–64 at 43.

52   See Pat Brereton, *Smart Cinema, DVD Add-Ons, and New Audience Pleasures* (New York: Palgrave Macmillan, 2012).

53 Fay, "Seeing/Loving Animals," 61.

54 *Winged Migration* did very well at the box office, making $11.7 million in the United States (placing it seventh in all-time box office receipts among documentaries) and another $32 million worldwide.

55 Cubitt, *The Cinema Effect* (Cambridge, MA: MIT Press, 2005), 70–71.

56 Ibid., 91–92.

57 Cubitt, *EcoMedia*, 36.

58 Ibid., 36–37, 39.

59 Ibid., 31. ·

60 Ian Christie, "Introduction: Rediscovering Eisenstein," in *Eisenstein Rediscovered*, ed. Christie and Richard Taylor (London: Routledge, 1993), 1–30 at 24.

61 Daniel Morgan, "The Place of Nature in Godard's Late Films," *Critical Quarterly* 51, no. 3 (2009): 1–24 at 3.

62 For example, Henry Giroux, "Animating Youth: The Disnification of Children's Culture," http://www.henryagiroux.com/online_articles/animating_youth.htm; Matthew Roth, "Man Is in the Forest: Humans and Nature in *Bambi* and *Lion King*," *Invisible Culture* 9 (2005), http://www.rochester.edu/in_visible_culture/ Issue; Matthew Roth, "Lion King: A Short history of Disney-Fascism," *Jump Cut* 40 (1996): 15–20.

63 Douglas Brode, *From Walt to Woodstock: How Disney Created the Counterculture* (Austin: University of Texas Press, 2004); David Whitley, *The Idea of Nature in Disney Animation* (Burlington: Ashgate, 2008).

64 Whitley, *The Idea of Nature in Disney Animation*, 9.

65 MacDonald, "Up Close and Political," 8.

66 Matt Cartmill, "The Bambi Syndrome," in Cartmill, *A View to a Death in the Morning: Hunting and Nature Through History* (Cambridge, MA: Harvard University Press, 1993); Ralph H. Lutts, "The Trouble with *Bambi*: Walt Disney's Bambi and the American Vision of Nature," *Forest and Conservation History* 36 (1992): 160–71; A. Waller Hastings, "Bambi and the Hunting Ethos," *Journal of Popular Film and Television* 24, no. 2 (1996): 53–59.

67 Lutts argues this in "The Trouble with Bambi."

68 Whitley makes the case for this in *The Idea of Nature in Disney Animation*.

69 Cartmill, *A View to a Death in the Morning*, 162.

70 Lutts, "The Trouble with Bambi," 161.

71 Ibid., 162.

72 Hastings, "*Bambi* and the Hunting Ethos."

73 Whitley, *The Idea of Nature in Disney Animation*, 74.

74 The first criticism is David Ingram's; see his *Green Screen: Environmentalism and Hollywood Cinema* (Exeter: University of Exeter Press, 2004). The Lutts quote is from "The Bambi Syndrome," 169. The Chaudhuri quote is from "Animal Geographies: Zooësis and the Space of Modern Drama," in *Performing Nature: Explorations in Ecology and the Arts*, ed. Gabriella Giannachi and Nigel Stewart (Bern: Peter Lang, 2005), 103–18 at 105.

75 Whitley, *The Idea of Nature in Disney Animation*, 77

76 Ibid., 73.

77 Nils Lindahl Elliot, *Mediating Nature: Environmentalism and Modern Culture* (New York: Routledge, 2006), 189–90.

78 The term is Cynthia Erb's from *Tracking King Kong: A Hollywood Icon in World Culture* (Detroit: Wayne State University Press, 1998), 63. Donna Haraway's account of King Kong is found in her *Primate Visions: Gender, Race, and Nature in the World of Modern Science* (New York: Routledge, 1989), 160–62.

79 In his classic study *The Philosophy of Horror, Or Paradoxes of the Heart* (New York: Routledge, 1990), Noel Carroll argues on behalf of the "thought theory" of fiction, whereby our emotional responses to fiction are "built on our capacity to be moved by thought contents and to take pleasure in being so moved" (83). My view is different insofar as it emphasizes that what we see and hear is never "fiction"—it consists of *real* visual and auditory contents—and that while the narrative sense we make of these things may be "fictional" in that we think of them as a "mere story," our being drawn into the story is the same *kind* of thing as our being drawn into a story we believe may be "real." In other words, it is only at the level of thirdness, where we consider the actual meaning of the story, that we separate the *real* from the *fictional*. But by this point our experience of becoming emotionally drawn into the sound-images and narrative cannot be merely eliminated; it has to be interpreted away.

80 Robin Wood, *Hitchcock's Films Revisited*, rev. ed. (New York: Columbia University Press, 2002), 155.

81 Stacy Alaimo, "Discomforting Creatures: Monstrous Natures in Recent Films," in *Beyond Nature Writing: Expanding the Boundaries of Ecocriticism*, ed. Karla Armbruster and Kathleen Wallace (Charlottesville: University Press of Virginia, 2001), 287–96 at 289.

82 Alaimo, "Discomforting Creatures," 294.

83 Gilles Deleuze and Félix Guattari, "1730: Becoming-Intense, Becoming-Animal, Becoming-Imperceptible," Chapter 10 in *A Thousand Plateaus: Capitalism and Schizophrenia*, trans. Brian Massumi (Minneapolis: University of Minnesota Press, 1987). See also Margot Norris, *Beasts of the Modern Imagination: Darwin, Nietzsche, Kafka, Ernst, and Lawrence* (Baltimore: Johns Hopkins University Press, 1985); Steve Baker, *The Postmodern Animal* (London: Reaktion, 2000); and Nato Thompson, ed., *Becoming Animal: Contemporary Art in the Animal Kingdom* (Cambridge, MA: MIT Press, 2005).

84 For simplicity's sake, I am referring to non-human animals in this chapter mostly just as "animals," though of course this is not meant to deny that humans are a particular type of animal.

85 Angela Creager and William Jordan, eds., *The Animal/Human Boundary: Historical Perspectives* (Rochester: University of Rochester Press, 2002); Lorraine Daston and Gregg Mitman, eds., *Thinking with Animals: New Perspectives on Anthropomorphism* (New York: Columbia University Press, 2005); Erica Fudge, *Animal* (London: Reaktion Books, 2002); Tim Ingold, ed., *What Is an Animal?* (London: Unwin Hyman, 1988); Howard Morphy, *Animals into Art* (London: Unwin Hyman, 1989); Nigel Rothfels, ed., *Representing Animals* (Bloomington: Indiana University Press, 2002); Roy Willis, ed., *Signifying Animals: Human Meaning in the Natural World* (London: Unwin Hyman, 1990).

86   Laura Hobgood-Oster, *Holy Dogs and Asses: Animals in the Christian Tradition* (Urbana: University of Illinois Press, 2008); Dorothy Yamamoto, *The Boundaries of the Human in Medieval English Literature* (New York: Oxford University Press, 2000).

87   Matthew Calarco and Peter Atterton, eds., *Animal Philosophy: Essential Readings in Continental Philosophy* (London: Continuum, 2004); Steven Clark, "Is Humanity a Natural Kind?," in Tim Ingold, ed., *What Is an Animal?* (London: Unwin Hyman, 1988); Raymond Corbey, *The Metaphysics of Apes: Negotiating the Animal–Human Boundary* (New York: Cambridge University Press, 2005); Adrian Franklin, *Animals and Modern Cultures: A Sociology of Human–Animal Relations in Modernity* (London: Sage, 2005); Barbara Noske, *Humans and Other Animals: Beyond the Boundaries of Anthropology* (London: Pluto Press, 1989); Jennifer Ham and Matthew Senior, eds., *Animal Acts: Configuring the Human in Western Society* (New York: Routledge, 1997); Adrian Ivakhiv, "Re-animations: Instinct and Civility after the Ends of 'Man' and 'Nature,'" in From *Virgin Land to Disney World: Nature and Its Discontents in the USA of Yesterday and Today*, ed. Bernd Herzogenrath (Amsterdam/New York: Rodopi, 2001), 7–32; Molly Mullin, "Mirrors and Windows: Sociocultural Studies of Human–Animal Relationships," *Annual Review of Anthropology* 28 (1999): 201–24; Rothfels, *Representing Animals*; Cary Wolfe, *Zoontologies: The Question of the Animal* (Minneapolis: University of Minnesota Press, 2003).

88   Giorgio Agamben, *The Open: Man and Animal*, trans. Kevin Attell (Stanford: Stanford University Press, 2004).

89   See Erb, *Tracking King Kong*. Viewer reviews on websites such as Amazon.com, Rotten Tomatoes, Metacritic, IMDb, and Mubi, as well as blogs focusing on specific genres, directors, and perspectives on cinema, provide a wealth of data for analysis.

90   Kathryn Elizabeth Kasic, "Perspective in Wildlife Films," MFA thesis, Montana State University, Bozeman, 2007, 11.

91   Documentaries have rarely been seen by major film studios as promising much box office success, but this situation saw a sea change in 2004, when Michael Moore's *Fahrenheit 9/11* broke through the $100 million barrier. (Though falling into a somewhat different genre, *Everest* [1998] had broken the same barrier.) My figures here are taken from http://www.the-numbers.com/market/Genres/Documentary.php, accessed January 12, 2008, http://www.rottentomatoes.com, and http://www.imdb.com.

92   Katie McGoldrick and Emma Marris, "Green Activists Enlist Penguins to Save the World," *Nature* 444 (2006): 978–79; Jonathan Miller, "March of the Conservatives: Penguin Film as Political Fodder," *New York Times*, September 13, 2005; Marlene Zuk, "Family Values in Black and White," *Nature* 439 (2006): 917.

93   See Editorial, *New York Times*, 25 September 2005; American Public Media, *Living on Earth*, December 8, 2006.

94   Editorial, *New York Times*, 25 September 2005.

95   McGoldrick and Marris, "Green Activists Enlist Penguins."

96   Max Blumenthal, "Dobson and Medved Warned of Purported Pro-Gay 'Subtext' in *Happy Feet*," Media Matters for America, 15 December 2006.

97   Rebecca Wexler, "Onward, Christian Penguins: Wildlife Film and the Image of Scientific Authority," *Studies in the History and Philosophy of Biology and Biomedical Science* 39 (2008): 273–79 at 277.

98   Wexler, "Onward, Christian Penguins," 275.

99   See, for instance, Lorraine Daston and Gregg Mitman, eds., *Thinking with Animals: New Perspectives on Anthropomorphism* (New York: Columbia University Press, 2005).

100 The sites I reviewed included ChristianityToday.com, Focus on the Family's Pluggedinonline.com, Crosswalk.com, *American Catholic's* CatholicMovieReview .org, and the Catholic News Service (CatholicNews.com).

101 As skeptical commentators have pointed out, each of these arguments can be turned on its head. For instance, one might ask why a divine creator would give the penguins such difficult lives or how he could possibly sit by as species go extinct, as biologists claim they are doing at a rate unprecedented in human history.

102 Huckabee's campaign has been criticized by noted right-wing personalities, including Rush Limbaugh (as being about "class warfare") and the editors of the *Wall Street Journal* (who call his position "religious left"). See David Kirkpatrick, "Huckabee Splits Young Evangelicals and Old Guard," *New York Times*, 13 January 2008, 1, 18.

103 The reference is to Peter Singer's movement-catalyzing book *Animal Liberation* (New York: Random House, 1975).

104 Mark Bittner, "The Ordinance to Ban the Feeding of the Wild Parrots" (2007), http:// www.markbittner.net/writings /feeding_ordinance_1.html, accessed 10 December 2012.

105 A Yahoo discussion group called wildparrotfeeders, which had tried to build public support against the ban, was particularly active in 2007 and maintains a website at http://groups.yahoo.com/group/wildparrotfeeders. Other wild parrot support groups continue to work across the country.

106 Nick Jans writes that there was "not a single documented case of a bear being illegally killed inside park boundaries" for eighty years prior to 2004; see Ganz, *The Grizzly Maze: Timothy Treadwell's Fatal Obsession with Alaskan Bears* (New York: Dutton, 2005), 34. Ecologist Marc Gaede claims, however, that "Tim did protect his bears from poachers.... There is poaching in Katmai National Park because that's where the best trophy animals are in fact located. Alaskan professional poaching is a sophisticated business involving millions of dollars, crafty guides and probably the best bush pilots in the world."

107 See, for example, Ellen Brinks, "Uncovering the Child in Timothy Treadwell's Feral Tale," *Lion and the Unicorn* 32 (2008): 304–23.

108 This argument about the gaze of the bear "exhausting" any efforts to capture it is made by Benjamin Noys in a very perceptive treatment of the film; see Noys, "*Antiphusis*: Werner Herzog's *Grizzly Man*," *Film–Philosophy* 11, no. 3 (2007): 38–51 at 48, http://www.film-philosophy.com/2007v11n3/noys.pdf.

109 An archived version of this Web page can be found athttp://web.archive.org/ web/20060831142627/http://blog.nrdcactionfund.org/archives/2005/10/ timothy_treadwe.html, accessed 10 December 2012.

110 The last archived version retrievable at the time of writing this article contained 156 posts and was saved on 23 August 2006. The blog closed sometime afterwards.

111 See http://pets.groups.yahoo.com/group/TimothyTreadwell_Paths.

112 A fascinating, if at times vitriolic, exchange between Watson and *Anchorage Daily News* columnist Mike Doogan is reproduced on the Sea Shapherd website: http://www.seashepherd.org/editorials/editorial_031024_1.html.

113 At least this is Baele's claim, one that I could not verify.

114 "Sabrina," posted on TimothyTreadwell_Paths (see note 109), 29 March 2006.

115 "johngaltlives," posted on TimothyTreadwell_Paths, 29 March 2006.

116 "filmed everything": Kevin Sanders, "Night of the Grizzly: A True Story of Love and Death in the Wilderness," Bearman's Yellowstone Adventures (2008), http://www.yellowstone-bearman.com/Tim_Treadwell.html, accessed 30 March 2008; "planned a big movie": Herzog, interview with Devin Faraci, 8 August 2005, posted on TimothyTreadwell_Paths, 15 April 2006.

117 John Rogers, n.d., "The Myth of Timothy Treadwell," http://www.katmaibears.com/timothytreadwell.htm; Charlie Russell, "Letters from Charlie: Timothy Treadwell—Grizzly Man," Pacific Rim Grizzly Bear Co-Existence Study (2006), http://cloudline.org/treadwell.html, accessed 30 March 2008; Sanders, "Night of the Grizzly," accessed 30 March 2008.

118 Russell, "Letters from Charlie."

119 Rogers, "The Myth of Timothy Treadwell."

120 Sanders, "Night of the Grizzly."

121 The books include Jans, *The Grizzly Maze*; and Mike Lapinski, *Death in the Grizzly Maze: The Timothy Treadwell Story* (Guilford: Falcon, 2005).

122 Werner Herzog, interview with Marrit Ingman, *Austin Chronicle,* 19 August 2005; emphasis added.

123 Astrida Neimanis, "Becoming-Grizzly: Bodily Molecularity and the Animal That Becomes," *PhaenEx* 2, no. 2 (2007): 279–308 at 298.

124 Ibid., 298.

125 Ibid., 299.

126 Deleuze and Guattari, *A Thousand Plateaus,* 279.

127 Patricia Pisters, *The Matrix of Visual Culture: Working with Deleuze in Film Theory* (Stanford: Stanford University Press, 2003), 144.

128 Neimanis, "Becoming-Grizzly," 281.

129 Ibid., 291.

130 Alphonso Lingis, *Dangerous Emotions* (Berkeley: University of California Press, 2000), 29.

131 I am relying especially on Keith Hopper's reading of the film in "Hairy on the Inside: Revisiting Neil Jordan's *The Company of Wolves,*" *Canadian Journal of Irish Studies* 29, no. 2 (2003): 17–26.

132 Ibid., 22.

133 Laura Mulvey, in Pisters, *The Matrix of Cinema,* 166.

134 Rob Nelson, "The Dark Horse: Zoo," interview with Robinson Devor, *Antennae* 8, no. 2 (2008): 45–58 at 48.

135 Robert McKay, "A Dangerous Border," *Antennae* 8, no. 2 (2008): 60–64.

136 See Donna Haraway, *When Species Meet* (Bloomington: University of Minnesota Press, 2008), esp. Chapter 8, "Training in the Contact Zone."

137 That said, the DVD of the film, as is often the case, includes material that focuses on the making of the film, portraying the hardships undergone by the crew, their technical expertise and prowess, and so on. The DVD, then, provides a broader ethnographic strategy than the film alone.

138 Seung-hoon Jeong and Dudley Andrew, "*Grizzly Ghost*: Herzog, Bazin, and the Cinematic Animal," *Screen* 49, no. 1 (2008): 1–12.

139 On Derrida's ethic toward animals, see Leonard Lawlor, *This Is Not Sufficient: An Essay on Animality and Human Nature in Derrida* (New York: Columbia University Press, 2007). Levinas's philosophy of alterity, despite its name, tends to focus on commonality, since the thing that makes ethical action possible for Levinas is the "face" of the Other. In his writing, this generally means a human face (notwithstanding his account of the Nazi prison camp dog "Bobby"; see Matthew Calarco and Peter Atterton, *Animal Philosophy* [New York: Continuum, 2004], 45ff.), but animal rights philosophers have interpreted his work to include the face of other-than-human Others. See John Llewelyn, *The Middle Voice of Ecological Conscience: A Chiasmic Reading of Responsibility in the Neighborhood of Levinas, Heidegger, and Others* (New York: St. Martin's Press, 1991); and Barbara Jane Davy, "An Other Face of Ethics in Levinas," *Ethics and the Environment* 12, no. 1 (2005): 39–65. Representations of the face and especially of the eye become particularly potent sites for studying the potential breakdown of any human/animal differential "system."

140 Herzog claims that such characters find him: "He [Treadwell] discovered me. This kind of character somehow stumbles into my path." Interview with Ingman.

Notes to Chapter 6

1   Fredric Jameson, *Postmodernism, or, the Cultural Logic of Late Capitalism* (Durham: Duke University Press, 1991), ix.

2   Bill McKibben, *The End of Nature* (New York: Random House, 1989), 7.

3   Guattari, *Chaosmosis: An Ethico-Aesthetic Paradigm*, trans. Paul Bains and Julian Prefanis (Indianapolis: Indiana University Press, 1995), 20–21.

4   Joseph LeDoux, *The Emotional Brain: The Mysterious Underpinnings of Emotional Life* (London: Weidenfeld and Nicolson, 1996). This differentiation between primary and secondary brain circuits parallels a more general differentiation between affect and cognition. Psychologists such as Silvan Tomkins, Paul Ekman, and Robert Zajonc have argued that this points to two separate systems, the first of which acts more rapidly than (and relatively independently from) the second. Neuroscientists, including Antonio Damasio and Joseph LeDoux, have popularized this view of separate affective and cognitive systems—a view that has since spread to the social sciences, especially among "new affect theorists" such as Eve Kosovsky Sedgwick, Patricia Clough, Brian Massumi, and William Connolly. However, this "two systems" view is controversial and is not accepted by all psychologists and neuroscientists. Some, including Richard S. Lazarus, Alan Fridlund, James A. Russell,

Jose-Miguel Fernandez-Dols, and Lisa Feldman Barrett, prefer a more nuanced view or call for a new paradigm in the study of affect and cognition. For a summary and review of these critiques, see Ruth Leys, "The Turn to Affect: A Critique," *Critical Inquiry* 37 (2011): 434–72.

5   Influential works about trauma and its cultural impacts and representations include Cathy Caruth, *Unclaimed Experience: Trauma, Narrative, and History* (Baltimore: Johns Hopkins University Press, 1996); Cathy Caruth, ed., *Trauma: Explorations in Memory* (Baltimore: Johns Hopkins University Press, 1995; Shoshana Felman and Dori Laub, *Testimony: Crises of Witnessing in Literature, Psychoanalysis, and History* (New York: Routledge, 1992); E. Ann Kaplan, *Trauma Culture: The Politics of Terror and Loss in Media and Literature* (New Brunswick: Rutgers University Press, 2005); and Ruth Leys, *Trauma: A Genealogy* (Chicago: University of Chicago Press, 2000). On the visuality of trauma, see Jill Bennett, "On the Subject of Trauma," in her *Empathic Vision: Affect, Trauma, and Contemporary Art* (Stanford: Stanford University Press, 2005); Susan Sontag, *Regarding the Pain of Others* (New York: Farrar Straus and Giroux, 2003); E. Ann Kaplan and Ban Wang, *Trauma and Cinema: Cross-Cultural Explorations* (Hong Kong University Press, 2004); Janet Walker, *Trauma Cinema: Documenting Incest and the Holocaust* (Berkeley: University of California Press, 2005); and Allen Meek, *Trauma and Media: Theories, Histories, and Images* (London: Routledge, 2010).

6   Shoshana Felman and Dori Laub, *Testimony: Crises of Witnessing in Literature, Psychoanalysis, and History* (New York: Routledge, 1992), xvii.

7   Roger Luckhurst, "The Trauma Knot," in *The Future of Memory,* ed. Richard Crownshaw, Jane Kilby, and Antony Rowland (London: Berghahn Books, 2010), 191–206 at 192.

8   On the "traumatological aesthetic," see Philip Tew, *The Contemporary British Novel,* 2nd ed. (London: Continuum, 2007), xviii. On the culture "saturated with trauma," see Roger Luckhurst, *The Trauma Question* (London: Routledge, 2008), 2.

9   Janet Walker, "Trauma Cinema: False Memories and True Experience," *Screen* 42, no. 2 (2001): 211–16 at 214.

10   Shoshana Felman, "In an Era of Testimony: Claude Lanzmann's *Shoah,*" *Yale French Studies* 97 (2000), "50 Years of Yale French Studies: A Commemorative Anthology," Part 2: 1980–1998: 103–50 at 104.

11   E. Ann Kaplan, "Global Trauma and Public Feelings: Viewing Images of Catastrophe," *Consumption, Markets, and Culture* 11, no. 1 (2008): 3–24.

12   Jodi Dean's *Aliens in America: Conspiracy Cultures from Outer Space to Cyberspace* (Ithaca: Cornell University Press, 1998), and Elaine Showalter's *Hystories: Hysterical Epidemics and Modern Media* (New York: Columbia University Press, 1997), provide divergent but insightful analyses of these kinds of phenomena.

13   See Slavoj Žižek, *Welcome to the Desert of the Real* (London: Verso, 2002); Paul Virilio, *Ground Zero,* trans. Chris Turner (London: Verso, 2002); and Jean Baudrillard, *The Spirit of Terrorism,* trans. Chris Turner (London: Verso, 2003). See also Susannah Radstone, "The War of the Fathers: Trauma, Fantasy, and September 11," in *Trauma at Home: After 9/11,* ed. Judith Greenberg (Lincoln: University of Nebraska Press, 2003), 117–23 at 117.

14   Meek, *Trauma and Media,* 10.

15   Kaplan, "Global Trauma," 9.

16   John Sanders, *Studying Disaster Movies* (Leighton Buzzard: Auteur, 2009).

17   Until recently, the role of affect in risk perception had been underemphasized in favour of cognitive factors. This is now being challenged by researchers such as Antonio Damasio, Joseph Ledoux, Robert Zajonc, Seymour Epstein, George Loewenstein, and Paul Slovic. Anthony Leiserowitz provides a good overview of cognitive versus affective reactions to stimuli, with reference to the perception of environmental risks, in "Climate Change Risk Perception and Policy Preferences: The Role of Affect, Imagery, and Values," *Climatic Change* 77, nos. 1–2 (2006): 45–72. Leiserowitz's preferred terms are "analytic" and "experiential" processing. See also Paul Slovic, Melissa Finucane, Ellen Peters, and Donald G. MacGregor, "Affect, Risk, and Decision Making," *Health Psychology* 24, no. 4 (2005): S35–40.

18   There is, of course, much debate among scholars of risk perception regarding the relative roles played by thinking and feeling, or cognition and affect, and even regarding whether it makes sense to separate the two domains in this way. What I've summarized rather loosely resembles a position articulated (with somewhat different emphasis) by Mary Douglas and Aaron Wildavsky, and their followers in the "cultural theory of risk"; see Douglas and Wildavsky, *Risk and Culture: An Essay on the Selection of Technical and Environmental Dangers (Berkeley: University of California Press, 1982).* More broadly, I am echoing much of the more recent work on "neuropolitics" (as William Connolly has called it), though I do not wish to skirt its many criticisms. See Adrian Ivakhiv, "From Frames to Resonance Machines: The Neuropolitics of Environmental Communication," *Environmental Communication* 4, no. 1 (2010): 109–21, for a review of some of this literature.

19   Robin Murray and Joseph Heumann are therefore right to compare the film's affects with those of a number of eco-disaster films from the 1970s such as *Soylent Green* (1973), with its narrative of ecological decline and overpopulation. See Murray and Heumann, "Al Gore's *An Inconvenient Truth* and Its Skeptics: A Case of Environmental Nostalgia," *Jump Cut* 49 (Spring 2007), http://www.ejumpcut.org/archive/jc49.2007/inconvenTruth/text.html; and *idem,* "Conclusion," in *Ecology and Popular Film: Cinema on the Edge* (Albany: SUNY Press, 2009), 195–205.

20   *Soylent Green* has been well analyzed by Murray and Heumann and also by Pat Brereton, so I will not detail that film or other eco-themed films (e.g., *Silent Running,* 1971; *Omega Man,* 1971). See Murray and Heumann, "Al Gore's *An Inconvenient Truth*"; and Pat Brereton, *Hollywood Utopia: Ecology in Contemporary American Cinema* (Bristol: Intellect Books, 2005).

21   Americans' views about climate change are notoriously fickle, in part because of the power of the "skeptic" lobby in shaping media agendas. In Britain, the downturn in the public's assessment of the film was spurred by a debate over whether it should be distributed to public schools. After the Department for Education and Public Skills announced it would do so, a lawsuit was brought against the Secretary of State for Education and Skills. On its second hearing, the British High Court concluded that the film included nine "errors," which the

media subsequently played up as "inconvenient untruths." Many climate scientists disagreed with the ruling. See Felicity Mellor, "The Politics of Accuracy in Judging Global Warming Films," *Environmental Communication* 3, no. 2 (2009): 134–50. Another paper, which I reviewed for the same journal, included data on the change in views about the Gore film's claims.

22   See Anthony A. Leiserowitz, "Before and After *The Day After Tomorrow*: A U.S. Study of Climate Change Risk Perception," *Environment* 47, no. 3 (2004): 22–37; Fritz Reusswig, "The International Impact of *The Day After Tomorrow*," *Environment* 47, no. 3 (2005): 41–43, and Leiserowitz's response, 43–44; Fritz Reusswig, Julia Schwarzkopf, and Phillipp Pohlenz, "Double Impact: The Climate Blockbuster *The Day After Tomorrow* and Its Impact on the German Cinema Public," Potsdam Institute for Climate Impact Research (PIK) Report no. 93 (Potsdam: PIK, 2004), http://www.pik-potsdam.de/research/publications/.../.files/pr92.pdf; M. Aoyagi-Usui, "*The Day After Tomorrow*: A Study on the Impact of a Global Warming Movie on the Japanese Public," National Institute for Environmental Studies (NIES) Working Paper (unpublished), October 2004; Thomas Lowe et al., "Does Tomorrow Ever Come? Disaster Narrative and Public Perceptions of Climate Change," Draft Tyndall Working Paper (unpublished), October 2004; and Andrew Balmford et al., "Hollywood, Climate Change, and the Public," *Science* 17 (September 2004): 1713.

23   Leiserowitz, "Before and After *The Day After Tomorrow*," 26.

24   Ibid., 34.

25   Thomas Lowe et al., "Does Tomorrow Ever Come? Disaster Narrative and Public Perceptions of Climate Change," *Public Understanding of Science* 15 (2006): 435–57 at 435.

26   Ibid., 452.

27   Thomas Lowe, "Is This Climate Porn? How Does Climate Change Communication Affect Our Perceptions of Behaviour?," Tyndall Centre for Climate Change Research Working Paper no. 98 (Norwich: University of East Anglia, 2006), 24; emphasis added.

28   Leiserowitz, "Before and After," 31–32; Leiserowitz, letter, *Environment* 47, no. 3 (2005): 43–44.

29   See Matthew Nisbet, "Evaluating the Impact of *The Day After Tomorrow*: Can a Blockbuster Film Shape the Public's Understanding of a Science Controversy?," 16 June 2004, *Skeptical Inquirer Online,* http://www.csicop.org/specialarticles/show/evaluating_the_impact_of_the_day_after_tomorrow; and Lowe et al., "Does Tomorrow Ever Come?," 454.

30   Leiserowitz, "Before and After," 32.

31   E. Ann Kaplan, *Trauma Culture: The Politics of Terror and Loss in Media and Literature* (New Brunswick, NJ: Rutgers University Press, 2005), 1.

32   Fredric Jameson, *The Geopolitical Aesthetic: Cinema and Space in the World System* (Bloomington: Indiana University Press, 1992). See also *idem, The Political Unconscious: Narrative as a Socially Symbolic Act* (London: Routledge, 1981). The quote comes from Jameson, *Postmodernism, or, the Cultural Logic of Late Capitalism* (Durham, NC: Duke University Press, 1991), 4; emphasis in original.

33   Colin McCabe, "Preface" in Jameson, *The Geopolitical Aesthetic,* xi.

34   Jameson, *The Geopolitical Aesthetic*, 4.

35   Jameson, *Postmodernism*, ix.

36   Ibid., ix.

37   Bill McKibben, *The End of Nature* (New York: Anchor/Doubleday, 1990).

38   Immanuel Wallerstein, the founder of world-systems theory (on which Jameson draws, alongside other neo-Marxist historians and sociologists), has argued that the ecological crisis is a consequence of the process of capital accumulation that is inherent to the modern world-system; see Wallerstein, "Ecology and Capitalist Costs of Production: No Exit," in *The End of the World as We Know It: Social Science for the Twenty-first Century* (Minneapolis: University of Minnesota Press, 1999), 76–86. See also Jason Moore, "*The Modern World System* as Environmental History? Ecology and the Rise of Capitalism," *Theory and Society* 32 (2003): 307–77, for an insightful elaboration of an ecologized world-systems theory. James O'Connor and various contributors to the journal *Capitalism Nature Socialism* have developed related neo-Marxist arguments about the "second" (i.e., ecological) "contradiction" of capitalism.

39   Aldemaro Romero and Christian Jones, "Not All Are Created Equal: An Analysis of the Environmental Programs/Departments in U.S. Academic Institutions until May 2003," *Macalester Environmental Review*, http://altweb.astate.edu/electronicjournal/Electronic%20Journal/NotAllAreCreatedEqual%5B1%5D.2005.hannigan.pdf, accessed 10 December2012.

40   Andrew Ross, "The Drought This Time," in *Strange Weather: Culture, Science, and Technology in the Age of Limits* (New York: Verso, 1991), 193–249.

41   Paul Thomas Anderson, *Magnolia: The Shooting Script* (New York: Newmarket, 2000), 207. A relevant question for an ecocritic is whether any frogs were harmed during the production; the answer, apparently, is no: more than 7,900 rubber frogs were made for the film; the rest were created by computer graphics.

42   Jonathan Romney, "In the Time of Earthquakes," *Sight and Sound* (March 1994), 9.

43   That LA leads the pack in the imagination of natural catastrophe is demonstrated in Mike Davis, *The Ecology of Fear: Los Angeles and the Imagination of Disaster* (New York: Vintage, 1998).

44   Don DeLillo, *White Noise* (New York: Viking/Penguin, 1985).

45   Slavoj Žižek, "The Undergrowth of Enjoyment," *New Frontiers* 9, no. 7 (1989): 29.

46   I am indebted to Wendy Wheeler for pointing out these resonances undergirding Žižek's phrase.

47   Stephen Helmling, *The Success and Failure of Fredric Jameson: Writing, the Sublime, and the Dialectic of Critique* (Albany: SUNY Press, 2001), 13. See also Edmund Burke, *A Philosophical Enquiry into the Origin of Our Ideas of the Sublime and Beautiful*, ed. Adam Phillips, new ed. (Oxford: Oxford University Press, 1998); Immanuel Kant, *Critique of Practical Reason*, trans. Lewis Beck (New York: Macmillan, 1993); Thomas Weiskel, *The Romantic Sublime: Studies in the Structure and Psychology of Transcendence* (Baltimore: Johns Hopkins University Press, 1986).

48   David E. Nye, *American Technological Sublime* (Cambridge, MA: MIT Press, 1996).

49   Rob Wilson, *American Sublime: The Genealogy of a Poetic Genre* (Madison: University of Wisconsin Press, 1991).

50   Jerry Aline Flieger, "The Listening Eye: Postmodernism, Paranoia, and the Hypevisible," *Diacritics* 26, no. 1 (1996): 99. See also *idem,* "Postmodern Perspective: The Paranoid Eye," *New Literary History* 28, no. 1 (1989): 87–109.

51   Jean-François Lyotard, "The Sublime and the Avant-Garde," *Paragraph* 6 (1985): 1–18; *idem, The Postmodern Condition,* trans. Geoffrey Bennington and Brian Massumi (Manchester: Manchester University Press, 1986); *idem, The Inhuman: Reflections on Time,* trans. Geoffrey Bennington and Rachel Bowlby (Cambridge: Polity Press, 1991); and *idem, Of the Sublime: Presence in Question,* trans. Jeffrey Librett (Albany: SUNY Press, 1993).

52   Lyotard, *The Postmodern Condition,* 80ff.

53   Nicoletta Pireddu, "Beyond Figuration, Below the Threshold: Some Observations on Postmodernism and the Sublime," *Negations* 1 (1996), http://www.datawranglers .com/negations/issues/96w/96w_pireddu.html.

54   Helmling, *The Success and Failure of Fredric Jameson,* 112; though I am told this point was made by William Wordsworth in his 1805 Preface to the *Lyrical Ballads.*

55   Jameson, *Postmodernism,* 38; cf. Flieger, "The Listening Eye" and "Postmodern Perspective."

56   Stacy Alaimo, "Discomforting Creatures: Monstrous Natures in Recent Films," in *Beyond Nature Writing: Expanding the Boundaries of Ecocriticism,* ed. Karla Armbruster and Kathleen Wallace (Charlottesville: University Press of Virginia, 2001), 291.

57   Theodore Roszak, *The Voice of the Earth: An Exploration of Ecopsychology* (Grand Rapids, MI: Phanes Press, 2001), 320.

58   This is not to suggest that the mind is a blank slate, but rather that whatever propensities humans are born with vary from individual to individual and co-evolve with their environments from the first moments of embryonic development to the final breaths of mature adulthood. They do not represent a unified and clearly demarcated "species being," whether it be that of Jung's archetypal unconscious or the genetic templates proposed by sociobiologists or evolutionary psychologists. I also do not intend to imply that Jungian notions are irredeemably "essentialist." In the hands of James Hillman and others, as I will argue below, they are profoundly useful for understanding our relationship to symbols and images. On the utter intertwining of nature and culture, see Susan Oyama's groundbreaking *The Ontogeny of Information: Developmental Systems and Evolution,* 2nd rev. and exp. ed. (Durham, NC: Duke University Press, 2000).

59   Andrew Ross, *The Chicago Gangster Theory of Life: Nature's Debt to Society* (London: Verso, 1994), 171.

60   See, for example, Alaimo, "Discomforting Creatures"; and Fatimah Rony, "King Kong and the Monster in Ethnographic Cinema," in *The Third Eye: Race Cinema, and Ethnographic Spectacle* (Durham, NC: Duke University Press, 1996), 157–91.

61   Slavoj Žižek, "Children of Men: Comments by Slavoj Žižek," http://www .childrenofmen.net.

62   On database narratives, see Lev Manovich, *The Language of New Media* (Cambridge, MA: MIT Press, 2001). On forking-paths, multiple-draft, and modula narratives, see David Bordwell, "Film Futures," *SubStance* 31, no. 1 (2002): 88–104; and Edward Branigan, "Nearly True: Forking Plots, Forking Interpretations: A Response to

David Bordwell's 'Film Futures,'" *SubStance* 31, no. 1 (2002): 105–14. On modular narratives, see Allan Cameron, *Modular Narratives in Contemporary Cinema* (New York: Palgrave Macmillan, 2008). On puzzle films, see Warren Buckland, *Puzzle Films: Complex Storytelling in Contemporary Cinema* (Malden: Blackwell, 2009).

63 See, for example, Marina Hassapopoulou, "*Babel:* Pushing and Reaffirming Mainstream Cinema's Boundaries," *Jump Cut* 50 (2008), http://www.ejumpcut.org/archive/jc50.2008/Babel.

64 Kirk Boyle, "*Children of Men* and *I Am Legend*: The Disaster-Capitalism Complex Hits Hollywood," *Jump Cut* 51 (2009), http://www.ejumpcut.org/archive/jc51.2009/ChildrenMenLegend.

65 A.O. Scott, "The Ties That Bind America's Food Chain," *New York Times,* 17 November 2006.

66 Gregory Stephens examines this trope of "eating shit" in "Corn-Fed Culture: Living Large and 'Eating Shit' in *King Corn* and *Fast Food Nation,*" *Bright Lights Film Journal* 68 (2010), http://www.brightlightsfilm.com/68/68cornfedculture.php.

67 Tobias Grey, "'Darwin' Tells African Fish Tale," *Variety,* 20–26 June 2005.

68 A letter written to Sauper by the Executive Secretary of the Lake Victoria Fisheries Organization and by the Eastern Africa Regional Director of the IUCN argues that his film is as corrupt as he argues the fisheries to be (Thomas Maembe and Alice Kaudia, Letter of Hubert Sauper, 8 December 2005). A more fully developed version of this argument is presented in François Garçon, *Enquête sur le cauchemar de Darwin* (Paris: Flammarion, 2006). See also K.H. von Kaufman, "The Deathpond," *Futures* 39 (2007): 763–67. Garçon and Kaufman appear to lack the scholarly credentials of some of those whom Sauper has enlisted in his defence, such as fisheries biologist Les Kaufman and anthropologist Eirik Jansen; see Les Kaufman, "A Scientist's Letter on the Veracity of the Film, 'Darwin's Nightmare,'" 22 February 2006; and Jansen, "Evolutions recentes dans les usines de poisson d'Afrique de l'Est"; both at http://www.darwinsnightmare.com/reviews.htm, accessed 6 October 2011. But where biologists see crisis abetted by global forces, anthropologists and development researchers see much greater complexity. Thomas Molony, Lisa Ann Richey, and Stefano Ponte criticize the film for its "totalizing vision," which "reduces gender relations, sexuality, socio-economic change, homelessness, poverty and complicated vectors of disease transmission into stale tropes associated with Afro-pessimism," and conclude that the "ethically dubious" film "exploits the power imbalances it claims to critique." See Molony, Richey, and Ponte, "'Darwin's Nightmare': A Critical Assessment," *Review of African Political Economy* 34, no. 113 (2007): 598–608 at 599. The fate of the lake, meanwhile, remains uncertain: the perch have turned out to be cannibalistic upon smaller members of their own species (which doesn't bode well for continuation of the species), and eutrophication threatens to turn the lake's water into an undrinkable, protein-free disaster. For other historical perspectives on Lake Victoria and the Nile perch issue—most of them at least loosely supportive of Sauper's overall argument—see Tijs Goldschmidt, *Darwin's Dreampond: Drama in Lake Victoria* (Cambridge: MIT Press, 1998); A. Kent MacDougall, "Lake Victoria: Casualty of Capitalism," *Monthly*

Review 53 (2001): 38–42; and Robert Pringle, "The Nile Perch in Lake Victoria: Local Responses and Adaptations," *Africa* 75, no. 4 (2005): 510–38.

69 Molony, Richey, and Ponte, "'Darwin's Nightmare,'" 605; Economist Intelligence Unit, "Country Profile: Tanzania" (London: 2006), 17.

70 A.O. Scott, "Movie Review: *Darwin's Nightmare*," *New York Times*, 3 August 2005.

71 B. Ruby Rich, "Documentary Disciplines: An Introduction," *Cinema Journal* 46, no. 1 (2006): 108–15.

72 Olivier Barlet, "The Ambiguity of Darwin's Nightmare," trans. Kyana LeMaitre, Africultures.com, 8 August 2007, http://www.africultures.com/php/index .php?nav=article&no=5745.

73 Ilan Kapoor, "Troubled Waters: Crashing into *The Cove*," *Bright Lights Film Journal* 68 (May 2010), http://brightlightsfilm.com/68/68thecove.php.

74 Kapoor, "Troubled Waters."

75 Paul Cronin, ed., *Herzog on Herzog* (London: Faber and Faber, 2002), 249.

76 Nadia Bozak, "Firepower: Herzog's Pure Cinema as the Internal Combustion of War," *CineAction* 68 (2006): 24.

77 Werner Herzog, Roger Ebert, and Gene Walsh, *Images at the Horizon: A Workshop with Werner Herzog* (Chicago: Facets Multimedia, 1979), 21.

78 See Alain Badiou, *Being and Event*, trans. by Oliver Feltham (New York: Continuum, 2005).

79 William S. Burroughs, *The Naked Lunch*, 50th Anniversary Edition (New York: Grove Press, 2009), 199.

80 With its gross receipts of nearly $3 billion exceeding the gross national product of seventy-seven countries, it is, as Max Cafard observes, "the highest-grossing film of all time—in the U.S., in at least thirty-one other countries worldwide, and as far as we know, in the entire universe." See Max Cafard, "Intergalactic Blues: Fantasy and Ideology in Avatar," *Psychic Swamp: The Surre(gion)al Review* 1 (2010): 9–41 at 9.

81 Viewer polls conducted during the opening weekend showed that the 3-D effects were the largest draw and that all demographics gave the film a positive ("A" average) grade. See Neil Miller, "*Avatar* Opens to Big Returns, but Staying Power Is the Key," *Film School Rejects*, 21 December 2009, http://www.filmschoolrejects .com/news/avatar-opens-to-big-returns-but-staying-power-is-the-key.php.

82 Kvond, comment on "Avatar: Panthea v. the Capitalist War Machine," *Immanence* blog, 21 December 2009, http://blog.uvm.edu/aivakhiv/2009/12/21/avatar-panthea -v-the-capitalist-war-machine; *idem*, "Avatarship and the New Man: Reading Ideology, Technology, and Hope," *Frames/sing*, 21 December 2009, http://kvond.wordpress .com/2009/12/21/avatarship-and-the-new-man-reading-ideology-and-hope. On the other hand, Joshua Clover ("The Struggle for Space," *Film Quarterly* 63, no. 3 [2010]: 6–7) complains that most of the movie "looks like a series of Roger Dean album covers from 1970s prog-rock albums, set in motion. The technology is improving, but the achievement does not yet feel like a profound change in our experience of cinematic volume equivalent to Greg Toland's deep focus, the introduction of CinemaScope, or the onset of the Steadicam" (6). It is, in any case, the film's immersiveness in an alternative world that leads to "post-*Avatar* depression syndrome,"

discussed below. Some have found that world more edifying to the imagination than this one, which may not exactly bode well for the ecopsychological task that Gilles Deleuze described as the revival of "belief in this world." But, as others have argued, such reactions can also prompt action on behalf of this world.

83   Lisa Sideris, "I See You: Interspecies Empathy and *Avatar*," *Journal for the Study of Religion, Nature, and Culture* 4, no. 4 (2010): 457–77 at 465.

84   Ibid., 471.

85   See ibid., 472ff.

86   Robert Hyland, "Going Na'vi: Mastery in *Avatar*," *CineAction* 82–83 (2011): 10–16 at 12.

87   Catherine Grant perspicuously sifts through the many allegorical readings to be found online and in the press in "Seeing Through *Avatar*: Film Allegory 101," *Film Studies for Free,* 27 January 2010, http://filmstudiesforfree.blogspot .com/2010/01/i-see-you-on-avatar-and-allegory.html, accessed 26 September 2010. The Wikipedia article "Themes in Avatar" provides a thorough distillation of the film's many themes and interpretations. See http://en.wikipedia.org/wiki/ Themes_in_Avatar. The cinema analogy is my own addition, which I have not seen elsewhere, but which is consistent with the argument of this book.

88   Many of these responses, by commentators such as Glenn Beck and John Podhoretz, are documented on the Wikipedia "Themes in Avatar" article (see "Anti-Americanism" section).

89   See, for instance, Ross Douthat's op-ed "Heaven and Nature" in the *New York Times* (20 December 2009), http://www.nytimes.com/2009/12/21/opinion/21douthat1 .html?_r=3&th&emc=th, accessed 26 September 2010; Kathryn Reklis, "'New' Pantheism Enters the Oscar Race," *The Immanent Frame,* 1 February 2010, http:// blogs.ssrc.org/tif/2010/02/01/new-pantheism-enters-the-oscar-race; and Nathan Schneider, "The Religion of *Avatar*," *The Immanent Frame*, 30 December 2009, http://blogs.ssrc.org/tif/2009/12/30/the-religion-of-avatar. Echoing a common conservative sentiment, Douthat wrote that "the human societies that hew closest to the natural order aren't the shining Edens of James Cameron's fond imaginings" but are "places where existence tends to be nasty, brutish and short." More interesting than his assessment, however, was that nearly 90 percent of his online commenters disagreed with it, often vehemently, generally by sympathizing with the film's pantheism, which they saw as either something deeply American (and akin to Transcendentalism), or much more broadly religious (such as a mixture of animism and stewardship), or just eco-pragmatically commensensical. And while some of the Christian movie sites that typically like to bash Hollywood liberalism did trash *Avatar*, others (reviewers and commenters alike) were surprisingly positive about it. For the variations in responses, see David Outten, "Capitalism, Christianity, and AVATAR," *MovieGuide: The Family Guide to Movies and Entertainment,* 14 December 2009, http://www.movieguide.org/articles/main/capitalism-christianity-and-avatar -by-david-outten.html; Todd Hertz, "Avatar," *Christianity Today: A Magazine of Evangelical Conviction,* 14 December 2009, http://www.christianitytoday.com/ct/ movies/reviews/2009/avatar.html; and Joshua Moritz, "Science Fiction, ET, and the

Theological Cosmology of Avatar," *Theology and Science* 8, no. 2 (2010): 127–31. Moritz makes the case that the storyline in *Avatar* strongly echoes Lewis's *Out of the Silent Planet* and, less directly, the theology of Jurgen Moltmann. Defenders could also be found among more sophisticated conservatives, such as the localist Front Porch Republic. Even the libertarian Cato Institute has defended it as an argument on behalf of property rights, the very foundation of capitalism. See Ilya Somin, "Avatar and Property Rights in China," *The Volokh Conspiracy*, 14 January 2010, http://volokh.com/2010/01/14/avatar-and-property-rights-in-china; David Boaz, "The Right Has 'Avatar' Wrong," *Los Angeles Times*, Opinion, 26 January 2010, http://articles.latimes.com/2010/jan/26/opinion/la-oe-boaz26-2010jan26; and Caleb Stegall, "Avatar: Reviewing the Reviewers," *Front Porch Republic*, http://www.frontporchrepublic.com/2009/12/avatar-reviewing-the-reviewers.

90 James Der Derian, "'Now We Are All Avatars,'" *Millennium: Journal of International Studies* 39, no. 1 (2010): 181–86 at 182–83.

91 Slavoj Žižek, "Return of the Natives," *New Statesman*, 4 March 2010, http://www.newstatesman.com/film/2010/03/avatar-reality-love-couple-sex.

92 Todd McGowan, "Maternity Divided: *Avatar* and the Enjoyment of Nature," *Jump Cut* 52 (2010), http://www.ejumpcut.org/currentissue/mcGowanAvatar/text.html.

93 See, for instance, Vincent M. Gaine, "The Emergence of Feminine Humanity from a Technologised Masculinity in the Films of James Cameron," *Journal of Technology, Theology, and Religion* 2, no. 4 (2011): 1–41.

94 Renee Lertzman, "Desire, Longing, and the Return to the Garden: Reflections on *Avatar*," *Ecopsychology* 2, no. 1 (2010): 41–43 at 42.

95 Cafard, "Intergalactic Blues," 29, 10.

96 Ibid., 29.

97 Ibid., 25, 26. Cafard argues that planting trees is a mere ruse for product promotion and marketing, which helps explain why the film had partnered with McDonald's and Coca-Cola for promotion. He quotes the film's website: "By filling out and submitting this registration form [to adopt a tree] I understand and agree that Twentieth Century Fox Home Entertainment may send me information about upcoming products, promotions and services and may use information about my activities on Fox web sites to determine what products, promotions and services are likely to be of interest to me." "Until," he interprets, "they can plant something directly in your brain that determines what your interests are, they need a little bit of cooperation on your part to effectively track and check up on you" (27).

98 Cafard, "Intergalactic Blues," 31.

99 Ibid., 38.

100 Caleb Crain, "Don't Play with That, or You'll Go Blind: On James Cameron's *Avatar*," *n+1*, 1 January 2010, http://www.nplusonemag.com/dont-play-or-youll-go-blind, accessed 20 August 2011.

101 Kerin Friedman, "Avatar," *Savage Minds*, 24 December 2009, http://savageminds.org/2009/12/24/avatar, accessed September 30, 2010; David Price, "Hollywood's Human Terrain Avatars," *CounterPunch*, 23 December 2009, http://www.counterpunch.org/price12232009.html, accessed 30 September 2010.

102 E-ANTH listserv communication, 29 January 2010.

103 "Palestinians Dressed as Na'vi from the Film Avatar Stage a Protest against Israel's Separation Barrier," *The Telegraph*, http://www.telegraph.co.uk/news/picturegalleries/worldnews/7222508/Palestinians-dressed-as-the-Navi-from-the-film-Avatar-stage-a-protest-against-Israels-separation-barrier.html. Media theorists Henry Jenkins and Stephen Duscombe refer to such activist appropriations of popular media imagery as "participatory" and "spectacular" forms of cultural activism. See Jenkins, "Avatar Activism," *Le monde diplomatique* (English ed.), September 2010, http://mondediplo.com/2010/09/15avatar, accessed 27 March 2012.

104 *Huffington Post*, "Evo Morales Praises 'Avatar,'" 12 January 2010, http://www.huffingtonpost.com/2010/01/12/evo-morales-praises-avata_n_420663.html, accessed 26 September 2010.

105 See PRI's The World, "Avatar and the Amazon," 29 January 2010, reported by Melaina Spitzer, http://www.theworld.org/2010/01/avatar-in-the-amazon; "Avatar Is Stimulating Some Very Juicy Conversation ..." 27 January 2010, http://tom-atlee.posterous.com/avatar-is-stimulating-some-very-juicy-convers; and "Avatar and Making All the difference in the World," 12 February 2010, http://tom-atlee.posterous.com/avatar-and-making-all-the-difference-in-the-w.

106 Kathryn Hopkins, "Indian Tribe Appeals for Avatar Director's Help to Stop Vedanta,' *The Guardian,* 8 February 2010, http://www.guardian.co.uk/business/2010/feb/08/dongria-kondh-help-stop-vedanta, accessed 26 September 2010.

107 Pete Stanton, "China Pulls Avatar from Their Cinemas Fearing Civil Unrest," Moviefone.com, 19 January 2010, http://blog.moviefone.com/2010/01/19/china-bans-avatar-from-their-cinemas-fearing-civil-unrest, accessed 30 September 2010; Moon "Avatar Lands on a Wrong Mountain,' *China Decoded*, 4 January 2010, http://www.chinadecoded.com/2010/01/04/avatar-lands-on-a-wrong-mountain, accessed 30 September 2010.

108 Harold Linde, "Is *Avatar* Radical Environmental Propaganda?," Karl Burkart's blog, *Mother Nature Network,* 4 January 2010, http://www.mnn.com/green-tech/research-innovations/blogs/is-avatar-radical-environmental-propaganda, accessed 20 August 2010.

109 "SRK Means India for Cameron," *Times of India,* 20 March 2010, http://articles.timesofindia.indiatimes.com/2010-03-20/news-interviews/28139062_1_avatar-second-life-photo-op/2.

110 Jeremy Hance, "The Real Avatar Story: Indigenous People Fight to Save Their Forest Homes from Corporate Exploitation," mongabay.com, 22 December 2009, http://news.mongabay.com/2009/1222-hance_avatar.html; Rohini Hensman, "Of Avatar and Adivasis: How James Cameron's *Avatar* Relates to the Exploitation of Indigenous People of the World and India," Over the Top: Raising a Regional Ruckus (Himal SouthAsian), 28 January 2010, http://himalmag.com/blogs/blog/2010/01/28/of-avatar-and-adivasis. See also Žižek, "Return of the Natives."

111 Daniel Heath Justice, "James Cameron's *Avatar:* Missed Opportunities," *First Peoples: New Directions in Indigenous Studies,* 20 January 2010, http://www.firstpeoplesnewdirections.org/blog/?p=169.

112 Rachelle Gould, Nicole Ardoin, and Jennifer Kamakanipakolonahe'okekai Hashimoto, "'Mālama the 'āina, Mālama the people on the 'āina': The Reaction to Avatar in Hawai'i," Journal for the Study of Religion, Nature, and Culture 4, no. 4 (2010): 425–56 at 450, 452.

113 Jo Piazza, "Audience Experience 'Avatar' Blues," CNN Entertainment, 11 January 2010, http://www.cnn.com/2010/SHOWBIZ/Movies/01/11/avatar.movie.blues/index.html.

114 Matthew Holtmeier, "Post-Pandoran Depression or Na'vi Sympathy: Avatar, Affect, and Audience Reception," Journal for the Study of Religion, Nature, and Culture 4, no. 4 (2010): 414–24 at 415.

115 Dictionaries include Marki and Tirea Aean's Definitive Na'vi Dictionary and NeotrekkerZ's Na'vi in a Nutshell, both available at http://www.learnnavi.org. Field guides include Maria Wilhelm and Dirk Matheson's James Cameron's Avatar: An Activist Field Guide—A Confidential Report on the Biological and Social History of Pandora (London: HarperCollins, 2010). I speculated online on 21 December 2009, that it would not be long before Na'vi fan cults with appropriate garb and rituals took the place of the Klingon and Elvish reconstructionist clubs (and religious groups, for that matter), though it might take a sequel or two to generate more Na'vi vocabulary. Within a few months all these things had seemingly emerged, even without the sequels. See also Henry Jenkins, "Avatar Activism and Beyond," Confessions of an Aca-Fan, 22 September 2010, http://henryjenkins.org/2010/09/avatar_activism_and_beyond.html; idem, "Avatar Activism," Le monde diplomatique, http://mondediplo.com/2010/09/15avatar; and Britt Istoft, "Avatar Fandom as Nature-Religious Expression?," Journal for the Study of Religion, Nature, and Culture 4, no. 4 (2010): 394–413.

116 Istoft (see previous note) documents that the Web forums Avatar-forums.com and Naviblue.com had some 8,000 and 5,500 members each, respectively (it's not clear how many of these numbers overlapped), and that more than 850,000 posts had been logged on some 27,000 subjects within nine months of the film's release; see ibid., 401.

117 Holtmeier, "Post-Pandoran Depression or Na'vi Sympathy: Avatar, Affect, and Audience Reception," Journal for the Study of Religion, Nature, and Culture 4, no. 4 (2010): 414–24 at 416–18. See also Jenkins, "Avatar Activism."

118 Istoft argued that the technological violence "evoked little response" among the fan groups he studied; "Avatar Fandom," 411.

119 The quote here is from Cafard, "Intergalactic Blues," 33. I explored the connection between the Lacanian and Buddhist understandings of desires in a series of blog posts reviewing and responding to an article by John Clark. ("Max Cafard" is Clark's radical pen name.) See "Nagarjuna, Ecophilosophy, and the "Practice of Liberation," 14 November 2009, Immanence, http://blog.uvm.edu/aivakhiv/2009/11/14/nagarjuna-ecophilosophy-the-practice-of-liberation; and "Nagarjuna and Ecophilosophy, pt. 2," Immanence, 14 November 2009, http://blog.uvm.edu/aivakhiv/2009/11/14/nagarjuna-ecophilosophy-pt-2.

120 Renee Lertzman, "Desire, Longing, and the Return to the Garden: Reflections on Avatar," Ecopsychology 2, no. 1 (2010): 41–43 at 42.

121 Kaplan, "Global Trauma," 21; emphasis in original. See also Kelly Oliver, *Witnessing: Beyond Recognition* (Minneapolis: University of Minnesota Press, 2001).

122 Kaplan, "Global Trauma," 14, quoting John Leonard, "Not What Happened but Why" (review of Susan Sontag's *Regarding the Pain of Others*), *New York Review of Books*, February 23 March 2004.

123 See, for example, Andrew Light and Holmes Rolston III, *Environmental Ethics: An Anthology* (Oxford: Blackwell, 2003); and Michael Zimmerman et al., *Environmental Philosophy: From Animal Rights to Radical Ecology*, 4th ed. (Upper Saddle River, NJ: Pearson/Prentice-Hall, 2005).

124 The division of the normative sciences into aesthetics, ethics, and logic came relatively late in the development of Peirce's thought and is found in its most complete form in his writings and lectures from 1902 onward. See, for instance, the fifth of his Harvard Lectures on Pragmatism, "The Three Normative Sciences," in *The Essential Peirce: Selected Philosophical Writings*, vol. 2 (1893–1913), ed. Peirce Edition Project (Bloomington: Indiana University Press, 1998), 196–207; and "An Outline Classification of the Sciences," 256–62 in the same volume. For discussion of aesthetics and its relation to ethics and logic in Peirce, see Bent Sorensen and Torkild Leo Thellefsen, "The Normative Sciences, the Sign Universe, Self-Control and Relationality—According to Peirce," *Cosmos and History* 6, no. 1 (2010); Martin Lefebvre, "Peirce's Esthetics: A Taste for Signs in Art," *Transactions of the Charles S. Peirce Society* 43, no. 2 (2007): 319–44; Carl M. Smith, "The Aesthetics of Charles S. Peirce," *Journal of Aesthetics and Art Criticism* 31, no. 1 (1972): 21–29; and Herman Parret, ed., *Peirce and Value Theory* (Amsterdam: John Benjamins, 1994).

125 See Peirce, *Collected Papers* 5.129 and 8.256; and Herman Parret, "Peircian Fragments on the Aesthetic Experience," in *Peirce and Value Theory*, ed. Parret (Amsterdam: John Benjamins, 1994), 181ff.

126 This phrasing is Beverley Kent's, from *Charles S. Peirce: Logic and the Classification of the Sciences* (Kingston and Montreal: McGill–Queen's University Press, 1987), 165, 133. The book presents one of the most detailed examinations of Peirce's classification schema.

127 Kent, *Charles S. Peirce*, 170.

128 Peirce, *Collected Papers* 5.551; "The Three Normative Sciences," in *The Essential Peirce*, vol. 2, 203.

129 Kent, *Charles S. Peirce*, 154–55. Similarly, Whitehead spoke of the value of Discord for the development of Beauty (terms that he capitalized in *Adventures of Ideas*, 252ff.).

130 Peirce's thinking on beauty and ugliness, good and evil, and coherence and incoherence, retained some ambiguity right through to the end of his life. For instance, he wrote: "Man comes to his normal development only through the so-called *evil passions*, which are evil, only in the sense that they ought to be controlled, and are *good* as the only possible agency for giving man his full development" (330.[4], in Kent, *Charles S. Peirce*, 155). Evil is, in this sense, "perfection in God's eyes," but while people can move toward a God-like vision, they have not at present (if ever) attained that vision.

131 Needless to say, this paragraph barely scratches the surface of what such a Peirce-inspired triadic analysis might offer. I present it only to suggest some thoughts, but these require much more detailed development.

132 On cinematic excess, see Kristin Thompson, "The Concept of Cinematic Excess," in *Narrative, Apparatus, Ideology,* ed. Philip Rosen, 130–42 (New York: Columbia University Press, 1986). Coming at it from a rather different theoretical direction, filmmaker and theorist Raul Ruiz speaks of the excess that allows a film to escape its own "central conflict," the linear narrative trajectory that would tame it of its value. See Ruiz, *The Poetics of Cinema,* trans. Brian Holmes (Paris: Dis Voir, 1995), 11.

133 Daniel Frampton, *Filmosophy* (London: Wallflower Press, 2006), 38.

134 Carl Plantinga, "Affective Counterpoint and *The Thin Red Line,*" *Projections* 4, no. 2 (2010): 86–103 at 93.

135 See, for instance, the arguments proposed by Robert Heilbroner, *An Inquiry into the Human Prospect, Updated for the 1980s* (New York: W.W. Norton, 1980); and William Ophuls, *Ecology and the Politics of Scarcity* (San Francisco: W.H. Freeman, 1977).

136 This question of the politics of process-relational philosophies is hardly a settled one. All three of the thinkers mentioned (Whitehead, Peirce, and Deleuze) manifested strong democratic if not anarchistic (in the case of Deleuze) leanings, and others on my list (see Chapter 2)—Spinoza, for instance, or the Daoists—count similarly among history's canonic democrats and freethinkers. But there were process-relational thinkers whose political preferences were not nearly as clear. For a few avenues into this topic, see Anne Fairchild Pomeroy, *Marx and Whitehead: Process, Dialectics, and the Critique of Capitalism* (Albany: SUNY Press, 2004); Randall C. Morris, *Process Philosophy and Political Ideology: The Social and Political Thought of Alfred North Whitehead and Charles Hartshorne* (Albany: SUNY Press, 1991); Michael Halewood, *A.N. Whitehead and Social Theory: Tracing a Culture of Thought* (London: Anthem, 2011); Lara Trout, *The Politics of Survival: Peirce, Affectivity, and Social Criticism* (New York: Fordham University Press, 2010); and Ian Buchanan and Nicholas Thoburn, eds., *Deleuze and Politics* (Edinburgh: Edinburgh University Press, 2008).

137 See Uri Hasson et al., "Intersubject Synchronization of Cortical Activity During Natural Vision," *Science* 303, no. 5664 (2004): 1634–40; *idem,* "Neurocinematics: The Neuroscience of Film," *Projections* 2 (2008): 1–26; and Jessica Hamzelou, "Brain Imaging Monitors Effect of Movie Magic," *Human Brain* 2777 (September 8, 2010).

138 In *Poetics of Cinema,* filmmaker and theorist Raul Ruiz argues that it is precisely this escape from a film's "central conflict"—the failure to contribute to the linear narrative trajectory of that central axis—that constitutes the cinematic "excess" that makes a film a good film. Ruiz's films, like those of other Surrealists and Baroque aesthetes, celebrate their "perverse" elements, allowing them to flourish and proliferate. *Avatar* does not do this. In terms of the research mentioned in "neurocinematics," *Avatar* follows traditional Hollywood narrative formulas. Furthermore, brain scans indicate that 3-D movie viewers have higher general brain

activation than 2-D movie viewers, which suggests that *Avatar* would have elicited particularly strong similarities of brain response in viewers. See previous note.

139 Oddly enough, however, Tarkovsky does not appear in Harry Tuttle's timeline of "Unspoken Cinema (Contemporary Contemplative Cinema)," http://unspokencinema.blogspot.com/2009/06/ccc-timeline-2008.html. But his work is often acknowledged by denizens of the movement.

140 On the debates over "slow cinema," see See Matthew Flanagan, "Towards an Aesthetic of Slow in Contemporary Cinema," *16:9* 29 (November 2008), http://www.16-9 .dk/2008-11/side11_inenglish.htm; Harry Tuttle, "Slower or Contemplative?" *Unspoken Cinema,* 17 March 2010, http://unspokencinema.blogspot.com/2010/03/slower-or-contemplative.html; Nick James, Editorial: "Passive Aggressive," *Sight and Sound,* April 2010; Steven Shaviro, "Slow Cinema vs. Fast Films," *The Pinocchio Theory,* 12 May 2010, http://www.shaviro.com/Blog/?p=891; and Manohla Dargis and A.O. Scott, "In Defense of the Slow and the Boring," *New York Times,* 3 June 2011, http://www.nytimes.com/2011/06/05/movies/films-in-defense-of-slow-and-boring.html. On "post-continuity," see Steven Shaviro, *Post Cinematic Affect* (Ropley: John Hunt / zerO books, 2010); and *idem,* "Steven Shaviro's Post-Cinematic Affect," *In Media Res,* 29 August–2 September 2011, http://mediacommons.futureofthebook.org/imr/theme-week/2011/35/steven-shaviros-post-cinematic-affect-august-29-sept-2-2011. In debates over cinematic slowness and speed, one commonly cited datum is some variation of the following: that shot length has steadily decreased in popular films from an average somewhere between five and nine seconds in American films of the 1970s, to less than two seconds in such recent popular fare as *The Bourne Supremacy* (2004) and *The Bourne Ultimatum* (2007).

141 The school of thought known as "object-oriented philosophy" has sometimes objected to the idea that a process-relational ontology, such as Deleuze's or a Buddhist relationalism, is adequate for ecology. Philosopher Graham Harman in particular has maintained that an ontology in which everything is relational process cannot account for the existence of actual *objects,* and that this is an ethical pitfall and weakness of relational philosophies. The problem with Harman's argument is that it assumes that reality can only be found in substantive things, not in events and encounters. Process-relational philosophy argues that reality in its full ethical significance is only found in actual events and encounters. *This moment* is the significant moment, because it is the moment in which I (or another) can act. The same will be the case in the next moment, which will then be *this* moment. And the same is the case for you in the moment you can identify as this moment. The "I" who is acting and the "you" I am acting in response to are significant in part because we have a future we aspire to and a past we remember, but it is only the processual openness of each of us that makes us ethically significant for another. (And positing an "I" does not necessarily commit me to a substantialist notion of the self. "I" can be part of a series of processes in which identity, the "I-ness" of the "I," emerges from moment to moment through relations of subjectivation–objectivation.) I deal with this debate between process-relational and object-oriented approaches in a forthcoming book; I have also discussed it on numerous occasions on my blog, *Immanence* (blog.uvm.edu/immanence).

142 The concept of "time-pressure" is Tarkovsky's; see Andrei Tarkovsky, *Sculpting in Time*, trans. Kitty Hunter-Blair (Austin: University of Texas Press, 1989), 117. Deleuze refers to it in *Cinema 2: The Time-Image* (Minneapolis: University of Minnesota Press, 1989), 42. See also David George Menard, "A Deleuzian Analysis of Tarkovsky's Theory of Time-Pressure," which appeared in *Offscreen* in two parts, beginning here: http://horschamp.qc.ca/new_offscreen/deleuzian_pressure.html.

143 Deleuze, *Cinema 2*, 78–83 at 98.

144 Ibid., 81.

145 Henry Corbin, "Mundus Imaginalis, or, the Imaginary and the Imaginal," *Spring* (1972): 1–19.

146 James Hillman, *Archetypal Psychology: A Brief Account* (Dallas: Spring Publications, 1983), 6.

147 Ibid., 5, 16.

148 The resonance between Hillman's notion of the image and Bergson's, discussed in Chapter 2, should be fairly obvious. The differences, while also significant, are beyond the scope of this book.

149 Ibid., 16.

150 James Hillman, "On Mythic Certitude," *Sphinx: A Journal for Archetypal Psychology and the Arts* 3 (1990): 224–43 at 230.

151 James Hillman, "Back to Beyond: On Cosmology," in *Archetypal Process: Self and Divine in Whitehead, Jung, and Hillman,* ed. David Ray Griffin (Evanston: Northwestern University Press, 1989), 213–31 at 226. See also *idem, Archetypal Psychology,* 14, 34. For an updated, neo-Jamesian argument espousing a pluralistic universe, see William Connolly, *A World of Becoming* (Durham, NC: Duke University Press, 2010).

152 James Hillman, *Re-Visioning Psychology* (New York: Harper Colophon, 1975), 40.

153 Hillman, "Back to Beyond," 253; *idem, Archetypal Psychology,* 9.

154 A more conservative Jungianism might be the one articulated in Anthony Stevens's *Archetype Revisited: An Updated Natural History of the Self* (London: Brunner-Routledge, 2002).

155 Some 600 million people, or one in five humans alive, participated as the spectatorial third party to that contact, either by radio or by television. See Andrew Chaikin, "Live from the Moon: The Societal Impact of Apollo," in *Societal Impact of Spaceflight,* ed. Steven Dick and Roger Launius (Washington: NASA Office of External Relations, History Division), 53–66 at 55.

156 It is known more prosaically by its NASA designation as image AS8-14-2383. See Benjamin Lazier, "Earthrise; or, The Globalization of the World Picture," *American Historical Review* 116, no. 3 (2011): 602–30.

157 Al Reinert, "The Blue Marble Shot: Our First Complete Photograph of Earth," *The Atlantic,* 12 April 2011, http://www.theatlantic.com/technology/archive/2011/04/the-blue-marble-shot-our-first-complete-photograph-of-earth/237167, 24–25.

158 Stefan Helmreich, "From Spaceship Earth to Google Ocean: Planetary Icons, Indexes, and Infrastructures," *Social Research* 78, no. 4 (2011): 1211–42 at 1218, 1221. This article provides an illuminating Peircian account of Google Earth and its blue relative, Google Ocean. Helmreich describes the latter in terms of what

Peirce called an "existential graph," a "logical diagram that conjoins multiple representations, real and fictive, and multiple semiotic registers, iconic, indexical, symbolic, which can operate independently of one another (in different layers) while still forming part of a composite," yet characterized, in Helmreich's account, by a peculiar weightlessness (1235–36).

159 For a concise overview of the cultural meanings of the space race, see Emily Rosenberg, "Far Out: The Space Age in American Culture," in *Remembering the Space Age: Proceedings of the 50th Anniversary Conference,* ed. Steven Dick, vol. 4703 of NASA SP, 157–84 (Washington, DC: National Aeronautics and Space Administration, Office of External Relations, History Division, 2008). See also Chaikin, "Live from the Moon."

160 Lazier, "Earthrise," 606. See also Yaakov J. Garb, "The Use and Misuse of the Whole Earth Image," *Whole Earth Review* (March 1985), 18–25; and Denis Cosgrove, "Contested Global Visions: One-World, Whole-Earth, and the Apollo Space Photographs," *Annals of the Association of American Geographers* 84, no. 2 (1994): 270–94.

161 The literature on film-philosophy, including debates over whether film can qualify *as* a form of philosophy, has erupted in recent years. For a few glimpses of it, see the online journal *Film-Philosophy*; see also its founding editor Daniel Frampton's *Filmosophy*; Thomas Wartenberg, *Thinking on Film: Film as Philosophy* (New York: Routledge, 2007); and Havi Carel and Greg Tuck, eds., *New Takes in Film-Philosophy* (New York: Palgrave Macmillan, 2011).

162 Ignatiy Vishnevetsky, "'The Tree of Life': A Malickiad," *Notebook*, 26 May 2011, http://mubi.com/notebook/posts/the-tree-of-life-a-malickiad, accessed 15 October 2011.

163 "those who've written": Emerson, in A.O. Scott, "Summer Cinema Worth Debating," *New York Times,* 28 August 2010, Arts and Leisure section, 1 and 13 at 13.

164 Kent Jones, "Light Years: Terrence Malick Returns to the Landscape of His Childhood and Sees All the Way to Eternity in His Immense New Film," *Film Comment* 47, no. 4 (2011): 24–29; "doesn't move forward," "bursts of attentively," 29; "the film's signature action," 28.

165 G. Roger Denson, "Terrence Malick's 'The Tree of Life' Plays Garden of Eden to the Family of Man," *Huffington Post*, 6 June 2011, http://www.huffingtonpost.com/g-roger-denson/terrence-malicks-tree-of-_b_868895.html, accessed 6 October 2011.

166 Jeff Reichert, "The Tree of Life: Children of the Evolution," *Reverse Shot* 29, http://reverseshot.com/article/tree_life_children_evolution, accessed 15 October 2011.

167 Charles Darwin, *On the Origin of Species by Means of Natural Selection, or the Preservation of Favoured Races in the Struggle for Life* (London: John Murray, 1859), 489–90. Just as Darwin added the words "by the Creator" in later editions to appease his Christian critics, so *The Tree of Life* seems suited for such multiple readings, though these are easily explainable as artifacts of the time and characters depicted in the film. Witness the ease with which a movie depicting the Big Bang, the evolution of life, and the mind's quest for meaning in dreams and fantasies has

been taken on by Christian commentators as depicting Christian themes. Some of these themes are, admittedly, fairly evident: quotes from the Book of Job, the musical 'requiems, ideas of guilt and repentance, direct address to a deity, and the resurrection-and-afterlife "flavour" of the film's final beach scenes. See Brett McCracken, "The Tree of Life," *Christianity Today,* 27 May 2011, http://www .christianitytoday.com/ct/movies/reviews/2011/treeoflife.html; and Church of the Holy Cross Palermo, "Movie Night at Holy Cross: The Tree of Life," *Chaplaincy News,* http://www.chiesaanglicanapalermo.it/news_treelife.html.

168 For an interpretation of these images in light of art history, see Melissa Tamminga, "Something Rotten in the State of Things: *Melancholia,*" *A Journal of Film,* 18 November 2011, http://ajournaloffilm.blogspot.com/2011/11/memento -mori-melancholia-lars-von-trier.html.

169 J. Hoberman, "Lars von Trier's *Melancholia.* Wow." *Village Voice,* 18 May 2011. Or see Betsy Sharkey, "Lars von Trier's 'Melancholia' is—gasp—hopeful," *Los Angeles Times,* 11 November 2011.

170 I take this idea of ontogeny and eschatology from Richard Corliss's review, "*Melancholia:* Lars von Trier's Tree of Death," *Time,* 18 May 2011.

171 Slavoj Žižek, "Nature and Its Discontents," *SubStance* 37, no. 3 (2008): 37–72 at 68.

172 Slavoj Žižek, "Censorship Today: Violence, or Ecology as a New Opium for the Masses," Lacan.com, http://www.lacan.com/zizecology1.htm.

Notes to Afterword

1 William E. Connolly, *Pluralism* (Durham, NC: Duke University Press, 2005), 91.

2 Steven Shaviro, *Post-Cinematic Affect* (New Alresford, UK: John Hunt Publishing, 2010), 63.

3 Gilles Deleuze, *Cinema 2: The Time-Image,* tr. H. Tomlinson and R. Galeta (Minneapolis: University of Minnesota Press, 2007), 166–67.

4 See Pat Brereton, *Smart Cinema, DVD Add-Ons, and New Audience Pleasures* (Basingstoke: Palgrave Macmillan, 2012).

5 D.N. Rodowick, *The Virtual Life of Film* (Cambridge, MA: Harvard University Press, 2007), 27.

6 Lev Manovich, *The Language of New Media* (Cambridge, MA: MIT Press, 2001), 78–79.

7 Ibid., 86.

8 Lev Manovich, "What Is Cinema?" in *The Digital Dialectic: New Essays on New Media,* ed. Peter Lunenfeld (Cambridge, MA: MIT Press, 2000), 174.

9 Niels Niessen, "Lives of Cinema: Against Its 'Death,'" *Screen* 52, no. 3 (2011): 307–26 at 317.

10 Rodowick, *The Virtual Life of Film,* 86–87.

11 Coover, "On Verité to Virtual: Conversations on the Frontier of Film and Anthropology," *Visual Studies* 24, no. 3 (2009): 235–249 at 244.

12 Jean-Pierre Geuens argues that the magic and ritual of cinema has been lost, replaced by an emphasis on total control. To him, this represents a nihilistic

"distrust of the everyday world"; see Geuens, "The Digital World Picture," *Film Quarterly* 55, no. 4 (2002): 16–27 at 21. Kristen Daly, on the other hand, focuses on the possibilities opened up by digital cinema: long takes, an "aesthetic of the non-cut," the computer-camera as collaborator, a Web browser aesthetic, and the possibility for "a way of production that can be organic to both the place and people of that place, producing an innovative, spontaneous and intimate aesthetic"; see Daly, "New Mode of Cinema: How Digital Technologies Are Changing Aesthetics and Style," *Kinephanos Journal*, Fall 2009, http://www.kinephanos.ca.

13   Francesco Casetti, *Eye of the Century: Film, Experience, Modernity,* trans. Erin Larkin and Jennifer Pranolo (New York: Columbia University Press, 2008), 107.

14   Casetti, *Eye of the Century,* 173.

15   Ibid., 188.

16   Shaviro, *Post-Cinematic Affect* (Hampshire: John Hunt Publishing, 2010), 132.

17   Cited in ibid., 136.

18   Ibid.: "the contours of the prison," 14; "swells and contracts," 11; "singularity," 12; "long string," 13; "posthuman," 20; "puts on and takes off personas," 23; "for keeps," 24; "whatever she encounters," and "track[ing] and embrac[ing] the transmutations," 30; "the chronic condition," 31.

19   Manovich, *The Language of New Media,* 301.

20   Ibid.: "raw material for further compositing," 301; "an isolated accident," 308; "Born from animation," 302, italics his.

21   Wheeler Winston Dixon, "Twenty-Five Reasons Why It's All Over," in *The End of Cinema as We Know It: American Film in the Nineties,* ed. Jon Lewis (London: Pluto Press, 2001), 356–66.

22   Nadia Bozak, *The Cinematic Footprint: Lights, Camera, Natural Resources* (New Brunswick, NJ: Rutgers University Press, 2012).

23   As Stefan Jovanovic puts it, "more than any other art, the cinema has died repeatedly and with great regularity over the course of its relatively brief (just over one century) existence." Jovanovic, "The Ending(s) of Cinema: Notes on the Recurrent Demise of the Seventh Art, Part 1," *Offscreen* 7, no. 4 (2003), http://www.horschamp.qc.ca/new_offscreen/death_cinema.html. See also Michael Witt, "The Death(s) of Cinema According to Godard," *Screen* 40, no. 3 (1999): 331–46.

24   Vilém Flusser, *Towards a Philosophy of Photography* (London: Reaktion Books, 2000), 33.

INDEX

world-making, 6, 9–13, 23; and process-
relational thought, 43. *See also* cinema;
cosmomorphism; Martin Heidegger; poiesis
world-productiveness, three registers
of, 67. *See also* animamorphism;
anthropromorphism; geomorphism
world-systems theory, 388n38
World, The (*Shijie,* Jia Zhang-ke, 2004), 103–4
Worth, Sol, 147

X-Files, The, 22, 161, 274

Yong-kyun, Bae, 112

Zhang-ke, Jia, 101–4; film techniques, 104
Žižek, Slavoj, 272; and 9/11, 261;
anamorphosis and, 276; criticism of racism

in *Avatar,* 288; psychoanalytic pessimism,
323–24; and Tarkovsky's cinematic
materialism, 16–18, 340; and the traumatic
kernel, 28. *See also* anamorphosis; the Real;
trauma
Zone the in *Stalker,* 14–18, 241, 283–84. *See
also* Andrei Tarkovsky
Zone of cinema: nature of, 21, 22; otherness
and, 21, 244
Zone, the, 283, 287, 300, 304, 321, 323;
and landscapes of radical otherness, 244;
as liminal space, 17; as meeting ground of
image and sound, 17; as metaphor, 321;
metaphysics of, 16, 28; movement into,
284. *See also* contact zones
Zoo (Devor, 2007), 242–43, 246
zoo-ethnographic intervention, 243

Environmental Humanities Series

Environmental thought pursues with renewed urgency the grand concerns of the humanities: who we think we are, how we relate to others, and how we live in the world. Scholarship in the environmental humanities explores these questions by crossing the lines that separate human from animal, social from material, and objects and bodies from techno-ecological networks. Humanistic accounts of political representation and ethical recognition are re-examined in consideration of other species. Social identities are studied in relation to conceptions of the natural, the animal, the bodily, place, space, landscape, risk, and technology, and in relation to the material distribution and contestation of environmental hazards and pleasures.

The Environmental Humanities Series features research that adopts and adapts the methods of the humanities to clarify the cultural meanings associated with environmental debate. The scope of the series is broad. Film, literature, television, Web-based media, visual art, and physical landscape—all are crucial sites for exploring how ecological relationships and identities are lived and imagined. The Environmental Humanities Series publishes scholarly monographs and essay collections in environmental cultural studies, including popular culture, film, media, and visual cultures; environmental literary criticism; cultural geography; environmental philosophy, ethics, and religious studies; and other cross-disciplinary research that probes what it means to be human, animal, and technological in an ecological world.

Gathering research and writing in environmental philosophy, ethics, cultural studies, and literature under a single umbrella, the series aims to make visible the contributions of humanities research to environmental studies, and to foster discussion that challenges and reconceptualizes the humanities.

SERIES EDITOR
Cheryl Lousley, English and Film Studies, Wilfrid Laurier University

EDITORIAL COMMITTEE
Adrian J. Ivakhiv, Environmental Studies, University of Vermont
Catriona Mortimer-Sandilands, Tier 1 CRC in Sustainability and Culture,
Environmental Studies, York University
Susie O'Brien, English and Cultural Studies, McMaster University
Laurie Ricou, English, University of British Columbia
Rob Shields, Henry Marshall Tory Chair and Professor,
Department of Sociology, University of Alberta

FOR MORE INFORMATION, CONTACT
Lisa Quinn
Acquisitions Editor
Wilfrid Laurier University Press
75 University Avenue West
Waterloo, ON   N2L 3C5
(519) 884-0710 ext. 2843
Email: quinn@press.wlu.ca

Books in the Environmental Humanities Series
Published by Wilfrid Laurier University Press

Animal Subjects: An Ethical Reader in a Posthuman World
Jodey Castricano, editor / 2008 / 324 pp. / ISBN 978-0-88920-512-3

Open Wide a Wilderness: Canadian Nature Poems
Nancy Holmes, editor / 2009 / 534 pp. / ISBN 978-1-55458-033-0

Technonatures: Environments, Technologies, Spaces, and Places in the Twenty-first Century
Damian F. White and Chris Wilbert, editors / 2009 / 282 pp. /
ISBN 978-1-55458-150-4

Writing in Dust: Reading the Prairie Environmentally
Jenny Kerber / 2010 / 276 pp. / ISBN 978-1-55458-218-1 (hardcover),
ISBN 978-1-55458-306-5 (paper)

Ecologies of Affect: Placing Nostalgia, Desire, and Hope
Tonya K. Davidson, Ondine Park, and Rob Shields, editors / 2011 / 360 pp. /
illus. / ISBN 978-1-55458-258-7

Ornithologies of Desire: Ecocritical Essays, Avian Poetics, and Don McKay
Travis V. Mason / 2013 / 305 pp. / ISBN 978-1-55458-630-1

Ecologies of the Moving Image: Cinema, Affect, Nature
Adrian J. Ivakhiv / 2013 / 432 pp. / ISBN 978-1-55458-905-0

Avatar and Nature Spirituality
Bron Taylor, editor / forthcoming 2013 / 376 pp. / ISBN 978-1-55458-843-5

Sustaining the West: Cultural Responses to Western Environments, Past and Present
Liza Piper and Lisa Szabo-Jones, editors / forthcoming 2014 /
ISBN 978-1-55458-923-4